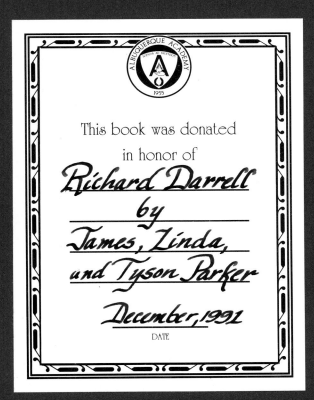

The Golden Age of Painting in Spain

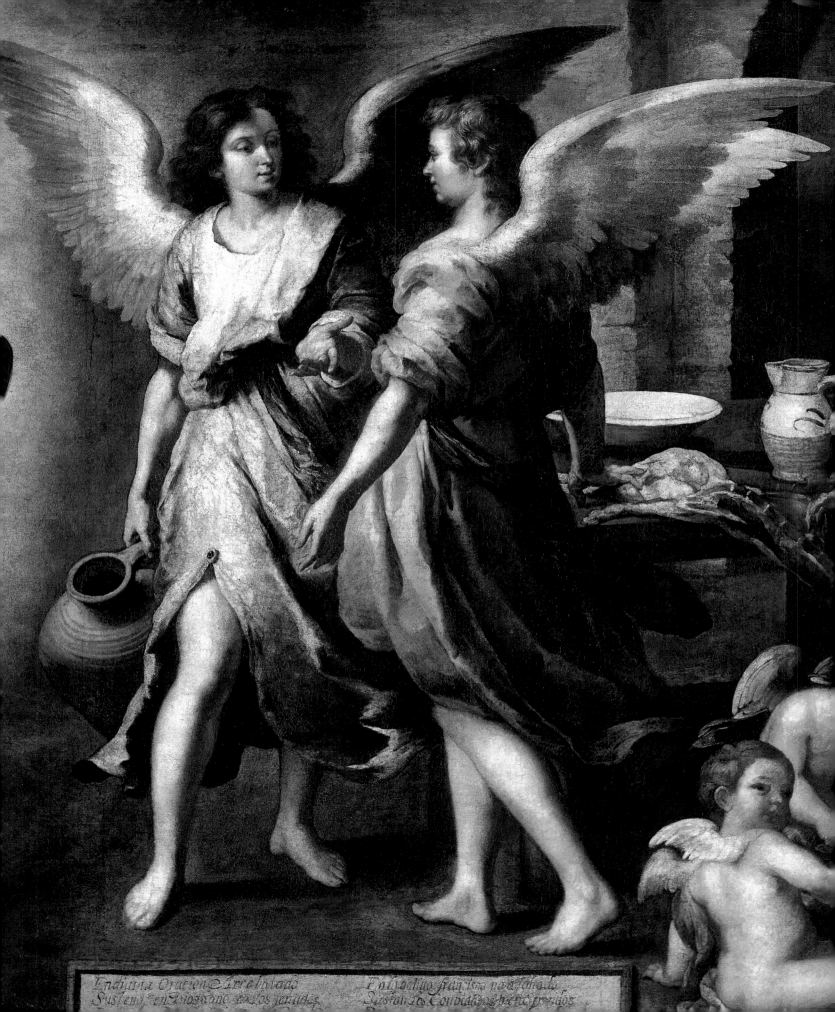

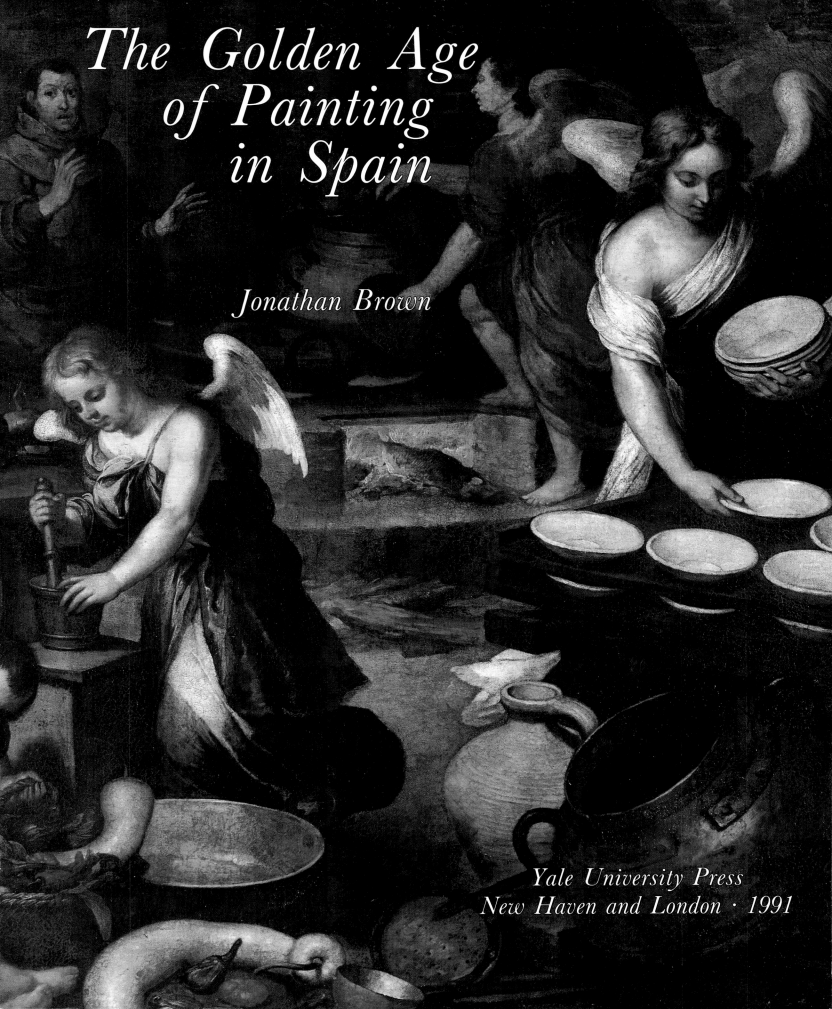

The Golden Age
of Painting
in Spain

Jonathan Brown

Yale University Press
New Haven and London · 1991

To Sandra,
for these twenty-five years

Frontispiece: Bartolomé Murillo, "*Angels' Kitchen*," 1646, Paris, Musée du Louvre (detail of pl. 227).

Designed by Gillian Malpass
Set in Linotron Bembo by
Excel Typesetters Company, Hong Kong
Printed in Spain by
Heraclio Fournier, S.A., Vitoria

Library of Congress Cataloging-in-Publication Data

Brown, Jonathan, 1939–
    The Golden Age of painting in Spain/
    Jonathan Brown.
        p.   .cm.
    Includes bibliographical references and index.
    ISBN 0-300-4760-6
    1. Painting, Spanish.   2. Painting, Modern
    — Spain.   I. Title.
ND804.B74   1991
    758.6'09'03 — dc20   90-12564
                                                          CIP

Photographic Acknowledgments

Except for the following, photographic material has been supplied by the owners or by Jonathan Brown and is reproduced courtesy of the copyright owners:

Arxiu Mas: 5, 7, 8, 9, 10, 11, 12, 14, 15, 20, 21, 23, 25, 26, 27, 38, 40, 43, 45, 46, 52, 80, 84, 96, 100, 101, 107, 108, 137, 138, 141, 143, 165, 223, 241, 242, 253, 254, 261, 285, 289; Courtesy of the Trustees of the National Gallery, London: 16, 112, 200, 209, 262; Scala: 28, 67; Fotografías de Francisco Javier Muñoz Gonzalez: 29, 30; Courtesy of the Hispanic Society of America: 47, 274; Cliché des Musées Nationaux, Paris. Photo R.M.N.: 74, 92, 146, 220, 222, 227, 233, 235; Studio Grafico Gaeta, Naples: 161, 175; Soprintendenza Per I Beni Artistici e Storici di Napoli: 176; Photo © Gilbert Mangin: 174; Artothek: 266, 285; Ali Meyer: 277.

Contents

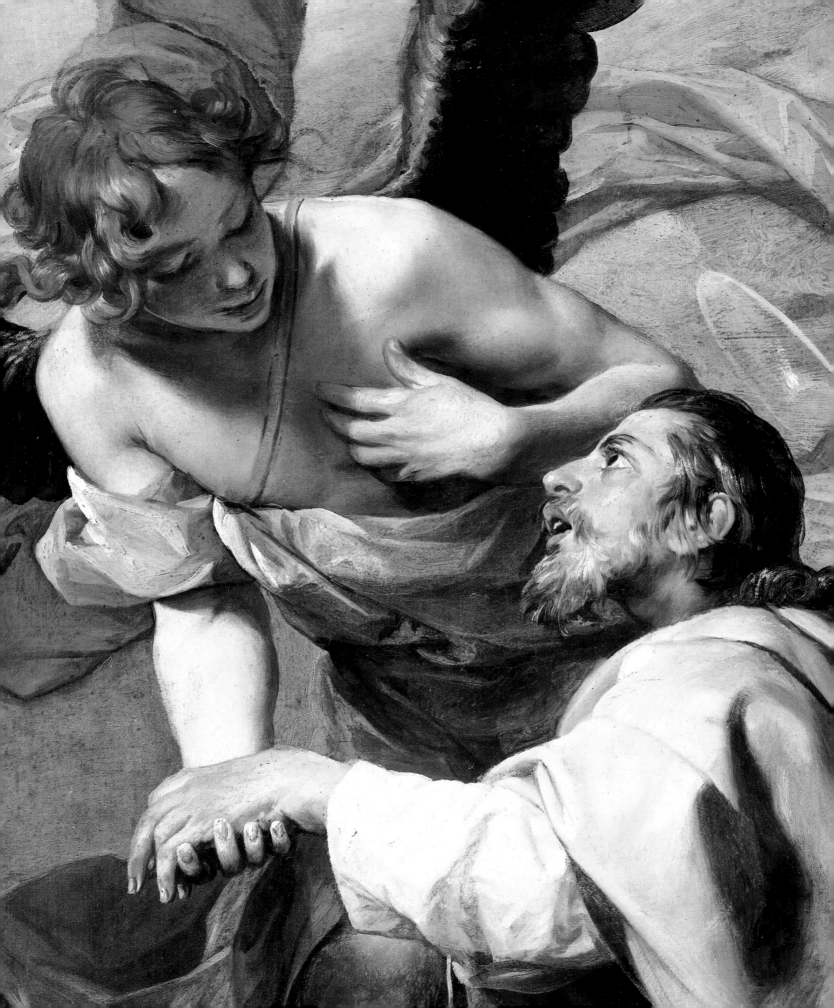

Preface

IN RECENT YEARS, there has been a phenomenal growth of interest in Spanish art. Among the factors contributing to this development are two that I believe to be especially important. The first is the global "art boom," the potent combination of social, economic, and cultural forces that has transformed the visual arts from a pastime of the elite into a preoccupation of the public at large. The second, which is unique to Spain, involves the dramatic changes set into motion by the death of General Francisco Franco in 1975. When I began the study of Spanish art in the late 1950s, memories of the Spanish Civil War were still fresh in the minds of my older compatriots, and my choice of field seemed dubious at best, if only because it entailed traveling to what was called "Franco's Spain." Now, some fifteen years after Franco's death, Spain has become a model for nations attempting the difficult transition from a closed to an open society.

The surge of interest in Spanish art has provided a powerful stimulus to the study of its greatest period of painting, universally known as the Golden Age, which is here defined as beginning with the reign of the Catholic Monarchs (1474) and extending to the end of the Habsburg dynasty (1700). Over the last years, an impressive number of monographs and documents concerning the period have been published and many important exhibitions have been organized, especially on the seventeenth century. (The sixteenth has only recently begun to attract interest.) Thus, the moment seems ripe to provide a synthesis that incorporates the mass of new information and to attempt to offer fresh perspectives on the special achievement of this important phase of European art.

In selecting a vantage point from which to survey the period, it is possible that I have been affected by observing the reincorporation of Spain into the community of European nations. However, I have long been convinced that the Golden Age of painting in Spain should be understood in relation to its nourishing sources in other regions of Europe, especially Italy and Flanders, large parts of which were ruled by the Spanish Habsburg monarchy.

The study of artistic influence and interchange has tended to be neglected, in part because of a long-standing bias of western culture, which originated in the Renaissance, in favor of novelty and uniqueness. The emphasis on innovation in particular makes it very difficult to understand the phenomenon of artistic diffusion.★ Invention undeniably is important, but the way in which new ideas are spread and adapted is the other, and largely untold, part of the story of European art. It should no longer be regarded as an admission of defeat or inferiority to acknowledge that one artistic center has been powerfully influenced by another, or

★However, anthropologists have a well-developed method for studying the process of cultural diffusion, known as acculturation theory. For its application to the study of Spanish history, see Thomas F. Glick and Oriol Pi-Sunyer, "Acculturation as an Explanatory Concept in Spanish History," *Comparative Studies in Society and History* 11 (1969), 136–54.

Facing page. Detail of pl.156.

to suggest that painters were affected by the same societal forces as others in their milieu. On the contrary, these processes are immensely important for understanding how different cultures intersect and are stimulated to grow in new directions by mutual contact. The study of the dynamics of cultural interaction also makes it possible to discern how works of a given time and place acquire a common identity.

As the reader will see, I do not believe that artistic identity is generated by quasi-mythical national characteristics that endure over long periods of time. Not climate nor geography nor ancient history nor, to mention the most elusive factor of all, innate mental habits play a role in this book. My view of artistic development is more circumstantial. Art, to be sure, has its own concerns and traditions upon which painters draw, but the implementation of these ideas is affected by a variety of extrinsic factors. In Golden Age Spain, a hierarchical society if ever there was one, the patronage of secular and religious elites looms as the largest of these forces, but market conditions, social biases, and local customs are also important.

In organizing the book, I have sought to maintain a balance between narrative and interpretation. The emphasis is on the careers of the major painters, who were best able to perceive and interpret what was going on around them. But in order to clarify their responses to changing conditions, I have abandoned a monographic approach – one chapter per major artist – and tried to show how they functioned within their microcultures. Exceptions are made only for El Greco and Ribera, both of whom stand apart, although for different reasons, from their Spanish contemporaries. I hope that an inevitable loss of biographical continuity is compensated for by a gain in perceiving how these painters navigated the currents of their society.

This approach, and the desire to keep the book at a manageable length, has also compelled me to make choices, often painful ones, about what to include and what to leave out. Students of the period and admirers of the many fine secondary artists will certainly note the absence of particular favorites. Besides offering apologies to those who are thus disappointed, I can say only that, short of doubling the length of the book, or, indeed, writing another kind of book entirely, I could see no way to make the coverage complete. The same process of selection has required me to omit important works even by the artists discussed in these pages.

A prefatory word should be said about the annotations to the text. After considerable thought, I decided to keep these to a minimum lest the book be overwhelmed by bibliographical references. Thus, I cite the sources of quotations and otherwise refer the reader to recent publications where up-to-date bibliographies are listed or certain ideas are expounded in detail. Accordingly, the bibliography is not complete, although it should be helpful as a starting place for those wishing to explore the ideas and personalities presented in the text.

These ideas have been taking shape in my mind for many years, over the course of which I have benefited greatly from discussions with colleagues and students on both sides of the Atlantic. The list of those who helped is now so long that it is impossible to acknowledge every person individually, although my gratitude for the sharing of information and points of view is obviously immense. I would be remiss, however, if I did not explicitly thank those who assisted in the production of this book.

The handwritten drafts were somehow deciphered and typed by Lynda Emery. Once processed, the words were read by John H. Elliott, who after many years of staunch friendship deserved a better reward. His incisive critique helped immeasurably in focusing my ideas and sharpening my prose.

The typescript was made into a book with the care, imagination, and efficiency for which the London office of Yale University Press, under the direction of John Nicoll, has become renowned. I am most indebted to my editor, Gillian Malpass, for providing the best professional and moral support imaginable. Her colleague, Juliet Thorp, efficiently collected the photographs, a task as tiresome it is essential. Additional editorial work was expertly contributed by Brenda Gilchrist in New York.

I take pleasure in acknowledging the generous grant made by the Robert Lehman Foundation to Yale University Press in support of this publication. In particular, I thank Michael M. Thomas, who long ago urged me to write this book, and who became its advocate before the Trustees of the Foundation. Paul Guth, the Foundation counsel, was also a sympathetic supporter of the project.

Finally, I wish to express heartfelt appreciation to my friends and colleagues in Spain for their unstinting generosity and hospitality during the years that I have worked in their marvelous country. This book is meant to be a small downpayment on my enormous debt to each and every one of them.

Princeton, December 1989

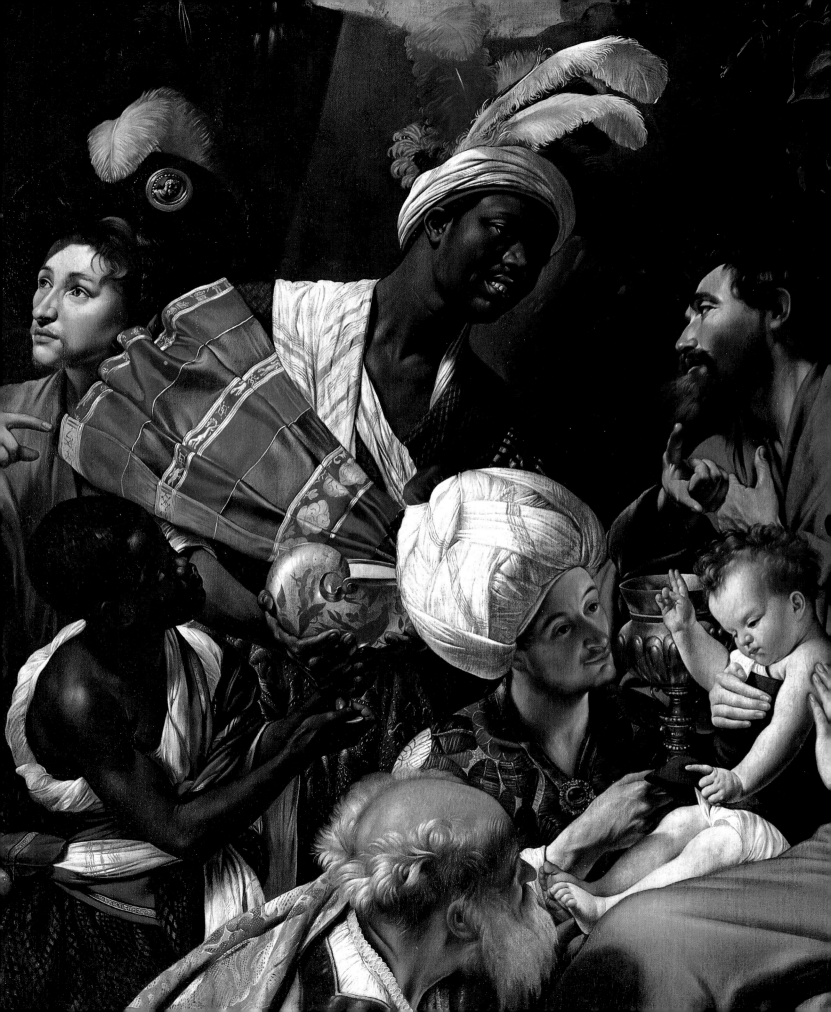

Introduction
The Frontiers of Spanish Art

THE GOLDEN AGE of painting in Spain was founded on a contradiction. In the sixteenth and seventeenth centuries, Spain was at the center of European politics and on the periphery of European art. As the leading political power for all but the last fifty years of the period, the monarchy was omnipresent and omnipotent in western Europe (and the New World). In Italy, Spanish viceroys governed the kingdoms of Naples and Sicily and the duchy of Milan and, at least for some of the time, influenced the client states of Genoa, Mantua, and Tuscany. In the north, during the sixteenth century, Spanish governors ruled over all of the Netherlands while maintaining the loyalty of the duke of Savoy. Even after the revolt of the northern Netherlands and the formation of the Dutch Republic in the later sixteenth century, Spain played a major role in the affairs of northern Europe. Spanish armies marched over the Italian peninsula and north along the Spanish Road through the Alps and up the Rhine to Flanders, as the southern Netherlands was called. Spanish diplomats were a conspicuous presence in the courts of Europe, rewarding friends and bribing enemies to protect the hegemony of His Catholic Majesty.

Spain dominated the politics of Europe, only to be dominated itself by the cultures of Italy and Flanders. The agents and ambassadors who had fanned out across Europe to defend the interests of the monarchy provided a return flow of ideas, objects, and information that made an enormous impact on those who stayed at home, artists and patrons alike. Works of art produced in other parts of Europe abounded in the Iberian peninsula, adorning palaces, country houses, and, of course, ecclesiastical institutions of every sort. Foreign artists also came to Spain, frequently in the sixteenth century, rather less frequently in the seventeenth.

These historical circumstances are self-evident, but their artistic consequences are not so patently clear, as witnessed by the fact that almost every history of Golden Age Spanish painting is confined to the study of Spanish artists. The late seventeenth-century painter Antonio Palomino knew better. His fundamental series of biographies entitled "El Parnaso español pintoresco laureado," published in 1724,[1] includes the lives of Titian, Rubens, and Luca Giordano, as well as those of Velázquez, Murillo, and Valdés Leal, despite the fact that Titian, for one, never set foot in Spain. It was obvious to Palomino, an eyewitness of the epoch, that neither these nor the other foreign artists patronized by the ruling classes could be excluded from the history of painting in his country.

Yet excluded they were, and merely on the adventitious grounds of nationality. The first serious accounts of Spanish art were written in the nineteenth century and reflected the rising importance of nationalism in contemporary political and cultural thought. Accordingly, the history of Spanish painting came to be understood as the

1. Detail of pl. 90.

1

history of Spanish painters, of those artists who had spent all or most of their lives working within what were in fact the political boundaries of the nineteenth- and twentieth-century state. Thus, it was easily forgotten that Rubens and Giordano, for example, had been subjects of the Spanish crown.

Once the political and geographical frontiers of the Spanish Habsburg monarchy are restored to their full extent, Spain's position on the periphery of artistic events becomes clearer. In this period, certain regions of Flanders and Italy were acknowledged as generative centers of the art of painting, and their connections with Spain facilitated the commerce of pictures in both the financial and the artistic sense. Waves of influence from these regions periodically washed over the country, but little was swept away with the tide (except to the American colonies). Of course, in this respect, Spain was hardly unique among the artistic regions of Europe. It could even be argued that the Spanish experience was typical, since the evolution of painting in many parts of Europe depended on the transmission and absorption of ideas and fashions from Italy. Yet if the development of painting in Spain was typical, it is by no means easily comprehensible.

The problem is bound up with a cultural bias that assigns primacy to innovation and invention. Indeed, the terms "center" and "periphery" unavoidably carry implicit qualitative connotations, which are related to another set of loaded terms – "original" and "derivative." While it would be foolish to attempt to reverse the judgmental implications of these words, much can be done to restore a sense of balance by seeking to understand the process of cultural diffusion, a process that has held little interest for historians of art. Spanish painters of the Golden Age were well acquainted with the work of artists in Italy and Flanders, although they by no means followed their examples uncritically. Choosing to retain certain qualities while rejecting others completely, they transformed what they decided was useful into a new stylistic synthesis. Spanish painting is inconceivable without Italy and Flanders, but it is not simply a regional school of Italian or Flemish art.

Spain's position as a receiver of artistic impulses from abroad imparted a distinctive rhythm to the development of its painting. The traditional view of stylistic development, which follows conventional notions of the history of Italian Renaissance and Baroque painting, is commonly understood as a coherent, progressive phenomenon based on the self-conscious pursuit of a certain set of artistic ideals. Stated schematically, Giotto inspired Masaccio who inspired Michelangelo who inspired Annibale Carracci. The irrelevance of this model for the study of Spanish painting is graphically illustrated in the works of three important artists who worked in Castile between 1500 and 1680 – Juan de Flandes (pl. 3), Juan Fernández de Navarrete (pl. 55), and Francisco de Herrera the Younger (pl. 215). It takes only a moment to see that these pictures are not connected by any cohesive set of artistic goals.

These works are characteristic of Spanish painting of the Golden Age, which evolved in an arhythmic pattern often imposed by powerful patrons, who at times almost forcibly implanted foreign ideals into the native soil. Yet these sudden shifts of style were not uniformly experienced at the same time in every part of the country. Local clients and institutions, with their own needs and traditions, could ignore or resist novelty for a while, if they eventually succumbed to the new fashions. Thus, at a given moment, and as a result of an unequal rate of diffusion and absorption of external artistic forces, there could be an astonishing variety of stylistic modes in diverse centers of the peninsula. This was especially true in the sixteenth century, when it makes more sense to speak of Catalan or Castilian or Valencian or Andalusian painting rather than Spanish painting. Even within a single region, eclecticism seemed to prevail over uniformity until about the year 1600.

The possibilities, however, were not infinite, and three broad phases of style can be discerned in the period 1474–1700. Of these, the first, which ended around 1555, is the most complex and difficult to appreciate. Within the space of a few decades, Spanish artists were confronted by a myriad of painters and paintings from Italy and the north, representing the styles now known as the Early and High Renaissance and mannerism. From the tangle of artists and styles emerged two painters of great originality, Alonso Berruguete and Pedro Machuca, both of whom were trained in central Italy in the early 1500s. However, upon their return to Spain, they shifted their activities to sculpture and architecture respectively, and only occasionally executed a work in their initial metier. Other painters of talent were active in the period, but a mere handful was able to effect a truly profound transformation of their sources.

The beginning of the second phase can be dated to 1556, when Philip II ascended the throne. Philip was an extraordinary patron and connoisseur, who had cultivated his tastes in Italy and Flanders and then set out to impose them on his Spanish subjects. Over the long years of his reign (1556–98), he imported distinguished painters from Italy and Flanders, who introduced current styles into Castile and trained a new generation of native artists. By establishing a permanent court in Madrid, the king changed the artistic map of Spain and began the process of centralization that reached its climax in the next century. Yet even his rule over the artistic dominions of Spain was not absolute. In nearby Toledo, a small group of ecclesiastics and theologians was able to support the career of El Greco, a painter who did not conform to the prevailing taste in Castile and failed to find favor with the king.

The impetus provided by Philip II opened the way for the golden age of seventeenth-century Spanish painting, which began to take shape during the reign of his son, Philip III (1598–1621). This monarch's favorite, the duke of Lerma, was the major patron at court and was especially interested in the "reform" painters of Tuscany, who provided a crucial ingredient to the formation of the powerful style of Spanish naturalism. The influence of other important Italian painters active around 1600, notably Caravaggio and Annibale Carracci, was of little consequence.

The next important development was initiated around 1630, when paintings by Peter Paul Rubens began to be collected on a large scale by Philip IV (1621–65), and these eventually provided the inspiration for a new phase of the Golden Age. By the later years of Philip's reign, a revolution in taste was underway, in which Flemish painting captured the attention of painters in Madrid and Seville, the remaining centers of major artistic activity. Until the end of the century, which brought a new dynasty to the Spanish throne and with it another radical shift of taste, the painters of Madrid and Seville found novel ways to interpret Rubens's energetic style of painting, incorporating elements from Italian artists as well.

The changes in artistic style and taste that occurred during the Golden Age may at first seem puzzling, if not arbitrary. However, beneath the confusing shifts of direction is a constant element – that of the relationship of patrons and painters. The influence of patronage on artistic production is, of course, a universal phenomenon in this period, but in Spain, as in many other regions of Europe, the patrons were not the junior partners. On the contrary, their predominance resulted from the marked difference in their and the artists' social prestige and economic power, which operated to the artists' disadvantage. The case of Philip II provides the clearest instance of the exercise of political and economic strength in the field of art. Having decided that his needs could not be satisfied by the talent available in Spain, the king commissioned works from painters in Italy and Flanders and eventually brought practitioners from those lands to his peninsular realms. At the start of his reign,

Philip employed Titian and Antonis Mor as his principal painters and later used only those Spaniards whose style had been shaped by the foreigners.

Philip is important also because he established the crown as the greatest individual source of artistic patronage. In the first half of the sixteenth century, the centers of patronage were more diffuse and tended to be located in the major institutions of the church. The archbishops of Toledo and Seville, who controlled great wealth, easily rivaled and probably outdid the rulers, Isabella the Catholic and Charles V, in the sponsorship of major artistic projects. Members of important aristocratic families, notably the several branches of the Mendoza, were patrons of the greatest magnitude, especially in the realms of sculpture and architecture.

Royal power was institutionalized by the king through the creation of a corps of royal painters. Once Philip had decided to settle in Madrid, he began to refurbish and expand the royal houses, and thus it was convenient to have a certain number of artists in place to carry out the numerous and sometimes menial tasks of pictorial decoration. The number of *pintores del rey*, or royal painters, was not fixed; it fluctuated according to the needs of the moment and the means of the purse. Similarly, the stipends and perquisites varied from case to case, which meant that time was squandered in rivalry and bickering. These frequent disputes were referred to the Committee of Works (Junta de Obras y Bosques), which had jurisdiction over the royal painters, except for the one who was first among equals, the *pintor de cámara* (painter of the privy chamber, hereafter called court painter for the sake of convenience). This privileged person belonged to a section of the household called the *furriera*, and had access to favors and rewards beyond the reach of the royal painters. Nevertheless, all the artists with royal appointments were regarded as being at the pinnacle of the profession; they had received the royal seal of approval, which established their prestige among secular and ecclesiastical patrons alike, and this allowed them to dominate the market, especially in and around Madrid.

Although individual members of the church and aristocracy never ceased to be important patrons, there is no doubt that they were surpassed by the monarchs who took a serious interest in the visual arts, notably Philip II and Philip IV. In addition, these two kings were responsible for fostering the extraordinary interest in art collecting, the significance of which has only recently been perceived. Yet even now it is apparent that the impressive collections gathered by the rulers, and also by high churchmen and aristocrats, greatly affected the development of Spanish painting.

These collections helped to broaden the horizons of Spanish painters, who traveled abroad infrequently compared with the painters of Holland, France, Flanders, and even the German states. But the interest in collecting had a still more profound impact in that it imposed limits on the thematic repertory of Spanish painters. It has often been observed that Spanish painting of the Golden Age is largely restricted to religious subjects (mostly from the New Testament), portraiture, and still life, in that order. Absent, or nearly absent, are mythological and allegorical subjects, scenes of the daily activities of every class of society, and landscapes, townscapes, and seascapes. Although such paintings abounded in Spanish collections, they had been executed in Italy and Flanders. The preference on the part of collectors for versions of these subjects by foreigners, which began to emerge in the sixteenth century, effectively reduced the demand on local painters.

Thus, the home market was confined mainly to an ecclesiastical clientele, which, as ministers and guardians of the faith, was bound to give precedence to content over form. The churchmen, especially those in the provinces, tended to be both conservative and imitative in their artistic tastes. In this way, a curious situation came to pass, whereby the advanced sector of collectors indirectly strengthened the power of the conservative sector of patrons over the artists in their employ. The evidence of this power is readily found in contracts between painters and churchmen, as, for instance, in the 1628 contract between Francisco de Zurbarán and the prior of the Merced Calzada of Seville. The decisive clause, which is replicated in many similar documents, required the painter "to make twenty-two paintings of the story of St. Peter Nolasco [pl. 145] to adorn the second cloister where the refectory is, putting in each one the figures and other things that the prior orders me to do, be they few or many."[2] As a further control, the prior provided the artist with a set of engravings of scenes of the saint's life executed in Rome a few years earlier, which was to serve as a model.

This zealous if typical example of ecclesiastical patronage helps to explain the long duration of given stylistic modes within a particular center and the markedly different rhythm of artistic evolution in various parts of the peninsula. In addition, it illustrates an important characteristic of the working procedures of Spanish painters – their extensive use of prints as compositional sources. In the last forty years, scholars have identified a multitude of prints by northern and Italian artists that were appropriated with little if any variation by painters in Spain. Furthermore, the numerous publications of artists' inventories show that a print collection was a standard component of the atelier. When painters died and their possessions had to be sold, their prints were often snapped up by their colleagues.

This practice was followed by artists all over Europe and was by no means limited to Spain. It is fair to say, however, that its frequency among Spanish artists is truly phenomenal and cannot be taken for granted. The search for an explanation begins with the obvious: prints have traditionally served as vehicles for the transmission of artistic information, a purpose that was all the more important when painters were not accustomed to travel to other lands. During the sixteenth century, Spanish artists were on the move a great deal and foreign painters often came to work in the leading centers of the peninsula. But in the next century, the traffic dropped considerably and this made the print a necessity for discovering what was happening in the world outside. The use of prints could be promoted as much by the patrons as by the painters. As mentioned, church officials, with their overriding concern for orthodoxy, seem to have regarded the print as a kind of iconographical insurance policy which guarded them against unwelcome innovations or deviations from the doctrinal norm introduced by painters purely for artistic reasons. This control over composition in the name of orthodoxy was bound to have an influence on practice, albeit a subtle one. *Invenzione*, that quality of mental agility in composition praised by Italian theorists as a sign of the great artist, is also stressed by the major writers on art of the first half of the seventeenth century, Vicente Carducho and Francisco Pacheco. In practice, however, only a few artists were given scope to demonstrate their powers of invention in composition. The point is illustrated in the careers of two of the most inventive painters, Velázquez and Ribera. Velázquez left Seville for Madrid in search of an enlightened secular patron, while Ribera explicitly refused to return from Naples to his native Spain. The positive aspect of this situation was that the close relationships between the clergy and the painters contributed much to the ability of Spanish artists to evoke with matchless power and sincerity the beliefs of the Catholic church.

The reaction of the painters to the limiting conditions of the marketplace was decidedly ambivalent. A small, but articulate, sector resented its subordinate social and economic position and the lack of reliable support from the highest levels of secular patrons, who were often less encumbered by religious and moral considerations. Eugenio Cajés, a leading painter in Madrid during the first third of the seventeenth century, gave voice to this dissatisfaction in an encounter with an unidentified Italian painter called "Pedro Antonio," who was visiting Seville and

Madrid. In a letter dated 5 May 1610 to a fellow painter in Rome, Bartolommeo Cavarozzi, this Pedro Antonio reported his impressions of artistic life in Spain:

> And what most surprised me was to see how little Spaniards esteemed their own native painters. I was also disappointed to see how two very ordinary Flemish painters, whose works were all bright colors and nothing more, had acquired a great reputation, although in our country they would not have cast a shadow.

Puzzled by this situation, he sought an explanation from Cajés, who gave this revealing answer:

> Dear Sir, there are many reasons for it, and the first is the little confidence we have in ourselves, and in particular in this profession of drawing. To those who know little of the profession, it seems as if we are not apt in it. And because there are so few intelligent people among the masses, [our talent] never comes to be known. The second cause is that all the gentlemen [*señores*] who go abroad from Spain attempt to bring back great quantities of pictures from foreign provinces, but they take nothing with them when they leave, which, if it were done, would make the value of our talents known.[3]

Here Cajés points a finger directly at the aristocratic preference for imported works of art (even while defensively impugning the taste of the collectors) and the resulting, and now well-known, indifference of the foreign markets to works by Spanish artists.

About twenty years later, a greater artist, Jusepe de Ribera, offered another perspective on the plight of Spanish painters in their society. When asked why he did not leave Naples and return to his native Spain, he is said to have replied:

> My dear friend, I have a strong impulse to go, but judging from the experience of many well-informed and truthful persons I find this drawback. During the first year, I would be received there as a great painter, but in the second year, no one would pay attention to me because when people know you are around they lose respect for you. This is confirmed because I have seen some works by excellent Spanish masters that were held in low esteem [in Spain]. Thus, I judge Spain to be a loving mother to foreigners and a very cruel stepmother to her own sons.[4]

Even the greatest painter of them all, Velázquez, encountered the same bias and had to go to extraordinary lengths to achieve the social recognition and prestige he so earnestly desired and so greatly deserved.

In the face of these prejudicial circumstances, ambitious members of the painters' community tried to raise the status of their profession through both argumentation and action. A consequence of this campaign was the creation of a formidable body of theoretical literature that centered on the struggle to raise painting to the status of a liberal art.[5] The principal treatises were written by Pacheco, Carducho, and Antonio Palomino, three painters who were versed in Italian theory and had some knowledge of the status of the artist in Italian society. In their treatises, they tried to change the climate of opinion by rehearsing the standard arguments in support of the nobility of painting: that it was an intellectual pursuit, not a manual craft; that it had been patronized and even practiced by kings, princes, and nobles; that it was a suitable and glorious adornment of a great nation.

In a more practical vein, Carducho devoted considerable energy to attempting to establish an academy of art under the patronage of the king. The earliest evidence of the plan dates to 1603, but it was not until 1624, when Carducho enlisted the support of the count-duke of Olivares, that the dream nearly became a reality. Carducho's plan was enormously ambitious: the proposed academy would not only train but also license painters, whether or not they had received the academic education. Yet just when success was at hand, the project unexpectedly foundered and sank into oblivion. Carducho offered a laconic explanation of the failure in his treatise, *Diálogos de la pintura*: "It was suspended because of certain qualities, not on the part of Painting or its partisans, but because of the opinions and particular judgments on the parts of those of the faculty (more's the pity!)."[6]

Reading between the lines of this convoluted sentence, it appears that the rigorous program of education and strict licensing procedures did not correspond to the working conditions of the majority of painters, who earned a modest living as artisans and craftsmen, producing inexpensive devotional images, restoring damaged paintings, evaluating collections, and acting as dealers in old and new works of art. The image of Velázquez standing proudly at his easel in *Las Meninas* (pl. 198) needs to be corrected by the more familiar sight of the art trade represented in José Antolínez's candid view of a picture jobber (pl. 285), flogging the works of the reticent painter in the background. An academy was not only irrelevant to these painters, it was dangerous to their interests because it threatened their right to work and the existence of the apprentice system.

Apprentice painters usually began their education around the age of twelve, following the execution of a contract with a licensed master.[7] The contract established the length of the apprenticeship – four years was the norm – and the obligations of both parties. Masters were required to give room, board, and unrestricted tutelage in the art, for which they were paid a stipulated amount by the apprentices' parents or guardians. Apprentices were to be treated as pupils, not as household servants, and were required to perform menial work only insofar as it was related to the task of painting. As they gained in proficiency and experience, apprentice painters became increasingly useful to the master, and it was not uncommon for them to become shop assistants once the contract had expired. The apprentice system may not have had a fixed curriculum, but at least it gave some control over artistic education to individual masters, control that the academy proposed to abolish. And the academy also threatened to eliminate one of the most important organisms of the painter's way of life, the artistic dynasty, in which members of a family worked together and supported the careers of the younger generation. The best-known examples are the father-and-son combinations of Vicente and Juan Maçip (called de Juanes); El Greco and Jorge Manuel Theotocopoulos; Francisco and Juan de Ribalta; Francisco and Juan de Zurbarán; and the two Francisco de Herreras. Antonio Ricci and his sons Juan and Francisco (called Rizi) span almost a century of activity in Madrid. In other instances, marriage provided the connecting link – Velázquez married the daughter of his master, Pacheco. About twenty-five years later, in 1632, his own daughter Francisca married his assistant Juan del Mazo. A more complicated family relationship linked a large group of Sevillian painters, who played a dominant role in artistic life from the late sixteenth to the late seventeenth century. This dynasty began when the daughter of Vasco Pereira married Anton Pérez. The daughter of this couple married Juan del Castillo, a major figure in Seville during the 1630s and 1640s. Castillo's relations went in all directions. He was the nephew of Pablo Legot; his second wife was a close relative of Alonso Cano; and, finally, he was a cousin by marriage of Bartolomé Murillo, who became his apprentice.

Artistic dynasties are by no means unique to Spain, which in fact produced none to equal the most famous of all, the Brueghel family in Flanders. Indeed, they are a logical by-product of the closed society of the period, which fostered clannish groupings. But when combined with an equally potent master-apprentice relationship and the generally conservative clientele, they reduced the momentum for change within the realm of art by academies or other extrinsic forces furthered. Perhaps this is why a dominant patron was required to alter the course of artistic events from above and outside the established order.

Thus, the international scope of the monarchy helped to condition the art of Spanish painters. Spanish rulers and aristocrats knew their way around the wider world of European painting and treated with major foreign artists. The energy and money thus diverted from the home market inevitably changed the conditions of local production, and it is these altered conditions that fostered the distinctive character of Spanish painting of the Golden Age.

1

The Arrival of the Renaissance
1480–1560

Castile

THE YEARS SPANNED by the reigns of Ferdinand and Isabella (1474–1516) and of their grandson, the emperor Charles V (1516–56), were years of unrivaled complexity for the art of painting in Spain.[1] In some measure, the variety and the rapid changes of styles can be explained by the lack of a permanent court. Until the queen's death in 1504, Ferdinand and Isabella traveled incessantly to establish their authority over the areas of Castile that had rejected the queen's claim to the crown and to complete the reconquest of the last Iberian lands from the Moslems of Granada. Charles V was another wanderer, but on a much grander scale. Through the dynastic marriage arranged by Ferdinand between his daughter Juana and Philip the Fair of Burgundy, Charles, their son, became heir to a European empire, the defense of which led him to travel all over the continent and even into Africa. His prolonged absences from Spain allowed the traditional centers of artistic patronage within the church to retain their power and independence.

The church, however, was far from a monolithic institution. At the summit were the archbishops and bishops, of whom some, like those of Toledo, Seville, and Burgos, had great wealth at their disposal and were able to impose their tastes on artistic projects in their dioceses, even when this meant a break with the patronage of their predecessors. The next level was occupied by distinguished churchmen, usually to be found in the ranks of the cathedral chapters. Many of these canons were well educated and well traveled and commissioned important works of art for the decoration of the mother church and its satellites. Then there were the religious orders, which blossomed in the triumphant surge of faith that followed the conquest of Granada, and which developed their own traditions of artistic patronage. The last constituent group of the church was the parish priests and heads of various educational and eleemosynary institutions, who had less money at their disposal and tended to follow the lead of the metropolitan patrons, usually with some delay. The diversity of taste among these various centers of patronage allowed an extraordinary variety of painting styles to flourish simultaneously and sometimes caused abrupt shifts of direction to occur within a single center, even within a single commission, as newly imported styles arrived from abroad in quick succession.

Perhaps the royal court would have become a more significant center of the arts had Isabella lived to a greater age, for she seems to have been the dominant figure in matters of patronage. On the other hand, her taste, although exquisite, was somewhat conservative. When the Catholic Monarchs came to the throne, the influence of Flemish art in Castile had become all-pervasive. Architects and sculptors from northern lands were directing and executing the work at the great cathedrals of

Burgos, Toledo, and Seville, and huge numbers of paintings and tapestries were continually arriving from the artistic centers of the Netherlands for Castilian clients and collectors.

Thus, when Ferdinand and Isabella began to devote part of their considerable energies and intelligence to artistic patronage, they naturally looked to the north. An early indication of their interest in painting is found in a letter of 23 December 1486 written by Ferdinand to Jerónimo González, who was being sent to Naples to explore the possibility of marriages for their son and daughter. Then, as later, proposals of dynastic alliances by marriage were facilitated by the exchange of portraits. But Ferdinand did not have a painter equal to the task and instructed González to promise delivery of the portraits as soon as a qualified painter could be found: "It would please us greatly to send portraits of our princess and most illustrious prince, which would have been sent with you were it not that we lacked such a painter here. But we will quickly order them to be painted and they will be sent."[2] It took longer than expected to find a suitable artist, but in 1492, the first Spanish-court portraitist of the modern era was appointed. He was a native of Estonia.

Michel Sittow was born in the Baltic city of Reval (the modern Tallinn) in 1468 and had gone to Bruges around 1484 to learn the art of painting.[3] There he stayed until 1491, becoming a master of the elegant chiseled style that is characteristic of the so-called Ghent-Bruges school. Sittow was in Spain by 30 March 1492, when his name first appears in the royal accounts as "Melchior Alemán," "alemán" ("German") being a catchall term applied indiscriminately by Spaniards to anyone from northern Europe, and he stayed until the death of Isabella. Not much remains of Sittow's production for the Spanish court, although presumably he was kept busy making portraits in aid of Ferdinand's diplomatic and political machinations.

By 1496, Sittow had been joined by another artist trained in the Ghent-Bruges school, who is known as Juan de Flandes (John of Flanders)[4] and is a still more shadowy figure than Sittow. The only indications of his early life are his style as a painter and the name given him in Spain, which indicates his place of origin. Even his twenty-three years in Castile are sparsely documented and known mostly through contracts and official records. He is first recorded in the payrolls of Isabella's servants in 1496, and stayed on at court until her death eight years later. Little remains of this period of activity, except for part of the magnificent work of art known as the Polyptych of Isabella the Catholic. This polyptych fully justifies the use of the term – it originally comprised forty-seven small panels (each measuring about 0.21 × 0.15 meters). Approximately twenty-seven survive, of which two were executed by Sittow. Indeed, a comparison of Sittow's *Assumption of the Virgin* (pl. 2) with Juan de Flandes's *Temptation of Christ* (pl. 3) immediately reveals their common origins in the art of Hugo van der Goes and his follower the Master of Mary of Burgundy, whose precise, delicate style of miniature painting they adapted to works in oil on panel. If any distinction is to be made between the two painters, it would rest on Flandes's extraordinary effects of light, a warm, vibrant light that is markedly different from the cooler tones used by contemporary painters in the Netherlands.

Following Isabella's death, Sittow returned to the north and plied his talents at the courts of Philip the Fair, Margaret of Austria, and Christian II of Denmark, finally returning to Reval, where he died in 1526. Juan de Flandes decided to remain in Castile, seeking commissions from ecclesiastical clients. After a brief spell in Salamanca, he attracted the attention of a major patron, Juan Rodríguez de Fonseca, the bishop of Palencia.

Fonseca belonged to a noble family, several of whose members occupied ecclesiastical dignities in the fifteenth and sixteenth centuries and became active patrons of

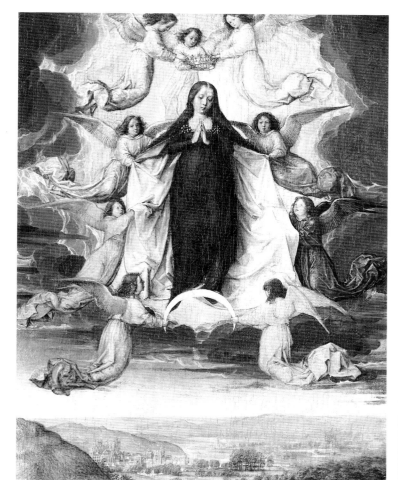

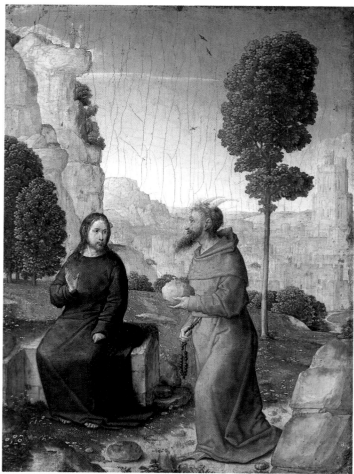

2. Michel Sittow, *Assumption of the Virgin*, ca. 1495. Washington, National Gallery of Art, Ailsa Mellon Bruce Fund (1965), panel, 0.21 × 0.16m.

3. Juan de Flandes, *Temptation of Christ*, ca. 1500. Washington, National Gallery of Art, Ailsa Mellon Bruce Fund, panel, 0.21 × 0.16m.

the arts. Bishop Fonseca, an important figure in the government of Ferdinand and Isabela, might have come to know Juan de Flandes during his prolonged stays at court. His taste for Flemish painting had already been sharpened by a trip to the Netherlands in 1505, when he was nominated to report the news of Isabella's death to Juana and Philip. Although often absent from his Palencian see, he provided funds for the decoration of the cathedral, principally for the completion of the high altar, which had been started by his predecessor.

The altar, which is still intact, is an early example of the Plateresque style and was originally intended to contain only sculpture by the Burgundian master Felipe de Vigarny. However, Fonseca decided to expand the commission with ten paintings by Juan de Flandes, who signed the contract on 19 December 1509 and completed the work a year or so before his death in 1519.[5]

The scale of the retable and distant placement of the panels required Juan de Flandes to adapt his miniaturist's technique to a larger format. *Christ Carrying the Cross* (pl. 4), for example, measures 1.16 × 1.48 meters, or five times higher and ten times wider than the panels of the Polyptych of Isabella the Catholic, but the results are equally satisfying. The firm modeling of forms and the refined, painstaking execution remain unchanged, and the figures are effortlessly enlarged to fill the more ample format. There is even a concession to the Spanish taste for evoking the real world through specific details. Near St. Veronica, who kneels at the right, is a basket of newly laundered bedsheets, twisted into a neat, spiral coil. The ploy of casting Veronica in the role of a laundress is an ingenious way to explain how she

11

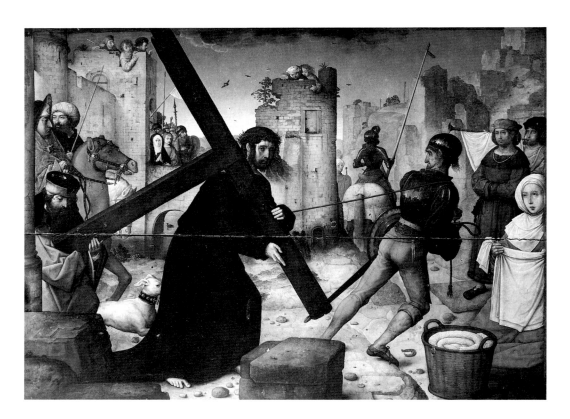

4. Juan de Flandes, *Christ Carrying the Cross*, 1509–18. Palencia, cathedral, panel, 1.16 × 1.48m.

came to have a cloth available to wipe the brow of Christ as He made his arduous way up the mount of Calvary.

For all its appeal and mastery, the style of Juan de Flandes would have been passing out of fashion in the advanced sectors of taste when the painter died. As a matter of fact, it had been superseded not once, but twice, by newer currents of influence from abroad, which were already in evidence by the time Juan de Flandes entered the queen's service. The earliest of these is represented by Pedro Berruguete, whose documented career covers no more than half his life.[6]

Berruguete probably was born in the 1450s in Paredes de Nava, a prosperous agricultural town to the north of Palencia. His early training seems to have been acquired in this region and was grounded in the Hispano-Flemish manner, a forceful, somewhat brittle Spanish interpretation of mid-fifteenth-century Netherlandish painting. As the sources indicate and his works confirm, at some point Berruguete made his way to Italy, although probably not to Urbino, as is often thought.[7] By 1483, he was once again in Spain and in the employ of the cathedral of Toledo.

Unfortunately, almost nothing survives of Berruguete's work in Toledo. However, the lessons learned in Italy are apparent in the *Beheading of the Baptist* (pl. 5), which forms part of an altarpiece in the parish church of Santa María del Campo, near Burgos. As this picture shows, Berruguete's Italian experience did not fundamentally alter the innate Flemish character of his art, which is evident in the stylized figures and faces. But the spatial illusionism of the tiled anteroom and the carefully wrought architecture of the banquet hall beyond, including, of course, the classicizing architectural details, are explained by his study of central-Italian quattrocento painting. This synthesis of Flanders and Italy formed the basis of the artist's mature style and is best seen in Avila, which was to be his base of operations from 1499 until his death in 1503.

Berruguete's principal patron in this city was the Dominican monastery of Santo

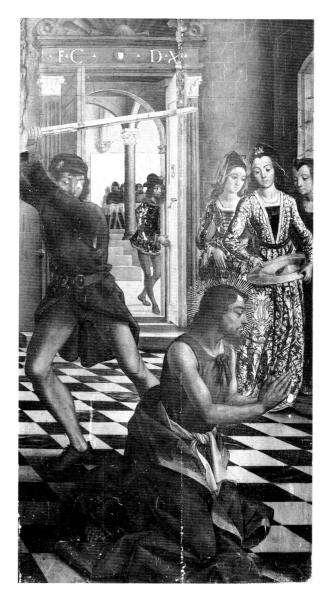

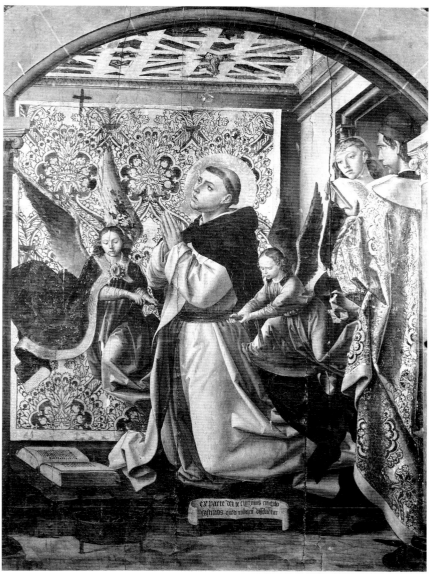

Tomás, where he created paintings for the main altarpiece, dedicated to St. Thomas Aquinas, and two subsidiary altars, dedicated to St. Peter Martyr and St. Dominic, and which contain his most Italianate works. Santo Tomás had been funded by a testamentary bequest of the royal treasurer in 1479 and constructed between the years 1482 and 1493, under the direction of Fray Tomás de Torquemada, notorious as the founder of the Castilian Inquisition. Ferdinand and Isabella were also patrons of the monastery, and eventually chose to bury their son, Prince Juan, in front of the main altar after his premature death in 1497.

The importance of the new foundation and its powerful patrons was not lost on Berruguete, and he rose to meet the challenge. The paintings in the principal altarpiece are especially sumptuous, in part because of the lavish, if somewhat anachronistic use of tooled gold backgrounds, which was probably stipulated in the contract. One of the best is the *Temptation of St. Thomas Aquinas* (pl. 6), which shows the pious man resisting the temptations of a seductress who retreats from the monastic cell through a doorway. St. Thomas's virtue is rewarded by two angels, who tie a symbolic belt around his waist, a token of his chastity.

The scene is framed by an arch, which opens into a narrow space, meticulously

5. Pedro Berruguete, *Beheading of the Baptist*, ca. 1490. Santa María del Campo, parish church, panel, 1.02 × 0.75m.

6. Pedro Berruguete, *Temptation of St. Thomas Aquinas*, ca. 1500. Avila, Santo Tomás, panel.

defined by a patterned ceiling. Yet for all the attention to perspective, the cell is too small for the occupants; there would hardly be room for the saint to stand after rising from his prayers. And the golden background cloth establishes an opaque plane that conflicts with the illusion of depth created by the ceiling. The unresolved duality of the composition is emphasized by the inclusion of naturalistic vignettes, notably the angel who braces a leg against the saint's waist in order to pull the belt as tight as possible.

The best-known picture from Santo Tomás represents St. Dominic seated in the middle of a high tribune, pardoning a heretic from death at the stake (pl. 7). For all the good intentions of glorifying the holy man, the picture now seems to be less a testimony to the mercy of the saint than an unforgettable record of Torquemada's Inquisition. The artist makes the connection with the contemporary world practically inevitable by clothing the figures in the costume of his time, although the event occurred in the thirteenth century. It is not merely this anachronism that gives the picture its power, however, but the disarmingly informal tone with which the story is presented. The execution at the right proceeds with the callous indifference of institutionalized murder. In one corner, there is a small stack of firewood standing ready to feed the blaze. A jailer sits just above the woodpile, holding a new victim by a cord around the neck, while resting his head on his hand in a gesture of boredom and stifled impatience. The inquisitors are situated high above the crowd, elevated in body if not in spirit, making idle conversation and vacantly staring into space. One of them no longer even manages to stay awake and sleeps a deep sleep, untroubled by the terrible scene that unfolds just a few feet away. Berruguete steps out of his comfortable role as the faithful painter of exemplary sacred stories and offers a bitter taste of contemporary life, expressed in the impartial but chilling prose of a chronicle.

The artist's death late in 1503 caught him in the midst of the execution of the main altarpiece of the cathedral of Avila, and after a hiatus of two years and the nomination of a successor who immediately died himself, a new artist was hired to finish the job. He was called Juan de Borgoña (John of Burgundy) and had come to Spain around 1495, when he is documented at the cathedral of Toledo.[8] As his Spanish name indicates, he was considered to be a native of Burgundy, which, to judge by his earliest known works, is quite probable. The records of Toledo cathedral archive show that Borgoña's first task was to assist Berruguete in painting the frescoes of the main cloister. Soon he was producing independent works such as the altarpiece of the Immaculate Conception, located in the chapel of this vocation, constructed in 1502. The *Annunciation* (pl. 8) offers little that could not have been derived from his Burgundian training.

Yet when Borgoña painted the same scene for the altarpiece in Avila cathedral in 1508 (pl. 9), he was obviously a different artist, one who had become conversant with central-Italian painting of around 1500. This radical transformation might best be explained by a trip to Rome, perhaps in the years 1505–6, when the artist's name disappears from the published records of Toledo cathedral[9] – a trip that converted Borgoña into an Italianate artist, particularly with respect to his understanding of perspective. Northern elements still linger in his art, notably the figure proportions and nervous, linear treatment of the drapery, and these would never entirely disappear. However, when compared with the scenes by Berruguete in the same altarpiece (pl. 10), it is clear that a new chapter in the Castilian Renaissance has begun. The immediate juxtaposition of the panels of Berruguete and Borgoña in the Avila cathedral high altar shows it happening within the confines of a single commission.

The death of Berruguete opened new possibilities for Borgoña at the cathedral of Toledo as well, where he had the good fortune to coincide with one of the great

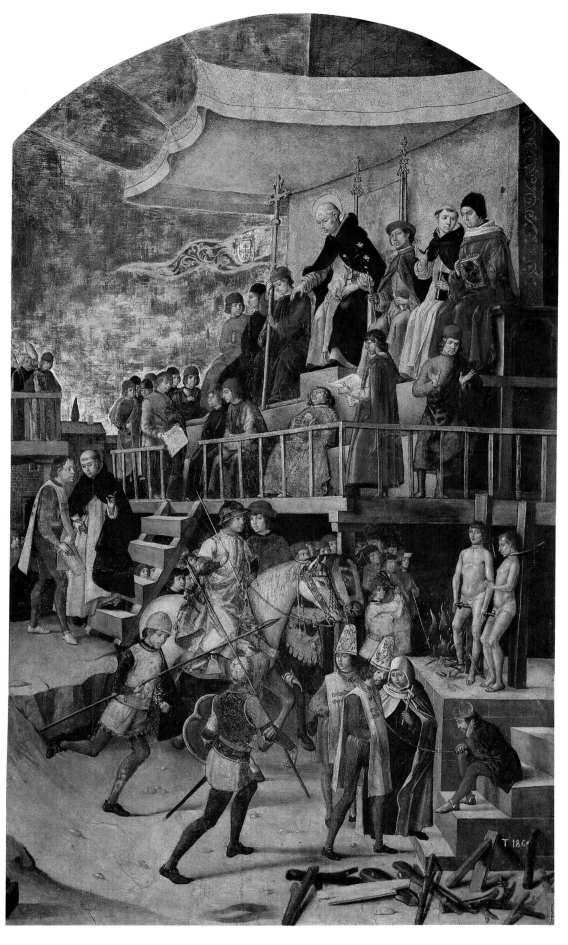

7. Pedro Berruguete, *St. Dominic Pardons a Heretic*, ca. 1500. Madrid, Prado, panel, 1.54 × 0.92m.

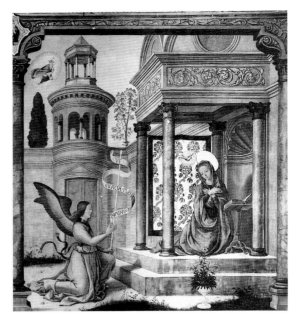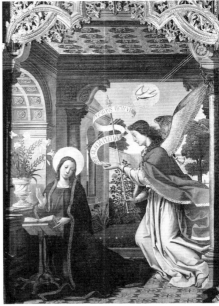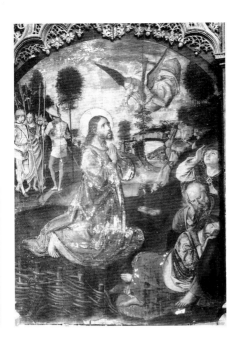

8. Juan de Borgoña, *Annunciation*, ca. 1502. Toledo, cathedral, chapter room, panel.

9. Juan de Borgoña, *Annunciation*, ca. 1506. Avila, cathedral, panel.

10. Pedro Berruguete, *Agony in the Garden*, ca. 1503. Avila, cathedral, panel.

figures of the epoch, Cardinal Francisco Jiménez de Cisneros (1436–1517). In addition to his multifarious activities as churchman and statesman, Cardinal Cisneros was a notable patron of the arts, an interest that came into play after he succeeded Cardinal Mendoza as archbishop of Toledo in 1495. It may have taken him time to discover the talents of Borgoña, in part because Berruguete was still in place as the cathedral's painter, but when at last in 1509 he offered him a commission, it was of incomparable scope and importance: the fresco decoration of the chapter room and its small antechamber.

The antechamber fresco, which is without precedent in Spain, is a purely decorative, non-figural composition made up of still life and natural elements (pl. 11), and forms part of a colorful ensemble of richly carved doorways and an elaborate gilt ceiling. An illusionistic architectural framework opens onto a vista of a lush garden of flowers and fruit trees, with birds sitting in the branches and flying overhead. Vases and urns rest on a ledge and define the foreground plane of the composition. The model for this scheme has been identified with Domenico Ghirlandaio's frescoes in Santa Maria Novella, Florence, although there the garden landscape occurs within the narrative context of the Last Supper. The difficulty in finding an exact prototype suggests that the artist converted rather than copied existing ideas from a variety of types of Italian landscape painting.

Beyond the small anteroom is the chapter room (pl. 12), which Borgoña frescoed between 1509 and 1511 with eight Marian scenes on the lateral walls and three scenes of the Passion and a large Last Judgment on the end walls. In the chapter room, the viewer enters the artistic world of late quattrocento Tuscany, although the illusionistic columns dividing the lateral compartments are crowned by a typically Toledan architectural feature called a "zapata." Many of the scenes of the Virgin's life take place within complicated classicizing architectural settings (pls. 8 and 13), although, in one instance, the nave of a Gothic church is depicted. Whatever architectural style is employed, the masterful use of perspective provides a spacious setting for the calm, controlled narration of episodes from literary sources.

The three Passion scenes, which, although separated by columns, unfold in a continuous landscape that arises and falls gently to the left, strike a mood of profound but subdued sorrow. In depicting the body of Christ in the *Descent from the Cross* (pl. 15) and the *Pietà*, Borgoña reached back to his Burgundian origins to retrieve bony,

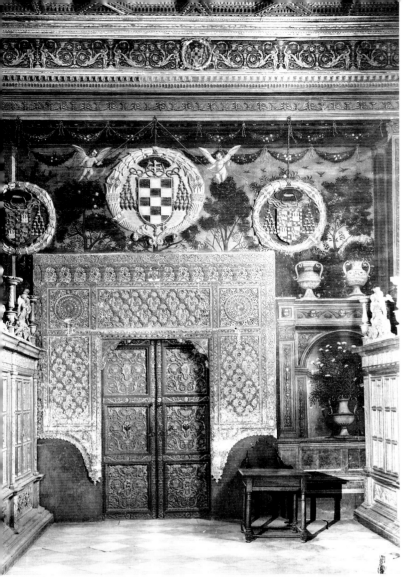 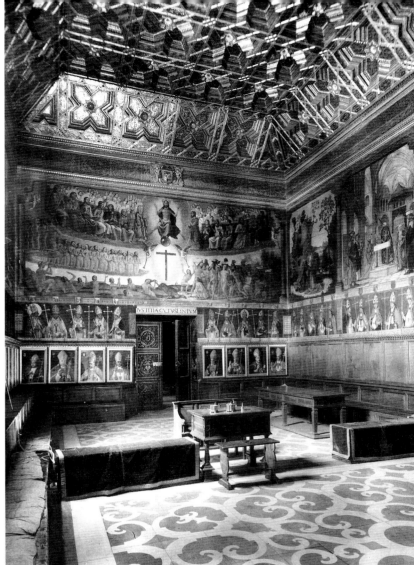

angular figure types, which succeed in evoking the viewer's pity and pain at the sight of the ultimate sacrifice.

The grand finale of the cycle is achieved in the *Last Judgment*, which spans the entire rectangular space above the entrance (pl. 14). In the upper zone sits Christ the Judge, symmetrically flanked by the Virgin Mary, St. John the Baptist, and the Apostles. Beneath the heavenly judge, the nude figures of the blessed and the damned are displayed in a composition of unremitting clarity. The damned are helpfully labeled with the names of the seven deadly sins in accord with established medieval practice, while those who are saved kneel in neatly ordered ranks, hands clasped in prayer and thanksgiving. With their garments removed and bodies uncovered, the figures can no longer hide the northern origins of their artistic creator: the smooth, lightly muscled men and the women with schematically rounded abdomens show little of the central-Italian interest in the correct rendering of anatomy. The lack of drama and pathos in the representation of this climactic moment of universal history reveals the essence of Borgoña's imperturbable style.

The frescoes in the chapter room clinched Borgoña's reputation as the leading painter in Castile, and over the next twenty-five years he established a virtual monopoly of commissions in the archdiocese of Toledo and amassed considerable wealth. Following his death in 1536, his pupils and assistants prolonged the hegemony of his style until nearly the middle of the century. Perhaps his success

11. Juan de Borgoña, antechamber of chapter room (general view), 1509. Toledo, cathedral.

12. Juan de Borgoña, chapter room (general view), 1509–11. Toledo, cathedral.

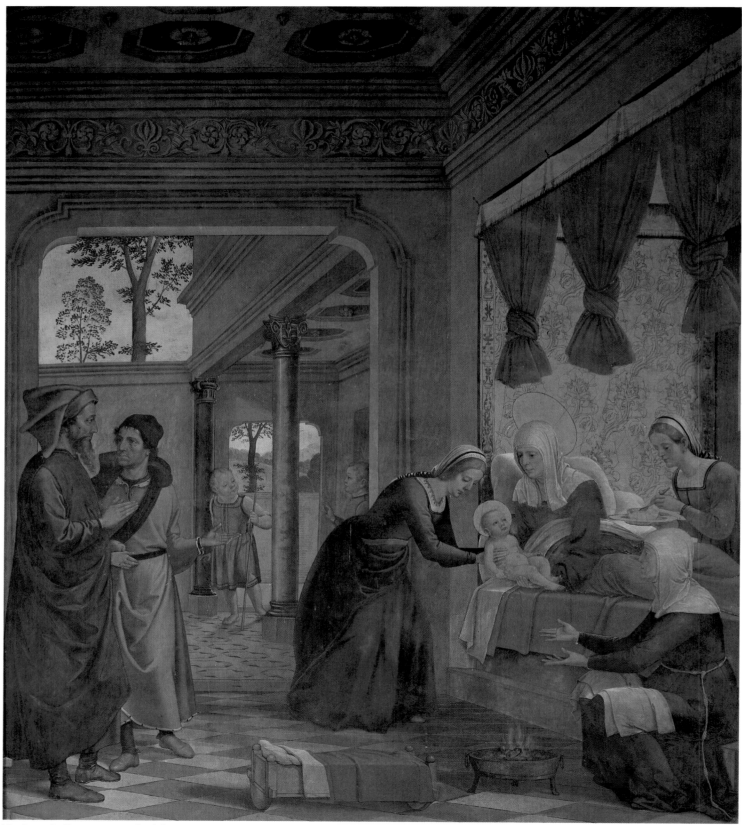

13. Juan de Borgoña, *Birth of the Virgin*, 1509–11. Toledo, cathedral, chapter room, fresco.

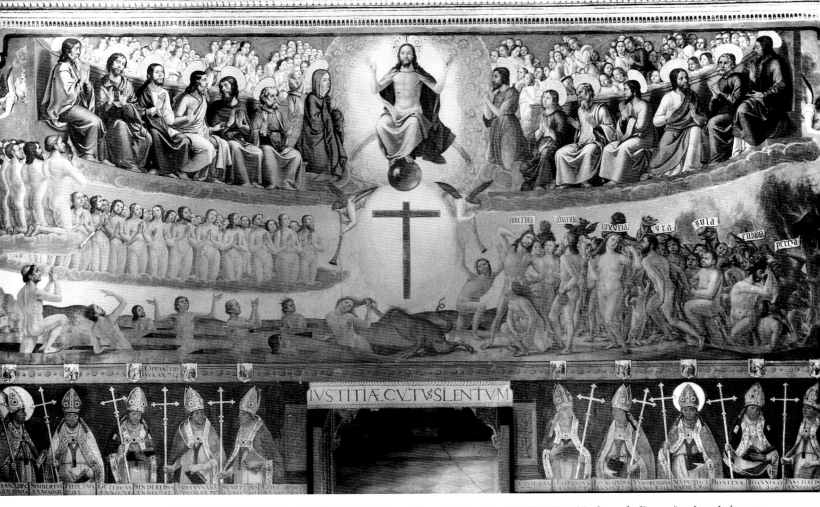

Within the Last Judgment fresco, the following inscriptions appear:

soberuia · abaricia · luxuria · yra · gula · embidia · pereza

OPPASITRVSVS·AN·714

IVSTITIÆ·CVLTVSSLENTVM

14. Juan de Borgoña, *Last Judgment*, 1509–11. Toledo, cathedral, chapter room, fresco.

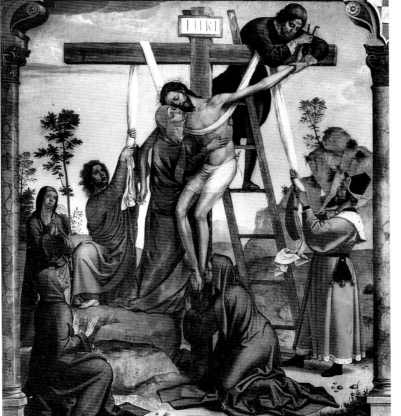

I·N·R·I

15. Juan de Borgoña, *Descent from the Cross*, 1509–11. Toledo, cathedral, chapter room, fresco.

would have been diminished during his life had not the leading practitioner of the next wave of Italian painterly style been diverted to other artistic activities. As will be seen below, however, Alonso Berruguete, who returned to Spain from Italy in 1517, eventually put his painter's brushes aside in favor of the sculptor's chisel.

Valencia

As part of the crown of Aragon, which controlled an important commercial empire in the Mediterranean, Valencia was in closer contact with Italy during the fifteenth century than was Castile. Yet prior to the last quarter of the century, the mercantile connections had little impact on artistic trade. Admittedly, knowledge of Valencian painting of this period is sketchy. Rodrigo de Osona the Elder is thought to have enjoyed a certain reputation as a painter and his few remaining works show some knowledge of North Italian painting, but he is too slight a figure to support a strong case for the influence of Italian painting in Valencia.

The lack of qualified painters in the region is indicated by the actions of the cathedral chapter following the destruction of the main chapel in 1469. Once the fabric was rebuilt, the canons started to look for a painter to create a new fresco decoration. They apparently had little faith in the local talent, because their first move was to bring to Valencia from Salamanca an Italian named Dello Delli, who died in 1471, before he was able to execute the work. However, in the following year, another Italian painter arrived and changed Valencian painting almost overnight.

The impact of Paolo da San Leocadio, as he is called, resembles developments in Castile, where a chain of stylistic continuity was broken by a painter from abroad, supported by a powerful patron. Since more is known of the circumstances that brought Paolo to Spain, the process of change in Valencia can be seen with greater clarity.

The artist was born in Reggio Emilia at an uncertain date, conventionally given as around 1445–50, and almost certainly learned his art from the Ferrarese painters Cosimo Tura, Francesco del Cossa, and Ercole Roberti.[10] The impetus to go to Spain was provided by Cardinal Rodrigo Borja (the future Pope Alexander VI), a member of a noble family of Gandía, a town near Valencia. Cardinal Borja returned to the city from Rome as papal legate in 1472 and brought with him two painters, Paolo da San Leocadio and Francesco Pagano. It may be that Cardinal Borja (or Borgia) had received an appeal from the canons of Valencia for help in finding a painter to decorate the sanctuary. In any event, this is what Paolo and Francesco agreed to do in a contract signed on 28 July 1472. Thus, through the good offices of Cardinal Borja, the Italian Renaissance landed in Valencia.

Little remains of the cathedral frescoes, which were finished in late 1481, but Paolo's style of this period can be seen not only in a signed painting of the *Virgin and Child with Saints* (pl. 16), but also in the *Virgin and Child with Sts. Benedict, Bernard, and a Donor* (pl. 17), known as the "*Virgin of the Knight of Montesa.*" The attribution of the latter picture has been debated, although the identification of the donor with Luis Despuig tends to suggest that Paolo was the author. Despuig was elected master of the Order of Montesa in 1472, which coincides with Paolo's arrival in Valencia and helps to secure the attribution, especially because no other painter in the city was capable of producing a work of such high quality. The solid sense of form and the sure control of spatial effects, if unexceptional in North Italian painting of the period, are entirely novel elements in the context of Valencian art.

Paolo seems to have stayed in the city until 1484 and then left the region, not

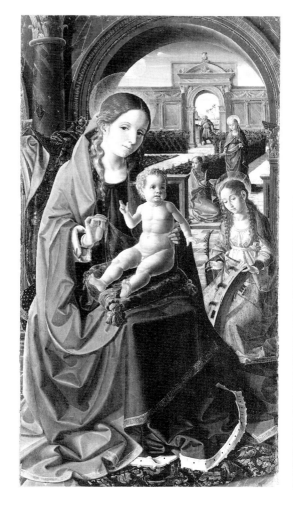

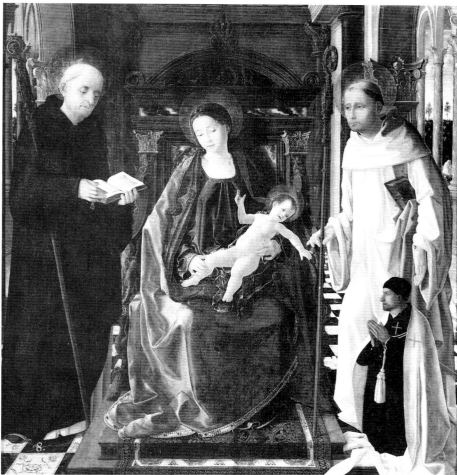

returning until 1493, when he was married in Valencia. It is assumed that he went back to Italy, although this trip is not documented. In 1501, he made a fateful decision to serve as the painter to the duchess of Gandía, the widow of a bastard son of Pope Alexander VI.[11] He moved to Gandía and stayed until 1513, executing altarpieces for local churches and convents in a style that increasingly displays conspicuous elements of Flemish painting. When he returned to Valencia, it was to discover that the arrival of yet another style had made him an anachronism. He lived until around 1520, working toward the end in the provincial town of Villareal de los Infantes and producing paintings with his workshop that are best described as rustic.

Paolo's successors, Fernando Llanos and Fernando Yáñez, also had come from Italy, although they were born in Spain, in the region of La Mancha. Llanos is listed first in the documents of their joint commissions and therefore probably was the older of the two, although the birth date of neither is known.[12] From their style, it is apparent that the two nearly homonymous Spaniards spent time in Florence and were powerfully influenced by Leonardo da Vinci, who had returned from Milan in April 1500. In fact, between 30 April and 10 August 1505, a certain "Ferrando Spagnuolo" received payments for assisting the master in the execution of the *Battle of Anghiari* in the Palazzo della Signoria. The painter in question must have been Yáñez, as proved by the recent discovery of the first known work of his Italian period (pl. 18).[13] This picture combines motifs from three compositions by Leonardo and places them against a bright landscape derived from Flemish painting, an idea found in paintings of Raphael and Fra Bartolommeo. Yáñez continued to draw on

16. Paolo da San Leocadio, *Virgin and Child with Saints*, before 1472. London, National Gallery, panel, 0.46 × 0.26m.

17. Paolo da San Leocadio, *Virgin and Child with Sts. Benedict, Bernard, and a Donor*, 1472–82. Madrid, Prado, panel, 1.02 × 0.96m.

Leonardo's vocabulary for the rest of his career, re-using motifs such as the extended, foreshortened hand of the Virgin until they became clichés.

Llanos was equally receptive to Leonardo's art, but was able to interpret it with greater force and imagination. Once established in Spain, the two "Fernandos" would lead Valencian painting through a rapid transition from the Emilian quattrocento to the Tuscan High Renaissance. Indeed, Yáñez and Llanos were the first non-Italian painters to assimilate the style of the High Renaissance and practice it in a foreign land.

Although the motives for their return to Spain remain enigmatic, Llanos and Yáñez are first mentioned in Valencia in a document of 1506, receiving payments for an altarpiece in the chapel of Sts. Cosmas and Damian (now dedicated to St. Catherine) in the cathedral. Early in the next year, on 1 March 1507, they contracted for the work that is indisputably their masterpiece. This is a series of twelve panel paintings that serve as shutters for the altarpiece of the cathedral sanctuary. The altar is dedicated to the Virgin Mary; thus, six exterior panels represent all but one of the Seven Joys of the Virgin, while the six interior panels depict scenes from her life.

The division of labor for these large panels (each measuring about 1.94 × 2.27 meters) although not specified in the contract, is fairly easy to determine because the two painters were not possessed of equal gifts. Llanos, the greater and more eclectic artist, complemented his knowledge of da Vinci with the study of other Florentine and even Venetian painters, while Yáñez remained the faithful disciple of Leonardo. For instance, his *Rest on the Flight into Egypt* (pl. 19) recycles the exact pose of the Virgin and Child in his Florentine *Holy Family*. Judging by his other paintings for the sanctuary, he is also less inventive in his compositions and weaker in his handling of forms than his senior partner.

The influence of Leonardo on both artists is evident in the distinctive facial and figure types. Da Vinci's famous sfumato, or soft shadow, is another important characteristic that the Spaniards imitated. However, each painter interpreted Leonardo's lessons in markedly different ways, as seen in a comparison of two similar compositions, the *Birth of the Virgin* by Yáñez (pl. 21) and the *Death of the Virgin* by Llanos (pl. 22). Yáñez places the scene in a broken, fragmented setting that verges on the incoherent and terminates at the far right in a distant view of two large arched but totally unrelated structures. The foreground figures seem somewhat limply drawn and are arranged in a gently swaying, slightly unstable rhythm, a hallmark of his style.

Llanos owes both more and less to Leonardo. He has appropriated, of course, the figure types, but also seems to have been aware of Leonardo's fascination with the grotesque and unusual. The apostle hunched over a book at the lower right could be derived from one of Leonardo's study sheets of people with idiosyncratic features. Yet the insistent monumentality of the architectural and human forms brings Llanos closer to the earlier works of Andrea del Sarto and Fra Bartolommeo, which, in fact, he anticipates. Compared with Yáñez's picture, his is severe and controlled. The architectural background takes the form of a triple arch, utterly devoid of ornamentation, which opens at the center to a view of the Virgin and the Apostle Thomas. In front of the arch, large-scale figures are consumed by grief. Most eloquent is the figure of St. John, who is seated on a carefully chiseled block of stone, holding his head in his hand as if wiping the tears from his eyes. Although his face is concealed, the depth of his feeling is unmistakable.

In Llanos's *Presentation of the Virgin* (pl. 20), the architecture becomes a protagonist of the composition, and fills the space with its eccentric design of shifting levels and focal points. According to apocryphal histories of the Virgin's life, she was taken to the temple prior to her fourth birthday. As she ascended the fifteen steps at the

18. Fernando Yáñez de la Almedina, *Madonna and Child with Infant St. John*, ca. 1505. Washington, National Gallery of Art, Samuel H. Kress Collection, panel, 0.78 × 0.64m.

22

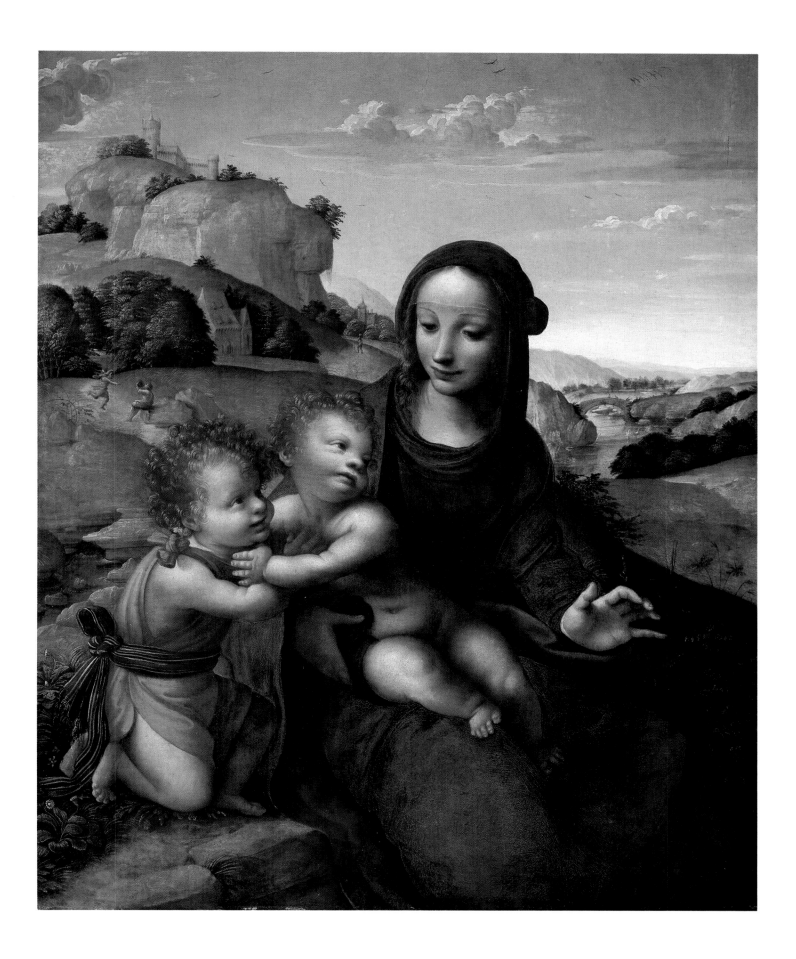

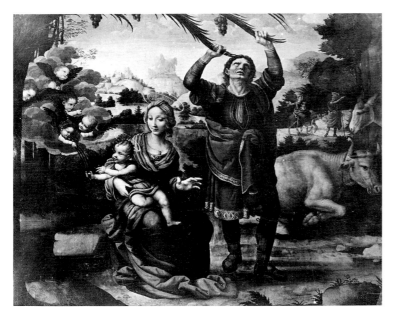
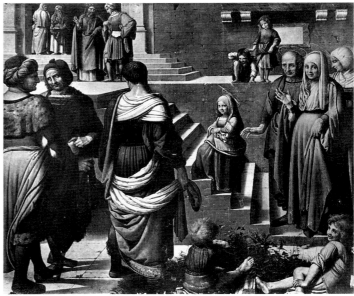

19. Fernando Yáñez de la Almedina, *Rest on the Flight into Egypt*, 1507–10. Valencia, cathedral, panel, 1.94 × 2.27m.

20. Fernando Llanos, *Presentation of the Virgin*, 1507–10. Valencia, cathedral, panel, 1.94 × 2.27m.

entrance, she miraculously recited from memory the fifteen psalms of David, while all present watched in amazement. The peculiar stepped composition is therefore motivated in part by iconographical considerations,[14] but at the same time shows that, even at this early date, Llanos was beginning to understand how the classical style of Renaissance painting could be used in strangely expressive ways.

After the completion of the altar shutters later in 1510, the two painters ended their collaboration, but they continued to share lodgings until 1513. Thereafter they drifted apart and entered a period of decline. Llanos eventually settled in Murcia and painted diluted versions of his early manner. Yáñez went to Barcelona for a while, but returned to Valencia where he stayed until around 1523. On 17 March 1525, he is documented in Cuenca, working for the canon Gómez Carrillo de Albornoz on the decoration of his family chapel in the cathedral, which was finished in 1531.[15] In these final, ghostly paintings, he regained his momentum and, although continuing to repeat the poses and gestures of Leonardo, liberated the dark, discordant emotions being unleashed at just this time by Pontormo and Rosso Fiorentino.

Catalonia

Up the coast from Valencia, in the principality of Catalonia, Italian Renaissance painting was establishing another beachhead. Catalonia was the most important region of the kingdom of Aragon, which during the fourteenth century had been a prosperous Mediterranean state. During the fifteenth century, however, Aragonese power began to decline, reduced by plague, agrarian unrest, and civil war, and by the middle of the century, the Catalan economy was showing serious signs of weakness as well. Catalonia, like Valencia, its junior partner in the crown of Aragon, was oriented toward the east and especially toward Italy, where it controlled the kingdom of Naples and Sicily. These commercial and political connections opened the principality and its two major artistic centers, Barcelona and Gerona, to the influence of Italian painting.

Although elements of Italian Renaissance painting had started to filter into Catalonia by 1500, the first painter to demonstrate a fuller mastery of the style is Pedro Fernández, who until recently was known to art historians as "Pseudo Bramantino."[16] He was born in Murcia, perhaps around 1480, and by about 1500 or

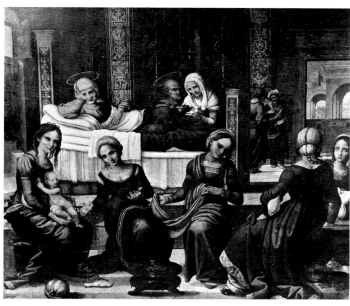

21. Fernando Yáñez de la Almedina,
Birth of the Virgin, 1507–10. Valencia,
cathedral, panel, 1.94 × 2.27m.

22. Fernando Llanos, *Death of the
Virgin*, 1507–10. Valencia, cathedral,
panel, 1.94 × 2.27m.

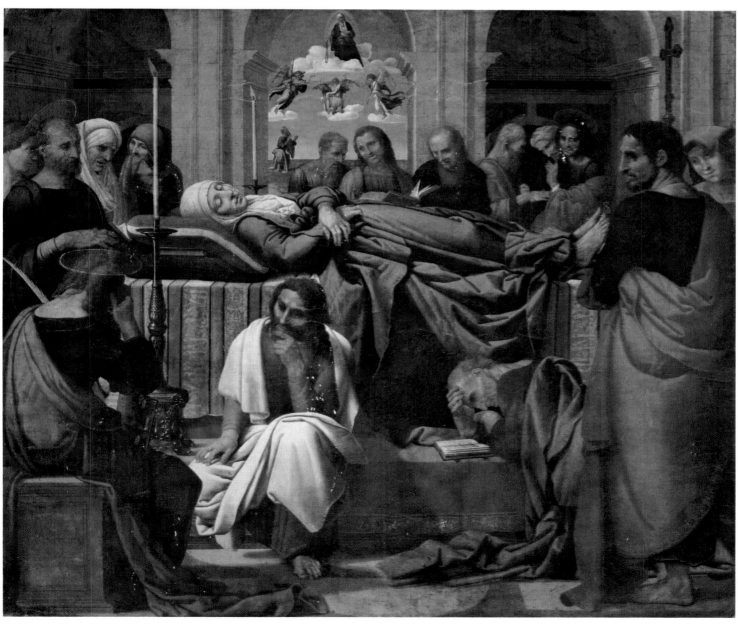

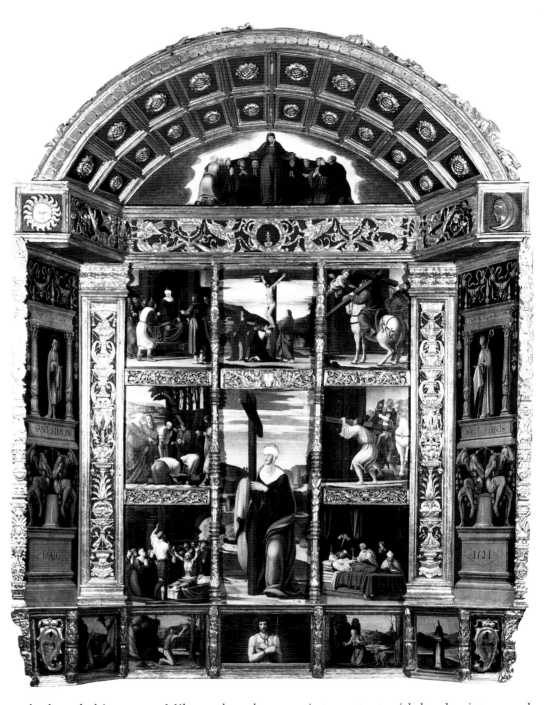

23. Pedro Fernández, altarpiece of St. Helen, 1519–21. Gerona, cathedral.

so had made his way to Milan, where he came into contact with local painters such as Bramantino and Andrea Solario, who were followers of Bramante and Leonardo respectively. Fernández, who seems to have received his early training from a Flemish or Hispano-Flemish artist, absorbed and transformed these powerful impulses into a linear, brittle Italianate style that is entirely distinctive and strangely beautiful. From Lombardy he went south to Rome, and then to Naples, where he was active from 1508 to 1512 and became a leading artist of the city. Over the next half dozen years, he lived in Rome and again in Naples, finally returning to northern Italy by around 1518.

In the following year, Fernández was once more on Spanish soil, executing an altarpiece dedicated to St. Helen in the cathedral of Gerona, in collaboration with a

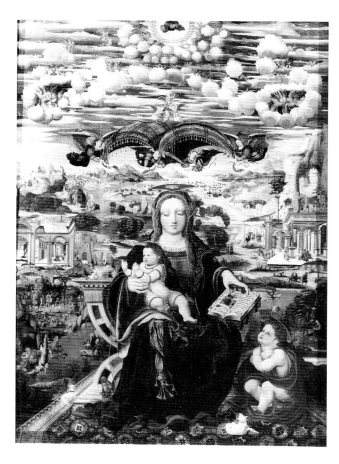

24. Joan de Burgunya, *Virgin and Child with St. John in a Landscape*, ca. 1520. Barcelona, Museo de Arte de Cataluña, panel, 1.81 × 1.27m.

local painter (pl. 23).[17] The panels for this altarpiece show a somewhat attenuated version of the artist's Italian manner; the figures are taller and thinner, the handling of the drapery has gone somewhat flaccid, and the strange, pinched facial types have become normalized. In their totality, the paintings nevertheless reveal the idiosyncratic interpretation of Italian art that is characteristic of Spanish artists in this period, which will be commented on below. After the completion of this work in 1521, Fernández disappears from view.

His most important follower was Joan de Burgunya (his name is given in Catalan to distinguish him from Juan de Borgoña), a native of Strasbourg who was active in Barcelona, Gerona, and Valencia from 1510 to around 1525 and is a true artistic magpie.[18] A representative painting is the *Virgin and Child with St. John in a Landscape* (pl. 24), a remarkable amalgamation of compositional motifs from Albrecht Dürer and Marcantonio Raimondi, and of stylistic sources from Flemish and Italian painting. It is as heterogeneous a picture as can be found anywhere in Europe at this time.

For all their diversity, the early sixteenth-century painters of Castile and Aragon adopted a common attitude toward Italian painting, which they understood more as a repository of motifs and ideas than as a coherent, self-conscious system of artistic values. As outsiders to this system, they felt free to pick and choose elements that seemed attractive, refashioning them so they could be understood by Spanish patrons. Quotations from classical architecture did not have to be archaeologically correct when used purely for decorative purposes. The rules of perspective could be loosely interpreted to create an impression of spaciousness but not to control the proportions of the figures. In other words, the Spanish painters of this period understood the classical style as an option, not as an imperative. Working on the interface between two artistic cultures – the Hispano-Flemish and the Italian – they produced an original synthesis of the two that renovated the surface of the existing style without disturbing its expressive core.

Seville

The evolution of painting in Seville in the early fifteenth century was considerably less dynamic than in Castile, Valencia, and Catalonia. In 1508, Alejo Fernández settled in Seville and for the next thirty-seven years was almost unchallenged as the pre-eminent master.[19]

Although his origins are uncertain, it appears that the painter's father was from northern Europe and his mother, from Spain. Whether Alejo was born in the north or in Córdoba (the date would be around 1475) is equally unclear. On a few occasions, he is referred to by that catchall term, "alemán," suggesting that his Spanish contemporaries considered him to be of foreign stock. Certainly, the evidence of his style points in that direction, for there was little novelty to be found among the late-Gothic painters who were working in Córdoba and Seville in the final decades of the fifteenth century. To them, it must have seemed that Fernández had indeed come from another world.

The first known paintings by Fernández, who had taken his wife's last name, indicate his familiarity with Italian as well as Flemish art. In the *Last Supper* (pl. 26), the central panel of a triptych thought to have been painted in Córdoba, the architectural setting is a competent exercise in linear perspective, and the architecture, too, is thoroughly Italianate. Yet the figures could only have been painted by an artist trained in the Netherlands and acquainted with the work of Quentin Metsys.

In 1508, Fernández was called to Seville by the cathedral chapter to execute paintings for the rood beam of the main chapel. This commission, of which four panels exist, immediately established his reputation, although in the wider context of Italian and Netherlandish art the style is quite conservative. The *Adoration of the Magi* (pl. 25) in fact is based on a print by Martin Schongauer, the first of hundreds of paintings by Sevillian masters of the Golden Age to rely on northern prints for their compositional sources. In this picture, the use of gold in the drapery and the rich colors are combined with refined drawing and competent perspective, an amalgamation that would have satisfied the taste of the canons for art at once novel and familiar.

An exceptional work is the so-called *Virgin of the Navigators* (pl. 27), one of the few paintings that reflect the Spanish conquest of America. It is curious that the eventful history of the conquest and the subsequent colonization of the New World were largely ignored by the leading Spanish painters and their patrons. There are no great portraits of the *conquistadores* and navigators, and few representations of their remarkable achievements. The absence of such paintings is even more noteworthy in Seville, which since 1503 had been the seat of the House of Trade (Casa de Contratación), the body that governed commerce with the New World. There is no satisfactory explanation of this phenomenon, especially since the events of the exploration and conquest were reported in numerous publications by Spanish writers.

Fernández's picture was created for an altarpiece in the chapel of the Casa de Contratación, probably in the 1530s, and is derived from a devotional image known as the Madonna of Mercy, in which the Virgin protects the faithful under the ample folds of her mantle. In the lower part of the work, the small ships of the Indies fleet

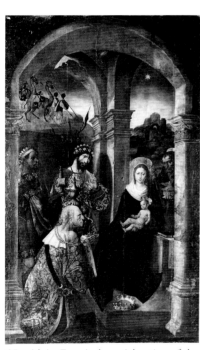

25. Alejo Fernández, *Adoration of the Magi*, 1508. Seville, cathedral, panel, 2.97 × 1.75m.

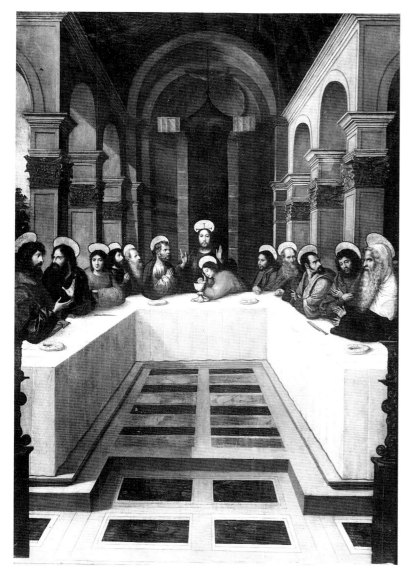

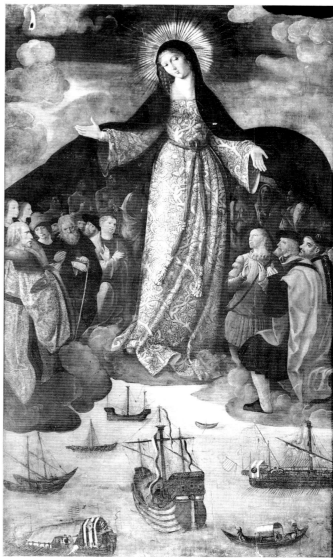

lie at anchor, waiting for the navigators to embark after receiving the blessing. Although the seamen appear to be specific individuals, none has been securely identified.

Fernández's unrivaled prestige ensured the domination of his style until a few years before he died in 1545, thirty-seven years after settling in Seville. In some ways, his monopoly of the marketplace resembles the position of Juan de Borgoña, whose manner of painting remained in vogue in Toledo until at least the middle of the century. After a period of rapid change and frequent innovation that began in the 1480s and lasted until about 1520, the art of painting in Castile was becalmed. This turn of events is partly explained by a lost generation of painters who might be called the "missing mannerists."

26. Alejo Fernández, *Last Supper*, ca. 1505. Zaragoza, El Pilar, panel.

27. Alejo Fernández, *Virgin of the Navigators*, 1530–40. Seville, Alcázar.

The "Missing Mannerists"

Alonso Berruguete and Pedro Machuca were two artists of remarkable originality who resided in central Italy during the critical years when the mannerist style was

29

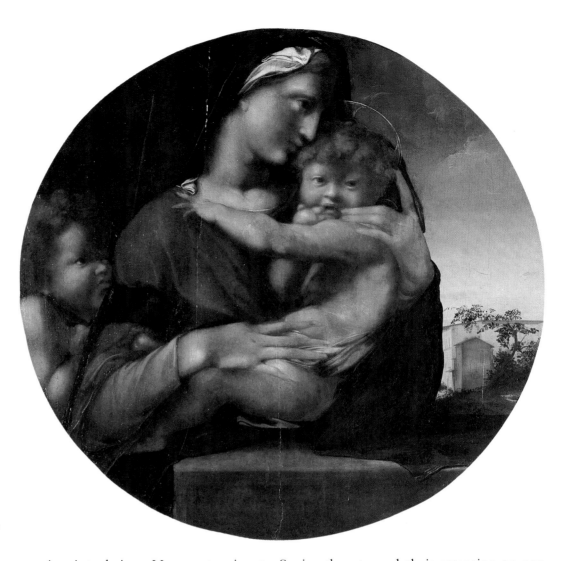

28. Alonso Berruguete, *Madonna and Child with the Young St. John*, 1510–15. Florence, Palazzo Vecchio, panel.

coming into being. Upon returning to Spain, they turned their attention to one of the sister arts – for Berruguete it was sculpture, for Machuca, architecture – although both continued to execute pictures from time to time. As will be seen, the diversion of their energies away from painting had profound consequences for the younger generation of Castilian painters, who were deprived of knowledge of the latest Italian style by the defection of their logical masters.

Alonso, the son of Pedro Berruguete, was born in Paredes de Nava around 1485.[20] Presumably his father provided Alonso's initial training as a painter and encouraged him to go to Italy, where he must have spent a good ten years, probably leaving Castile soon after his father's death in 1503. Little is know of Berruguete's activities in Italy, although it is clear that the experience was decisive for his art. According to Vasari, he was in Rome around 1507 and made a copy of the antique sculpture group *Laocoon and His Sons*, which had been discovered a year before. It is generally accepted that he is the person mentioned in two letters written by Michelangelo in the summer of 1508 requesting that a young Spaniard be allowed to study the cartoons for the *Battle of Cascina* in Florence. Berruguete was again in Florence in 1512 when Michelangelo, now mentioning his first name, made inquiries about his health on behalf of a Spaniard in Rome. By 1518, the painter had returned to Castile to commence his career as an independent artist.

Many pictures have been attributed to Berruguete's Italian period and much has been claimed for them.[21] These claims, which situate the artist in the vanguard of early mannerism, are often supported by the questionable attribution of eccentric, unclassical paintings, which seem to lack true stylistic unity. One of the plausible candidates for his authorship is a tondo of the *Madonna and Child with the Young St. John* (pl. 28), which both reflects and distorts the style of Michelangelo. The intimate embrace of the two figures and the ambiguous gesture of the Child, who places a finger in the side of His mouth, are characteristic of the unstable world of early Florentine mannerism. Without knowing the exact date of this picture or more about his life in this crucial period, Berruguete can be regarded only as a supporting player in the unfolding drama of mannerism.

Upon his return to Spain, Berruguete established two goals: one was to be an important painter, the other was to be an important person. During the next ten years, he struggled to achieve these ambitions, and strangely had more success with the latter than the former. While in Florence and Rome, Berruguete had been impressed not only by the works of the leading artists but also by their way of life, and in particular by how the best of them were improving their position in society. These artists, and to some extent their patrons, were coming to regard painting as an intellectual activity, a notion that was far from being accepted in Spain in the early sixteenth century and that would in fact be a point of contention throughout the Golden Age.

Berruguete did not have many illusions about gaining recognition simply by producing superior works of art. To be sure, he had a high opinion of his own achievements and must have been the first Spanish artist to promote himself without modesty. In a letter of 1532 written to a colleague, Andrés de Nájera, he announced with pride the completion of one of his masterpieces, the grandiose altarpiece for the monastery of San Benito in Valladolid:

> Sir, I have completed this work for San Benito. The altarpiece is installed and with such perfection that I am very content. And I know well that when you see it, you will be very pleased because although you have seen the good things that are in Spain, this is such that you will see how great the difference is.[22]

(Nájera, by the way, was unmoved by the statement and, as the evaluator for the monastery, strongly criticized the piece.)

These are brave words indeed, but Berruguete was not foolish enough to rely on words alone. He knew that society valued wealth more than talent and thus set out to make himself rich. In 1523, he obtained the appointment of clerk of the criminal court in Valladolid, which provided him with a guaranteed annual income. Although the job had serious responsibilities, Berruguete treated it as a sinecure, causing endless, bitter quarrels with the officers of the court. Three years later, he married into a prosperous merchant family and eventually accumulated enough money to purchase a small seigneury near Valladolid. Thus, in 1542, he became the lord of Villatoque, where he maintained a country house until 1557, when a financial reversal forced him to relinquish the property. Two years later, his finances restored, he purchased Ventosa de la Cuesta, where he reigned until his death in 1561.

Berruguete's career as a painter was not to be so successful, although it began brilliantly enough. His return from Italy coincided with the first visit of Charles V to Castile, and Berruguete was somehow able to obtain the appointment of royal painter, a title that promised more than it delivered. Almost at once, he was given the substantial commission to decorate the Capilla Real in Granada, the funerary chapel of Ferdinand and Isabella. Yet in 1526, the details of the commission were still not resolved, and Berruguete, tired of being a frustrated royal painter, decided to turn to sculpture.

Behind this decision lay two considerations. Charles V was often absent from Spain, which left Berruguete as a royal painter without a court. The alternative clientele was ecclesiastical, but in Castile the major church decorations, in keeping with late medieval practice, were sculptural, not pictorial. Painted altarpieces were commissioned, of course, but only when the patron was not able to afford sculpture. These market conditions compelled Berruguete to turn from painting to sculpture.

In the long run, this decision had important consequences for the evolution of painting in Castile. Berruguete was the obvious leader of the next generation of painters, and his retreat into the art of sculpture eliminated a potent source of change. Although he was not without some influence on younger painters such as Juan de Villoldo (active 1548–70), the probable author of several pictures ascribed to Berruguete's Italian period, and Cristóbal Herrera (documented in 1544), these artists worked in the towns and villages of old Castile, not the major centers, and never entered the artistic mainstream, which continued to be occupied by the school of Juan de Borgoña.

Berruguete's change of vocation did not mean that he became a full-time sculptor. For one thing, he continued to make paintings for altarpieces in which the two media were combined. Moreover, Berruguete's sculptural work was entirely two-dimensional and thus conceived pictorially. It is even possible that he participated only in the design and did little of the actual carving.[23] For this reason, it is legitimate to include both paintings and relief sculpture in a consideration of his powerful but unconventional style.

29. Alonso Berruguete, *Adoration of the Magi*, 1526–32. Valladolid, Museo Nacional de Escultura, wood relief, 1.34 × 1.06m.

30. Alonso Berruguete, *Nativity*, 1526–32. Valladolid, Museo Nacional de Escultura, panel, 1.44 × 0.98m.

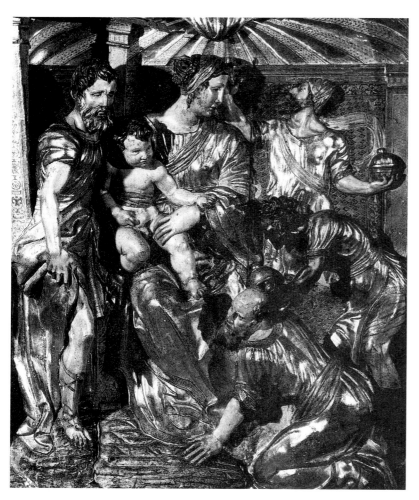

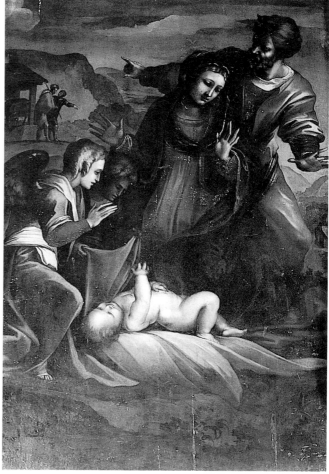

Once back from Italy, Berruguete broke free of the constraints of the classical Renaissance style and let his imagination run free. In assessing his sculpture, however, it must be remembered that it was made to be seen in the context of an altarpiece placed at a considerable distance and height from the viewer and subject to varied and often marginal conditions of light. Before Berruguete, sculptors tended to ignore these conditions and fabricate retables as if they were readily accessible to the worshipper. The result was often magnificent but invariably static. Berruguete's idea was to generate the sensation of ceaseless, pulsating movement, which he did by exaggerating the contorted figural canon of the mannerist style to an unprecedented degree, compromising and even abolishing the rational space of linear perspective and making it secondary to the volume of the figures. In his hands, the sacred drama of Christian history acquires an overpowering sense of urgency and emotion, as if the actors were in a headlong rush for salvation.

The *Adoration of the Magi* (pl. 29), one of the reliefs from the San Benito altarpiece, offers a restrained version of Berruguete's agitated style. The Madonna and Child, as the most important figures, fill the crowded central space and are modeled in a way that is faintly evocative of classical sculpture. To the left, and rendered in a smaller scale, the figure of St. Joseph is wedged against the frame; inexplicably he raises his garment to reveal a leg. The three kings are ranged along the other side, one on top of the other, schematically carved and greatly reduced in size. The figure in the background, executed in low relief, is strangely animated. He looks upward, his body represented frontally, his head in profile. In one hand he holds a jar of incense, which he appears about to launch like a projectile into space.

Berruguete's art achieves even greater distortions of space and scale in the more pliant medium of painting. In the *Nativity* (pl. 30), also part of the San Benito altarpiece, the flattened, dematerialized figure of the Virgin makes a gesture of surprise, while St. Joseph motions dramatically to the background where the shepherds stand in waiting. The Christ Child lies in front of them, His head thrown back, raising an arm as if appealing to His mother for help. In this novel, imaginative interpretation of the Gospel, the arrival of the Savior on earth arouses frenzied, almost overwhelming excitement.

The career of Pedro Machuca in some ways resembles that of Berruguete.[24] He was from Toledo and worked in central Italy during the 1510s. Berruguete had returned to Spain in 1517; Machuca had come back by 1520; and both transformed their experience of Italian painting into highly personal forms of expression. At first, Machuca worked exclusively as a painter in Jaén and Granada, where he settled. Subsequently he came into contact with Luis Hurtado de Mendoza, marquis of Mondéjar and governor of the Alhambra, who in 1520 appointed the artist to the regiment of light cavalry quartered in the grounds of the palace. A more transcendental appointment came in the years following 1526, when Charles V decided to build a palace on the Alhambra, which was to be designed and supervised by Machuca. From then until his death in 1550, Machuca devoted himself principally to the construction of that extraordinary monument of Renaissance architecture.[25] Nevertheless, he kept up the practice of painting, accepting commissions for the altarpieces of village churches in the region. The few surviving examples of his later work indicate that he often left the execution to his assistants.

Machuca's style as painter and architect leaves no doubt that he had lived in Rome. The key picture for understanding his artistic origins is the *Virgin of Souls in Purgatory* (pl. 31), which is signed and dated on the verso: PETRUS MACHUCA HISPANUS TOLETANUS FACIEBAT A.D. MCCCXVII, and was therefore done while he was still in Italy. The subject, which is rare in Spanish art, is the Virgin offering the milk from her breast to assuage the suffering of the souls in Purgatory. This picture demon-

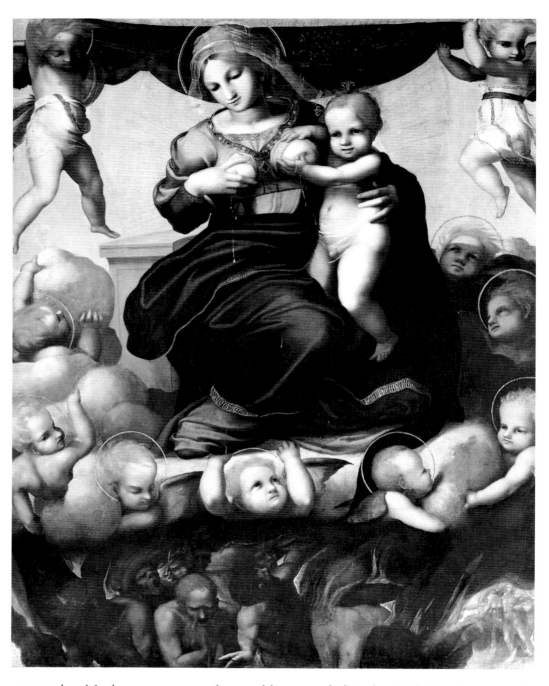

31. Pedro Machuca, *Virgin of Souls in Purgatory*, 1517. Madrid, Prado, panel, 1.67 × 1.35m.

strates that Machuca was more thoroughly grounded in the High Renaissance style than Berruguete; it has even been hypothesized that he was a member of Raphael's workshop and participated in the decoration of the Vatican loggias.[26] Yet some parts of the picture, notably the distorted, dancing putto in the upper right, prove that Renaissance classicism was like a second language to Machuca rather than his native tongue. Thus, once back in Spain, he gradually lost his foreign accent and, as in the case of Berruguete, produced exotic, hybrid paintings that place a higher value on expression than on correctness.

In the *Deposition* (pl. 32), thought to have been painted in the early 1520s,[27] the Italian veneer is starting to wear thin, as the figures grow flatter, their anatomy, more schematic. At the same time, the facial expressions are more intense, as in the center group, where St. Mary Magdalene, waiting to receive Christ's body, and the man at the foot of the cross, who holds the corpse, open their mouths wide, emitting

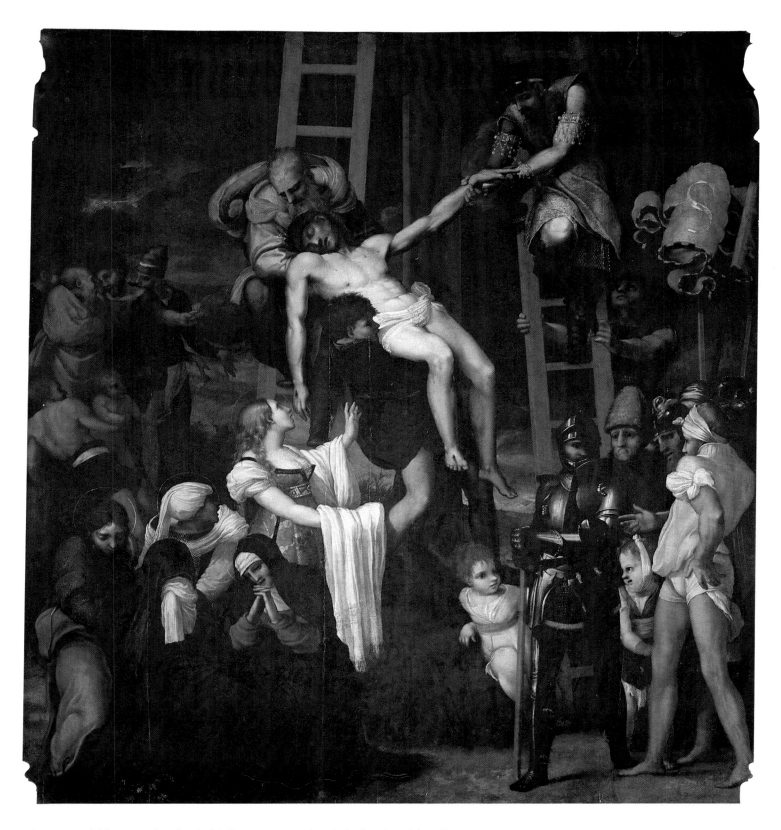

almost audible sounds of grief. The group at the right is a jumble of strange types – a soldier in full armor, an old man in a tall fur hat with a conspicuous grimace on his face, a youth in short pants, standing self-consciously with a hand on his hip. Under the dark, midnight sky, the scene of death acquires a peculiar intensity.

Perhaps the paintings of Machuca and Berruguete would have been inimitable

32. Pedro Machuca, *Deposition*, 1520–25. Madrid, Prado, panel, 1.41 × 1.28m.

after all, even if their authors had not turned to other arts – too personal and complex to offer inspiration to those of lesser talent. Be that as it may, they provide another instructive example of how Spanish painters in this period devised their personal construction of Italian sources, in this instance seizing upon the eccentric expressionism of early mannerism and carrying it to extremes of distortion that were never attained in Italy itself.

Art and Empire

Of equal importance for the development of Spanish painting in the early sixteenth century were the dynastic marriages between the princes of Spain and the house of Habsburg. In the successive years of 1496–97, the infante Juan, the only son of Ferdinand and Isabella, married Margaret of Austria, daughter of Maximilian I and Mary of Habsburg, while the Catholic Monarchs' daughter Juana married the Habsburg's son, Archduke Philip. Neither marriage was fated to last long: the infante Juan died a mere seven months after the ceremony; Philip the Fair survived until 1506, long enough to become the father of four children, one of whom, Charles of Ghent, only six at the time, was to inherit the vast European and American domains of his grandparents. Ferdinand the Catholic governed Spain until his death in 1516, when Charles claimed his Spanish inheritance and joined it to the Habsburg lands in the Netherlands, Burgundy, and Germany. The artistic consequences of empire for Spain, if overshadowed by military, political, and economic events, are nonetheless worthy of note.

During the fifteenth century, northern art and artists were well known in Castile. Indeed, Isabella had made a notable collection of Flemish paintings and tapestries,[28] in addition to securing the services of Michel Sittow and Juan de Flandes. When Castile and the Low Countries were incorporated under a single ruler, the contacts between the two regions were increased, and the importance of Flemish art in Spain was intensified.

These contacts occurred on several levels, starting with the imperial family itself. Despite his unquestioned pre-eminence in European politics, the emperor Charles V was not the central figure in the process of artistic transmission, although he had a part to play. His military campaigns did not permit the leisure or tranquility needed to establish a tradition of artistic patronage, although he and his advisers were exceptionally shrewd in using the arts for political propaganda.[29] Rather, it was his aunt Margaret of Austria who initiated the Habsburg patronage of the visual arts in the sixteenth century.

In 1507, Margaret established her residence in Mechelen (Malines), a town midway between Brussels and Antwerp, where she established a great center of art and learning.[30] During the succeeding years, she acted as the guardian of her young nephew Charles and as governor of the Netherlands, a position that she held until her death in 1530, which made her a commanding figure among the art patrons of the region. From an early age, Margaret had collected works of art; once settled in Flanders, she expanded her activities considerably. As a patron, she employed Bernard van Orley, Jan Gossart, Jan Cornelisz Vermeyen, Jan Mostaert, and Michel Sittow, and acquired works by the great fifteenth-century Flemish artists. For instance, she owned Jan van Eyck's *Arnolfini Wedding Portrait* (London, National Gallery), a version of Hieronymus Bosch's *Temptation of St. Anthony* (now unidentifiable), and Roger van der Weyden's "Miraflores Altarpiece" (Berlin), one of several paintings acquired from the collection of Queen Isabella. Another of the princess's interests was illuminated manuscripts, of which she made an important collection.

Many of these works were bequeathed to her niece and successor as governor of the Netherlands, Mary of Hungary, the sister of Charles V, who acquired works of art as avidly as her aunt.[31] Mary patronized Bernard van Orley and Jan Vermeyen and added new names to the list of royal painters, including Pieter Cocke van Aelst and Michel Coxcie. Among the additions to her picture collection were several major works, notably Jan van Eyck's *Madonna of Canon van der Paele* (Bruges, Groeninge Museum) and Roger van der Weyden's *Descent from the Cross* (Prado). In her later years, as will soon be seen, she discovered the genius of Titian and became one of his best clients.

The example of the Habsburg princesses inspired several of their Castilian courtiers, such as Diego de Guevara (died 1520), who was the chamberlain of Philip the Fair and then entered the service of Margaret of Austria.[32] Guevara owned the *Arnolfini Wedding Portrait*, which he bequeathed to Margaret, and was one of the original collectors of the paintings of Hieronymus Bosch.

Another of this group was Mencía de Mendoza, the third wife of Henry III of Nassau, who was a member of the inner circle of Charles V and was himself a collector of note and owner of Bosch's most famous picture, the *Garden of Delights* (Prado).[33] Countess de Mendoza, who spent most of the 1530s in the Netherlands, became a serious collector of Flemish art, buying works by Jan Gossart, Bernard van Orley, and Martin van Heemskerck, as well as the panels of Bosch that were especially coveted by Spanish and Flemish aristocrats. After the death of her husband in 1538, she returned to Spain, bringing her collection to Valencia, where she settled after marrying the viceroy, the duke of Calabria.

As for the emperor, it is generally agreed that he was not as devoted or refined a collector as his aunt or his sister. His interest in Flemish painting, in fact, was largely determined by their examples. But his extensive travels in Italy in the 1520s and 1530s gave him an opportunity they were denied – to see the best masters of the Renaissance, one of whom in particular caught his eye, Titian. Thus began an almost hereditary interest in the works of the artist who was destined to have a crucial and lasting impact on painting in Spain.[34]

Charles V had first been introduced to Titian by Duke Federico Gonzaga in October 1529, but the meeting was not fruitful. However, Gonzaga persisted and brought the two together again in Mantua in November 1532. On this occasion, Titian triumphed by painting a portrait of the emperor in armor (now lost), for which he was rewarded not only with a large payment but also with a patent of nobility.

During the ensuing years, Titian provided the emperor with additional works. However, the climactic moment in the relationship arrived in 1548, when Titian joined Charles in Augsburg and stayed with him for eight months. The major work executed during this period was *Charles V on Horseback* (pl. 33), which became a key piece in the iconography of the Spanish Habsburgs. This portrait was not kept by the emperor, but passed into the hands of his sister Mary, who from this time became a more eager patron of Titian than was Charles. Between 1548 and 1554, she acquired a series of nineteen portraits by Titian and his assistants, as well as the impressive series of the fallen giants of antiquity, *Tityus* and *Sisyphus* (both in the Prado) and *Tantalus* and *Ixion* (lost), which she installed in her palace at Binche. As a result of this dual patronage, Titian became the unofficial court painter of the Habsburgs and was granted pensions that by 1550 amounted to 500 ducats per year.

Charles met Titian for the final time in Augsburg in November 1550, and commissioned a painting of the Last Judgment (or *Gloria*) (pl. 34), in which the emperor and other members of the royal family appeal to Christ for salvation. When he

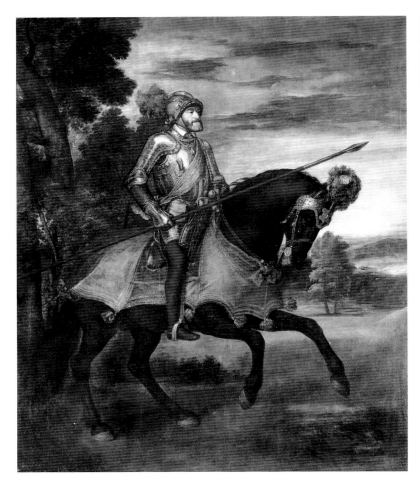

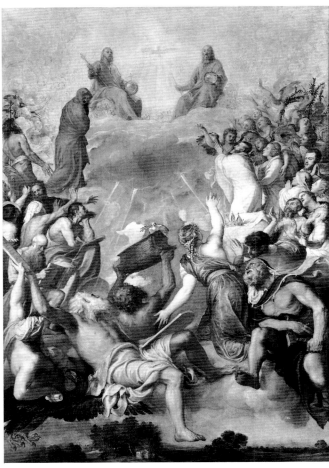

33. Titian, *Charles V on Horseback*, 1548. Madrid, Prado, canvas, 3.32 × 2.79m.

34. Titian, *Last Judgment* (or *Gloria*), 1551–54. Madrid, Prado, canvas, 3.46 × 2.40m.

retired to the monastery of Yuste in 1556, Charles took seven canvases by Titian with him, but he loved the *Last Judgment* best and gazed upon it as he died.

Through the patronage of Charles and Mary, Titian made his entry upon the scene of Spanish art. The emperor and his sister both died in 1558, bequeathing their art collections, including all the works by Titian, to the emperor's son, Prince Philip, later Philip II, who would become an even more devoted admirer of the artist. At Titian's death in 1576, a sizable part of his output had come to rest in Philip's palaces and country seats, and there they remained, emitting silent but powerful signals to future generations of Spanish painters and patrons.

2
The Revolution of Philip II

PHILIP II HAS SUFFERED the fate of those whose enemies become their biographers. Bent on seeing his flaws and the errors of his ways, many of these authors, especially outside Spain, have drawn a vivid, malign portrait of the most powerful man of the epoch. A bigot and an oppressor, a fanatic and a murderer – these are only some of the terms applied to this austere, forbidding man. Even writers who have been sympathetic, who have attempted to understand the king as a complex, uncertain person, compelled to act by the powerful forces that shaped his temper and his times, have had little success in altering the image of Philip as the "black spider in his bleak cell at the Escorial."

This ruler would seem to be an unlikely candidate to reshape the history of Spanish painting, and yet this is what he did. Philip was an extraordinary patron, who used his enormous power and wealth to transform the development of painting in Spain by importing the art and artists of Flanders and Italy on an unprecedented scale.[1] By the end of his long reign (1556–98), Spanish painting was about to enter its most famous golden age.

Philip was born in Valladolid in 1527 and lived in Castile for his first twenty-one years. His education, although late to begin, was excellent. Learned tutors versed him well in ancient languages, geography, history, mathematics, and architecture. In addition, he developed lasting interests in music, art, and book collecting, and became adept at hunting and riding. The first evidence of his engagement with the visual arts appears around 1540, when a book of large sheets of plain paper was purchased, "which His Highness has asked for so that he could paint in it." Philip's practice of painting was still active in 1557, when the Venetian ambassador noted that he "knew something of sculpture and painting, which he likes to exercise to distract himself." This observation confirms Philip's personal experience of the arts he would patronize.

The turning point in Philip's artistic education occurred between 1548 and 1551, when he made an extended trip to Italy, Germany, and the Netherlands, the purpose of which was to become acquainted with the foreign lands and people he was destined to rule. This journey transformed his taste and understanding of the visual arts and launched him on a career as a great patron. Philip's Italian itinerary did not include Venice, Florence, or Rome, the leading centers of art and culture, although he did visit Genoa, Milan, and Mantua, where he saw the work of such important masters as Mantegna, Leonardo, Perino del Vaga, and Giulio Romano. It was in Milan, late in 1548, that he first made contact with the artist he loved best, Titian. In the portrait made on this occasion (pl. 35), Titian represented the prince in an elegant, understated composition that established an enduring model for portraiture at the court of the Spanish Habsburgs (see below, pls. 84 and 116).

Philip and Titian met again in Augsburg in 1550–51 for the second and last time. Despite his preoccupation with his work for Charles V and Mary of Hungary, the painter found time to curry the favor of the prince, with whom he planned a series of

35. Titian, *Philip II in Armor*, 1548. Madrid, Prado, canvas, 1.93 × 1.11m.

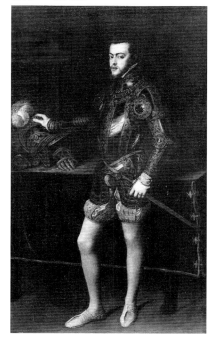

39

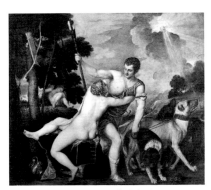

36. Titian, *Venus and Adonis*, 1511–54. Madrid, Prado, canvas, 1.86 × 2.07m.

about ten pictures, including the "Poesie," the six mythologies that count among his greatest works. In the following year, Titian sent to Spain two independent pieces, the *"Pardo Venus"* (Paris, Louvre) and *St. Margaret* (El Escorial), and by 1562, had finished the "Poesie." These were delivered to the king, along with other important pictures such as *Venus and Adonis* (pl. 36), and together form the first significant group of mythological pictures to enter the royal collection. It was only to be expected that Philip's artistic encounters in Italy and Flanders (he made a second trip to the north in 1554–59), and especially his close association with Titian, would cause him to look anew at the painters who were at work in his Spanish realms. What he saw did not appeal to the tastes he had cultivated during his foreign travels.

Spanish Painting at the Mid-Century

In Castile, where Philip had been raised, the stage was occupied by Alonso Berruguete, who was working mostly in Toledo in the 1540s and 1550s. The other notable artist in the Imperial City was Juan Correa de Vivar (ca. 1510–66), the leading pupil of Juan de Borgoña.[2] In his works of the 1530s, Correa had hewn closely to the style of his master, and it was not until the following decade that he began to incorporate, if somewhat tentatively, elements of the style of Raphael, derived mostly from the prints of Marcantonio Raimondi. At his best, as in an *Annunciation* of about 1550 (pl. 37), Correa produced graceful compositions with finely wrought details. However, a sizable portion of his output was destined for village churches in the countryside around Toledo and Madrid – places like Dos Barrios and Cenicentos – for which he was liable to take shortcuts or consign the execution to his workshop.

It would be easy to ignore the works for these and other small places in Castile, works that were intended for rural audiences interested in novelty but not always experienced enough to judge quality as it was judged in the metropolitan centers. However, the byroads of Spanish painting should not be shunned, for they lead to a deeper understanding of the phenomenon of stylistic diffusion.

During the sixteenth century, the provincial regions of Castile experienced a wave of prosperity that, among its effects, led to the construction and renovation of numerous churches. This period of expansion increased the demand for new examples of devotional art, some of which was met by the major artists. Still, there was plenty of work left over for those painters who straddled the line between artist and artisan. Although their number is almost beyond counting, and their identities sometimes lost in the passage of time, many were capable of producing striking works of art.

For the most part, these painters worked at a considerable remove from their foreign sources. Their initial training was usually in the Hispano-Flemish style, which meant that their understanding of the language of northern art had already been altered by translation into a local dialect. The knowledge of the increasingly fashionable painting of Italy was accommodated not so much by the study of the originals as by the work of painters such as Pedro Berruguete and Juan de Borgoña, or perhaps by more current models of style provided by Llanos, Yáñez, and Pedro Fernández, which, of course, offered idiosyncratic versions of Italian painters such as Leonardo da Vinci. Another important source of visual information was prints – particularly those after compositions by Raphael and Michelangelo – which seem to have been as common as paint brushes in the ateliers of Spanish artists. The confluence of these currents produced what might be called a "secondhand

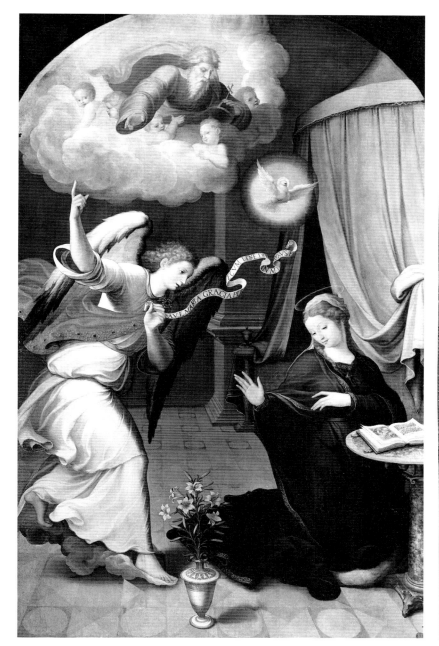

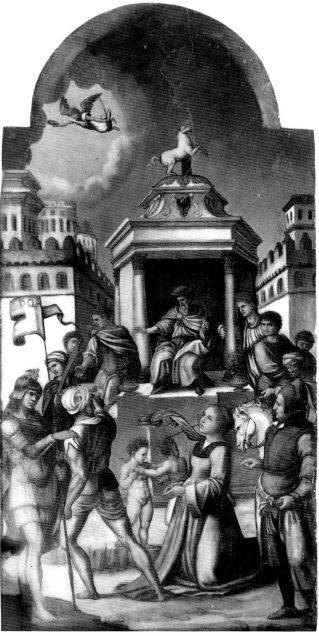

Renaissance," which can be exemplified in the work of Juan Soreda, who was employed at the cathedral of Sigüenza in the 1520s.[3]

Soreda's principal work for the cathedral is the altarpiece of Santa Librada, produced between 1526 and 1528, which is a catchall of Italian motifs expressed in a mixed Italo–Flemish style. For instance, the *Decapitation of Santa Librada* (pl. 38) stitches together elements from three prints after Raphael: the executioner and the horseman come from Agostino Veneziano's 1517 engraving after *Christ on the Road to Calvary* (known as the "*Pasmo di Sicilia*" and now in the Prado); the angel in the sky is an exact quotation from Marcantonio's version of the master's *Martyrdom of St. Cecilia*; and the figure seated on the throne was taken from Veneziano's print of 1516 after the *Blinding of Elymas*, one of the tapestries of the Acts of the Apostles created for the Sistine Chapel.[4] It is interesting to see how rapidly these prints found their way to a place like Sigüenza, and more interesting still, the difference in style

37. Juan Correa de Vivar, *Annunciation*, ca. 1550. Madrid, Prado, panel, 2.25 × 1.46m.

38. Juan Soreda, *Decapitation of Santa Librada*, 1526–28. Sigüenza, cathedral, panel.

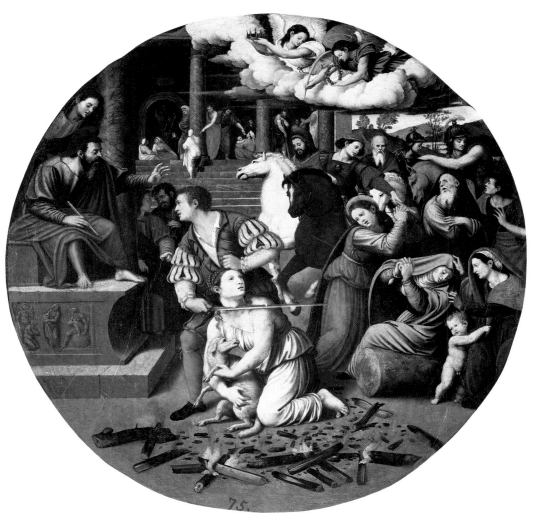

39. Vicente Maçip, *Martyrdom of St. Agnes*, 1540–50. Madrid, Prado, panel, 0.58m. diameter.

between the borrowed and the borrower. The place where Soreda received his training is not known, but, as the two-dimensional figure style, diffuse composition, and irregular perspective show, it must have been in Spain. It is easy to dismiss such vernacular paintings as provincial, yet this is unjust and suggests that our criteria may need to be revised in order to validate images of such sincerity and vitality.

To the east, in Valencia, the influence of Tuscan and Roman painting of the High Renaissance was undiminished during the late sixteenth century. After Llanos and Yáñez left the city, their place was taken by Vicente Maçip (ca. 1475–1550), the founder of an artistic dynasty that lasted into the early 1600s.[5] This family style enjoyed unbroken success in the region and proved resistant to significant changes over the eighty years that it endured.

While the paintings of Maçip have points of contact with Llanos and Yáñez, they demonstrate new elements in his style acquired through works from Italy. For example, the *Martyrdom of St. Agnes* (pl. 39), executed in the 1540s for an altarpiece in the convent church of San Julián, Valencia, displays the knowledge, undoubtedly derived from prints, of Raphael's Stanza d'Eliodoro and the tapestries of the Sistine Chapel. More direct contact with Italian painting was gained through four important works by Sebastiano del Piombo brought to Valencia around 1521 by Jerónimo Vich y Volterra, ambassador of Ferdinand and Charles V to the Holy See.[6] These included *Christ Carrying the Cross* (Prado) and a triptych that comprised the

42

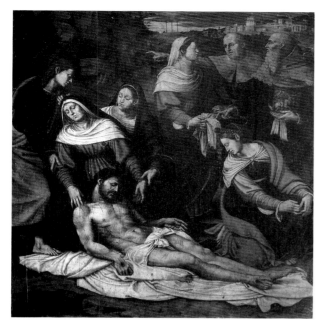

40. Vicente Maçip, *Lamentation*, ca. 1530. Segorbe, cathedral, panel, 1.50 × 1.73m.

Pietà (signed and dated 1516; Leningrad, Hermitage), the *Descent into Limbo* (Prado), and the *Appearance of Christ to the Eleven Apostles* (lost). Macip's *Lamentation* (pl. 40), which forms part of the altarpiece for the cathedral of Segorbe, his major commission and executed around 1530, is obviously adapted from Sebastiano's version of the subject. However, Maçip's knowledge of current Italian painting goes no further than Sebastiano's generation.

The conservatism of Valencian painting can best be explained by the extraordinary success of the Maçip dynasty. Vicente lived a long life, continuing to work until incapacitated by old age and poor health in the 1540s. By then, his son, called Juan de Juanes (born ca. 1510),[7] was thoroughly schooled in his father's ways and kept the family business going until he died in 1579, when it was taken over by his own offspring. Although it has been suggested that Juanes traveled to Rome in the 1560s, his style is completely contained within the parameters of his father's art.

Juanes's mature career coincided with the beginning of the Counter Reformation and its renewal of the Catholic faith. In particular, Juanes was inspired by the new spirit of personal prayer and devotion that culminated in the great Spanish mystics St. Theresa of Avila and St. John of the Cross. In the spiritual exercises, as Ignatius Loyola called them, the worshipper, through an intense effort of prayer and imagination, sought to come into the closest possible contact with the Holy Family and the saints, and several of Juanes's paintings illustrate the new faith in action. The best example depicts the Venerable Mosén Bautista Agnesio (or Anyes), a Valencian cleric and theologian, who kneels at one side of the composition, which is centered on the Virgin and Child with saints (pl. 41).[8] The Venerable Agnesio believed that he was a descendant of St. Agnes and claimed to have seen her in a vision, in which he placed a wedding ring on her finger, the event represented in Juanes's picture.

Juanes was especially adept at creating inspiring devotional images of Christ, the most famous of which represents the Savior holding the Eucharistic wafer. The figure is excerpted from the artist's celebrated composition, the *Last Supper* (pl. 42), itself an obvious paraphrase of Leonardo's masterpiece, a copy of which was at that time in the cathedral of Valencia. By showing Christ with the wafer, Juanes asserts the truth of the doctrine of transubstantiation, then an issue of heated controversy between Catholics and Protestants. In this expressive image, a gentle Christ offers the fruits of His sacrifice to those who will follow His teachings and example. As shown by the countless repetitions of the composition, some made even in the present century, this image of the Savior successfully provided inspiration and consolation to legions of the faithful.

If the painters of Castile and Valencia seem to have taken little notice of the Italian style known as the *maniera*, which flourished in Rome in the second third of the century, it was a different story in Seville. While Alejo Fernández survived almost until 1550, his hegemony was threatened in 1537, when a Flemish artist arrived in the city. Pieter Kempeneer, known to Spaniards as Pedro de Campaña, was born around 1503 in Brussels, where presumably he received his artistic training.[9] By 1529, he was in Bologna working on the decorations for the triumphal entry of Charles V, which preceded his coronation as Holy Roman Emperor. For a while thereafter, Kempeneer was employed by Cardinal Grimani in Venice. On the evidence of his Spanish works, the decisive impact on his style was made by followers of Raphael – Polidoro da Caravaggio, notably – who, like Kempeneer himself, spent much of the 1530s wandering through Italy in the troubled period following the Sack of Rome in 1527.[10]

Kempeneer's decision to move to Seville may have been determined by the prospect of working for the growing community of Flemings, who had come to participate in the Indies trade. However, most of his documented commissions came

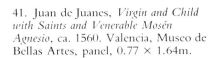

41. Juan de Juanes, *Virgin and Child with Saints and Venerable Mosén Agnesio*, ca. 1560. Valencia, Museo de Bellas Artes, panel, 0.77 × 1.64m.

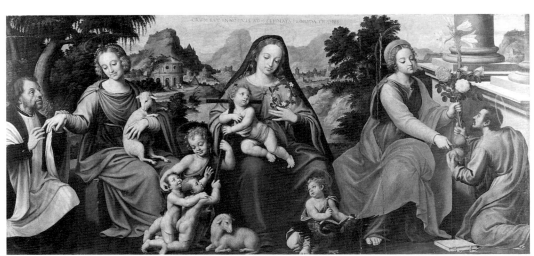

42. Juan de Juanes, *Last Supper*, ca. 1560. Madrid, Prado, panel, 1.16 × 1.91m.

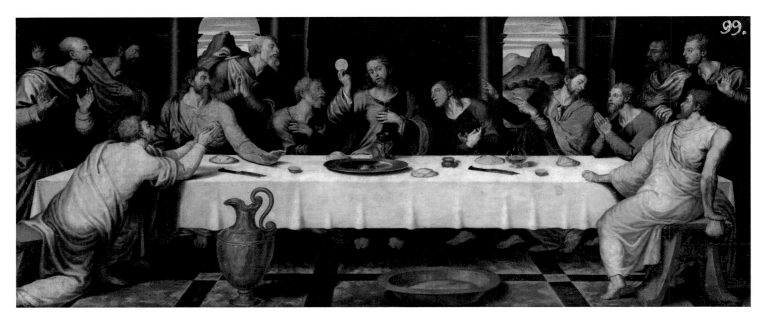

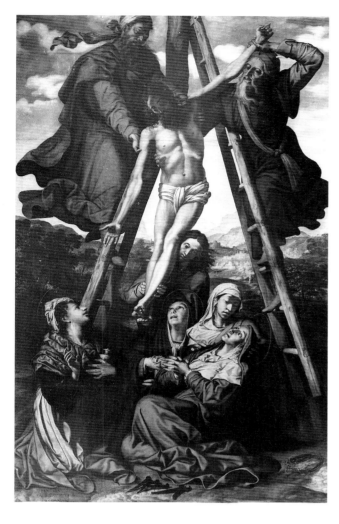

43. Pieter Kempeneer, *Descent from the Cross*, 1540–50. Seville, cathedral, panel, 3.20 × 1.91m.

from Spanish clients, who were quick to appreciate the novelty and quality of his art, which would have looked very advanced indeed when compared with the work of Fernández.

During his stay in Seville, which extended to 1562, Kempeneer enjoyed great success and attracted commissions from all over the region, although his best work was done for patrons in the metropolis. Unfortunately, little remains from the first ten years of this period, except the *Descent from the Cross* (pl. 43), an undated painting for the funerary chapel of a local magistrate, formerly in the church of Santa María de Gracia. The contrast of this powerful painting with the delicate, even-tempered style of Fernández is self-evident. While the composition is derived from a Roman source, a print by Marcantonio Raimondi, the style, and particularly the angular figure of Christ, reveals the artist's Flemish heritage. This synthesis of northern and southern stylistic elements is entirely characteristic of the generation of Flemish painters who visited Italy in the first quarter of the century, as is the expressive, emotional tenor of the scene.

During the 1550s, Kempeneer executed his two major surviving commissions, the altarpiece of the Purification in the cathedral (1555) and the grandiose retable for the parish church of Santa Ana (begun in 1557). The altarpiece of the Purification, consisting of ten panels, adorns the funerary chapel of Diego Caballero, a veteran of the conquest of Peru, who had served in the colonial administration on Hispaniola.[11] The donor and members of his family are represented in two of the predella panels,

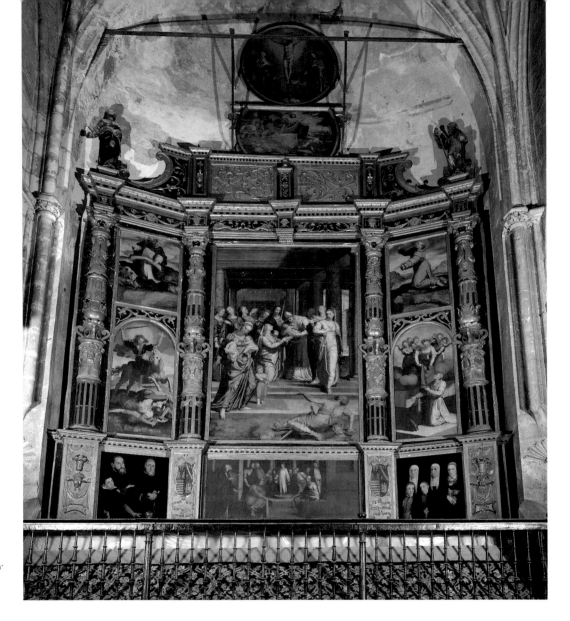

44. Pieter Kempeneer, *Purification of the Virgin*, 1555. Seville, cathedral, panel, 3.13 × 2.10m.

which are fine examples of Flemish portraiture and constitute an unusual record of the middle class of Spanish society (pl. 44).

The *Purification of the Virgin*, the centerpiece of the retable, is a work of considerable sophistication. The basic composition, to be sure, is based on a print by Dürer, which has been reframed in a carefully rendered classical structure. Surrounding the central scene are personifications that embody the virtues of the Virgin Mary – Charity, Justice, Fortitude, Faith, and Hope among them. Charity offers assistance to a lame man, conspicuously posed in one corner, who provides a demonstration of the painter's skill at drawing the figure. Strange to say, this work evinces a more thorough grasp of current Italian art than the *Descent from the Cross*, which was done shortly after the artist arrived in Seville some twelve years earlier. The figures are more solidly drawn, the treatment of the drapery more rigorous and adapted to the contours of the body, the colors more subtly nuanced and shaded than in the earlier work. Unlike other painters who had come to Spain from Italy and gradually lost their grasp of Italian style, Kempeneer seems to have become a more Italianate painter, as if he had in some way refreshed his knowledge of the sources. Yet there is no record that he ever returned to Italy.

One explanation for the renewal of Kempeneer's style can be found in the work of

46

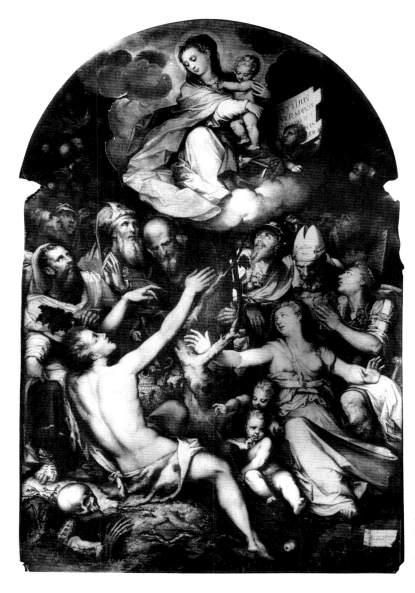

45. Luis de Vargas, *Allegory of the Immaculate Conception*, 1561. Seville, cathedral, panel, 0.75 × 1.83m.

another Italianate painter, Luis de Vargas.[12] Vargas, a native of Seville, was born around 1505 and is known to have spent a considerable time in Italy. However, his activities are not recorded until 1550, when he returned definitively to Spain where he worked until his death in 1567. The duration of his stay abroad is uncertain; it has even been theorized that he went to Italy on two separate occasions. The first trip, undertaken when he was still a young man, would have ended in 1534, when he came home and remained for about seven years. Supposedly, he then went back to Italy until 1550. In any event, the few remaining works of his final period of activity make it virtually certain that he was in Florence and Rome in the 1540s, and that he came into contact with Giorgio Vasari, Francesco Salviati, and Perino del Vaga, three important practitioners of the *maniera* style. The evidence of these contacts is found in the *Allegory of the Immaculate Conception*, signed and dated 1561, which decorates a minor chapel in Seville cathedral (pl. 45). This painting depends on Vasari's version of the same subject, painted in 1540–41 for the church of the Santissimi Apostoli, Florence, and represents the transmission of original sin from Adam, the nude figure in the lower left, through successive generations via the Tree of Jesse, culminating in the Virgin Mary, the first person to be created without mortal sin. Vargas's mastery of the artful style of the *maniera* is convincing –

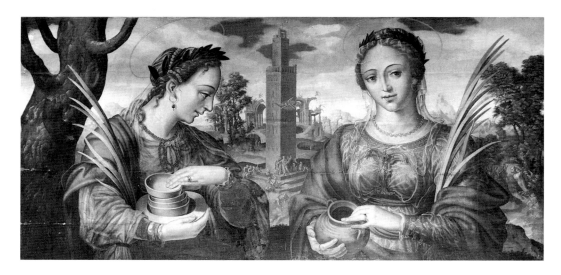

46. Ferdinand Sturm, *Sts. Justa and Rufina*, 1553–55. Seville, cathedral, panel, 0.79 × 1.62m.

the off-key, pastel colors, the crowded, airless space, the studied complexity and variety of poses all derive from this source, and these in turn were assimilated by Kempeneer.[13] The relationship between the two artists is best seen by comparing the figure of Adam in Vargas's painting with the contorted pose of the beggar splayed across the right-hand corner of Kempeneer's *Purification*.

Another Flemish painter active in Seville during the middle years of the century was Ferdinand Sturm, or Hernando Esturmio, a native of Zieriksee (Zeeland), who came to the city in the same year as Kempeneer.[14] Sturm's Spanish career is well documented until his death in 1556, and he obviously enjoyed a considerable measure of success, although his thriving practice was founded more on his business acumen than on the quality of his art. It is generally agreed that his best work is to be found in the altarpiece of the Evangelists in Seville cathedral, a commission of 1553 from Sebastián de Obregón, the bishop of Morocco. In one of the predella panels, representing Sts. Justa and Rufina with the tower of the cathedral in the background (pl. 46), Sturm displays the flat, rigid style that he had learned in his native land in the 1520s.

Sturm was clearly no match for Kempeneer as an artist, but his very lack of pretension served him well in the special conditions of the Sevillian art market. As an analysis of artists' contracts from the period has shown, the clientele cared more about price and content than style and quality.[15] For example, commissions for altarpieces were sometimes put up for bid among the local painters, following a set procedure. The client would hire an artist-consultant to draft the specifications, which were then published with the date of the auction. The system is seen at work in an auction for the right to execute an altarpiece intended as a gift to the monastery of San Francisco. On 13 July 1539, four painters appeared to bid – Sturm, Kempeneer, Juan Ramírez, and Pedro Martín.[16] Ramírez opened the bidding at one hundred ducats, and Kempeneer countered with ninety. Sturm entered the contest at eighty ducats, only to be undercut by Ramírez with seventy-five. However, Sturm was not to be bested, and made two lower bids, finally winning the contract at sixty-five.

The contract thus won left the artist little room for initiative. It runs to several pages and stipulates both the subjects and the specific motifs to be included in each composition, not to mention the materials to be employed. Adherence was enforced by a system of staggered payments, which gave the client the chance to approve the work as it progressed.

In the contract for the altarpiece of the Evangelists, Bishop Obregón ordered that the central scene, the Mass of St. Gregory, be represented in the "customary manner" ("como es de costumbre de pintar tal historia"). This condition, which is repeated in other contracts, effectively reduced or eliminated the possibility of invention. Sturm solved the problem as requested, by copying a print of Albrecht Dürer. As has been seen before, and will be seen over and again, the use of prints was standard among the painters of Seville; one explanation for the practice is provided in this contract, that is to say, the wishes of a conservative clientele that prized the proven orthodoxy of familiar formulas and was largely uninterested in what is now called artistic creativity. The balance of power in artist-client relations was tipped heavily in favor of those who were paying, not those who were painting, and change thus came slowly to the art.

The final artist in this sweep of the artistic horizon at mid-century is certainly the most renowned. Luis de Morales has always been known as "El Divino," a term that, strictly speaking, is more appropriate to his habitual subject matter than his artistic personality.[17] Yet Morales is beyond question one of the great devotional painters of the period. He spent his working life in Badajoz, where he was probably born at a date that has been set as early as 1509 and as late as 1519. Capital of the region of Extremadura, Badajoz in the sixteenth century was a remote and isolated town of ten to twelve thousand inhabitants and the seat of a small, poor diocese. Morales is first documented there around 1539, and was still plying his trade as late as 1585, when he would have been in his mid- to late seventies.[18]

During his heyday, Morales's artistic domain extended along the border of Extremadura and Portugal, and he executed several commissions from important churches in the area, including the cathedral of Badajoz and the monastery of Santo Domingo in Evora (Portugal). He was also employed by parish churches in the villages and towns of the region, places like the one suggestively named Arroyo del Puerco (Brook of Pigs, which later understandably was changed to Arroyo de la Luz, or Brook of Light), where animal husbandry was the principal activity.[19] However, most of his pictures were produced for individual clients who visited the workshop and ordered replicas of the devotional compositions for which the artist became famous. Morales was a fast worker: in 1548, several fellow artists had occasion to observe that he could complete a picture in two days; as a result, the number of paintings from his brush is very considerable.

Thus described, these circumstances do not seem propitious for significant artistic activity. But during the 1550s and 1560s, Badajoz was visited by a succession of distinguished churchmen who headed the diocese.[20] Francisco de Navarra, the bishop from 1545 to 1556, had studied in Toulouse and Paris and was present at the first sessions of the Council of Trent. His successor, Cristóbal Sandoval y Rojas, was one of the most important Spanish ecclesiastics of the period. He had attended the second session of the Council and, upon his arrival in Badajoz, determined to put the new tenets of the faith into action. In particular, Sandoval encouraged spiritual renewal through the emotional, personal devotion espoused by Loyola in the *Spiritual Exercises*, and thus unleashed a powerful local variety of mystical practice known as illuminism.

This fervent brand of religious expression was encouraged by the next bishop, Juan de Ribera, who occupied the see from 1562 to 1569. Ribera, the illegitimate son of a Sevillian magnate, the duke of Alcalá, was a man of great learning and intense faith, who maintained close contact with the mystical writers St. John of Avila and Fray Luis de Granada. The fervor fostered by Sandoval and Ribera eventually was perverted by corrupt religious advisers, who manipulated female practitioners, called "beatas," into highly dubious practices, with the result that the movement was suppressed by the Inquisition in 1576. At its inception, however, the renewal of

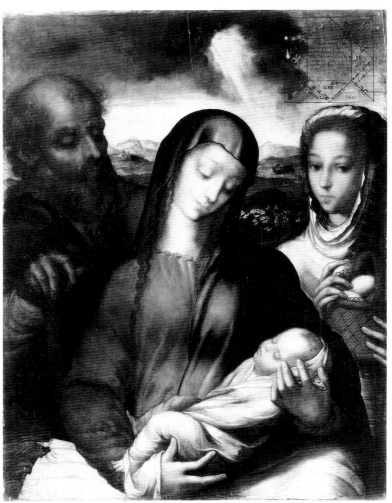

47. Luis de Morales, *Holy Family*, 1562–69. New York, Hispanic Society of America, panel, 0.91 × 0.67m.

faith sponsored by the two bishops was genuine and pure, and Morales became its knowing interpreter.

The consequences of Morales's contacts with Bishop Ribera can be observed in a painting that reflects the peculiar mixture of devotion and recondite learning that characterized Ribera's faith. Although nominally representing the Holy Family (pl. 47), the iconography has been expanded by a number of unusual motifs typical of the initial phase of the Counter Reformation, when new approaches to Catholic devotion were being devised.[21] The figure at the right offers a rather conventional expansion of the content; she holds a basket of eggs, symbol of the germ of life and regeneration of the world that began with the birth of Christ. Just behind the main group, in the landscape, a shepherd receives the news of the Savior's birth, while farther back stands a small, low tower, labeled "Turris Ader," the Tower of Ader. This motif, a landmark of Bethlehem, is described in Erasmus's *Commentary on the Gospel of St. Luke*, a source that, with other writings by Erasmus, was soon to be placed on the Index of Prohibited Books by the Inquisition.

The strangest feature is the diagram in the upper right, which has been shown to be a version of the horoscope of Christ published by Girolamo Cardano in his *Commentaria in Claudium Ptolomaeum* (Basel, 1554).[22] The potent combination of magic, astrology, and Christian theology embodied in this scheme quickly became suspect, and Cardano was accused of heterodoxy by the Inquisition of Bologna in 1571 and sent to prison; the horoscope was also deleted from all successive editions of the text.

48. Luis de Morales, *Pietà*, 1560–70. Madrid, Real Academia de Bellas Artes, panel, 1.26 × 0.98m.

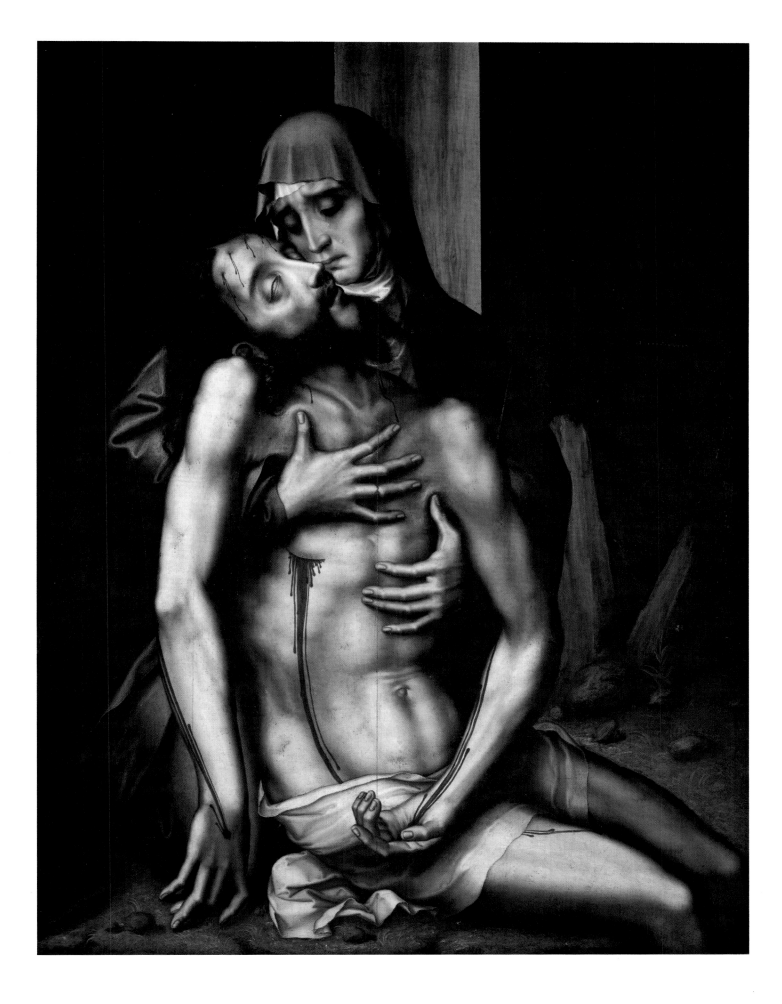

To be sure, this painting, replete as it is with arcane references, is unusual among the vast production of Morales and his workshop. Most of his clientele preferred simplified compositions comprising a few figures, dramatically illuminated and posed against a dark or neutral background, the purpose of which was to arouse feelings of tragedy in the viewers and even move them to tears. At times, it seems as if Morales was inspired by the mystical texts then so popular in the region. For instance, a comparison has been drawn between Morales's *Pietà* (pl. 48), which came from the Jesuit church in Córdoba, and a passage from Fray Luis de Granada's *Libro de la oración y meditación*. Although later in date (1586) than the picture (1560–70), it evokes the spiritual experience of a pious viewer:

> The Mother strongly clasps the lacerated body to her breast . . . resting her face among the thorns of the sacred head, visage against visage, the face of the Mother colored with the blood of the Son, that of the Son bathed with the tears of the Mother.[23]

No Spanish painter was ever to surpass Morales in expressing the passionate, personal faith of the mystical writers. It may be that his very isolation from new stylistic influences enhanced his effectiveness as a devotional artist, allowing him the freedom to develop his peculiar mode of painting without the distractions of novelty. The origins of this distinctive style are far from being understood. Elements of the manner of Leonardo da Vinci are readily discernible in his mature paintings, but they are not sufficiently potent to suggest that he had extensive firsthand knowledge of the art of the Florentine master. In any event, his way of painting the human figure in no way relates to central-Italian painting of the early sixteenth century, and is much closer to Flemish painting of the period. This quality has led to the hypothesis that Morales learned to paint in Seville, studying with Kempeneer. That he had clients in Seville is well established, as is the fact that his paintings were acquired by high-ranking patrons in Toledo, where, had he traveled there, he would have been in touch with Alonso Berruguete. It is even remotely possible that he spent time as a youth in Naples, which from about 1510 onwards was visited by a succession of painters from other parts of Italy, who contributed various elements to the incredibly heterogeneous style of the local artists. Among the visitors was Leonardo's Milanese follower Cesare da Sesto who resided in the city from 1513 to 1518 and created a local school headed by Andrea Sabatini. Only the discovery of documents of his early years can settle the questions that surround Morales's beginnings as a painter. Wherever these transpired, once settled in Badajoz, he never varied his perfect formula for communicating the religious passions that briefly energized this remote and desolate corner of Spain.

The New Court Art

On 25 August 1559, Philip II boarded a ship in Flanders to return to Spain after a five-year stay in the north. The trip had been more than eventful. In July 1554, he had traveled to London to marry Mary Tudor, a short-lived, unhappy marriage that ended with Mary's death in 1558. Of greater and more lasting import was the abdication of the emperor in Brussels in 1556, which made Philip the king of the largest monarchy in the western world, even after the division of the empire among the Austrian and Spanish branches of the Habsburg family. French pretensions to European hegemony were crushed by the Spanish army at the Battle of St. Quentin in 1557, and the succeeding Treaty of Cateau–Cambrésis officially sealed Philip's political power in Europe. The man who had left his native land as a prince in 1554 now returned home to govern as a mighty ruler.

To control more effectively the affairs of this far-flung empire, Philip decided to abandon the peripatetic style of kingship of the Catholic Monarchs and Charles V in favor of a fixed court. In 1561, he transferred his residence from Toledo to Madrid, where he remained for the rest of his life, never again leaving Spain, except to claim the crown of Portugal in 1580–82.

The decision to establish a permanent residence in Madrid had a profound and lasting impact on many spheres of Spanish life, including the arts. By concentrating the enormous financial resources of the crown in one place, Philip was able to convert this small town into the pre-eminent artistic center of his Spanish realms. Although the practice of painting would continue to flourish for a while in other regions, eventually the court, with its rewards of wealth and prestige, proved to be an irresistible attraction to artists from all over Spain.

The gradual centralization of patronage provided the king with the means to control artistic practice on an entirely new scale. Before Philip came to the throne, individual patrons were able to introduce new artists and styles into their circle of influence, but their impact often did not outlast their lives, resulting in the sporadic patterns of artistic development described above. Abetted by the length of his reign (1556–98), Philip sponsored changes that took hold and endured well into the seventeenth century.

None of this would have been possible had the king not been an exceptionally keen and informed patron of the arts.[24] His native interest in painting and architecture had been deepened, and his discernment sharpened, by the time spent abroad in the 1550s, when he had become familiar with some of the best in Italian and Flemish painting. Upon returning home, Philip must have decided that the painters in his Spanish realms could not measure up to the achievements of the foreigners, for none of them was called to court. While Juanes stayed in Valencia, Correa in Toledo, and Morales in Badajoz, Kempeneer was allowed to return to Brussels in 1562, where he headed a tapestry factory until his death in 1580.[25] With Titian as his unofficial court painter, Philip's taste not only had become sophisticated, but had been spoiled for the work of lesser artists.

Yet Titian refused to leave Venice, compelling the king to recruit foreigners to serve the immediate needs of the court. The first step he took was to employ a portraitist, there being none in Spain who had achieved distinction in the genre. Portraits were an essential component of court art: they presented the image of the royal family at home and abroad, especially because the exchange of portraits was an established diplomatic courtesy and custom. When Philip left Flanders in 1559, he was accompanied by one of the best portrait painters, Antonis Mor.[26]

Mor had been introduced into the court of Mary of Hungary by Cardinal Antoine Perrenot-Granvelle, one of the emperor's principal counselors and a major collector, and it was there that he met Philip during the prince's first stay in Flanders. In 1554, when Philip went to London for his marriage to Mary Tudor, he brought Mor to paint the queen's portrait (pl. 49), a representative work that reveals the essence of his style. In keeping with the prevailing manner of court portraiture, Mor is concerned with physiognomic accuracy but not with expression. This is a reticent image, devoid of allegorical paraphernalia, that emphasizes the social distinction of the sitter instead of her personality. However, the austerity is somewhat relieved by the attention paid to the costume and jewelry, which are rendered with a technique of dazzling exactitude. The effect of understated majesty perfectly expressed Philip's concept of kingship and led to the appointment of Mor as royal painter.

Contrary to expectations, Mor did not remain for long in Spain, although the

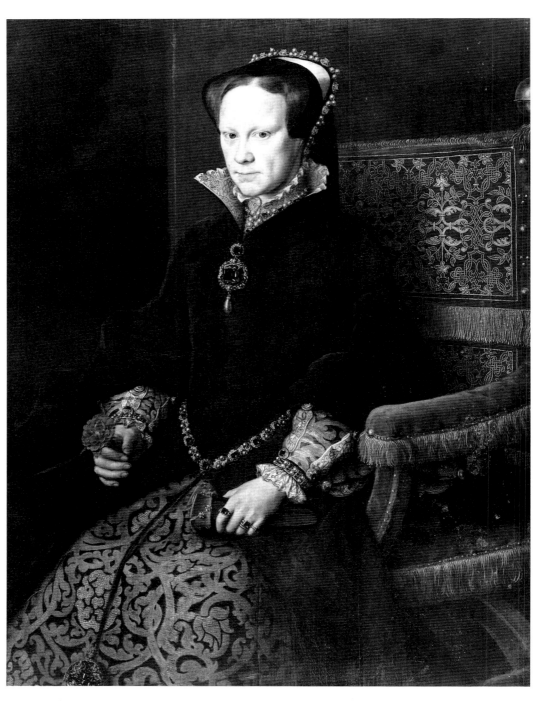

49. Antonis Mor, *Mary Tudor*, 1554. Madrid, Prado, panel, 1.09 × 0.84m.

reasons for his return to the north in 1560 are not certainly known. Among the few paintings attributed to this period is the *Portrait of the Jester Pérejon* (Prado), an early example of a subject that would remain popular at the court of the Spanish Habsburgs. Although Mor continued to sign paintings with the title "Painter to Philip II," he was of no use as a court portraitist *in absentia*.

Fortunately, Mor had trained a gifted Spanish disciple, Alonso Sánchez Coello (ca. 1531–88), who was able to continue and, in some ways, to enrich the inherited portrait formula.[27] Although born near Valencia, Sánchez Coello went to Portugal in his youth and started to learn the art of painting. There he attracted the attention of the king, Juan III, who sent him to Flanders in 1550 to study with Mor. Sánchez Coello returned to Portugal in 1552, and remained at the Lisbon court until 1555, at which time he was sent on a mission to Valladolid. He decided to

54

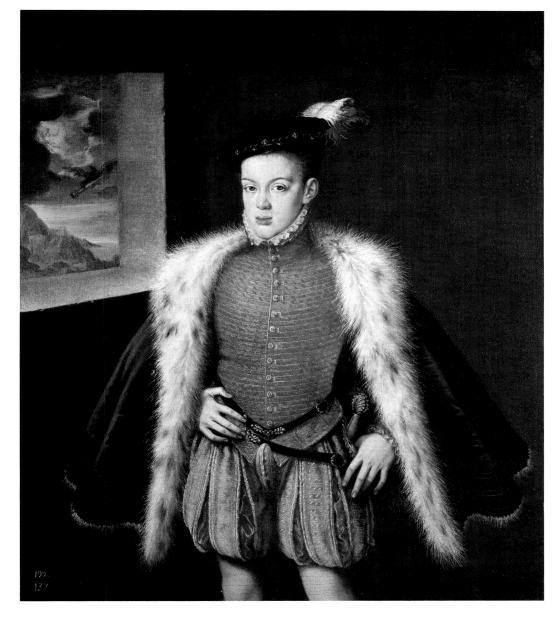

50. Alonso Sánchez Coello, *Infante Carlos*, ca. 1565. Madrid, Prado, canvas, 1.16 × 1.02m.

settle in Spain and entered the service of Philip II, for whom he worked until his death.

Sánchez Coello's reputation as a portraitist has been diminished by the innumerable copies and imitations that wrongly bear his name. While his debt to Mor is evident, Sánchez Coello brings distinctive qualities to the court portrait, notably a refined, subtle sense of color and a sharp eye for light and texture. In his best-known portrait, that of the ill-fated infante Carlos (pl. 50), the silken, wispy feel of the ermine trim is exquisitely rendered and exemplifies the opulent surface effects favored by the artist. Through the open window are seen the regal symbols of Jupiter and an eagle clutching a column in its claws.

Besides a portrait painter, and perhaps even more importantly, Philip needed history painters to carry out the artistic program that he initiated once he had settled in Madrid. In addition to the Alcázar of Madrid, Philip had inherited palaces and country houses in the surrounding region, which he began to enlarge, renovate, and embellish. Among these were the Casa de Campo, a suburban casino with gardens, just across the Manzanares River from the Alcázar; the Palace of the Pardo, a

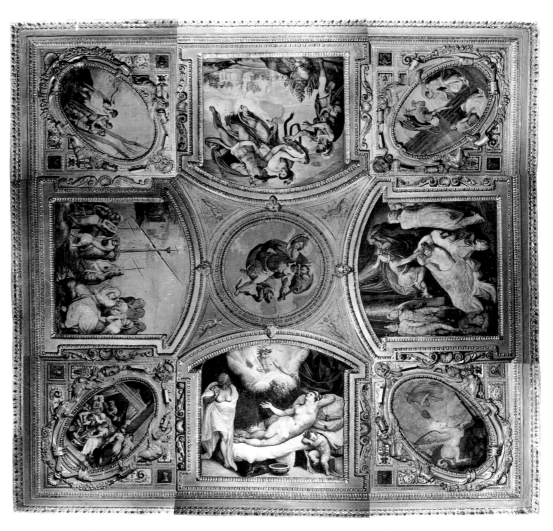

51. Gaspar Becerra, *Perseus and the Golden Fleece*, 1562–67. El Pardo, fresco.

hunting lodge some miles to the north, in the foothills of the Guadarrama Mountains; and the Palace of Aranjuez, a country retreat with extensive gardens that lay to the south and was used in the spring. Philip would make several additions to this stock of royal properties, one of which, the Escorial, would become the centerpiece of his patronage and the greatest artistic enterprise of Habsburg Spain.[28]

The planning of the Escorial began shortly after Philip's return from the north, and construction commenced in April 1563. Several years would pass before the painters were called into action, and in the meanwhile, Philip concentrated his attention on the redecoration of the Alcázar and the Pardo. During his absence from Spain in the years 1554–59, Philip's architects had effected certain additions and reforms to the Alcázar in an attempt to modernize the essentially medieval palace.[29] Although the Alcázar was destroyed in 1734 and replaced by the present Royal Palace, there is written information indicating the nature of the work. In effect, Philip wanted to duplicate the elaborate interior decorations of frescoes and ornamental stucco work that he had admired in the palaces of Genoa in 1549. By good fortune, he was able to find an experienced artist to direct the work who was no farther away than Valladolid. Surprisingly, he was a Spaniard.

However, Gaspar Becerra owed little of his training to Spanish masters.[30] Said to have been born in Baeza (Jaén) around 1520, Becerra had made his way to Italy and by the mid-1540s was working with Vasari, whom he assisted in the execution of that frenetic piece of mannerist painting known as the Hall of One Hundred Days (the time it took to execute the fresco) in the Cancelleria Palace, Rome. From there, he went on to assist another key painter of the *maniera* style, Daniele da Volterra, in the decoration of the Rovere Chapel in Sta. Trinità dei Monti.

Becerra stayed in Italy until around 1557, having become an adept practitioner of the *maniera* style, and then came back to Spain, settling in Valladolid. His first major commission, however, was a work of sculpture, the altarpiece for the cathedral of Astorga. By 1562, he had come to the attention of the king, who appointed him royal painter on 26 November, at the elevated annual salary of 600 ducats. Becerra was ordered to concentrate on painting frescoes in the king's quarters of the Alcázar and in the Pardo. Although the Madrid frescoes are lost, the subjects are indicative of a new interest in allegory and included the Four Seasons and the Liberal Arts, which were surrounded by stucco frames presumably designed by Becerra and executed by his Spanish assistants.

Fortunately, a portion of his fresco paintings at the Pardo has survived, representing the legend of Perseus and the Golden Fleece (pl. 51) This introduced the sophisticated, technically complex *maniera* style into Spain just at the time when Luis de Morales was reaching the height of his career in Badajoz. The contrast between the art of court and country could not have been more sharply drawn.

Becerra's tenure as royal painter soon terminated; he fell ill in 1567 and was dead on 23 January 1568.[31] Philip, as impatient a patron as ever lived, had already begun to despair of his slow pace and in 1567, had recruited new artists to expedite the work. They all came from Italy and comprised the first of several waves of Italian painters who from this moment on monopolized the major royal commissions. Thus, the next significant phase of the history of Spanish painting would be in large part a phase in the history of Italian painting.

The most important of this group was the Genoese architect Giovanni Battista Castello, il Bergamasco.[32] When Philip summoned him to court, Castello was already in Spain, decorating one of the most unusual monuments of the sixteenth century, the palace of the marquis of Santa Cruz in Viso del Marqués.[33] Santa Cruz, a famous admiral of the royal fleet, possessed seignorial lands on the border of Extremadura and Andalusia, where the appearance of water is likely to be a mirage. In this dusty village, he built an imposing palace, which was decorated by the Bergamasco team as though it were on the Strada Nuova of Genoa (pl. 52).

Bergamasco entered the king's service on 5 September 1567, and in the following year was allowed to bring assistants and members of his family from Italy. These included his stepson, Nicolò Granello, and the brothers Giovanni Maria and Francesco da Urbino. Castello's young son, Fabrizio, also accompanied the team, all of whose members would settle permanently in Spain and continue to work at court. Unfortunately, Bergamasco himself died in 1569, having been able to oversee the completion of the decorative projects in the Alcázar, but with dozens of ambitious plans still on the drawing board.

Two more masters recruited in Italy to assist in the decorative projects were Romulo Cincinnato, a Florentine pupil of Francesco Salviati, and Patrizio Cascesi of Arezzo. They departed Rome on 1 October 1567, having agreed on a two-year contract, but never went back to their native country, remaining at court to form part of Philip's artistic team.

Throughout the 1560s, as Italian painters began to assemble in Madrid, the greatest of them all, Titian, continued to provide pictures for the king, who was by now his most important patron.[34] In 1562, Titian delivered the last of the "Poesie," the *Rape of Europa* (pl. 53), thus completing the Augsburg commission of 1550. From now on, most of his paintings for the king were of religious subjects, beginning with the *Last Supper* (El Escorial), which arrived in 1564 and was inexplicably

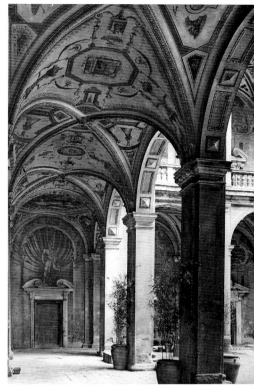

52. Giovanni Battista Castello and assistants, palace of Santa Cruz (general view), Viso del Marqués, 1560–70, fresco.

53. Titian, *Rape of Europa*, 1559–62. Boston, Isabella Stewart Gardner Museum, canvas, 1.78 × 2.05m.

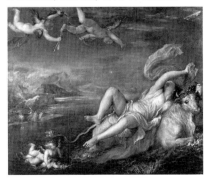

ordered by the king to be cut down in size. Three years later, Titian produced one of the great pictures of his later years, the *Martyrdom of St. Lawrence* (El Escorial), a subject specifically ordered for the building complex at the Escorial, which was dedicated to the holy martyr. Even into the 1570s, the aged painter continued to supply masterpieces of religious art, notably the *Allegory of Lepanto* (Prado), *Spain Coming to the Aid of Religion* (Prado), and *St. Jerome* (El Escorial), all completed in 1575, a year before he died. In the first two of these pictures, Titian seems to have been responding to the growing militancy of Philip's defense of the faith against the Protestants, an attitude that was to dominate the decoration of the Escorial.

The Painters of the Escorial

Although this impressive structure has come to be known as the monastery of the Escorial, it was built for a different function. Charles V had died without specifying a place of interment, charging his son to make suitable arrangements. As stated in the letter of foundation (1567), the Escorial was to serve that exalted purpose. In Philip's mind, it was fitting that the body of the greatest ruler of post-antiquity should be entombed in a site of imperial grandeur, which would also serve as the final resting place for his successors.

With the burial of the royal corpses now satisfactorily arranged, there was a still more important mission to accomplish – the care of their souls. This was assigned to the brothers of the Hieronymite Order, who were to occupy a large monastery in the southern half of the structure. Also to be included in the building were a seminary and a palace, where future kings and queens could reside while they contemplated the greatness of their ancestors and prayed for their salvation. The masses and devotional exercises were to occur in the royal chapel, called the basilica, placed in the center of the structure.

The Escorial was planned during the final session of the Council of Trent, which would redefine the dogma and spirit of the Catholic faith, a faith that Philip, following the example of his father, believed himself chosen to uphold and defend. And as the construction was in progress, the defense of the faith acquired new urgency with the revolt of the northern Netherlands, which posed a grave threat to the spiritual domain of Catholicism and the temporal domain of the Spanish Habsburgs. By the time the pictorial decoration was beginning, and during all the time it was being executed, Philip was occupied with preserving the supremacy of the faith in his inherited lands. This terrible and costly struggle found its reflection in the paintings and frescoes commissioned for his dynastic monument.

Planning for the decoration of the basilica, the physical and spiritual center of the Escorial, began before the final architectural design had been drafted. Philip chose as the principal artist a Spanish painter who had worked in Italy, Juan Fernández de Navarrete, known as "el Mudo" because he was deaf–mute from a very early age. Navarrete was born in the northern town of Logroño, presumably around 1540, and was appointed royal painter on 6 March 1568.[35] Very little is known of his earlier life; Father José Sigüenza, eyewitness and chronicler of the creation of the Escorial, claimed that he had studied in Rome, Florence, Venice, Milan, and Naples, thus naming every major artistic center of Italy. Judging from the trial piece he executed for the king (pl. 54), it is conceivable that he was in Rome in the 1550s, especially because Pellegrino Tibaldi, who came to work in the Escorial in 1586, claimed to have known him in Italy. Tibaldi was active in Rome from the mid-1540s to the mid-1550s, more or less the time when Navarrete might have been there.

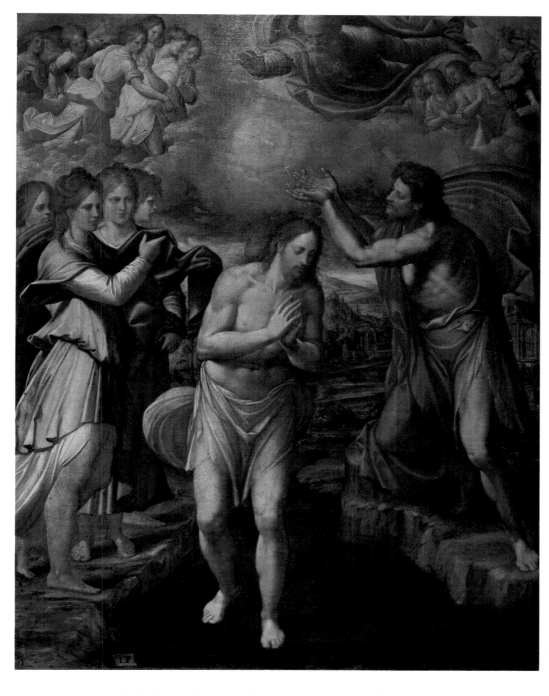

54. Juan Fernández de Navarrete, *Baptism of Christ*, ca. 1568. Madrid, Prado, panel, 0.49 × 0.37m.

Navarrete worked for the king in fits and starts; right from the beginning of his tenure he was plagued by poor health, complaining of stomach problems of a kind that today might be treated by a psychologist rather than a physician. Yet when he was feeling fit, he was a productive painter. For example, after returning from a year's leave of absence that had begun in August 1569, he was able to deliver four paintings to the Escorial in 1571, including the *Martyrdom of St. James* (pl. 55), perhaps his most admired work. The chief attraction to Father Sigüenza was the restrained verisimilitude of the martyr's execution. "The attitude and movement of the knife passing through the neck of the apostle [is done] with such propriety and naturalism that those who see it will swear that he is already starting to expire."[36] Sigüenza here gives voice to the criteria by which the painters of the Escorial would be judged: clarity of exposition and credibility of detail.

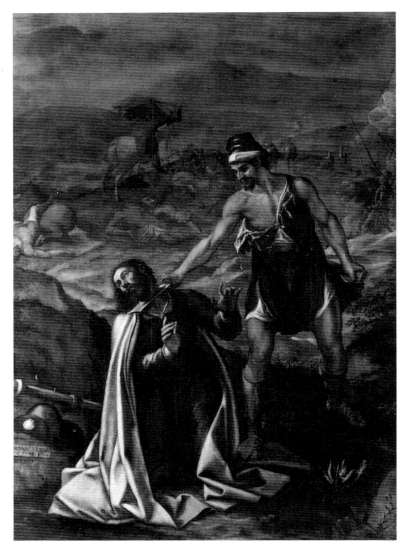

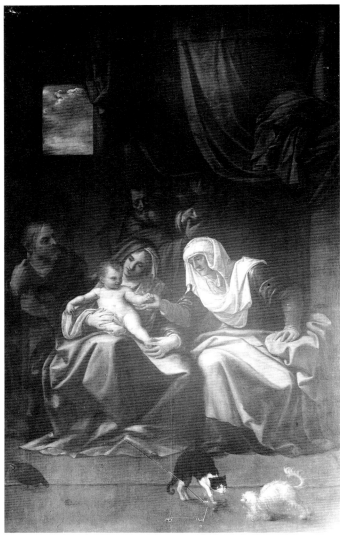

55. Juan Fernández de Navarrete, *Martyrdom of St. James*, 1569–71. El Escorial, canvas, 3.40 × 2.10m.

56. Juan Fernández de Navarrete, *Holy Family*, 1569–71. El Escorial, canvas, 3.50 × 2.10m.

On 21 August 1576, Navarrete signed the contract for his major commission, thirty-two paintings for the subsidiary chapels of the basilica, the construction of which was just then commencing.[37] Each was to represent a pair of saints in a landscape setting, the ensemble forming an affirmation of the efficacy of saints as divine intercessors and models of human conduct. The contract laid down the standard conditions, vesting approval of the finished pictures in the king or his representative. In addition, there was a special clause that reads as follows: "And in said pictures he may not put cat or dog or any other indecent figure; all must be saintly and inspire devotion."[38] This safeguard was not solely the result of an obsessively orthodox mentality; in an earlier painting of the *Holy Family* (pl. 56), Navarrete had shown a slice of animal life in the foreground. Sigüenza had thought it funny – "they make one feel like laughing" – but the king was not amused.

Navarrete lived to complete only eight of the commissioned paintings; his health failed once again early in 1579, and on 28 March, he died in Toledo. Sigüenza's wistful valedictory seems appropriate for an artist whose unspectacular virtues make it easy to minimize his important contribution to shaping the painting of his time – "If only he had lived, we would have been spared knowing all these Italians, although we would not have known the good that we had lost."[39] Put another way, Navarrete had invested the devotional picture with the dignity, sobriety, and realism required by the Spanish church of the Counter Reformation.

After his death, most of the remaining altarpieces were assigned to three painters, Sánchez Coello, Luis de Carvajal, and Diego de Urbina, the first of whom produced some important pictures. The religious paintings of Sánchez Coello have always taken second place to the portraits, and not without reason, for they sometimes lack the immediacy and incisiveness of his images of individual persons. In the basilica altarpieces, however, he is able to effect a remarkable synthesis between the divine and the human.[40] For example, in *Sts. Stephen and Lawrence* (pl. 57), dated 1580, it seems as if the artist had employed real people as models. These are not abstract types, based on a preconceived ideal, but ordinary men with irregular, individualized features. The appearance of these rather plain, if elegantly posed, human beings, wearing richly ornamented, sculpturesque vestments, is a striking departure from the norm of idealized religious painting and would be an inspiration to the next generation of Spanish artists.

The altarpieces of Luis de Carvajal (ca. 1556–1607) are not nearly as accomplished or original.[41] He was an artist from Toledo, who is recorded in Rome in 1577 and was called to the Escorial in 1579, where he worked at intervals over the next thirteen years. Lacking the refinement of Sánchez Coello, his versions of the paired saints are often stolid and immobile, although, on occasion, the very lack of grace and the true-to-life appearance effectively conjure up believable images of the heroes and scholars of the faith (pl. 58).

During the early 1580s, as the construction of the Escorial was nearing completion, Philip began to contemplate the vast, empty expanses of walls and ceilings that needed to be covered with frescoes, and of necessity turned to the recognized

57. Alonso Sánchez Coello, *Sts. Stephen and Lawrence*, 1580. El Escorial, basilica, canvas, 2.35 × 1.85m.

58. Luis de Carvajal, *Sts. Isidore and Leander*, ca. 1582. El Escorial, basilica, canvas, 2.35 × 1.85m.

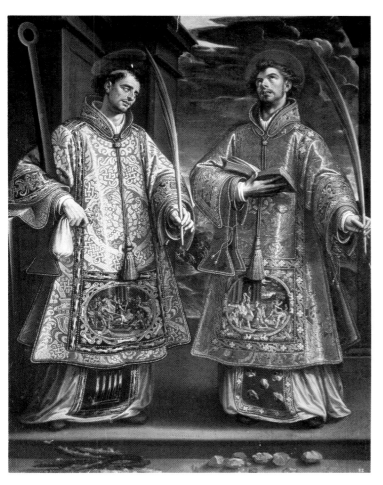

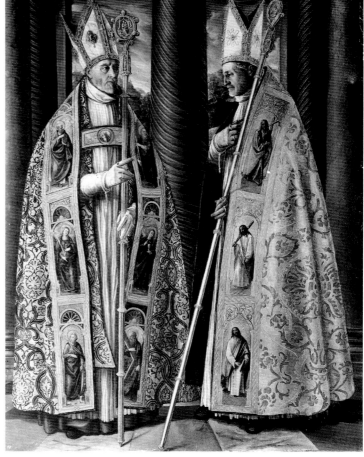

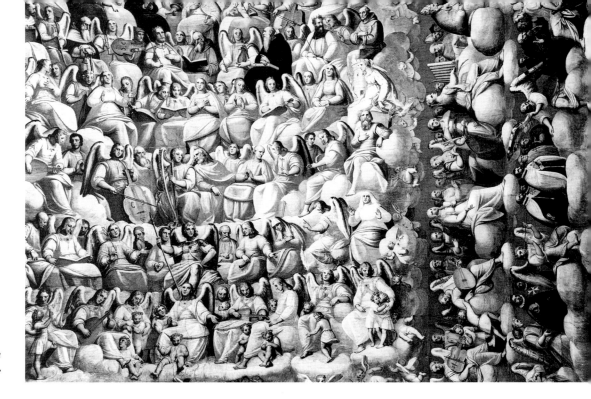

59. Luca Cambiaso, *Holy Trinity in Glory* (detail), 1584–85. El Escorial, fresco.

masters of the art, the painters of Italy. Right at hand he had the holdovers of the Bergamasco regime, Granello, Fabrizio Castello (now grown to maturity and appointed royal painter on 26 June 1584), and the Urbino brothers, both of whom, however, had died by the end of 1582. Romulo Cincinnato was another who remained on the payroll and was available for fresco commissions.

The Genoese painters were assigned to paint the two chapter rooms and had begun to work in the anteroom as early as 1575, finishing late in 1581. During the rest of the decade, Granello and Castello, assisted by two new arrivals, Lazzaro Tavarone and Orazio Cambiaso, diligently painted frescoes for the chapter rooms and the sacristy of the monastic complex. At the same time, they executed the impressive Hall of Battles in the Queen's Quarter of the palace, where the major military victories of the reign were memorialized in the first pictorial cycle glorifying the secular achievements of a Spanish monarch.[42]

Granello was chosen for an even grander assignment, the decoration of the vault of the choir in the basilica, but almost at once the king decided to look for a more renowned artist. In 1583, he engaged the services of the Genoese painter Luca Cambiaso (1527–85), who was appointed royal painter on 19 November 1583.[43] Cambiaso, already advanced in age, may have been attracted to Spain by the promise of extraordinary remuneration – Philip was famous for his generous treatment of artists. He worked for less than two years before he died, assisted by a team comprising his son, Orazio, and Lazzaro Tavarone. All three must have labored day and night to complete this enormous commission.

The choir vault (pl. 59) was executed between May 1584 and April 1585 and is a work of remarkable rigidity and lifelessness, characteristics that, if Italian sources are credible, were recognized by Cambiaso himself, who blamed the results on his theological advisers. The painting represents a heavenly glory with row after row of saints and angels adoring the Holy Trinity, while along the sidelines are figures in contemporary costume aspiring to join the ranks of the blessed. Sigüenza, ever ready with an apposite remark, attributed the debacle to the haste with which Cambiaso completed the fresco, motivated, in his opinion, by the artist's bad luck at gambling. "He painted his own portrait at the entrance to heaven. May it please

God that he be seen inside it! But I have my doubts, because he was in a great hurry to make money and even more to leave it here."[44] Although it would be easy to criticize Cambiaso's paintings for the Escorial (he also executed the fresco of the major chapel and four altarpieces that are considerably more successful), it must be recognized that he seems to have satisfied the king's taste for utter clarity and legibility in religious painting.

Following the death of Cambiaso, Philip brought two more eminent Italians to the Escorial, Federico Zuccaro and Pellegrino Tibaldi, the first of whom started to work in 1585, the second, in 1586. Zuccaro (ca. 1542/3–1609) had been recommended as the painter for one of the most important sites, the altarpiece of the main chapel of the basilica.[45] The initial contract had been signed several years earlier, in January 1579, and involved three artists: the architect Juan de Herrera, who was to design the framework; the sculptor Leone Leoni; and the painter Navarrete. Following Navarrete's death just two months later, Philip began a search for a new painter, considering in turn Cambiaso, Veronese, and Tintoretto. Cambiaso's trial piece was a failure and neither Veronese nor Tintoretto was disposed to leave Venice. Thus, the king settled on Zuccaro, who had bargained for the huge salary of 500 escudos per year.

From the first, Zuccaro's arrogance offended the king's men, and this set the stage for the troubles to come. The artist began with the most important work of all, the paintings for the high altar of the basilica. Late in 1586, he advised the king that he had completed them and solved the problem that had plagued his predecessors – the lack of legibility resulting from the distance between the spectators and the altarpiece. Sigüenza reported the outcome of the fateful encounter:

> The king spent a while in looking at them. Then he asked if what was in a basket held in two hands by a shepherd, as an offering to the recently delivered Virgin Mother, was correct. He [Zuccaro] said yes. All who found themselves present noted it, understanding that the king had paid little attention to the rest, and that it seemed improper that a shepherd, who had come running in the middle of the night from tending his herd, could have so many eggs, especially if he did not keep chickens.[47]

The offending eggs, it should be mentioned, are an entirely conventional symbol of regeneration and often appear in representations of this subject (pl. 47).

Zuccaro was given another chance to prove himself with the frescoes in the principal cloister, but once again failed and was sent home with his assistants. Later, reflecting on the debacle, the king refused to draw the obvious conclusion, and, in a characteristic lapidary phrase, lightly tinged with irony, exculpated the artist: "The blame does not belong to him, but to him who sent him this way."

It now seems evident that Zuccaro was unfairly judged. Admittedly, his paintings are not immortal works of art, but they do show the mastery of an impressive range of skills and effects. For instance, the *Annunciation* (pl. 60), which serves as the shutter to one of the reliquary altars, displays grace and movement in the figures and composition, and strikes an effective balance between the solemn encounter of Gabriel and Mary and the active scene of the heavenly glory above. In the foreground there is a deftly executed still life of flowers in vases. Regardless of the king's opinion, the Spanish painters who saw Zuccaro's work found much in it to admire, and he became a vital inspiration to the next generation.

Pellegrino Tibaldi (1527–96), undoubtedly a better artist than Zuccaro, enjoyed greater success.[48] Upon his arrival at the Escorial, Tibaldi resumed full-time work as a painter, which had been somewhat in abeyance during the preceding twenty years, when he served as the architect of the city and province of Milan (under Spanish rule

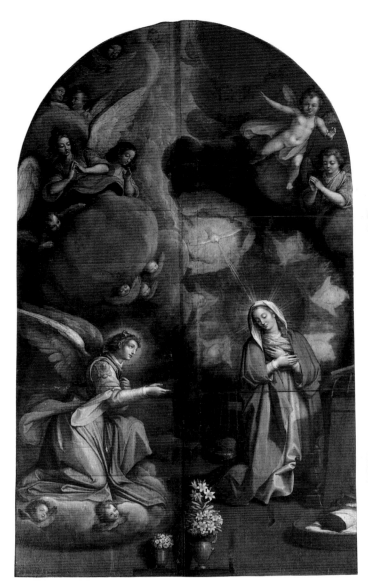

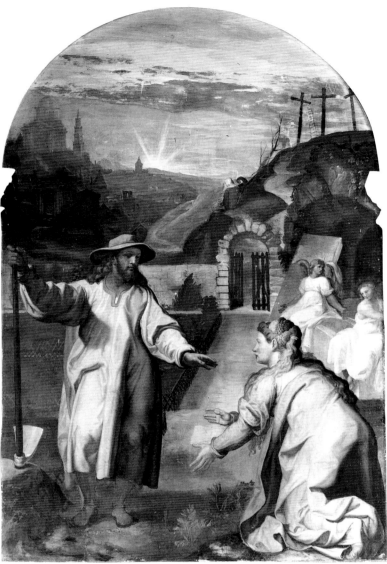

60. Federico Zuccaro, *Annunciation*, 1585–86. El Escorial, basilica, panel.

61. Pellegrino Tibaldi, *Christ Appearing to Mary Magdalene*, 1593. El Escorial, Imperial Staircase, fresco.

since 1556). His first assignment was to complete the frescoes of the cloister, inauspiciously begun by Zuccaro and company. This work was done primarily by assistants, except for the compartments on the Imperial Staircase (completed in 1593), where Tibaldi effected a thorough synthesis of the monumental figure style of the Roman Renaissance and the coloristic subtlety of Venice (pl. 61).

From there he moved to the Escorial library,[49] the masterpiece of his Spanish period, and executed the ceiling fresco (1590–91) with the assistance of Bartolommeo Carducci (discussed in chapter 4 under the hispanicized form of his name, Bartolomé Carducho), one of Zuccaro's assistants, who had stayed behind and continued to work for the king. The iconography was devised by Father Sigüenza and is an encyclopedic exposition of Philosophy and Theology, combining allegorical and historical subjects. The ceiling is a compendium of figure painting in the grand manner, which the Spanish artists at the Escorial would study with profit.

Finally, Tibaldi tackled the main altar and attempted what none of his predecessors had succeeded in doing – to satisfy that most exigent of patrons, Philip II. By 1592, when Tibaldi set to work, the king may have recognized that time was running short if he ever wished to intone a prayer before the completed altar. Thus, it was decided to deploy five of the pictures executed by Zuccaro and three new

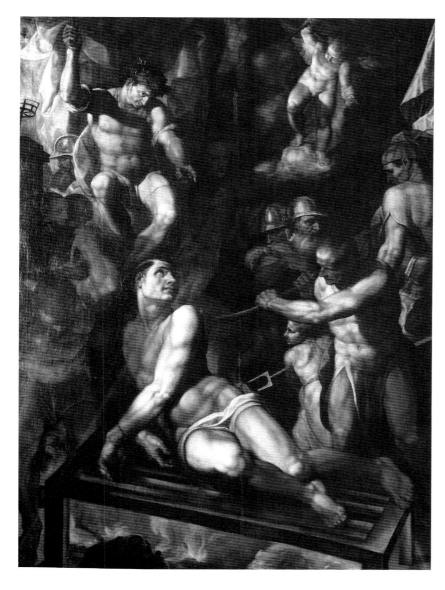

62. Pellegrino Tibaldi, *Martyrdom of St. Lawrence*, 1592. El Escorial, basilica.

works by Tibaldi – the *Adoration of the Shepherds* (eggless, of course), the *Adoration of the Magi*, and the *Martyrdom of St. Lawrence*. In the last-named composition (pl. 62), which turns back the clock to the period of the Roman *maniera* style, the saint is grilled to a turn by the executioner's forked spear, resulting in a rather bizarre culinary interpretation of the text. Philip might well have been expected to object to this violation of decorum, as he had done when shown El Greco's *Martyrdom of St. Maurice and the Theban Legion* (pl. 68), but if he did, no record exists.

In 1595, Tibaldi, having finished his work at the Escorial, returned, a rich man, to Italy. The decoration was now substantially complete and, for all the trials and errors, can be reckoned an artistic success, if not a triumph. Prior to evaluating the consequences of this enormous pictorial undertaking, it is necessary to look at the other important aspect of Philip's involvement with the visual arts, the formation of his great collection of pictures.

The Royal Collection

Philip began his collection with an important headstart, the legacy of works inherited from his father, Charles V, and his aunt, Mary of Hungary, which came

65

into his possession in 1558.[50] The emperor, who did not own many pictures, had taken some of the best to the monastery at Yuste, where he retired after his abdication. Of these, the most important were the works by Titian, including the *Gloria* (pl. 34) and portraits of the emperor and the empress. In quite a different vein were the four erotic mythologies by Correggio – *Leda and the Swan* (Berlin), *Ganymede*, *Io* (both in Vienna), and *Danäe* (Rome, Borghese Gallery) – which the emperor had received from Federico Gonzaga. Now considered among the master-pieces of the Renaissance, their frank sensuality made Philip uneasy, and he gave away two of them to his secretary, Antonio Pérez.

The pictures owned by the queen of Hungary were more numerous and important. She, too, possessed canvases by Titian, which included a large gallery of portraits (pls. 33 and 35), and several history paintings. Mary was also a devoted admirer of Flemish painting, and had masterpieces by Jan van Eyck and Roger van der Weyden.

Philip's artistic taste was modeled on the example of these illustrious forebears. Works by Titian formed the nucleus of his collection; Philip possessed the largest group of the master's pictures assembled by an individual collector in the sixteenth century. Besides these, he had examples of other Venetians, including Tintoretto, Veronese, Sebastiano del Piombo, Palma il Vecchio, and several by Jacopo Bassano and his followers. The rest of the Italian school was not very well represented. There were a pair of pictures by Federico Barocci; four attributed to Raphael (none of which has been traced), plus three copies of the *Transfiguration*; one composition ascribed to Leonardo (and now given to Bernardo Luini; Prado), as well as a copy of the *Last Supper*; one, to Andrea del Sarto; another, to Francesco Salviati; and a religious subject by Parmigianino. Most of the other Italian pictures owned by the king were made by the artists he had brought to Spain.

As for Netherlandish painters, Philip loved Bosch best of all, a taste he surely acquired from the collectors at the Flemish court, who were the principal patrons of that eccentric genius. Like these courtiers, many of them Spaniards, Philip was fascinated by the bizarre, complex imagery of Bosch, which, it is assumed, he understood in the same terms as Sigüenza, that is, as moralizing allegories. In 1596, he bought nine panels attributed to Bosch from the heirs of Ladrón de Guevara, a descendant of Diego de Guevara, an early and avid collector of these strange paintings. These panels included such famous compositions as the *Haywain* (El Escorial), the *Table with the Seven Deadly Sins* (Prado), and two versions of the *Temptation of St. Anthony* (perhaps the two in the Prado).[51] (Philip eventually owned about a dozen examples of this last-named subject by Bosch and his school.)

The king also tried to acquire pictures by famous Flemish painters of the fifteenth century, although they were harder to find. Nevertheless, he did manage to obtain panels by the Master of Flémalle (*Marriage of the Virgin*, Prado), Dirk Bouts (Triptych of the Virgin, Prado), and several by Patinir. In addition to the primitives, Philip bought pictures by the Flemish painters of his own century, such as Jan van Scorel, Jan Gossart, Bernard van Orley, Michel Coxcie – the latter being a particular favorite.[52] He even tried to keep pace with the newer developments; five years before he died, he sent to the Escorial several anonymous paintings that, as described in the inventory, were genre scenes in the manner of Pieter Brueghel the Elder and Pieter Aertsen: "a wedding [scene] done in Flanders, with diverse costumes, . . . a Flemish canvas with a man and woman eating in a tavern, and another woman cooking the meal, and many things and cooking utensils painted from life."[53]

The importance of the royal collection derives in equal measures from its size and quality. Although the number of paintings is difficult to calculate precisely, it is known that, at Philip's death, there were about 1,150 paintings at the

Escorial, about 300 at the Alcázar of Madrid, and perhaps 100 at the Pardo, totaling roughly 1,500 in all. If it is assumed that about 200 came from the collections of Charles V and Mary of Hungary, then it can be conservatively estimated that Philip collected over 1,000 pictures. This scale of acquisition is unprecedented in the history of picture collecting and represents the start of a new era – the era of the mega-collector, which was established in the seventeenth century.

The range of the collection was also impressive, if uneven. Emphasis fell heavily on Titian and the early Flemings; the Italian fifteenth century was almost entirely missing, while the High Renaissance was present only in token numbers, and often in copies rather than originals. Yet despite the unevenness, it was now possible for Spanish painters, at least for those who could gain admittance to the royal seats, to study a representative sample of the major achievements of Italian and Flemish painting and to derive a fairly complete idea of the artistry of Titian. Indeed, the royal collection implicitly elevated Titian to the place of honor among European painters.

In its totality, the importance of Philip as a patron and collector of paintings was immense. The most apparent result of his activities was to transfer the art of painting in Spain from a provincial to an international arena. Father Sigüenza may have wished to have been "spared knowing all these Italians," but they laid the foundations for a new phase of Spanish painting by introducing the grand manner of the Italian Renaissance. This was a notable development, but it had an unexpected consequence. Philip's generous patronage of foreign artists and his eager pursuit of their paintings made it seem as though they were essentially superior to the natives. Given the prestige of the monarch, it was only natural that the members of the elite would try to follow his example. Thus, as the frontiers of the Spanish art market were expanded, the painters of Spain found themselves competing at a disadvantage with foreign talent.

The centralization of patronage at the court accomplished by Philip was another development of transcendental importance. Slowly but surely, the regional centers found they could no longer retain a hold on the best talent. It was not only the money that attracted the provincial painters to Madrid, but the prospect of fame and glory in a society that revolved around the figure of the king. As the seventeenth century advanced, vital centers of painting such as Valladolid, Valencia, and Toledo declined in importance, leaving only Seville as a rival to Madrid. Philip's record of accomplishment as a patron was not to be surpassed in the later history of Spanish art and would be virtually unimpeachable if only he had recognized the worth of the one painter of genius who crossed his path, Domenikos Theotocopoulos, El Greco.

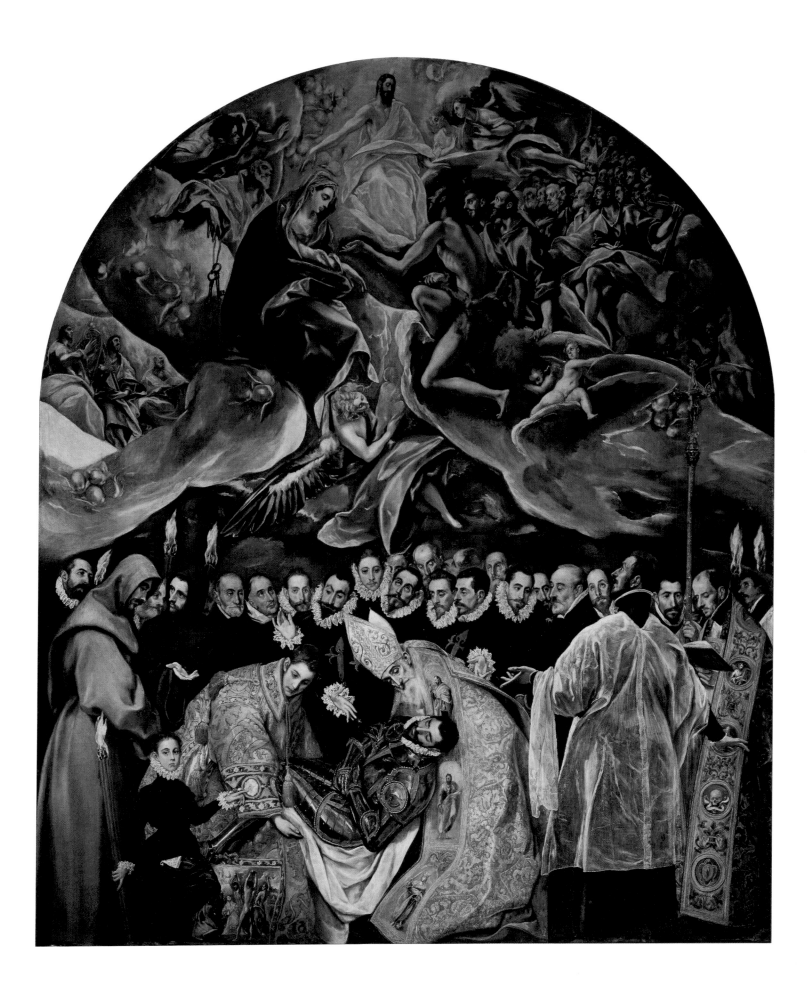

3
El Greco

THE CAREER OF Domenikos Theotocopoulos is by any measure one of the strangest in the history of art.[1] Born into the post-Byzantine world and trained as an icon painter, he moved to Italy and gradually relearned his art by studying the masters of the Renaissance. However, he had to go to Spain, that crucible of artistic acculturation, to find the success that had eluded him in Venice and Rome.

Theotocopoulos was born around 1541 in Candia (now Heraklion), capital of the island of Crete, then a possession of the Venetian Republic, and was trained by a local painter who is possibly identifiable as John Gripiotis.[2] Like Gripiotis, Theotocopoulos painted *alla greca* and *alla latina*; that is to say, he made gold-ground icons in the traditional Byzantine manner as well as small-scale pictures in a hybrid Greco–Italian style. None of his Byzantine-style works has been identified, but the recent discovery of a signed Greco–Italian painting, *Death of the Virgin* (pl. 64), although damaged, demonstrates how he, like other Cretan painters, had timidly assimilated the Renaissance style of Italy.[3] El Greco, as Theotocopoulos came to be known, quickly rose to a position of eminence among the painters of Crete; by 1563, he was already known as "maistro." As subsequent events reveal, he was a man of high ambitions, well educated, and of restless spirit, with professional and social aspirations that could not be fulfilled in his native land. Given the close contacts between Venice and Candia, it would have seemed logical for El Greco to move to the capital of the Republic in search of the fame and fortune that, in fact, were slow to come his way.

El Greco stayed in Venice for only a short period of time – he seems to have settled in the city in 1567 and moved to Rome three years later – but, from an artistic point of view, it was eventful. In Candia, El Greco could have seen a few works by or after some of the leading Venetian painters of the moment, especially Titian and Tintoretto, which are known to have existed in Cretan collections. In Venice, he was able to study the best paintings by these masters, and possibly became acquainted with the artists themselves, leading him to transform his style. The Byzantine manner was suppressed, partially to re-emerge in the artist's last years, and his "Latin" style was modified and modernized, a process that took considerable time and effort.

By November 1570, El Greco was in Rome where, thanks to the intervention of the miniaturist Giulio Clovio, he was given lodgings in the palace of Cardinal Alessandro Farnese. El Greco hardly seems to have made a mark in the competitive artistic world of Rome. In 1572, he was admitted to the Academy of St. Luke, but in the modest category of a "painter on paper."[4] Although he executed a few pictures for private clients, there was no public commission of consequence, no important patron to sponsor his career. Despite the lack of support, El Greco never ceased to study and to improve his art, thoroughly assimilating the work of the best Italian masters.

By a fortunate accident of survival, El Greco's opinions of the leading sixteenth-

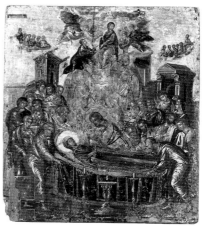

64. El Greco. *Death of the Virgin*, before 1567. Syros, Church of the Dormition, panel.

63. El Greco, *Burial of the Count of Orgaz*, 1586–88. Toledo, Santo Tomé, canvas, 4.80 × 3.60m.

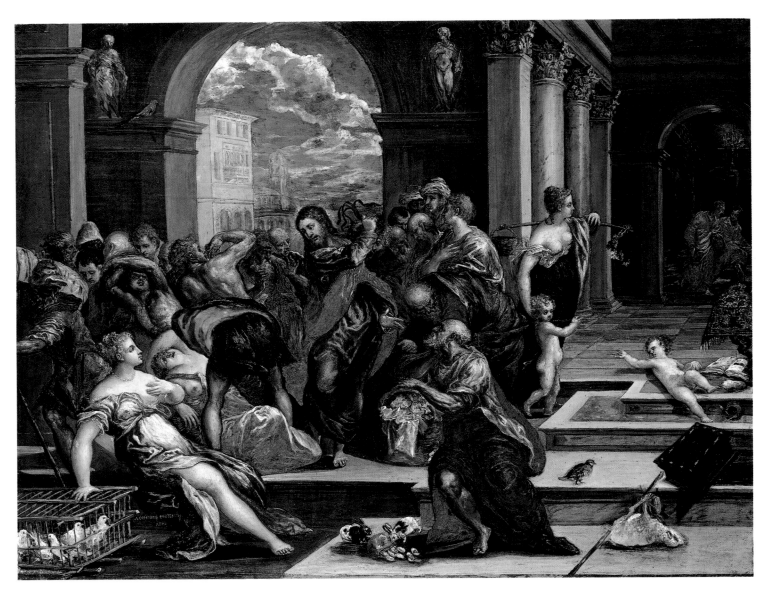

65. El Greco, *Purification of the Temple*, 1567–70. Washington, National Gallery of Art, Samuel H. Kress Collection, panel, 0.65 × 0.83m.

century Italian painters have been preserved in the marginal comments he wrote in his personal copy of Vasari's *Lives of the Artists*. These leave no doubt about his intense admiration for Titian and his great respect for Tintoretto.[5] After essaying a number of small-scale compositions in their manner (for instance, the *Pietà*, Philadelphia Museum of Art, and the *Annunciation*, Prado), El Greco attempted the more complex *Purification of the Temple* (pl. 65), in which he sought to bridge the gulf between Crete and Venice. This painting is an undisciplined exercise in the standard techniques of Renaissance painting – perspective, composition, gesture, figure drawing – bonded by the rich, saturated colors of Venice. It also demonstrates that the new style did not come easily; the composition is crowded and clumsy, marred by the overlapping of figures and the spongy rendering of anatomy. Although the elaborate architectural setting is dignified and enhances the illusion of space, it lacks a unified point of view and contains several stylistic solecisms.

A few years later, in Rome, El Greco produced another version of the same composition, with significantly better results (pl. 66), especially in the handling of the figures. This improvement can be attributed to the study of Michelangelo, an artist about whom El Greco was ambivalent. As noted in the margins of his copy of Vasari, El Greco believed that Michelangelo was deficient as a colorist and therefore

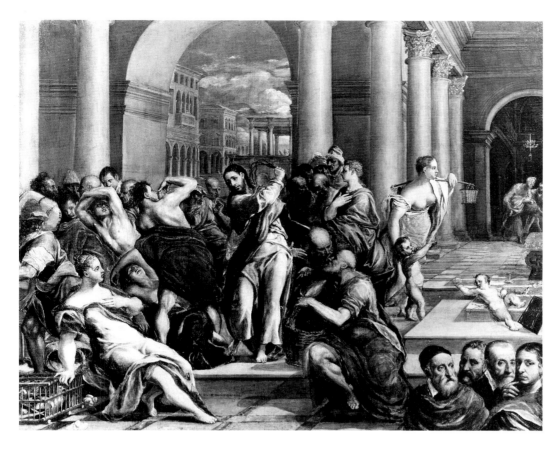

66. El Greco, *Purification of the Temple*, 1570–76. Minneapolis, Institute of Arts, canvas, 1.17 × 1.50m.

as a true painter. On the other hand, he could not restrain his admiration for Michelangelo's inspired treatment of the human form. "This is what he knew how to do best, and he did it better than anyone," he wrote.[6] Thus, Michelangelo is among the artists in the pictorial "footnote" inserted in the lower right corner, second from the left in the group that includes Titian, Giulio Clovio, and, in all probability, Raphael. Except for Clovio, who was portrayed for reasons of friendship, the acknowledgment of these famous practitioners as sources of inspiration is not surprising for a painter seeking to master the grand manner of Renaissance painting.

From outward appearances, the Roman years of El Greco seem to have led him nowhere; in fact they would lead him to Spain. Within the walls of the Farnese Palace, El Greco met the cardinal's librarian, Fulvio Orsini, renowned as the greatest living scholar of classical antiquity. Orsini, an important collector in his own right, acquired several works by El Greco, whose knowledge of Latin and Greek (a facility not uncommon among Cretans of the middle class) would have eased his acceptance into the circle of classical scholars, theologians, and artists that Orsini had gathered around him. One of this number was a young Spanish priest, Luis de Castilla (in Rome 1571–75), who became a lifelong friend and supporter of the artist.[7]

That Luis de Castilla specifically invited El Greco to come to Spain is possible, if not certain. It may be that the artist also had hopes of working for Philip II, who was then actively recruiting painters to work at the Escorial. Perhaps these two factors persuaded El Greco to gamble on finding in Spain the patronage that had eluded him in Rome. In any event, by July 1577, he was in Toledo, now thirty-six years old and about to begin the first significant commission of his career.

This commission came from the most important ecclesiastical patron in Spain, the cathedral of Toledo, and seems to have been arranged by Luis de Castilla, whose father, Diego, was dean of the chapter. Given El Greco's lack of experience in large-scale religious painting, Diego de Castilla had to take his (illegitimate) son's recommendation on faith, a faith that was amply rewarded.

The *Disrobing of Christ* (pl. 67), the painting in question, was executed for the sacristy of the cathedral and is the artist's first masterpiece.[8] The subject is rare in western art and must have been chosen to accord with the function of the room, where the priests changed into their vestments. While the theme is more frequent in Byzantine art, there is no exact precedent for El Greco's composition, which contains several unusual features, notably the man in armor, the person pointing his finger toward Christ, and the Three Marys. However, these and other curious motifs are explained by reference to the Passion as narrated in the Gospels of John and Luke. El Greco simply compressed several episodes into one moment. Thus, the man in armor is either Pilate or Herod; the figure who points is one of the priests who accuses Christ; and even the Three Marys are alluded to in both of the Gospels.

By any reckoning, the *Disrobing of Christ* is a strange and wonderful combination of real and abstract elements. The composition is a crowded, airless mass of gigantic figures and disembodied heads, which are pressed together around the body of Christ. Almost every hint of the natural setting has been eliminated; only a tiny patch of brown earth and a few scattered pebbles are seen at the feet of Christ. Yet in the midst of these unnatural elements, there are several uncannily realistic details, notably the man in armor, whose gleaming metal breastplate is a tour de force of naturalism. Much of the picture's power is generated by the exceptionally confident and audacious sense of color, which intensifies this vital component of Venetian painting. The figure of Christ is clad in a robe of vibrant red, which forces all eyes to gaze upon Him and detaches Him from the crowd. The daring use of rich color to define space instead of linear perspective reveals a pictorial imagination of the highest order and brings the meaning of the picture to the fore with unmistakable clarity – the physical and spiritual beauty of Christ as He prepares to sacrifice Himself for the sake of humanity.

The reaction of the cathedral chapter to this picture was not what the artist might have expected. Instead of applause there was rancor, which was caused by two issues: price and propriety. In sixteenth- and seventeenth-century Castile, the value of an altarpiece was customarily determined by a procedure called *tasación*, or evaluation. *Tasación* was simple in theory: the artist and patron each nominated an appraiser or team of appraisers (*tasadores*) who independently set a value on the finished work. In the event of an irreconcilable difference, the final determination was made by an arbitrator. Despite the appearance of fairness, *tasación* worked against the artist because it required him to invest his time, skill, and money in advance of payment, leaving him nothing to hold over the patron in the event of a grievance. El Greco did not have the power to change the system but, unlike most other artists working in the kingdom, he fought against being the hapless victim of its inequities.[9]

El Greco's refusal to compromise with the chapter, and with other patrons for whom he worked later in his career, was motivated in the first instance by pecuniary considerations. His overhead expenses were high and so was his standard of living. He had seen the best painters of Italy – Titian was a conspicuous example – residing in splendid houses and attended by servants. This extravagant way of life, however, was not mere self-indulgence; it reflected the superior social status of artistic activity, something in which El Greco strongly believed. Then as now, price and worth were inextricably linked in the system of social values, and El Greco was well aware of the dangers of selling cheap.

However, the art market in Spain, and in Toledo especially, did not favor the acceptance of El Greco's novel ideas. The church was too strong a patron for artists

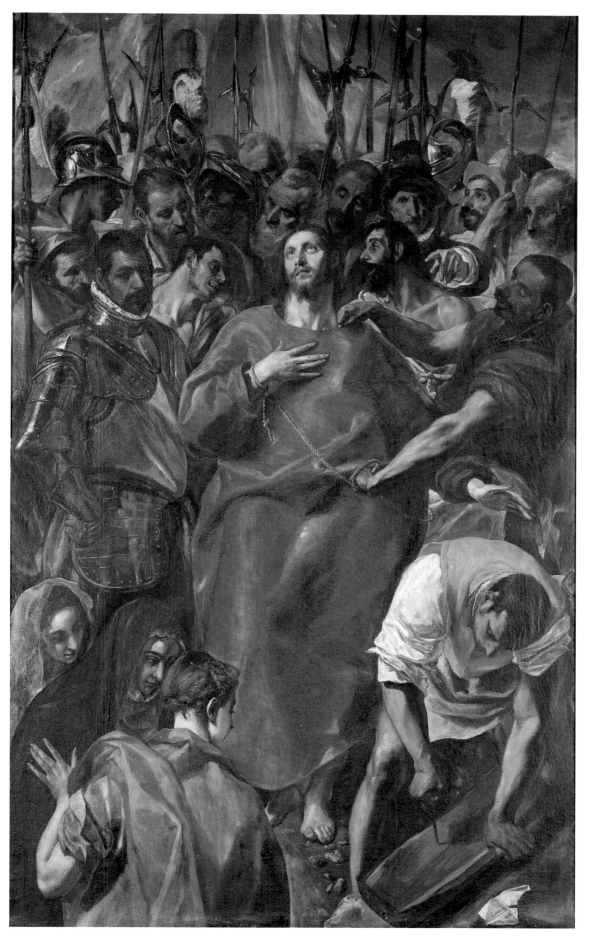

67. El Greco, *Disrobing of Christ*, 1577–79. Toledo, cathedral, sacristy, canvas, 2.85 × 1.73m.

of the rank and file to resist, and they prudently took what was offered in the hope of receiving new commissions. The painters of Toledo had not even troubled to form a guild or corporation to defend their interests. Thus, El Greco's only recourse was to the law, that notoriously inefficient, expensive way to achieve justice. As a proud man, El Greco was quick to sue and slow to settle, but settle he did, worn down by a legal system that favored those with the most time and money to spend in litigation. El Greco fought the first battles in the long campaign of Spanish painters to have their work regarded as an art, not a craft, and emerged a glorious loser.

In the case of the *Disrobing of Christ*, the two evaluations were miles apart, 900 versus 228 ducats. After bickering for two and a half years, the artist accepted a mere 250, having wasted time and money and, what is worse, having antagonized a powerful patron. Yet the defeat was not total. The canon in charge of the cathedral fabric had accused the artist of impropriety, objecting to the presence in the lower left corner of the Three Marys and to the fact that the head of Christ was not uppermost in the picture. El Greco refused to make changes; short of starting anew, it would have been impossible to do so. Even so, these elements are not impious except by the strictest standards of Counter Reformation theology. The fact that the picture was installed in the intended place and has remained there to this day proves that El Greco's imaginative composition falls within the bounds of orthodoxy, even if his rebellious conduct had offended some of the canons. At the time, the loss of the cathedral's favor might not have seemed a disaster because, in the very next year, he received a commission from the most important patron of all, Philip II.

The death of Navarrete in 1579, as has been seen, necessitated recruiting a new group of artists to finish the altarpieces of the Escorial basilica, and El Greco had the good fortune to be chosen as one of this number. Not a great deal is known about the royal commission to paint the *Martyrdom of St. Maurice and the Theban Legion* (pl. 68) except that it was completed by the autumn of 1582, that its price was disputed by El Greco, and that it was not acceptable to the king, who almost at once ordered a replacement to be made by Romulo Cincinnato. El Greco had certainly done his best to create a sophisticated, up-to-date picture in the *maniera* style, a strange choice of idiom given his passionate dislike of some of its leading Italian practitioners, including Giorgio Vasari, whom he seems to have met in Rome and come to hate. He also used the opportunity to demonstrate his mental acuity by deftly commingling early Christian and contemporary history.[10]

St. Maurice was the leader of an Egyptian legion of the Roman army whose members chose to die for the Christian faith rather than sacrifice to pagan gods. The martial career of St. Maurice had led to his adoption as the patron of infantry soldiers, a fact that inspired El Greco to include portraits of some of Philip's best generals in various parts of the composition. Wedged into the space between St. Lawrence and the standard bearer are two bearded men. The older of the pair, wearing an armored breastplate, is Emmanuel Philibert, duke of Savoy, who had commanded the Spanish troops at the battle of St. Quentin, the event that originally inspired the king to build the Escorial. Emmanuel Philibert, who had died in August 1580, was also the grand master of the military order of St. Maurice. To his right, nearest the saint, is Alessandro Farnese, prince of Parma, who at that moment was fighting with distinction against the Dutch heretics in the Netherlands. A further reference to a Spanish general is found in the background, where St. Maurice and his troops are suffering martyrdom by decapitation. Just behind St. Maurice is a portrait of Don Juan de Austria, the victor of Lepanto and bastard son of the king, who had died in 1578 and been reburied at the Escorial in May 1579.

For all the care expended in thought and execution, the picture failed to please the

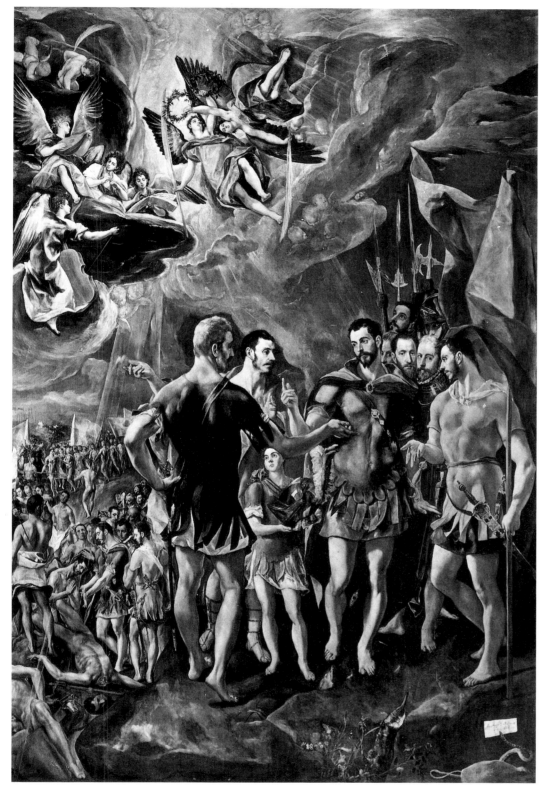

68. El Greco, *Martyrdom of St. Maurice and the Theban Legion*, 1580–82. El Escorial, canvas, 4.48 × 3.01m.

king, who surely would have considered the presence of sixteenth-century generals in a third-century history to be a serious "error," and there were other problems as well. Some years later, Father Sigüenza obliquely explained what had gone wrong, stating that the picture lacked what he called "reason" and "nature." He elaborated by saying that "the saints have to be painted so that they do not quell the desire to pray before them, but, rather, inspire devotion, because this has to be the principal effect and end of painting."[11] In other words, El Greco had failed the litmus test of Counter Reformation painting because his martyrs were not true to their nature and thus did not inspire devotion.

The meaning of this statement is not exactly transparent, but the intention becomes clearer when El Greco's version of the scene is compared with the replacement provided by Cincinnato (pl. 69). As revealed at once, this work, while no less mannered than El Greco's, places the scene of martyrdom where it belongs, in the center foreground, and not as an afterthought, as it were, along the margins of the composition. In El Greco's picture, St. Maurice and his officers almost appear to be debating the merits of martyrdom rather than freely accepting their glorious fate. To a patron who pondered the propriety of a shepherd holding a basket of eggs, the marginalization of the martyrdom was bound to be regarded as unforgivable. And he would have wanted even less to do with an artist who haggled over his generous norms of compensation. In four short years, El Greco had succeeded in alienating the king of Spain and the canons of Toledo, the wealthiest and most powerful patrons of the secular and religious realms of the monarchy. His grandiose ambitions now a thing of the past, El Greco was forced to join the ranks of the contract painters of Toledo.

The life of a contract painter was nothing if not precarious. Unlike a royal artist, who enjoyed an annual stipend and thus a modicum of financial security, the ordinary painter was continually on the prowl for new commissions to keep himself and his workshop solvent. Luckily, El Greco had an important advantage, namely entry into the ecclesiastical elite of Toledo provided by Luis and Diego de Castilla, who awarded El Greco a second major commission soon after he began to paint the *Disrobing of Christ*. This was the execution of the altarpieces in the church of Santo Domingo el Antiguo.[12]

Santo Domingo, a convent of Cistercian nuns, had been chosen by Don Diego to serve as the burial chapel for himself, his son, and Doña María de Silva, a noblewoman who had lived in the convent for some thirty years and possibly had been the mother of Luis de Castilla. On 8 August 1577, El Greco signed a contract, which stipulated the execution of six pictures for the main altarpiece, and one apiece for the two lateral altars. The final payment was received on 27 July 1578, although the pictures for the lateral altarpieces were still incomplete; in all likelihood they were finished by the time Don Diego celebrated the first mass in the new church on 27 September 1579.

The complex iconography of the three altars is dedicated to the theme of salvation through Christ, which is presented in both doctrinal and liturgical terms. Christ's sacrifice and its acceptance by God the Father form one level of meaning. Associated with this idea is the role of the Virgin Mary as the effective advocate of man before Christ the Judge. The second level of meaning validates the celebration of the mass as the true re-creation of Christ's sacrifice. These fundamental Roman Catholic ideas were elaborated with a truly symphonic complexity, which resulted from the close, continuing collaboration between artist and patron. Indeed, the contract of 1577 specified that the painter had to follow the instructions of Don Diego without exception. "And whatever is said must be done, without any appeal except to the wishes of said dean."[13] Nevertheless, Diego de Castilla was not an artist and it was therefore left to El Greco to find a suitable way to communicate the main points, which he did with uncommon brilliance of thought and artistry.

The subjects of the side altars, the *Adoration of the Shepherds* and the *Resurrection*, represent the beginning and end of Christ's life on earth and allude to the full

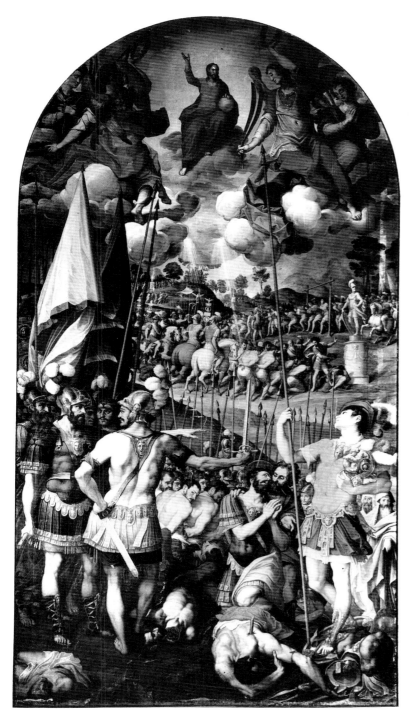

69. Romulo Cincinnato,
*Martyrdom of St. Maurice
and the Theban Legion*,
1582–83. El Escorial,
basilica, canvas.

celebration of the mass, because Christ is born again at every consecration of the host and resurrected at the conclusion of the office. To emphasize this idea, both paintings originally rested directly on the altar-tables, reinforcing their liturgical meaning.

In the *Adoration* (pl. 70), El Greco employs several effects to make the point. One is the central placement of the naked body of the Christ Child on an altar–like manger, around which the Virgin, St. Joseph, and the shepherds kneel in fervent prayer. The conspicuous representation of the unclad body of Christ was a standard reference to the mystery of the Eucharist, and thus both the biblical event and its

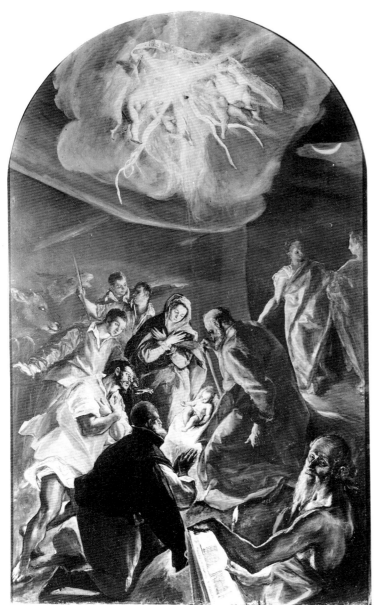

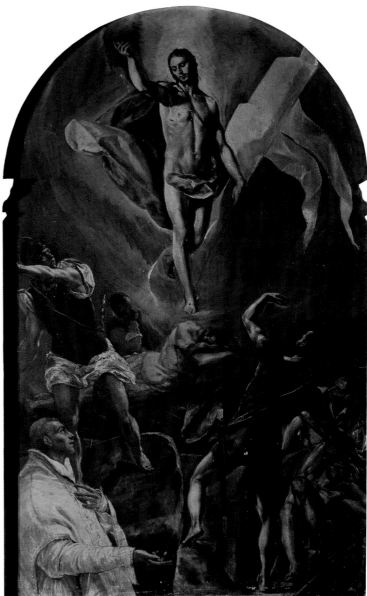

70. El Greco, *Adoration of the Shepherds*, 1577–79. Santander, Emilio Bótin, canvas, 2.10 × 1.28m.

71. El Greco, *Resurrection*, 1577–79. Toledo, Santo Domingo el Antiguo, canvas, 2.10 × 1.28m.

liturgical translation are at once communicated to the viewer. The artist also concentrates all the radiance on the infant's body, as if He were the source of illumination, a supernatural reference that focuses attention on the most important element of the composition and emphasizes the extraordinary nature of the event – Christ's willingness to become a man as a necessary stage in the sacrifice that makes salvation possible. As specified in the contract, St. Jerome stands in the lower right-hand corner, testifying to his belief, also upheld by Diego de Castilla, that the church must make its benefits equally available to all its members, especially the poor, represented here by the shepherds.

In the second side altar, El Greco depicted the Resurrection (pl. 71), the proof, as it were, that the benefits of Christ's sacrifice would be conveyed to mankind. (Once again the figure of a saint is to be found, this time, St. Ildephonsus, the patron of Toledo.) The composition for this scene is based on a work by Michelangelo, to whom El Greco sometimes turned for inspiration. In this instance, it was a drawing, now in Windsor Castle, which the artist had seen in Rome, in the collection of his friend Giulio Clovio. Although El Greco was in most respects an inventive painter,

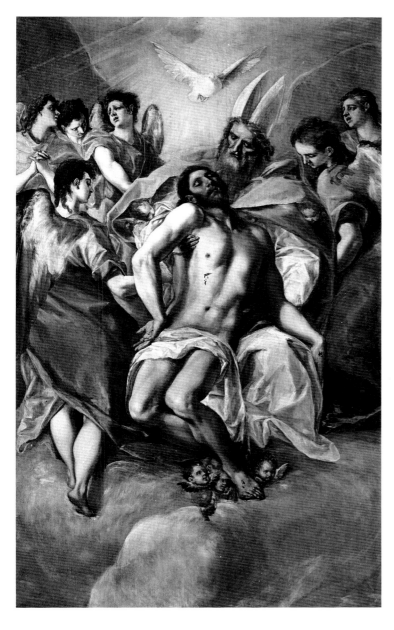

72. El Greco, *Trinity*, 1577–78. Madrid, Prado, canvas, 3.00 × 1.78m.

he was not loath to use works by other artists as a repertory of poses, gestures, and even entire compositions, and possessed a collection of 200 prints and 150 drawings, which he referred to as the need arose.[14] The influence of Michelangelo is found not only in the composition, but also in the figure of Christ, who is set in the spiraling pose made popular by the great sculptor.

The main altar contains two large pictures and a number of smaller ones. At the top was a painting, now called the *Trinity* (pl. 72), that more precisely illustrates the acceptance by God the Father of Christ's sacrifice, thus indicating that Christ's death is effective for redemption. Because the painting depicts the realization of the Christian's hope of salvation, it was especially suitable for inclusion in a funerary chapel. In this painting, too, El Greco incorporated motifs from the works of other artists: the basic composition comes from a print by Dürer, and the position of Christ's right arm depends on Michelangelo's statue of Duke Lorenzo de' Medici, in the Medici Chapel, Florence. However, the brilliant, original colors and the convincing emotion imparted to the figures subsume the sources into a moving example of religious art.

The final large-scale work, the largest of all, is the brilliant *Assumption* (pl. 73), which glorifies the Virgin as advocate before Christ. Diego de Castilla had specifically entrusted his soul to the care of the Virgin, and therefore her looming presence is an essential part of a program that advocates the patron's hope for justification and salvation. The principal visual source for this composition is Titian's famous *Assumption* in the church of the Frari, Venice, but once again El Greco reworked his primary material to emphasize a doctrinal point. The most important change involves the perspective, which is distorted so that the Virgin is seen from below while the Apostles are viewed at eye level. This adjustment increases the sense of upward movement, which is essential to demonstrating that the bodily assumption of the Virgin into heaven prefigures the resurrection of all mortals who will be saved.

The pictorial decoration of Santo Domingo set a pattern for El Greco's major commissions by providing his patrons with a sophisticated, dazzling artistic display of their religious convictions and spiritual aspirations. In the future, virtually all his major clients would be learned churchmen like Diego de Castilla, who would establish the program for the decoration and rely on the artist to cast it in a formal idiom that interpreted the essential doctrinal message. To some degree, El Greco's friends and patrons constituted a world of culture similar to the one he had known in the Farnese Palace, a world in which artists, theologians, and antiquarians met as equals and shared ideas.[15] The Toledan counterpart of Fulvio Orsini was Antonio de Covarrubias, a humanist and theologian, whom El Greco called a "miracle of nature" because of his extraordinary knowledge. Another close friend was Pedro Salazar de Mendoza (ca. 1550–1627), who had received a doctorate in canon law and wrote prolifically on theology, the classics, genealogy, geography, history, and literature.[16] His admiration for El Greco is attested by the ownership of several paintings, including the *View of Toledo* (New York, Metropolitan Museum of Art), and the commission in 1596 for a series of works for the hospital of San Juan Bautista, of which he was administrator.

The churchmen of Toledo also frequently provided the models for El Greco's portraits, which subtly combine the realistic and spiritual facets of his art. These works are likenesses, to be sure, but they are infused with a powerful sense of character and emotion. The moving bust-length portrait of Antonio de Covarrubias (pl. 74) was painted around 1600, after the sitter had lost his hearing. Isolated from the world, he is forced to live in his mind. Yet the quiet, brooding expression is played off against the restless folds of his costume, conveying the sense of a person whose inner resources are more than adequate to save him from despair.

By contrast, the portrait of Francisco de Pisa (pl. 75) reveals a tough-minded churchman who opposed the publication of the writings of St. Theresa of Avila, which he found to contain "many things that appear to contradict true and correct doctrine as well as the good use of mental prayer."[17] The sitter's gaunt, craggy features and pallid complexion are intensified by his black mantle, which is scored by slashing white highlights, and the perfect imitation of a luxurious fur collar. Pisa and Covarrubias exemplify the learned ecclesiastics who provided contacts and contracts for El Greco and encouraged his extraordinary flights of artistic imagination in the service of Counter Reformation Catholicism.

No picture better captures the essence of El Greco's art than his most famous, the *Burial of the Count of Orgaz* (pl. 63), which was painted for his own parish church, Santo Tomé.[18] Gonzalo Ruiz de Toledo, count of Orgaz, was a Toledan nobleman who had lived in the fourteenth century and acquired renown as a donor to religious institutions. Before he died, he had willed certain rents from the village of Orgaz to the church of Santo Tomé, where he had elected to be buried. These were duly paid

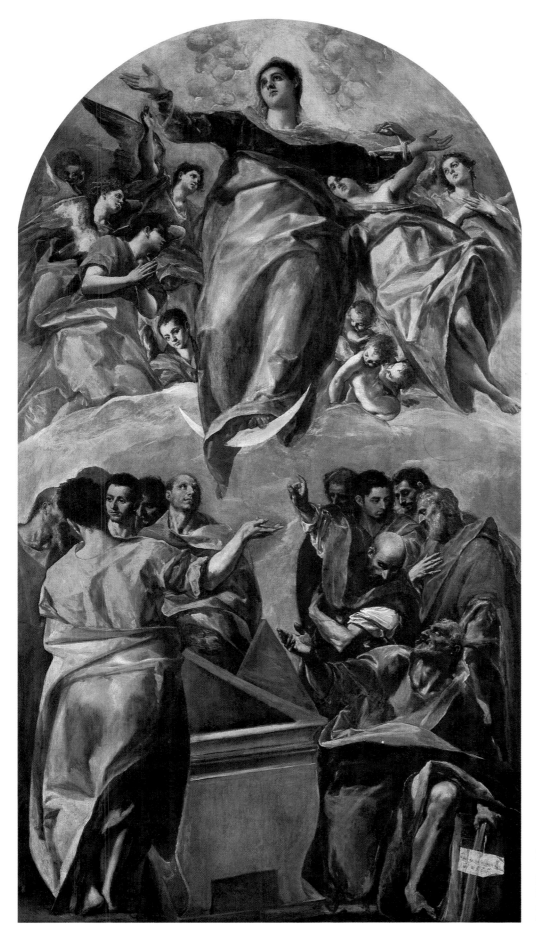

73. El Greco, *Assumption of the Virgin*, 1577–78. Chicago, Art Institute, Gift of Nancy Atwood Sprague in memory of Albert Arnold Sprague (1906.99), canvas, 4.01 × 2.29m.

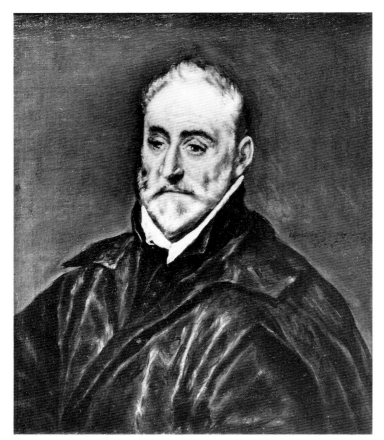 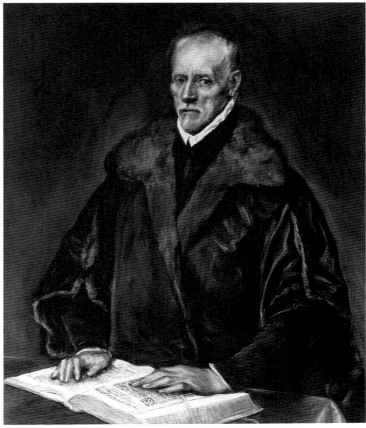

74. El Greco, *Antonio de Covarrubias*, ca. 1600. Paris, Musée du Louvre, canvas, 0.65 × 0.52m.

75. El Greco, *Francisco de Pisa*, ca. 1610–14. Fort Worth, Kimbell Art Museum, canvas, 1.07 × 0.90m.

until 1564, when the villagers ceased their remittances. In order to force the town to honor its obligation, the parish priest instituted a successful lawsuit that restored the income to the church, and with the proceeds initiated a project to refurbish the count's burial chapel, including a commission for El Greco to paint what has come to be considered as his masterpiece.

The contract signed by the artist in 1586 specifies some, but not all, of the details included in the picture:

> On the canvas shall be painted a procession of the priest and clerics, who were performing the office for the burial of Don Gonzalo Ruiz. And [also to be painted are] St. Augustine and St. Stephen, who descended to bury the body of this knight, one holding the head and the other the feet, placing him in the tomb. And around are many people who were watching and above all of this shall be painted an open heaven of glory.[19]

These rather general instructions account for the central deposition scene and the row of spectators. However, they make no reference to the doctrinal points embodied in the picture or to several other important features, which presumably were discussed by the principals, perhaps with the advice of El Greco's learned friends.

The most striking aspect of the composition is the juxtaposition of the imaginative vision of heaven with the burial scene, in which all the figures are garbed in contemporary costumes and presumably represent distinguished citizens of El Greco's Toledo. The explanation for the combination of the eternal and the mundane is found in the picture itself. At the lower left is the figure of a small boy, thought to be El Greco's son, Jorge Manuel, who points toward the funeral. His gesture is one that was commonly used in religious painting to signify that a lesson was being taught, and here the lesson concerns good works as indispensable to ensure the justification and eventual salvation of the soul. (Justification is the means by which the soul is brought into a saving relation with God.) The doctrine of good works was hotly contested by Protestants, who denied their efficacy as a means to redemption and salvation. This picture makes it clear that good works work. For, above the entombment, an angel holds the soul of Gonzalo Ruiz for judgment, while the Virgin and St. John appeal for its salvation. Flanking Christ the Judge are the saints who through their good works have already won a place in heaven, one of which is being reserved for the count of Orgaz.

If the doctrine of good works is timeless and universal, then the apparent anachronism of the sixteenth-century audience is explained. El Greco's contemporaries observe the miracle not in wonder or amazement, but with the solemn, knowing expressions of those who bear witness to an eternal truth, which is as valid for the sixteenth century as it was for the fourteenth and as it will be forever.

The dichotomy in style between the upper and lower parts has often been noted and indeed is one of the most remarkable features of the painting. In the lower zone, El Greco meticulously reproduces the appearances of persons and objects, as seen in the glistening armor of the deceased knight, the gray and lifeless pallor of the corpse, and the dazzling representation of the ecclesiastical vestments. More extraordinary still is the transparent rochet that is worn by the priest who stands in the right foreground and that clings to the black cassock beneath. The heavenly scene, by contrast, is far more abstracted. Strange, thin clouds support figures of inordinate height, notably the almost endless body of St. John the Baptist, while a strange, unreal light flickers over the surfaces.

This peculiar synthesis of the real and super-real is essential to El Greco's art, as he himself explains in the notations he wrote in the margins of his copy of the 1556 edition of Vitruvius's *De Architectura*. Although fragmentary and incohesive, as marginal notations are wont to be, these writings reveal the intellectual basis of El Greco's style and practice.[20]

For El Greco, painting, and not architecture or sculpture, was the superior art form, because it alone could reproduce every aspect of reality. The re-creation of reality was defined by El Greco not merely as the process of imitation: he considered sight to be a rational faculty by which the experienced and gifted painter could transform what he saw into a beautiful work of art. This process of transformation did not rely on mechanical rules and procedures, such as geometry, but rather on the judgment of an artistic intellect trained in the vision of nature.

In El Greco's conception of painting as the imitation and improvement of nature, color and light became the pre-eminent elements of the art. Thus, he prized Titian above all painters and found Michelangelo, however admirable as a draftsman, at fault because he was deficient in these other respects. The effective imitation of color and light posed the greatest challenge to the painter, and anyone who could overcome this maximum difficulty was entitled to be considered a great artist, for only thus could the entire range of natural phenomena be depicted and the full expression of beauty be achieved.

Once painters had achieved the mastery of color and light, and, of course, the mastery of form, they had it within their power to represent not only the visible, but also the "invisible," in this case the divine beings of heaven. El Greco assumed that the natural world was an imperfect reflection of the heavenly; thus, the same powers of vision that enabled artists to understand the visual world permitted them to imagine the unseen celestial realm.

As conceived by El Greco, neither the natural nor the celestial realm was static or immobile, qualities that he believed were antithetical to the beautiful. Beauty implied life, and life was movement in all its complexity and variety, to be captured through the use of elongated figures, drawn with twisting poses, severe foreshortenings, and sinuous outlines, so that they appeared to be in a state of perpetual flux.

Although presented schematically, and without reference to his own words, El Greco's ideas of beauty, if not original in themselves (they draw heavily on an eclectic range of Aristotelian and Neo-Platonic writers as well as on artistic theoreticians from both the Venetian and Tuscan schools), were carefully considered and applied to his paintings. In the *Burial of the Count of Orgaz*, to return to this masterpiece, El Greco put them into practice, demonstrating how he could imitate this world and envision the next, endowing both with movement and variety – in short, with life. Despite his steadfast adherence to this personal canon of beauty, El Greco's style was not immutable, but continued to evolve in the direction of increasing abstraction and complexity. Put in different terms, what might be called the naturalistic component was gradually displaced by the imaginative.

A logical starting place for an analysis of El Greco's later phase is the commission of 1596 for the church of the Colegio de Doña María de Aragón in Madrid, a seminary for training Augustinian preachers.[21] Doña María de Córdoba y Aragón (d. 1593) was a wealthy noblewoman of exemplary piety who decided to found a religious establishment in the capital, which would serve as her final resting place. The eventual decision to construct and endow a seminary of the Augustinian order was influenced by her spiritual advisor, an almost legendary holy man named Alonso de Orozco. The Blessed Alonso (1500–91; beatified in 1882) was an ascetic, visionary, and man of charity who in his day was venerated as a saint.

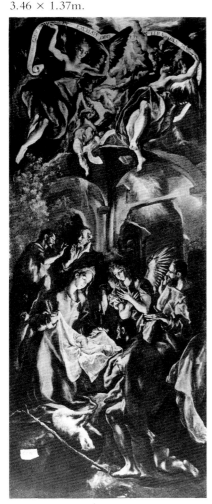

76. El Greco, *Adoration of the Shepherds*, 1596–1600. Bucharest, Rumanian National Museum, canvas, 3.46 × 1.37m.

Both Doña María and Alonso died before the seminary was completed, and the work was brought to a conclusion by her executor, Jerónimo de Chiriboga, and the rector, Fray Hernando de Rojas. The decision to commission El Greco to provide the pictures for the main altarpiece was probably determined by Chiriboga, who was a canon of the college of Talavera la Vieja, for which El Greco had worked just a few years before. Chiriboga had served in the administration of Cardinal Quiroga, archbishop of Toledo (1577–94), and was often in residence in Toledo, where he would have moved in the same circle as many of the artist's friends.

The program for El Greco's commission, in the first instance, was determined by the function of the church as a burial chapel for Doña María and the Blessed Alonso. In her will, Doña María made the care of her soul a requirement for the tenancy of the Augustinians, stipulating that their leasehold would expire if they neglected to pay the "rent" of sixteen daily masses in her favor. Doña María also provided for the burial of the Blessed Alonso in the church, and it was his extensive writings that served as the basis for the content of the altarpiece.

The original disposition of the altarpiece is a matter for conjecture; it was dismantled early in the nineteenth century and was never fully described or depicted. It does seem likely, however, that it comprised four images: the *Incarnation* (Villanueva y Geltrú, Museo Balaguer); the *Baptism of Christ* and the *Crucifixion* (both Prado), and the *Adoration of the Shepherds* (pl. 76). In his writings, Alonso constantly refers to these four events to explain his devotion to the Eucharist and to exemplify the vows of chastity, poverty, and obedience required of those who took holy orders. Thus, as a group, the paintings express the dual purpose of the foundation – to work for the salvation of the founder's soul and to prepare young men for careers as preachers. Although the author of the program is not mentioned in the documents, it is likely to have been Fray Hernando de Rojas, who was the confessor of the Blessed Alonso and devoted to his memory. This would explain

84

the use of many motifs derived from the writings of Alonso de Orozco, which otherwise do not appear in El Greco's work.

Some of these features are seen to good advantage in the *Adoration of the Shepherds*, which was also the subject of one of the lateral altarpieces in Santo Domingo el Antiguo. In both commissions, this choice was motivated by the desire to illustrate Christ's love of the poor, but in the college altarpiece, it also reflected Alonso's conviction that the shepherds exemplified the efficacy of the monastic vow of poverty. Like Diego de Castilla, Alonso believed in the eucharistic dimension of the Nativity:

> Here is the mystery of the Nativity. Thus, Bethlehem, the house of bread, is the church, and the crib is the holy altar where the Child is lying, wrapped in humble clothes, which are the "accidents" of bread and wine. Here come the angels singing "Gloria," just as they came there.[22]

Another common element in the two *Adorations* is the group of heavenly angels, holding aloft a banner with the Latin words of praise "Glory to God in the highest, and on earth peace among men" (Luke 2:14), a quotation reflecting the belief that good Christians would enjoy the proclaimed peace when they rested in the grace of God after death. This theme is entirely appropriate to the function of the churches as burial chapels.

But the *Adoration of the Shepherds* for the college has novel features, which were generated by adherence to Alonso's writings. For example, the presence of the angel, which is unique among El Greco's versions of the theme, corresponds to Alonso's belief that celestial beings joined the shepherds in the worship of the Child and became the brothers of the men in their mutual adoration of the Lord.

Through such pictorial references to Alonso's writings, El Greco sought to illustrate the pious man's meditations on the life of Christ, meditations that combine major theological ideas with a detailed representation of the Gospel text. Even some of the tenor of Alonso's prose has been absorbed by the artist, which accounts for the high-keyed emotionalism of this version of the *Adoration*. In comparing the style of the two paintings, executed some twenty years apart, it is easy to see the changes – the more elongated figure style, the more drastic compression of space, and the increased abstraction of naturalistic detail, all of which heighten the other-worldly quality of the scene. Although certain elements have remained essentially unchanged, notably the studied elegance of pose, the love of complicated fore-shortenings, and the bold contrasts of light and shadow, the innovations are striking nonetheless.

It is tempting to attribute these changes entirely to the visionary writings of the Blessed Alonso and thus to validate the longstanding belief that El Greco was a mystical painter. However, it is important to give equal weight to the constants as well as the novelties of the late style. While executing the paintings for the college, El Greco, as in all his commissions, attempted to express both the letter and the spirit of the patron's directives, and to find an appropriate visual equivalent for the doctrinal program; but obviously he could not reinvent his means of expression for every new commission. While the heightened intensity of these paintings owes something to the textual sources that lie behind them, these sources only accelerated El Greco's progress along a path of increasing pictorial abstraction, which he followed almost to the day he died.

About a dozen years later, El Greco returned to the subject of the Adoration of the Shepherds in a painting charged with personal significance that was destined for the altar above his tomb in Santo Domingo el Antiguo. As proof of his unflagging affection for the artist, Luis de Castilla had granted him permission to be buried at the same site as his parents, and where Luis himself was to be interred. In this, one of the last works of the artist, the deliberate and consistent transformation of nature into art reaches a climax (pl. 77).

Alongside this very late painting (ca. 1610–14), the *Adoration* for the college of Doña María appears almost realistic. Here all vestiges of nature have been eradicated and the gigantic, flame-like figures crowd together in an indeterminate setting. With great subtlety, the artist confounds the definition of solid and void. On the ground just to the right of the kneeling shepherd is a patch of white that seems to read as a space, but that, on close scrutiny, becomes legible as the form of the symbolic sacrificial lamb. In front of the same figure, and placed at an impossibly close distance, is another strange configuration that is eventually recognizable as a disembodied ox-head with curved horns. (The ox was a traditional symbol of the Hebrews, who meekly genuflect before the founder of the New Order.) The spectral light effects, the uneven, sketchy application of paint, the sudden shifts in perspective, all familiar features of the earlier works, are here exploited with new daring by an artist approaching seventy years of age. A dozen years after the start of a new century and a new artistic era, El Greco resolutely continued to explore the possibilities of artistic ideas pondered throughout his long career as a painter.

The visionary character of the late works has often been attributed to the influence of the mystics of Spain, an explanation that simplifies a complex phenomenon, especially now that it is known that El Greco's contacts with the mystics were non-existent.[23] On the contrary, his patrons and friends, as members and defenders of the institutional church, regarded the mystics as marginal and even potentially dangerous to orthodox practice. Furthermore, El Greco's writings show that his art was a meditated, not spontaneous, form of expression and firmly rooted in Italian theory. This accounts for the remarkable consistency of his development over the thirty-eight years he lived in Toledo.

However, for all their importance, El Greco's artistic concepts are not sufficient in themselves to provide an understanding of an art that may fairly be called unique. Other conditions had to exist that would permit him to bring these ideas to fruition, and one of these surely was his initial training as a Byzantine painter. As can be seen in his earliest works, El Greco was essentially an outsider to the conventions and practices of Renaissance painting, the standard elements of which he might have regarded not as the immutable laws of art but simply as another way to make pictures, which could be altered as necessary. Beneath the polished veneer acquired through the study of Titian and Michelangelo was an icon painter who had been trained in a tradition with little investment in naturalism or anatomical drawing or linear perspective. Under the right conditions, this Byzantine heritage could re-emerge and recombine with all that had been learned in Italy.[24]

El Greco was fortunate to find these conditions in Toledo, where there were no painters who could approach his artistic brilliance and power. For most of his career, the competition was typified by a painter like Luis de Carvajal (pl. 58), clearly no match for him. And it was not until the very last years of his life that El Greco witnessed the arrival of Juan Bautista Maino (see chapter 4), who brought the innovative style of Caravaggio from Rome to Toledo.

In addition to this essentially negative feature of Toledan artistic life was something much more positive: the network of friends and patrons who stood by this gifted but quarrelsome artist. Luckily, their loyalty was matched by their learning and sophistication, and thus they were able to appreciate and enrich El Greco's constantly deepening understanding of his art.

It is possible that El Greco would have enjoyed comparable success as a painter of allegories in Prague, of mythologies in Haarlem, of portraits in Fontainebleau, places

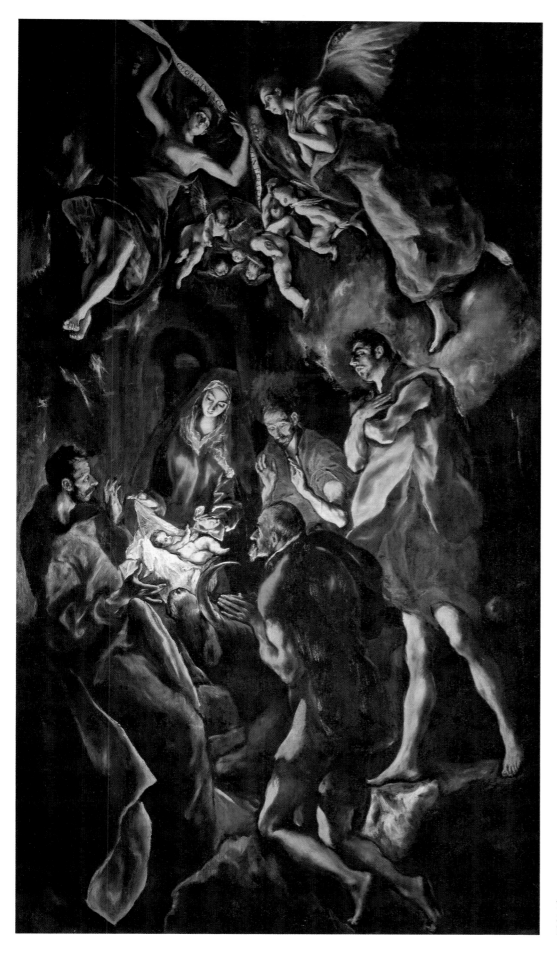

77. El Greco, *Adoration of the
Shepherds*, ca. 1612–14. Madrid,
Prado, canvas, 3.20 × 1.80m.

that, like Toledo, were tolerant and even admiring of a non-classical art. However, the upper reaches of the Toledan ecclesiastical establishment had already become accustomed to the supercharged expression of Christian history through the sculpture of Alonso Berruguete. The points of contact between these two individualistic artists are easy to detect if not to evaluate. It is too convenient to say that the painter was inspired to remake his manner of painting after contemplating Berruguete's sculpture in the choirstall and archbishop's throne of the cathedral. Rather, it can be suggested that Berruguete's independent stance toward the classical tradition of Renaissance art and the expressive distortions of his style prepared the Toledan elite for El Greco's non-normative painting. Without in any way shaping El Greco's approach, Berruguete's flamboyant, exaggerated style created a climate of taste that was propitious for the migrant artist from Crete.

The decision to settle in Toledo had another consequence, which was to convert El Greco into the quintessential painter of the Spanish Counter Reformation. El Greco's career coincided with the moment when the church was struggling not only to defend itself as an institution against Protestantism, but also to renew the Catholic faith as the sole means to perfection and salvation. The archbishops of Toledo in the late sixteenth century, as the spiritual leaders of Spain, were zealous in applying the new norms of Catholicism in their see.[25] El Greco accepted the tenets of the renewed orthodoxy and became a knowing interpreter of its doctrine.

The paintings of El Greco served another important purpose: they provided consolation and inspired devotion. Part of El Greco's achievement resides in his invention of a pictorial language that glorified, dramatized, and vivified the faith on which everything depended. By visualizing the mysteries of Catholicism in a brilliant and affecting rhetorical style, he emulated the preachers of the age, such as Fray Hortensio Félix de Paravicino, a great admirer of the artist and the subject of one of his best portraits (Boston, Museum of Fine Arts). These priests sought to arouse the spirit of the faithful with glittering discourses that artfully led the spirit to contemplate the road to glory blazed by Christ, which they too might travel if only they would follow in His footsteps.[26]

This expression of personal faith, with its occasional excesses, stands apart from the institutional faith required by Philip II for the decoration of the Escorial. Not that the king was indifferent to the spiritual component of Catholicism: among his subjects, none was more devout than he. But as the recognized leader of the secular forces of Catholicism, he was required to provide a perfect example of orthodoxy, especially in the monument he was constructing to glorify the Catholic majesty of his dynasty. El Greco's bid for the monarch's favor, the *Martyrdom of St. Maurice*, singularly miscalculated what was at stake at the Escorial. Thus, having failed to win the patronage of the king, he retreated to Toledo and the company of learned, pious men, there to create the pictures that inspired their yearning for salvation and satisfied their taste for exciting works of art.

4
Crosscurrents in Castile
1598–1621

IN ART, AS IN POLITICS, the reign of Philip III (1598–1621) seems to suffer by comparison with those that came before and after. Philip II and Philip IV stand high among the patrons and collectors of their day, while the Philip in between is scarcely visible as a presence in the world of art, or anywhere for that matter. As his father had foreseen, Philip III lacked the talent and temperament to govern a country facing enormous military and economic problems. The new king himself had few illusions about his capacity to govern, and quickly turned the administration of the monarchy over to an ambitious aristocrat, Francisco de Sandoval y Rojas, soon elevated to the title of duke of Lerma. In addition to seizing the portfolios of government, Lerma became the dominant figure in the patronage of art.[1]

Lerma had entered the court of Philip II in 1574, when the artistic activities of the monarch were reaching their zenith, and was deeply impressed by the works being collected and commissioned. Lacking Philip's opportunities as a connoisseur and powers as a ruler, Lerma was content initially to follow the old king's example, employing painters who had worked for him and acquiring pictures by authors sanctioned by their presence in the royal collection. Whereas Philip II brought painters from Italy, Lerma preferred to bring them from the Escorial. But if the duke was a more cautious patron, he was by no means unaware of important changes that occurred in Italy during his twenty-year tenure in office.

The impact of Lerma's patronage on the art of painting is still imprecise, in part because it is not well studied, in part because it defies easy categorization. In some aspects, Lerma was an artistic conservative. He left the tradition of Habsburg portraiture largely as he found it, probably because the formulas devised by Antonis Mor and Titian had by then become iconic. In contrast, his taste in religious painting was outward-looking. To be sure, he did not make sweeping changes in the corps of royal painters, as Philip II had done, preferring to support the artists already on the payroll when he came into office, and thus facilitating the formation of family dynasties within the ranks. However, these dynasties were not allowed to become monopolies, since Lerma and other courtiers were interested also in the different types of naturalist painting that were emerging in Florence, Venice, and Rome around the turn of the century. The Lerma years, in fact, mirror that dynamic period of Italian painting spanning 1580–1610, when manifestations of late mannerism, nascent naturalism, and reborn classicism appeared side by side. Only the conclusion of the period is different because the most advanced styles, represented by Caravaggio and Annibale Carracci, did not find much of a following in Spain. The taste of the Lerma period may therefore be described as progressive but not revolutionary, formative but not definitive, and thus needs to be viewed from more than one vantage point.

Lerma's first task upon winning the favor of the young king was to improve the depleted financial condition of his own house. Impoverished patrons can afford only poor art, if any at all. Lerma has long been renowned as an extraordinary opportunist, and with good reason. By 1602, after only four years in power, he had accumulated titles, offices, and grants that were producing an annual income of around 200,000 ducats, enough to buy and commission works of art and a good deal more. He immediately began to assemble an art collection that grew to immense proportions and was distributed among the houses he built or acquired in Madrid, Valladolid, and Lerma, his seignorial town, where he started to construct an ambitious urban complex. However, as early as 1606, Lerma began to disperse the collection for reasons that are still unfathomable. In part, he seems to have been cashing in his investment, which he accomplished by selling one of his Valladolid palaces to the king, complete with furnishings and decoration, for an inflated price. And by 1617, a year before his fall from power, he had divested himself of roughly eighty percent of the works in his possession.

Lerma's interest in masters of the sixteenth century was heavily influenced by the royal collection and therefore centered on the Venetians, especially Titian, Veronese, and Tintoretto. Unlike Philip II, Lerma was unable to obtain many originals by these masters and had to be content with copies, a not uncommon occurrence in the period just prior to the sales of numerous important Italian collections in the 1620s. An unusual feature of his collection were the copies after such early mannerists as Pontormo, Parmigianino, and Fra Bartolommeo.

Of greater interest are the paintings by contemporary artists purchased or commissioned by the duke. The best of these, of course, was Rubens, who visited the Spanish court at Valladolid in 1603. Rubens was not unimpressed by Lerma as a connoisseur, although he tended to speak well of those in power. As he commented on 24 May 1603, "he [Lerma] is not without knowledge of fine things, through the particular pleasure he has in seeing every day so many splendid works by Titian, Raphael, and others . . . in the king's palace, the Escorial, and elsewhere."[2] Rubens painted several works for Lerma, including the famous equestrian portrait (Prado), a picture that the duke sold to the king in 1607 with the contents of his country house near Valladolid. Lerma also owned a series of Apostles by Rubens, which he kept. However, once Rubens had left the country, the duke seems to have lost contact with him.

Lerma's interest in the art of the day was focused elsewhere, particularly on the group of Florentine painters today known as the reformers,[3] a term that describes their rejection of the complex mannerist style practiced in the second third of the century and their attempts to evoke the new spirit of Counter Reformation Catholicism. The precursor of the movement in Spain had been Federico Zuccaro, whose paintings for the Escorial basilica became a point of reference for the next generation of painters and patrons. These pictures helped to provide a new pictorial vocabulary, but their insistent classicism and emotional neutrality (the latter imposed by Philip II) were not entirely suitable for an age of greater religious fervor. It was left to Zuccaro's one-time assistant Bartolomé Carducho to provide the essential models for the new religious painting.

Carducho, in fact, was himself a Florentine (baptized as Bartolommeo Carducci), born around 1560.[4] In 1578, still a young painter, he joined the workshop of Zuccaro, who was then in Florence to execute the frescoes in the dome of the cathedral. Deciding to cast his lot with Zuccaro, Carducho traveled to Rome as part of a team of assistants, including Domenico Cresti, il Passignano (1559–1638), and worked there during the early 1580s before returning to Florence. Then in 1585, he made the fateful decision to accompany Zuccaro to the Escorial, where he worked

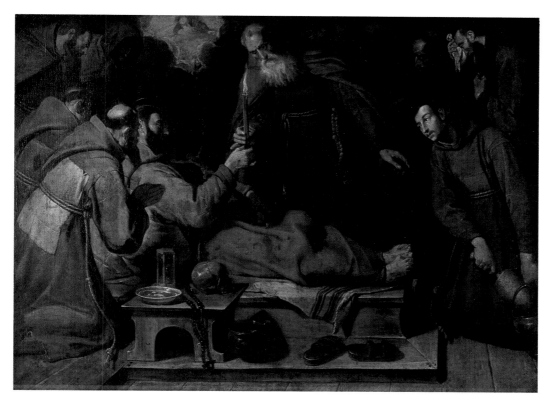

78. Bartolomé Carducho, *Death of St. Francis*, 1593. Lisbon, Museu de Arte Antiga, canvas, 1.15 × 1.53m.

on the frescoes in the main cloister. After Zuccaro's dismissal, Carducho chose to remain in Spain.

During the next ten years, Carducho worked occasionally for the king and found a few private patrons. In order to supplement his income, he became a picture importer of some consequence. Given his Florentine origins, he naturally turned to compatriots to supply his stock, among them il Passignano and Gregorio Pagano, two of the better-known reform painters.[5] This commerce proved to be a bonanza for all concerned. Indeed, in 1605, Passignano's pupil, the Sienese Pietro Sorri (1556–1622), formed a company with his nephew Sallustio Lucchi to ship paintings from Livorno to Cartagena, from where presumably they were sent to Carducho in Madrid.[6]

For Carducho, the benefits of this commerce were to be artistic as well as financial. His luck as a painter finally turned on 8 August 1598, when Philip II appointed him royal painter. A month later the prickly old king was dead and Carducho was set for life. By then, and as a result of his dealings with Florence, he had himself become an excellent reform painter and was ready to make the most of the possibilities offered by the new regime.

The extant work by Carducho is not very large and dates almost entirely from the last ten years of his life. But while wandering in the wilderness of disfavor, he painted two extraordinary pictures that demonstrate both his indebtedness to Florentine colleagues and his great importance to the formation of a new style of religious painting at court. The earlier of the two works is the *Death of St. Francis* (pl. 78), which, were it not signed and dated 1593, could easily be placed a good thirty years later. In this composition, Carducho builds a moving, humanized narrative on the armature of the classical style. The composition is nearly symmetrical, the figures carefully drawn and posed, the gestures and expressions exquisitely calibrated to evince deep, internalized grief. Even more than his Florentine models, Carducho individualizes the physical traits of the figures, much as Sánchez Coello had done in his altarpieces in the Escorial basilica. The rough, appealing humanity of the Franciscans seems to be the artist's response to the Spanish taste for a new realism in devotional pictures which would only increase in the years to come.

Carducho's potent use of light is another notable innovation: it intensifies the presence of the figures and glances off the inanimate objects, endowing each with a characteristic texture. The saint's scuffed, worn sandals, an earthenware chamber-pot, a bowl of thin broth, a tawny human skull, and an hourglass with the sands of time running out – all are depicted with an authentic feel that draws the viewer into the unfolding drama of the saint's pious death.

Two years later, Carducho executed the *Descent from the Cross* (pl. 79) for San Felipe el Real, Madrid, which is fully in line with the tendencies of the Florentine reformers. The arresting play of light and shadow, soon to become a commonplace in the leading centers of Spanish painting, effectively underscores the pathos of the scene, and only the rich colors of the costumes alleviate the suffocating gloom of this supremely tragic moment.

Carducho's activities as a painter and merchant clearly played an important part in reorienting artistic taste at court toward the style of the central-Italian reformers, and may well have encouraged a few painters from Italy to try their luck in Spain. Orazio Borgianni (ca. 1575–1616) was in Spain at two different periods.[7] The first stay lasted from about 1598 to 1602, when he went back to his native Rome. He was again in Madrid by June 1603, when he signed a petition to the king for support of a painters' academy. By October 1607, he had returned home, where he remained until his premature death nine years later.

There is little information about Borgianni's activities in Spain, and only a few paintings can securely be identified with either period of activity. His best-known Spanish commission was not executed until after he had left for good, and consists of several altarpieces for the monastery of Portacoeli, Valladolid, thought to have been done around 1613–14. In other works of this period, Borgianni was beginning to show the effects of his study of Caravaggio, but the Portacoeli pictures are still entirely within the mainstream of the reform movement favored by the court. (The patron was Rodrigo de Calderón, an important member of Lerma's inner circle.[8])

About the time that Borgianni was departing Spain, his compatriot Angelo Nardi arrived in Madrid, where he spent the rest of his long life (1584–ca. 1665).[9] Nardi was born in a Tuscan village and received his training in Florence. Around 1600, he went to Venice for a while, finally settling in Spain around 1607. There he found a ready audience for his mellifluous synthesis of Florentine and Venetian stylistic elements and, during the reign of Philip III, attracted important commissions, notably the entire pictorial decoration of the church of the Bernardine convent in Alcalá de Henares, begun in 1619. Among these pictures are the best of Nardi's Spanish production, which show how he adapted to his new clientele by emphasizing the realism of his figure types (pl. 80). In the reign of Philip IV, Nardi succeeded in obtaining an honorary appointment as royal painter, although he painted much as he had done at the start of his career.

By 1610, the reform style, tailored to the requirements of Spanish taste, had become the quasi-official style of the court of Philip III and, as will be seen, proved resistant to fresh impulses from Italy, especially those generated by Caravaggio, Carracci, and their followers. Bartolomé Carducho, who had done his work well, had also, before he died in 1608, trained a successor, his younger brother, Vicente.

Vicente Carducho was born in Florence around 1576 and thus was almost a generation younger than his brother, with whom he went to Spain in 1585.[10] Vicente owed not only his art but his early success to Bartolomé. In 1601, the duke

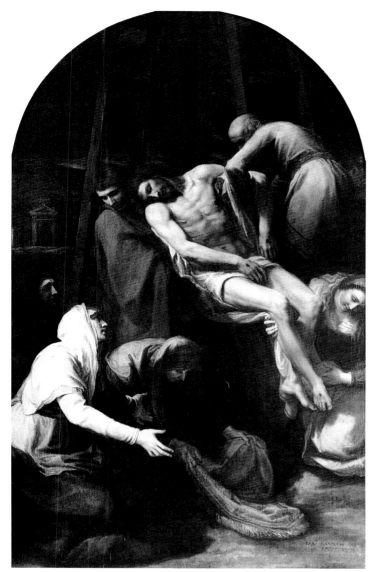

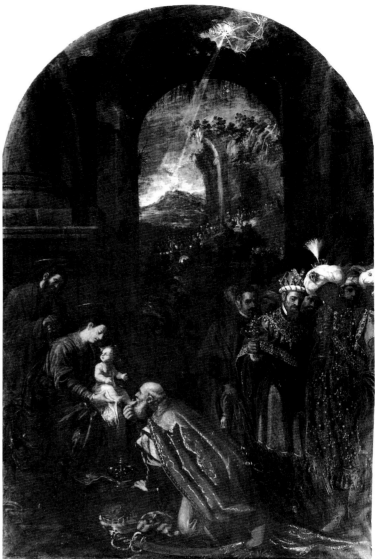

79. Bartolomé Carducho, *Descent from the Cross*, 1595. Madrid, Prado, canvas, 2.63 × 1.81m.

80. Angelo Nardi, *Adoration of the Magi*, 1619–20. Alcalá de Henares, convent of Las Bernardas, canvas, 3.00 × 1.90m.

of Lerma decided to move the court from Madrid to Valladolid. The move proved unsatisfactory and, in 1606, the court returned permanently to Madrid. During this five-year hiatus, Vicente, who was then collaborating with Bartolomé, began to attract the patronage of Lerma and ultimately was appointed to his brother's place as a royal painter on 28 January 1609, a place he maintained until his death almost thirty years later in 1638. This long tenure and his success as an artist assured Carducho a pre-eminent place among the painters of Madrid, despite the fact that he was supplanted in the royal favor by Velázquez during the 1620s.

The earliest known works of the artist, which date to 1606, are logically indebted to the example of his brother. Vicente proved to be a very faithful disciple indeed, perpetuating Bartolomé's Florentine manner into the mid-1620s. In 1610, he executed *St. John Preaching* (pl. 81), a painting with pastel colors, a complex composition, and studied poses that still has a vestigial mannerist air. Six years later he painted an *Annunciation* (pl. 82), a balanced, dignified work of art that reveals his gradual assimilation of the reform style, which culminated in the later 1620s when, as will be seen in chapter 6, he began to introduce greater realism into his pictures and reached the pinnacle of his artistic achievement.

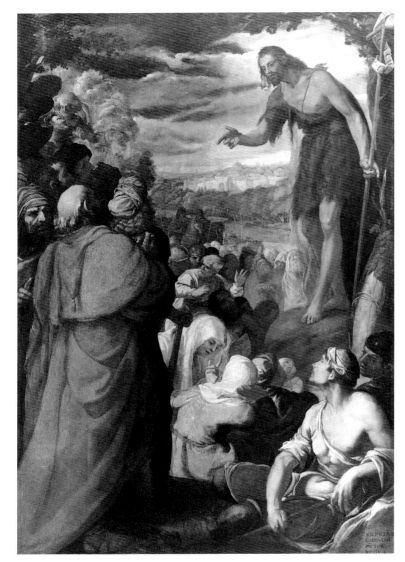

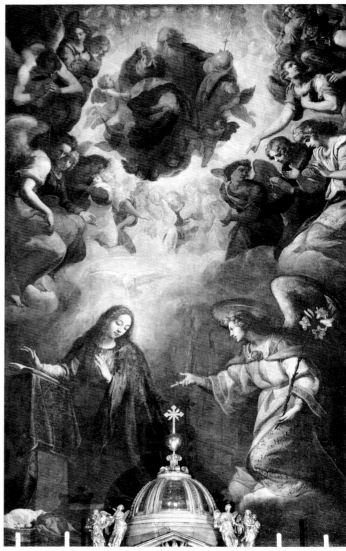

81. Vicente Carducho, *St John Preaching*, 1610. Madrid, Real Academía de San Fernando, canvas, 2.69 × 1.80m.

82. Vicente Carducho, *Annunciation*, 1616. Madrid, Convento de la Encarnacíon, canvas, 4.16 × 2.54m.

Carducho's importance as a painter was equaled, and perhaps exceeded, by his activities as a spokesman for the dignity of the artistic profession in Spain. Although he had left Florence while still a boy, he felt a powerful attraction to its literary and artistic culture and became an avid student of its writings; at his death he owned a library of about 300 books, the largest of any Spanish artist of the period (by comparison, Velázquez owned about 160), and there is reason to believe that he had read them all. Carducho's literary interests led him to form friendships with leading men of letters at court, including Lope de Vega and Juan de Jáuregui, a distinguished poet and amateur artist, and to cultivate an elegant style of writing.

For Carducho, these literary activities were undoubtedly important in their own right, but they had another dimension. Like El Greco, but with much greater discipline and determination, Carducho wanted to improve the mediocre status of the artist in Spanish society, a condition that, curiously, was aggravated by the duke of Lerma's treatment of painters. For all his interest in the arts, Lerma had fixed and none-too-generous ideas about what painters should be paid, and, accordingly, one of the first acts of his regime was to reduce the salaries of the royal painters. Another instance of this tight-fisted attitude, and one that directly affected Carducho, was the lengthy process that followed the completion of the decoration of the Pardo Palace in 1612.[11] In the evaluation, the crown's representative determined a price that was only half the amount proposed by the appointee of the painters, who included Carducho. Rather than compromise, the royal agents invited a lawsuit, which they contested vigorously for more than three years until the painters at last capitulated, complaining that they were "conquered and finished" ("rendidos y acabados"). This style of patronage led Carducho and his colleagues to believe that the only hope of changing the system was to organize themselves into a corporate entity under the patronage of the king himself. Thus, from an early date in the reign, they began to plan a royal academy of art, which, through a rigorous educational program, would elevate the metier of painting to the status of a liberal profession.[12]

The first attempt to constitute an academy dates to 1603, when a group of painters in Madrid, some of whom (Borgianni and Eugenio Cajés, for example) had had contacts with the academies of Florence and Rome, sent a petition to the king, requesting his support. Carducho, then with the court in Valladolid, was not among the signatories, but there is every reason to believe that he was sympathetic to the cause.

Not surprisingly, the petition went unheeded, but the painters persisted, motivated by the need and desire to improve their social status. In November 1606, another group, this time including Carducho, signed an agreement with the monastery of San Bartolomé de la Victoria, by which the painters were allotted space to house their academic establishment. The later history of this initiative is still unknown, but presumably it was not glorious because in 1624 Carducho launched another attempt to incorporate an academy, which was intended to revolutionize the practice of painting in Spain. Carducho had first obtained the support of the count-duke of Olivares, the favorite of the new king, Philip IV, and then drafted a bold, new constitution, which he submitted to the Cortes (the representative body of the towns of Castile) for approval.

The proposed constitution vested broad powers in the academy, which was to have jurisdiction not only over painters but also over architects, tapestry-weavers, silver- and goldsmiths, metalworkers, gardeners, and masons. A rigorous program of education was prescribed, including classes in anatomy, perspective, mathematics, geometry, physiognomy, and astronomy. In most respects, the plan for the academy followed Italian models, but there was one significant novelty – a proposal to license all practitioners of the art by means of an examination based on the academy's course of study. Those who failed were to be prohibited from practicing their arts in the kingdom of Spain.

This document, which set lofty standards for the profession, also erected high barriers for the artisan-painters, who constituted the majority of the artistic community. It must have seemed to them that an attempt was being made by an elite group to monopolize the field and thus to control if not curtail their livelihoods. As Carducho himself later admitted, opposition from within the ranks proved sufficient to put an end to the plan, and the artists of Spain remained without a formal, state-sponsored academy until the middle of the eighteenth century.

Despite his disappointment at the failure of the academy, Carducho never wavered in his dedication to the concept of painting as a liberal art, fully entitled to the respect of a society that stubbornly persisted in regarding it as a craft. From 1625 to 1633, he led a successful campaign to repeal a sales tax, the *alcabala*, which the Council of Finance had levied on paintings, thus reducing them to the legal status of general merchandise.[13] However, the most enduring monument to Carducho's advocacy of the nobility of art is his famous treatise, *Diálogos de la pintura*, published in Madrid in 1633.[14]

Implicit in the text is the need for the aspiring painter to be thoroughly educated in

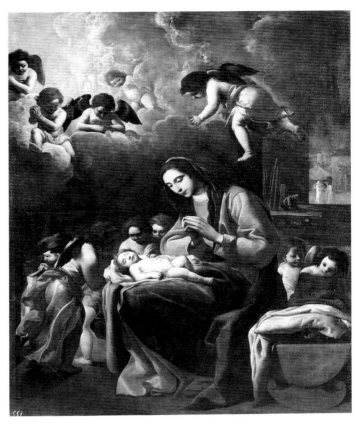

83. Eugenio Cajés, *Virgin and Child With Angels*, ca. 1618. Madrid, Prado, canvas, 1.60 × 1.35m.

the history and theory of the visual arts. Carducho's ideas of beauty derive from the major Italian theorists, especially Lomazzo and Zuccaro. He believed that good painting was based on good doctrine and that good doctrine in turn was founded on rules that allowed the painter to represent a perfected nature, free from the flaws that occurred in everyday life. Like the classical theorists who wrote in Italy later in the century, Carducho regarded naturalist art as unsatisfactory, because it accepted nature's imperfections without seeking to improve or subject them to the processes of a higher intellectual order. Although he recognized the genius of Caravaggio, he feared that his example would inspire – indeed, was inspiring – less talented painters to abandon the good and true principles of idealizing art.

Although the theory is considerably more developed and complex than this brief summary would suggest, Carducho fundamentally believed that good painting was governed by rules and thus was capable of being taught and learned. Once mastered, this idealized art was bound to serve the highest moral purpose, which, in the context of Counter Reformation Spain, was to lead people to God. By codifying the practice and purpose of art in this way, Carducho sought to establish a school of painting of which the academy was to have been the logical fulfillment. When the plan for the academy failed to develop, he tried to make his workshop serve this purpose, and with some success.

Throughout most of his career, Carducho worked closely with Eugenio Cajés (1574–1634), the son of the Tuscan painter Patrizio Cascesi, who had come to work at the Escorial in 1567.[15] After an apprenticeship with his father, Cajés probably went to Rome, residing there in the mid-1590s and surely making contact with members of the reform school of painting. Upon his return to Madrid, he began to collaborate with his father, who facilitated his entry into the circle of royal painters, and in 1607, he joined that unhappy team of painters who were contracted to paint the fresco decorations in the Pardo Palace. In keeping with the emerging pattern of dynastic succession, Cajés was named to fill his father's place as royal painter in 1612, and he remained a fixture at the court until his death.

Cajés and Carducho were friends from an early age and remained close associates throughout their lives, collaborating on several commissions and dedicating themselves to the advancement of their profession, while establishing a position as the most powerful among the royal painters. They also shared a similar outlook on the art of painting, resisting the forces of change that gathered momentum around them. A painting by Cajés of 1630 does not look very different from one executed fifteen years earlier. Like Carducho, he remained faithful to the artistic models of his youth, although his choice of sources was somewhat different: he tended to avoid the sculpturesque style preferred by Carducho in favor of a softer, blander art influenced by Correggio and characterized by sweetness of expression and gentle, flowing lines. The *Virgin and Child with Angels* (pl. 83), done around 1618, can serve as a prototype of his style, which was more effectively employed in devotional pictures than in dramatic narrative compositions, and perfectly expresses the religiosity of the king, known as Philip the Pious.

Neither Carducho nor Cajés was called upon to paint royal portraits; this remained the province of specialists, who were bound by traditions and formulas that left little room for innovation or novelty, except to reflect the changing fashions of apparel. When Philip III ascended the throne, his portraitist was awaiting him, Juan Pantoja de la Cruz, who had been appointed royal painter in the final years of Philip II's reign.[16] Pantoja's early career is not well documented, but it is known that he was born in Valladolid in 1553 and studied with Sánchez Coello, whose path as a portraitist he scrupulously followed at the start of his career. However, in his later years, he enriched his style by absorbing new ideas from contemporary Flemish painters, including Rubens. Pantoja's portraits of the duke and duchess of Lerma (pl. 84) are painted in a freer technique and endow the sitters with greater psychological vitality than is found in the implacable portraits of Sánchez Coello.

Following Pantoja's death in 1608, the responsibility for portraits at court was divided among a number of painters, most of whom have yet to be studied. The senior painter was Santiago Morán (active 1597–1626), who succeeded Pantoja in the office of royal painter; to date, not one of his portraits has been identified. Only slightly less obscure is Bartolomé González (1564–1627), appointed as royal painter in 1617, whose portraits of the royal family are vigorous and direct, if unpolished. Also active in this period were Rodrigo de Villandrando, the author of an arresting portrait, *Philip IV as Prince and the Dwarf Soplillo* (pl. 85), and Pedro Antonio Vidal. Now regarded as marginal figures in the period, these painters were still in place as royal portraitists in 1623 when Velázquez was appointed to their number.

The duke of Lerma remained in power until 1618, when a group of rivals, headed by his own son, the duke of Uceda, forced him into a retirement dignified by a cardinalate. His retreat from the world, if dictated by forces beyond his control and assuaged by material comforts carefully arranged in advance, is probably not to be regarded with total cynicism. There is no reason to doubt the sincerity of his faith, which is mirrored in the paintings he collected and commissioned. The penchant toward realism tempered by decorum in the works of the Carduchos, for instance, was well suited to the new mood of Catholic devotion that followed the harsh years of militancy under Philip II, when it looked as though the Protestants might just win control of Christendom. The reform style was to endure unchallenged in Madrid until well into the reign of the next ruler.

However, in nearby Toledo, long a major and independent center of artistic activity, there was an audience receptive to all kinds of innovation. Although Philip II had removed the court from Toledo to Madrid in 1561, the city continued to

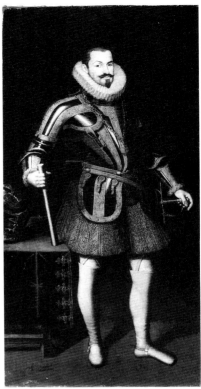

84. Juan Pantoja de la Cruz, *Duke of Lerma*, 1600–10. Toledo, Fundación Lerma, canvas.

85. Rodrigo de Villandrando, *Philip IV as Prince and the Dwarf Soplillo*, ca. 1616. Madrid, Prado, canvas, 2.04 × 1.10m.

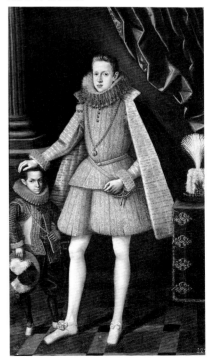

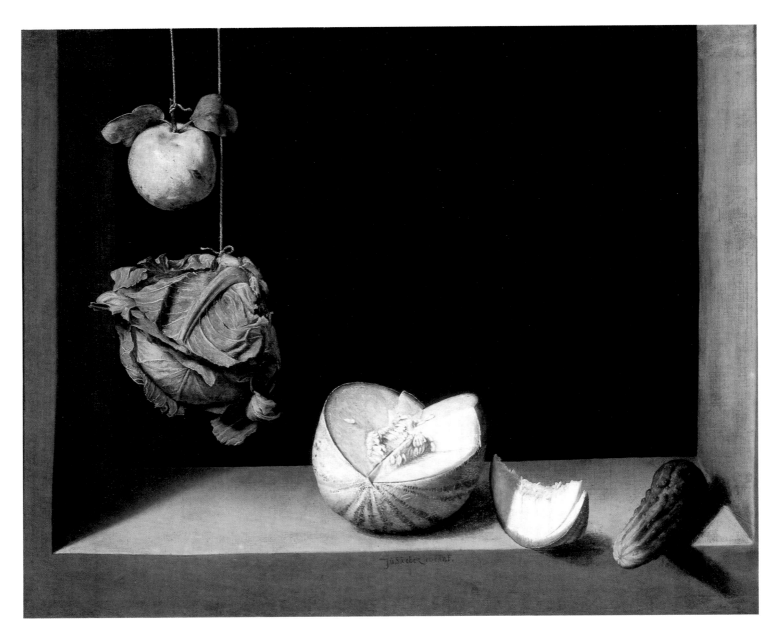

86. Juan Sánchez Cotán, *Still Life With Quince, Cabbage, Melon and Cucumber*, ca. 1600. San Diego, Museum of Art, canvas, 0.69 × 0.85m.

flourish economically and culturally into the early years of the seventeenth century, thanks to the wealth of the cathedral and the prosperity of the cloth industry, which permitted an enlightened elite to cultivate an interest in the visual arts. The most striking evidence of their taste for the new is the appearance of still-life painting, a genre that was just beginning to emerge as an independent artistic category in the closing years of the century. The first documented reference to a still-life painting in Toledo dates to 1590, when nine "canvases of vegetables" were listed in the inventory of a Toledan nobleman, Alonso Téllez de Girón.[17] Although still lifes were destined to become popular with a broad segment of the public, they were initially collected by an educated minority, who fancied the new, and probably somewhat shocking, idea that the most ordinary elements of the natural world could be converted into works of high art. Thus, for example, the cardinal-archbishop of Toledo, García de Loaysa Girón, a famous bibliophile and scholar of Latin and Greek, owned numerous still lifes, which were inventoried in his collection when he died in 1599.

Toledan artists were quick to capitalize on the rising demand for these works,

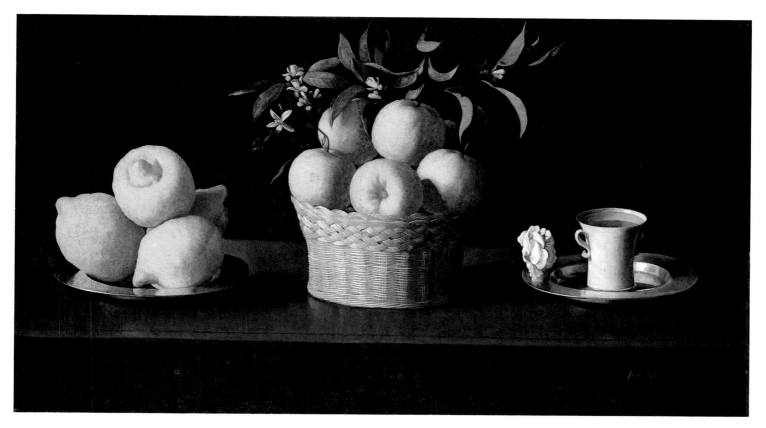

87. Francisco de Zurbarán, *Still Life*, 1633. Pasadena, Norton Simon Museum of Art, canvas, 0.60 × 1.07m.

which were inspired by paintings from northern Italy. The first to add them to his repertory was Blas de Prado (ca. 1545–99), a rather ordinary figure painter whose still lifes made a great impact on his contemporaries, although none is known today.[18] Prado was making still lifes in 1593, the year he showed his paintings of fruit to Francisco Pacheco in Seville. But the most famous Toledan practitioner of the genre was Juan Sánchez Cotán, who is thought to have been the pupil of Blas de Prado.

Sánchez Cotán (1560–1627) was primarily a religious painter of modest fame and attainments.[19] His still-life compositions, on the other hand, although few in number, are now regarded as among the greatest ever painted. As a point of departure, Sánchez Cotán probably used Italian still lifes of the kind done by the Milanese painters Fede Galizia, Panfilo Nuvolone, and Carlo Antonio Procaccini, as well as the works by his master, which he endowed with an ineluctable sense of presence and mystery. His trick, as it might have been termed by contemporary theorists, was to frame the objects in what appears to be the opening of a window (the exact identity of the architectural configuration is uncertain), placing some of the fruit and produce on the ledge while suspending other pieces from an invisible hook above (pl. 86). A powerful light sharply delineates contours and greatly enhances the perception of surfaces and textures, yet somehow fails to illuminate the background space, which is submerged in deep shadow. The resulting tension between the real, the super-real, and the unreal endows these humble objects with a power disproportionate to their status in the natural order.

In 1603, Sánchez Cotán entered the Carthusian order and virtually stopped painting still lifes. By then, he had both legitimized the genre in Spain and established a prototype that remained in vogue in Toledo even into the 1640s, as seen in paintings by followers such as Alejandro de Loarte (late 1590s–1626) and Cristóbal Ramírez de Arellano (active in the 1630s and 1640s). It also filtered into the south and was adopted by Francisco de Zurbarán, whose *Still Life* of 1633 (pl. 87) is one of the few that rekindles the mysterious, complex emotions that Sánchez Cotán managed to evoke in this unprepossessing artistic genre.

The situation of religious painting in Toledo was considerably more complex, as older painters continued to practice alongside younger artists who were trying out new ideas. At the head of the senior group was El Greco, who lived until 1614, pursuing his personal aesthetic to its conclusion. El Greco had only one true disciple, his son, Jorge Manuel, who produced a debased version of his father's manner into the 1620s. Otherwise, there were few painters who could adapt El Greco's idiosyncratic style to suit the changing tastes of the wider market. The practitioners of what might be called the "plain" style of the Escorial painters were more numerous. Until his departure for Granada in 1603, Sánchez Cotán based his art on that of Luca Cambiaso, while Luis de Velasco (died 1606) and Blas de Prado were similarly attuned to the Italian masters employed by Philip II. New elements in this varied landscape were: Caravaggio, whose only authentic Spanish follower had a brief, brilliant career in Toledo; the reform style, which was as popular in Toledo as in Madrid; and that immense, amorphous phenomenon known as the Bassanos.

The main supporter of the new tendencies in religious art was Cardinal Bernardo Sandoval y Rojas (pl. 88), archbishop from 1599 to 1618.[20] Cardinal Sandoval was the uncle of Lerma, who had arranged for his promotion to the primatial see of Spain as a means to ensure the support of the church and to provide access to the wealth of the archdiocese. This ploy proved a miscalculation because the cardinal was no mere puppet, either as an ecclesiastic or a politician. In 1618, he joined forces with Lerma's opponents and helped to cause his fall from favor.

Cardinal Sandoval's patronage of the visual arts has as yet been defined only in the broadest terms, but the available evidence suggests that he was a well-informed patron of painting with distinctly progressive tastes. He made a sizable collection of pictures, including several still lifes, and, during his tenure, acquired works by followers of Caravaggio. In fact, it is only in Toledo that any concentration of paintings from Caravaggio's immediate circle was known in Spain at an early date in the seventeenth century.

One indication of Cardinal Sandoval's interest in Caravaggism is a commission of around 1613 for Carlo Saraceni (ca. 1585–1620), a close follower of the innovative Italian master.[21] In 1604, Sandoval decided to convert the Capilla del Sagrario in the cathedral into his funerary chapel. The principal decoration was frescoes by Carducho and Cajés, who were to paint an altarpiece to accompany what were called the "other three that have been brought from Rome." These were the compositions by Saraceni, which remain in the chapel – the *Martyrdom of St. Eugene*, *St. Leocadia in Prison*, and the *Miracle of St. Ildephonsus*. The origins of this commission are unknown, but there was a painter then working in Toledo who might have known Saraceni in Rome, Juan Bautista Maino, the most important Spanish follower of Caravaggio and, indeed, the only Spanish painter profoundly affected by his art.[22]

Maino was born in Pastrana (Guadalajara) in 1578, the son of a Milanese father and Portuguese mother, who was in the service of the princess of Eboli. Knowledge of Maino's stay in Italy is based on the brief mention of a seventeenth-century writer, who refers to him as a disciple of Annibale Carracci and friend of Guido Reni, which, if accurate, would date his Roman sojourn to the first five or six years of the century. By January 1608, Maino had returned to his native town, where he painted a *Trinity* for a lateral altar in the church of the Franciscanas Concepcionistas, a work that lends credibility to his putative friendship with Guido Reni.[23]

By March 1611, Maino had moved to Toledo and was working for the cathedral, restoring a fresco in the cloister. A commission for an original work – now

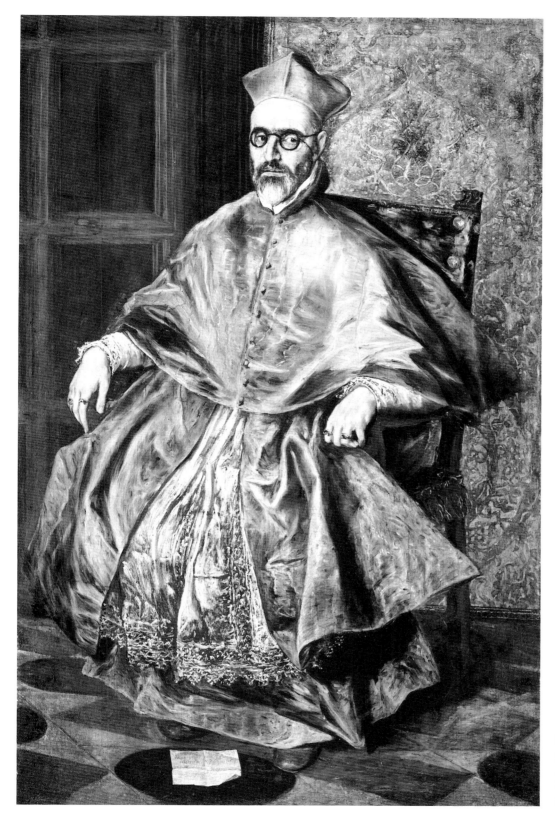

88. El Greco, *Cardinal Bernardo Sandoval y Rojas*, ca. 1600. New York, Metropolitan Museum of Art, Bequest of Mrs. H. O. Havemeyer, 1929. The H. O. Havemeyer Collection, canvas, 1.71 × 1.08m.

unfortunately lost – soon followed. A year later, Maino was hired by the Dominican monastery of San Pedro Mártir to paint the main altarpiece of the church and the frescoes inside the entrance portal, under the choir. The altarpiece decoration

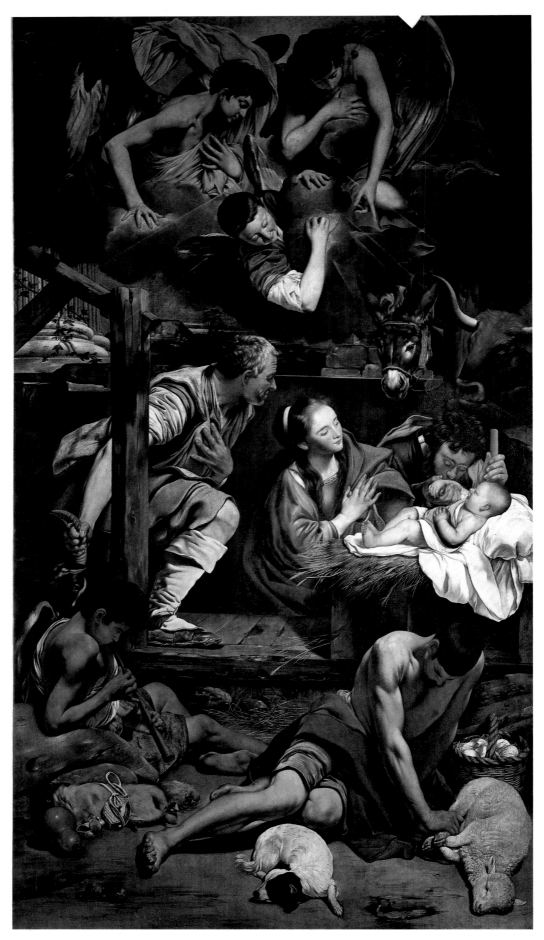

89. Juan Bautista Maino, *Adoration of the Shepherds*, 1612–13. Madrid, Prado, canvas, 3.15 × 1.74m.

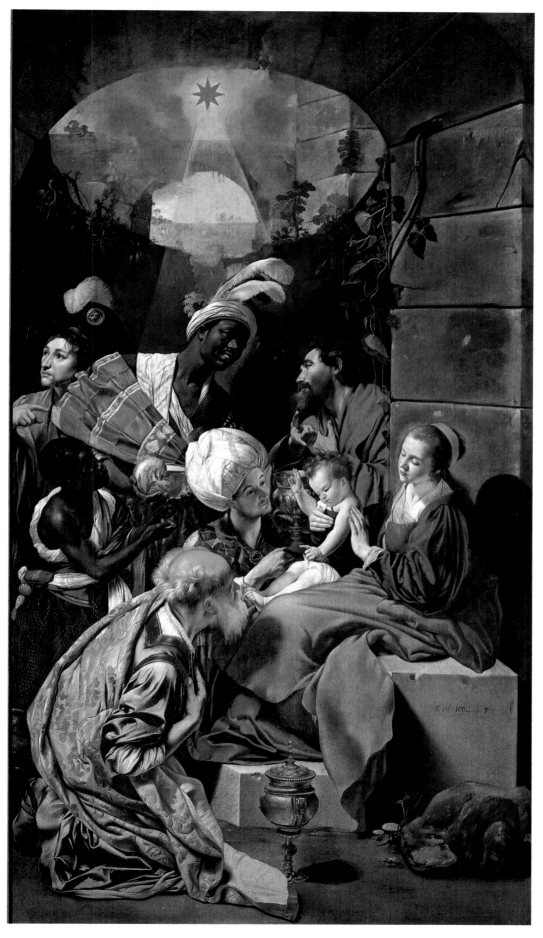

90. Juan Bautista Maino, *Adoration of the Magi*, 1612–13. Madrid, Prado, canvas, 3.15 × 1.74m.

consists of four large paintings – the *Adoration of the Shepherds* (pl. 89), the *Adoration of the Magi* (pl. 90), the *Resurrection* (Villanueva y Geltrú, Museo Balaguer), and the *Pentecost* (Prado) – and two small works for the predella, *St. John the Baptist in a Landscape* and *St. John the Evangelist in a Landscape* (both Prado).

The Adoration of the Shepherds is the work of a painter fully immersed in the art of Caravaggio. Maino appropriated not only Caravaggio's distinctive human types, seen especially in the angels and the shepherd in the right corner, but also his characteristic use of light and his love of intricate, studied compositions. Furthermore, Maino was able to fathom Caravaggio's dazzling surface effects and comprehend his profoundly human sense of religious feeling. In the most moving passage of the painting, St. Joseph kneels beside the Christ Child and tenderly, almost reverently, kisses His wrist, subtly fusing feelings of paternal love and spiritual revelation. In this work, Maino reproduces the flamboyance of Caravaggio's early Roman style, exaggerating it by heightening the luster and brilliant color of the exotic costumes, an effect that he possibly appropriated from the Dutch and Flemish "Caravaggisti," who were in Rome at the same time.

Maino's artistic career virtually came to an end on 20 June 1613, when he professed as a Dominican in the very monastery of San Pedro Mártir. A few years later, he moved to Madrid and was appointed the drawing master of Prince Philip, the future Philip IV. Maino seldom picked up his brushes from 1613 to the day he died in March 1641, but when he did (pl. 129), his brilliance was undiminished.

The change in Maino's vocation from painter to friar had more than personal ramifications. During the first quarter of the seventeenth century, painters from Holland, Flanders, and France descended upon Rome en masse and were entranced by Caravaggio's emotional, theatrical brand of naturalism, which they reinterpreted and then brought home. Among Spanish painters, however, Maino alone was able to assimilate this distinctive mode of expression. (The little-known Pedro Núñez del Valle was in Rome in 1613–14, and returned to Madrid with an attenuated Caravaggesque style.) Thus, when he ceased to paint, the line from Caravaggio to Castile went dead. It is true that a few authentic pictures by Caravaggio and several copies were brought to Spain at an early date, primarily by the viceroys of Naples and other noblemen who visited the city, which would have made Spanish painters aware of the phenomenon now called Caravaggism.[24] But divorced from their artistic culture and context, these pictures would have lost their generative power and could have inspired only superficial copies, not a sweeping revolution in the art of painting.

Nor was the only recorded visit to Spain of an Italian follower of Caravaggio any more consequential. In 1617, the Roman painter Bartolommeo Cavarozzi came to court in the company of Giovanni Battista Crescenzi (see chapter 6), returning home in early 1619.[25] There are no signs that any painters in Madrid were moved by Cavarozzi's art. His painting of the *Mystic Marriage of St. Catherine* (Prado), one of the few attributable to his Spanish period, inspired two or three copies, but otherwise there are no traces of his presence. Upon close analysis, all the putative points of contact between the Spanish naturalists and Caravaggio – notably, the use of powerful effects of light and the unidealized figure types – are more reasonably explained by reference to the reform style of painting, itself an important source for the art of Caravaggio.

After the retirement of Maino, the field was left open for Luis Tristán (ca. 1590–1624), a painter of strange and unequal talents.[26] Tristán's formative years coincided with the period of maximum heterogeneity in Toledan painting and, rather than choose among the available options, he embraced them all. He began his artistic training with El Greco around 1603, and three years later went to Italy, where he remained until 1611, when he is again documented in Toledo. Upon his return, Tristán picked up new mannerisms from Carducho, Cajés, and Maino, which he added to his eclectic repertory of pictorial expression.

A characteristic work of this fusion is the *Adoration of the Shepherds* (pl. 91), painted in 1620, which seeks to translate the compositional types and figural proportions of El Greco into the more realistic language of Maino. The kneeling figure at the right is almost a quotation from El Greco's compositions of the same subject (for instance, Valencia, Colegio del Patriarca), while the young boy standing behind him was inspired by Maino.

For all his study of these two painters, Tristán seldom came close to matching their polish and sophistication. In many of his works, he combines a certain awkwardness of technique with a sometimes astounding naturalism. The result can be grating but peculiarly effective, as in *St. Louis of France Distributing Alms* (pl. 92), which draws a brutal distinction between the rich and the poor. The magnificent, over-sized figure of the saint looms above the beggars, who are as much reduced in size as in fortune. Their misery is transmitted through crippled bodies and ravaged faces, as they cringe in the shadows along the margins of the canvas. Tristán's abrasive naturalism obviously struck a responsive chord among the religious orders and parish churches that were the mainstay of his career.

91. Luis Tristán, *Adoration of the Shepherds*, 1620. Cambridge, Fitzwilliam Museum, canvas, 2.33 × 1.15m.

92. Luis Tristán, *St. Louis of France Distributing Alms*, 1615–20. Paris, Musée du Louvre, canvas, 2.45 × 1.83m.

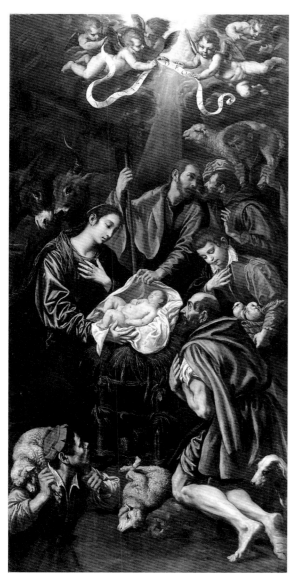

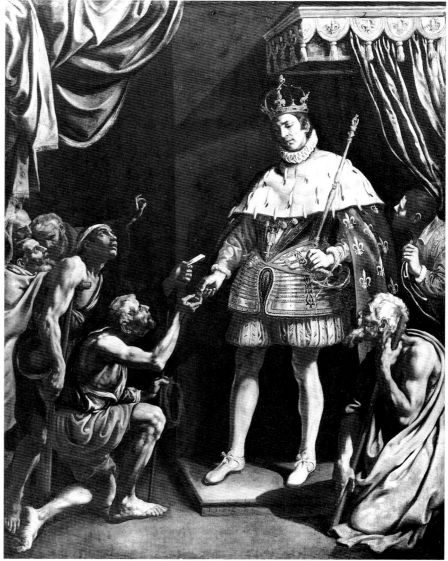

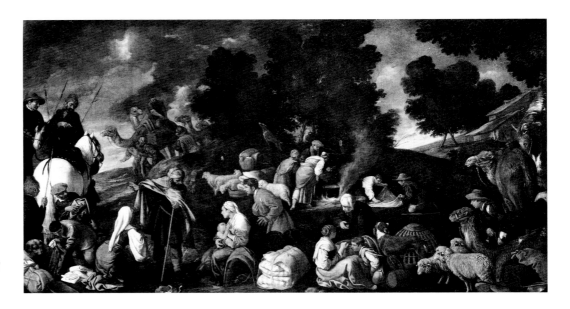

93. Pedro Orrente, *Jacob Overtaking Laban*, 1630–40. Madrid, Prado, canvas, 1.16 × 2.09m.

The last painter of consequence to work in the Imperial City was Pedro Orrente, who commuted between Murcia, where he was born and spent long periods of time, Valencia, where he died, and Toledo, where he resided at various periods during his life.[27] Orrente was born in 1580 of part French, part Spanish stock. It is not known where he received his training, although his first documented work, executed in 1600, was for a village church in the province of Toledo, suggesting that he was apprenticed in the region. Thereafter he seems to have gone to Venice, where he was in contact with the Bassano family. By 1616, he was residing in Valencia, but a year later had moved again to Toledo, where he spent further time between 1628 and 1631. Otherwise, he lived in his native Murcia, until the final years of his life (1644–45), which were passed in Valencia.

Orrente was a highly absorbent painter, and his style is tinctured with a variety of Italian and Spanish hues. The influence of the Bassanos has long been recognized as the predominant characteristic of his art, and throughout his career, he painted vast quantities of Old Testament scenes in their manner. The popularity of this subject, which deploys rustic types in a realistic setting with fruits, vegetables, livestock, and still-life objects, had been established in Spain before Orrente went to work. Philip II owned several examples, but it was not until the end of the sixteenth century that they started to pour into Spain. Not surprisingly, Bartolomé Carducho was among the principal importers. On 20 April 1596, he received payment for another popular Bassano subject, twelve paintings of the months, which he had sold to a city councillor in Seville.[28] Carducho may also have had a hand in supplying the duke of Lerma with his substantial collection of paintings by the Bassanos, which eventually reached a total of twenty-five.

These biblical subjects became the staple of Orrente and his workshop, a representative example of which is *Jacob Overtaking Laban* (pl. 93). To some extent, the artist was trapped by the easy success of genre. He succumbed to the demand and hired assistants to satisfy it, making himself rich but paying a high price, a noticeable decline in quality in the works associated with his name.

More impressive are a few pictures done just after his return from Italy, when he was in the vanguard of Spanish painting. Around 1616, during his first stay in Valencia, he created a *St. Sebastian* (pl. 94) for a private chapel in the cathedral which contains a crepuscular landscape in the Venetian manner and figures that might well be derived from the work of the followers of Caravaggio in Naples.

In the following year, Orrente painted his masterpiece for Cardinal Sandoval, the

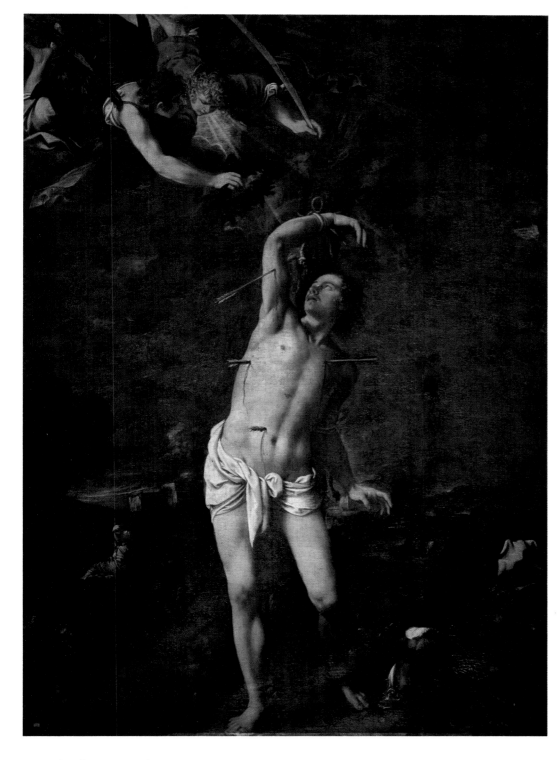

94. Pedro Orrente, *St. Sebastian*, ca. 1616. Valencia, cathedral, canvas, 3.06 × 2.19m.

Miracle of St. Leocadia (pl. 95), in which the saint returns from the dead to thank St. Ildephonsus for his devotion to the Virgin. Although the canon in charge of the cathedral fabric had refused to pay for a picture that, in his view, had not been commissioned and was not needed, he was overruled by Sandoval, who ordered that Orrente be given 1,500 reales. With its dramatic use of light, its realistic figure types, and its overt Italianisms, it is easy to see why the picture appealed to the sophisticated tastes of the cardinal–collector.

The death of Sandoval in 1618 may conveniently be taken as the moment when

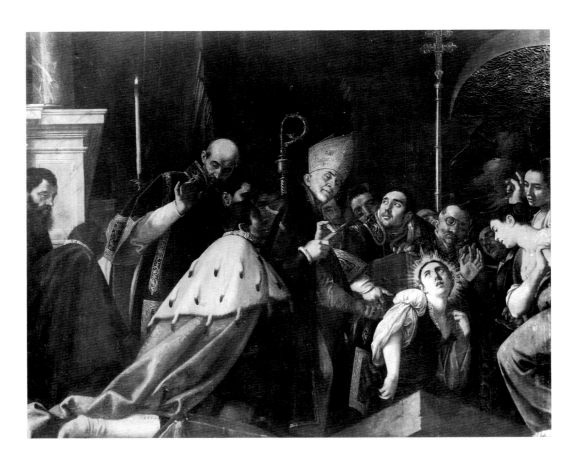

95. Pedro Orrente, *Miracle of St. Leocadia*, 1616. Toledo, cathedral, canvas, approx. 2.50 × 3.00m.

Toledo ceased to count among the major centers of pictorial activity in Spain. The accelerating decline of the city as a manufacturing center and the consequent reduction in wealth and population were in fact more significant. Allied to these factors was the enlightened and generous patronage of Philip IV. With the start of his reign in 1621, there were diminishing incentives for good artists to remain in Toledo, and by the middle years of the century, the official painters of the cathedral were routinely being drawn from the ranks of Madrid artists.

The third important center of reform painting arose not in Castile, but in Valencia, which had become an active artistic center during the long rule of the archbishop, the Blessed Juan de Ribera, who had been the patron of Luis de Morales in Badajoz in the 1560s. In 1569, he was appointed to the Valencian see, where he governed for over forty years, until his death in 1611. As in Badajoz, Archbishop Ribera promoted a renovation of the faith in accord with the spirit of the Council of Trent, which in turn inspired the building and decoration of every kind of religious institution.

The focal point of Ribera's patronage was the Colegio de Corpus Christi, a seminary he founded for the education of the clergy.[29] The construction of the college (also known as the Colegio del Patriarca, a reference to Ribera's ecclesiastical title of Patriarch of Antioch) was begun in 1586, and it was inaugurated on 8 February 1604, in the presence of Philip III and the duke of Lerma. For the main decoration of the chapel, Ribera employed the Genoese mannerist Bartolomé Matarana, who had come to Spain in 1573 to work in Cuenca for the count of Priego.[30] By 1597, when he started to cover the walls with frescoes, his style was about to pass from fashion.

The change in taste was sponsored by the archbishop himself, who formed a considerable collection of canvases by current Italian and Spanish painters, often through the medium of copies. Among the works he owned were paintings by and after El Greco, Sánchez Cotán, Pantoja, and Orrente; and by and after Giovanni Baglione and Caravaggio, among the Italians. The work after Caravaggio is a copy of the *Crucifixion of St. Peter* (Rome, Santa Maria del Popolo), which was acquired by the patriarch toward the end of his life. This picture, one of the earliest copies of a work by Caravaggio to reach Spain, inspired a few replicas by the painters of Valencia, none of whom, however, achieved a deeper understanding of its purpose or used it for further inspiration. Caravaggism failed in Valencia for the same reason that it failed in Castile and elsewhere in Spain – it was famous as a phenomenon but little understood as a style. When change came to Valencian painting, it came from Madrid, not Rome, and in the person of Francisco Ribalta, the leading painter of Valencia during the first third of the seventeenth century.[31]

Ribalta was born in 1565 in Solsona in the principality of Catalonia, and moved to Barcelona as a young child. In the early 1580s, he went to Madrid, where he remained for almost twenty years, befriending some of the royal painters but never landing a job at court himself. In 1599, he decided to go to Valencia, perhaps in the hope of finding work at the Colegio de Corpus Christi. In any event, he soon attracted the attention of Archbishop Ribera, for whom he painted several important pictures. By the time of his death in 1628, Ribalta monpolized the production of painting in Valencia and his hegemony was extended into the later years of the century by his followers.

Ribalta appeared in Valencia at a moment of transition in the art of painting. Although Juan de Juanes had died twenty years before, his manner was being kept alive by his son, Vicente Maçip Comes (ca. 1555–ca. 1607), and others. However, a new alternative had been introduced around 1580 by Juan Sariñena (ca. 1545–1619), a painter of Aragonese origins, who arrived in Valencia after a five-year stay in Italy.[32] Although little is known of Sariñena's activities in Italy, he seems to have been in Rome and come into contact with reform painters such as Scipione Pulzone and Marco Venusti. The novelty of Sariñena's paintings, with their simple compositions and incipient naturalism, was noticed by Archbishop Ribera, who immediately began to patronize the artist. In 1591, Sariñena received his most important commission, which came from the Generalitat, the governing body of the region. This was for the decoration of the Sala Nova, or council room, which consists of a series of portraits of the deputies conducting the affairs of state. Although inspired by earlier representations of the Venetian Senate, the life-size portraits, executed on the walls in oil, constitute one of the few artistic testimonies to civic life in the reign of the Spanish Habsburgs.

To some extent, Sariñena opened the way for Ribalta, who would eventually displace him as the principal painter of Valencia. Yet Ribalta, although clearly a more gifted artist, was not necessarily more innovative. Having spent his formative years in Madrid in the 1580s and 1590s, he owed a great deal to the Italian painters employed by Philip II, who were of the same vintage as the ones seen by Sariñena in Rome. Ribalta's first works in Valencia, notably the large altarpiece for San Jaume Apóstol in Algemesí, started in 1603, are a potpourri of compositions and poses borrowed from artists as diverse as Navarrete, Juanes, Titian, Dürer, and Zuccaro (pl. 96). In 1612, Ribalta appears to have gained access to the paintings by Sebastiano del Piombo owned by the heirs of Jerónimo Vich, and in the succeeding years motifs from these compositions frequently appear in his work.[33] He continued this eclectic painting until around 1620, when a marked change of style occurred.

This transformation was long thought to be the result of Ribalta's direct contact with the art of Caravaggio in Rome, and supposedly was proved by a small-scale copy of Caravaggio's *Martyrdom of St. Peter* (Mombello, Principe Pio di Savoia). A

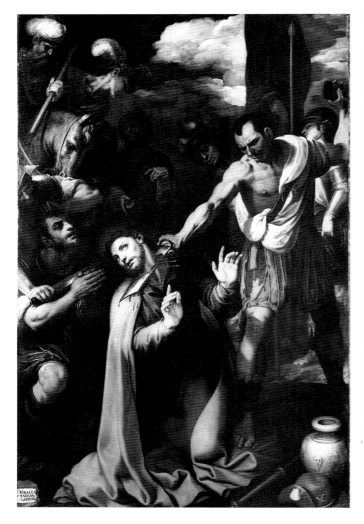

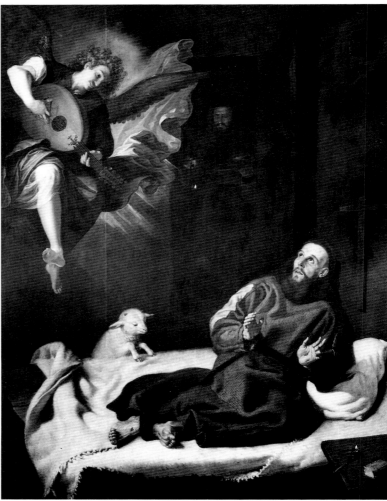

96. Francisco Ribalta, *Martyrdom of St. James*, 1603. Algemesí, San Jaume Apostol, panel, 2.00 × 1.30m.

97. Francisco Ribalta, *St. Francis Comforted by a Musical Angel*, ca. 1620. Madrid, Prado, canvas, 2.04 × 1.58m.

98. Francisco Ribalta, *Christ Embracing St. Bernard*, 1625–27. Madrid, Prado, canvas, 7.58 × 1.13m.

recent, more plausible, hypothesis suggests that Ribalta, like other artists in Valencia, had based his version on the replica already in the Colegio de Corpus Christi,[34] and that the change in style is more convincingly attributed to an important shift in the religious climate of Valencia.[35] This change was precipitated by the expulsion of the Moriscos from Spain, which occurred between 1609 and 1614. The Moriscos, who were the unassimilated remnant of the Islamic population, comprised about a third of Valencia's inhabitants and were mostly employed as laborers on noble estates. Their expulsion, on grounds that they would never become true Catholics, had a ruinous effect on the regional economy and plunged it into a depression.

The death of Archbishop Ribera in 1611 struck another hard blow to the faithful. He had ruled the archdiocese so long and so wisely that he was regarded as a saint and protector. Without his support and example, many Valencians turned to extreme forms of spiritual devotion, which centered on a local priest, Father Francesc Simó, a visionary and performer of dubious miracles. Ribalta, in fact, painted a picture of one of Father Simó's famous visions (London, National Gallery), which, like all representations of the priest, were ordered by the Inquisition to be removed from public view in 1619.

After about 1612, Ribalta's art begins to reflect the heightened, anguished spirituality of the city, but it was not until a visit to Madrid around 1620 that he found the way to channel the religious fervor into great works of art. In Madrid, Ribalta experienced the Italianate naturalism of the Carducho brothers. Indeed,

110

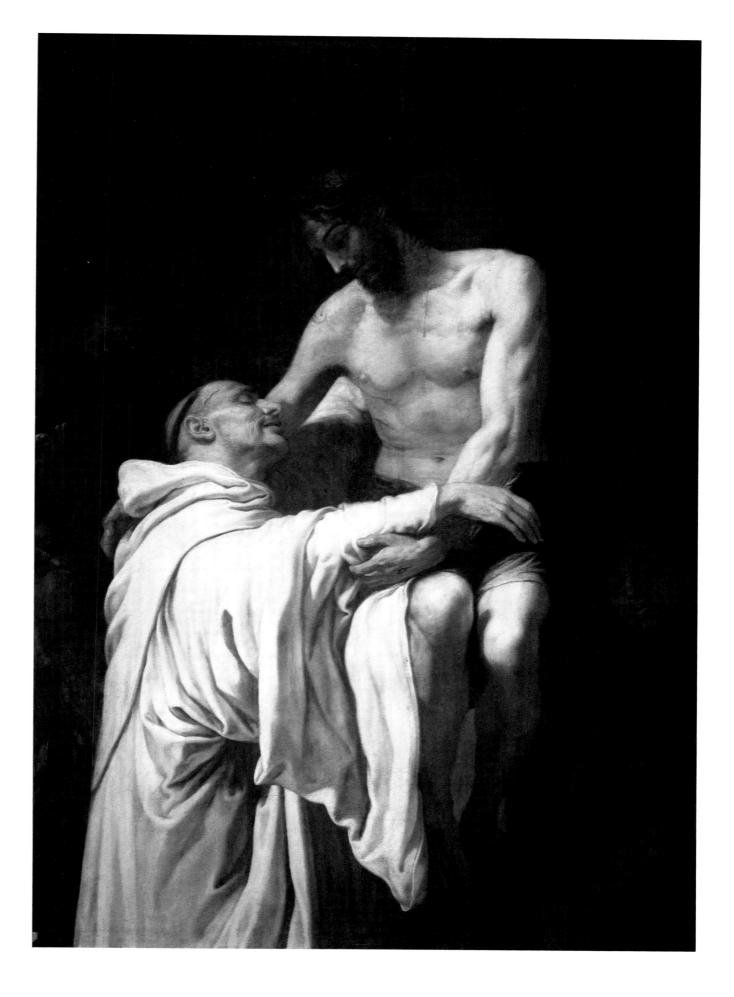

his *St. Francis Comforted by a Musical Angel* (pl. 97), painted around 1620 for an altar in the church of the Capuchinos of Valencia, is a direct descendant of Bartolomé Carducho's *Death of St. Francis* (pl. 78). This painting is purged of all vestiges of mannerism and uses the powerful force of light to enhance the presence of figures and objects alike. It also displays a new fluidity and confidence in composition and draftsmanship: the angel, dramatically framed by fluttering drapery, points the lute like a crossbow at the recoiling body of the saint, who is startled by the heavenly intruder.

In a more solemn vein is *Christ Embracing St. Bernard* (pl. 98), which came from the Cartuja de Porta Coeli, Valencia, and was painted in the mid-1620s. Here, perhaps for the first time, a Spanish painter was able to realize the full potential of the naturalist style to communicate profound religious feelings. The depiction of St. Bernard's rapturous vision is perfectly calculated to achieve maximum effect. The saint is represented as a gaunt figure with prominent cheekbones and deep-set eyes. He embraces Christ, and his mouth forms a half smile that communicates the holy rapture suffusing his body and soul. As Christ descends from the cross to meet him, St. Bernard's body goes limp and needs to be supported by the Savior. Under the tightly focused light, the figures seem palpable. Exercising superb control of the composition and every detail, Ribalta succeeds in externalizing this powerful religious experience, making it seem real but not commonplace.

The influence of Ribalta's later style was not to be denied for almost the rest of the century; he represents both the acme and the end of innovation in Valencian painting. There were worthy followers, to be sure, notably his son, Juan (ca. 1596–1628), who unfortunately died at an early age, outliving his father by only nine months, and Jerónimo Jacinto de Espinosa (1600–67), who effectively perpetuated the Ribalta style well into the second half of the century.[36] But thereafter Valencia seems to have been bypassed by painters with something new to offer and gradually lost its vitality as an artistic center.

The causes of this gradual decline are undoubtedly related to the economic consequences of the expulsion of the Moriscos, which would have lessened the appeal of Valencia to painters from the outside. And even if foreign painters had been tempted to try their luck, they would have encountered the resistance of local artists, who were determined to eliminate the competition of foreigners by means of a college of painters.[37] This college was formed in 1607 by a group including Ribalta and Sariñena and was intended to replace the guild with an organization that would exercise tight control over the activity of painters. Among its statutes was one that prohibited non-Valencian artists from working within the region. Guild members vigorously resisted the legitimacy of the college, fearing restraint of trade, and in due course persuaded the king to revoke the constitution in 1616. The royal edict seems to have been ignored because the college was still in existence in 1686, when the members fought against the incorporation of a local art academy. It is true that some artists found a way to circumvent the ban; Pedro Orrente was able to return to work in Valencia in 1644. For the most part, however, the Valencian painters kept their monopoly intact and their art insulated from the stimulating effects of new colleagues and ideas.

By contrast with the period of Philip II, when a powerful patron shaped artistic production to his desires, the age of Philip III seems incoherent and contradictory. The king and the duke of Lerma were active patrons of religious art and showed a tendency to prefer paintings that expressed sacred history and doctrine in human terms, a tendency that was kindled by their experience of Italian reform painting. "Naturalism" is the convenient word to define this taste, but it is all too imprecise. The painters at court either sensed or were instructed about the need for a decorous treatment of religious themes – Carducho is the spokesman for that attitude – and this placed a limit on the extent to which the divine could be humanized. In the provinces, however, there was a greater tolerance for commingling the worlds of the flesh and the spirit, and a quicker interest in the most extreme form of naturalism, still-life painting. Despite the conservative tendencies of court patronage, there is no doubt that attitudes about the mission and manner of painting in Castile were profoundly changed between 1598 and 1621, and these attitudes would continue to exert an important influence on artistic production for years to come.

In one respect, the reign of Philip III, and particularly the regime of the duke of Lerma, made an unequivocal difference. During the period of Philip II, the nobles had been kept away from the seat of government; Lerma welcomed them back and, by his own extravagant example, encouraged them to spend the money that they might otherwise have lost to inflation. If the king was excessively pious, the nobles were correspondingly profligate. Whatever the long-term effects of their prodigality upon the health of the economy, it was only beneficial to the arts, both visual and literary. In short, the conspicuous expenditure of wealth that is a pre-condition for every golden age of art was well and truly initiated at the court of Philip III.

Unfortunately, Madrid's growth as an artistic center eventually sapped the energy of the regional centers. Painters would still find plenty of work in the towns; but the work was provided almost exclusively by the religious sector, which was conservative in taste, sometimes inattentive to quality, and unwilling to pay good prices. For painters who believed in the nobility of their profession, more was needed, more even than money. This was prestige, an intangible quality that, as everyone recognized, was uniquely in the king's gift. Madrid, then, became the destination of Spain's most ambitious painters, and even Seville, the one city that still had the resources to compete, was unable to keep all of its greatest talents at home.

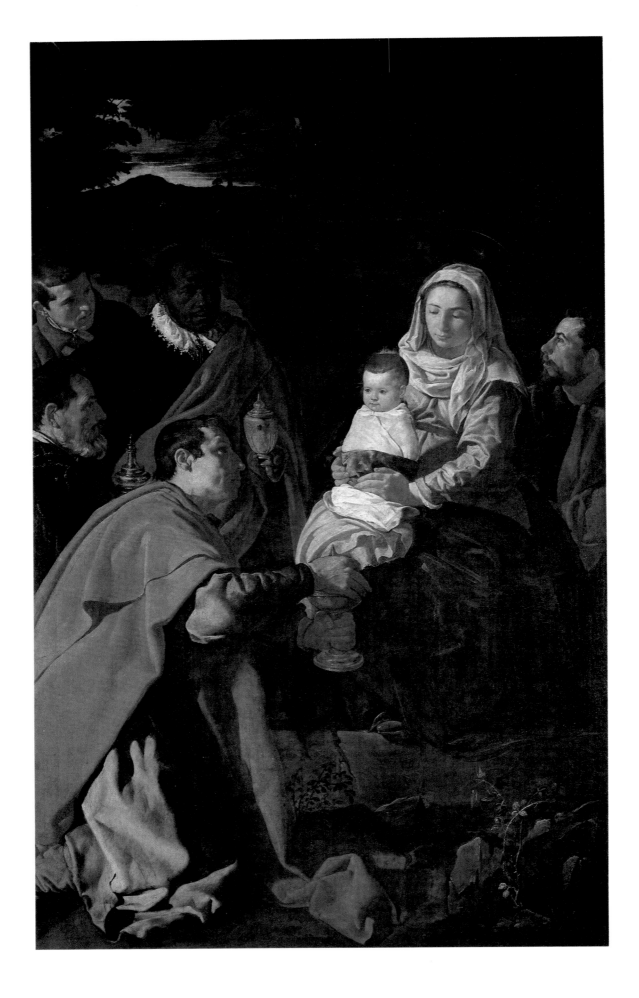

5
Nascent Naturalism
Seville 1575–1625

IN THEORY, SIXTEENTH-CENTURY Seville should have been one of the most propitious places in Spain for the art of painting. As the exclusive port for trade with the New World (despite its inland location), Seville had prospered and grown into the largest city of the peninsula. It was a cosmopolitan center with a sizable colony of merchants from other parts of Europe, especially Flanders and Genoa, whose relations with the Spanish crown gave their citizens entry into the lucrative Indies trade.

Yet somehow the energy and vitality of commercial life failed to affect the artistic sector, or at least the community of painters, until after 1600.[1] The prevalent style of painting changed, to be sure, but the change was slow and minimal compared with the rapid, profound shift that occurred in Madrid during the reign of Philip II. An important reason for the difference was the patronage. In Seville, the church in all its aspects dominated the artistic scene and the secular population was content to follow its lead. There is still much to be learned about aristocratic and corporate patronage in Seville during this period, but what is known does not suggest that these sectors of the community acted with much autonomy. Only one aristocratic family distinguished itself over several generations as patrons of the visual arts: the Enríquez de Ribera, titled first as the marquises of Tarifa and then as the dukes of Alcalá.

In the absence of a counterweight to the influence of the church, of an independent vision of what the art of painting might be and what it might accomplish as a means to enhance reputation and broadcast fame, a closed system of artistic activity was fostered, which the painters inevitably came to support as strongly as the patrons. The workings of this system are illustrated by Vasco Pereira, a painter born in Lisbon in 1535 and active in Seville from about 1561 to his death in 1609.[2] Over the course of his long career, Pereira achieved a position of eminence in Seville rivaled only by Alonso Vázquez and Francisco Pacheco. Thus, his artistic conduct can be taken as exemplary.

In the main, Pereira seems to have regarded painting more as an artisanal than a professional activity. Yet he was by no means an unlettered craftsman: at his death, he owned a library of 241 titles, a very considerable number for someone who was not a professional man of letters. However, as a painter he was a jack-of-all-trades and a willing servant of his masters, simply because there was no other way to proceed. His contracts with various ecclesiastical institutions could more rightly be called suffocating than binding, vesting power in the patron over the stipulation of the subject, the details of the composition, even, at times, the colors to be used, and, of course, the amount to be paid. Unlike the patrons of Castile, who were occasionally surprised by the generous outcome of a *tasación*, those of Seville committed the painters to a set fee in advance and, as has been seen above, liked to pit the artists against each other in auctions for the lowest price.

99. Diego de Velázquez, *Adoration of the Magi*, 1619. Madrid, Prado, canvas, 2.03 × 1.25m.

115

The emphasis on content over form had other important consequences. For instance, patrons could be indifferent to what might be called the master's touch, the distinctive quality of execution that, in theory, distinguished the painter of talent from the second rater. In a contract of 1582 with the parish church of La Magdalena, it is stated that the central image could be painted "by the hand of Pereira or by his son-in-law."[3] As far as compositions were concerned, there was a preference for the tried and true, either as represented in existing paintings or, more frequently, in prints that the patron could examine beforehand. From the early 1500s until the end of the seventeenth century, Sevillian artists and their patrons assigned more authority to compositions in prints than to the powers of the imagination, a point dramatically illustrated by Pereira, whose death inventory lists no fewer than 2,407, some of which may have been intended for shipment to the New World. It is no surprise then that, for example, his *Annunciation* (1576) for San Juan Bautista, Marchena, is a faithful copy of a composition by Titian as recorded in the print by Cornelis Cort. This commission, incidentally, originated with a secular patron, the duke of Arcos, and shows how the aristocrats fell right into the prevailing pattern established by the church.

In this one-sided contest with their patrons, the painters defended themselves as best they could to earn a decent living. One obvious way was to restrain competition through guild restrictions. In 1599, when Pereira was elected as a governor of the guild, Seville had fewer than thirty master painters to serve a city that had a population of around one hundred thousand and that numbered among its ecclesiastical establishments almost forty monasteries and convents as well as parish churches, hospitals, and almshouses, not to mention the most important of all, the cathedral.[4]

Another way to earn a good living was to industrialize production through the formation of a company. The painters' company was essentially a mercantile association, established to exploit the peculiarities of the Seville marketplace. The relative indifference to quality opened the way to the manufacture of paintings through the pooling of labor and expenses and the sharing of profits. The company sought church and other commissions and produced dozens of inexpensive devotional images that were sold directly from the workshop. Painters also capitalized on the booming export market to Spanish America, where the demand for cheap paintings was insatiable.

Pereira is recorded as a partner in three companies.[5] The first was formed with Alonso Vázquez in 1592, for the purpose of executing a number of frescoes and over fifty paintings for a local monastery. Pereira entered into a second company in 1598, this time with his son-in-law, Antón Pérez, which lasted four years and then was renewed for another four. The practice of incorporating family members into the company, or at least the workshop, not only made economic sense but served to establish dynasties of painters, which were a characteristic of artistic life in Seville and provided a powerful competitive advantage to their members. Family companies and dynasties could cut costs and thus prices, exploit long-established contacts among the patrons, and expand their markets through strategic matrimonial alliances. The Pereira dynasty, as mentioned before, is a notable case in point. A granddaughter from the union of his daughter with Antón Pérez married the painter Juan del Castillo, who was himself a cousin by marriage of the mother of Bartolomé Esteban Murillo; this was the glorious culmination of the Pereira family tree.

A further effect of these restrictive practices was to close the market to foreign artists, who had dominated painting in Seville from the start of the century. Only one outsider of note worked in Seville in the sixteenth century after the departure of

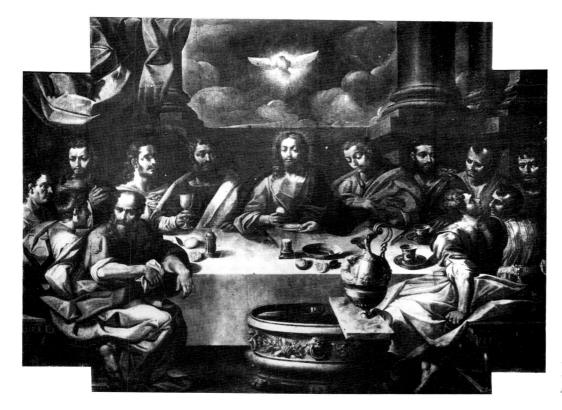

100. Pablo de Céspedes, *Last Supper*, 1595. Córdoba, cathedral, 2.66 × 4.09m.

Pieter Kempeneer in 1562; this was the Italian Matteo Pérez da Lecce (known in Spain as Mateo Pérez de Alesio), who, as his name suggests, was probably of Spanish origin anyway. Pérez da Leccio stopped in Seville in 1583–84 on his way to Peru, where he died around 1615.[6] From about 1568 to 1576 and again from 1581 to 1583, the artist had worked in Rome, executing, among other things, some of the frescoes in the Oratorio del Gonfalone with Jacopo Bertoia, Raffaellino da Reggio, and Federico Zuccaro. Not much is known of his career in Seville, and his major work can hardly be called representative. This is the towering fresco of *St. Christopher* in the cathedral, signed and dated 1584 and measuring almost nine meters high. In addition to being the largest figure painted in the period, the *St Christopher* is a competent example of central-Italian painting of the late sixteenth century.

Another painter schooled in Rome, although Spanish by birth, was Pablo de Céspedes, Spain's first artist-theorist, who worked intermittently in Seville from 1585 to his death in 1608.[7] Céspedes was born in Córdoba around 1548 and studied ancient languages at the university of Alcalá before going to Rome around 1570. There he became acquainted with Federico Zuccaro, a surprisingly omnipresent figure in the history of Spanish painting of the period. (The two would meet again in 1587 at the remote monastery of Guadalupe, surely the most improbable chance encounter in the history of sixteenth-century art.) During his years in Rome, Céspedes received a few commissions, notably frescoes for Santa Trinità dei Monti, which are still preserved. After his return to Córdoba in 1577, he was appointed to a benefice in the cathedral, which he enjoyed to the end of his life.

From time to time, Céspedes would travel to Seville – his first known visit occurred in 1585 – where he became acquainted with Francisco Pacheco and was given a commission to paint frescoes in the chapter room of the cathedral. The few attributable paintings of his Spanish period were executed in the 1590s, of which the *Last Supper* of 1595 is a typical example (pl. 100). Although lacking the discipline of his Roman frescoes, the painting displays the same conspicuous interest in the human figure and an elevated narrative tone.

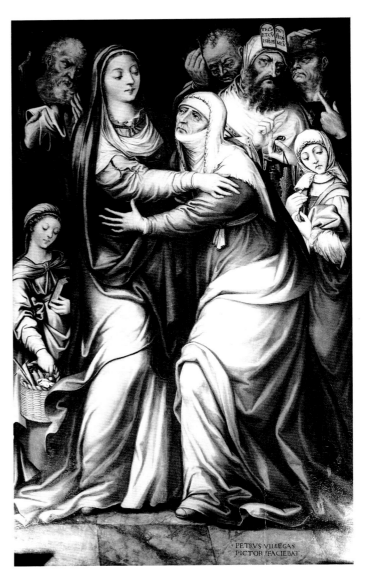

101. Pedro de Villegas,
Visitation, 1566. Seville,
cathedral, canvas glued on panel,
1.90 × 0.98m.

The impact of this updated version of Roman style on the local painters was limited but not insignificant. Following the departure of Kempeneer and the death of Luis de Vargas (1567), the leading painter was Pedro de Villegas (1519–96), who was at his peak in the 1560s and 1570s, when he painted the altarpiece of the Visitation in the cathedral (pl. 101), a work that closely adheres to the models of Kempeneer.[8] By the end of the next decade, the sculpturesque style of Pérez da Lecce and Céspedes had left its mark on the younger generation. However, of greater importance was the work – also based on Roman sources – of northern painters such as Martin de Vos and Martin van Heemskerck. The resulting hybrid of Italian and Flemish elements became the dominant mode of expression until well into the seventeenth century and is first observable in the work of Alonso Vázquez, who worked in Seville from 1588 until his departure for Mexico in 1603.[9] His *Last Supper* (pl. 102), painted for the Carthusians of Santa María de la Cuevas, is a pastiche of poses and motifs borrowed from prints by or after Heemskerck, de Vos, and Cornelis Cort. In fact, the stylistic correspondence to the paintings by these northern late mannerists is close enough to suggest that Vázquez had been able to study their works, perhaps in the collections of the resident Flemish community, if not in Flanders itself.

118

In addition to Pereira and Vázquez, another painter of significance emerged in the closing decades of the century, Francisco Pacheco, the most well known, although not the most talented, of the group (Vázquez was the better artist). Pacheco is perhaps best understood as a cultural phenomenon; indeed, the quality of his painting leaves little choice. But as a chronicler and shaper of artistic culture in Seville, he is of the greatest importance.

Pacheco was born in 1564 in Sanlúcar de Barrameda, the son of a seafaring family.[10] He and his three brothers were orphaned at an early age and adopted by their uncle, also named Francisco, who was a learned canon of Seville cathedral. Canon Pacheco's literary and scholarly interests were transmitted to the young Francisco, who was apprenticed to an obscure local painter, thus beginning an artistic career that would span part or all of seven decades.

Pacheco started to make his mark on the local scene in the 1590s. In 1599, he was elected as a governor of the painters' guild, and in 1600, he received a major commission for the large cloister of the Order of Mercy, which he shared with Alonso Vázquez. These pictures represent episodes from the lives of the founders, St. Peter Nolasco and St. Raymond Nonnatus, and one of Pacheco's compositions shows the Mercedarians redeeming Christian captives from the Turks (pl. 103), with St. Raymond of Pennafort in the background. It does not take long to see that Pacheco's painting represents the triumph of tenacity over talent. The stiff poses, the disjointed composition, the fixed expressions, the dry execution are, alas, all self-evident. Pacheco has taken his sources – the late mannerist painting of Rome and Flanders – to a final, gelid climax. However, if his style is cold, it is also clear, and for the guardians of orthodoxy in Seville's ecclesiastical establishment, many of whom were Pacheco's friends, this was sufficient.

In fairness, multi-figure compositions were never Pacheco's forte, although with the passing of time he did manage to sharpen his artistic skills. A milestone in his career occurred in 1611, when he traveled to Castile, visiting Madrid, the Escorial, and Toledo, a trip that provided the opportunity to study the paintings in the collections of the crown and aristocracy and to meet important fellow painters, including Vicente Carducho and El Greco. And in the same year, upon his return home, he accepted Diego de Velázquez as his apprentice. It was only a few years before the pupil was imparting to the master some of his skills as a naturalist painter.

As a result, Pacheco's paintings of the 1610s and 1620s represent a notable advance

102. Alonso Vázquez, *Last Supper*, 1588–1603. Seville, Museo de Bellas Artes.

103. Francisco Pacheco, *Mercedarians Redeeming Christian Captives*, 1600. Barcelona, Museo de Arte de Cataluña, canvas, 2.00 × 2.50m.

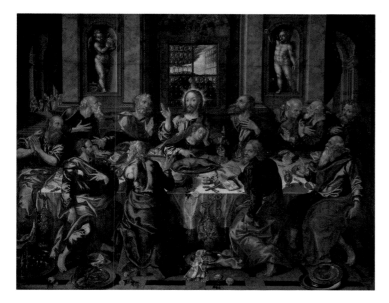

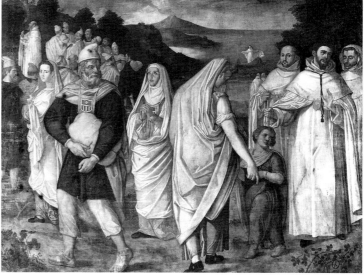

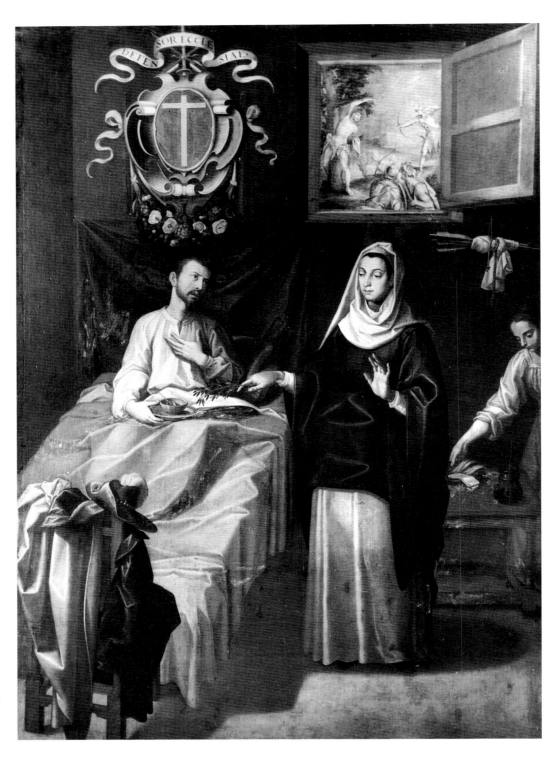

104. Francisco Pacheco, *St. Sebastian Attended by St. Irene*, 1616. Formerly Alcalá de Guadaira, hospital, canvas, 2.92 × 2.16m.

over the work of the earlier years. A good example is *St. Sebastian Attended by St. Irene* (pl. 104), signed and dated 1616, which has a novel composition, combining an interior and exterior scene. The principal action is set inside a room where the saint rests in bed, recovering from his wounds. St. Irene is treating the patient with a bowl of medicinal soup and a sprig of herbs, which, to judge from his lively expression of gratitude, work as well as a miracle drug. An effective touch of realism is the saint's clothing, thrown carelessly over a chair at the foot of the bed. The background scene, framed by an open window, shows the attempted execution of the martyr, which is copied line for line from a print by Jan Muller after a painting by Hans van Aachen. Pacheco, like all his contemporaries, was a faithful follower of northern prints.

Pacheco reached his peak as an artist in these years and then commenced a slow decline. His advancing age – he died in his eightieth year – and a new generation of artists headed by Zurbarán and Alonso Cano took their toll on his standing as a painter. In any case, his activity as a practitioner was equaled if not surpassed by his interests in artistic theory and Catholic doctrine, which he fostered within the context of his academy.[11]

The academy of Pacheco, which was modeled in structure on the neo-Platonic academies of Renaissance Italy, was an informal association of theologians, poets, antiquarians, and other writers organized in the 1560s by the humanist Juan de Mal Lara and then continued by a group including Pacheco's uncle. Following the death of Canon Pacheco in 1599, the painter Pacheco assumed a role of leadership in the academy and invited a new generation of scholars to join. Among the most important new members was the third duke of Alcalá, Fernando Enríquez de Ribera (1583–1637), a notable collector and patron of the visual arts. In 1603, Pacheco executed an elaborate mythological ceiling painting for the duke's Seville palace, known as the Casa de Pilatos.[12]

While the academy continued to be interested in studies of classical antiquity and poetics, during Pacheco's tenure, heavy emphasis was placed on Catholic doctrine as applied to painting. Pacheco's almost obsessive concern with orthodoxy is reflected in his treatise, *Arte de la pintura*, published posthumously in 1649.[13] This book is the labor of almost four decades; it was started around 1600 and brought to completion by 1638, although the publication was mysteriously delayed for another eleven years. Compared with Carducho's *Diálogos*, the *Arte* seems a less organized and coherent work, in part because the author was as much interested in practice as theory. But Pacheco's informal approach has its advantages, notably the innumerable anecdotes about the personalities and events of his time, including the development of his pupil and son-in-law, Diego de Velázquez.

The *Arte* is divided into three books and a lengthy appendix, which constitutes a book in itself. Books One and Two develop the theme of painting as a noble and liberal art through the demonstration (in Book One) of its antiquity and grandeur. Painting, it is argued, was habitually patronized and practiced by kings, princes, noblemen, and high-ranking ecclesiastics, whose lofty social status guaranteed the nobility of the art. In Book Two, a theory of painting is expounded, in part to advance the idea that it is the equivalent of poetry and the other liberal arts founded on theoretical precepts.

Book Three is devoted to artistic practice and constitutes the most complete source of information on the techniques of painting written in Spain before the eighteenth century.[14] Here too, however, Pacheco is guided by his ambition to improve the status of the art, restricting his discussion to techniques and materials deemed appropriate to the profession, while deleting others that, because they contained base elements (urine is the worst offender), argue against his case.

Into a fourth section, called "Adiciones a algunas imágenes," Pacheco decanted his life's study of what would now be called Counter Reformation iconography. Pacheco counted among his friends the best theological scholars of Seville, and he pressed them into service to help establish the orthodox formulas for the major themes of Catholic art. He firmly believed that the principal aim of painting, and its principal glory, was to excite the faithful "to adore and love God and to cultivate piety," and his zeal was rewarded by his appointment in 1618 as overseer of sacred images by the Seville Inquisition.

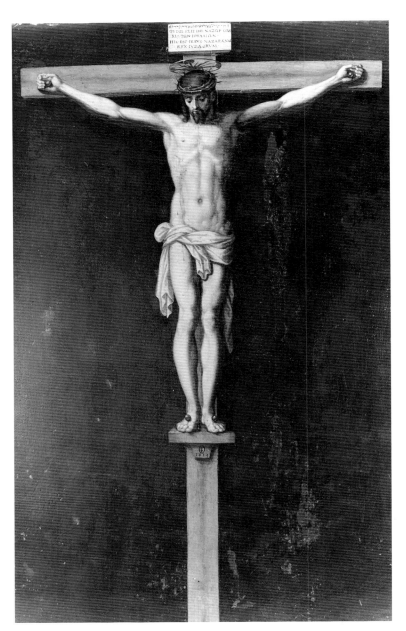

105. Francisco Pacheco,
Christ on the Cross, 1614.
Granada, Fundación
Gómez–Moreno, panel,
0.58 × 0.37m.

The most famous example of Pacheco's concern with strict orthodoxy is the discussion of whether Christ had been crucified with three nails or with four.[15] To clarify the question, he solicited an opinion from the poet-scholar Francisco de Rioja, who was later to become the royal librarian. As shown by his *Christ on the Cross* (pl. 105) – one of the most effective images painted by the artist – the correct answer is four, and for the next generation, Sevillian painters followed the dictum with unswerving dedication.

Pacheco's consuming interest in religious imagery was inspired in the first instance by his desire to defend and glorify the faith. From this conviction flowed another desire of almost equal importance: the ennoblement of painting as an art. Entrusted as it was with the power to seek "eternal glory and [the obligation] to dissuade man from vice and to lead him to the cult of God Our Lord," painting was a partner in the greatest human endeavor, and, therefore, its practitioners were entitled to be treated with every respect. This argument was hardly new to the theory of Renaissance art, but it took great courage and determination to argue it in the Seville of Vasco Pereira, where painting was regarded by patrons and practitioners alike as a manual, marginal skill. Furthermore, Pacheco put his theory into practice through his academy, whose members included not only the best minds, but also the most distinguished noblemen of Seville. To see painters and poets and potentates working together as friends and colleagues, meeting one week in Pacheco's house and the next in the Casa de Pilatos, made the concept of the noble artist a reality. While Pacheco did not succeed in revolutionizing the relationship between painters and their clients, he certainly helped to strengthen the position of the artists with higher ambitions.

Another example of Pacheco's endeavor to ennoble painting is the *Libro de descripción de verdaderos retratos de ilustres y memorables varones*,[16] which was never published during his lifetime. As the title indicates, the book is a compilation of portraits – and splendid portraits they are – of famous men, who were mostly from Seville despite the sweeping claim of the title. Included are the portraits of Luis de Vargas, Pieter Kempeneer (pl. 106), and Pablo de Céspedes, all of whom are shown dressed as gentlemen, without paintbrushes, palettes, or other signs of their profession, and who are given equal status with the practitioners of the traditional liberal arts.

The theoretical section of the *Arte*, Book Two, is the least satisfying and suffers in comparison with the closely reasoned arguments of Carducho. Pacheco was thoroughly versed in Italian theory and perhaps somewhat overwhelmed by it, for quotations and paraphrases from the major works fill many of the pages. In the main, Pacheco believed in the idealizing purpose of art. The painter begins with the direct observation of nature and then corrects the defects and improves the flaws by using his judgment and learning. This was Pacheco's fundamental conviction, yet he was no dogmatist; how could he be when, right before his eyes, the young Velázquez was painting impressive pictures that recorded nature as it appeared? And Pacheco's beliefs were further altered when his gifted pupil and son-in-law was appointed at an early age as royal painter, a position to which the older man had long aspired. During Pacheco's lifetime, Velázquez went on to achieve unprecedented status and honors at court. By what must have seemed an incredible paradox, the painter of appearances had validated the nobility of the art. Velázquez's triumph was irresistible and, with good grace, Pacheco expanded his criteria of excellence to include the best of the new naturalist painters, or at least those who did not pose a threat to his livelihood.

It has often been noted that Francisco de Zurbarán is conspicuously absent from the pages of *Arte de la pintura* and that Juan de Roelas, a key figure of the early 1600s, is mentioned only to be censured. Pacheco could afford to smile on the good fortune of his son-in-law, but his tolerance was limited when it came to painters who departed from the canons of idealized art and were also credible rivals. Pacheco's peak of activity coincided with the period when Sevillian painting began to experience changes comparable to those that occurred in Madrid and Valencia during the reign of Philip III. An old guard, headed by Pacheco, included several painters who still worked in the Italo-Flemish style of the late sixteenth century. A typical representative of this group is Juan de Uceda (ca. 1570–1631), an occasional collaborator of Pacheco, and one of Velázquez's examiners for admission to the painters' guild in 1616.[17] Uceda's *Two Trinities* of 1624 (Seville, Museo de Bellas Artes) shows him to be a graceful practitioner of the static compositional formulas and polished surfaces favored by artists of his generation.

Younger artists kept this manner alive well into the 1630s. Juan del Castillo (ca. 1590–ca. 1657),[18] although a near contemporary of Velázquez, Zurbarán, and

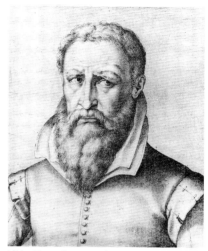

106. Francisco Pacheco, *Pieter Kempeneer*, 1600–20. From *Libro de . . . verdaderos retratos*, Madrid, Lázaro Galdiano.

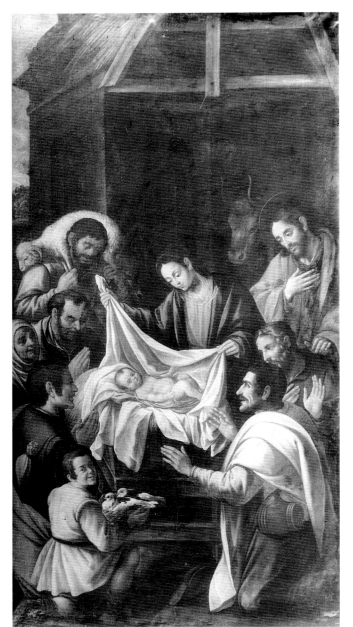

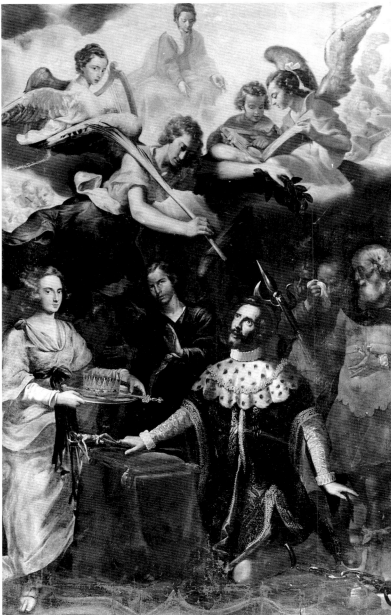

107. Juan del Castillo, *Adoration of the Shepherds*, 1630. Seville, Museo de Bellas Artes, canvas, 3.68 × 1.98m.

108. Alonso Vázquez and Juan de Uceda, *Death of St. Hermengild*, 1603–4. Seville, San Hermenegildo, canvas, 4.92 × 3.40m. (detail).

Alonso Cano, never modernized the style he derived from the work of Vázquez, Pereira, and Pacheco. The *Adoration of the Shepherds* (pl. 107), painted for the church of Monte Sión, Seville, a commission of 1636, looks to have been done a good thirty years earlier, despite the fact that it is nearly contemporary with a version by Zurbarán (pl. 150), in which an inventive artist revitalizes a standard pictorial formula by applying the novelties of naturalism. Despite the popularity of the Italo-Flemish style, newcomers and new ideas could not be excluded from the market-place, and the first to invigorate the practice of painting in Seville was Juan de Roelas.[19]

The events of Roelas's early years are still a mystery. He was probably born around 1560, but his work is unknown until 1597, when he signed and dated a print of the *Elevation of the Cross*. In the following year, he is recorded as a citizen of Valladolid and a member of the clergy. Roelas stayed in Valladolid until 1603, at which time he accepted a chaplaincy at the Colegiata of Olivares. Almost at once, he began to work as a painter in nearby Seville, and, by 1606, he was so well regarded

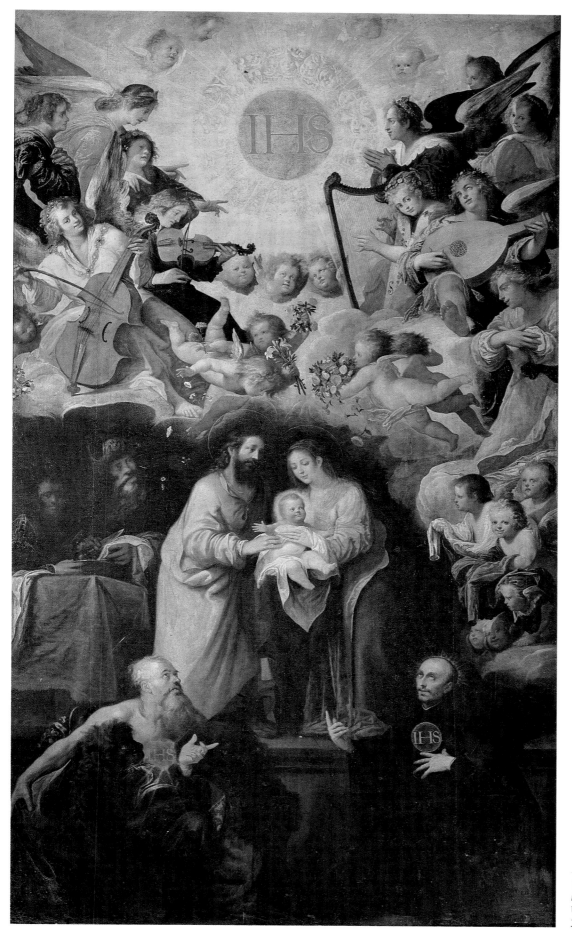

109. Juan de Roelas, *Adoration of the Name of Jesus*, 1604–5. Seville, University chapel, canvas, 5.74 × 3.35m.

that he relinquished his benefice and moved to the city. During the next ten years, Roelas became a commanding figure in the art world, executing significant commissions for the cathedral and several local churches. In 1617, Roelas decided to try his luck at court and applied for a position as royal painter. His application failed, but he lingered in Madrid until 1621, the date he returned to his chaplaincy at Olivares, where he died in 1625.

The style introduced by Roelas into Seville was not a radical departure from the work of the established local painters, which is probably why he found favor among traditionally minded ecclesiastical patrons. For instance, his first commission, the central painting for the main altarpiece in the Jesuit church, executed in 1604–5 (pl. 109), is divided into heavenly and earthly zones, following a formula that was popular throughout Catholic Europe and especially in Seville. In these same years, it was employed in the *Death of St. Hermengild* for the hospital of San Hermenegildo (pl. 108), begun by Vázquez and finished by Uceda. But the differences between the two compositions should not be minimized. Roelas's is in every way a more fluid, assured performance. The two parts of the composition flow smoothly together, whereas in the painting by Vázquez and Uceda, they are kept distinctly separate, like the floors of a two-story house. The figures in Roelas's work are rounded in form and move with easy grace, their expressions are lively and varied, and the controlled play of light and shadow increases the dramatic effect. In addition, Roelas's textured brushstroke, with its rich impastos and abundant highlights, is far more effective in animating the surface than the tight, lacquered finish of his colleagues.

The origins of Roelas's style have always been puzzling. It has sometimes been suggested that he studied with the Italian painters at the Escorial in the 1580s, although it is difficult to link him with any of these masters. More frequently, a stay in Italy has been postulated, with Venice as the destination of choice. On close analysis, however, the connection of Roelas with the Venice of Tintoretto, Veronese, and the Bassanos hardly seems credible. If indeed Roelas studied anywhere in Italy, a good case could be made for Naples, where painters like Girolamo Imperato and Luigi Rodríguez, both active in the 1590s, offer a certain similarity to Roelas.[20] (One of Imperato's paintings was installed in Santa María de la Vid, Burgos, around 1592.) Naples also attracted minor Flemish painters from whom the Spaniard could have acquired his penchant for landscape backgrounds in the northern manner.

Wherever his art was formed, the mature Roelas excelled at creating monumental altarpieces replete with figures and teeming with incident. The *Death of St. Isidore* of 1613, painted for the church of San Isidoro, is the best example of his mastery of this demanding type of commission. He also brought new life to smaller, more intimate religious subjects, such as the *Vision of St. Bernard*, executed for the hospital of San Bernardo in 1611 (pl. 110). Here the saint is represented in a study that is furnished with a shelf lined with parchment-bound books. In front of the bookcase is a realistic glass vase holding symbolic lilies. St. Bernard is a portrait-like type with a narrow head, a sharp nose, and sunken eyes, and his face expresses silent rapture as the Virgin's milk bathes his forehead. Roelas was able to capture as no Sevillian artist before him the intense piety, earthy realism, and love of spectacle that characterized the devotional practices of Andalusia, and thus he made a profound impact on many younger painters, notably Francisco de Zurbarán.

If Roelas combined novelty and tradition in a discreet, familiar way, the other innovative painter of the period seems totally disconnected from the artistic world of Seville. This, of course, is Diego de Velázquez, whose break with an existing local stylistic tradition must be the most radical in the entire history of Renaissance and Baroque art.[21] His *Adoration of the Magi* (pl. 99) comprises a collection of very ordinary people cast in the roles of the Holy Family and the Three Kings. In this

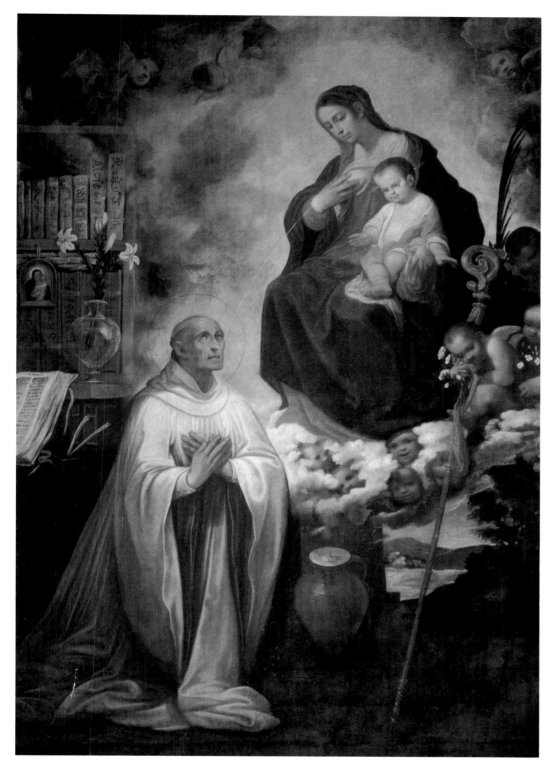

110. Juan de Roelas, *Vision of St. Bernard*, 1611. Seville, Hospital de San Bernardo, canvas, 2.52 × 1.66m.

painting, the distinction between the world of the spectator and the world of the holy personages is almost entirely obliterated, as if the artist were using a shock technique to emphasize the moment when the son of God consents to become a man. However, Christ's future sacrifice is subtly implied by the thorny vegetation in the lower right and the heavy, broken slab of stone on which Mary rests her feet, perhaps an allusion to the lid of the tomb and thus to the Resurrection.

127

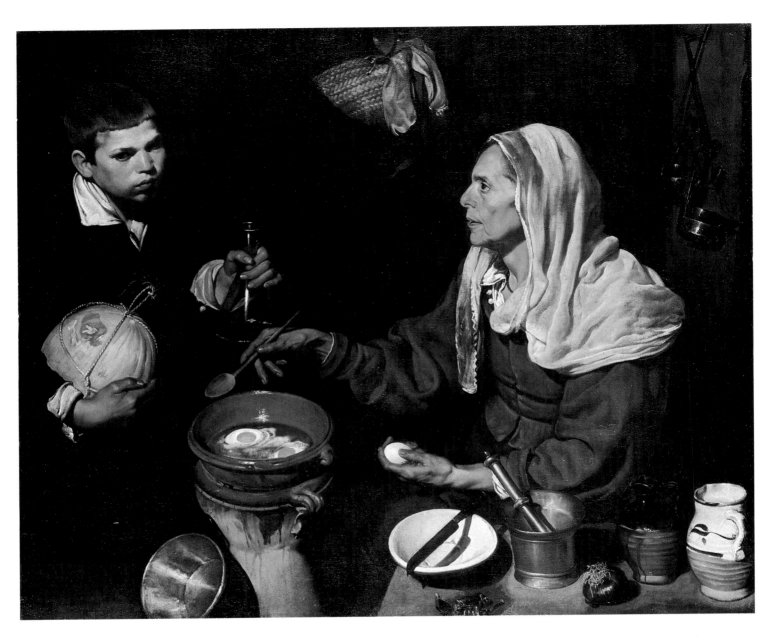

111. Diego de Velázquez, *Old Woman Cooking Eggs*, 1618. Edinburgh, National Gallery of Scotland, canvas, 0.99 × 1.69m.

Nothing in Sevillian painting, past or present, prepared the way for this extraordinary artist, who was born in Seville in 1599, only twenty years before he executed the *Adoration of the Magi*. Velázquez's formative years were neither eventful nor unusual. In December 1610, he became the apprentice of Pacheco, and in 1617 was admitted to the painters' guild. A year later he married Pacheco's daughter Juana. By 1621, he had hired an apprentice, acquired a rental property, and was beginning to establish a local reputation. Yet, despite this conventional curriculum vitae, his pictures are entirely original creations.

As a matter of fact, the *Adoration of the Magi* is one of the less adventurous early pictures. At least, there were numerous local versions for the artist to study and criticize while formulating his own interpretation. Much more inventive are several genre scenes for which there are no known precedents in Seville. *Old Woman Cooking Eggs* (pl. 111) is not the earliest of these pictures, but it is a particularly brilliant example. Using a powerful, focused light, itself a novel feature, Velázquez creates a tour de force of naturalistic painting in which different shapes, textures, and

128

surfaces are miraculously brought to life. The artist's eye has observed and recorded every telling detail, down to the thin sliver of glowing coals that warm the eggs which are absent-mindedly tended by the woman.

Another of his innovations is the treatment of religious subjects as genre paintings populated with mundane figures in contemporary dress and in commonplace settings. In *Christ in the House of Mary and Martha* (pl. 112) of 1618, a young servant girl grumpily grinds spices in a mortar, while an older woman points an admonishing finger in her direction. Seen through a window in an adjacent room, Christ speaks to Martha, who complains that she is "about much serving," while her sister Mary sits at His feet and righteously listens to His words. The inversion of scale between the worldly and divine components of the composition and the loving, lingering attention paid to the beautiful but somewhat distracting still-life details might conceivably have brought the Inquisition to the door had not the inspector of paintings been Pacheco, the artist's proud teacher.

Velázquez also showed a precocious talent for portraiture. In 1620, the indomitable Mother Jerónima de la Fuente, a Franciscan from the convent of Santa Isabel, Toledo, arrived in Seville en route to the Philippines, where she planned to establish a house of the order. Although sixty-six years old, she is portrayed by Velázquez as unafraid of the hazards of her mission. She holds the Crucifix firmly in her grasp, as if preparing to batter the heathen into submission (pl. 113).

This group of early works proclaims Velázquez's prodigious gifts and his enormous self-confidence in breaking with the existing patterns of painting in Seville. Finding little of use in the work of his compatriots, he turned his eyes outward to those unfailing sources of inspiration for Spanish painters: the arts of Italy and Flanders. The genre scenes, for example, have their origins in a tradition

112. Diego de Velázquez, *Christ in the House of Mary and Martha*, 1618. London, National Gallery, canvas, 0.60 × 1.04m.

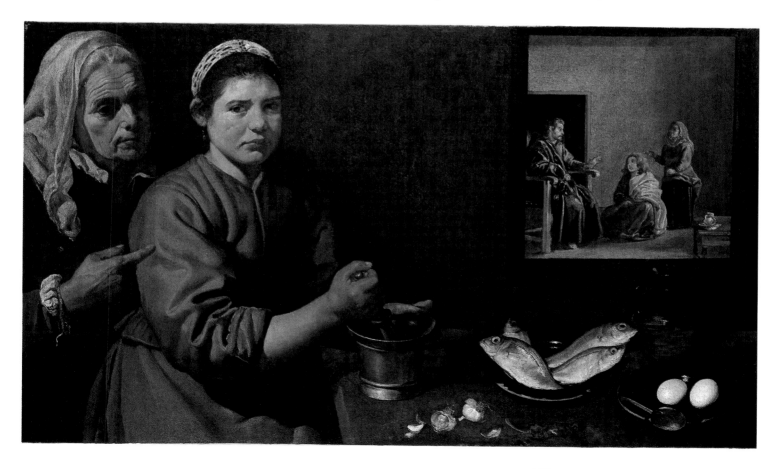

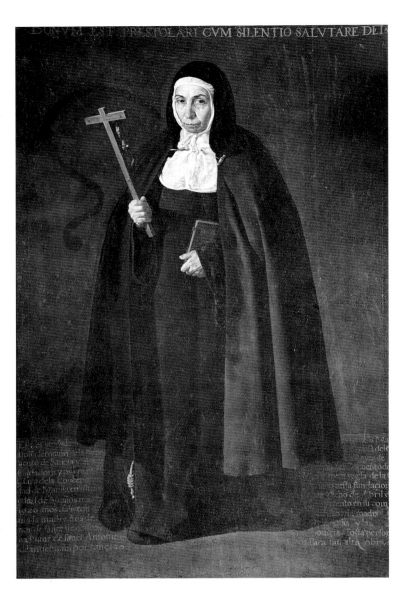

113. Diego de Velázquez, *Mother Jerónima de la Fuente*, 1620. Madrid, Prado, canvas, 1.60 × 1.10m.

initiated in the 1550s by the Flemish painter Pieter Aertsen and continued by artists both in Flanders and in northern Italy, such as Vincenzo Campi. The inverted religious compositions also can be traced to the Aertsen circle through the medium of engravings, which were available to an artist working in a city that was flooded with these inexpensive images. Taking these prints as a point of departure, Velázquez cleared away most of the objects and focused on the remainder with unremitting intensity.

It is probable that Velázquez saw paintings as well as prints by Flemish and Italian masters. By the closing years of the sixteenth century, Flemish genre paintings were being inventoried in several Madrid collections, beginning with that of Philip II. The 1600 inventory of the collection of Juan de Borja, count of Ficallo, included "three panels of fruit sellers" and a "kitchen canvas from Flanders," while the collection of Iñigo López de Mendoza, fifth duke of Infantado, contained at his death in 1602 several examples, among them a "cocina vieja de Marta y María" ("an old kitchen with Martha and Mary").[22]

These paintings were not within reach of the young Velázquez, but comparable works were known in Seville. For example, the duke of Alcalá commissioned a painting from Alonso Vázquez (pl. 114) that is an amalgamation of Flemish religious

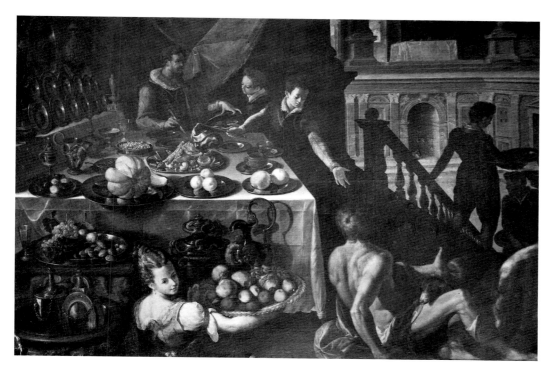

114. Alonso Vázquez, *Lazarus and the Rich Man*, 1588–1603. Whereabouts unknown.

and secular imagery. Alcalá had been at court in 1597–98 and again in 1608, and almost certainly saw northern paintings of every kind. The fact that he owned two genre paintings by Velázquez suggests that he may have helped to import the fashion for these subjects to Seville.[23]

This taste for pictorial novelties is characteristic of enlightened Spanish collectors around the turn of the century, a time when genre and still-life subjects were just becoming popular in Spain and were prized by those with a taste for the new. In particular, they seem to have appealed to erudite collectors such as Alcalá, who owned several still lifes by the Antequera artist Antonio Mohedano as well as the genre scenes by Velázquez. Such collectors may have regarded these compositions as recreations of the antique genre paintings described in Pliny's *Natural History*. In 1623, when Velázquez went to Madrid for the second time, he brought the *Waterseller* (London, Wellington Museum) as a gift to his sponsor, Juan de Fonseca y Figueroa, a royal chaplain from Seville who was renowned for his learning and was the author of a treatise on ancient painting. To the artist, the gift and the recipient were evidently well matched.

The trip to Madrid of 1623 had been preceded by another in 1622, which had the same objective – to attract the attention of the king and gain an appointment as royal painter. For much of his life, Velázquez had lived under the same roof as a leading proponent of the nobility of painting and heard endless arguments and discussions on the subject. Once persuaded of this truth, he would have come to see that the world outside the walls of Pacheco's academy, that is, the art market of Seville, was bound to regard the theory as so many empty words. Accordingly, Velázquez set his sights on Madrid and the court, where he hoped to win the favor of the shy youth who had just become the most powerful monarch in Europe.

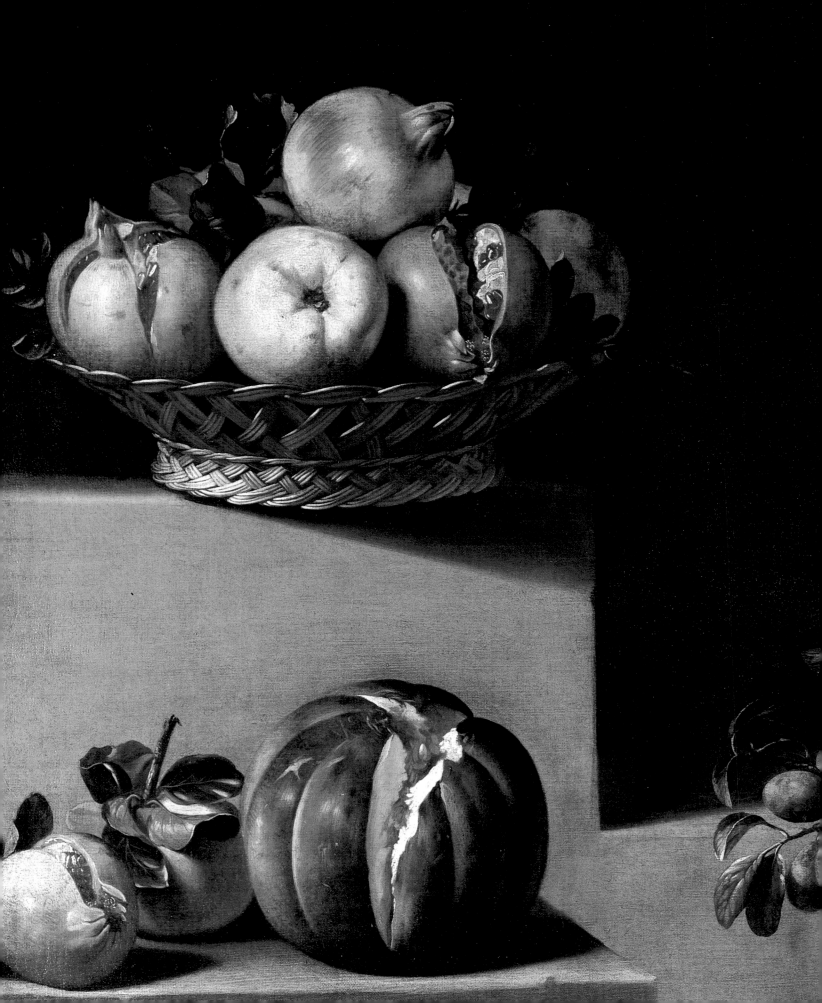

6

The Dawn of a New Golden Age Madrid 1620–1640

THE REIGN OF PHILIP IV (1621–65) is justly famous as a golden age of painting in Spain, matched only by that of Philip II, which, by coincidence, it virtually equaled in duration. Like his grandfather, Philip IV had a deep love of the art of painting and the resources to indulge it on a grand scale. Inspired by his example, the leading nobles, many of whom spent time abroad in the service of the monarchy, became avid, discerning collectors and helped to transform Madrid into one of the liveliest art markets in Europe. Philip's reign was equally notable for the accomplishments of the painters of Madrid, many of whom, however, tended to perpetuate the "official" style forged under Philip III. Even in the palace, where conditions for innovation were more propitious than in the ecclesiastical sector, the acceptance of novelty did not occur all at once, as the new artistic star, Diego de Velázquez, would quickly discover.

Velázquez's entry to the court had opened with the death of Philip III, whose reign had lasted for twenty-three years and had been marked by the drift and decline of the monarchy's power in Europe. The new king, Philip IV, was a young king; he was only sixteen years old when he ascended the throne and still unformed as a person and ruler alike. His lack of confidence and experience provided the opportunity for Gaspar de Guzmán, the count-duke of Olivares, an ambitious aristocrat who had been carefully planning for the day when he could capture the king's favor, to take hold of the reins of government and begin to rebuild the monarchy.[1]

During the 1610s, Olivares had spent time in Seville and become acquainted with members of Pacheco's circle, including the painter himself. After he came to power, he called upon these Sevillian friends to serve in the government and royal household, and their arrival at court provided Velázquez with the opportunity to advance his career.[2] Thus, in 1622, he traveled to Madrid for what would prove to be a vain attempt to gain a foothold at court. Discouraged but not defeated, he returned to Madrid the following year and, with the assistance of Juan de Fonseca and other friends from Seville, he was given the opportunity to execute a portrait of the king (pl. 116), a picture that he reworked extensively a few years later. The portrait was favorably received and the desired appointment obtained: on 6 October 1623 Velázquez was named royal painter with a salary of twenty ducats a month plus payment for individual works as executed.

When Velázquez joined their ranks, the royal painters numbered six, all holdovers from the previous regime. By this time, Vicente Carducho and Eugenio Cajés had become pre-eminent, although in title the obscure portraitist Santiago Morán held the higher office of court painter. Years of unchallenged hegemony had allowed these two painters to continue to work in the reform style learned from their Italian

115. Detail of pl. 120.

133

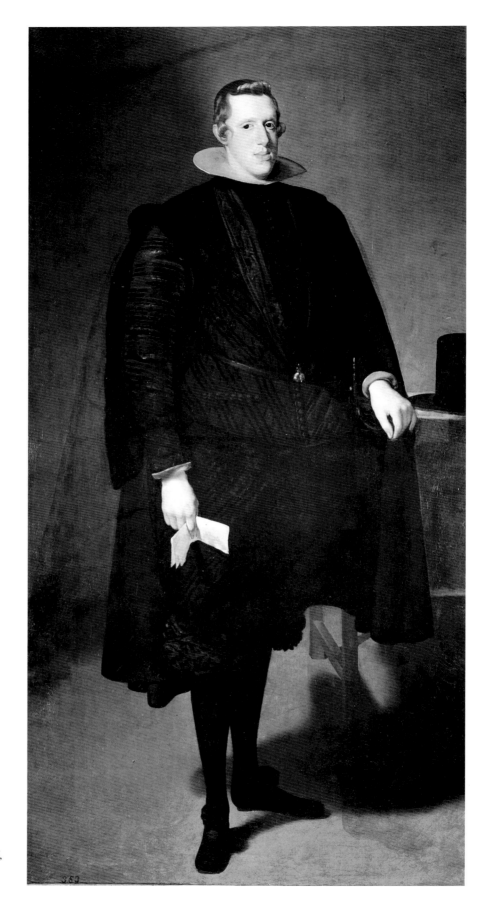

116. Diego de Velázquez, *Philip IV*,
1623–26. Madrid, Prado, canvas,
1.98 × 1.02m.

relations at the close of the previous century. By 1620, Cajés had reached a plateau; although he lived until December 1634, his best work had been done by the time Velázquez reached Madrid. Carducho, on the other hand, was far from being finished either as a painter or as a spokesman for the nobility of his art. During the 1620s, he made his greatest effort to organize the state academy of the arts and fought strenuously for the repeal of the *alcabala* on works by living painters.

Carducho also continued to develop as an artist, gradually accommodating a greater degree of naturalism into his monumental style. After the installation of Velázquez at court, Carducho seems to have received fewer commissions from the crown, but his standing among ecclesiastical patrons, in whom Velázquez had little interest, continued to grow, culminating in his most important commission and greatest work. On 29 August 1626, he signed a contract with the Cartuja del Paular, a Carthusian monastery in the Sierra Guadarrama, north of Madrid, for fifty-six pictures.[3] Twenty-seven of these were to represent scenes from the life of St. Bruno, the founder, and another twenty-seven were to depict episodes from the lives of illustrious Carthusians, with two additional canvases containing the coats of arms of the king and of the order. The contract stipulated the delivery of fourteen pictures a year, no small feat considering that the average dimensions are 3.45 × 3.15 meters. In the event, the series was not completed until 1632, but the rate of production is still impressive, especially given the elaborate preparatory stages undertaken by the painter.

Carducho was a proponent of painting as a process inspired by thought and guided by careful preparation; unlike his colleagues in Seville, he believed that painters should draw inspiration from their imagination and not the inventions of other artists. For the Paular commission, as in other works, he followed the Italian practice of making preliminary drawings for each composition and then refining individual passages in further studies.[4] Once a definitive solution to the pictorial problem had been found, he produced small oil sketches for the patron to approve and to guide the execution of the finished work. Although he certainly used assistants for the more routine parts of the commission – sizing and priming canvases, for instance – there is no evidence that he was aided in the execution of the principal parts of the compositions.

In its entirety, the series for El Paular is an impressive display of dignified pictorial narrative that ranks as a major creation of the seventeenth-century classical style of religious painting. The tenor of the histories is elevated and dignified and thus perfectly suited to illustrate the heroes of Catholicism's most ascetic order. In most of the scenes, Carducho employs a frieze-like composition, placing monumental figures against rigorously ordered backgrounds of classical architecture or placid landscapes. The expression of emotion is carefully calibrated and restrained, but never dull or routine. However, the actors in Carducho's sacred dramas are not the ideal types employed by French and Italian classicists that were derived from antique sculpture and the great paintings of the High Renaissance, notably the Roman frescoes of Raphael and Michelangelo. Rather, his protagonists are given individualized features in keeping with the long-standing preference of Castilian painters. The resulting synthesis between the real and ideal imparts a sense of actuality and decorum to Carthusian history.

The episodes from the life of St. Bruno unfold in a steady, measured rhythm. In the depiction of the founder refusing the nomination as archbishop of Reggio da Calabria, Carducho invents a balanced composition, centered around the ecclesiastical regalia proffered to the monk by Pope Urban II (pl. 117). The pope announces the appointment by extending his arms in semaphore fashion, one pointing to the saint, the other to the miter, staff, and vestments placed on a low table. St.

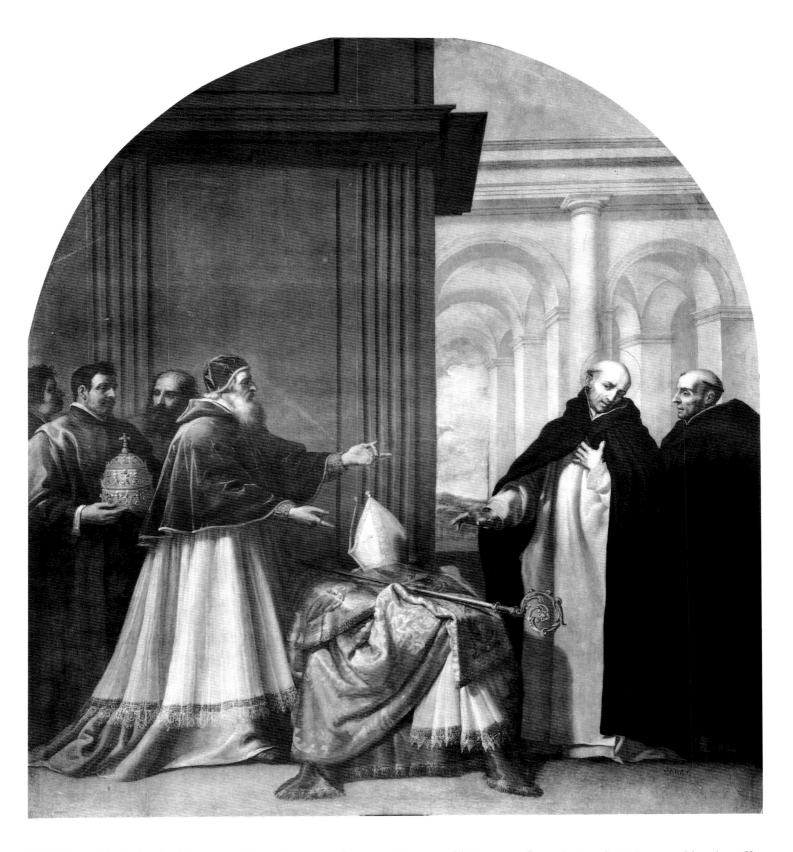

117. Vicente Carducho, *St. Bruno Refuses the Archbishopric of Reggio da Calabria*, 1626–32. Madrid, Prado, canvas, 3.45 × 3.15m.

Bruno's pose and expression reveal his sense of perplexity; he is honored by the offer but unwilling to abandon his life of prayer, manual labor, and fasting to pursue an active ministry. Behind the figures, a setting of Doric architecture, the severest classical order, emphasizes the seriousness of the moment.

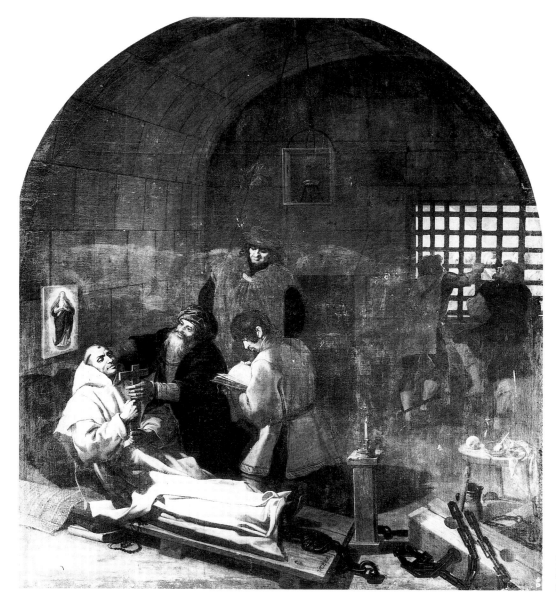

118. Vicente Carducho, *Death of
Brother Lauduino*, 1626–32. Poblet,
monastery, canvas, 3.45 × 3.15m.

The scenes of miracles and martyrdoms are more dramatically conceived. One of
the most effective (pl. 118) is the death of Brother Lauduino (or Lanuino), one of St.
Bruno's original companions who was captured by Guibert, the anti-pope, and
ordered to recognize his authority. When Lauduino refused to comply, he was put
into prison, where he died of privation in 1100. To heighten the dramatic impact of
the saint's final moments, Carducho selects a viewpoint from inside the cell, a
gloomy, vaulted place sealed off at the rear by a heavy grill. A blaze of light
illuminates the deathbed, where the drawn, haggard monk, assisted by two men,
clutches a crucifix to his breast as he draws his last breath. Scattered about the
floor are chains and shackles; on two small tables there are a candle and some vessels
with meager rations of food and water. In this painting, Carducho revives the spirit
of his brother's *Death of St. Francis* (pl. 78) and makes it grand and authoritative
through ambitious effects of space and light.

In 1626 and 1627, the ranks of the royal painters were depleted by the deaths of
Santiago Morán and Bartolomé González respectively, which initiated a scramble
for the appointment to those prestigious posts. Morán's place as court painter was
filled by Velázquez in 1627 or 1628. In a solicitous if futile gesture, Velázquez

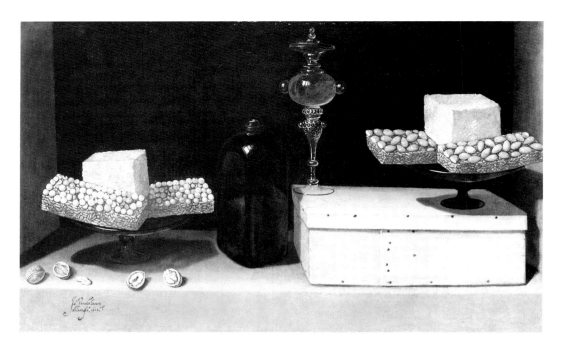

119. Juan van der Hamen, *Still Life with Sweets*, 1622. Cleveland, Museum of Art, John L. Severance Fund (80.6), canvas, 0.58 × 0.97m.

petitioned the king to appoint his father-in-law to the position vacated by Morán, but was refused. As for González's place, there were twelve applicants of distinctly uneven accomplishments.[5] Four are known in name only – Francisco de las Cuevas, Antonio de Monreal, Antonio de Salazar, and Francisco Gómez. Others had been on the fringes of the court and were now looking for a regular position; these included the Italians Angelo Nardi and Julio César Semini, and Juan de la Corte, a battle painter from Flanders. Two more of the contenders were descendants of painters who had served Philip II: Felipe Diricksen was the grandson of the topographical artist, Anton van den Wyngaerde, while Félix Castelo was the grandson of G. B. Castello, il Bergamasco, and the son of Fabrizio, who also had served Philip II and then Philip III as royal painter.[6] Another two enjoyed the advantage of having been the pupils of Carducho and Cajés: Pedro Núñez del Valle and Antonio Lanchares.[7] The final contestant was the great still-life painter Juan van der Hamen y León.

A committee comprising Cajés, Carducho, and Velázquez was formed to rank the four most qualified candidates. Cajés and Carducho voted for Lanchares, Castelo, Nardi, and Núñez del Valle, in that order. Velázquez concurred, except that he reversed the order of Castelo and Nardi. In the end the committee's deliberations came to nothing, because the position was suppressed in one of the many false economies with which the government vainly tried to fight off bankruptcy. Nonetheless, the competition is useful for assessing the art of painting in Madrid in the late 1620s, and what it shows is a situation approaching stagnation. The contenders fall roughly into three categories – the descendants of earlier royal painters, the disciples of the older incumbents, and a smattering of minor Flemish and Italian artists who had drifted to Madrid hoping to find the success that had eluded them at home. The only painter now considered to be significant, Juan van der Hamen, did not even appear on the short list.

Van der Hamen (1596–1631) was born in Madrid, the son of a Flemish nobleman who had left his native land in the late 1580s.[8] The family – Juan was one of three brothers – was well-to-do and provided its offspring with sound educations. Lorenzo, the eldest, became a priest and established a reputation as a scholar and historian. Juan was trained as a painter and, by 1619, was producing still lifes for the king. His earliest examples indicate that he had studied the still lifes of Spanish and Flemish artists alike: in some of these works, van der Hamen employs the chaste,

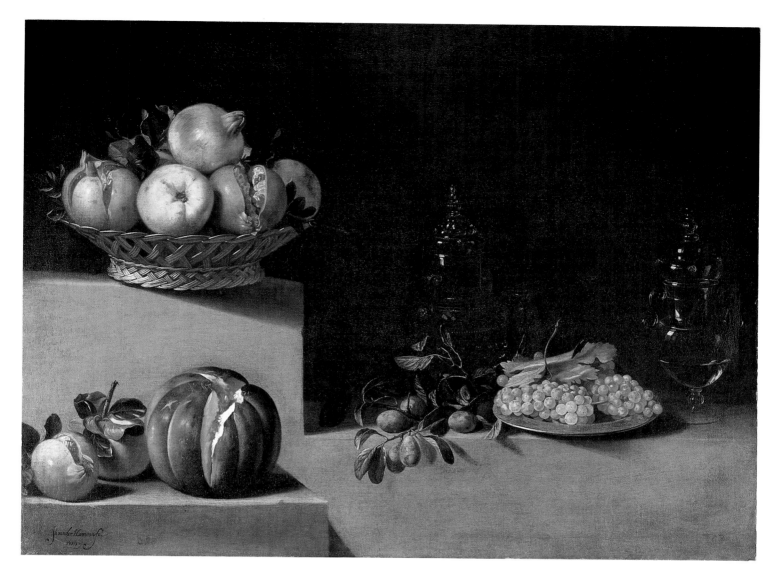

120. Juan van der Hamen, *Still Life with Fruit and Glassware*, 1626. Houston, Museum of Fine Arts, canvas, 0.84 × 1.11m.

dramatic compositional format of Sánchez Cotán; in others, he imitates the more opulent paintings of the young Frans Snyders, which seem to have entered Spanish collections soon after they were made. However, the costly objects depicted by van der Hamen reflect his popularity with a clientele that with justice can be called the carriage trade, the upper classes of court society. A composition of 1622 (pl. 119) shows a fine Venetian goblet filled with wine and flanked by expensive, sweet confections. In keeping with these high-class foodstuffs, van der Hamen uses a technique of considerable refinement and delicacy. Tiny highlights, made with small, pointed dabs of the brush, flicker over the sugary granules of the sweetmeats, and smoothly blended strokes produce a convincing illusion of the changing pattern of woodgrain.

In 1626, van der Hamen made his still lifes more varied and complex by placing objects on different levels (pl. 120).[9] This new type of composition seems to have originated in Rome during the early 1620s and is seen in works attributed to Tomasso Salini and Agostino Verrocchi. It is not certain how van der Hamen became familiar with these pictures, although it has been suggested that they were brought to his attention by the renowned Roman collector and connoisseur Cassiano dal Pozzo, who accompanied Cardinal Francesco Barberini on a mission to Madrid precisely in the year of 1626. However, van der Hamen's use of this scheme differs from that of the Roman painters, who liked to scatter a profusion of inanimate objects over the surface. Van der Hamen drastically reduces the number of elements and arranges the remainder into exquisitely balanced, asymmetrical compositions, strongly lit in the Spanish manner. This allows him to concentrate on the rendering of each individual object and thus to enhance the sensation of corporeality and texture.

Van der Hamen's still lifes are now considered among the finest ever painted, and thus, it seems strange that none of the royal painters saw fit to include him on the short list of candidates for González's post. Perhaps his skill in still-life painting, then held to be an amusing but inferior category of artistic endeavor, lowered his standing in the eyes of the selectors. However, van der Hamen was equally excellent as a figure painter and portraitist. In fact, according to Cassiano, Cardinal Barberini preferred his portraits to those of Velázquez. Writing in his diary on 28 July 1626, Cassiano noted that he had summoned van der Hamen to paint a new portrait of the cardinal, who was displeased with the one already completed by Velázquez.[10] Van der Hamen, in other words, had the makings of a serious contender for royal favor, especially because he was of noble descent and already established in the household as a member of the Burgundian Guard (*archeros del rey*). His failure to make the final list of contenders for the vacant place of royal painter therefore may have been the consequence of too much talent and promise, not too little. This is merely speculation, but it does fit into a larger pattern of competition and jealousy that afflicted the young Velázquez in his initial years at court.

The first evidence of Velázquez's struggle to consolidate his position is somewhat oblique but credible, given the way in which he, a young outsider, had jumped ahead of incumbent and aspiring royal painters alike. For example, the name of Velázquez is nowhere to be found in the treatise of Carducho, who by right of his long, distinguished service to the crown would have expected to cap his career with the appointment as court painter. Somewhat more specific is the reference by Pacheco to Velázquez's equestrian portrait of Philip IV (lost), a work exhibited in public in 1626; Pacheco states that the picture "won the admiration of the court and the envy of artists."[11] Many years later, an acquaintance of Velázquez, the Aragonese painter Jusepe Martínez, referred to the tension between the young painter and his senior colleagues by noting that the older artists accused him of being able to paint only heads and, by implication, not entire compositions.

Palomino reports that the rivalry culminated in a competition held in 1627, involving Velázquez, Carducho, Cajés, and Nardi, each of whom produced a composition of the Expulsion of the Moriscos from Spain by Philip III (all lost).[12] The judges of the contest were Fray Juan Bautista Maino and Giovanni Battista Crescenzi, a Roman nobleman who had arrived in Madrid in 1617 and become a powerful figure in artistic circles at the court of Philip IV.[13] As sympathizers with "modern" painting, they declared Velázquez the winner, and his painting was duly installed in a major state room in the palace. This victory was confirmed by further appointments as Usher of the Privy Chamber (7 March 1627) and court painter (first mention of this title, 18 September 1628). From then on, Velázquez's pre-eminent position in the hierarchy of royal painters was unassailable.

Yet Velázquez's triumph over his rivals does not imply that their criticisms were unfounded. The masterpiece of the 1620s, the *Feast of Bacchus* (pl. 121), is undoubtedly a brilliant interpretation of a theme probably known to Velázquez in a print by Hendrik Goltzius.[14] Bacchus is depicted as offering the gift of wine, an elixir that provides temporary respite from the common man's struggle for existence. As in the *Adoration of the Magi* (pl. 99), the realism of the figures is heightened to reduce the distance between the realm of art and the world of experience, and so

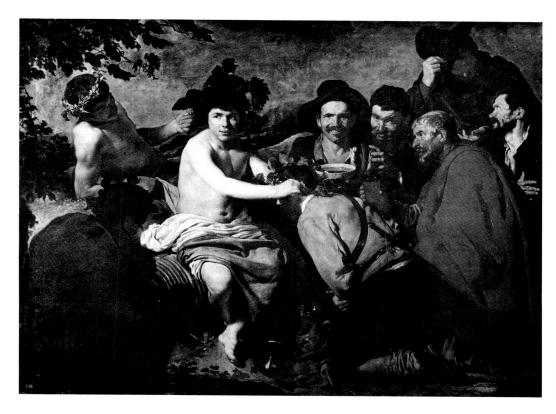

121. Diego de Velázquez, *Feast of Bacchus*, 1629. Madrid, Prado, canvas, 1.65 × 2.27m.

compelling are these sunburnt peasants that certain infelicities in the picture, such as the overcrowded composition and the uncertain definition of space, are in no way obtrusive. However, it must be admitted that Velázquez's technique cannot quite keep pace with his soaring imagination. The need to improve his skills seems to have become apparent during the visit of Peter Paul Rubens to Madrid in 1628–29.

Rubens's second visit to the court is one of the major events in the history of seventeenth-century Spanish painting.[15] Before 1628, paintings by Rubens were to be found in a few Madrid collections, including that of the monarch. After his departure, the number would be considerably augmented by several large commissions from the king, who was captivated by Rubens's artistry and thereafter became his most important client. During the 1630s, Philip accumulated the vast collection of works by Rubens and his disciples that provided new pictorial models for the artists of Madrid.

The pictures completed by Rubens while he was still at court would surely have made a deep impression on Velázquez, as well, and even had consequences for his self-esteem. Rubens's equestrian portrait of the king, for instance, known only in a copy (Florence, Uffizi), was evidently considered superior to the one executed by Velázquez in 1626, which was removed to make room for the new version. To his credit, Rubens was not interested in supplanting Velázquez at the Spanish court; he generously shared his knowledge with his young colleague, particularly his admiration for Titian, which he demonstrated by making spirited copies of masterpieces by the Venetian in the royal collection. Through these copies, Rubens revived the paintings of Titian as a force in Spanish painting, and no one was more impressed than Velázquez. Rubens may also have had a hand in persuading the monarch to send his protégé to Italy. At any rate, the turn of events suggests that this is so. Rubens left Madrid for the north in May 1629, and less than two months later a royal license was granted to Velázquez to travel to Italy, where, according to the ambassador of Parma, he was "going to perfect his art."

141

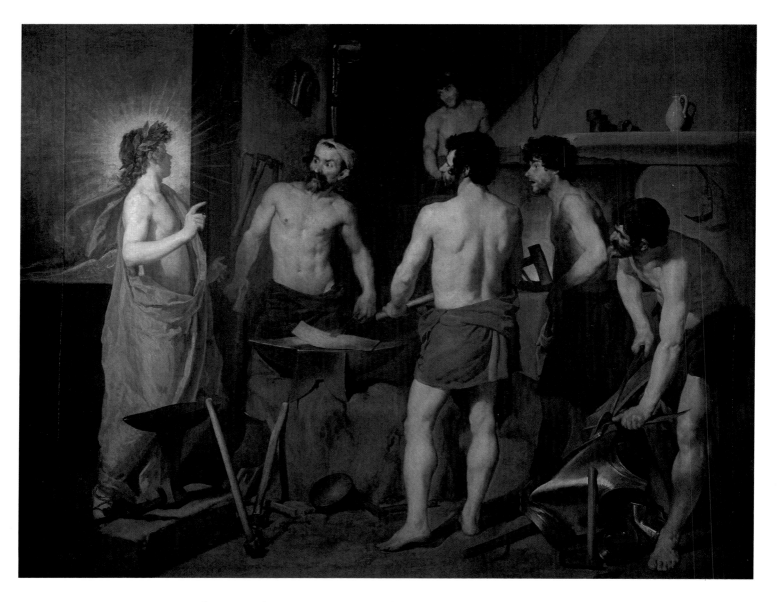

122. Diego de Velázquez, "*Forge of Vulcan*," 1630. Prado, Madrid, canvas, 2.23 × 2.90m.

Velázquez was in Italy for just over a year, and when he returned to Madrid his art had indeed been perfected.[16] Pacheco provides a schematic itinerary of the trip, which included short stays in Venice, Ferrara, Cento, and Naples, with most of the time spent in Rome. The Roman experience seems to have been crucial, for there Velázquez could study the grand manner of Italian painting, exemplified by Raphael and Michelangelo, and meet the best practitioners then active in the city – Pietro da Cortona, Andrea Sacchi, Domenichino, Giovanni Lanfranco, to name the most famous. Velázquez synthesized these experiences in two history paintings in the Italian manner, the "*Forge of Vulcan*" and *Joseph's Bloodied Coat Presented to Jacob* (pls. 122 and 123), works that demonstrate his mastery of Italian classicizing art, including such techniques as dramatic gesture and expression, illusionistic space, accurate anatomical draftsmanship – indeed, all the elements that had previously confounded him and exposed him to hostile criticism. A greater psychological unity is also observable. In the "*Forge of Vulcan*," Apollo transmits the news of Venus's infidelity to her husband, Vulcan, whose sense of shock brings the work of the Cyclops to a halt. Yet the artist did not fall completely under the sway of the Italians; in the "*Forge of Vulcan*," Velázquez retains his earlier interest in depicting the texture

142

and look of objects, from the molten, red piece of metal on the forge to the bright, cool armor of the breastplate. In these pictures, Velázquez paid homage to the great masters of Italian painting, and, having learned his lessons, he proceeded to devise a new pictorial language of his own.

Upon his return to Madrid, Velázquez encountered a new atmosphere at court. The count-duke of Olivares, faced with an impetuous king eager to lead his army into battle against the French in Italy or the Dutch in the Netherlands, and besieged by rising opposition to his regime at court, had decided to initiate a lavish program of artistic display in the hope of distracting the sovereign. These efforts were to be centered on the construction of a new pleasure palace on the eastern border of Madrid, which came to be known as the Buen Retiro.[17] Here theatrical plays and spectacles would be staged, tournaments and jousts would be organized, and painting, sculpture, and tapestry would be displayed. Beginning in 1630 with a modest renovation of the royal apartment in San Jerónimo, the project was expanded in 1632 and again in 1633, culminating in a sizable if unpretentious complex of buildings surrounded by enormous gardens adorned by fountains, alleys, and hermitage chapels. Once the structure was finished, Olivares was faced with the mammoth problem of decorating the new palace, a problem that was solved by importing

123. Diego de Velázquez, *Joseph's Bloodied Coat Presented to Jacob*, 1630. El Escorial, Nuevos Museos, canvas, 2.17 × 2.85m.

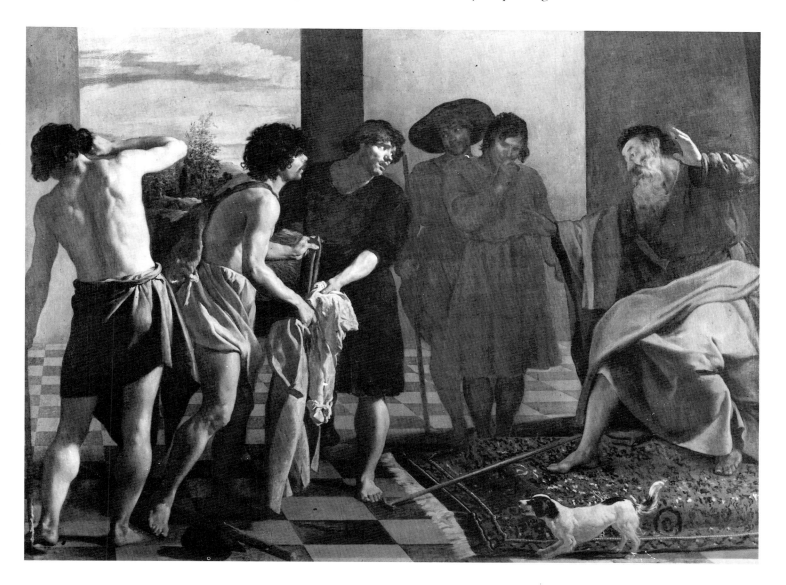

hundreds of pictures from Italy and Flanders and by commissioning as many works from local artists as they could paint. The imported paintings are best discussed in another context and will be included in chapter 9. As for the works by royal artists and their disciples, the decoration of the Retiro was the major event of the 1630s and thus is a microcosm of court painting during the decade.

Not surprisingly, the generational struggle played out in the 1620s was continued during the 1630s, except that now Velázquez was much better armed. The earliest of his contributions to the decoration of the Retiro is the luminous *St. Anthony Abbot and St. Paul the Hermit* (pl. 124), his first picture with an extensive landscape background. It was installed in the hermitage chapel of San Pablo by spring, 1633.[18] Before the trip to Italy, Velázquez had generally used an opaque, red priming layer over which he applied thick pigments; this technique produced a dark and somber tonality. Here, however, he uses a ground of reflecting lead-white, which is applied so thinly that it barely covers the nubby weave of the linen canvas. This procedure, when coupled with the application of diluted pigments, creates an evocative play of silvery light and transparent forms. While the foreground figures are solidly and correctly drawn, those in the background are rendered merely by notational brush-work. When pitted against a sparkling work like this, the paintings of Carducho and Cajés suddenly began to look very old-fashioned.

Nowhere are the differences between the royal painters more sharply drawn than in the Hall of Realms, the principal ceremonial room of the Buen Retiro Palace.[19] Spanish palace decoration during the reign of Philip IV tended to be loosely programmed in comparison with Italian examples. There is no counterpart to Cortona's decorations in the Barberini Palace, Rome, or the Pitti Palace, Florence, in which the history and virtues of a ruling family are exalted in clever, complicated allegories. However, the paintings of the Hall of Realms, executed in 1634–35, offer an exception to the rule, for here the count-duke and his advisers invented a coherent if straightforward program designed to magnify the power of the Spanish monarchy.

The principal element is twelve paintings of important military victories of Philip IV's reign, which demonstrate the invincibility of Spanish arms. These are complemented by ten scenes of the life of Hercules, who was claimed by the Spanish Habsburgs (and virtually every other ruling house of Europe) as the founding ancestor of the dynasty. The final component is a group of equestrian portraits of Philip III and Margaret of Austria, Philip IV and Isabella of Bourbon, and the heir to the throne, Baltasar Carlos (born on 17 October 1629), which embodies the idea of dynastic legitimacy and succession.

The division of responsibility for the twenty-seven paintings and the works themselves mirror the prevailing artistic trends of the moment. Unexpectedly, the largest share went to Francisco de Zurbarán, then the leading painter of Seville. The motives for his summons to court are not clear: perhaps they were to include a subject of the king from outside Madrid or try out a painter whose fame had come to the attention of people at court. In any event, Zurbarán painted an idiosyncratic series of Hercules scenes (discussed in chapter 7) and the *Defense of Cádiz*, and then returned home. Velázquez, as court painter, obtained a generous share of the work – all five equestrian portraits and the *Surrender of Breda* (pl. 130). Most of the remaining pictures were assigned to the old guard and their followers. Carducho obtained the commission for three battle paintings, while his pupil Félix Castelo was awarded one. Cajés was given two subjects, but died only four months after he started to work; his canvases were completed by his assistants Antonio Puga and Luis Fernández. Also assigned two compositions was Cajés's follower José Leonardo. In other words, Cajés and Carducho had succeeded in securing eight of

124. Diego de Velázquez, *St. Anthony Abbot and St. Paul the Hermit*, 1633. Madrid, Prado, canvas, 2.60 × 1.92m.

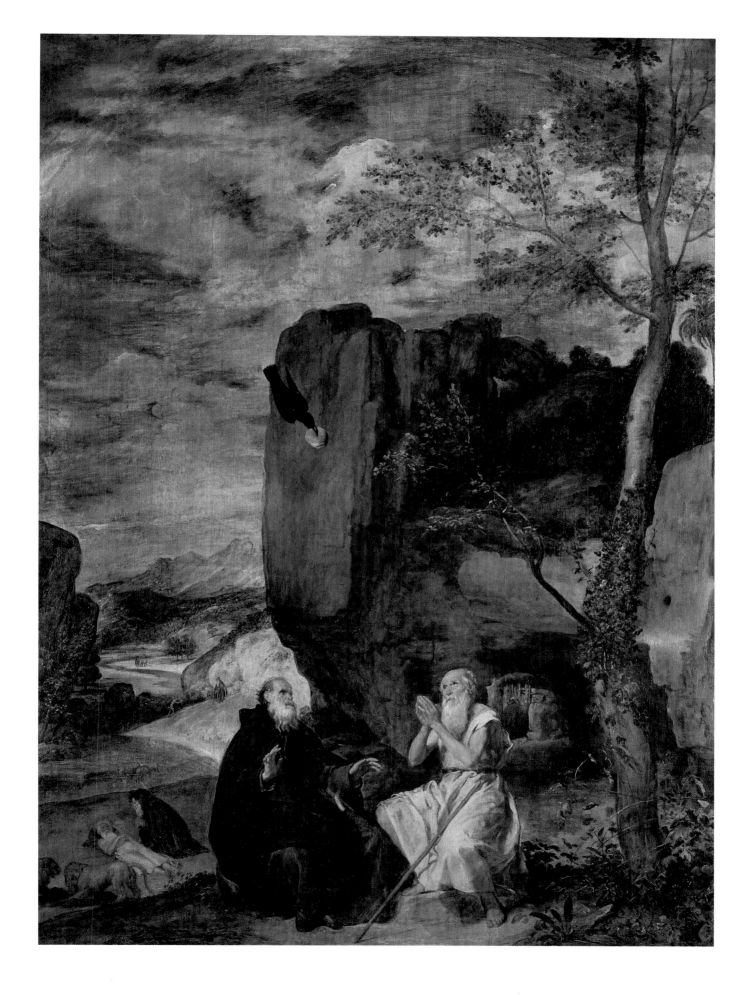

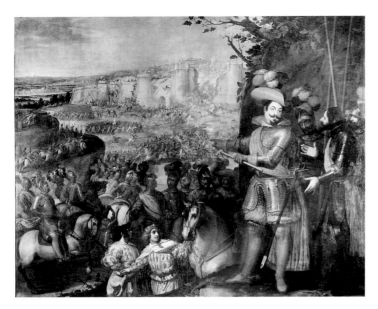

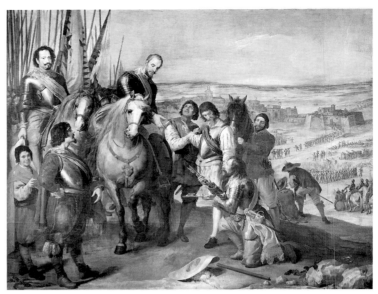

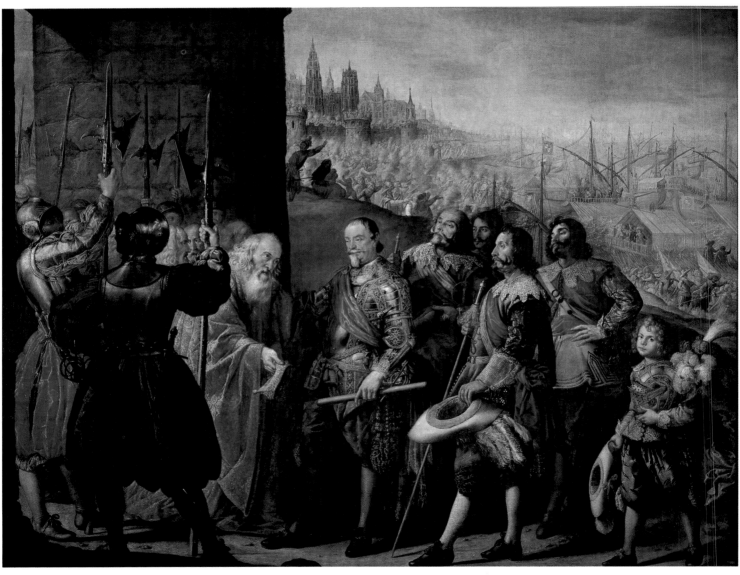

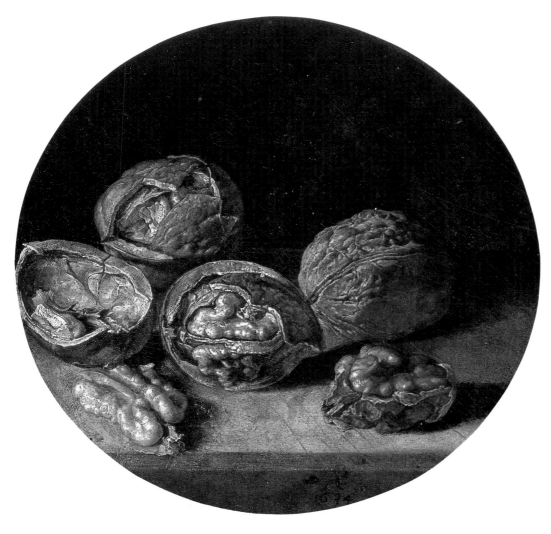

128. Antonio de Pereda, *Still Life of Walnuts*, 1634. Spain, private collection, panel, 0.21m. diameter.

the twelve battle pictures for themselves and their faithful. The two remaining works fell into the hands of Maino, who had not painted for many years, and Antonio de Pereda, a young outsider who was promoted by Giovanni Battista Crescenzi, the architect of the palace.

In composition, all but two of the battle paintings follow a scheme exemplified by Carducho's *Siege of Rheinfelden* (pl. 125), which features a general (here the duke of Feria) in the foreground directing a military engagement unfolding in the distance. This rigid pattern of organization was derived from sixteenth-century battle scenes and accounts for the somewhat archaic flavor of these works. However, the two engagements depicted by José Leonardo (pl. 126), the best of Cajés's followers, succeed in conveying a sense of the flow and movement of troops and suggest that he was a painter of considerable promise, which unfortunately was not to be fulfilled.

Leonardo was born in Calatayud in 1601 and moved to Madrid in 1612,[20] where he probably was the apprentice of Pedro de las Cuevas, famous as a teacher of young painters but almost unknown as an artist himself. Nevertheless, Leonardo's earliest works, which are in the altarpiece of the church of Santiago, Cebreros (Avila), of 1625, are patently influenced by Cajés. After completing his pictures for the Hall of Realms, Leonardo received occasional assignments from the crown, but his application to fill the place vacated by Carducho's death in 1638 was rejected.

125 (facing page top left). Vicente Carducho, *Siege of Rheinfelden*, 1634. Madrid, Prado, canvas, 2.97 × 3.57m.

126. (facing page top right). José Leonardo, *Surrender of Jülich*, 1634–35. Madrid, Prado, canvas, 3.07 × 3.81m.

127. (facing page bottom). Antonio de Pereda, *Relief of Genoa*, 1634–35. Madrid, Prado, canvas, 2.90 × 3.70m.

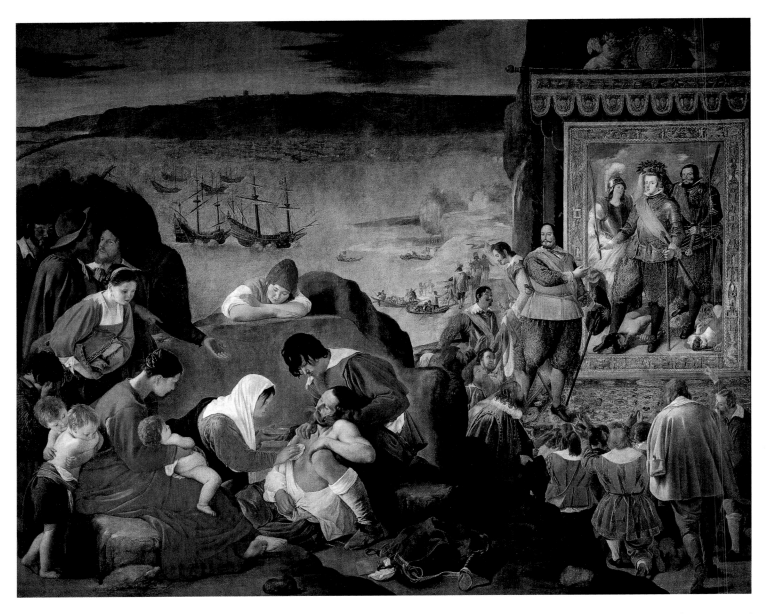

129. Juan Bautista Maino, *Recapture of Bahía*, 1634–35. Madrid, Prado, canvas, 3.09 × 3.81m.

Through his work at the palace, Leonardo came into contact with Velázquez and began to imitate, if tentatively, the master's technique. Unfortunately, in the 1640s, just as he was beginning to achieve a deeper understanding of Velázquez's style, he suffered a mental breakdown and painted no more. Eventually, he was committed to the hospital of Nuestra Señora de la Gracia, an insane asylum in Zaragoza, where he died around 1652.

The other painter new to the court scene was Antonio de Pereda, the youngest of all the artists and author of the *Relief of Genoa* (p. 127).[21] Born in Valladolid in 1611, Pereda first studied with his father. In 1622, he moved to Madrid, where he was a pupil of Pedro de las Cuevas. Soon after becoming an independent master, he attracted the attention of an important protector, Giovanni Battista Crescenzi. As a still-life painter himself, Crescenzi would certainly have admired Pereda's extraordinary facility in this genre, as evinced in the riveting *Still Life of Walnuts* (pl. 128), signed and dated 1634.[22] This small picture miraculously transforms a humble dry fruit into a strangely moving, universal statement on the wonders of nature. Pereda employs the same microscopic vision in certain passages of his battle painting, the *Relief of Genoa* (p. 127), particularly in the silvery reflections of the pikemen's armor. However, the rest of the composition falls into the pattern used by the older court artists; in fact, there is a marked similarity between the figure styles of Pereda and Carducho. He received the final payment from the crown for this work on 15 June 1635, and final it was. Crescenzi had died a month or two earlier and, without his protection, the painter lost his access to the court forever. He soon managed, however, to establish himself with an ecclesiastical clientele and was able to thrive by giving a new, lustrous surface to old compositional formulas.

In contrast with the formulaic treatment favored by the other painters, Velázquez and Maino break fresh ground in their battle compositions,[23] the *Surrender of Breda* and the *Recapture of Bahía*, which share a common premise by interpreting the clash of arms as a clash of emotions. In the other artists' battle scenes, the principal actors are set into ritual poses, self-consciously discussing strategy with subordinates or directing troop movements with broad, sweeping gestures. The fighting occurs at a safe distance from headquarters, well out of the range of the commanders. For Maino and Velázquez, however, war inflicts pain, the physical pain of being

130. Diego de Velázquez, *Surrender of Breda*, 1634–35. Madrid, Prado, canvas, 3.07 × 3.70m.

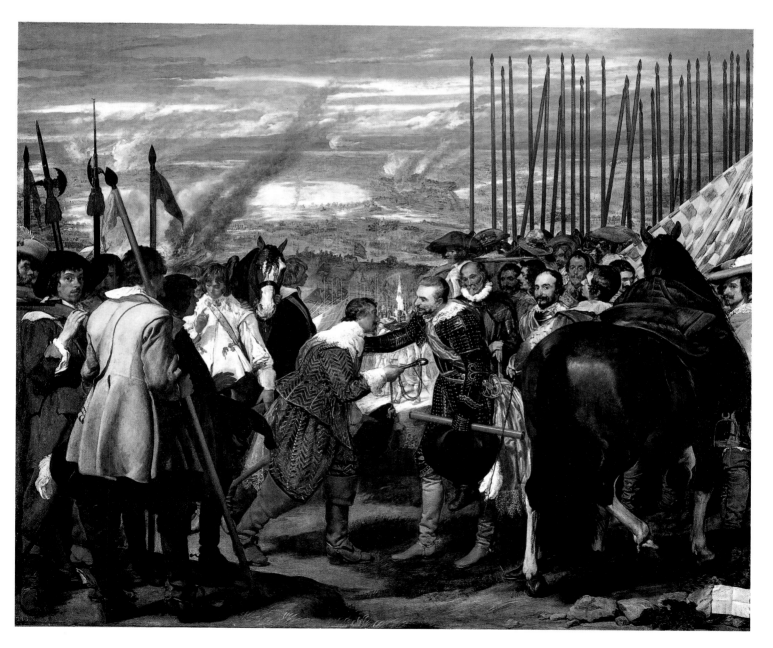

wounded, the psychological pain of suffering defeat. Although the narrative action of their pictures was inspired by two theatrical works – Calderón de la Barca's *El sitio de Breda* and Lope de Vega's *El Brasil restituido* – each artist enriches the text in a significant way. Maino includes the count-duke's portrait to glorify the minister as the author of the victory (pl. 129). A more telling addition is the wounded soldier, who evokes a Christian martyrdom in order to arouse admiration and compassion for those who risk their lives in defense of the monarchy. The *Recapture of Bahía* is painted in Maino's crisp, burnished manner, which he effortlessly revived for the occasion.

Velázquez's *Surrender of Breda* (pl. 130) interprets an event in the war with the United Provinces from the vantage point of an eyewitness.[24] Although this version of the surrender is largely fictitious – the keys to the fortress were never handed over by Justin of Nassau to the Spanish general Ambrogio de Spinola – Velázquez makes it seem real. Flouting the usual formula for surrender scenes, in which the vanquished meekly genuflects before the victorious, Velázquez represents Spinola as having dismounted from his horse to meet the Dutch commander on equal footing. Instead of accepting the token of surrender, he places a hand on the Dutchman's shoulder, offering the consolation of one soldier to another, and seems to speak the climactic line of Calderón's play: "Justin, I accept them [the keys] in full awareness of your valor; for the valor of the defeated confers fame upon the victor." On either side, the Spanish and Dutch soldiers restlessly move in place and observe the act of capitulation, reflecting each in his way on the fortunes of war.

The decoration of the Hall of Realms is a line of demarcation in the history of art at the court of Philip IV. Cajés died as he was executing his share of the work and Carducho died three years later; thus, the old guard passed away. Neither of their positions as royal painter was filled for some time, perhaps because of the edict of 1627, prohibiting the appointment of new salaried painters; and their followers and disciples were employed thereafter by the crown only on a piecemeal basis. As a consequence, Velázquez was now able to turn his dominance into a monopoly and to rebuild the corps of painters with artists of his choice. The first of these appointments was made immediately after the death of Carducho when Alonso Cano, Velázquez's fellow apprentice in Seville, was called to Madrid to serve as painter to the count-duke, thus circumventing the proscription of new royal painters. Five years later, Velázquez's son-in-law Juan Martínez del Mazo was named as painter to Prince Baltasar Carlos. The new order was now becoming formally installed and would be further strengthened by other appointments in the years to come.

As the decoration of the Hall of Realms was being completed, the king and the count-duke began another, smaller construction. This was a hunting lodge in the grounds of the Pardo Palace, known as the Torre de la Parada, which consisted of a series of small rooms clustered around a central tower.[25] The decoration of these rooms was provided principally by Flemish painters, led by Rubens and his shop, an event that should not pass without comment. Great numbers of works by foreign painters had been installed in the Retiro, which must have elicited the admiration of the king and made him realize that he did not have to rely exclusively on the painters of Madrid to do his bidding. Flemish painters, after all, were his subjects, as were those of Naples and Milan, and could be commissioned to provide works for the decoration of the royal houses. Beginning with the Torre de la Parada, Philip was as apt to use paintings by non-Spanish as Spanish artists and for his major galleries, only the foreigners would do. The one exception to this growing preference, of course, was Velázquez, who had thoroughly assimilated the language of Italian art and whose pictures could stand comparison with the best from abroad.

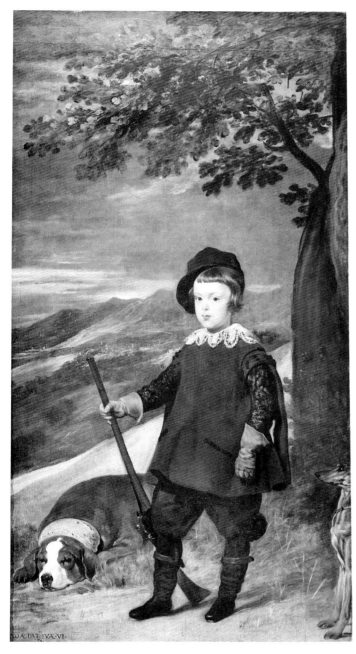

131. Diego de Velázquez, *Baltasar Carlos as Hunter*, 1636. Madrid, Prado, canvas, 1.90 × 1.03m.

Velázquez executed several paintings for the Torre, including the large hunting piece known as the *Tela Real* (London, National Gallery); portraits of the king, the prince, and the cardinal-infante Ferdinand in hunting garb (Prado); three antique subjects, *Aesop*, *Menippus*, and *Mars* (Prado); and two renderings of dwarfs (Prado), all of which were executed between 1636 and 1640.[26] The royal portraits, intended to be hung in the Galería del Rey amidst several Flemish hunting scenes, are the only images of the royal family in which the rigid etiquette of the court is in any way relaxed. Certainly the most captivating is *Baltasar Carlos as Hunter* (pl. 131), which shows the prince's diminutive figure standing confidently beneath an impromptu canopy formed by the branch of a tree, while a large hunting dog, wearied from its exertions, sleeps soundly at his feet. In the background, which is quickly brushed in with long, dragging strokes, Velázquez creates a mountainous landscape as seen toward the end of a cool, gray autumn day.

151

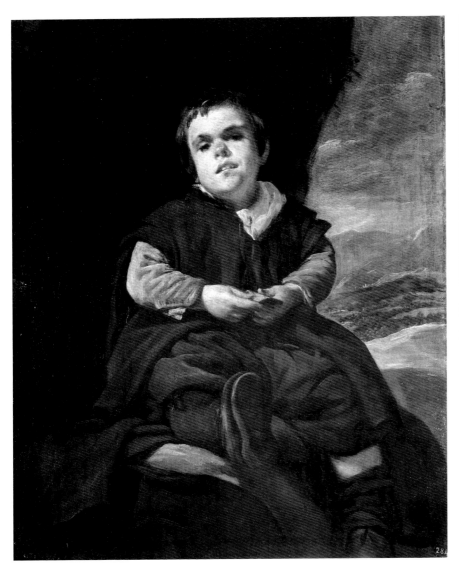

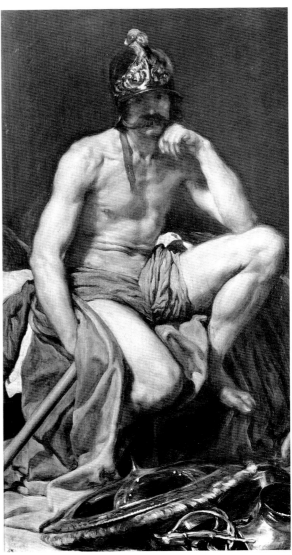

132. Diego de Velázquez, "*Francisco Lezcano*," 1636–40. Madrid, Prado, canvas, 1.07 × 0.83m.

133. Diego de Velázquez, *Mars*, ca. 1640. Madrid, Prado, canvas, 1.67 × 0.97m.

Velázquez's official portraits provided no opportunity to examine the inner life of the sitters; what mattered was their status, not their state of mind. But when he painted portraits of jesters and dwarfs, who were on the margins of court society, he was free to experiment. For instance, in one of the jester portraits for the Retiro (pl. 151), Velázquez tests the frontiers of spatial illusionism by placing the figure against an undefined, radically flattened backdrop. In two superb examples of informal portraiture, which were created as overdoor compositions for the Torre, he explores new realms of human character. These are the images of the dwarfs, *Diego de Acedo, "El Primo"* and *"Francisco Lezcano"* (pl. 132).[27] The portrait of Lezcano shows a boy afflicted with what is now called called Down's Syndrome. His head lolls to the left, slightly out of control, as he absently fingers a deck of cards and stares vacantly into space. The keen psychological insight of this work, achieved through an objective but somehow sympathetic presentation of the sitter, makes it one of the most moving portraits of the seventeenth century.

Velázquez demonstrates comparable brilliance as a portraitist of imaginary subjects in the lively, amusing images of the ancient philosophers Aesop and Menippus. An even better example of his deadpan sense of humor is *Mars* (pl. 133),[28] which catches the god of war in an uncharacteristic moment of embarrassment and chagrin. Vulcan, having been apprised of Venus's infidelity with Mars (the event depicted in

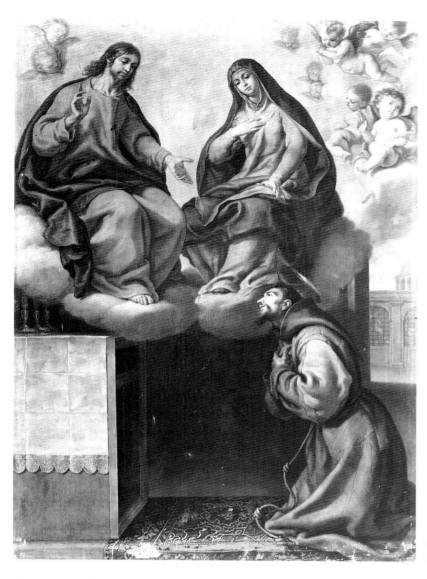

134. Félix Castelo,
Vision of St. Francis,
1630–40. Madrid,
San Jerónimo,
canvas, 2.50 × 1.90m.

the "*Forge of Vulcan*"), seeks his revenge by trapping the faithless lovers in the act. As they begin their amorous exertions, they are ensnared by a finely wrought metal net, while the gods of Olympus, who have been invited to witness the scene, mock them. Velázquez depicts Mars seated on the edge of the bed after everyone has left, trying to make sense of the unexpected dénouement of his affair. Striking the traditional pose of the melancholic, his face half-hidden in shadow beneath the tilted helmet, he looks bemused and puzzled. With its urbane wit and stylistic sophistication, this painting shows that, by 1640, Velázquez was in a class by himself among the painters of Madrid, both in title and in talent.

Velázquez is also unusual in his avoidance of the ecclesiastical market. After becoming a royal painter, he executed very few religious paintings, and then only on commission from the crown and high-ranking members of the government. For other artists, however, church commissions were the staff of life. The religious patrons of Madrid, as in other parts of Spain, did not care to take chances either with the form or content of devotional images, and thus, until around 1650, when the dramatic style of Rubens finally achieved acceptance, the existing formulas for religious painting were scrupulously followed.

In this domain, the example of Carducho was sovereign. Félix Castelo's *Vision of St. Francis* (pl. 134), probably painted in the 1630s, offers a clear-cut example of the

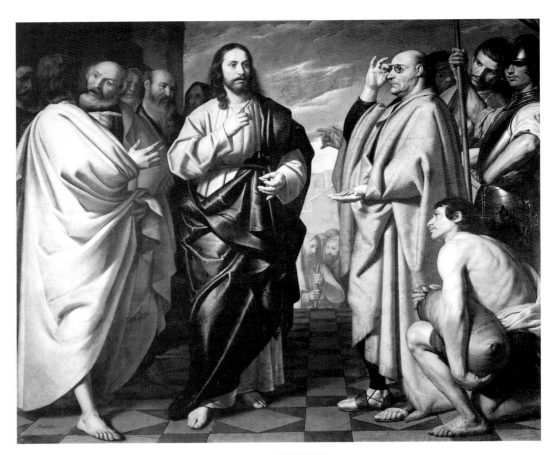

135. Antonio Arias, *Tribute Money*,
1646. Madrid, Prado, canvas,
1.91 × 2.30m.

136. Antonio de Pereda, *St. Joseph
and the Christ Child*, 1654. Madrid,
Palacio Real, canvas, 2.10 × 1.55m.

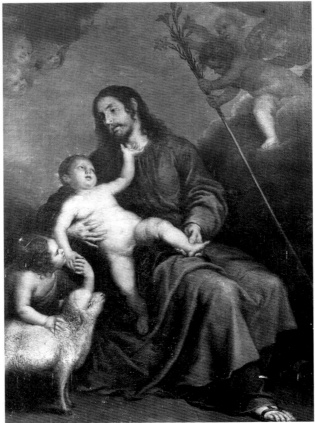

phenomenon. Even during his lifetime (before 1600–52), Castelo was perceived as Carducho's most faithful disciple, and he never deviated from his master's paradigm, although he outlived him by almost fifteen years.

Another generative center was the workshop of the mysterious Pedro de las Cuevas, the teacher of several productive artists, some of whom were influenced to a certain degree by the Flemish and Italian works available in Madrid. Their paintings often display more dynamic compositions, brighter palettes and a sharper sense of realism than those of their older contemporaries, but always within the framework of the Carducho-Cajés stylistic model. Two examples of the Cuevas school, the *Tribute Money* (pl. 135), dated 1646, by Antonio Arias (ca. 1614–84),[29] and Pereda's *St. Joseph and the Christ Child* (pl. 136), dated 1654, demonstrate the continued vitality of this style through the 1640s and into the 1650s.

Among this group of conservative painters, there is one who stands apart as a creator of exceptional religious images, which rank among the most deeply felt of the Spanish Golden Age. This is Fray Juan Rizi, who was born in Madrid in 1600, the son of the Italian painter Antonio Ricci of Ancona.[30] The elder Ricci had come to Spain with Zuccaro in 1585 and presumably was the teacher of his son, who also was impressed by the works of Carducho. From an early age, Juan Rizi showed signs of deep religious faith, writing a book on the Virgin Mary, to whom he was especially devoted, when only seventeen years old. This led him to join a religious order in 1627, when he entered the famous Benedictine monastery at Montserrat, where he professed in 1628. Fray Juan later studied at the University of Salamanca and became a devoted student of theology and letters.

The revolt of the Catalans in 1640 forced Rizi to leave Montserrat and move to Madrid, where he was enlisted as the drawing master of Prince Baltasar Carlos. He soon discovered that palace life was not to his liking and in 1642, was named confessor at Santo Domingo de Silos. During the next twenty years, he moved from one monastery of the order to another, partly to satisfy the demand for his services as a painter. He was in Madrid again around 1659–62, when he wrote a treatise on architecture and the geometry of painting entitled *Pintura sabia*.[31] In 1662, Rizi left Spain for Italy and after spending some years in Rome, settled at the mother house in Monte Cassino, where he died in 1682.

The chroniclers of the abbey of Monte Cassino describe the extreme piety and abnegation practiced by Fray Juan in his final years. He assiduously attended offices both day and night, nourished himself, when not fasting, on a diet of vegetable broth, and never closed the window of his cell, even during the winter months. It would be too simplistic to say that his paintings reflect these spiritual practices, but they are certainly unconventional and moving works of religious art.

All of Rizi's surviving pictures were done between 1642 and 1662 and are remarkably consistent in style and expression. His most ambitious commission, executed around 1653 for the monastery church of San Millán de la Cogolla (still *in situ*), consists of the high altar with eight pictures and several lateral altars with depictions of notable Benedictines.[32] The leitmotif is the visionary appearances of Christ and the Virgin Mary to members of the order, which Rizi captures with undeniable power and authenticity.

His formal vocabulary tends to be simple: the compositions are dominated by a few heavily robed figures set in a shallow space and illuminated by strong beams of light. These paintings, if firmly within the matrix of the Carduchos, are not simply illustrations of sacred narratives; they succeed in reproducing the overwhelming, all-encompassing religious experience described in contemporary mystical writings. In the *Vision of St. Aurea* (pl. 137), Rizi interprets the mystical appearance of the Virgin as a powerful corporeal encounter. The nun's cell is

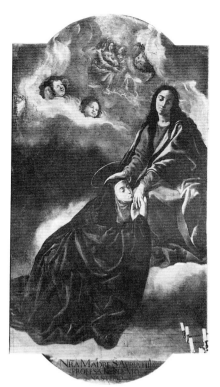

137. Fray Juan Rizi, *Vision of St. Aurea*, ca. 1653. San Millán de la Cogolla, monastery, canvas.

138. Fray Juan Rizi, *Stigmatization of St. Francis*, 1656–59. Burgos, cathedral, canvas.

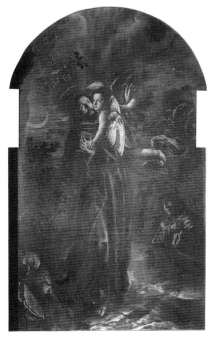

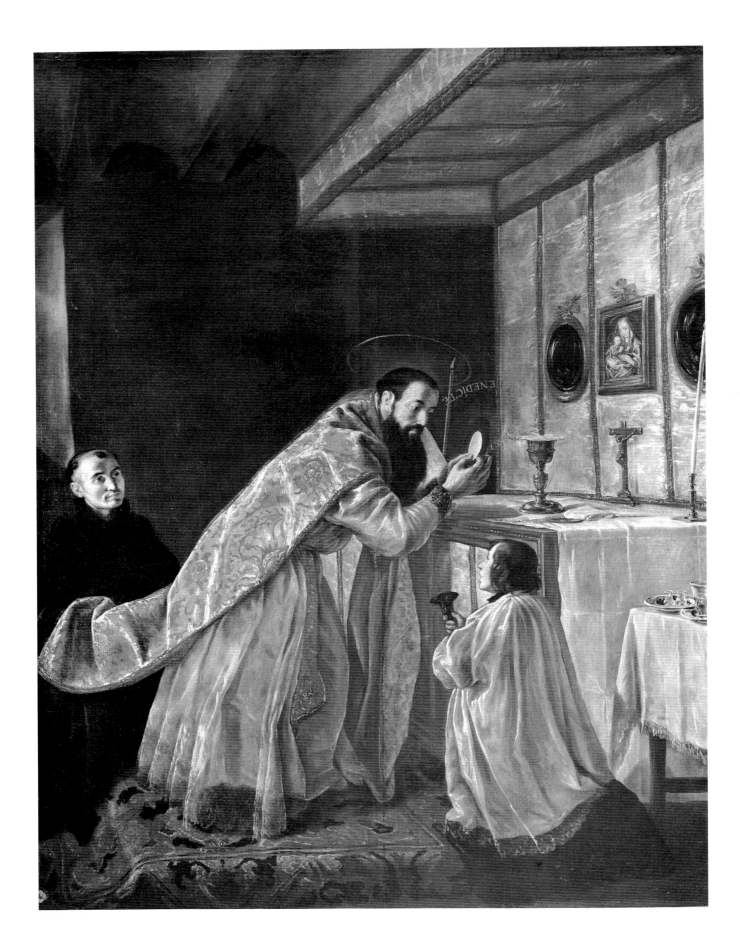

invaded by banks of clouds, broken here and there by angels and putti. St. Aurea extends her body forward and grasps the outstretched hand of the Virgin, raising it to her lips. By continuing the contour of the saint's back into the left side of the Virgin Mary, Rizi makes their union seem complete. Even the peculiar, wide-eyed expressions help to heighten the ecstatic, other-worldly effect.

Rizi's *Stigmatization of St. Francis* (pl. 138), painted for the retrochoir of Burgos cathedral between 1656 and 1659, is another work of rare imagination and intensity. The event takes place in the dark of night and is lit only by the sliver of a crescent moon. From out of the shadows, an angel alights on St. Francis, impressing the stigmata by a touching of the hands, while brushing its cheek against that of the astonished holy man.

The somber tones of the Benedictine habit predominate in Rizi's paintings, but his superb gifts as a colorist sometimes come to the fore, as in the *Last Mass of St. Benedict* (pl. 139), which is replete with vivid passages of still life. Executed in the 1650s for the monastery of San Martín, Madrid, the picture combines Rizi's customary sacral solemnity with unwonted chromatic richness.

The departure of Rizi for Rome in 1662 is a convenient way to mark the end of a long tradition of religious painting in Castile, the beginning of which could be dated almost exactly seventy years earlier in 1593, when Bartolomé Carducho painted the *Death of St. Francis* (p. 78). The internal consistency of this style is at once remarkable and understandable, because it provided the devout with a meaningful expression of their religious convictions and aspirations. Austere yet grand, the best of these pictures are rooted in reality but lead the soul upward to God. Through years of practice, this special style conveyed the essence of the powerful, sober faith that permeated every aspect of daily life in that providentialist society.

139. Fray Juan Rizi, *Last Mass of St. Benedict*, 1650–60. Madrid, Real Academia de San Fernando, canvas, 2.81 × 2.12m.

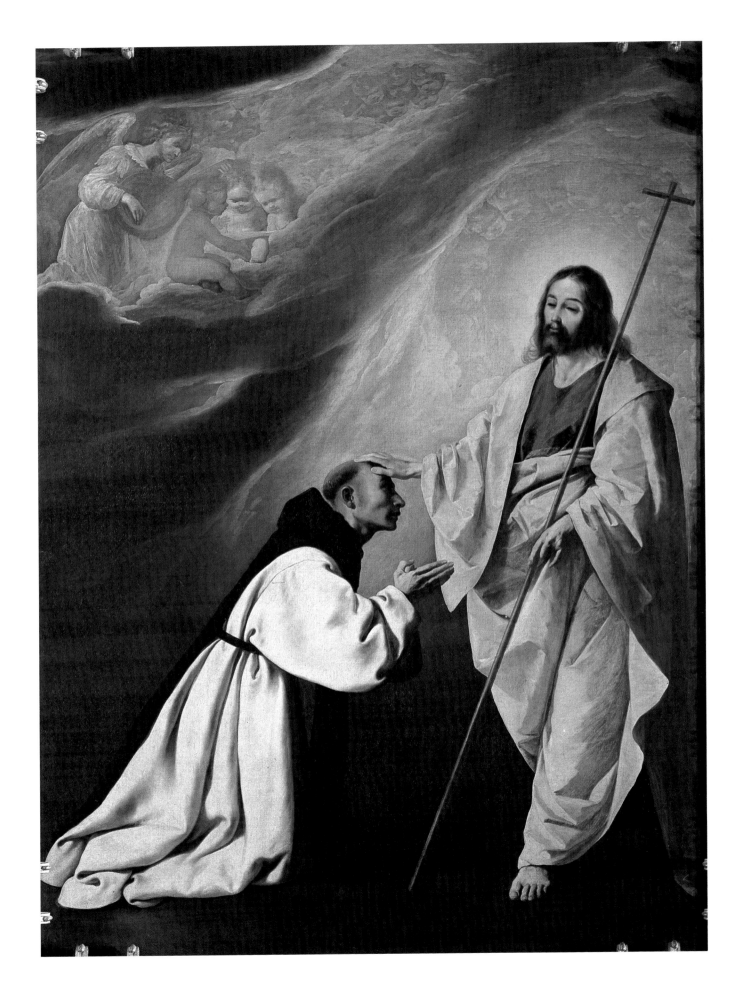

7

The Art of Immediacy
Seville 1625–1640

TOWARD THE YEAR 1620, painting in Seville appeared to be entering an especially rich period. In several substantial works, Roelas had renovated religious painting, and the young Velázquez was establishing himself as an artist of unprecedented originality. But within the space of five years, all this changed. Velázquez left the city for good in 1623, and, two years later, Roelas died. Nevertheless, the impact of these painters, if attenuated, continued to be felt by means of their pictures, and these were complemented by a new source of artistic ideas, the works of Jusepe de Ribera, which were imported by the duke of Alcalá during the 1630s. This heterogeneous collection of sources provided the inspiration for a group of young artists who succeeded in forging a new synthesis of the conventions inherited from their predecessors and a growing taste for naturalistic effects. As a result, religious painting, and there was almost no other kind, was revitalized in Seville at this time as it never was in Madrid.

The changes are exemplified in the career of Francisco de Herrera, who was born in the city around 1590 and was therefore Velázquez's senior by roughly nine years.[1] As a matter of fact, Palomino claims that Herrera was Velázquez's first master, although this assertion has never been substantiated. Herrera's father was a miniaturist, who presumably instructed his son in the art of painting. However, his earliest works are two engravings dated 1609 and 1610, which demonstrate a mastery not only of the technique but also of the vocabulary of the sixteenth-century Flemish ornamental print. Herrera's first paintings date from 1614, when he executed twelve scenes from the History of the True Cross, commissioned by the Brotherhood of the True Cross for its chapel in the monastery church of San Francisco. One of the few surviving pictures, the *Vision of Constantine* (pl. 141), is a standard example of the late *maniera* style, with its complicated arrangement of space, studied elegance of pose, and off-key colors.[2] A painting of the Pentecost (Toledo, Museo y Casa del Greco), signed and dated 1617, can be characterized in much the same way.

The heavy attrition of pictures from Herrera's early years makes it difficult to reconstruct his evolution, but by the mid-1620s he had revised his style by following the models of Roelas and Velázquez. The first instance of this change is found in his most ambitious commission, the decoration of the church of the Franciscan Colegio de San Buenaventura. Herrera began working for the college in 1626, when he frescoed the nave and dome of the small chapel with portraits of famous doctors of the order, which are accompanied by painted emblems extolling the glories of their sacred learning.[3] These imaginary portraits have aggressively individualized features and bear no resemblance to the bland, idealized facial types of his earlier works. The point of departure for this radical change seems to be Velázquez's genre scenes, but Herrera has transformed the ordinary into the ugly.

140. Francisco de Zurbarán, *Vision of Brother Andrés de Salmerón*, 1639–40. Guadalupe, monastery, canvas, 2.90 2.22m.

159

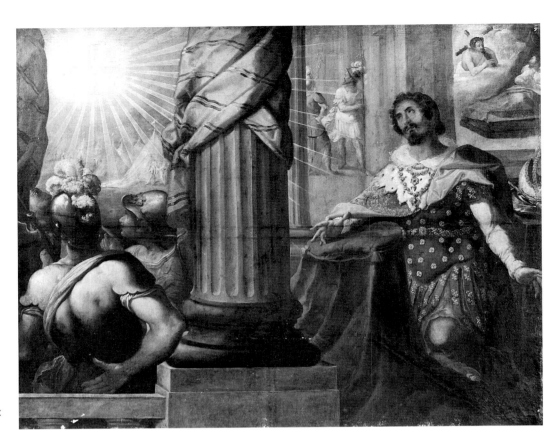

141. Francisco de Herrera the Elder, *Vision of Constantine*, 1617. Seville, Hospital de la Caridad, canvas, 2.40 × 2.70m.

Nevertheless, his patrons seem to have been satisfied and, upon the completion of the frescoes in 1627, they immediately commissioned the artist to paint six pictures of St. Bonaventure's life to decorate the walls of the church.[4] In the event, and for reasons shortly to be discussed, Herrera completed only four of the projected works, in which his brutal style of realism becomes even more abrasive. For example, in *St. Bonaventure Entering the Franciscan Order* (pl. 142), Herrera arranges a row of friars diagonally in front of an altar but makes little attempt to relate the figures to each other; instead each head is individualized as though the artist were determined to call attention to what is, after all, a powerfully unattractive group of people. That vital modicum of restraint exercised by Velázquez has been eliminated; as a result, there is a violent collision between the abstract realm of the art work and the accidental reality of the mundane.

It may be that Herrera had overstepped the boundaries of propriety; he certainly never again cut so close to the bone of reality. In any case, after four pictures had been finished, the Franciscans decided to expand the number to eight and invite another artist to intervene. This was Francisco de Zurbarán, who in 1629 was assigned the remaining four pictures. The reasons for changing artists in midstream are not documented, although the raw style of Herrera's pictures may have had something to do with it. More likely, however, it resulted from a confluence of two circumstances. Herrera had agreed to finish all six paintings by mid-August 1629 or forfeit the contract. This schedule, given the pressure of other commitments, was not very realistic, but then most painters, and especially Herrera, often fell behind in their work and were usually granted extensions. However, the deadline coincided with Zurbarán's definitive move to Seville and the start of a career that would rise from humble beginnings to spectacular heights.

Zurbarán was born in 1598 in Fuentedecantos, an agricultural village in Extremadura, where his father kept a shop.[5] He must have displayed a precocious talent

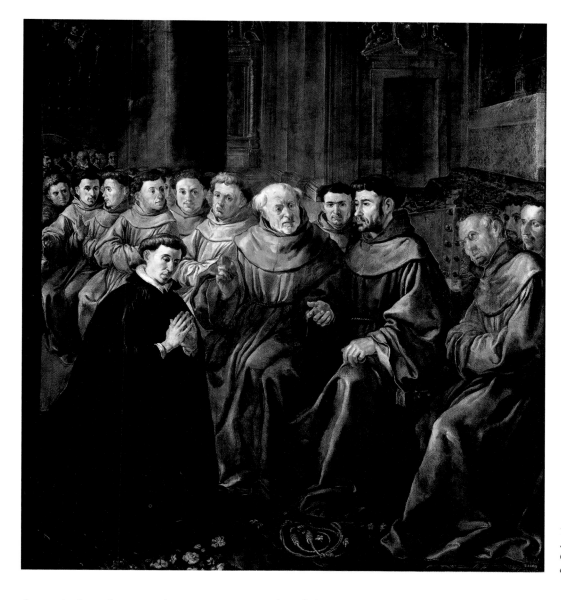

142. Francisco de Herrera the Elder, *St. Bonaventure Entering the Franciscan Order*, 1627–29. Madrid, Prado, canvas, 2.35 × 2.15m.

for painting, because in January 1614, his father made the effort to take him to Seville and apprenticed him to Pedro Díaz de Villanueva, an artist not otherwise known. Three years later, the apprenticeship ended and the newly fledged artist, perhaps daunted by the prospect of finding a place among the clannish painters of Seville, moved to the Extremaduran market town of Llerena, where he set up shop and married the daughter of a modest family. During the next ten years, he lived the life of an artisan-painter, accepting whatever commissions came his way. None of the works of this period has been identified, making it impossible to evaluate his early style.

Around 1624, Zurbarán's wife, María Páez, died, and a year or so later he married Beatriz de Morales, who belonged to a prominent family of landowners and merchants. The marriage immediately improved the artist's social and financial status and probably started him thinking about returning to Seville. Another incentive to try his luck there would have been the death of Roelas, which occurred at about the same time as Zurbarán's second marriage. On 16 January 1626, he signed a contract with the Dominican monastery of San Pablo in Seville, agreeing to execute a large number of pictures for a small amount of money. The contract stipulates a total payment of 4,000 reales for twenty-one paintings of diverse sizes, which amounts to

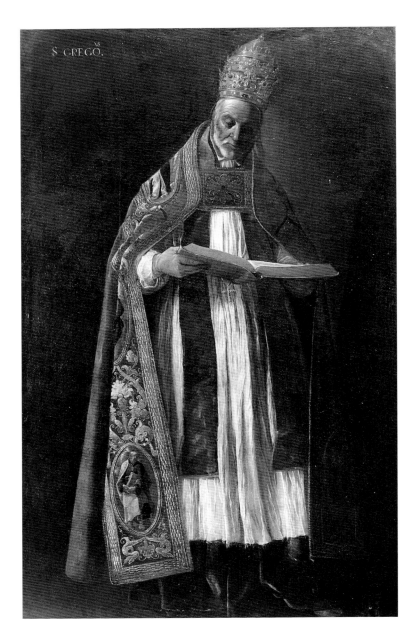

143. Francisco de Zurbarán, *St. Gregory*, 1626. Seville, Museo de Bellas Artes, canvas, 1.98 × 1.25m.

an average of about 250 reales apiece.[6] By comparison, Herrera's 1627 contract with the Franciscans provided him with 900 reales per picture, suggesting that Zurbarán was offering concessionary terms in order to gain a foothold in Seville.

Zurbarán's determination to work for a monastery was equally shrewd, for these religious communities were a rapidly expanding, dynamic sector of the market. Around 1600, there were approximately forty religious houses in and around the city; by 1649, the number had risen to nearly seventy, and well outnumbered the twenty-eight parish churches.[7] Monastic patrons, of course, were unremitting in their requirements for orthodoxy, and so Zurbarán, like other painters, had to accept the absolute control of the prior. The relevant clause of his contract with the Dominicans reads as follows: "And if some of them [the pictures] do not satisfy the said Father Prior, they can be returned to me and I agree to accept one, two, or more paintings, which I agree to do over again."[8]

Unfortunately, most of the pictures for the Dominicans have vanished or suffered heavy damage, but one of the survivors, *St. Gregory* (pl. 143), shows the powerful style that Zurbarán displayed to his new audience. The format of a full-length figure

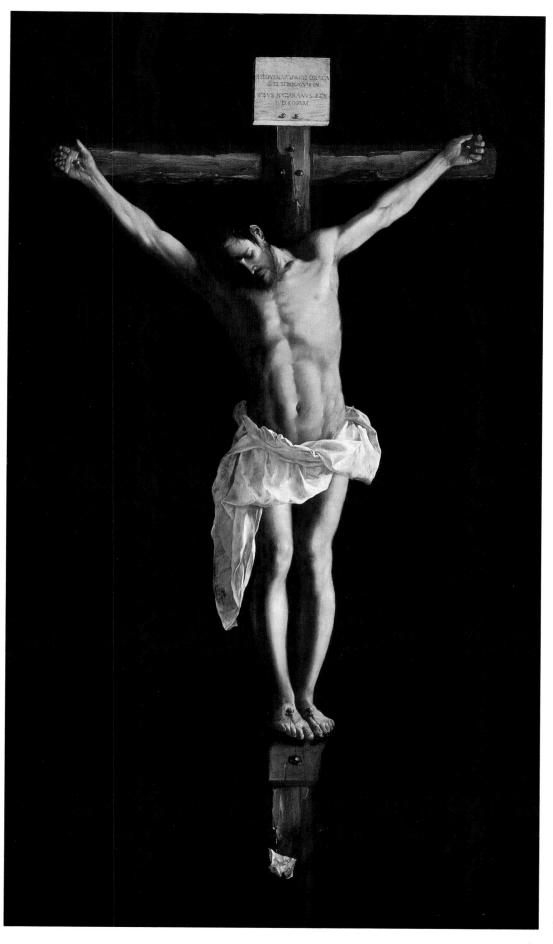

144. Francisco de Zurbarán, *Christ on the Cross*, 1627. Chicago, Art Institute, Albert A. Waller Memorial Fund (1954.15), canvas, 2.91 × 1.65m.

standing against a dark background was fairly common in Seville (among the many examples are Pacheco's *St. Dominic* of ca. 1605–10, in the Museo de Bellas Artes, Seville, or Roelas's *St. Rodrigo* of ca. 1607–9, in Santa Isabel, Marchena). Zurbarán enriched the formula through the intensification of light, which accentuates the sense of presence, and the use of realistic human types, both elements probably derived from the early works of Velázquez. However, unlike Velázquez, Zurbarán emphasizes the splendor and magnificence of the garments, as in the finely embroidered cassock, which is realized with exquisite attention to detail. This compelling combination of sober realism and opulent surfaces was to become a hallmark of his style.

In 1627, while still resident in Llerena, Zurbarán painted a picture for the Dominicans that made him famous, the spectacular *Christ on the Cross* (pl. 144), which was placed in a small oratory chapel and made a strong impression.[9] The model for this work is Pacheco's composition of 1614 (pl. 105), in which Christ is depicted as crucified with four nails. However unimpeachable its orthodoxy, this static format tended to neutralize the emotion of the more traditional three-nailed Crucifixion, where the body is twisted in pain and anguish. Zurbarán overcame the problem by insinuating a slight but powerful pull to the left, cradling Christ's head against His shoulder and reinforcing the movement with the hanging fold of the loincloth and the asymmetrical placement of the shadow. Although the body of Christ is preternaturally still, the composition has become subtly dramatic, a drama that is increased by the overpowering light, which heightens and then transforms the real into the super-real, thus expressing the dual nature of Christ.

Christ on the Cross may be appreciated as a brilliant exercise in form and light; it was also perfectly calculated to attract the ecclesiastical clientele of Seville. Zurbarán's lucid compositions and monumental figures were familiar elements to his prospective employers, who were also receptive to his spectacular realism, which made the familiar look new again and increased the power of the spiritual message by directly appealing to their senses. The success of this new approach is confirmed by the increased demand for the artist's work.

On 24 August 1628, Zurbarán signed a contract with the Order of Mercy for twenty-two scenes of the life of the founder, St. Peter Nolasco.[10] Peter Nolasco was not in fact canonized until a month later, on 30 September, but in preparation for the event a suite of prints illustrating his life had been engraved, and this was delivered to Zurbarán for use as a model. In this instance, and throughout his career, Zurbarán, like the other artists of Seville, borrowed compositions from prints, often by northern artists. However, his powers of adaptation are of a very high order, as can be seen in *St. Peter Nolasco's Vision of the Crucified St. Peter* (pl. 145).[11] This painting follows the print quite faithfully, but the principal change makes all the difference. In the engraving, the crucified apostle is seen from the side, and thus only part of his body is visible. However, Zurbarán positions him frontally, which allows him to increase the realism of the visionary experience. In the inverted position of the upside-down crucifixion, the apostle's blood runs to his head, causing the veins of his temples to swell and his eyeballs to distend under the increased pressure. St. Peter Nolasco reacts to this corporeal apparition with surprising calm: his hands form a parenthesis in the air, framing his silent amazement.

Zurbarán's share of the work for the Colegio de San Buenaventura was executed even while the Mercedarian pictures were in progress,[12] and, when finished, his four paintings faced the ones by Herrera across the narrow space of the chapel, inviting the viewer to compare them. Indeed, Zurbarán's *St. Bonaventure at the Council of Lyon* (pl. 146), which echoes the composition of Herrera's *St. Bonaventure Entering the Franciscan Order* (pl. 142), almost seems designed for this purpose. Both

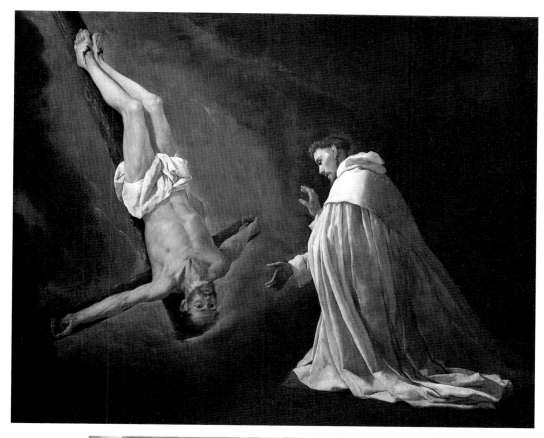

145. Francisco de Zurbarán, *St. Peter Nolasco's Vision of the Crucified St. Peter*, 1628. Madrid, Prado, canvas, 1.79 × 2.23m.

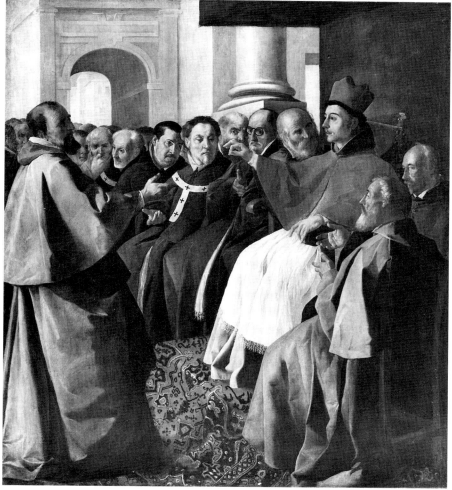

146. Francisco de Zurbarán, *St. Bonaventure at the Council of Lyon*, 1629–30. Paris, Musée du Louvre, canvas, 2.50 × 2.25m.

painters use arbitrary, somewhat illogical architectural settings which are not quite in scale with the figures. While Zurbarán utilizes large, legible forms – a triumphal arch, a single column – to anchor the composition, Herrera employs more complicated architecture which proves somewhat distracting and unbalanced. Although it is fair to say that both paintings deviate significantly from the standards of the Italian grand manner, Zurbarán's undeniably achieves greater dignity and decorum, without sacrificing the requisite degree of credible naturalism. Perhaps this terminology is anachronistic, but the conclusions drawn by contemporaries from this confrontation undoubtedly favored Zurbarán. Herrera's career now reached a plateau; he would still be employed by a few important ecclesiastical patrons in the 1630s, precisely the period when Zurbarán became the pre-eminent painter of Seville.

His rise to prominence was sealed by an important event that occurred at a meeting of the city council of Seville held on 27 June 1629. One of the councillors, Rodrigo Suárez, rose to speak and explained that Zurbarán had come from Llerena to paint for the Order of Mercy and also had executed the *Christ* in the sacristy of San Pablo. Suárez's next statement was truly extraordinary. "Presupposing," he said, that "painting is not among the lesser ornaments of a republic, but rather one of the greater . . . , the city should attempt [to persuade] Francisco Zurbarán to remain here to live,"[13] although no salary or living allowance could be provided. The motion was supported by three members of the council and duly passed. This was a remarkable triumph for Zurbarán and for the art of painting in Seville, which for the first time was being acknowledged as an "ornament of the republic" rather than as what would today be called a service industry. Unfortunately, Zurbarán's success was not greeted with due applause by those who logically had the most to gain, the painters of Seville. As in Valencia and Madrid, the requirements of the profession conflicted with the rules of the guild, and the painters chose to defend what they had rather than to risk something theoretically better but potentially damaging to their livelihoods.

Thus, on 25 May 1630, the guild officers, led by Alonso Cano and accompanied by a constable, visited Zurbarán's shop, demanding that he pass the examination required of all painters who wished to practice in Seville.[14] (Obviously Zurbarán had left Seville for Llerena immediately after completing his apprenticeship, and was not duly licensed. For that matter, Herrera had somehow avoided the requirement and was compelled to take the examination in 1619, five years after accepting his first important commission.) Rather than comply with a demand that, he suspected, was motivated solely by professional jealousy, Zurbarán appealed to the city council, arguing that its invitation superseded the guild regulations.

The council's ruling has yet to be discovered, but an action of 8 June establishes that the guild's challenge had been dismissed. On that date, the councillors empowered the *asistente* (the royal representative), the viscount of Corzana, to commission from Zurbarán a picture of the Virgin of the Immaculate Conception, to be placed in a room of the town hall (present whereabouts unknown). Thus, the guild was twice a loser: it failed to stop the advance of Zurbarán's career and retarded the definition of a higher conception of artistic activity.

With the support of the council and the success of his previous works, Zurbarán was now firmly established as the most prestigious painter in Seville, and his business flourished accordingly. In 1630, he painted an important picture for the Jesuits, the *Vision of St. Alonso Rodríguez* (Madrid, Academia de San Fernando), and this was just a start. By the end of the decade, his workshop was executing orders from every corner of Andalusia and was exporting pictures to the American colonies.

Indeed, word of the painter's reputation soon reached the court, resulting in the invitation to participate in the decoration of the Hall of Realms. Clearly, great things were expected, for on 12 June 1634, Zurbarán was paid 200 ducats on account for paintings of the Twelve Labors of Hercules. Eventually this commission was somewhat modified: the Hercules scenes were reduced to ten and a battle painting, the *Defense of Cádiz* (Prado), was added, all of which were completed by 13 November, the date of the final payment.[15] Zurbarán's battle scene is a competent work, conforming to the model followed by every painter save Maino and Velázquez, but perhaps coming closest to Pereda's *Relief of Genoa*, with its splendid treatment of the costumes.

The Hercules scenes, on the other hand, have elicited diverse opinions; they are regarded by some as deficient interpretations of the ancient legend and by others as totally original conceptions of this venerable theme.[16] Hercules was the classical hero *par excellence*, whose deeds of strength and perseverance in the face of adversity, and whose transfiguration into god-like status, made him an indispensable figure in princely iconography. Antique images of Hercules abounded, preserved in monumental and small-scale sculpture, and it took considerable courage for Zurbarán to depart from these familiar classical prototypes.

However one chooses to explain these works, there is no denying their tremendous impact. Nothing comes easily to Zurbarán's Hercules; he is presented as a powerful, awkward figure, who needs to strain every muscle in order to defeat his enemies (pl. 147). Unlike the Hercules paintings by other famous artists of the period – Annibale Carracci, Guido Reni, Rubens – Zurbarán's do not follow a

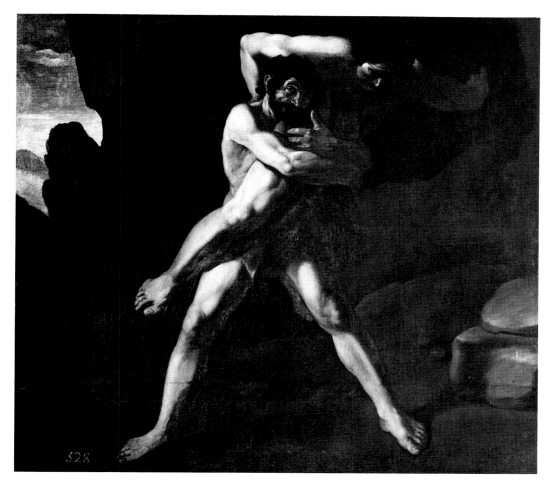

147. Francisco de Zurbarán, *Hercules and Antaeus*, 1634–35. Madrid, Prado, canvas, 1.36 × 1.53m.

167

classical prototype, the most familiar of which was the so-called *Farnese Hercules*. Instead, he imagines Hercules as a common man with uncommon strength. As in his religious paintings, Zurbarán strives to achieve an immediate impact by exploiting a set of artistic conventions that were commonly used by the painters of Seville.

This "art of immediacy," as it may be called, was the culmination of a system of representation that had been gathering strength since the late sixteenth century and offered an alternative to the conventions of Italianate painting. The Sevillian painters were certainly familiar with Italian classical painting, at least through prints if not original canvases, but they viewed it, for various reasons, with detachment. Certainly the clannish organization of the artistic community helped to foster and perpetuate this alternative system of representation. And the relative indifference to artistic theory – Pacheco being the exception that proves the rule – also implied a relative indifference to the ideals and procedures promulgated by the more literate artists of Italy (and of course Flanders), who were determined to put painting on the same intellectual footing as the sister art of poetry. Another factor was the lack of direct contact between the painters of Seville and artists from other parts of Europe. After the middle of the sixteenth century, Sevillian painters remained at home and were seldom visited by colleagues from abroad. Finally, the decisive role played by conservative ecclesiastical patrons offered little incentive for novelty or change, except at a slow, gradual pace. However, this resistance to change was not mere willfulness, but arose from the overarching requirement for accuracy and legibility in the representation of sacred subjects. Orthodoxy was sanctioned by usage and not by artifice. Thus, the artistic traditions of Seville became self-referential and singleminded, reaching their climax in Zurbarán's two greatest commissions – the main altarpiece of the Cartuja of Jerez de la Frontera and the paintings for the sacristy of the monastery of Guadalupe, both done in the same short period from 1638 to 1640.

Although the exact date of his return to Seville is uncertain, Zurbarán's stay in Madrid seems to have ended by early 1635. There really was no reason to remain at court; no offer of a royal appointment was forthcoming and, in any case, it could not have provided a great improvement over his lucrative practice in Seville, where he continued to receive new orders from both inside and outside the city – from Nuestra Señora de la Granada in Llerena (1636), from the parish church in Marchena, the Franciscan monastery of Arcos de la Frontera (1637), and, around 1638, from the Carthusians of Jerez.[17]

The Carthusian commission consisted principally of two parts: five large and two small canvases for the monumental altarpiece of the church, and eight portraits of distinguished members of the order, accompanied by two images of angels with censers, which were installed in a narrow passageway leading to a small room behind the altar where the host was kept. Four of the major altarpiece paintings depict the Infancy of Christ and, for sheer magnificence of color and spectacle, they are unsurpassed in the artist's work.

For the sake of analysis, two of these pictures can be discussed, the *Adoration of the Shepherds*, which is signed and dated 1638, and the *Adoration of the Magi* (pls. 149 and 150). Perhaps the easiest way to interpret the style of the *Adoration of the Shepherds* is by comparison with a version that exemplifies the classical tradition of representation, the one by Domenichino painted around 1607–8 and based on a design by Annibale Carracci (pl. 148).[18] Domenichino is concerned equally with drama, decorum, and design. In terms of iconography, the painting depicts the solemn moment of the Nativity with its joyful sequel, the Adoration of the Shepherds, and is organized around the illuminated figure of the Christ Child, beside whom three

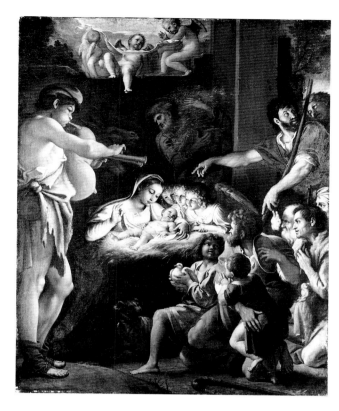

148. Domenichino, *Adoration of the Shepherds*, 1607–8. Edinburgh, National Gallery of Scotland, canvas, 1.43 × 1.15m.

angels stand in reverent adoration. The shepherds, who approach the manger, react in studiously differentiated ways to the wonderful sight. At the left, a piper supplies a theatrical touch, while, in the background, St. Joseph hurriedly enters the scene carrying a bale of hay to feed the animals. Despite the shallow space, all the figures are smoothly integrated into the composition. The light effects and colors are subtly modulated, and the forms are carefully modeled and anatomically correct.

Zurbarán uses an entirely different means of composing, one that can also be found, for example, in Juan del Castillo's *Adoration* of around 1636 (pl. 107) and that is in fact a staple procedure of Sevillian painters. In this scheme, the space is preempted by massive figures; indeed, it seems that ambient space comprises the area that remains empty after the figures have been put into place. This is very different from the conventional construction of perspective, which is always done with reference to the scale and placement of the figures, resulting in a composition dominated by large figures that fill the front plane, where they impose themselves on the viewer's attention.

Another crucial difference is found in the conception of the human types. Zurbarán's painting is inhabited by rough, plain countryfolk, who have been toasted by the sun and beaten by the weather, not the sculpturesque, classicizing demigods depicted by Domenichino. In compliance with the strict local rules for religious imagery, all the figures are fully clothed, and no distracting virtuoso touches like Domenichino's half-clad bagpiper are permitted. Zurbarán seeks to establish an atmosphere of quiet reverence and concentrates attention on the upper bodies and faces; anatomical correctness is not essential to this enterprise and therefore he does not attempt to show the legs below the knees, leaving them to be furnished in the viewer's imagination. Instead, he dwells on the smallest inanimate details – the woolly fleece of the lamb, matted with caked, dried mud; the rough weave of the multi-colored mantle covering the bed of straw; the dry, bony shells of the eggs – and makes them come to life. Despite the considerable distance that originally

149 (following page). Francisco de Zurbarán, *Adoration of the Shepherds*, 1638. Grenoble, Musée de Peinture et de Sculpture, canvas, 2.67 × 1.85m.

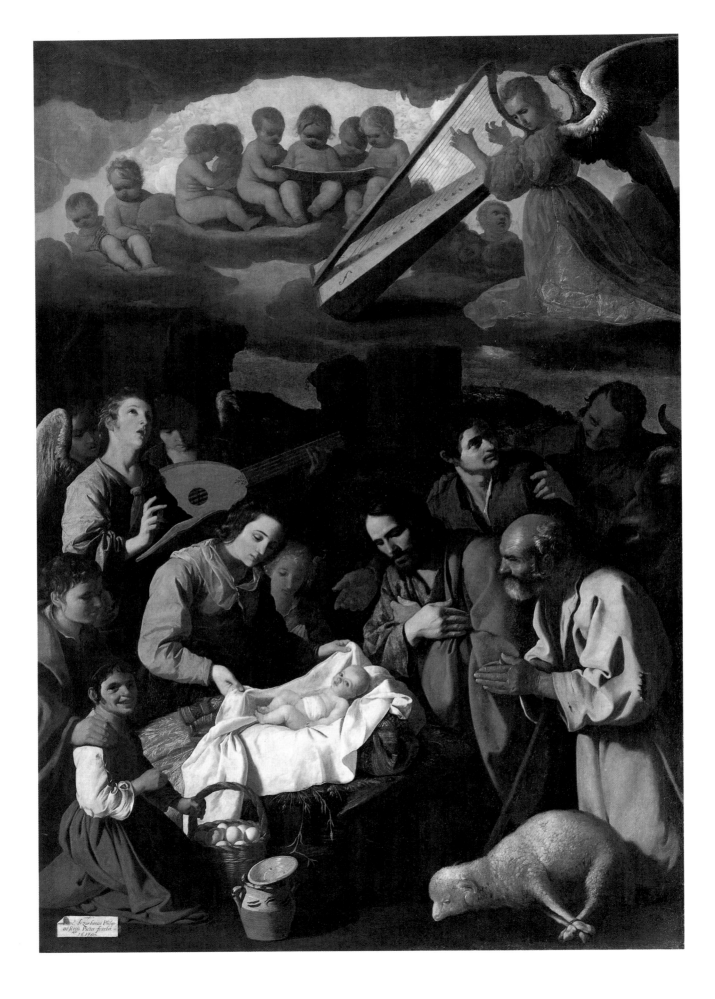

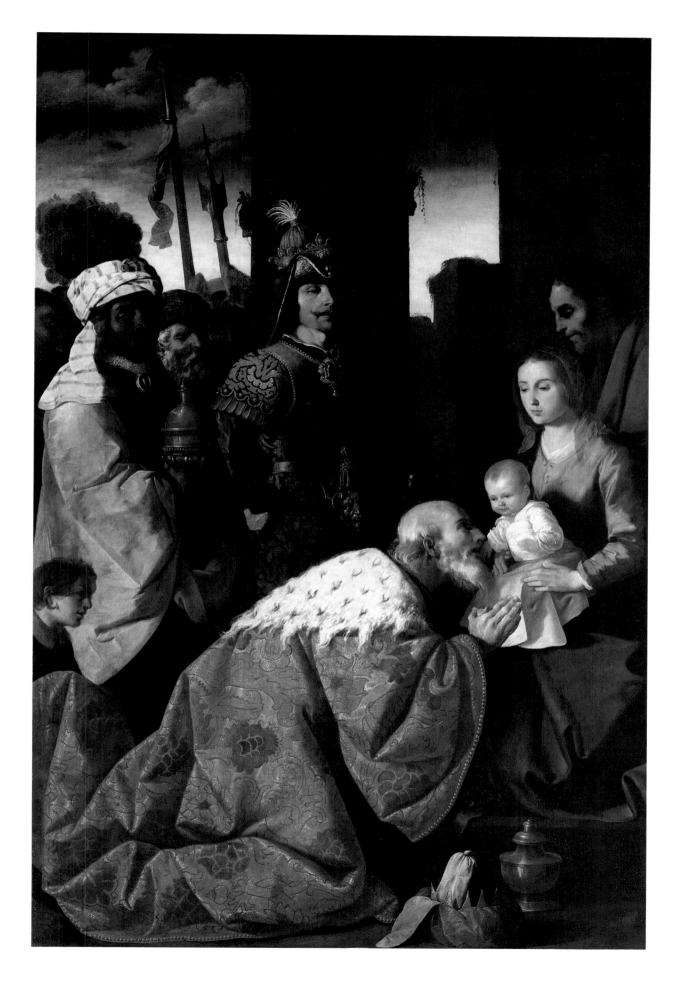

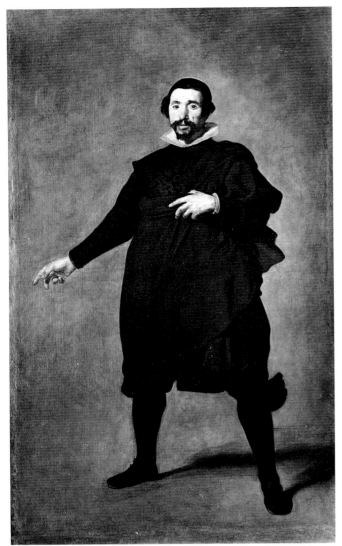

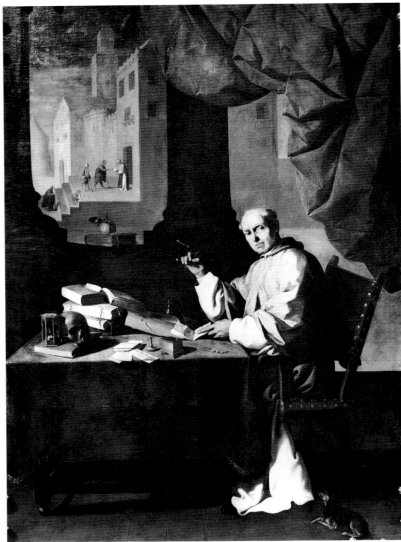

151. Diego de Velázquez, *Pablo de Valladolid*, 1635–40. Madrid, Prado, canvas, 2.09 × 1.25m.

152. Francisco de Zurbarán, *Bishop Gonzalo de Illescas*, 1639–40. Guadalupe, monastery, canvas, 2.90 × 2.22m.

150 (previous page). Francisco de Zurbarán, *Adoration of the Magi*, 1639–40. Grenoble, Musée de Peinture et de Sculpture, canvas, 2.64 × 1.76m.

separated the spectator from the picture, Zurbarán stresses the tactile, palpable qualities in order to enhance the sense of reality. By eschewing complicated artifice and imbuing the aesthetic traditions of Sevillian painters with a new sense of immediacy, Zurbarán achieves a direct, unaffected presentation of the story and a powerful interpretation of its spiritual significance.

The *Adoration of the Magi* (pl. 150) is a de luxe version of the composition employed by Velázquez (pl. 99), a variant of which is used also by Pablo Legot (1598–1671), a Netherlandish painter who came to Seville around 1610 and pursued an active career until he became a government official in Cádiz.[19] His *Adoration of the Magi*, painted for the parish church of Lebrija in the 1630s, is of interest primarily to demonstrate how this composition had become almost obligatory. Zurbarán takes this scheme as his point of departure and enriches it by substituting rich, colorful costumes for the plain serges worn by the magi of Velázquez and Legot, although fundamentally the paintings are similar in their use of large figures, the suppression of illusionistic space, and the air of high solemnity. Velázquez, who was trained from the start in this alternative mode of painting, later would consciously exaggerate its conventions in his revolutionary jester portrait (pl. 151), in which he reduces space to a neutral element in picture-making.

172

After producing a trial piece for the Hieronymite monastery of Guadalupe in 1638, Zurbarán signed a contract on 2 March 1639, which obligated him to supply eight pictures for the sacristy, each portraying a noted brother of the order.[20] These paintings remain in their original place and constitute the best surviving example of a series of monastic history painted in the seventeenth century. As usual, the artist agreed to follow the instructions of the prior, who planned what might be called a Hieronymite hall of fame. However, unlike other monastic cycles, which normally included the most famous brothers of the order, here the protagonists were restricted to members of the Guadalupe house, as a way to commemorate and emphasize its importance in the religious and secular history of the kingdom of Castile.

The spiritual achievements of the Guadalupe Hieronymites are exemplified in the *Vision of Brother Andrés Salmerón* (pl. 140), in which Zurbarán's art of immediacy attains a pinnacle of intensity and feeling. Set in an indeterminate space that is flooded with amber light, the scene is divided by swirling, cyclonic clouds which accompany the appearance of Christ. In the shallow foreground zone, a mystical encounter takes place between two towering figures. Christ, garbed in a bright pink robe, reaches out and gently touches the forehead of Brother Andrés, who is posed in strict profile, hands clasped in a reverential attitude. The absence of external expression seems to turn all emotion inward, making the experience truly ineffable.

The importance of the Hieronymites in the world of affairs is illustrated by Brother Gonzalo de Illescas, a bishop of Córdoba and councillor of Juan II of Castile (d. 1454). As befits his high rank, Gonzalo is presented in a splendid setting (pl. 152), decorated with a magnificent red cloth draped in thick, heavy folds. This man of the world is surrounded by the things of the world, which are artfully arranged on the table before him. Yet the background is drawn in an arbitrary perspective, trailing off inconclusively to the right and jutting into contradictory angles formed by the buildings to the left. In keeping with established practice, the important elements of the composition are overemphasized, the lesser elements made distinctly subordinate.

Adjacent to the sacristy is a small chapel dedicated to St. Jerome, for which Zurbarán furnished a group of as yet undocumented paintings, presumably made around 1640. Some of these pictures, largely executed by the workshop, were destined for the small altar, but on the side walls are two large, magnificent compositions by the master himself, the *Scourging of St. Jerome* and the *Temptation of St. Jerome* (pl. 153). The latter is a curious but compelling work; as rendered by Zurbarán, the plain features and heavy proportions of the temptresses are far from enticing. Yet St. Jerome reacts to their blandishments with a broad, sweeping gesture that is like a bony hieroglyph of abnegation inspired by faith. This figure is also notable for a different reason: its obvious relationship to the art of Jusepe de Ribera, which became known in Seville during the 1630s and helped to enrich the local style of painting.

The earliest indications of Zurbarán's interest in Ribera can be detected in the altarpiece of St. Peter for the cathedral of Seville, which he executed in the mid-1630s.[21] In the *Penitence of St. Peter*, for instance, the facial type with its deep wrinkles, half-open mouth, and wispy hair and beard is adapted from Ribera's etching of the same subject (1621). Zurbarán also could have seen Ribera's painting of this theme that was in the Colegiata of Osuna, a town only seventy kilometers from Seville. This picture belonged to a group of works by Ribera that had been assembled by the duke of Osuna, the patron of the church and the viceroy of Naples from 1616 to 1620.[22] But far more important for the introduction of Ribera's work into Seville were the pictures collected by the duke of Alcalá.[23]

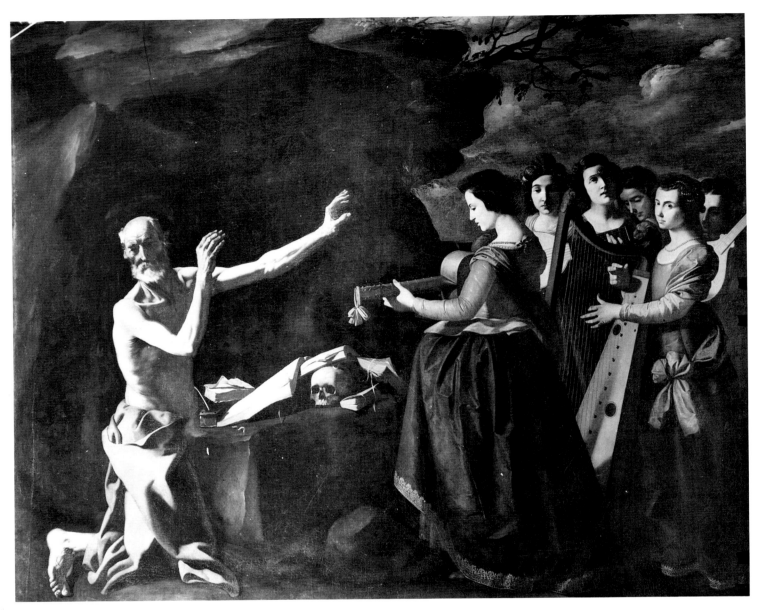

153. Francisco de Zurbarán,
Temptation of St. Jerome, ca. 1640.
Guadalupe, monastery, canvas,
2.35 × 2.90m.

Sevillian aristocrats do not seem to have collected paintings with the same zeal as their counterparts in Madrid. Alcalá's collection was therefore nearly unique in the city and was to have a considerable influence on the leading painters of Seville. It also provides an instructive example of a phenomenon to be considered fully in chapter 9 – the impact of picture collecting on Spanish painters.

Early in his career, as has been seen, Alcalá had been a member of Pacheco's academy and an active participant in the scholarly discussions fostered by that group. In 1618, he left Seville to commence a career in the service of the crown which eventually brought him to Italy. His first trip occurred in 1625–26, when he went to Rome as extraordinary ambassador to swear the king's obedience to the new pope, Urban VIII. During his stay, Alcalá became acquainted with such important collectors as Cardinal Ludovico Ludovisi, who gave him a version of Guido Reni's *Madonna Adoring the Christ Child* (original in Rome, Galleria Doria-Pamphili), and he also bought paintings by Artemisia Gentileschi, one of his favorite artists. Another interesting acquisition was a copy of Caravaggio's *Madonna of Loreto*, one of the three or four copies after works by this master available in Seville before 1630. As occurred earlier in the century at Valencia, the replicas seem to have aroused scant

174

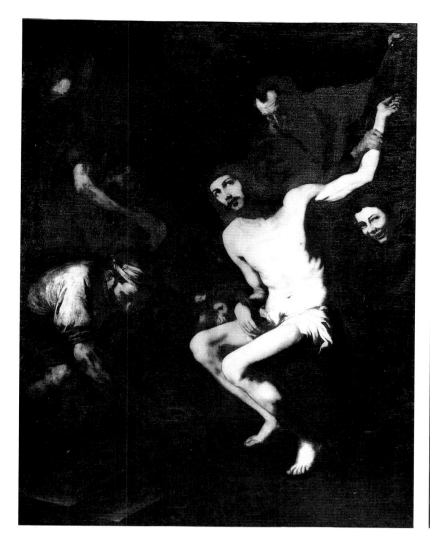

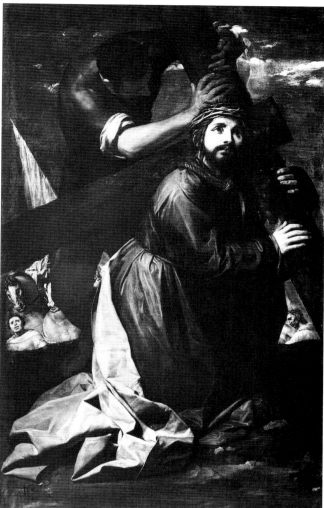

interest among local painters. From Rome, Alcalá went to Naples, where he encountered the art of Ribera, who had been living in the city since 1616. The viceroy, then the duke of Alba, made him a present of Ribera's large *Christ Being Prepared for the Cross* (pl. 154).

Alcalá returned to Seville and installed some of his new acquisitions in the Casa de Pilatos, while placing others in the large family chapel located in the Cartuja de Santa María de las Cuevas. He remained in the city for about three years, until February 1629, when he received the long-desired appointment as viceroy of Naples. Despite his brief tenure, which lasted only until 1631, the viceroy was able to make substantial additions to his picture collection, including more paintings by Ribera, his favorite artist.

The duke's new acquisitions were sent to Seville in 1631, among them further examples by Artemisia Gentileschi as well as single canvases attributed to Guercino and Reni. Yet allusions to the Italian works in Seville, either stylistic or iconographical, are rare, probably because they were grounded in a system of representation that was largely irrelevant to the local tastes. Alcalá's collection of paintings by Ribera, on the other hand, which was enlarged by five more acquisitions in Naples, struck a more sympathetic chord. Zurbarán's use of Ribera's models, while conspicuous, is largely confined to figure types; however, his contemporary and rival, Alonso Cano, achieved a much deeper understanding of the Neapolitan's art.

154. Jusepe de Ribera, *Christ Being Prepared for the Cross*, ca. 1625. Cogolludo, Santa María, canvas, 2.23 × 1.74m.

155. Alonso Cano, *Christ on the Road to Calvary*, 1637. Worcester, Art Museum, canvas, 1.66 × 1.01m.

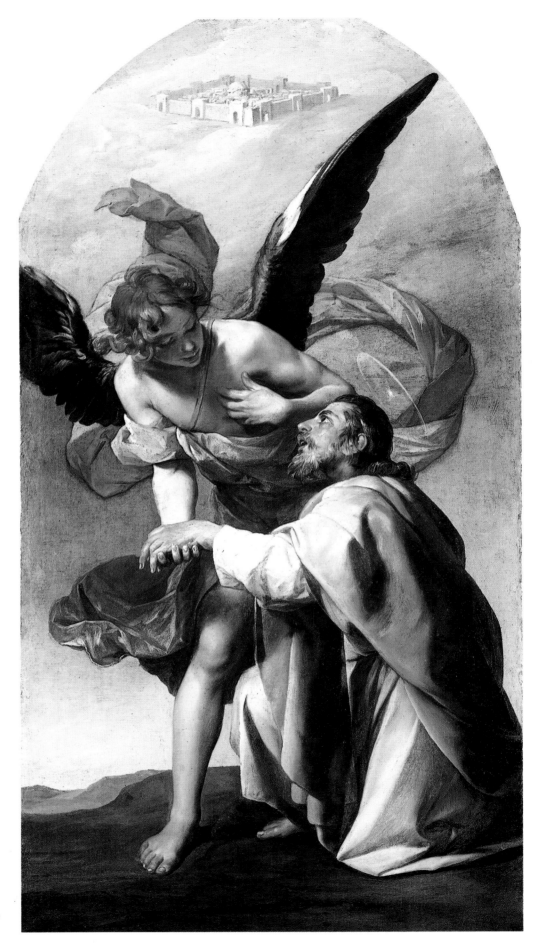

156. Alonso Cano, *St. John the Evangelist's Vision of the Heavenly Jerusalem*, 1635–36. London, Wallace Collection, canvas, 0.83 × 0.45m.

Cano is the odd man in Sevillian painting of the 1620s and 1630s, although his training was conventional enough.[24] The artist was the son of a designer and fabricator of altarpieces named Miguel Cano and was born in Granada in March 1601. In 1614, the family moved to Seville, where the young Alonso probably worked as his father's assistant. Two years later, he entered the workshop of Pacheco and there, of course, met Velázquez, who became his lifelong friend. He also learned the art of sculpture, possibly with Juan Martínez Montañés, the leading sculptor of Seville. Yet despite these credentials, Cano was far from being a typical Sevillian painter.

The problems of identifying the sources of his distinctive style seem almost insurmountable, in part because he devoted considerable energy to sculpture in the first phase of his career, and in part because very few pictures of his Sevillian period still exist. Given his training, Cano should have been in the mainstream of developments; not only had Pacheco been his master, but Juan del Castillo was a relation by marriage and Juan de Uceda was the father of his second wife. Nevertheless, his first-known figure paintings, admittedly done in the 1630s, do not seem to fit into their mold.

Cano's individuality is seen in *St. John the Evangelist's Vision of the Heavenly Jerusalem* (pl. 156), executed for the convent church of Santa Paula and contracted on 23 November 1635.[25] It is evident at once that the artist had mastered an Italianate manner of painting; the figure of the angel alone is sufficient to corroborate this observation. The partly clad body, the complicated, foreshortened pose, and the mastery of anatomical drawing are unique elements in Sevillian painting of the time, as are the deep perspective of the landscape and the delicate, translucent colors.

Cano's mastery of this facile, sophisticated style suggests that he had passed time in Italy, although there is not the slightest evidence that he left the city until his final departure in 1638, when he received a summons to join the count-duke's household as painter and *ayudante de cámara*. Perhaps he was simply uniquely receptive to the Italian paintings in the Alcalá collection. (His teacher, Pacheco, could have arranged his access to the Casa de Pilatos.) This notion tends to be confirmed by his knowing assimilation of Ribera's art, as seen in two works probably made around 1637 for an altarpiece in San Alberto, Seville – *Christ on the Road to Calvary* (pl. 155) and *Christ Before the Crucifixion* (Madrid, San Ginés). The paintings employ a similar composition, with large figures placed on a sort of terrace and half-length figures standing behind. Among the foreground group Cano includes the tormentors of Christ, who are preparing the instruments of his martyrdom, their faces carefully hidden from view as if to imply that they are anonymous, implacable agents of death. As will be seen in the next chapter, the "faceless executioner" is a stock motif of Ribera's religious compositions, and so for that matter are the half-length figures in the middle distance, framed by those in front (pl. 154). Thus, whereas Zurbarán imitated only the superficial aspects of Ribera's style, Cano sought to probe the deeper secrets of that great, transcultural artist.

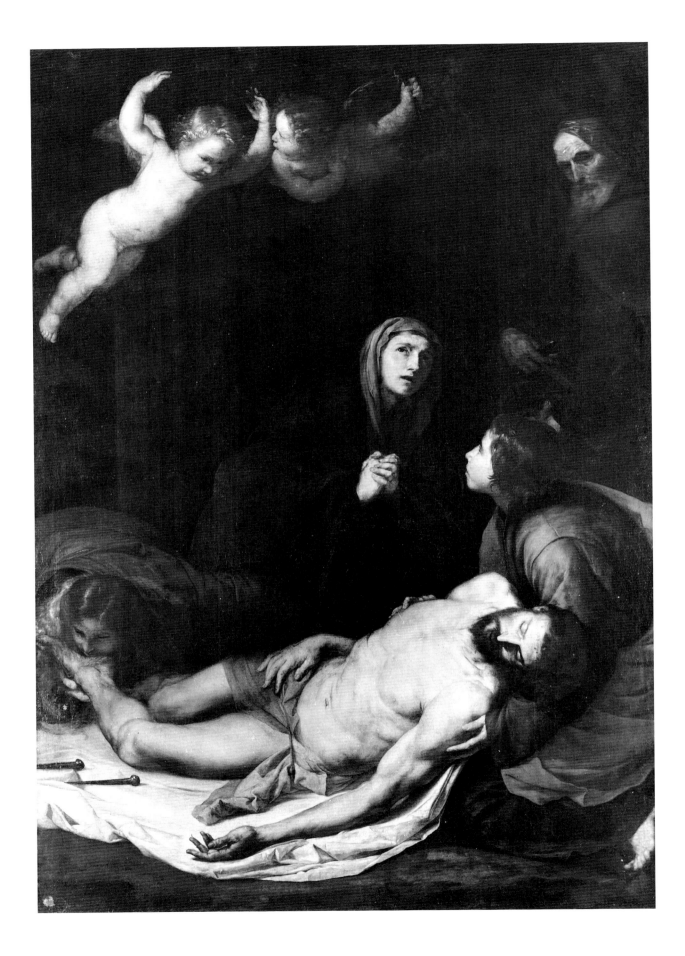

8

Jusepe de Ribera
A Spaniard in Italy

CLAIMED BY SPANIARDS and Italians alike, Jusepe de Ribera is a painter with a dual artistic citizenship.[1] Born in Játiva (Valencia) in 1591, he moved to Italy as a youth and by 1616 had settled in Naples, where he lived until his death in 1652. Ribera immediately established himself as the city's leading painter and exerted a profound influence on two generations of Neapolitan artists. "Lo Spagnoletto," as he is known in Italy, was much admired by Spanish patrons and collectors, but he was never tempted to return home for fear that those who favored him in Italy would scorn him in Spain. As he remarked in 1625 to Jusepe Martínez, "I judge that Spain is a pious mother to foreigners and a very cruel stepmother to her own native sons." Ribera was well informed about the precarious status of artists in Spanish society and thus preferred to remain in Naples, where his works were appreciated by Italians as well as by his countrymen.

Yet Ribera's art and career are tied to Spain in ways unparalleled by any other Neapolitan, or indeed Italian, painter of the period. The artist himself often insisted on his Spanish origins by signing his works, "Jusepe de Ribera, español." His ambivalent allegiance to the mother country – proud to be a subject, loath to be an inhabitant – was fostered by Naples's status as a Spanish territory governed by Spanish viceroys and officials, who were pre-eminent among the artistic patrons of the kingdom. In these circumstances, Ribera's claim of Spanish nationality afforded him an advantage when he sought the attention of the ruling elite. Furthermore, his naturalistic, accessible style of depicting religious subjects, although formed in Italy, was inherently appealing to clients who were accustomed to this type of representation in their native land. Thus, despite challenges to his hegemony by visiting painters from other parts of Italy, Ribera prospered in the heterogeneous marketplace of Naples.

Except for the date and place of his birth, the first third of Ribera's life is mostly a mystery. His parents were small-town artisans: Simón de Ribera was a shoemaker, who in 1588 had married Margarita Cuco, the daughter of another local shoemaker. Jusepe, the second of their three sons, was baptized on 17 February 1591. From that day to the twenty-fifth year of his life, Ribera's biography is a blank. The next record of his career dates from April 1615, when he is listed in the annual census of Rome, living on the Via Margutta, a street in the artists' quarter of the city.[2] When and where he arrived in Italy is not known, but it is almost certain that he spent time in Parma before moving to Rome. A letter from the painter Ludovico Carracci to a friend in Rome dated 11 December 1618 mentions a "Spanish painter who was a follower of the school of Caravaggio,"[3] and who had worked for Duke Mario Farnese in Parma, where he painted a *St. Martin and the Beggar* (lost, but known in copies). Other seventeenth-century sources confirm that this painter was Ribera.

157. Jusepe de Ribera, *Pietà*, 1637. Naples, San Martino, canvas, 2.64 × 1.70m.

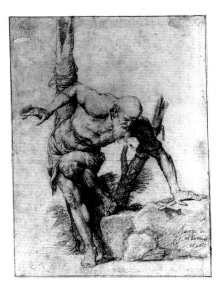

158. Jusepe de Ribera, *St. Albert*,
1626. London, British Museum, red
chalk on buff paper, 0.23 × 0.17m.

Ribera's apprenticeship is said traditionally to have occurred in Valencia, but even if this were true his fundamental training probably took place in Italy. This is suggested by his mastery in depicting the human figure, both in paintings and drawings. Throughout his career, Ribera was an avid draftsman in pen and ink and in red chalk,[4] and the chalk drawings in particular evince the approach of an artist trained in an Italian workshop. For example, in a study of St. Albert dated 1626 (pl. 158), Ribera solves a complex problem of figure drawing with an ease that is rarely matched by Spanish painters of the period. The technique is Italianate as well: thin, closely spaced lines and soft shadows are used to delineate the body and musculature.

Ribera's stay in Rome lasted only a few years; he is documented again in the census of April 1616, but within a couple of months he had left for good and moved to Naples. If a contemporary source is believable, Ribera led a disorderly life, until mounting debts forced him to depart in haste just a step ahead of his creditors.[5] Ribera's incessant need for money is said to have made him a productive painter; however, so far only one set of pictures from his Roman period has been identified, the Five Senses, supposedly made for a Spanish client.

The *Sense of Taste* (pl. 159), which typifies these pictures, is an ingenious representation of a theme made popular in the Netherlands during the late sixteenth century. Northern artists treated the subject as an allegory with classicizing figures.[6] However, Ribera rejects this model and takes a direct, naturalistic approach, embodying the sense of taste in a beefy, gluttonous type, poised to descend on a bowl of pasta and wash it down with a jug of wine. The artistic sources used for this composition are varied. Caravaggio's single-figure genre paintings were certainly important, although more for the composition and light effects than for the gritty, specific handling of the figure and still-life objects. These latter elements were partially derived from works seen in northern Italy, such as those by the Cremonese artist Vincenzo Campi, or the genre subjects executed by Annibale Carracci in Bologna. A more immediate source may be found in the Roman colony of northern artists, some of whose members lived in the same neighborhood as Ribera. (In the census of 1616, Ribera is recorded as residing in the "house of the Fleming," whoever that might have been.) Among this group were such painters as Terbrugghen, Baburen, and Honthorst. Ribera's affinity with Netherlandish artists was noted by an important contemporary collector, Marchese Vincenzo Giustiniani, who owned as many as thirteen of his works.[7] In the *Sense of Taste*, these affinities are evident in the ruddy tonality of the flesh and even more in the crude physiognomy and the palpable textures of the costume and objects. This wide-ranging appropriation of current artistic models is characteristic of Ribera, whose interest in Caravaggio was only one factor in the genesis of his sophisticated style. However, it was a factor that became increasingly salient after he had settled in Naples.

In May 1616, Ribera paid his dues to the Academy of St. Luke in Rome.[8] (He later signed certain pictures with his academic title.) Just two months later, he was in Naples and already at work because on 21 July, he received fifteen ducats for a *St. Mark* (unidentified), executed for the Genoese nobleman Marcantonio Doria, who had been a patron of Caravaggio.[9] In fact, painting in Naples had been revolutionized by Caravaggio's two brief stays, following his flight from Rome in May 1606. The first lasted from the autumn of 1606 to the spring of 1607, a short but productive period when the artist completed such important works as the *Seven Acts of Mercy* (Naples, Pio Monte della Misericordia) and the *Flagellation of Christ* (Naples, Capodimonte). The second stay, in 1609–10, ended with his melodramatic flight and death on the beach at Porto Ercole, and it was during this ten-month period that Caravaggio painted the picture for Marcantonio Doria, the *Martyrdom of*

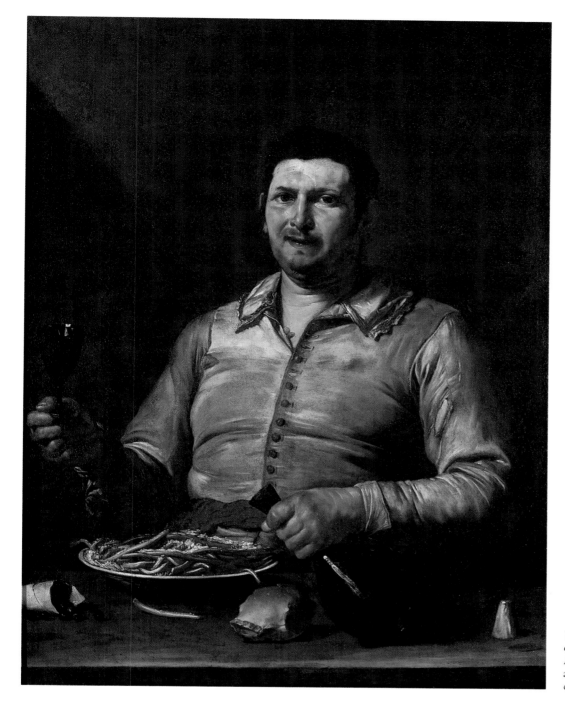

159. Jusepe de Ribera, *Sense of Taste*, ca. 1616. Hartford, Wadsworth Atheneum, The Ella Gallup Sumner and Mary Catlin Sumner Collection, canvas, 1.17 × 0.88m.

St. Ursula (Naples, Banca Commerciale Italiana),[10] a commission supervised by his agent, Lanfranco Massa, who was to be in contact with Ribera six years later. The similarities that presumably he perceived between the two painters were to intensify during the next period of Ribera's development.

Soon after settling in Naples, Ribera was employed by Pedro Téllez Girón, duke of Osuna, the first of eleven viceroys who governed during his career. Osuna had made his reputation as a warrior, not an aesthete, but he offered at least one commission to the artist, a series of four saints, the ones eventually installed in the Colegiata of Osuna.[11] Although poorly preserved, these paintings prove that during his initial years in Naples, Ribera's art was characterized by a powerful

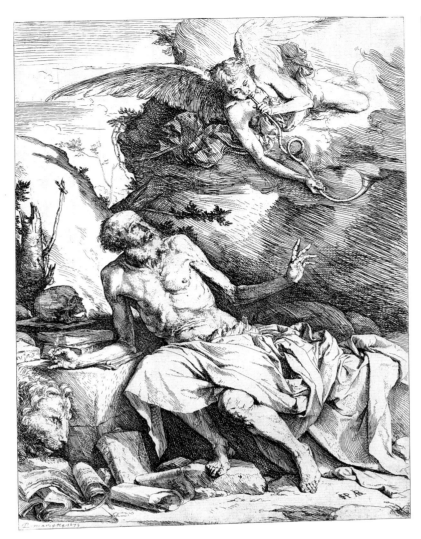

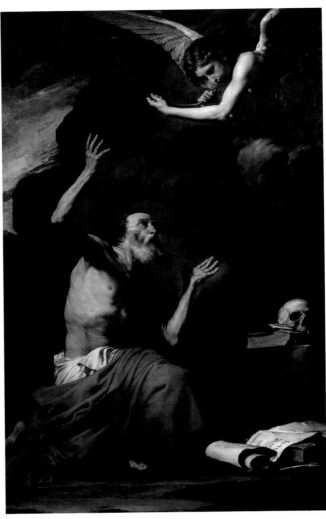

160. Jusepe de Ribera, *St. Jerome and the Angel*, 1621. Etching, 318 × 238mm.

161. Jusepe de Ribera, *St. Jerome and the Angel*, 1626. Naples, Museo e Gallerie Nazionali di Capodimonte, canvas, 2.62 × 1.64m.

realism of the figures, dramatic use of light and shadow, and confident handling of difficult poses.

These various commissions indicate that Ribera made rapid progress toward achieving the financial security that had eluded him in Rome. On 9 September 1616, he married Catalina Azzolino, the daughter of a prominent painter, and by 1622, he was recorded as the owner of a "casa grande." And in these years, he began to experiment with etching, a technique he soon mastered.[12] His first important etchings were made in 1621 and are variations of two compositions owned by the duke of Osuna, *St. Jerome and the Angel* (pl. 160) and the *Penitence of St. Peter*. For Ribera, this medium was a sideline that did not hold long his interest; all but one of his eighteen prints were created between 1620 and 1630, in the hope, it seems, of attracting new patrons. Whether the prints were an effective "marketing tool" is hard to judge, but they certainly contributed to spreading the artist's fame, and soon his compositions were being copied by painters, printmakers, and even sculptors all over Europe.

Except for the prints, not many works from the first ten years in Naples have been identified. It is not until around 1625–26 that Ribera's art begins to come into focus in several ambitious compositions, one of which is *St. Jerome and the Angel* (pl. 161), executed in 1626 for Santa Trinità delle Monache. The immediate source is Ribera's own print of 1621, which has been altered to heighten the dramatic impact of the angel, who rouses the saint from his studies by sounding the trumpet of the Last Judgment. More important is the level of technical maturity, as evinced in the richly textured brushwork that enlivens every square millimeter of the surface. The powerful contrast of light and shadow produces what contemporary theorists most admired about Ribera's painting – his "relievo," that ability to make two-dimensional objects seem as if they were projecting outward from the canvas. The brilliant red drapery over the saint's leg also provides the composition with an electrifying accent.

Another work of 1626 is the *Drunken Silenus* (pl. 162), painted for the Flemish merchant Gaspar Roomer. Roomer was a voracious collector – at his death in 1674, he had amassed around 1,500 pictures, including seven works by Ribera.[13] His taste also ran to the works of his countrymen, including Rubens, van Dyck, and a host of lesser figures, and it may be that Ribera was inspired in this, one of his few representations of an antique subject, to emulate the earthy, sensual style of his northern colleagues. The soft, sagging belly of Silenus is unquestionably a highlight of Ribera's pictorial career, and the hirsute, dusky satyrs who ply the besotted figure with wine make an effective contrast to his smooth, rounded form.

In the *Martyrdom of St. Andrew*, which is dated 1628, Ribera emerges as a mature painter of religious subjects (pl. 163). The artist's point of departure is Caravaggio's *Crucifixion of St. Peter* (Rome, Santa Maria del Popolo), which invests Catholic hagiography with a profoundly human character through the use of commonplace, unidealized physical types. To meet the demand inspired by this successful formula, Ribera devised a standard "martyrdom" composition that he varied continually to avoid repetition. In the foreground, he places the martyr's semi-nude figure, usually arranged in a pose with difficult foreshortenings. The wrinkled skin, brushed with thickly textured strokes, is illuminated by a powerful light. A stock figure is the

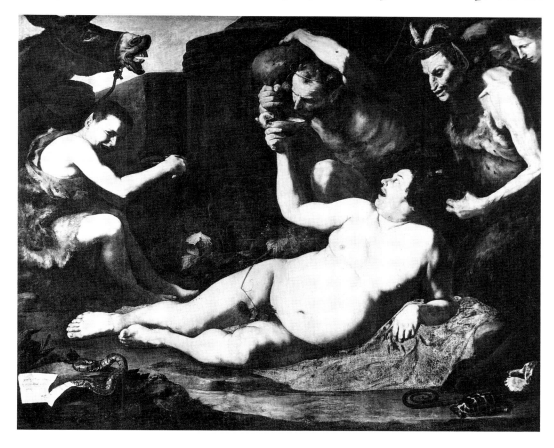

162. Jusepe de Ribera, *Drunken Silenus*, 1626. Museo e Gallerie Nazionali di Capodimonte, canvas, 1.85 × 2.29m.

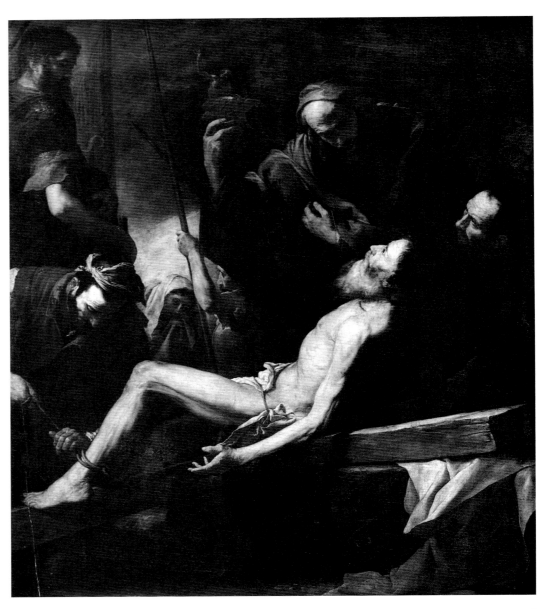

163. Jusepe de Ribera, *Martyrdom of St. Andrew*, 1628. Budapest, Szépmüvészeti Múzeum, canvas, 2.85 × 1.83m.

executioner, depicted in the guise of an anonymous laborer, who wears a ragged bandana around his forehead and prepares the instruments of torture and death. Large human bodies occupy most of the front plane, but there is a small opening into the background, where a group of onlookers, shown in half-length, witness the torment. Despite Ribera's undying and undeserved reputation as a specialist in gruesome martyrdoms, he invariably exercises restraint and emphasizes the unshakable faith of the victims, not the painful process that challenges their belief in the saving power of Christ.

In 1629, Ribera began to work for one of his major viceregal patrons, the duke of Alcalá.[14] They had first met in Naples in 1626, and when Alcalá returned as viceroy in July 1629, he took a serious interest in Ribera's art. Unlike his immediate predecessors, Alcalá was a man of cultivation and learning, and he quickly made an impression on the painter. An example of his influence is found in the paintings known as "beggar philosophers," several of which were in the duke's collection. This theme was original and daring; the idea was to depict famous philosophers of antiquity as ordinary men dressed in simple, often ragged garb. Ribera's *Democritus*, dated 1630 (pl. 164), interprets the famous smiling philosopher as a balding man with sunken eyes and bent, protruding ears. By means of this realistic equation, the vast distance between the antique and contemporary worlds is drastically reduced.

At the request of Alcalá, Ribera painted his most unusual work, *Magdalena Ventura with Her Husband and Son* (pl. 165).[15] A lengthy Latin inscription, which describes the circumstances of the commission, implies that it was executed to record a wonder of the natural world. Magdalena Ventura was from the Abruzzi, a region in the kingdom of Naples, and began to grow a beard when she was thirty-seven. Fifteen years later, the woman and her husband, a timid sort wearing an understandably befuddled expression, produced the infant she holds in her arms. As the inscription further attests, the picture was completed on 16 February 1631 by "JOSEPHVS DE RIBERA HISPANUS CHRISTI CRVCE INSIGNITVS," a characteristic reference to Ribera's prized nationality and to the Order of Christ received from Pope Urban VIII on 29 January 1626. In this unforgettable image, Ribera's uncompromising realism permits no escape from the unsettling force of this aberrative family portrait.

The fruitful partnership between Ribera and Alcalá came to a premature end when the duke was recalled to Madrid in May 1631. However, his successor was the formidable patron and collector, the count of Monterrey.[16] Unlike Alcalá, Monterrey had no pretensions to learning; he was interested in accumulating wealth,

164. Jusepe de Ribera, *Democritus*, 1630. Madrid, Prado, canvas, 1.25 × 0.81m.

165. Jusepe de Ribera, *Magdalena Ventura with Her Husband and Son*, 1631. Toledo, Museo Fundación Duque de Lerma, canvas, 1.96 × 1.27m.

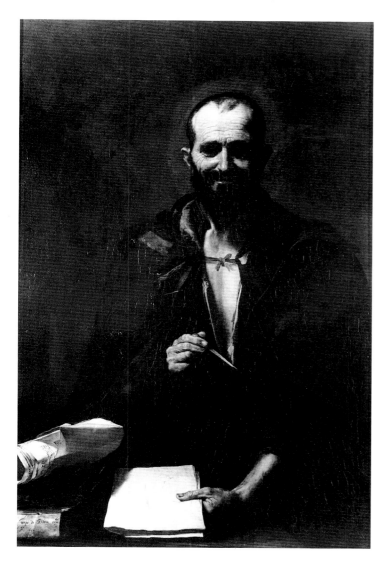

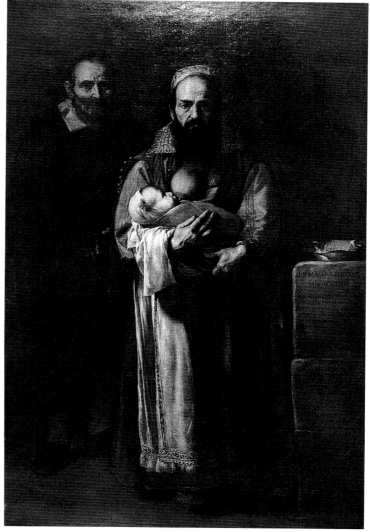

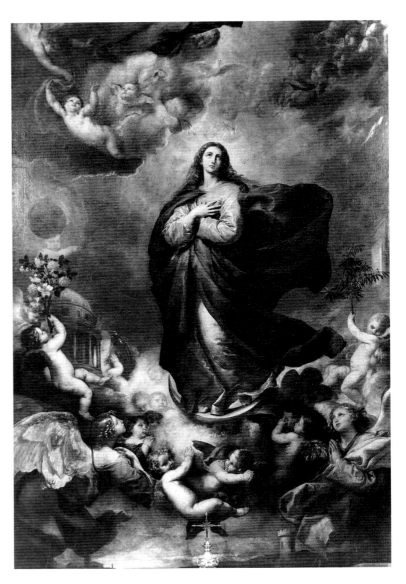

166. Jusepe de Ribera, *Virgin of the Immaculate Conception*, 1635. Salamanca, convent of Agustinas Descalzas, canvas, 5.02 × 3.29m.

although he did possess an indisputably keen eye for art. Before coming to Naples, Monterrey had been ambassador in Rome, and during his seven years as viceroy, he helped to promote an important development in Neapolitan art, away from Caravaggism and toward Roman-Bolognese classicism.

The foundations for this change were laid by Guido Reni, who was in Naples for a short stay in 1621–22, when he painted works for ecclesiastical patrons. Eight years later, Domenichino arrived to execute the most important commission the city had to offer, the decoration of the Cappella del Tesoro in the cathedral.[17] Finally, in 1634, Domenichino's great rival, Giovanni Lanfranco, came to town and soon found favor with Monterrey. While Lanfranco's presence seems to have been accepted by the local painters, Domenichino's proved to be intolerable, and he was mercilessly persecuted by jealous colleagues, Ribera among them. In Ribera's opinion, "Domenichino was not a painter, because he did not paint from nature, but was only an ordinary, good draftsman."[18] These are words that Ribera would later have to eat.

The impact of the Roman artists on Ribera becomes perceptible toward 1635, notably in the pictures commissioned by Monterrey for the church of the Agustinas Descalzas in Salamanca, which contained the family tombs.[19] The principal altarpiece is the *Virgin of the Immaculate Conception* (pl. 166), one of Ribera's largest

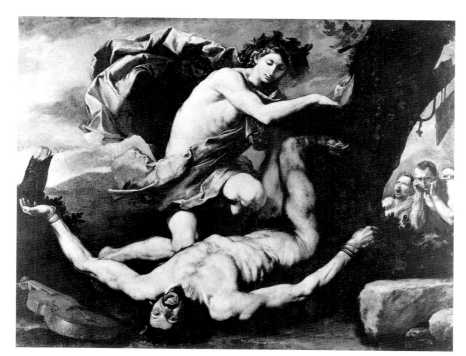

167. Jusepe de Ribera, *Apollo and Marsyas*, 1637. Naples, San Martino, canvas, 1.82 × 2.32m.

168. Jusepe de Ribera, *Apollo and Marsyas*, 1637. Brussels, Musée Royaux des Beaux-Arts, canvas, 2.02 × 2.55m.

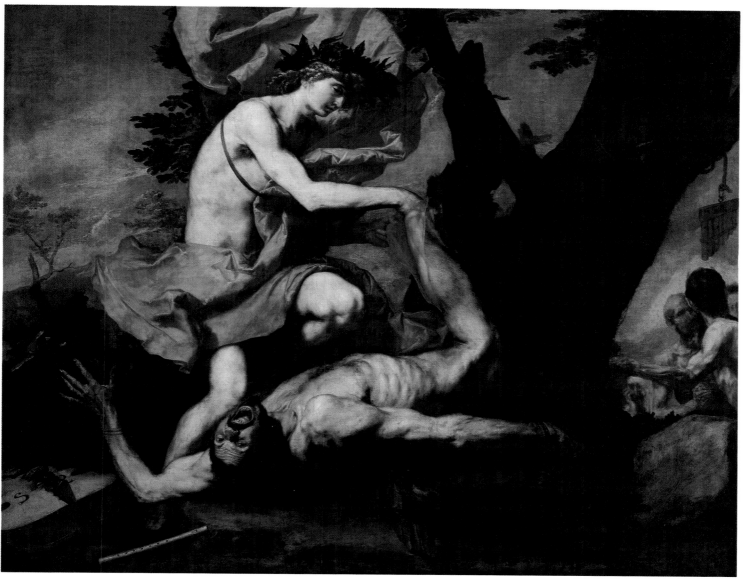

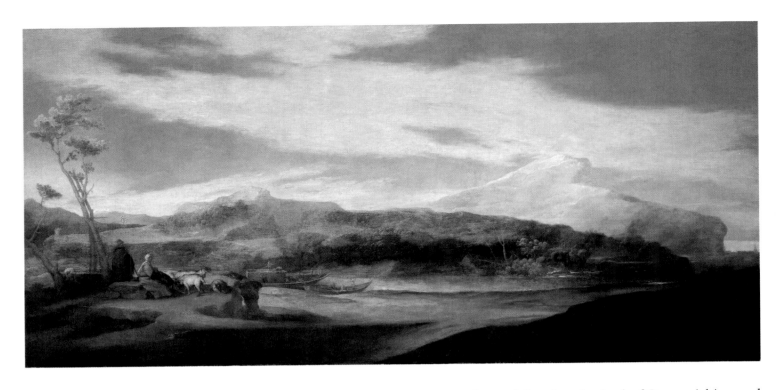

169. Jusepe de Ribera, *Landscape with Shepherds*, 1639. Salamanca, Dukes of Alba, canvas, 1.28 × 2.69m.

works, which is dated 1635. Here, Ribera, following the lead of Domenichino and Lanfranco, employs a lighter palette, abandoning the stark contrasts of light and shadow used in previous works. The dynamic symmetry of the composition and the solid architecture of the Virgin's body are also derived from the Roman painters. Without ever imitating Domenichino's rigorous abstraction of design and form, Ribera nevertheless appropriated many qualities of his style, and from Lanfranco's Neapolitan frescoes he learned to enliven his compositions by using animated poses.

Although Monterrey's collection of paintings by Ribera consisted mostly of religious works, he did own a few secular subjects. During the 1630s, Ribera created two popular mythological compositions: one was Venus and Adonis, a version of which was owned by Monterrey (unidentified); the other was Apollo and Marsyas. There are two extant versions of the latter, both executed in 1637, which offer a lucid case study of how Ribera incorporated the classical style into his art. In the first (pl. 167), possibly painted for Gaspar Roomer, Ribera created a dynamic composition along a diagonal axis running from the head of the satyr and up the trunk of the tree. The placement of the figures follows the formula used in the scenes of martyrdom: the victim is splayed across the foreground while an executioner administers the torture. Standing in the distance and seen through a small, triangular "window," a few satyrs cover their ears to dull the terrible sound of Marsyas's agony.

In the second version (pl. 168), the classicizing elements take control. The figures are placed farther back in space, which reduces their proximity to the viewer, and Apollo, represented in strict profile, stands in an almost upright position. The drapery, instead of swirling around the figure, forms a kind of backdrop to the god, who intently peels away the satyr's skin with clinical detachment. To be sure, Ribera has not surrendered completely to the classical style: the explicit act of flaying makes no concession to understatement. Thus, Ribera creates a dynamic balance between his powerful realism and the features of color and design appropriated from the Roman artists who were now finding favor with the clientele of Naples.

Under the influence of the Romans, Ribera experimented briefly with a new type of painting, the landscape. Two splendid examples, done in 1639 and only recently

188

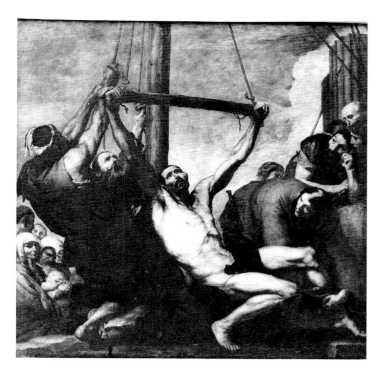

170. Jusepe de Ribera, *Martyrdom of St. Philip*, 1639. Madrid, Prado, canvas, 2.34 × 2.34m.

discovered, were apparently acquired by Monterrey after his return to Spain (pl. 169).[20] Ribera often included simple if evocative vistas in his backgrounds, which consist of little but distant mountains under a limpid, blue sky streaked with cirrus clouds. In these extensive landscapes of 1639, he creates compositions of a powerful simplicity and compelling atmosphere which imply a knowledge of land-scape painting in Rome. Ribera does not truly imitate Claude and his followers, but rather applies their warm effects of light to the sterner, architectonic compositions of the Bolognese practitioners, such as Carracci and Domenichino. This synthesis is new and original, and provided the initial inspiration to Salvator Rosa, who was then just starting his career in Naples.

Monterrey departed Naples in November 1637, to be replaced by the duke of Medina de las Torres, who governed until May 1644. Following the lead of his predecessors, Medina acquired paintings by Ribera, although it is sometimes difficult to associate them with existing works.[21] At his death in 1668, he owned four subjects known in multiple versions: the *Nativity*, the *Liberation of St. Peter*, *Jacob*, and a canvas described simply as *Venus*, possibly *Venus and Adonis*. Medina also obtained paintings by Ribera for the royal collection, which by 1700 contained over sixty of his works.[22] In fact, Ribera was one of the few painters of the seventeenth century, and one of only two Spaniards, whose works were avidly collected by Philip IV.

The first painting to enter the royal collection was an unidentified *Nativity* of 1630. In 1634, several were purchased for the Retiro from private collectors in Madrid, and two years after that, a pair of his works (now lost) was installed in the New Room of the Alcázar. The major pieces datable from the viceregency of Medina include the *Martyrdom of St. Philip* (pl. 170), done in 1639. This painting, which commemorates the king's patron saint, contains the usual elements of a Ribera martyrdom scene, but this is no set piece; it is a tour de force of figure painting. Like a great sail billowing in the wind, the saint's sprawling body is hoisted by a pair of executioners, who strain with all their might to lift the heavy weight. Two groups of spectators placidly watch at a respectful distance, serving as a counterforce to the strenuous exertions of the tormentors.

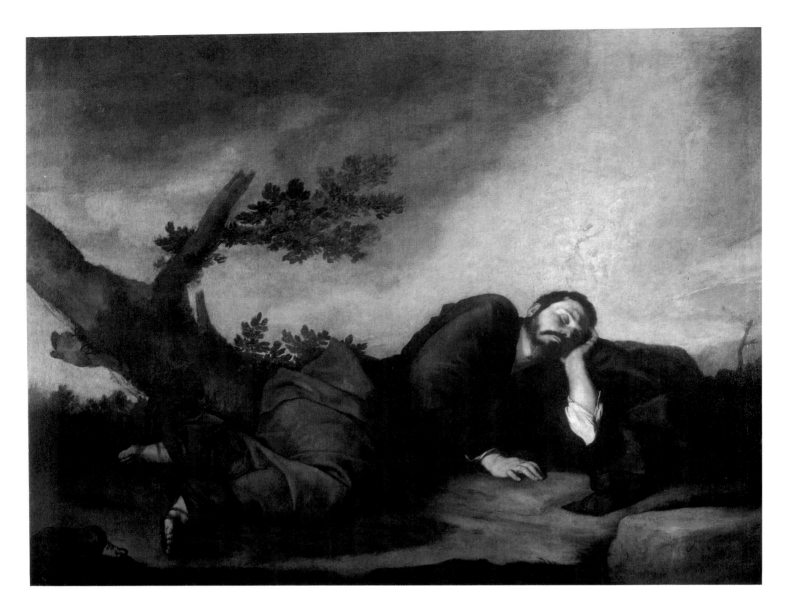

171. Jusepe de Ribera, *Dream of Jacob*, 1639. Madrid, Prado, canvas, 1.79 × 2.33m.

In 1639, the artist produced another powerful masterpiece in the same vein for Medina, the *Dream of Jacob* (pl. 171). Here the composition is daringly reduced to a simple right angle turned on its side, one arm of which is formed by the tree stump, the other, by the slumbering, inert figure of Jacob. His head is illuminated by a broad beam of light, in the midst of which angels, their forms so delicately brushed as to be almost invisible, descend the heavenly ladder. In this quiet but strangely powerful scene, as in the *Martyrdom of St. Philip*, Ribera turns the rigorous geometry of the Roman classical style into the lyric poetry of naturalism.

For all their importance, the viceroys constituted only one sector of Ribera's clientele. Of equal significance were the religious institutions of Naples, among which the Carthusians rank first. The Carthusian house of San Martino was a leading artistic patron and had always employed the best painters, sculptors, and craftsmen for the decoration of its sumptuous church. In 1637, the monks initiated a new decorative campaign by hiring Lanfranco to execute frescoes, which were finished less than two years later. Their relationship with Ribera, which began at the same time, was to last much longer and unfortunately took a considerable toll on both parties.[23] But the beginnings were happy enough.

The first work to be completed was a *Pietà* for the sacristy, for which the artist

190

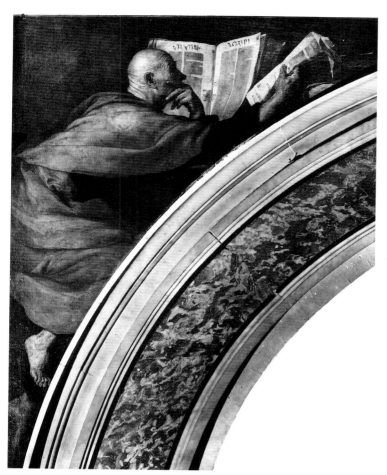

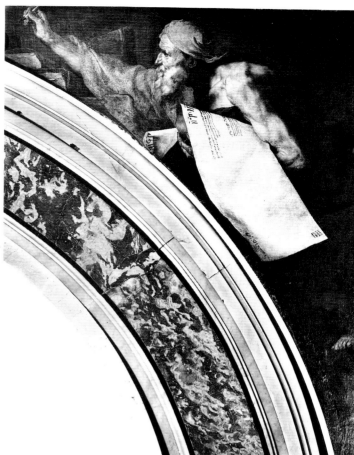

received the generous sum of 400 ducats (30 October 1637). In this painting, Ribera revives the dramatic chiaroscuro employed in the 1620s (pl. 157). As a matter of fact, he was always prepared to revive his original manner, if so required by patrons or circumstances. However, the emotional tone is decidedly different, achieving an unprecedented depth of feeling and pathos. Equally novel is the studied elegance of the pose and proportions of Christ's body, a characteristic sometimes attributed to the impact of van Dyck, who had been in Sicily and possibly Naples in the 1620s, and whose pictures began to trickle into Neapolitan collections in the late thirties.

This picture was a success and led to the commission of several new works in 1638. These included a series of Old Testament prophets for the spandrels of the nave arcade, to be paid at the rate of 80 ducats per figure; half-length representations of Moses and Elias, at 50 ducats apiece; and a large, multi-figured version of the *Communion of the Apostles*, for which a down payment of 1,000 ducats was made.

The prophets were painted over the next five years and rank among the artist's most brilliant works. The format of the spaces – right triangles with curved hypotenuses – posed a difficult problem, and Ribera's solution was to treat the curve as a support for the figures. Perhaps any competent painter would have arrived at the same idea, but the next step was not quite so easy. The challenge Ribera set for himself was to create a veritable portrait gallery of Old Testament characters; that is, twelve figures with distinctly different appearances and personalities. No less taxing was the problem of varying the poses and gestures to avoid monotony and provide a sense of movement. The splendid results can be judged, for example, in the still unidentified figure with a shaved head (pl. 172), who intently studies the books

172. Jusepe de Ribera, *Prophet*, 1638–43. Naples, San Martino, canvas, 2.65 × 2.35m.

173. Jusepe de Ribera, *Prophet*, 1638–43. Naples, San Martino, canvas, 2.65 × 2.35m.

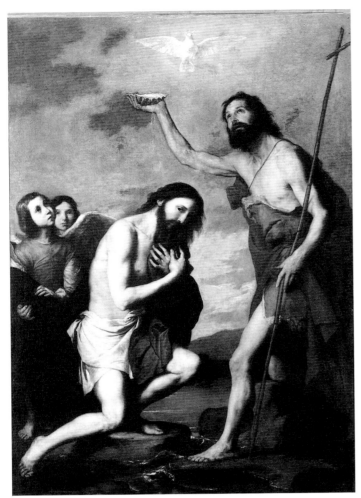 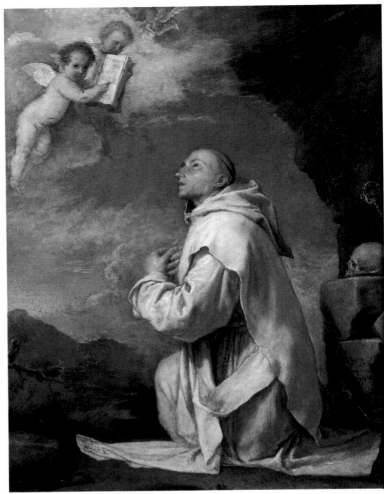

174. Jusepe de Ribera, *Baptism of Christ*, 1643. Nancy, Musée des Beaux-Arts, canvas, 2.35 × 1.60m.

175. Jusepe de Ribera, *Vision of St. Bruno*, 1643. Naples, Museo e Gallerie Nazionali di Capodimonte, copper, 0.38 × 0.27m.

before him, or the aged prophet (pl. 173), draped with one of his scrolls, who lunges toward the inkwell placed high above him.

Having finished this commission, Ribera turned his attention to the *Communion of the Apostles*, a work of great size and complexity. But no sooner had he started than he was stricken with an incapacitating ailment. The exact nature of his affliction, which occurred around 1644, is not clear, but it continued to plague him for several years, making it impossible for him to work except intermittently. Not until the autumn of 1650 had he fully recovered from what he called "my long and troublesome infirmity."[24] There is no convenient time to become seriously ill, but Ribera's malady occurred just as his inspired fusion of naturalism and classicism was reaching a peak. Two beautiful works of 1643 exemplify this climactic moment: the *Baptism of Christ* (pl. 174) and the *Vision of St. Bruno* (pl. 175). Now this development of his art came to a halt.

During 1644–45, Ribera was virtually unable to paint, although his workshop continued to function. Finally, in 1646, he returned to the practice of his profession, if in a reduced capacity. On 16 September 1646, he received 1,000 ducats upon completing a painting for the Cappella del Tesoro,[25] the splendid chapel dedicated to St. Januarius, the city's patron. The decoration of the chapel, Domenichino's major Neapolitan enterprise, was left unfinished when he died in 1641. (Members of his family were convinced that he had been poisoned by an accomplice of the painters of Naples.) Ribera's task was to furnish a large painting of the *Miraculous Escape of St. Januarius from the Fiery Furnace*, which was to be executed on the unusual support of silver-plated copper and might well be called "Domenichino's Revenge" (pl. 176).

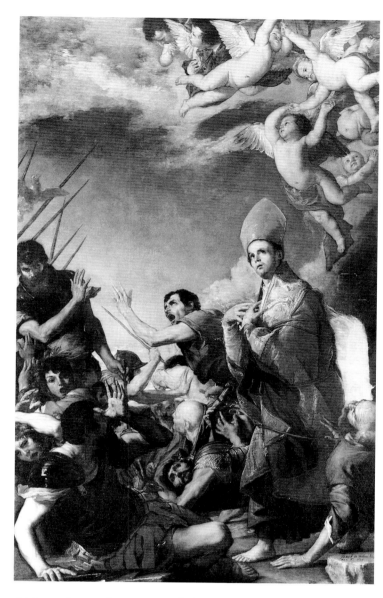

176. Jusepe de Ribera, *Miraculous Escape of St. Januarius from the Fiery Furnace*, 1646. Naples, San Gennaro, Cappella del Tesoro, copper, 3.20 × 2.00m.

Although poorly preserved, it constitutes Ribera's capitulation to the grand manner of Bolognese-Roman classicism. The ponderous, studied composition, rhetorical gestures, and studied expressions are quite foreign to Ribera's subdued, understated manner and were used, undoubtedly, because he was at pains to conform to the altarpieces and frescoes of his despised rival. Yet this uncharacteristic painting was to prove more than an academic exercise; necessity may have forced Ribera into Domenichino's corner but, unlike St. Januarius, he did not emerge unscathed from the tribulation.

During the remaining months of 1646 and through the following year, Ribera slowly continued his recovery. On 22 November 1646, he received 200 ducats on account from the incumbent viceroy, the duke of Arcos, for a *Virgin of the Immaculate Conception* (destroyed) to be installed in the chapel of the viceregal palace.[26] Only a few canvases datable to 1647 now exist, the most notable of which is a small group acquired by the Sicilian collector Antonio Ruffo.[27] Then his work was interrupted by a famous event in Neapolitan history, the revolt of Masaniello, a violent uprising of the overtaxed, underfed populace against the authority of the crown, which began in July and was not quelled until April of the following year, when the king's illegitimate son, Juan José of Austria, took command of the city from Arcos and defeated the rebels. Ribera painted an impressive portrait of the young general on horseback, set against a panoramic view of the Bay of Naples (Madrid, Palacio Real).

At last, in 1651, he was able to return to the long-delayed *Communion of the Apostles* for San Martino. As an anonymous informant reported to the monks, Ribera was eager to finish the work, "to show the world that he was alive, not dead," and that "he was doing it with great pleasure [in order] to recover his extinct reputation."[28] These sentiments are not mere hyperbole, because the *Communion of the Apostles* is Ribera's most ambitious painting (pl. 177).

177. Jusepe de Ribera, *Communion of the Apostles*, 1651–52. Naples, San Martino, canvas, 4.00 × 4.00m.

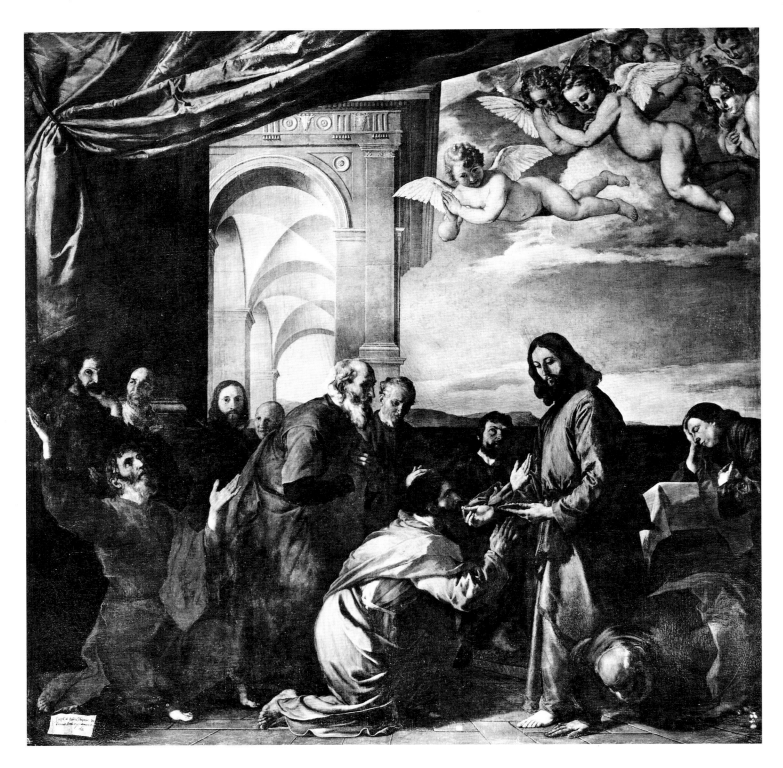

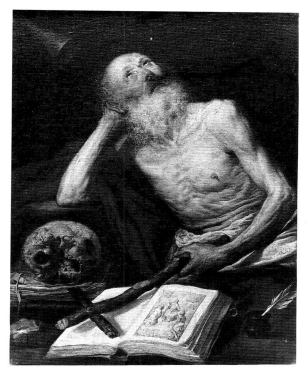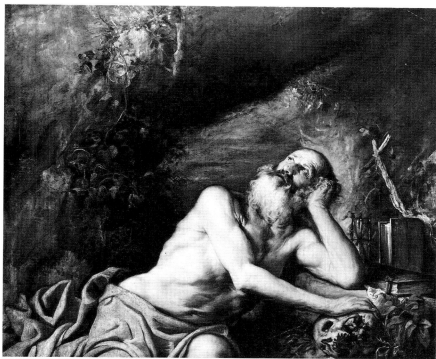

178. Antonio de Pereda, *St. Jerome*, 1643. Madrid, Prado, canvas, 1.05 × 0.84m.

179. Diego Polo, *St. Jerome*, 1640–50. Munich, Alte Pinakothek, canvas, 1.28 × 1.10m.

The idiom chosen by Ribera for his comeback, and what would be his final commission, is related to the *Miraculous Escape of St. Januarius*, that is to say, to the grandiloquent manner of Renaissance classicism. In 1625, Ribera had told Jusepe Martínez that he desired to return to Rome to contemplate the pictures he had seen in his youth, particularly "the histories of the immortal Raphael painted in the holy palace [of the Vatican]. He who studies these works will be a true and consummate painter."[29] Now, many years later, and after the 1646 encounter with the art of Domenichino, he again sought inspiration from this fundamental source.

The imposing architectural setting, consisting of a monumental portico, sets the tone for this inspired essay in the classical style. At the left, a large red curtain, gathered at the middle, is pulled back to reveal a measured composition in which Christ and the apostles are deployed in a frieze-like arrangement. In the center, Christ solemnly dispenses the unleavened bread to a prayerful apostle, thus instituting the holy sacrament of the Eucharist. A kneeling, gray-bearded figure opens his arms to the heavens, emphatically acknowledging the miraculous event. Judas stands alongside, lost in thought as he ponders the imminent consequence of his treachery. At the far right, the innocent John slumbers at the table, while Peter reverently genuflects at the feet of Christ. The *Communion of the Apostles* is a weighty subject rendered in a noble style, a "true and consummate" history painting in the grandest tradition of the grand manner. It is also unmistakably a work of its maker, because Ribera, remaining faithful to his essence, has imbued every character with a portrait-like quality, thus reconciling the two major trends of early seventeenth-century Italian painting. With this last, great effort accomplished, Ribera's life soon drew to a close and he died on 2 September 1652.

The death of Ribera marks the end of a period in Neapolitan painting in which his art was supremely influential. His output also resonated in the workshops of Spain, thanks to the pictures that were imported by the viceroys and other Spaniards who had been in Italy. These collectors owned every sort of work by Ribera – mythologies, portraits, "beggar philosophers," landscapes, and Old and New

Testament themes. But Spanish artists tended to imitate only his religious subjects, this being the type of painting in demand by their clientele. One subject in particular became popular, the depictions of penitent saints, whose rugged physiognomies proved irresistible.

Most of those who borrowed motifs from Ribera worked in the 1630s and 1640s, when many of his works were imported into Madrid. The decline of his production after 1643 and a subsequent shift in taste lessened his appeal to later Spanish painters. Typical of the reception of Ribera's art are three versions of his most imitated composition, St. Jerome and the Trumpet of the Last Judgment, which was known from paintings, and even more from the two prints of 1621.[30] The paintings by Francisco Collantes, Antonio de Pereda, and Diego Polo (pls. 178 and 179) hew closely to the composition but are less convincing as imitations of the style, which depends on local sources. As has been discussed in the previous chapter, Ribera's influence was keenly felt in Seville, particularly by Francisco de Zurbarán and Alonso Cano.

Thus, in the end, Ribera's insistent claims of Spanish heritage had the desired effect. Spanish painters and patrons were drawn to a master whose direct approach to the visible world coincided with their native artistic predilections. However, the more subtle aspects of Ribera's style, and especially his inspired confrontation with classicism, were inevitably lost in transmission to Spain, where the classical style was largely peripheral and where the complexities of his technique could not really be duplicated any more effectively than in Naples. In any case, by the 1650s, Spanish painters and their clients were finally abandoning their interest in naturalistic painting and becoming attracted to the dynamic art of Rubens, whose works were eagerly being acquired in a new wave of collecting that swept the Spanish court during the reign of Philip IV.

9
Collectors and Collections

ON 5 AUGUST 1638, the English ambassador, Sir Arthur Hopton, wrote to London concerning a recent exchange of portraits. The Spaniards, it seems, were dissatisfied with the quality of the images of Charles I and Henrietta Maria, and, by way of explanation, Hopton provided the following observation:

> They are now become more judicious in and affectioned unto the art of painting than they have been or than the world imagines. And the king within this 12 month had gotten an incredible number of ancient and the best modern hands. . . . And in this town is not a piece worth anything but the king takes and pays very well for them. And in his imitation the Admirante [the duke of Medina de Rioseco, Admiral of Castile], don Lewis [Luis] de Haro, and many others are making collections.[1]

The foundations of the phenomenal upsurge in picture collecting experienced during the epoch of Philip IV had been laid by Philip II and the duke of Lerma, but Hopton was surely correct in perceiving that the interest in fine pictures was attaining new heights in the 1630s, inspired by the growth of the royal collection.

Philip IV's interest in the art of painting probably was innate; like many a great collector, his love of pictures had an obsessive quality that cannot be acquired through instruction alone.[2] However, while prince, he did have the benefit of a superb drawing master in the person of Fray Juan Bautista Maino, who helped to sharpen his eye. Nevertheless, Philip's passion for painting was slow to develop because in the first years of his reign, he was occupied with his overwhelming responsibilities as ruler and had little time to devote to his magnificent hereditary collection. It required the visits of three great figures from abroad involved with the arts to stimulate his love of fine pictures.

In 1623, the prince of Wales (later Charles I) and the duke of Buckingham made their novelesque, incognito trip to Madrid in quest of the hand of the king's sister, the infanta María. It is easy to imagine how Philip would have been impressed by this handsome, urbane English prince who enthusiastically made his way through the royal palaces and private houses of Madrid, buying pictures as he went. The prince may have left Spain without a Spanish princess, but at least his artistic aspirations were not entirely thwarted. Philip made him a present of several pictures, the most famous of which were Titian's *Pardo Venus* (Paris, Musée du Louvre) and *Charles V with a Hound* (pl. 180). Charles purchased another painting by Titian at one of the estate sales (*almonedas*) that formed the heart of the bustling art market. Finally, he was promised Titian's "Poesie," those great mythological pictures painted for Philip II, as soon as the match was final. Philip went so far as to have them crated, but never sent them to England.

Three years later, two important Italian connoisseurs arrived in town, Cardinal Francesco Barberini and his secretary, Cassiano dal Pozzo. Barberini, who was

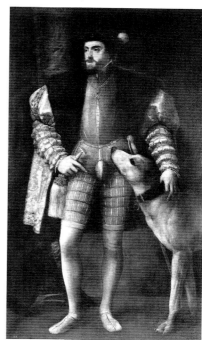

180. Titian, *Charles V with a Hound*, 1532–33. Madrid, Prado, canvas, 1.92 × 1.11m.

slightly older than the king, still had his great days as a collector to come, but he was already knowledgeable in the arts and offered another model worthy of emulation. Dal Pozzo was an equally formidable devotee of painting and during the next decade would become one of the most discerning collectors and patrons in Rome. His sometimes critical remarks on painters at the Spanish court, including Velázquez, may have helped to focus the king's attention on his own collection.

The last of the foreign visitors must be ranked first in importance for the development of the king's artistic tastes. This was Peter Paul Rubens, who, as has been seen, arrived at court in August 1628. Rubens, then at the height of his career as an artist, had come to Spain as a diplomat, attempting to plan a peace with England. Knowing of the king's interest in pictures, he was armed with gifts, eight splendid creations of his own, which were promptly installed in an important state room in the Alcázar. In moments borrowed from official business, Rubens painted additional pictures in a workshop in the palace, where Philip would watch him at work and deepen his understanding of the art. When Rubens returned home in the spring of 1629, Philip's education as a connoisseur was over. He had begun with drawing lessons from Maino, taken courses in princely collecting from Charles I and Francesco Barberini, and completed his education with postgraduate work in the studio of Rubens. With this impressive schooling behind him, the royal aesthete was prepared to commence his career as a collector.

Philip's evolution as a connoisseur in the 1620s and 1630s is graphically illustrated by the pictorial decoration of the so-called New Room (Salón Nuevo) of the Alcázar, an imposing gallery in the southern wing reserved for important occasions of state. The New Room would undergo periodic changes of decoration during Philip's reign, and thus is a useful barometer of the evolution of his taste.[3]

The first stage can be dated to 1623, when a number of paintings were moved from the palace of El Pardo to the Alcázar, including several works by Titian, which became the nucleus of the new decoration. There was also one work by Rubens done in collaboration with van Dyck (*Ulysses Discovers Achilles among the Daughters of Lycomedes*, Prado) and the now-lost equestrian portrait of Philip IV by Velázquez. To these were added recent paintings by Carducho and Cajés and a couple of representations of events from the reign of Philip III. With these pictures on the walls, the New Room was an interesting but not inspiring place to visit. At least, this is the opinion of Cassiano dal Pozzo, who was impressed only by the paintings of Titian.

Two years later, however, the decoration of the New Room entered a new phase, which began with the installation of the eight paintings by Rubens given to the king, most of which have disappeared. This stage of the room's development continued until 1636 and is characterized by an emphasis on paintings by living Italian and Flemish masters. Works by Domenichino (pl. 181), Camillo Procaccini, and Orazio Gentileschi (*Finding of Moses*, Prado) led the Italian contingent. Rubens's pictures were supplemented by van Dyck's *Cardinal Infante Ferdinand* (Prado), the first of several portraits by this master to enter the royal collection. These new acquisitions eclipsed the paintings by Spanish artists, as seen by the fact that canvases by Velázquez and Carducho were retired, while only Ribera, as much an Italian as a Spanish master, was given wall space.

The pattern of Philip's collecting in the thirties was thus established in the New Room – it was to center on works by contemporary artists from Flanders and Italy. This development was accelerated by the ambitious construction programs of the 1630s; paintings were needed to decorate the walls of the new buildings, and needed without delay. Between 1634 and 1640, about a thousand were gathered by the viceroys, ambassadors, and crown officials, who received their orders from the

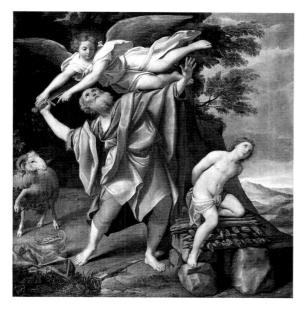 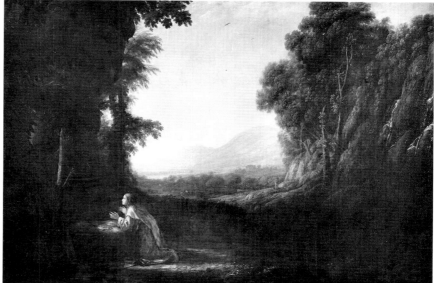

count-duke of Olivares. Obviously, rare old pictures were not available in such quantity, compelling the agents to concentrate on the work of contemporary artists.

The Buen Retiro posed the biggest problem because of its size.[4] The acquisitions in Spain were directed by Jerónimo de Villanueva, the protonotary of Aragon, and by the count of Castrillo, president of the Council of Indies. Villanueva bought paintings from aristocratic collections and made the payments for the Hall of Realms. He also bought works from Pedro Orrente, Francisco Collantes, a landscape specialist, and the battle painter Juan de la Corte.

The Italian acquisitions were the responsibility of the marquis of Castel Rodrigo, the ambassador to the Holy See, and the count of Monterrey, the viceroy of Naples. Castel Rodrigo was instrumental in assembling one of the most striking pictorial ensembles of the seventeenth century – a gallery consisting of about fifty large-scale landscapes by northern artists working in Rome, including Claude Lorrain (pl. 182), Nicolas Poussin, Jan Both, Herman Swanevelt, and Gaspard Dughet.[5] In Naples, Monterrey commissioned paintings by Giovanni Lanfranco (scenes of Roman history), Domenichino (*Emperor's Exequies*), and Massimo Stanzione (*Worship of Bacchus*; all in the Prado), which were sent to Madrid in the late 1630s.

In the north, the king's brother and governor of Flanders, the cardinal infante Ferdinand, was in charge and flooded the Rubens workshop with commissions. For the Retiro, he obtained more than a hundred paintings, including landscapes, allegories of the seasons and months of the year, hunting scenes, and illustrations of Aesop's Fables. Rubens himself produced the luminous *Judgment of Paris* (pl. 183), a painting much admired by Ferdinand despite his characteristically Spanish reservations about the fleshy goddesses.

Rubens's workshop also received orders for the Torre de la Parada.[6] In May 1638, a large shipment of pictures arrived in Madrid, many of which were intended for the hunting lodge, and which included illustrations from Ovid's *Metamorphoses*, hunting scenes, and animal pictures. Rubens himself painted only a few of these works (pl. 184); the majority were done by assistants and collaborators, among them Jacob Jordaens, Erasmus Quellinus, and Frans Snyders.

The 1630s were ebullient years of collecting that could never be repeated. So many paintings were acquired that the king is sometimes lost in the shuffle of canvases. However, during the 1640s, all this changed when the emphasis on

181. Domenichino, *Sacrifice of Isaac*, 1627–28. Madrid, Prado, canvas, 1.47 × 1.40m.

182. Claude Lorrain, *Landscape with St. Mary of Cervello*, 1635–38. Madrid, Prado, canvas, 1.62 × 2.41m.

199

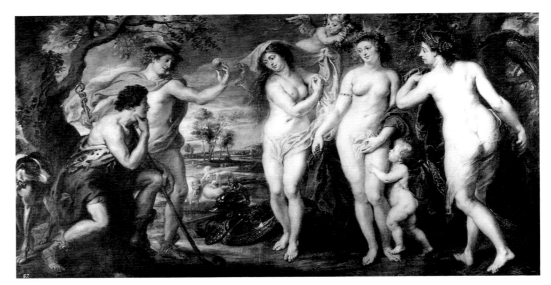

183. Peter Paul Rubens, *Judgment of Paris*, 1638–39. Madrid, Prado, canvas, 1.99 × 3.79m.

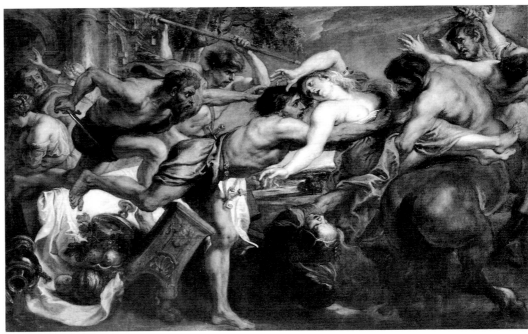

184. Peter Paul Rubens, *Rape of Deidamia*, 1636–38. Madrid, Prado, canvas, 1.82 × 2.90m.

quantity gave way to quality, and the king concentrated on purchasing works by Rubens and by masters of the Venetian school.

The first opportunity to enrich the holdings of Rubens's work was provided paradoxically by the painter's death, which occurred in May 1640.[7] Rubens had retained many of his own pictures and made a choice collection of canvases by other artists, all of which were put on the market by his heirs later in the year. Philip was advised of the impending sale in a letter of 24 September 1640 from the cardinal infante, who enclosed a memorandum of the pictures and advised the king to make his selection. Philip acted quickly, and the cardinal infante purchased thirty-two works, which were later sent to Madrid. Over half were by Rubens himself, including some of his finest easel paintings – for example, the *Rest on the Flight into Egypt* (pl. 186) and the *Peasants' Dance* (Prado). Philip also bought the copies after Titian that Rubens had created before his very eyes in 1628–29. As for works by other masters, the king acquired Titian's moving late *Self-Portrait* (Prado), van Dyck's *Arrest of Christ* (pl. 185), and Elsheimer's *Judith and Holofernes* (London, Wellington Museum).

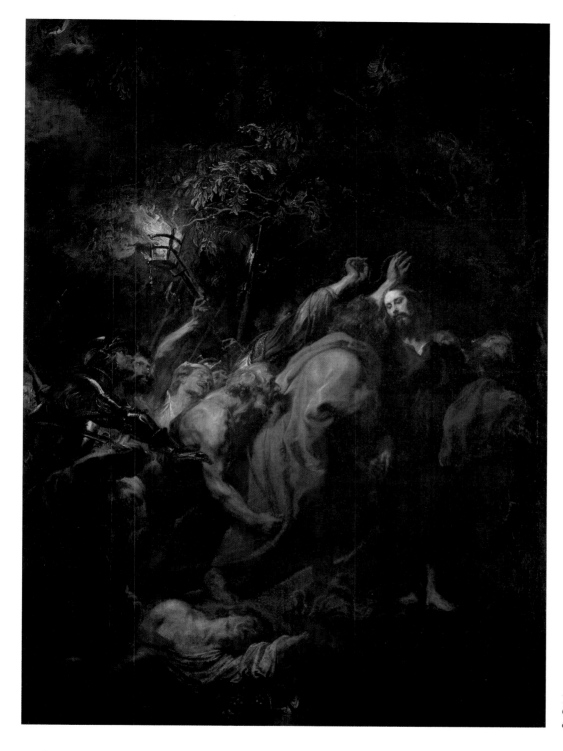

185. Anthony van Dyck, *Arrest of Christ*, 1618–20. Madrid, Prado, canvas, 3.44 × 2.49m.

The possession of these splendid canvases inspired Philip to create a "memorial" room in the Alcázar, known as the Octagonal Room, the decoration of which consisted of twenty paintings by Rubens and van Dyck and several large-scale bronze statues.[8] Unfortunately, except for the statues (Madrid, Palacio Real), most of the contents were consumed by a fire in 1734, which seriously damaged this sector of the palace.

The start of work on the Octagonal Room had been preceded by minor alterations in the New Room. In 1639, the king had ordered four more paintings from Rubens for this gallery, some of which were left unfinished at the artist's death. They were

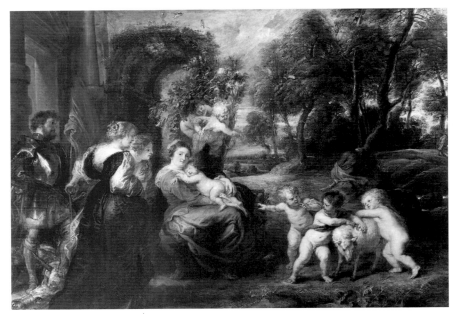

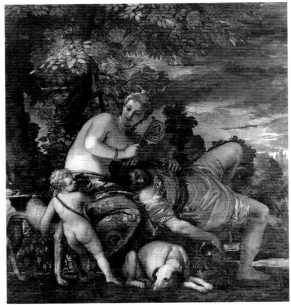

186. Peter Paul Rubens, *Rest on the Flight into Egypt*, 1630–40. Madrid, Prado, panel, 0.87 × 1.25m.

187. Paolo Veronese, *Venus and Adonis*, ca. 1580. Madrid, Prado, canvas, 2.12 × 1.91m.

188. Raphael, *Holy Family*, ca. 1518. Madrid, Prado, panel, 1.44 × 1.15m.

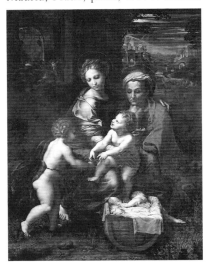

completed by his assistants and sent to Madrid by the cardinal infante. In 1643, the sculptor Antonio de Herrera executed mirror frames in the shape of double-eagles, which led to the renaming of the room as the Hall of Mirrors.[9] During the construction of the Octagonal Room, nothing of consequence was done in the Hall of Mirrors, but soon after the small room was finished, Philip turned his attention to the large. One consequence of the new project was the second trip of Velázquez to Italy, which was authorized on 25 November 1648. Two months later, the artist started the journey from which he would not return until June 1651. During his long absence, he acquired numerous bronze sculptures and bronze and plaster casts of antique statuary for use in the Hall of Mirrors and other palace rooms, as well as a few choice Venetian paintings, notably Veronese's *Venus and Adonis* (pl. 187) and *Cephalus and Procris* (Strasbourg, Musée des Beaux-Arts).

Even as Velázquez was pursuing his mission in Italy, Philip was seeking to purchase paintings from the collection of Charles I of England which were offered for sale by the Commonwealth after the king's execution in 1649. Philip's interest in buying Charles's pictures was so avid as to be unseemly.[10] His first inquiry actually predates the capture of the English monarch by a year. In a letter of 30 June 1645, the king instructed his English agent to buy paintings from the collections of the king and the duke of Buckingham.[11] The letter is interesting as the only known set of instructions from Philip to a representative in the field, and not surprisingly it gives priority to the Venetian masters.

As it happened, Philip had confused the sale of Buckingham's collection, which eventually was restored to his heirs and sold in the Netherlands, with that of the king. But four years later, when the English royal collection came onto the market, the Spaniards were ready. In part to conceal the monarch's involvement, the buying was done by his minister, Luis de Haro, the successor to Olivares, who collaborated with the ambassador in London, Alonso de Cárdenas. Cárdenas's principal sources of supply were the creditors of Charles I, who had accepted pictures as payment for the royal debts. Periodically, Cárdenas would send a list of available works to Haro, and once the treasures had arrived in Madrid, the minister offered many of the best works to the king, who employed Velázquez and Angelo Nardi to evaluate the attributions and quality.[12] In this way, Philip acquired some of his major pieces, including versions of the Holy Family by Raphael (pl. 188) and Andrea del Sarto, Tintoretto's magnificent *Christ Washing the Feet of the Apostles*, Dürer's *Self-Portrait*,

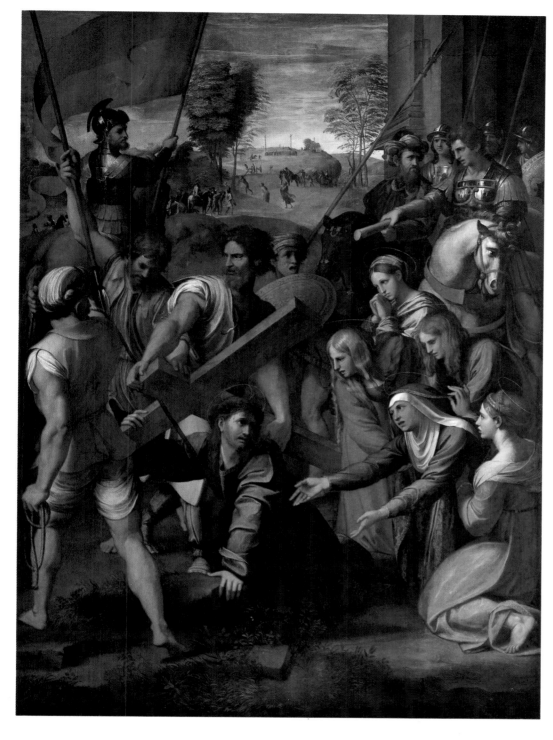

189. Raphael, *Christ on the Road to Calvary*, ca. 1517. Madrid, Prado, canvas, 3.18 × 2.29m.

and several major works by Titian, notably the very portrait of Charles V (pl. 180) that he had given to the prince of Wales in 1623 (all now in the Prado).

During the 1650s, Philip and Velázquez continued to refine the decoration of the Hall of Mirrors, which achieved its definitive form some thirty years after the initial project had been launched in what was then called the New Room.[13] This gallery was, in effect, the king's hall of famous painters, and the contents help to define his mature artistic taste. It is immediately apparent that Philip had a great eye for quality, and that he favored the rich, coloristic manner of the sixteenth-century Venetians and those who followed their example. There were twenty-seven paint-

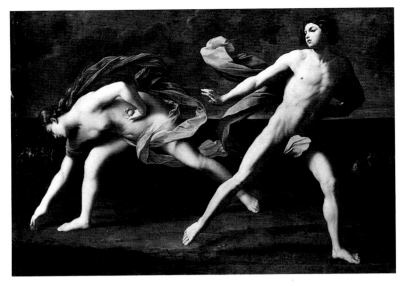 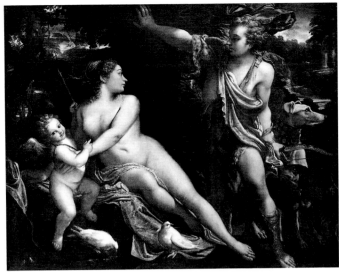

190. Guido Reni, *Atalanta and Hippomenes*, 1618–20. Madrid, Prado, canvas, 2.06 × 2.97m.

191. Annibale Carracci, *Venus and Adonis*, 1588–90. Madrid, Prado, canvas, 2.06 × 2.97m.

ings in the room, including four by Tintoretto, three by Titian, two by Veronese, and one by the Bassano shop, for a total of ten. This was also the number of canvases by Rubens (some done with the assistance of the leading members of his shop), a number that reflects both the king's admiration of the painter and the greater availability of his works. Only two Spanish subjects were represented, Velázquez by five pictures and Ribera by two. The choice of these painters would not be disputed today, but in effect the king was exercising a remarkable bias against native talent, past and present. Obviously, Philip owned innumerable works by the painters of Spain, but there is much to indicate that he (unfairly) relegated them to a secondary place in his hierarchy of artistic merit, thus perpetuating a bias that never ceased to trouble the more ambitious among them.

Philip continued to make acquisitions almost to the end of his life. In 1661, he bought Raphael's famous *Christ on the Road to Calvary* (pl. 189), for which he paid an enormous sum, in part as a perpetual grant to the monastery of Santa Maria del Spasmo, the owner of the picture. And in 1664, a year before he died, he acquired thirty-nine paintings from the heirs of Marchese Giovanni Francesco Serra, a Genoese nobleman who had been a general in the Spanish army.[14] Included in this lot were Guido Reni's *Atalanta and Hippomenes*, Annibale Carracci's *Venus and Adonis* (pls. 190 and 191), and Parmigianino's *Count of San Secondo* (all in the Prado).

These are some of the highlights of Philip's career as a collector. By the time his long reign drew to a close, the royal collection had grown enormously in quantity and quality alike; it is not an exaggeration to say that it had become the largest and finest in Europe. In the Alcázar alone, the king had accumulated, through inheritance, purchase, and gifts, this impressive roster of masterpieces: seventy-seven paintings attributed to Titian; sixty-two, to Rubens; forty-three, to Tintoretto; forty-three, to Velázquez; thirty-eight, to Brueghel the Younger; thirty-six, to Ribera; twenty-nine, to Veronese; twenty-six, to the Bassano family. And these numbers only begin to reveal the wealth of the royal collection. At the death of Charles II in 1700, the combined inventories of the twelve palaces and country seats totaled 5,539 paintings.[15] An estimate of the share acquired by Philip is difficult to calculate, but it may have been as much as fifty percent. No wonder that a French visitor to Madrid in 1667 was astounded by the pictures displayed in the Buen Retiro alone:

In the palace we were surprised by the quantity of pictures. I do not know how it is adorned in other seasons, but when we were there we saw more pictures than

192. Peter Paul Rubens, *Immaculate Conception*, ca. 1628. Madrid, Prado, canvas, 1.98 × 1.37m.

204

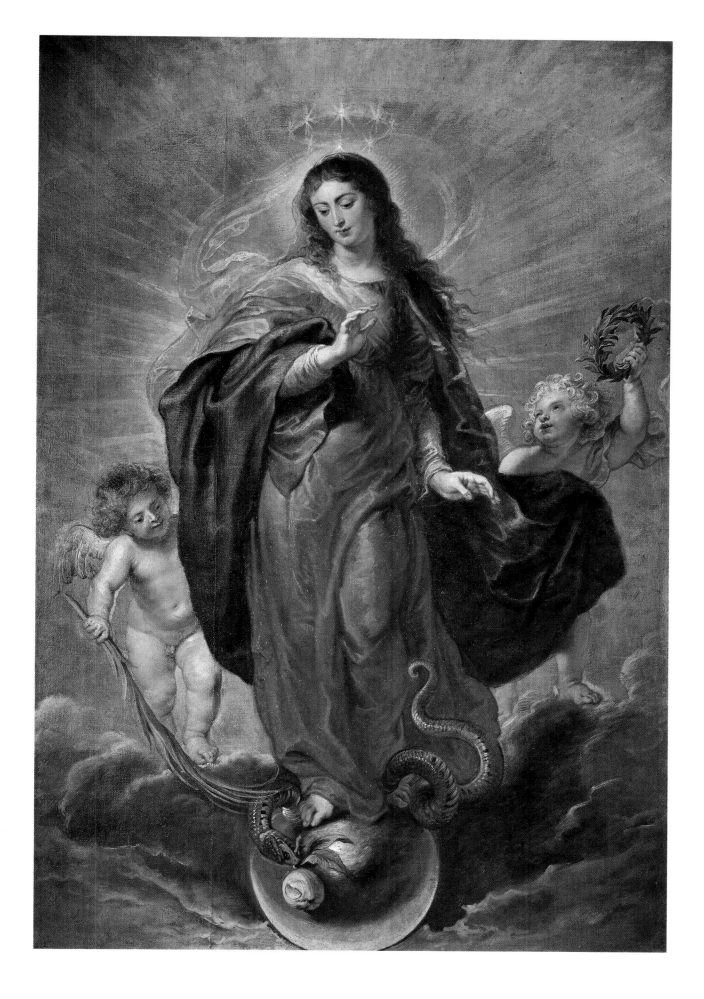

walls. The galleries and staircases were full of them, as well as the bedrooms and salons. I can assure you, Sir, that there were more than in all of Paris. I was not at all surprised when they told me that the principal quality of the deceased king was his love of painting, and that no one in the world understood more about it than he.[16]

The king's "affection" for pictures, as Sir Arthur Hopton had observed in 1638, was emulated by his courtiers, who amassed large collections and helped to turn Madrid into one of the most active picture markets in Europe. This phenomenon is demonstrated by the collecting activities of the count-duke's relatives, who used their connections to accumulate great personal fortunes, part of which they expended on pictures. These aristocrats were genuine connoisseurs, but they were also genuine opportunists, who recognized that it could do no harm if they gave the king a good picture from time to time.

The most spectacular member of the "clan," as it was known to contemporaries, was Olivares's cousin Diego Messía, the marquis of Leganés.[17] As a youth, Leganés had served as a page in the archducal court at Brussels and later embarked on a military career, commanding the Spanish army in Flanders (1603–35), Milan (1635–41), and Catalonia (he is the figure on horseback at the far left in plate 126). Leganés's military service in Flanders and Italy gave him the opportunity to collect, while Olivares provided him with funds by means of royal favors and benefices. His beginnings as a collector were modest enough; in 1630, his inventory lists a mere eighteen works, eleven of which were ascribed to Titian. Twelve years later, the total had increased to well over 1,100 pictures, among them masterpieces by Rubens (pl. 192) and van Dyck, as well as a generous share by lesser Flemish masters, including Snyders, Peter Snayers, Gaspar de Crayer, and Joos de Momper. Leganés also collected the Flemish primitives, among them van Eyck, Metsys, Patinir, and van der Weyden. His Italian paintings were almost as numerous and included attributions to Titian, Raphael, Veronese, and the Bassanos, with a smaller representation of contemporaries. Spanish painters made up the smallest group, but Leganés's taste was not to be faulted, for he concentrated on pictures by Velázquez, Ribera, and van der Hamen. As the connoisseurs in Madrid would have been quick to notice, Leganés's collection emulated that of the king.

Another notable member of the collecting clan was Manuel Acevedo y Zúñiga, the count of Monterrey, who was well connected to Olivares through marriage – each man had married the other's sister.[18] Monterrey's artistic interests were stimulated by his stay in Italy from 1628 to 1637, when he served successively as ambassador to the Holy See and viceroy of Naples. Little is known about his time in Rome, but when he moved to Naples in 1631, he became a prominent patron. Monterrey's tenure coincided with the decoration of the Retiro, and he was instrumental in commissioning paintings by Domenichino, Giovanni Lanfranco, Artemisia Gentileschi, and Massimo Stanzione, whose works he acquired for his own collection. However, the principal beneficiary of his patronage was, of course, Jusepe de Ribera. The count owned thirteen works by this master and commissioned him to paint pictures for the family chapel in the church of the Agustinas Descalzas, Salamanca.

Monterrey returned to Madrid in 1638, bringing his personal collection and, in addition, two great pictures for the king, Titian's *Bacchanal of the Andrians* and the *Worship of Venus* (pls. 193 and 194), a gift from Niccolò Ludovisi, prince of Piombino. Soon after his arrival, he built a picture gallery in the garden of his house, where he installed 265 paintings (there were others in his palace in Salamanca), among them works by Titian (indispensable to any ambitious Spanish collector), Borgianni, Cambiaso, Pordenone, and Salviati.

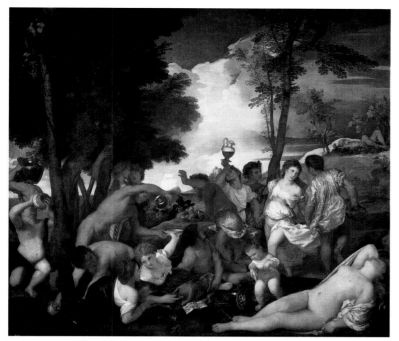

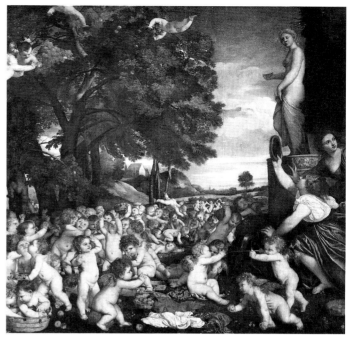

193. Titian, *Bacchanal of the Andrians*,
1518–19. Madrid, Prado, canvas,
1.75 × 1.93m.

194. Titian, *Worship of Venus*,
1518–19. Madrid, Prado, canvas,
1.72 × 1.75m.

195. Raphael, *Madonna of the Fish*,
ca. 1513. Madrid, Prado, canvas,
2.15 × 1.58m.

Monterrey was succeeded in Naples by yet another relative of Olivares, Ramiro de Guzmán, the duke of Medina de las Torres, who had married the count-duke's daughter María in 1624.[19] Although the marriage ended prematurely with María's death in 1626, the young nobleman retained the favor of his father-in-law and prospered. Medina was not the most avid of collectors; at his death in 1668, he owned a mere ninety-six works, which, by the generous standards of the day, is a small number. Except for a few compositions by Ribera, most are unattributed, suggesting that the duke was not a dedicated connoisseur. His greatest coup was struck on behalf of the king, Raphael's *Madonna of the Fish* (pl. 195), which Medina virtually stole from San Domenico, Naples, over the vigorous protests of the prior, who was finally silenced by expulsion from the kingdom.

A far more substantial collector was the count-duke's nephew Luis de Haro, the marquis of Carpio. He succeeded as royal favorite in 1647, four years after Olivares was forced to retire and, with the reins of government securely in hand, amassed a fortune, part of which he spent on an important collection of paintings and tapestries.[20] The extent of this collection is bound to remain uncertain pending the discovery of his death inventory, but Haro's participation in the Commonwealth sale and further acquisitions from the famous collection of the earl of Arundel leave no doubt that he was a major beneficiary of the massive dispersal of pictures following the end of the English Civil War. Haro, like other aristocrats, modeled himself after the king and thus preferred the sixteenth-century Venetians, especially Titian, Veronese, and Tintoretto. Another important part of the collection consisted of six works ascribed to Correggio, including the *Education of Cupid* (London, National Gallery), as well as pictures by Parmigianino, Barocci, and Raphael. His Flemish holdings are less well documented, although it is known that the king gave him Rubens's cartoons for the Eucharist tapestries and that he owned a few works by van Dyck.

Haro's interest in collecting was continued by his son, Gaspar, a notorious reprobate who, by 1651, although only twenty-two years old, owned as many as 331 pictures.[21] After a stormy early life, which included a plot to blow up the theater of the Buen Retiro, Haro redeemed himself and was sent first to Rome as ambassador and then to Naples as viceroy, where he formed one of the largest collections of the seventeenth century. At his death in 1687, he owned over 3,000 pictures, approximately 1,200 of which were kept in his houses in Madrid. It is impossible to describe a collection of this magnitude except to say that its very size compelled Gaspar to include a much wider assortment of artists than was usual.

The members of the Olivares clan were the most flamboyant collectors of the period, but there were many other noblemen who followed the fashion and started to collect pictures or to enlarge their patrimonial holdings. However, picture collecting was by no means confined to the high aristocracy.[22] Members of the ecclesiastical estate were often interested in pictures – Cardinal Sandoval is an earlier example of the phenomenon – although there was nothing in Spain to compare with the artistic proclivities of the Roman cardinals. A new class of collector emerged during the reign of Philip IV; this was composed of members of the royal bureaucracy who were enticed by the prestige enjoyed by owners of fine pictures. One example is Juan Alvarez, who administered the income from the royal salt mines in the region of Cuenca.[23] In addition to his salary, Alvarez presumably practiced the peculation that was considered almost a perquisite of office, and with the proceeds bought some 200 paintings, mostly by Spanish masters, which were inventoried at his death in 1668. A more impressive collector is the royal secretary, Francisco de Oviedo,[24] who, when he died in 1663, owned 128 pictures with attributions to Carlo Saraceni, Guido Reni, Caravaggio, Ribera, Carducho, and Navarrete el

Mudo. Pedro de Arce, a member of a royal honor guard (*montero de cámara*), is best known as the original owner of Velázquez's *Fable of Arachne* (pl. 204), which was only one of 208 paintings he possessed in 1664.[25] Arce's collection was large for persons of this rank, who on average had a hundred pictures or fewer, and it was more heavily weighted toward Spanish artists than were the great aristocratic collections.

The bottom of the scale was occupied by those who might be called picture consumers, people of modest means and standing who managed to accumulate no more than fifty pictures, which they used as devotional images or as an inexpensive form of interior decoration. Paintings, it must be remembered, could be very cheap as long as they did not pretend to be from the hand of a famous master. The quantity of data now available for the analysis of prices is immense and still to be studied systematically, but it is probably not misleading to take the 1653 inventory of the count of Monterrey as representative of price trends at mid-century. In this age before art historians, painters were customarily hired to appraise collections, and the heirs employed Antonio de Pereda for the purpose.

The cheapest pictures were small, anonymous works worth less than one hundred reales, or about nine ducats (there were eleven reales to a ducat). A *Veronica's Veil* was valued at sixty-six reales; a still life of fruit, at seventy-seven; a small landscape, at fifty. The expensive range comprised large, multi-figured compositions by renowned masters. In Monterrey's collection, the most valuable was *Venus, Mars, and Mercury* given to Pordenone and assessed at 8,100 reales. A work described as a "large picture of Venus and Adonis" by Ribera (an original is in Rome, a follower's version, in Cleveland) was assigned a value of 5,500 reales (this is the same as Velázquez's *Fable of Arachne* in the 1664 inventory of Pedro de Arce), while Titian's *St. Catherine*, now identified as the painting in the Museum of Fine Arts, Boston, came in at 4,950 reales. In general, 5,500 reales (500 ducats) was considered a substantial price, and so it was in an economy in which a well-to-do person received an annual income of 5,000 ducats and a royal painter earned a salary of 240 per year. For great noblemen, with extensive lands, numerous offices, and annual incomes in excess of 100,000 ducats, this price was affordable, but even their collections were studded with small, cheap landscapes, still lifes, and devotional paintings.

As the interest in picture collecting increased, so did the activity of the market. Knowledge of its workings is still scanty, particularly compared with other important centers such as Rome, Antwerp, Brussels, and Amsterdam. However, in Madrid, as wherever art was sold, the market was divided into two sectors, one that sold pictures by living local artists, and a second that dealt in works by masters who were deceased or foreign or both. (Paintings done on commission form a separate and distinct category.)

The market for local production was controlled by the artists themselves, who sold directly to the public from their workshops (see pl. 285), and by picture dealers. The *tratantes en pinturas*, as the dealers were called, sometimes functioned as brokers, buying large lots of canvases which they offered in town or shipped to the provinces.[26] In 1624, for instance, a certain Jorge Tineo sold 150 pictures with frames to a customer, possibly another dealer, from Estella, a town near Pamplona. These canvases were probably devotional pictures of artisanal quality which were frequently priced by the linear foot. In a transaction of 1622, Tineo sold a hundred framed pictures at twenty-nine reales the *vara* (just under a meter).

Merchants in Madrid are also known to have offered pictures for sale in open-air stalls. In 1620, Simón Fogo, described as a "dealer and master of painting," signed a four-year lease with the monastery of La Victoria (the same establishment that housed the nascent painters' academy in 1603), which entitled him to display

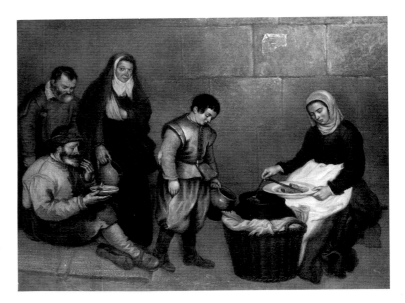

196. Attributed to Antonio Puga, *Poor People Eating*, 1630–40. Ponce, Museo de Arte, canvas, 1.19 × 1.60m.

paintings on an exterior wall of the church. It was in such places that consumers could buy paintings that had a functional rather than aesthetic purpose.

Pictures of quality tended to enter the market through estate sales (*almonedas*), which took place all the time. Estate sales were held for reasons that continue to prevail – to liquidate the real assets of a deceased person in order to settle debts and provide for the heirs. It was a sign of the rising importance and value of pictures that many of the major aristocratic collections were entailed, that is to say, incorporated into the permanent patrimony of the title. Both Leganés and Luis de Haro, for instance, adopted this course of action. Collectors of lesser means or greater indebtedness willed their pictures to be sold after they died, a procedure that began with an evaluation of the individual lots. Next, the date of the sale was advertised. Once it had begun, prospective purchasers were free to make lower offers if they questioned an attribution or if lack of interest made the seller receptive to a deal.

Although the size of the secondary market is beyond measure, it was obviously enormous and, as such, bound to have had an impact on the practice of painting, especially when the importation of works from abroad is also taken into account. One important effect was on the repertory of Spanish painters, which is largely devoid of several themes commonly found in seventeenth-century European painting, especially landscape, scenes of everyday life, and mythology.

Landscape specialists were rare in Spain; one example is Francisco Collantes, who

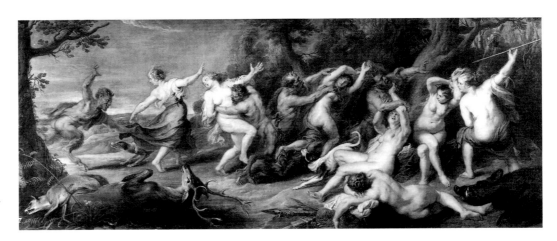

197. Peter Paul Rubens, *Diana and Nymphs Surprised by Satyrs*, ca. 1635–40. Madrid, Prado, canvas, 1.36 × 1.65m.

worked in Madrid in the 1630s and 1640s and produced a few excellent landscapes with figures, drawing on both Flemish and Italian sources.[27] Ignacio de Iriarte (1621–70), active in Seville from around 1642, is another, but very few of his works have been identified.[28] The Madrid painters Juan Martínez del Mazo and Benito Manuel Agüero (ca. 1626–70) painted fine landscape compositions modeled after the works by Claude and his colleagues in the Buen Retiro.[29] Similarly, Murillo produced magnificent landscapes with figures in his scenes from the life of Jacob (pl. 245). And Velázquez's incomparable views of the Villa Medici (pls. 202 and 203) are among the greatest landscapes of the century. However, even allowing for the occasional work by a principal artist, there is no denying that landscape painting played a distinctly secondary role in the output of Spanish painters.

Much the same can be said for genre paintings.[30] The best examples were produced by Velázquez (pl. 111) and Murillo (pl. 266), but these were brief episodes in careers devoted primarily to portraiture and religious subjects respectively. A splendid if tiny number of rough-hewn scenes of everyday life has been attributed to Antonio Puga (pl. 196), although his authorship is far from certain.[31] Otherwise, this class of painting was little cultivated in Golden Age Spain.

The relative paucity of mythological works by Spanish artists has usually been attributed to the influence of church doctrine, which regarded antique subjects as a pretext for representing the naked body and thus arousing the baser instincts of the viewer.[32] This explanation is plausible insofar as it concerns native painters, but it does neglect a crucial point – that quantities of mythological scenes were owned by private collectors, beginning with the king, who proudly displayed suggestive mythologies by Titian and Rubens on the walls of his palaces (pl. 197). In fact, as the inventories show, all the "missing" subject categories abounded in Spanish collections large and small, proving that there was a significant demand for secular subjects. However, this demand was satisfied primarily through imports, and once the fashion for Flemish landscapes or Italian mythologies had been established, there was to be no stopping it. This explains why Spanish painters were left at the mercy of ecclesiastical patrons except for portraits and still lifes, categories in which they often excelled. But considerations of fashion and the marketplace left them little opportunity to execute other secular subjects and compelled them to concentrate on sacred themes, whatever their private ambitions may have been.

The imported pictures, however, were not without benefits to painters who rarely traveled beyond the frontiers of Spain. The hundreds, if not thousands of paintings in Madrid, many of them superlative masterpieces, enabled the local practitioners to gain a wide acquaintance with foreign art, which would catalyze the formation of new styles of painting in Madrid and Seville.

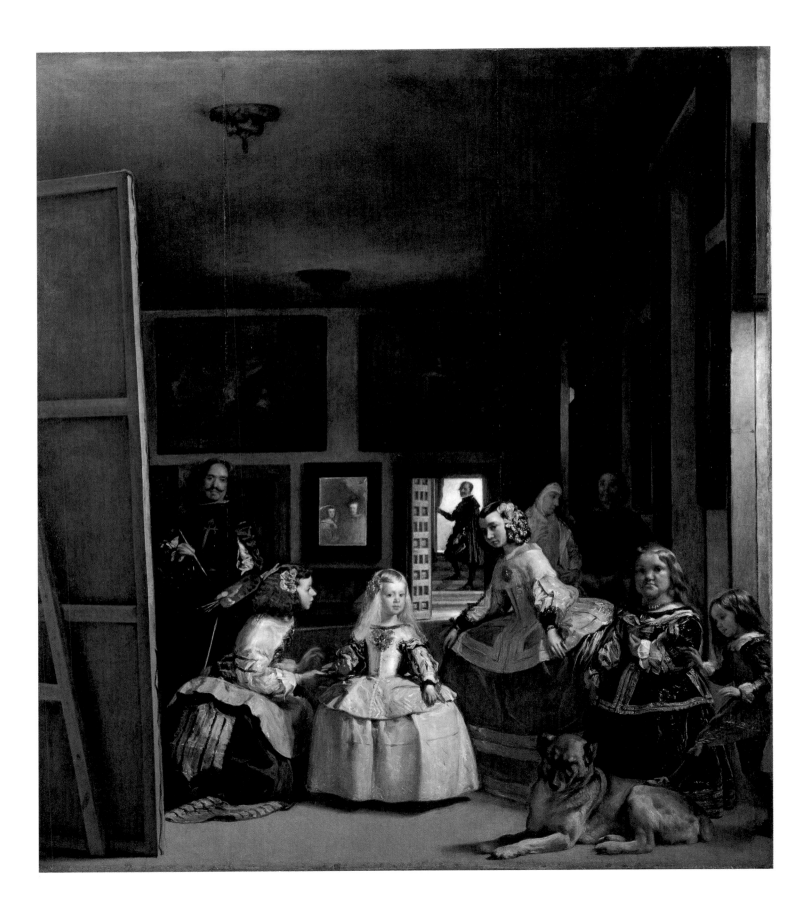

10

Painting in Transition Madrid 1640–1665

THE LATER YEARS of the reign of Philip IV were an unhappy time for the Spanish monarchy. By 1640, it had become clear that the ambitious reforms initiated by Olivares had failed to restore either the reputation or the finances of the crown. Foreign policy was also in ruins, the Spanish army and navy having lost ground in the long, costly wars against the Dutch and the French. Even heavier blows fell in 1640, when first the Catalans and then the Portuguese rebelled against the authority of the king. Catalonia would return to the fold in 1652, but Portugal was lost forever. Although Olivares was dismissed in 1643, the damage had been done, and during the last half of his reign, which ended in 1665, Philip became the remorseful witness of the decline of the great monarchy founded by his ancestors in the sixteenth century. Yet somehow these financial and military disasters did not make a lasting impact on the painters of Madrid. During this period, the foundations were laid for a remarkable efflorescence of the art that occurred in the second half of the century.

Velázquez and the Noble Art of Painting

The calamities that beset the king made the greatest impact on his painter.[1] Throughout the 1630s, Velázquez had been occupied with creating pictures for the Retiro and the Torre de la Parada, as well as with commissions for other clients. But around 1640, his production went into a steep decline, partly precipitated by the war with France. The two countries had declared war in 1635, and the revolt of the Catalans offered an opportunity to the French, who invaded the principality. This occupation of the homeland had to be answered, and whatever Spanish troops could be mustered took to the field, often led by the king himself. In every year from 1642 to 1646, Philip journeyed to Aragon to campaign against the enemy.

Philip's political and military problems were compounded by personal tragedies. On 6 October 1644, his beloved queen, Isabella of Bourbon, died, and two years later, almost to the day, the king suffered an even greater loss with the death of the heir, Prince Baltasar Carlos, then only seventeen years old. In the circumstances, there were few occasions when Velázquez was required to create pictures for his principal patron.

Only a single portrait of the king is datable to these years, the *"Fraga Philip"* (pl. 199), so called because it was painted in the town of this name during the Aragonese campaign of 1644.[2] The goal of this military operation was to recapture Lérida from the French, and in May, a siege was launched from nearby Fraga, where a workshop for the painter was constructed in a ramshackle house. Velázquez started

198. Diego de Velázquez, *Las Meninas*, ca. 1656. Madrid, Prado, canvas, 3.21 × 2.81m.

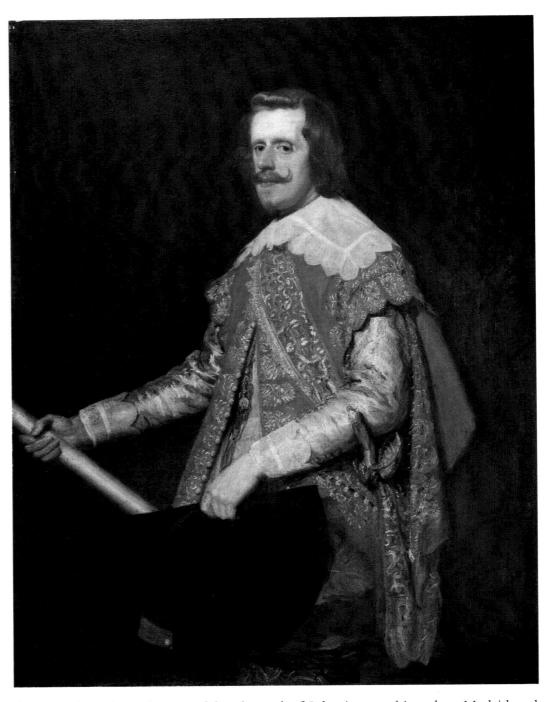

199. Diego de Velázquez, *Philip IV at Fraga*, 1644. New York, Frick Collection, canvas, 1.33 × 0.98m.

the portrait early in June, and by the end of July, it was shipped to Madrid and displayed in public on 10 August, just as Lérida was falling into Spanish hands.

Philip IV at Fraga is an exceptionally restrained image of the militant monarch, although it is in keeping with the tradition of understated portraiture favored by the Spanish Habsburgs.[3] The king of Spain was content to let his worldly power speak for itself, even when it was on the wane. Here, as in all his royal portraits, Velázquez shows the king wearing a fixed, impassive expression, which reveals nothing of his thoughts, feelings, or pretensions. The painter has therefore lavished his artistry on the costume. After his return from Italy in 1631, Velázquez had developed a new technique derived from his study of the late works of Titian and his observations of Rubens in 1628–29. He was impressed by the sketchy, notational brushstroke of these masters, which they used instead of the smoother, more precise technique

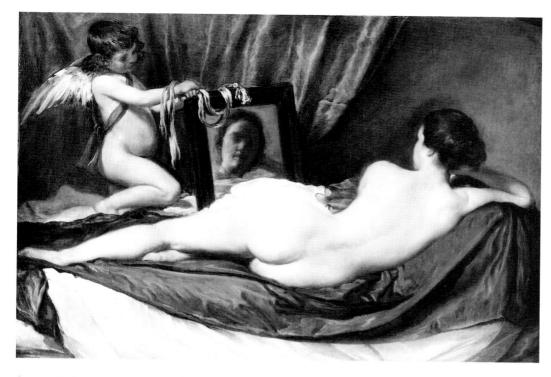

200. Diego de Velázquez, *Venus and Cupid*, ca. 1648. London, National Gallery, canvas, 1.23 × 1.77m.

favored by painters in the classical mode. Velázquez radically simplified this technique by thinning the ground layer to achieve greater luminosity and by employing irregular deposits of pigment to simulate the twinkling play of light on the surfaces.[4] The king's portrait at Fraga is a superb example of this audacious manner. While, at a distance, the geometrical design of the red coat fuses into a glistening pattern of gold and silver, at close range, it dissolves into unruly blobs and daubs of thick pigment.

The major picture of the 1640s was intended for the ne'er-do-well and fledgling collector Gaspar de Haro. This is the famous *Venus and Cupid* (pl. 200), which is listed in an inventory of his collection dated 1 June 1651.[5] The exact circumstances of the commission are unknown, but the painting almost certainly was done before November 1648. In that month, Velázquez departed for his extended trip to Italy and did not return until two weeks after Haro's inventory had been completed.

As has been seen, images of the female nude are exceptionally rare in the output of Spanish Golden Age painters, although not for any want of demand. The royal collection was richly endowed with such paintings as Titian's sensuous "Poesie," and many of Rubens's luscious images of naked women. As in other types of secular painting, the demand for this subject, which usually appeared in representations of antique texts, was satisfied by works of non-Spanish painters, none of whom, however, could match the exceptional intimacy of Velázquez's *Venus and Cupid*. By means of the suggestive pose, rich colors, and tantalizing use of the mirror, Velázquez makes the goddess of love into an irresistible object of desire.

Venus and Cupid, Philip IV at Fraga, and perhaps another seven or eight pictures constitute Velázquez's total extant production from about 1640 to the date of his departure for Italy. Averaged over a period of almost nine years, this amounts to little more than one picture every twelve months, an exceptionally low rate of production even for an artist known to his contemporaries as "phlegmatic." Neither war nor crisis is solely responsible for this dramatic decline in Velázquez's output. Another factor to be reckoned with was his increasing dedication to a new sphere of activity, the care and installation of the royal collection.[6] Despite the defeats and debacles of the 1640s, Philip IV remained interested in acquiring fine pictures, and as the collection grew ever more impressive, he decided to create carefully planned ensembles to accentuate its effect. Starting in 1643, the major galleries of the Alcázar and the principal rooms of the Escorial were redecorated under the supervision of Velázquez, and these projects consumed increasing amounts of time and inevitably reduced his production. However, the rewards were considerable, both in money and in prestige, and Velázquez was eager to enjoy them.

During the 1620s and 1630s, Velázquez had slowly been making his way up the hierarchy of household servants, and as he ascended the social ladder, he earned not only more money but also more of the confidence of the king. Although Velázquez could not aspire to the status of a grandee, his participation in the decorative projects afforded him a close, continual contact with the monarch, enjoyed by only a small number of courtiers. This association was crucial to his ambition to establish painting as a noble art and its practitioners as gentlemen.

It has already been observed that the nobility of painting had become a major issue in the seventeenth century[7] and that a small but articulate group of practitioners had constantly struggled to change the climate of opinion. The attempts to form a royal academy constitute one aspect of their efforts, but since this idea verged on monopoly, it was unacceptable to the many painters who could not or would not qualify for membership. Theoretical works that argued the case were another approach to the problem, but these arguments could be effective, if at all, only in the long term. Much more pressing and immediate was the battle against the imposition of the *alcabala* on works of painting. The *alcabala*, as mentioned above, was a general sales tax of ten percent levied on manufactured goods. Because pictures were classified in this category, painters were obliged to pay the tax, which they believed debased their art. Thus, from time to time, they brought suit against the Council of Finance to obtain exemption. The juridical arguments could be quite complex, but the fundamental issues were clear enough – painting was an art, not a craft, a profession, not a trade, and as such was exempt from a mercantile impost.

The most famous legal action in defense of painting was instigated in 1626, after the tax collector had attempted to exact the *alcabala* from a group of painters in Madrid,[8] among them Carducho and Cajés, neither of whom was disposed to capitulate without a fight. They engaged a lawyer to argue the case, and enlisted in their cause some of the leading figures in the literary world, including Lope de Vega and Lorenzo van der Hamen. (Carducho includes their opinions in an appendix to *Diálogos de la pintura*.) On 13 November 1630, the justices of the Council of Finance ruled that painters were exempt from tax on their own pictures, but would be liable when they or anyone else sold paintings by other artists. The painters considered this verdict to be unsatisfactory and pressed their suit, and on 13 January 1633, the appeals court ruled in their favor and exempted all paintings from the tax. This judgment, which took seven years to obtain, was breached a mere three years later. In 1636, the Council of Finance, hard pressed for revenues to fight the war against France, again levied the tax. The painters fought and won another victory, only to find the tax collector again knocking at their doors in 1640. And so it went for the rest of the century – taxation, litigation, exemption, followed again by new taxation. The nobility of painting, although a fine idea, was all too fragile to resist the urgent requirements of a bankrupt treasury.

Although Velázquez's name is notably absent from these interminable legal maneuvers, he was by no means indifferent to the outcome. In 1627, he had signed a petition of the painters' guild, then headed by his younger brother Juan, seeking exemption from a special one-percent tax. For some reason, he did not participate in the subsequent proceedings, although his position as court painter did not exempt him from the *alcabala*. Instead, he determined to work within the system in the hopes of establishing at least his own claims to nobility. Personal service to the king was his chosen course of action, and to this endeavor he now began to devote much of his time and energy.

The inception of Velázquez's career as court decorator can be dated to 9 June 1643, when he was appointed as assistant superintendent of private works (*obras particulares*). Earlier in the year, on 6 January, he had been promoted to *ayuda de cámara*, which provided entry into the king's private quarters, and as a result he was now well positioned to be in frequent contact with his monarch. The first decorative project, which was initiated in 1645, after the king had returned from the Aragonese campaign of 1644, was the Octagonal Room of the Alcázar. Extensively remodeled and decorated with hunting scenes by Rubens and monumental bronze statues of the Seven Planets, this section was completed in 1648. The king and the painter then turned their attention to the decoration of several other rooms, including the Hall of Mirrors.

Their guiding principle was to combine great paintings with statuary, following the model of Italian galleries. While the royal collection was certainly not wanting in pictures, works of sculpture, which had never been of primary interest to the Spanish kings, were in short supply. Thus, it was decided to send Velázquez to Italy to obtain casts, if not originals, of antique sculpture and other decorative pieces.

After leaving Madrid in late November 1648, he went to Venice to search for pictures, and then made his way to Rome, arriving in April 1649.[9] There he remained until November 1651, organizing a team of sculptors and supervising the making of casts. Given the pressure of work and time (the king was very eager for his return), he was able to paint but few pictures, mainly portraits of the papal court, beginning with the pope himself.

Velázquez's portrait of Innocent X (pl. 201) is one of his greatest. Although he employed a pose traditionally reserved for high-ranking ecclesiastics (pl. 88), he endowed the aged pontiff with unremitting psychological energy, in contrast to the emotionally neutral approach of his royal portraits. At the same time, he took the opportunity to enlist Innocent X's support for his greatest ambition, election to an order of knighthood. This plan met with success, for on 17 December 1650, the papal secretary of state wrote to the nuncio in Madrid instructing him to assist the artist's pretensions.

Besides attending to official duties and commissions, Velázquez did at least two paintings for his own pleasure. These are the views of the gardens of the Villa Medici, works of amazing spontaneity and virtuosity (pls. 202 and 203).[10] In the 1620s, a few northerners in Rome began to draw out of doors, a practice continued during the 1640s by Claude Lorrain, whose luminous landscape drawings of the countryside are the immediate forerunners of Velázquez's experimental works. But whereas Claude made drawings, Velázquez made paintings; in fact, these little canvases appear to be among the first landscapes executed in the open air. By appropriating the allusive technique of watercolor with its broad, summary treatment of forms, and working with subdued colors, he created almost palpable effects of light and atmosphere. It is unfortunate that Velázquez never attempted to expand his mastery of the genre, but once back in Madrid, he had little time to paint many pictures, except for the indispensable portraits of the royal family and a handful of other works.

Soon after his return, Velázquez was promoted to a higher office, that of *aposentador de palacio* (16 February 1652). The *aposentador* was charged with the maintenance of the king's quarters, a job that went hand in hand with the remodeling of the palace. The honor was great, but so were the responsibilities, and Velázquez now had even less time for painting, especially because the decorative projects were making increasing claims on his attention. Besides the rooms in the Alcázar, Velázquez was supervising the improvement of the Escorial. The work was started in 1654 and carried out with great intensity over the next two years. In October 1656, Philip paid a visit to the monastery to inspect the results, and they were spectacular. The sacristy and a chapter room had been turned into a veritable museum of great paintings, many of which had once belonged to the late Charles I of England.

Two years later, the final phase of the decoration of the Hall of Mirrors was launched with the arrival of the Bolognese fresco painters Agostino Mitelli and Angelo Michele Colonna, who were commissioned to execute a ceiling fresco above the magnificent canvases by the king's favorite artists – Titian, Veronese, Tintoretto, Rubens, and van Dyck. The only living painter deemed worthy of this company was Velázquez himself.

Velázquez had earned his reward, and now Philip was prepared to grant it. On 6

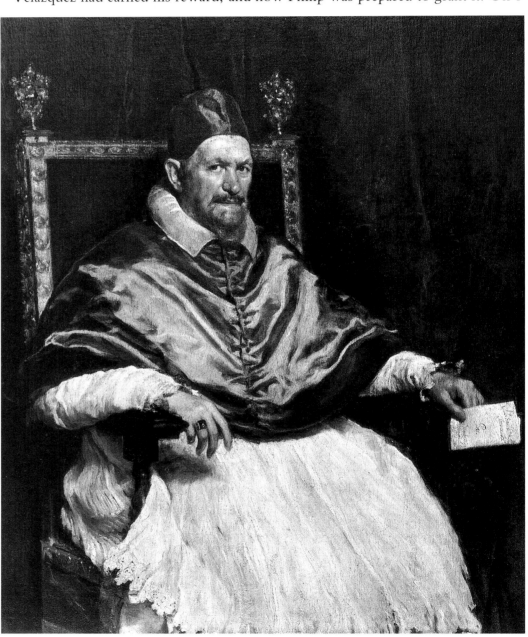

201. Diego de Velázquez, *Innocent X*, 1649–50. Rome, Galleria Doria–Pamphili, canvas, 1.40 × 1.20m.

218

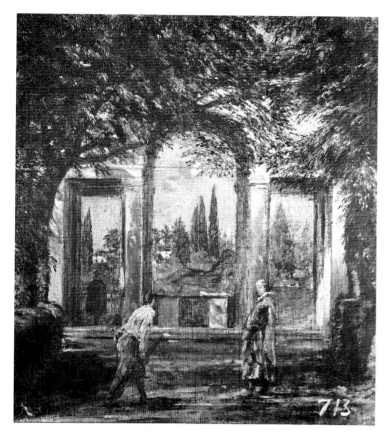

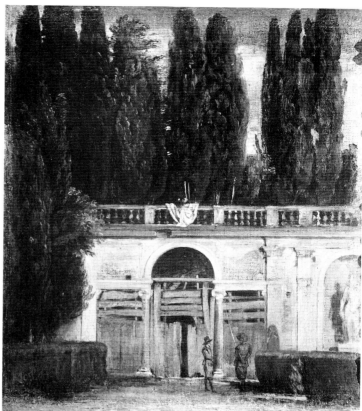

June 1658, he nominated the artist for a knighthood in the order of Santiago.[11] During the succeeding months, the Council of Orders looked into every corner of Velázquez's lineage and personal history, interviewing 148 witnesses in Seville, Madrid, and on the Portuguese border, near the site where his family had its origins.

The Council's verdict, rendered on 26 February 1659, must have come as a great surprise: it rejected the nomination on the grounds that the noble status of Velázquez's paternal grandmother and that of both maternal grandparents was unproven. There now seems to be no doubt that the genealogical evidence did in fact establish that both sets of Velázquez' grandparents belonged to a lower order of nobility. By inference, the true reason was Velázquez's profession. Painters were qualified for membership in the Order of Santiago, provided they did not accept payment for their works. Several of Velázquez's colleagues – Zurbarán, Cano, Carreño, and Nardi among them – gave statements to this effect, but everyone knew they were lying.

Velázquez could only have been shocked by the decision. The attempt to enhance his prestige had resulted in public humiliation. On 3 April, the Council advised the king that a papal dispensation would be needed to excuse the unproven nobility, and this was quickly obtained. However, the matter did not end there: on 3 August, the Council informed the king of a new genealogical flaw. Yet another papal dispensation was required, and when it arrived, the Council was compelled to admit Velázquez to the Order of Santiago (28 November 1659). The knighthood thus obtained was a pyrrhic victory. Without the king's unflagging support, Velázquez's application would have surely been rejected by those noblemen who refused to accept painting as a gentlemanly pursuit. For Velázquez, it validated his decision to devote his time to the personal service of the monarch. For the painters of Madrid, there was less to cheer about, since the process revealed that they were a very long

202. Diego de Velázquez, *Villa Medici, Pavilion of Cleopatra–Ariadne*, 1649–50. Madrid, Prado, canvas, 2.44 × 0.38m.

203. Diego de Velázquez, *Villa Medici, Grotto-Loggia Façade*, 1649–50. Madrid, Prado, canvas, 0.48 × 0.42m.

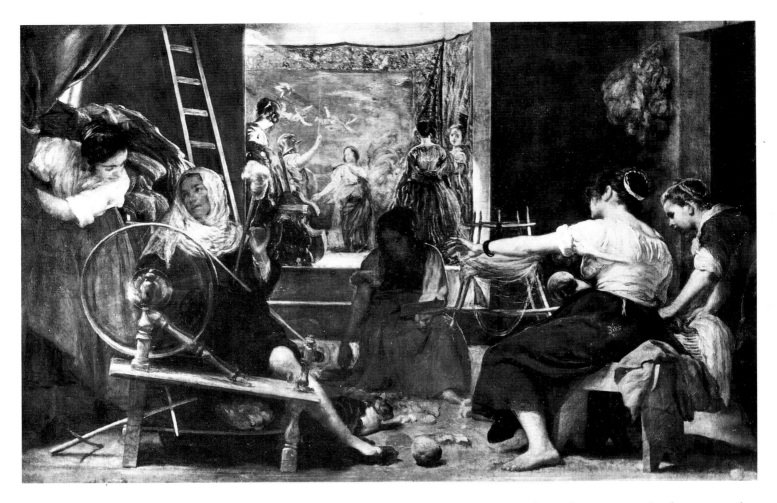

204. Diego de Velázquez, *Fable of Arachne*, ca. 1656–58. Madrid, Prado, canvas, 1.17 × 1.90m. (original size).

way from gaining social acceptance. It must have been recognized at once that Velázquez's admission to Santiago did not establish a precedent but was merely the exception that proved the rule.

In the years just prior to this affair, Velázquez painted his masterpieces: the *Fable of Arachne* and *Las Meninas*. A definitive interpretation of these allusive pictures is not to be had in this age of deconstruction, but a few observations on their historical circumstances, and especially their place in the trajectory of the artist's career, are indispensable. Although the paintings are not documented, it is generally agreed that they were done around 1656–58, at the time when Velázquez's ambitions for a knighthood were reaching a climax. His claims for the nobility of his art are firmly embedded in these multi-layered works.

The *Fable of Arachne* (pl. 204), which was owned by the court official Pedro de Arce, illustrates an episode from Ovid's *Metamorphoses*.[12] Arachne was a renowned weaver who challenged the goddess Minerva to a tapestry-weaving competition. Although the contest ended in a tie, Arachne was the ultimate loser. Minerva, first offended by Arachne's presumptuousness and then enraged by her choice of a subject that mocked Jupiter, punished the young woman by turning her into a spider.

Most earlier depictions of the myth represent the climax of the story, the metamorphosis of Arachne. In Velázquez's version, the action is centered on the previous moment in the narrative, when Arachne stands proudly in front of her great creation. This tapestry refers pointedly to the pretensions of painting as a noble activity. Although partly obscured, it is a copy of Titian's *Rape of Europa* (pl. 53), one of the "Poesie" then in the Alcázar. By quoting this famous work, Velázquez

220

implies that Titian, like Arachne, was a worthy rival of Minerva. If true, then painting had to be a divine, or at least a noble, art.

The copy of Titian's composition has another dimension. Titian was the favorite painter of Charles V and Philip II, who rewarded him with honors and emoluments. Charles, in fact, had granted him a knighthood in the Order of the Golden Spur, demonstrating that this greatest of rulers had accepted painting as a noble art. By quoting Titian in the *Fable of Arachne*, Velázquez, like a lawyer arguing his case, provides a famous precedent for his own aspirations.

In *Las Meninas* (pl. 198), the painter no longer resorts to subterfuge.[13] The king and queen appear in person, if discreetly reflected in a mirror, and bestow their approval on Velázquez and his art, as does the infanta Margarita. To avoid any confusion about the significance of the event, Velázquez sets the scene in the very suite of rooms where he did his work.[14] In a society that equated access to the king with high rank and favor, the significance of this visitation would have been blatant. Velázquez, the gentleman painter, stands confidently at the easel, basking in the glory of the monarch's person. And on his breast, the vibrant red cross of Santiago marks the artist as a nobleman.

The strongest support, however, for Velázquez's claims lies at a deeper level. In the artistic theory of the period, painters were warned against copying nature and urged to use it only as the initial step of the creative process. Carducho puts it this way:

> Nature has to be studied, not copied, and thus to make use of it, it then has to be thought about, speculating on the good and bad of its very essence, and on its accidents (or flaws). . . . And once art and science have been made of it, it will only serve to remind and awaken what has been forgotten. . . . And it may be useful to have it before you not simply to copy, but to study carefully, and to awaken the spirit of fantasy, arousing and bringing to mind dormant ideas. . . .[15]

Velázquez turns this notion on its head by creating a "perfect" work of art exclusively in naturalistic terms. Everything has been done to make it seem as though the events were happening right in front of the spectator, and yet each of the moves has been carefully calculated. *Las Meninas* is among the rare paintings that summarize the experiences of the past and predict the experiments of the future. If this masterpiece were not to be considered a noble work of art, then truly the cause was lost.

Velázquez's final days were consumed by his duties as *aposentador*. In 1659, Spain and France at last decided to end their long, exhausting war, and peace terms were arranged that included the marriage of Louis XIV to the infanta María Teresa. The final act of the treaty was a meeting between the French and Spanish rulers which occurred on 1 June 1660, on the Isle of Pheasants, a neutral site near the frontier. Velázquez was in charge of providing accommodations for the royal entourage along the route to the north and decorating the structure where the meeting would take place. This arduous work exhausted the last of his energy. He returned to Madrid on 26 June and just over a month later, died of a fever. His funeral was attended by dignitaries of the church and court, as befitted a person of his rank.

Painters of the Transition

Residing in the palace and unencumbered by the forces of the marketplace, Velázquez lived in splendid isolation from the larger world of painters. In these fortunate circumstances, he painted as he pleased and charted a path through

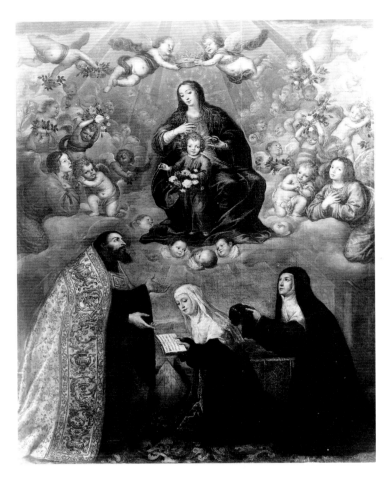

205. Antonio de Pereda, *Profession of Sor Ana Margarita to St. Augustine*, 1650. Madrid, Convento de la Encarnación, canvas, 2.97 × 2.30m.

unexplored artistic territory. Ordinary artists, on the other hand, lived ordinary lives, scrambling for commissions and taking whatever work was offered – restoring and repairing old pictures, evaluating collections, selling their canvases from the shops where they planted their easels. The history of their art is quite distinct from the career of Velázquez, but it is by no means uneventful.

In the 1640s, the gears of change began to grind. Painters who had established their styles and reputations in the previous decade continued to flourish, while younger artists were launching careers and widening their horizons. Despite the parlous conditions, there was work for all, as ecclesiastical institutions continued to demand paintings. The apparent contradiction between the decline of the monarchy and the stability of the need for religious paintings is not difficult to explain: ecclesiastical revenues often were derived from properties and donations largely unaffected by the problems of the monarchy. In addition, it was generally accepted that the patronage of a family chapel in a church or monastery furthered the quest for salvation, and private individuals sought to improve the odds by commissioning pictures that proclaimed their faith.

The death in 1638 of Vicente Carducho, a dominant figure in the ecclesiastical market, immediately opened the way for the older artists working in his shadow. One of these was Antonio de Pereda, who had seemed destined for a great career at court until the death of his protector, Giovanni Battista Crescenzi, in 1635 left him without a sponsor and forced him to turn to religious clients.[16] Like many a Madrid painter, he cast his net over all of central Castile, executing altarpieces for churches in Alcalá de Henares, Toledo, and Valladolid.

Pereda's main sources of support were the churches and monasteries of Madrid, who appreciated his hybrid style. While remaining faithful to the tradition of the Carduchos in his solid, carefully drawn forms and fondness for naturalistic details, he was also receptive to the growing interest in more dynamic compositions that emerged in the 1640s. In some ways, Pereda's position resembles that of Zurbarán in his later years: both painters perceived the need to remake their art in accordance with new norms of taste, but were unable to eradicate all traces of their initial manner.

A characteristic example of Pereda's transitional style is the *Profession of Sor Ana Margarita to St. Augustine* (pl. 205).[17] Sor Ana Margarita, the illegitimate daughter of the king, professed in the Order of the Agustinas Recoletas in 1650, an event commemorated in this picture of the same date. In the lower part, Pereda deploys the same architectonic forms used in the *Relief of Genoa* (pl. 127), rendering the rich clothstuffs in a technique bordering on hyper-realism, while in the scene of heavenly glory, he introduces the lively, active putti who energize this part of the canvas.

As a figure painter, Pereda attained only a partial synthesis between the old and the new. As a still-life painter, he was not obliged to reconcile the static with the mobile or the fugitive with the permanent, and the results are magnificent. In *Still Life with Fruit*, executed at mid-century (pl. 206), he revives the time-honored composition of objects arranged on a shallow ledge, illuminated by a strong light. Yet the nubby, granular textures and warm colors are new, distinctive elements in Spanish still-life painting. Pereda was able to find employment into the 1660s, but by the time he died in 1678 his compromise style had become archaic.

The 1640s were exceptionally eventful for another older artist, Alonso Cano.[18] Cano had moved to Madrid in 1638 to serve as painter to the count-duke and soon after his arrival, joined the team of painters working in the Gilded Hall of the Alcázar. Two years later, he accompanied Velázquez on a journey through Castile to collect paintings for the Buen Retiro.

Cano's employment at court was terminated in January 1643, when Olivares fell

206. Antonio de Pereda, *Still Life with Fruit*, 1650. Lisbon, Museu Nacional d'Arte Antiga, canvas, 0.75 × 1.43m.

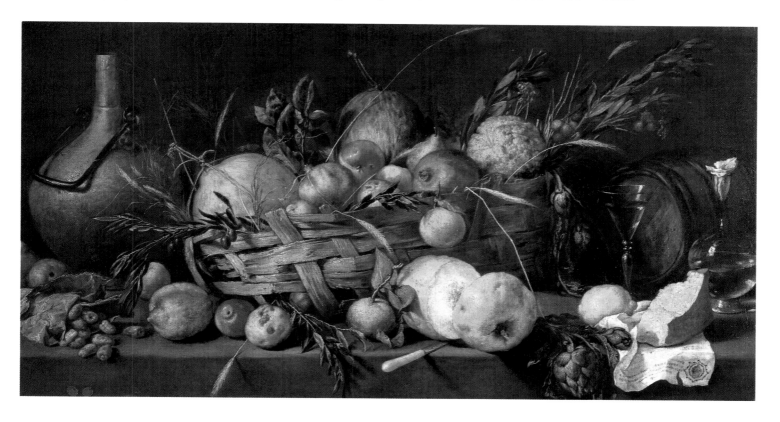

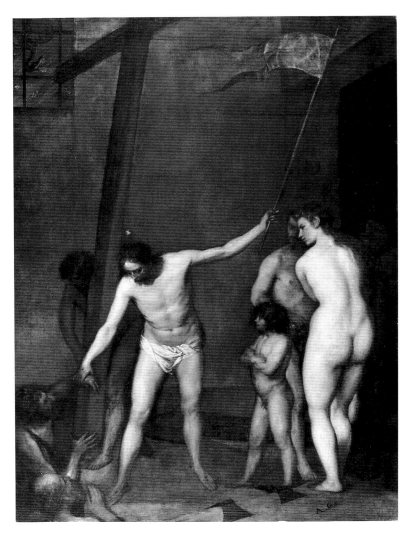

207. Alonso Cano, *Christ's Descent into Limbo*, 1645–50. Los Angeles, County Museum of Art, Gift of Miss Bella Mabury, canvas, 1.69 × 1.21m.

from power. He tried to recoup by applying for the position of principal painter at Toledo cathedral, but was unsuccessful. This misfortune was followed by disaster: on 10 June 1644, his wife, María Magdalena de Uceda, was brutally murdered in bed. Although the murderer was never identified, the authorities initially suspected that he had been hired by Cano. According to one account, the painter was questioned under torture before he was acquitted.

His life and career shattered, Cano sought refuge in Valencia, but by September 1645, after an absence of some fifteen months, he was back in Madrid. Over the next six years, Cano found work where he could, mostly doing devotional pictures. Contemporary sources depict him as a person who preferred talking to painting, which might explain his reduced output. Ultimately, he decided to make a new beginning in the place of his origins and on 11 September 1651, was appointed by the king as a prebendary in the cathedral of Granada. The canons ratified the appointment on 20 February of the following year, on condition that the painter be ordained within twelve months. As will be seen in chapter 12, this condition proved to be onerous, and Cano's retreat from the world did not bring him peace.

During his years in Madrid, Cano pursued his interest in the study of the human figure. He was an avid collector of prints and drawings, which he used as compositional sources and to enrich his repertory of poses and gestures. A good example is *Christ's Descent into Limbo* (pl. 207), a work of the later 1640s, which follows a print by Giulio Bonasone (active 1531–74). Cano smooths out Bonasone's angular

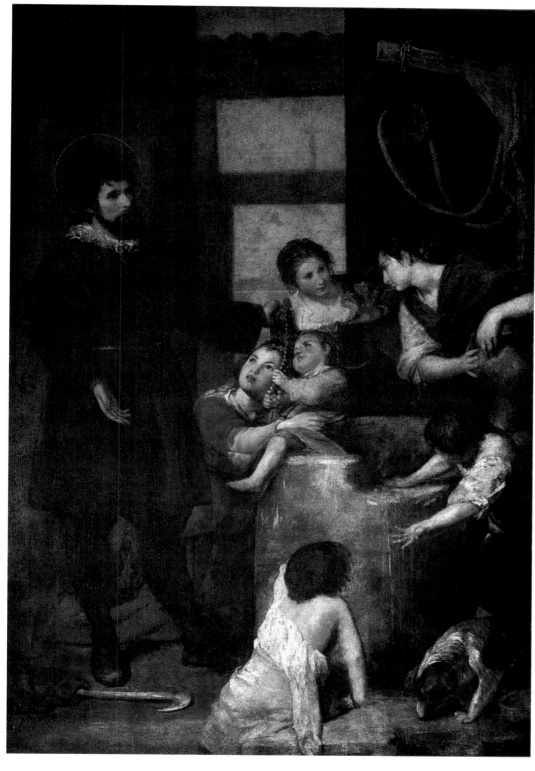

208. Alonso Cano, *St. Isidro and the Miracle of the Well*, 1640–50. Madrid, Prado, canvas, 2.16 × 1.49m.

forms and amplifies the scale of the figures, at the expense of relegating the souls in purgatory to a small corner of the picture.

This painting, although not in good condition, demonstrates how Cano's style changed after his move to Madrid. While in Seville, he created figures with crisp, precise outlines and hard, reflective surfaces. After 1638, there is a pronounced softening and loosening of his technique, the result of making contact with fresh sources of inspiration. Like many a painter of the time, Cano learned a great deal from studying the king's incomparable collection of works by Titian. For example, the figure of Eve in the *Descent into Limbo* presupposes an analysis of the female types found in Titian's *Danäe and the Golden Rain* (Prado), among others.

Another potent influence was Velázquez. More than any painter of the period, Cano was able to comprehend Velázquez's idiosyncratic technique of fractured brushwork, which he effectively imitates in *St. Isidro and the Miracle of the Well* (pl. 208), painted in the 1640s for Santa María de la Almudena.[19]

The painter most profoundly affected by Velázquez was his son-in-law Juan Martínez del Mazo.[20] Little is known of Mazo's life before he entered Velázquez's

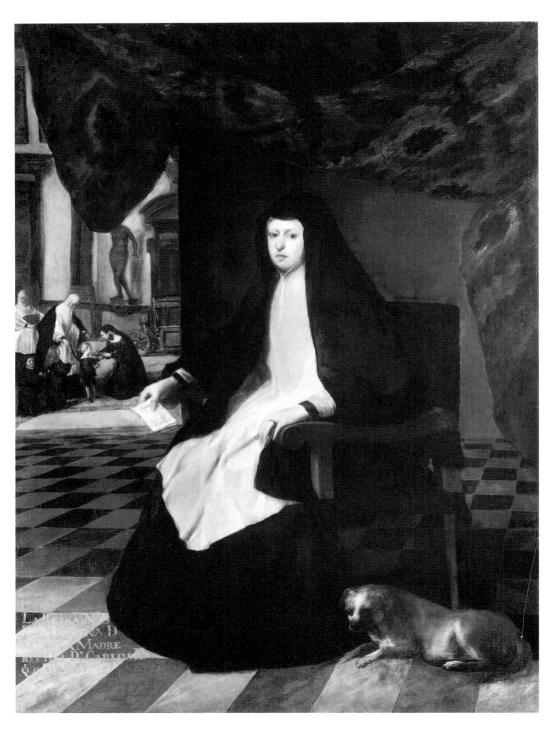

209. Juan Martínez del Mazo, *Queen Mariana*, 1666. London, National Gallery, canvas, 1.97 × 1.46m.

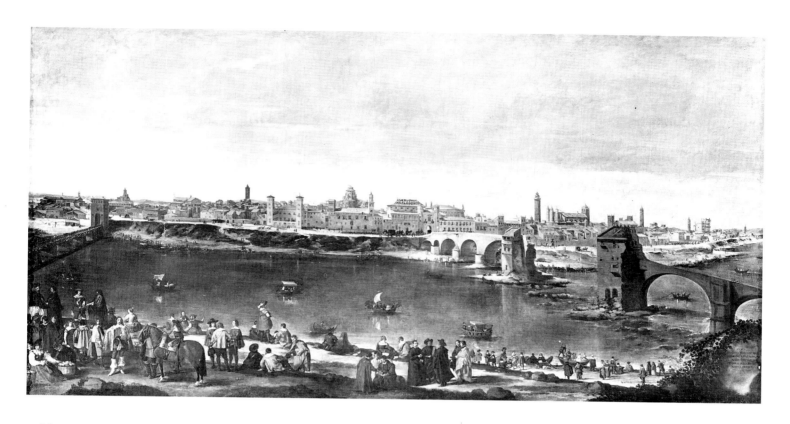

210. Juan Martínez del Mazo, *View of Zaragoza*, 1647. Madrid, Prado, canvas, 1.81 × 3.31m.

orbit. Apparently, he was born in the diocese of Cuenca around 1610–15 and went to Madrid to study painting. On 21 August 1633, he married Velázquez's elder daughter Francisca, the event that guaranteed his future success at court. Velázquez immediately arranged a royal appointment: on 23 February 1634, he transferred to Mazo his post of usher of the King's Chamber. Many years later, in 1657, Mazo was promoted to the rank of *ayuda de furriera*, which was incorporated in the section of the household headed by his father-in-law. In the same year, he traveled to Naples on family business, one of the few Spanish painters of his generation to make the trip. Mazo continued to reap the benefits of the relationship even after Velázquez's death. On 19 April 1661, he succeeded him as court painter and served until he died on 10 February 1667.

As Velázquez's principal assistant, Mazo was charged with making copies and versions of royal portraits. Thus, he came to depend on Velázquez for his art as well as his living, and "Mazo" has become the attribution of convenience for scores of rather terrible paintings which repeat compositions by the master. His quality is more fairly judged in a picture such as *Queen Mariana* of 1666 (pl. 209) which imaginatively expands the repertory of royal portraiture by using an identifiable setting, the Octagonal Room of the Alcázar. This composition became a stock in trade of Juan Carreño de Miranda, one of Mazo's successors as court painter.

Mazo found his own niche as a landscapist, an aspect of his work still awaiting definition, in part because his production was so varied. The most interesting landscapes depict hunting exercises and outdoor festivities, a type of painting only rarely executed by Spanish artists. His scenes of the royal hunt, such as the *Cacería del Tabladillo at Aranjuez* (Prado), are closely dependent on Flemish models, such as the ones executed by Peter Snayers for the Torre de la Parada. Another type of landscape occasionally done by Mazo is the topographical view, a superb example of which is the *View of Zaragoza* (pl. 210), painted in 1647. Mazo also studied the Roman landscapes in the Buen Retiro and produced distinctive interpretations of this poetic genre. These works are distinguished, and place the artist in the forefront of Spanish landscape painters.

A final category of Mazo's production hardly seems worthy of note – his copies of paintings by Titian and Rubens in the royal collection. These are fine pictures in their own right, executed with a lively sense of touch that elevates them above simple mimetic exercises. It is probably no coincidence that they also indicate the sources that would redirect the course of Spanish painting in the later years of the century.

The Presence of Rubens and Titian

The most important catalyst of the changes detectible in the 1640s was the art of Peter Paul Rubens.[21] Although Rubens had been known to Spanish collectors since 1603, it was not until his visit to Madrid in 1628–29 that he began to exert a powerful force on Spanish art. This development was initiated by a substantial increase in the number of his works available in Madrid. In addition to the paintings he brought for the king, and the ones executed during his stay, Rubens had designed the Eucharist tapestries for the convent of the Descalzas Reales.[22] These arrived in Madrid soon after Rubens himself and would make a powerful impression on those who saw the tapestries themselves or the original oil sketches and cartoons, which entered the collection of Luis de Haro around 1650.

It is curious that Rubens had no immediate impact on the artists of Madrid, except Velázquez. In part, this was because the famous Flemish painter had limited contact with his Spanish counterparts. Pacheco, although a biased source, confirms the point: "With painters he communicated but little. Only with my son-in-law (with whom he had corresponded before by letter) did he form a friendship. He greatly favored his works for their modesty and they went together to see the Escorial."[23] Another ten years would pass before the growing quantity of works by Rubens started to make their presence felt.

During the 1630s, and especially between 1636 and 1640, the year of Rubens's death, the king assiduously accumulated his paintings, notably the ones intended for the Alcázar and the Torre de la Parada. After the arrival of the works for the Torre in 1638, Philip ordered eighteen hunting paintings and four other compositions for the New Room of the Alcázar, which were in progress when the painter died. To these were added the eighteen pictures bought from Rubens's heirs in the 1640s. Thus, in about a dozen years, the number of Rubens's paintings in the royal collection had increased greatly.

Philip IV may have been the greatest Spanish collector of Rubens's pictures, but he was not the only one, or even the first, to prize his works. Leganés was an early enthusiast and acquired several important examples, some of which he later gave to the sovereign (pl. 192). Other canvases found their way into local churches, such as the *Martyrdom of St. Andrew* (Madrid, Real Diputación de San Andrés de los Flamencos), which was bequeathed to the Flemish hospital in 1639, and the *Mystical Contemplation of St. Augustine* (Madrid, Academia), which was in the Jesuit church in Alcalá de Henares.[24]

The originals were, of course, most highly cherished, but works by assistants, followers, and copyists were by no means disdained and appear in inventories, large and small. And for those who could not afford works in oil, there were the engraved replicas, which circulated widely and provided artists with a new repertory of compositions, poses, and motifs. It is often said that the photograph opened a new era of artistic diffusion, but the spread of Rubens's art in Spain suggests that prints could be just as effective a way to disseminate an artist's work.

Rubens also played a part in the rediscovery of Titian, the other moving force in the renovation of painting in Madrid.[25] Examples of Titian's work, of course, had long been prized by Spanish collectors, but they did not have a great influence on Spanish painters before 1640. Rubens's copies after Titian changed the indifference to eager interest by revealing the expressive possibilities of what was known as "sketchy" painting.[26] Velázquez was the first to grasp the point and was followed by many younger painters.

The most extraordinary example of the Titianesque is seen in a few works by the little-known Diego Polo, a painter who was born in Burgos around 1610 and died in Madrid some forty-five years later.[27] Polo's exceptional devotion to Titian's style and technique is unmistakable in the *Martyrdom of St. Lawrence* (Lille, Musée Wicar), which until only recently was considered to be a late work by the Venetian himself. The *Israelites Gathering Manna* (pl. 211) is a more independent creation, although the soft, warm colors and the open, pastose brushwork are still greatly indebted to Titian.

The novelty of Rubens and the profundity of Titian were enormously seductive in their own right, but the change in taste had deeper causes as well. One element, perhaps the crucial element, was a change in the tenor of religious spirit and practice. In the sixteenth century, Spain had established itself as the bulwark against the spread of Protestantism. The fusion of the monarchy's spiritual and temporal aspirations effected by Charles V and furthered by Philip II endowed Spanish Catholicism with a militant quality, which was inevitably reflected in the art of the period. In Seville and other places, the orthodoxy of paintings was surveyed by the Inquisition, which compelled artists to represent correct doctrine.

In the early years of the seventeenth century, however, the militant phase of the

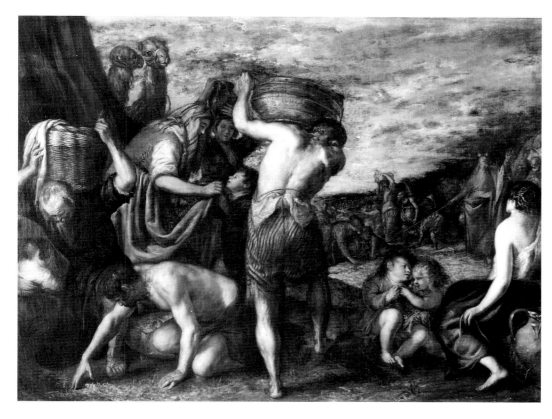

211. Diego Polo, *Israelites Gathering Manna*, 1640–50. Madrid, Prado, canvas, 1.87 × 2.38m.

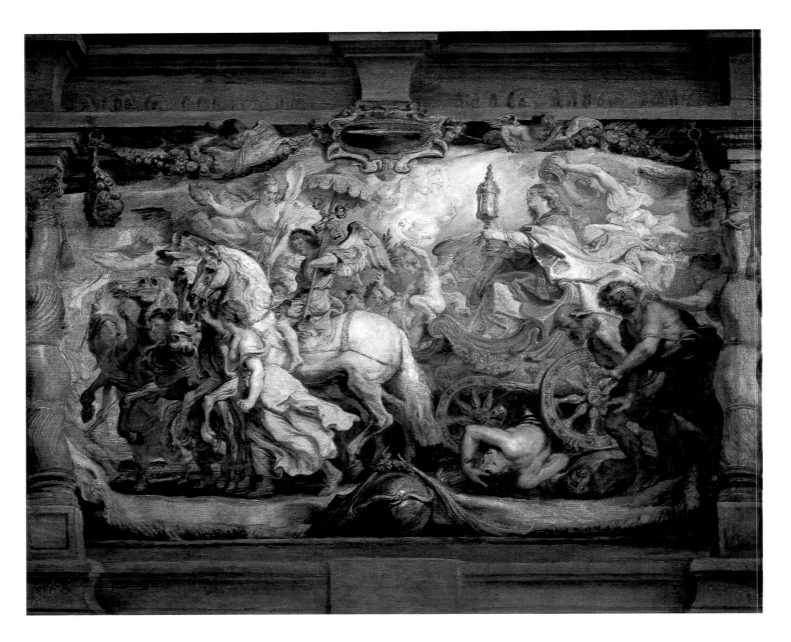

212. Peter Paul Rubens, *Triumph of the Church over Fury, Discord, and Hate* (oil sketch for Eucharist Tapestry), 1628. Madrid, Prado, panel, 0.86 × 0.91m.

Counter Reformation gave way in many parts of Catholic Europe to the wider practice of individual spiritual devotion. This type of worship had long been regarded with suspicion in Spain, where it was believed to border on heterodoxy and to pose a threat to the institutions of the church. Hence the caution and conservatism of ecclesiastical patrons in their artistic commissions. However, by the middle of the century, even Spaniards recognized that the Protestants had been contained if not defeated. In 1648, the monarchy signed the treaty of Münster with the Dutch and concentrated its forces on the conflict with Catholic France, which would last for ten more years. It was a different world when Spain made peace with heretical Protestants and waged war against brother Catholics.

Beyond these extrinsic considerations is the matter of artistic taste. For decades, the painters of Madrid had provided their patrons with eternal truths embodied in stable compositions, as if the confusion and mingling of forms would distract the viewer from the message. The paintings of Rubens offered a new, viable alternative by demonstrating that heightened color and pictorial energy did not necessarily

230

compromise the exposition of doctrine and dogma. The Eucharist tapestries in the Descalzas Reales were a convincing demonstration of the point. Although rich in symbols and complex in composition, they constitute a flawless, ringing exposition of a cardinal doctrine of the Catholic church (pl. 212), and the lesson was not lost on the guardians of religious life.

The career of one painter epitomizes the shifts in taste that occurred during the second part of the reign of Philip IV, that of Francisco Rizi (1614–85), the son of the Italian painter Antonio Ricci and brother of Fray Juan, who was fourteen years his senior.[28] By training as well as birth, Francisco, who also used the hispanicized version of the family name, was a member in good standing of the old guard – his master was Vicente Carducho.

Rizi's affinities with his teacher are evident in his earliest known work, the *Family of the Virgin* (Madrid, Condesa de Casa Loja), painted in 1640 for a priest in Madrid. At this point in his career, Rizi appeared to be poised to perpetuate the Carducho legacy. Every aspect of the painting, especially the facial and figure types, as well as the characteristic contrast of light and dark, derives from his teacher's style.

However, Rizi had other goals and a remarkable capacity to remake himself as an artist. He had worked on the decoration of the Gilded Hall in the Alcázar in 1639 and clearly used the opportunity to study the masterpieces in the palace and the latest works by Rubens and Velázquez. In 1645, he executed the *Adoration of the Magi* (Toledo, cathedral), in which the solid types and stable compositions of his first style are displaced by brighter colors, freer brushwork, and more animated poses.

By the end of the decade, Rizi was working steadily at court, although without an official appointment. Part of his time was dedicated to painting for the Buen Retiro theater, where his undeniable talent for scenographic decorative painting was developed. This is displayed in 1650, in what might be called the first High Baroque altarpiece painting in Spain, the *Virgin and Child with Sts. Philip and Francis* (pl. 213). The composition is enclosed within an illusionistic proscenium arch, behind which is seen a landscape vista drawn in the deep perspective of contemporary stage sets. The Virgin and Child are surrounded by a small army of fluttering putti, whose varied poses imitate the heavenly glories of Rubens. While the main figures are still firmly and solidly drawn, they have taken on a new sense of animation and movement.

Three years later, Rizi obtained the appointment of master painter of Toledo cathedral, for which he would execute several major works. He also expanded his activities outside the capital. In 1654, he agreed to execute two paintings for the main altarpiece of the cathedral of Plasencia and a year later, received a commission for the altarpiece of the parish church of Fuente el Saz (Madrid), which remains intact (pl. 214). The pictures for Plasencia and Fuente el Saz show a further development of Rizi's style, particularly the looser technique and the use of vibrant colors. At Fuente el Saz, he liberates himself from the compact brushstroke of the Carducho school and paints as if he were making large-scale oil sketches. The brush now seems to flicker over the surface, alighting briefly to indicate forms and shapes, while secondary figures in the background are treated as notational indications emerging from the shadows. At the same time, the colors are more brilliant and luminescent, imparting an air of pageantry to the scenes.

Another catalyst behind the change in Rizi's style is a daring, original painter, Francisco de Herrera the Younger, the son of Herrera the Elder,[29] and a seminal figure in both Madrid and Seville. Herrera was not a prolific artist, and several of his most important works, notably his frescoes, have not survived. But even on the available evidence, his significance is undeniable.

Herrera was a good deal younger than Rizi. He was born in Seville in 1627 and

213 (following page). Francisco Rizi, *Virgin and Child with Sts. Philip and Francis*, 1650. El Pardo, Capuchinos.

214 (page 233). Francisco Rizi, altarpiece, 1655. Fuente el Saz (Madrid), parish church.

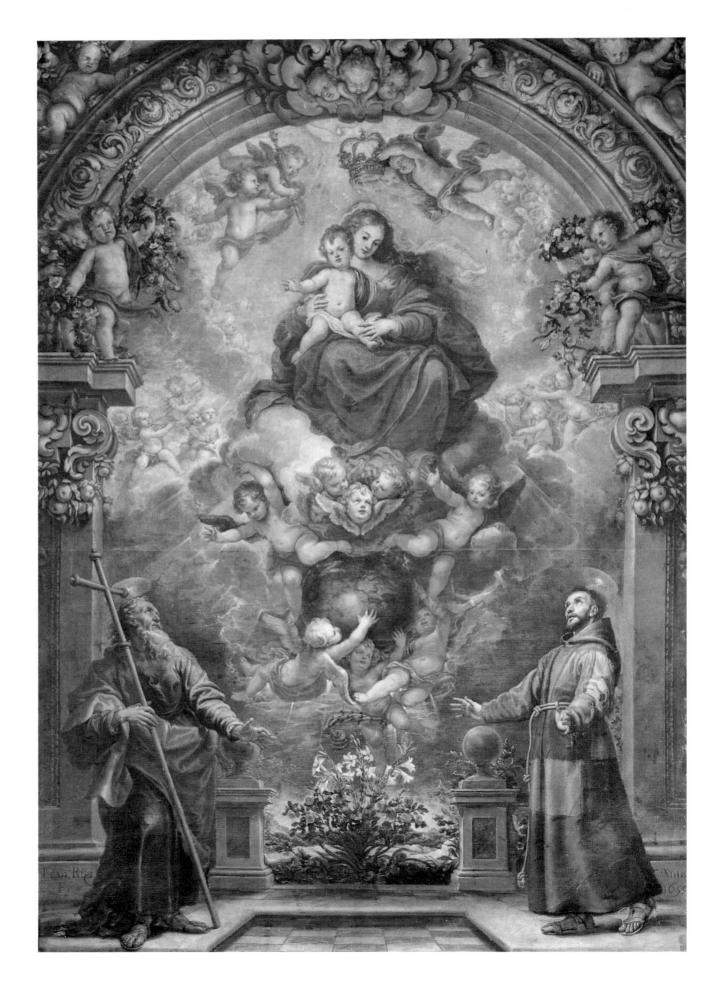

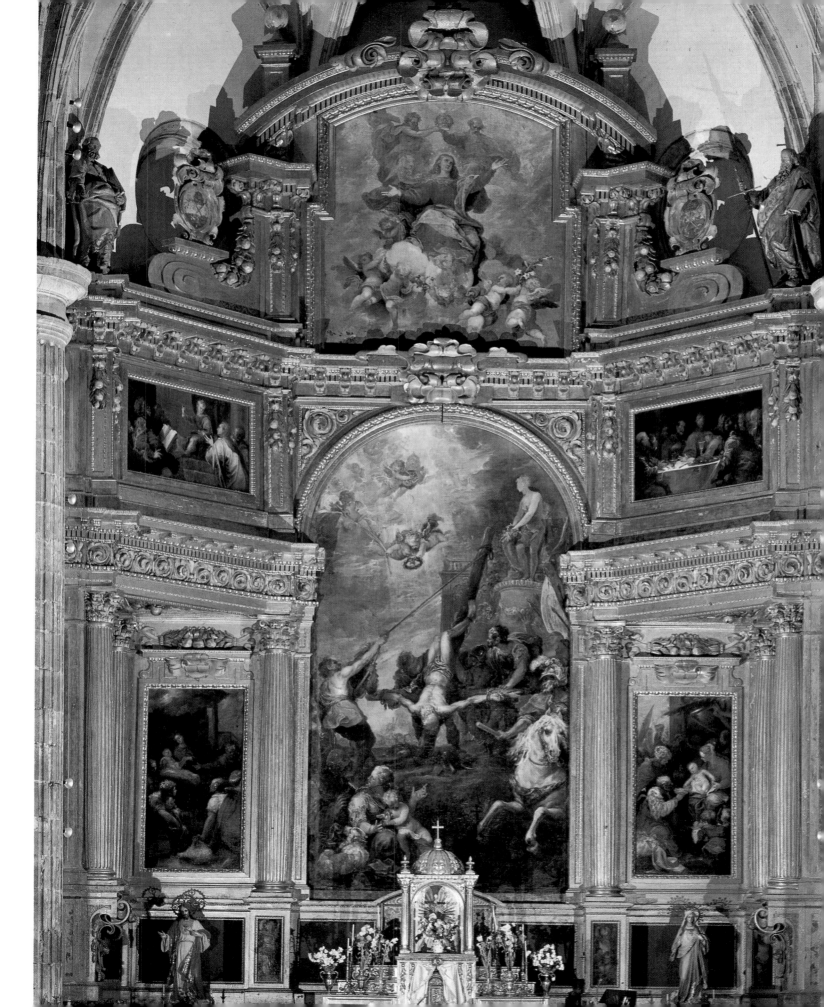

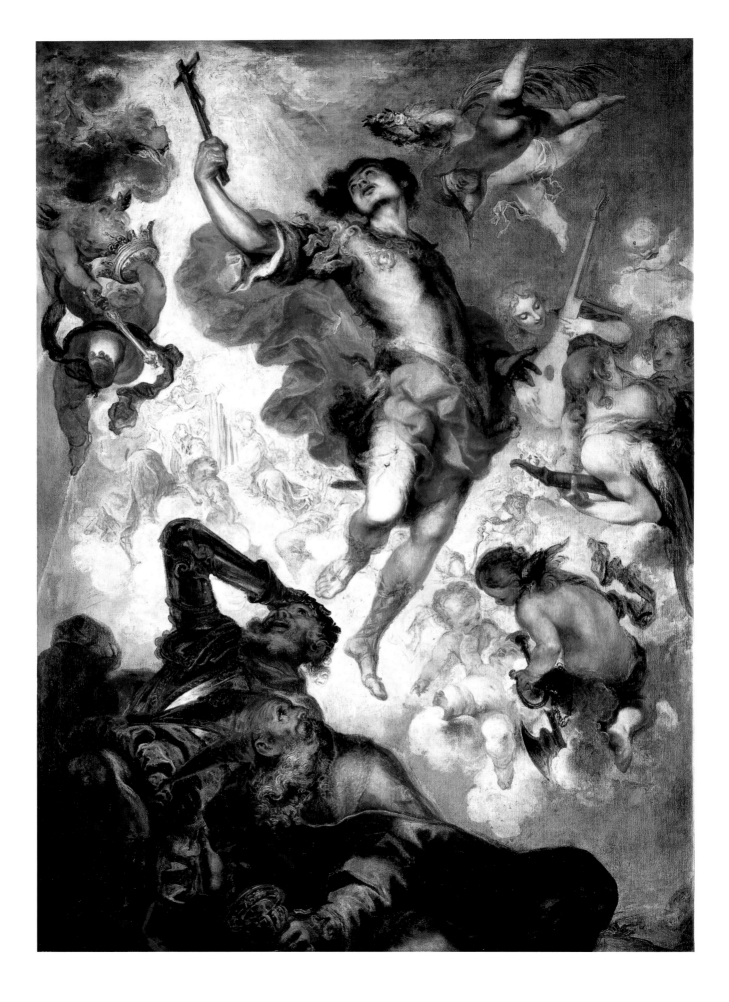

probably studied painting with his father, although little of his early life is documented. Palomino, who met Herrera in his later years, mentions that he rebelled against his quarrelsome father and fled to Rome, where he studied in the academy, became adept in architecture and perspective, and painted still lifes. This trip to Rome has never been substantiated and remains hypothetical.

However, on 17 July 1654, he was in Madrid, where he signed a contract for the altarpiece of the Carmelites of San Hermenegildo (now San José). Only the principal painting remains, but it is a brilliant work of art (pl. 215). The subject is the triumph of St. Hermengild, who died a martyr in prison rather than accept communion in the heretical Aryan faith of his father, Leovigild, the Visigoth king of Spain. St. Hermengild floats in glory above the shadowy figures of King Leovigild and the Aryan bishop, who cower before this irrepressible demonstration of the power of the true faith.

Herrera's painting is a tour de force of theatrical painting, a veritable showpiece of artistic virtuosity. As the documents prove, the entire commission, all fourteen paintings, was completed in just over three months. Palomino, who considered Herrera to be a vain, arrogant man, implies that he intended this work to teach a lesson in talent and showmanship, and in this he succeeded, for the dynamic composition and the amazing freedom of brushwork, especially in the angelic choir, won immediate converts to his style, Rizi among them. Unfortunately, Herrera had to abandon his career in Madrid at this moment; family business required him to return to Seville, where he would make an equal impact.

Meanwhile, Rizi continued to flourish. In 1656, he was appointed royal painter, the first new holder of the title since the death of Carducho eighteen years before, and he expanded his repertory by mastering the art of fresco painting. After the sixteenth century, this technique had virtually become extinct in Spain, and thus when the king wanted to have ceiling frescoes in the Alcázar, it was necessary to hire Italians. While in Rome in 1649–50, Velázquez had been ordered by Philip to secure the services of Pietro da Cortona. After Cortona had declined the offer, two of his collaborators, Angelo Colonna and Agostino Mitelli, accepted the proposal and arrived in Madrid in 1658.

The Italians were renowned specialists in *quadratura*, a type of fresco involving elaborate architectural illusionism, and at once were given several commissions in the Alcázar and the Buen Retiro. Sad to say, none of these frescoes has survived, but a preliminary model of the *quadratura* framework for a ceiling in San Pablo in the Retiro shows their approach (pl. 216),[30] which they taught to Rizi and Juan Carreño de Miranda. Rizi, with his experience as a stage designer, became adept in *quadratura*, while Carreño specialized in executing the figures. Thus, after Mitelli's death in 1660 and Colonna's return to Italy two years later, the two Spaniards were prepared to continue their work.

Rizi and Carreño launched their partnership in a fresco in the *camarín* of Nuestra Señora de Atocha, Madrid (1664), which, like the majority of such decorations in this period, has not survived. A year later, they undertook the decoration of the *camarín* of the Sagrario in Toledo cathedral, which is extant. At the same time, they began their most ambitious project, the cupola of San Antonio de los Portugueses, completed around 1668. This decoration, although repainted in the 1690s by Luca Giordano, is one of the best remaining examples of Baroque fresco painting in Madrid (pl. 217).

Preparatory drawings from Rizi's hand indicate that he planned both the illusionistic architectural framework and the principal scene, the vision of St. Anthony of Padua. Here, as in their other joint projects, Rizi was the dominant partner, designing the overall compositions and executing the complicated architectural

215. Francisco de Herrera the Younger, *Triumph of St. Hermengild*, 1654. Madrid, Prado, canvas, 3.28 × 2.29m.

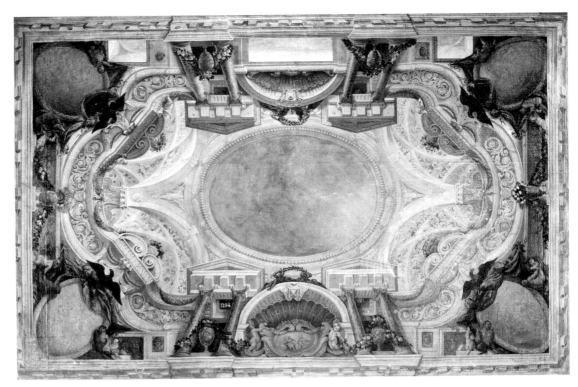

216. Angelo Colonna and Agostino Mitelli, design for a ceiling, 1658–60. Madrid, Prado, canvas, 1.87 × 2.81m.

217. Francisco Rizi and Juan Carreño, cupola, 1665–68. Madrid, San Antonio de los Portugueses.

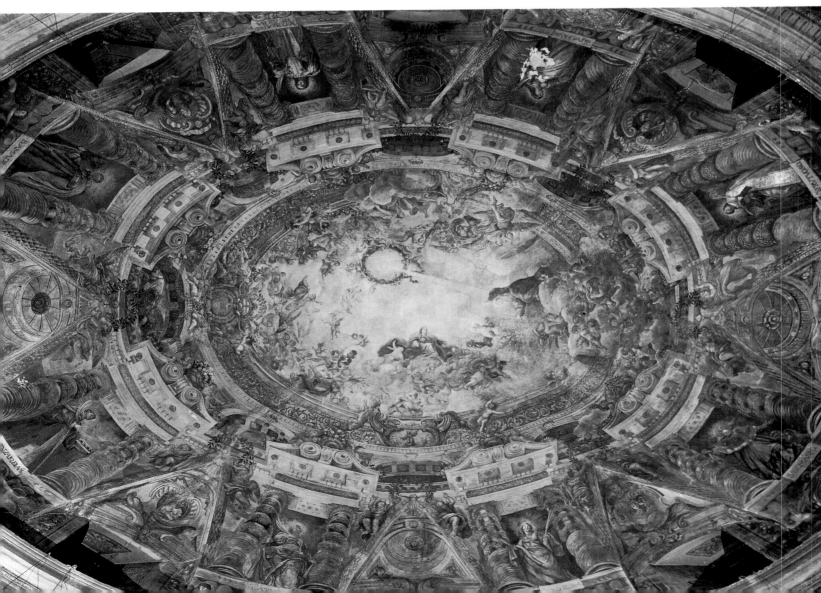

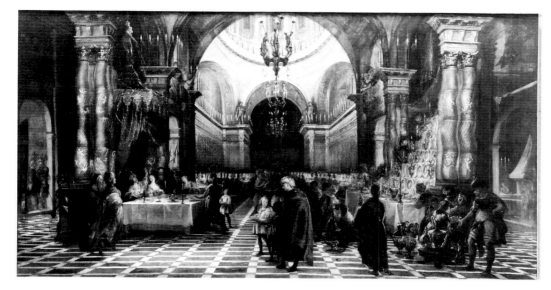

218. Juan Carreño, *Belshazzar's Feast*, 1647. Barnard Castle, Bowes Museum, canvas, 1.72 × 3.28m.

schemes, while Carreño painted the figures. However, there is no denying that Carreño is an excellent artist in his own right and in his own way.

Carreño was born a month before Rizi, on 25 March 1614, in Avilés (Asturias).[31] His father was an impoverished, somewhat eccentric member of the local gentry, who made a living as a picture dealer. Carreño accompanied his father to Madrid in 1625 and commenced an apprenticeship with Pedro de las Cuevas. Although he was an independent artist by the early thirties, there are no datable works before 1646, when he produced *St. Anthony Preaching to the Fish* (Prado), a work still tied to the previous generation.

In the following year, he executed *Belshazzar's Feast* (pl. 218), a curious painting derived mainly from the elaborate interior scenes of Frans Francken the Younger, although the man wearing a turban was lifted from an engraving by Lucas Vosterman after Rubens's *Adoration of the Magi*. This eclectic use of Flemish sources became habitual with Carreño, who lacked the inventiveness of Rizi but was a more seductive painter.

During the 1650s, Carreño fell increasingly under the influence of Rubens. The monumental *Assumption of the Virgin* (Poznán, Muzeum Wielkopolskie), done in the mid-fifties for the church at Alcorcón (Madrid), stems from prints after Rubens's *Assumption* in Antwerp cathedral, while *Santiago at the Battle of Clavijo* (Budapest, Szépmüvészeti Múzeum), signed and dated 1660, paraphrases Rubens's *St. George* (Prado), which Philip IV had acquired from the painter's estate. Carreño also attentively studied paintings by van Dyck, several of which were owned by the king. *St. Sebastian* (pl. 219), painted in 1656 for a private chapel in the convent of the Monjas Bernardas, imitates van Dyck's quasi-feminine treatment of the male nude, while the background is inspired by his warm, crepuscular landscapes. Later in his career, when he was court painter, Carreño would rely heavily on van Dyck as a model for portraiture.

In 1658, Carreño was hired as an assistant by Colonna and Mitelli and began his fruitful collaboration with Rizi. Rizi taught him how to handle the brush with greater facility and to develop an individual manner, using minute touches of pigment to produce scintillating highlights. He also assisted Carreño with his major commission of the 1660s.

In 1664, the Trinitarian order in Pamplona completed a new monastic complex and turned to Carreño and Rizi to paint the altarpiece for the church.[32] The Trinitarian order had been founded in the late twelfth century by the Frenchman

219. Juan Carreño, *St. Sebastian*, 1656. Madrid, Prado, canvas, 1.73 × 1.15m.

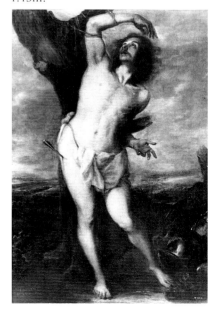

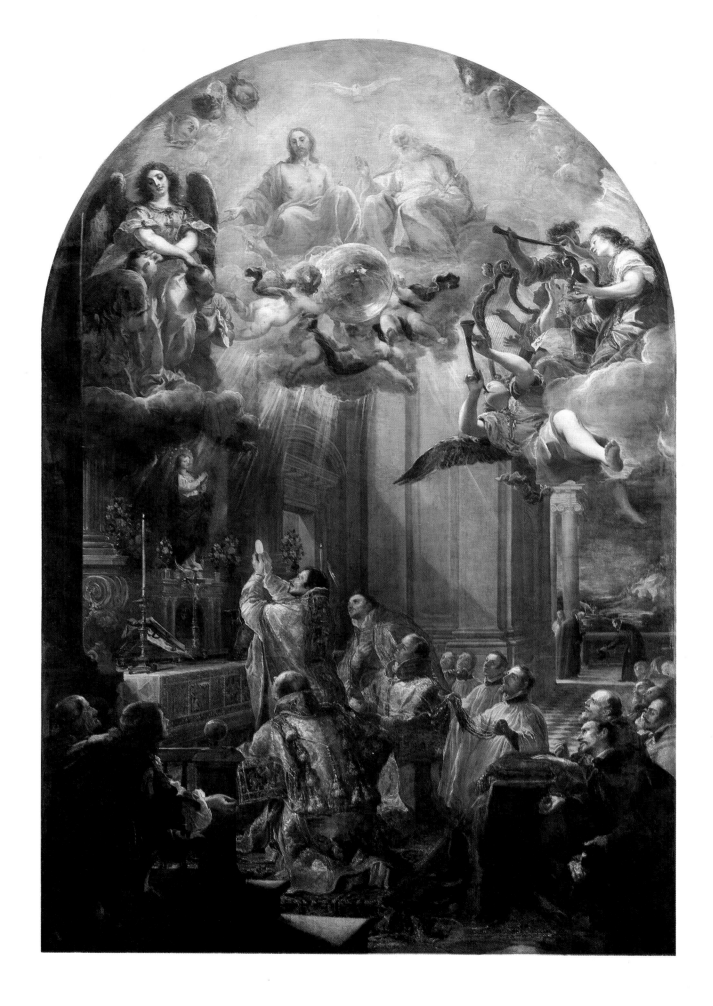

John of Matha, and the altarpiece illustrates a key moment in his career. As St. John raised the host during his first mass, he saw a vision of a young boy dressed in white (here converted into an angel), with arms crossed and hands resting on the heads of two prisoners, one a Christian, one a Moor. From this vision, the future saint divined his worldly mission, to establish a religious order devoted to the redemption of Christian prisoners.

The painting, which is signed only by Carreño and dated 1666 (pl. 220), demonstrates his mastery over a wide range of effects. The composition is set within a monumental space, opening at the right on a serene, luminous landscape. St. John of Matha is flanked by priests wearing rich, sparkling vestments woven with gold and silver threads. The onlookers focus their eyes on the priest, who lifts the sacramental wafer, and lean forward, drawn inexorably by the power of the incipient miracle. Above the throng, in the airy, upper reaches of the space, the artist demonstrates his command of movement and foreshortening. Of Carreño's supreme skill there can be no doubt, although it must be pointed out that the composition was designed by Rizi, in a drawing now in the Uffizi. This would seem to indicate that Carreño was merely the clever assistant of Rizi, the true master, but it would be more accurate to view this and their other collaborative works as if they were musical masterpieces, composed by Rizi and dazzlingly performed by Carreño. This painting represents the culmination of a partnership soon to dissolve; neither artist working alone would again be able to create a picture of this quality and complexity.

The *Mass of St. John of Matha* represents the triumph of the international Baroque style in Madrid. During the 1640s and 1650s, Rizi, Carreño, and Herrera consciously turned to the art of Flanders and Italy, seeking to give shape to the changing religious ideas and aesthetic tastes of their clientele. The stern, ascetic style of the first half of the century, with its unremitting realism, somber colors, and strong chiaroscuro, had been succeeded at last by an ebullient, colorful pictorial mode comparable to what was being produced in other European centers. As in the sixteenth century, the changes were catalyzed by the work of foreign artists. Whereas in the sixteenth century the transformations occurred principally through the interchange of artists between Italy and Spain, in the seventeenth century the importation of art works was a crucial factor.

This type of secondhand stylistic transmission had both advantages and limitations. Learning to imitate Rubens's art by studying his paintings was not the same as being a disciple or member of the workshop. The artists who worked directly with the master learned his manner through systematic study and close supervision. The painters of Madrid saw only the finished products, from which they selected the techniques and effects that most readily lent themselves to imitation. Rubens's powerful compositions, refulgent colors, and dashing brushwork were easily assimilable; his full-bodied figure style, which resulted from the long study of classical and Renaissance art, and his fecund interpretations of pagan and Christian history, were not as easily conquered. On the other hand, the Spanish painters were inspired but not limited by Rubens's art. With the exceptions of van Dyck and Jordaens, the Flemish followers of Rubens were stifled by his influence and could produce only pale imitations, whereas the painters of Madrid took the style at face value and, through the exercise of self-conscious virtuosity, turned it into an art of brilliant effects.

220. Juan Carreño, *Mass of St. John of Matha*, 1666. Paris, Musée du Louvre, canvas, 5.00 × 3.15m.

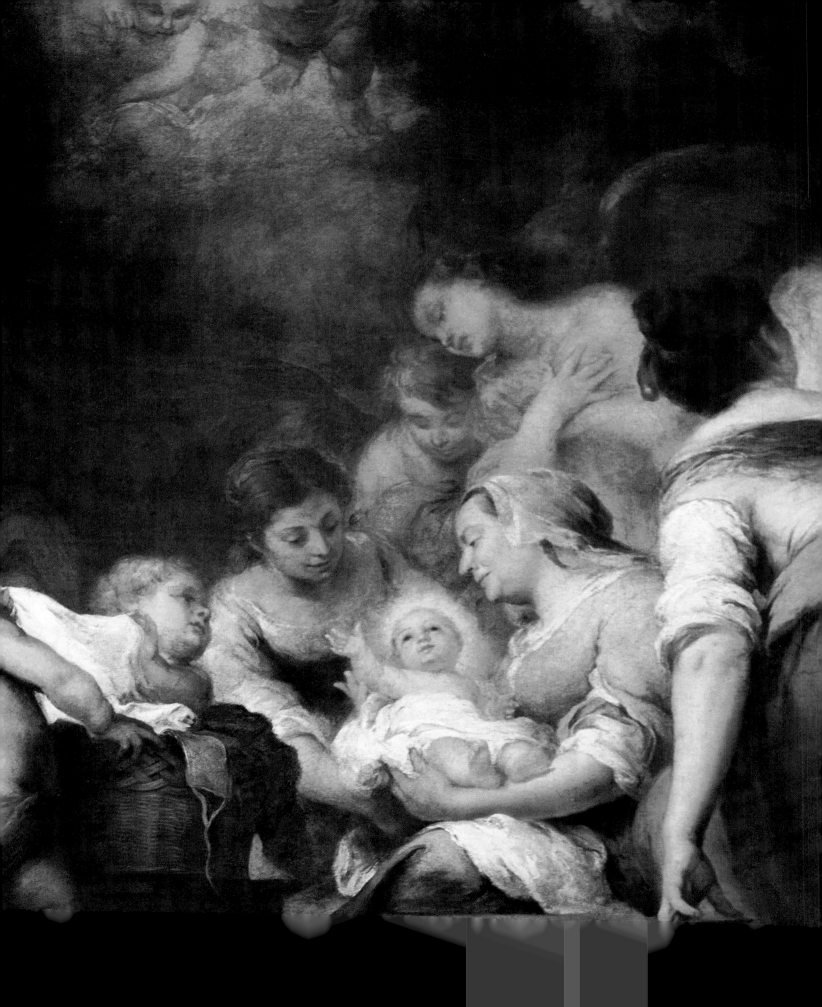

11

Seville at Mid-Century
1640–1660

THE MIDDLE YEARS of the seventeenth century were a time of suffering and hardship in Seville. To a certain extent, the city was a victim of the government's ruinous fiscal policies, which overtaxed the citizenry to support interminable foreign wars.[1] But there were local problems as well, especially with the Indies trade, the corner-stone of Sevillian prosperity. The progressive decline in silver remittances from the New World and the growing difficulties in protecting the shipping lanes started to take a heavy toll on the economy, a situation that was aggravated by the increasing importance of Cádiz as a port for the fleet. As the ships grew larger, Seville, an inland city, became harder to reach. In addition, the Guadalquivir River, its route to the sea, silted up, and the city could never organize an effort to dredge it. In these circumstances, Cádiz, which was directly on the Atlantic Ocean, seriously threatened Seville's monopoly of trade with the New World.

One reflection of these troubles was a declining population. At the height of its prosperity, which was attained around 1600, Seville had around 120,000 inhabitants and was one of the largest cities in Europe. As the economy contracted, the population inevitably decreased, and the slow, downward drift was dramatically accelerated by a violent episode of bubonic plague in 1649, which caused mass mortality on an unimaginable scale.[2] It is estimated that half the population perished in four terrible months, leaving only about 60,000 survivors. Three years later, Seville was racked by a dangerous uprising of the poor and famished, who came close to winning control of the city. By 1660, Seville had reached a point of no return. Although remaining the second largest city in Spain and still deriving benefits from foreign trade, it was no longer among the pre-eminent commercial centers of Europe.

The effects of decline and disaster on the production of painting are evident in the career of Francisco de Zurbarán. During the years 1638–40, Zurbarán executed the major commissions for the Carthusians of Jerez and the Hieronymites of Guadalupe. These pictures represent both the climax and the finale of his career as a monastic painter; after 1640, he received no new commissions of significance from the monasteries and convents of Andalusia.

This unexpected development was directly related to the contraction of the economy and population, which badly affected the institutional market for religious paintings. Even before the plague of 1649, the great period of expansion of Seville's religious communities was coming to a close. Here again, numbers tell the story.[3] Around 1620, Seville had thirty-three monasteries and twenty-seven convents. Another nine monasteries and one convent were established by 1649, but during the next fifty years only two or three more came into existence. The collapse of the economy and the impact of the plague also hit the existing religious communities

221. Detail of pl. 233.

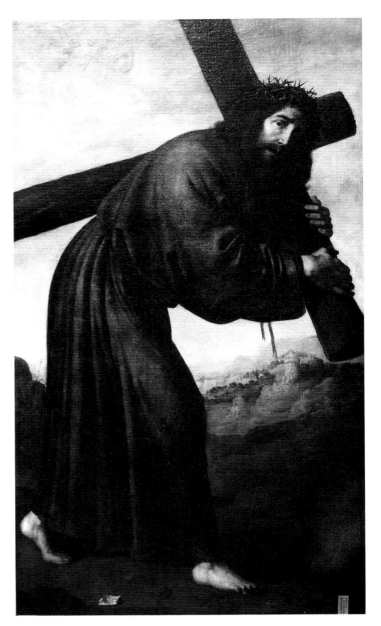

222. Francisco de Zurbarán, *Christ Carrying the Cross*, 1653. Orléans, cathedral, canvas, 1.95 × 1.08m.

hard; some were brought close to financial ruin, while others spent their income feeding the poor instead of adorning their churches. As Seville's economy gradually recovered strength, the ecclesiastical sector returned to the art market, providing new opportunities for a few favored painters. However, Zurbarán was not to be among their number.[4]

Fortunately, while unable to foresee it, the artist was prepared for this development. In the late 1630s, he had started to produce pictures for export to the New World, and he was now able to exploit this market.[5] These pictures were usually painted on speculation and consigned to a ship captain, who looked for buyers on the other side of the ocean. Given the lack of certainty as to whether the pictures would survive the perilous journey, there was little incentive to create masterpieces. Thus, most of them were executed by assistants, usually in series of twelve or more, permitting the buyer to decorate a church or chapel with a single purchase. Large consignments of paintings were sent abroad by Zurbarán in 1647 and 1649, and for ten years thereafter.

For the home market, Zurbarán and his workshop resorted to making devotional

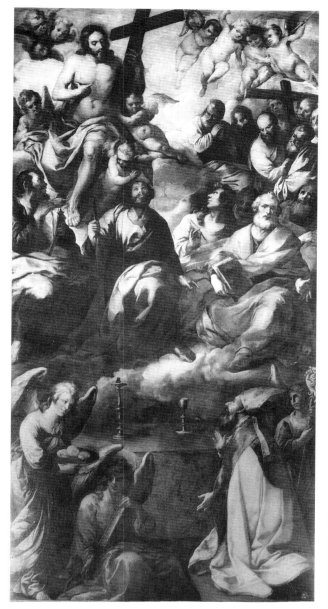

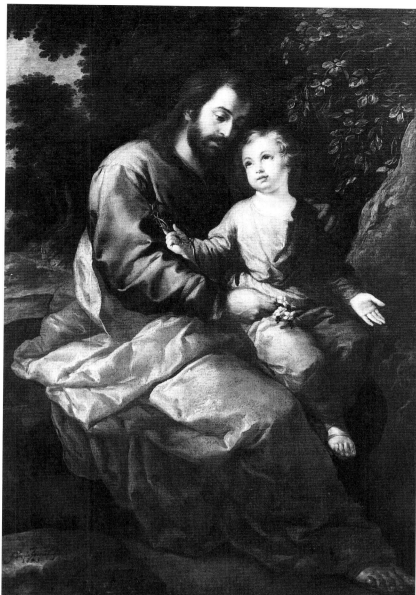

pictures for individual clients. Small in scale and simple in composition, these paintings were markedly different from the complex, doctrinal works created for the monasteries of Andalusia. Devotional pictures were not painted to glorify a religious order or to provide instruction in the major dogmas of Catholicism, but to appeal to clients who were now favoring images that aroused feelings of love toward the Virgin and Child, or pity at the sacrifice of the Savior. A representative work is *Christ Carrying the Cross* (pl. 222) of 1653, in which Christ, a figure of slender proportions, wearing a rich purple robe, is set against an idyllic landscape of grays and greens that unfolds beneath a rose-colored sky. He looks towards the spectator, beseeching pity and compassion.

A parallel development occurred in the work of Francisco de Herrera the Elder, Zurbarán's major competitor in the 1630s.[6] Herrera, who had been relegated to a secondary position after Zurbarán settled in Seville in 1630, continued to attract a few institutional clients such as the college of San Basilio, for which he executed an altarpiece in 1638–39.[7] The principal part of this ensemble, the enormous *Vision of St. Basil* (pl. 223), employs the two-storied composition that was standard for

223. Francisco de Herrera the Elder, *Vision of St. Basil*, 1638–39. Seville, Museo de Bellas Artes, canvas, 5.55 × 2.87m.

224. Francisco de Herrera the Elder, *St. Joseph and the Christ Child*, 1645. Budapest, Szépmüvészeti Múzeum, canvas, 1.65 × 1.15m.

243

church altarpieces in the early seventeenth century. Although Herrera still paints strongly individualized facial types, he has moderated the brutal naturalism of his earlier style (pl. 142).

In the forties, Herrera's production went into a decline, although he is known to have received the occasional commission from a religious order. *St. Joseph and the Christ Child* (pl. 224), done for the monastery of San José (Mercedarios Descalzos) in 1645, illustrates how the new devotional spirit was affecting Seville's monastic communities. Herrera made the necessary modifications to accommodate the new taste for quiet, sentimental art, but at the cost of the original, rough-hewn realism that made him a distinctive painter. Although the artist survived the plague of 1649, he must have concluded that the future in Seville was not very promising. In the following year, he moved to Madrid, where he died on 29 September 1654, at the very moment when his son was working on that standard-bearer of the new style, the *Triumph of St. Hermengild* (pl. 215).

Zurbarán decided to stay put. The plague had cost him the life of his son Juan, a still-life painter of considerable talent, who had left two small children to be cared for. The artist had started a new family of his own with his third wife, Leonor de Tordera, whom he had married in 1643, and in 1650, a son, Marcos, was born, the fourth of six children of the marriage. However, despite these new responsibilities, the artist's financial position appears to have remained stable, in part because he, like many an artist of Seville, owned the leaseholds of several properties, which he rented to subsidize his artistic income. It was only toward the middle of the decade that Zurbarán's position was threatened by young painters and fresh disasters.

Zurbarán's rival in the 1650s was Bartolomé Esteban Murillo, who would eventually supplant him as the city's principal painter.[8] Murillo was born in Seville in the final days of 1617, the youngest of fourteen children. His father, a barber-surgeon with a university education, died in 1627, and a year later his mother died too, leaving the eleven-year-old boy an orphan, although he had many relatives to

225. Bartolomé Murillo, *Heavenly and Earthly Trinities*, ca. 1640–45. Stockholm, Nationalmuseum, 2.22 × 1.62m.

226. Bartolomé Murillo, *San Diego de Alcalá Feeding the Poor*, 1645–46. Madrid, Real Academia de San Fernando, canvas, 1.72 × 1.83m.

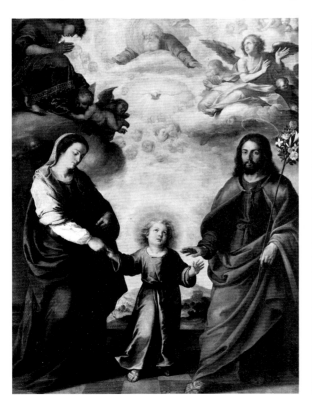

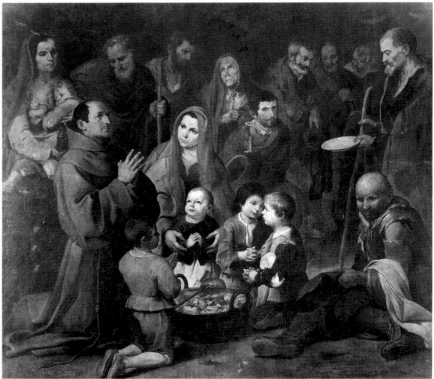

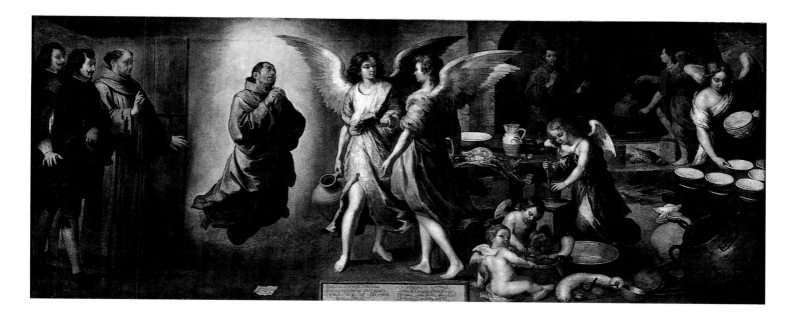

protect and assist him. He was adopted by an older, married sister, Ana, and trained as a painter by Juan del Castillo, a cousin by marriage.

The beginnings of Murillo's career are still obscure. In April 1633, having turned fifteen years old and completed his apprenticeship, he made arrangements to go to the New World, where he had family connections. It is not impossible that this voyage took place as planned; but whether it did or not, he was certainly working in Seville by the end of the decade.

The first pictures attributable to the painter have been dated to around 1640 and prove that he had already become an insatiable student of imagery. The *Heavenly and Earthly Trinities* (pl. 225) reads like an anthology of seventeenth-century Sevillian painting. The facial types are modeled on Cano, the sculpturesque drapery, on Zurbarán, the poses of the angels, on Juan del Castillo, while the restrained colors could have come from each and every one of them. Yet the painting is not a mere pastiche; all the parts are skillfully fused by a unifying gracefulness of pose and gentleness of expression.

Murillo's first major commission took him right into the heart of Zurbarán's territory. Around 1645, he began work on a series for the monastery of San Francisco el Grande, which depicts eleven episodes from the lives of famous Franciscans and was intended for one of the cloisters.[9] Inasmuch as the documentation is still to be found, nothing is known about how the artist obtained the commission, although it has been assumed that Murillo, like Zurbarán at the start of his career, offered a concessional price to entice the patron. Or it may be that, as a young artist, he could not command the same reward as a famous painter and thus was chosen to save money.

These paintings are by no means the work of an immature artist, although not all are equally successful. In *San Diego de Alcalá Feeding the Poor* (pl. 226), Murillo seems to have drawn the figures one by one, without attempting to unify the composition. But in the famous painting known as the "*Angels' Kitchen*" (pl. 227), which once bore a date of 1646 (now abraded), there is a greater narrative cohesion. Although the name of the protagonist is still somewhat uncertain, he may be the lay brother Francisco Pérez from the nearby town of Alcalá de Guadaira, who spent thirty years as an assistant in the kitchen of San Francisco el Grande. According to the story, he was much given to fervent prayer and one day became so lost in his

227. Bartolomé Murillo, "*Angels' Kitchen*," 1646. Paris, Musée du Louvre, canvas, 1.80 × 4.50m.

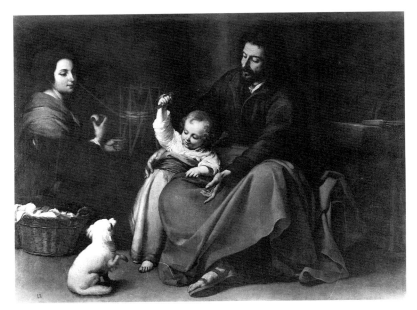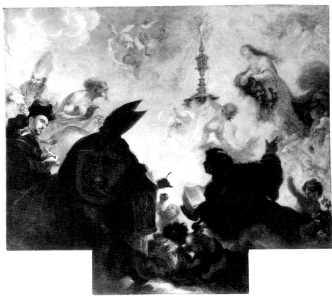

228. Bartolomé Murillo, *Holy Family with a Bird*, ca. 1650. Madrid, Prado, canvas, 1.44 × 1.88m.

229. Francisco de Herrera the Younger, *Allegory of the Eucharist and the Immaculate Conception*, 1655. Seville, Hermandad Sacramental del Sagrario, canvas, 2.69 × 2.95m.

devotions that he neglected his duties. Upon returning to consciousness, he was surprised to see that his chores had been miraculously accomplished.

Murillo has embellished the legend with irrestistibly charming details. Fray Francisco, who is bathed in an aura of golden light, floats above the ground in a mystical rapture. Next to him stand two exquisitely painted angels, with richly colored wings, while at the right putti and angels tackle the work of preparing the meal, grinding spices, stirring the hotpot, and setting the table in the midst of a delicious still life of vegetables and cookware (see frontispiece). Painted when the artist was approaching thirty years of age, the "*Angels' Kitchen*" announces the arrival of a new talent and temper in Sevillian painting.

During the succeeding years, Murillo catered to the rising demand for devotional pictures, of which he became an accomplished master. He did numerous versions of the Madonna and Child and other intimate scenes of the Holy Family, such as the domestic, playful *Holy Family with a Bird* (pl. 228), datable to around 1650. The origins of these pictures are not known; given their sheer number, it is conceivable that they were offered for sale in the artist's shop.

At the same time, Murillo was attracting a new group of clients, thanks in part to a family connection. Murillo's sister Ana and her husband had a daughter, Tomasa Josefa, who was only nine years younger than her uncle. On 10 July 1644, she contracted matrimony with a respectable but obscure young man, José de Veitia Linaje,[10] who, in 1649, was appointed to a minor post in the Casa de Contratación. Over the years, Veitia was to occupy increasingly important posts until he was called to Madrid in 1677 to become secretary of the Council of Indies and ultimately a secretary of the king.

Veitia was not in a position to commission works by Murillo, but he was certainly in a position to influence those who did. For example, he was a member of the Brotherhood of the True Cross, which possessed a chapel in San Francisco el Grande. This important confraternity owed its prominence to the fact that many of its members were rich foreign merchants. In 1652, the brotherhood asked Murillo to execute the *Immaculate Conception with Fray Juan de Quirós* (Seville, Archbishop's Palace), the initial payment for which was delivered to him by José de Veitia.[11] As the years passed, Murillo acquired many mercantile clients who were friends or associates of Veitia, suggesting that he was always ready to assist his relative.

An important milestone in the artist's career was reached in 1655, when Juan de Federigui, archdeacon of Carmona and canon of Seville, commissioned portraits of St. Isidore and St. Leander for the cathedral sacristy (*in situ*).[12] Little is known of Federigui's life, but two details are worthy of attention: his family was of Florentine origin, and he himself had been in Italy, where he served as a member of the privy chamber (*camariero segreto*) of Urban VIII.[13] In this respect, he was representative of a small, powerful group of the Sevillian oligarchy, who were of foreign descent and whose forebears had come to participate in the commerce with the New World. This colony of foreigners was a distinctive feature of Sevillian life, and their patronage of Murillo would have an important bearing on his career. On 19 May 1655, Archdeacon Federigui proposed his donation to the chapter and publicly praised the artist as "the best painter that there is today in Seville." Zurbarán might have wished to dispute this claim, but the number of sympathetic listeners was on the wane. However, in this same year, a serious competitor unexpectedly arrived from Madrid, the younger Francisco de Herrera.[14]

In an early source it is said that Herrera's ill-tempered father drove him from home while he was still a youth. The elder Herrera continued to torment his son from beyond the grave by dying without a will, which compelled Francisco the Younger to return to Seville to settle his father's estate. This would require several years, during which time Herrera set up shop and became a very successful painter.

Herrera's first public work indicates that he immediately attracted important patrons, and from within the cathedral precinct itself. On 19 December 1655, he was admitted to the prestigious Confraternity of the Most Holy Sacrament, which was attached to the cathedral parish and included many of the canons and prebendaries. At the next meeting of the brotherhood, on 6 January 1656, it was recorded that Herrera had painted a picture for the new chapter room, the *Allegory of the Eucharist and the Immaculate Conception* (pl. 229), which represents the Four Doctors of the Latin Church with Sts. Thomas Aquinas and Bonaventure as defenders of the confraternity's two principal devotions. Although the requirements of space and subject imposed certain limitations, the picture is a convincing demonstration of Herrera's feathery technique and animated manner of composition. Its greatest novelty is the heavenly scene, where putti twist and turn amidst the fluffy clouds in a tour de force of complex figure painting.

Prior to Herrera's arrival in Seville, Murillo himself had been exploring ways to animate and energize his compositions by using putti as visual ornamentation, as in the *Vision of St. Bernard* (Prado) and the *Miracle of St. Ildephonsus* (pl. 258). In Herrera's work, Murillo suddenly saw how to solve the problem and was inspired to create his first essay in the High Baroque style, the *Vision of St. Anthony of Padua* (pl. 230), which was installed in the cathedral baptistery on 21 November 1656. The chiseled ridges of St. Anthony's habit, emphasized by a pronounced contrast of light and shadow, are still typical of Murillo's early style. However, in the upper part of the picture, which contains a veritable explosion of putti and angels around the resplendent figure of the Christ Child, Murillo pays homage to Herrera the Younger.

The *Vision of St. Anthony* was an immediate success, and, only two weeks after its completion, a group of prebendaries petitioned the chapter to authorize a new commission for a picture of St. Francis by the artist. The canons assented to the proposal, but, quite unexpectedly, the commission was transferred to Herrera. By June 1657, Herrera's *Stigmatization of St. Francis* (pl. 231) had been placed in the spot once reserved for Murillo.

A comparison between Herrera's work and Murillo's *Vision of St. Anthony of Padua* is unavoidable: both are large-scale representations of Franciscan subjects and

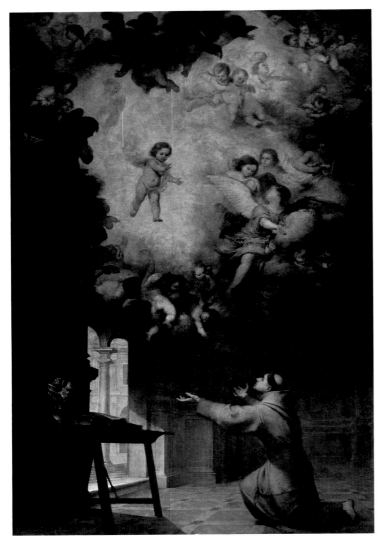

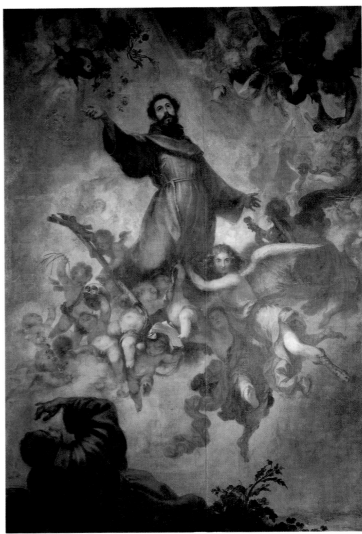

230. Bartolomé Murillo, *Vision of St. Anthony of Padua*, 1656. Seville, cathedral, canvas, 5.60 × 3.69m.

231. Francisco de Herrera the Younger, *Stigmatization of St. Francis*, 1657. Seville, cathedral, canvas, 5.70 × 3.63m.

contain a heavenly scene with a multitude of putti and angels. Murillo's picture is fundamentally an animated version of the traditional Sevillian formula for large altarpieces, with a clear demarcation between heaven and earth, while Herrera, following the model of his own *Triumph of St. Hermengild* (pl. 215), conceives the subject as a surging apotheosis of the saint, who is carried triumphantly aloft by a convoy of angels and putti.

The *Stigmatization of St. Francis* established a new standard in Seville. The dynamic composition, sketchy technique, rich, soft colors, and complicated poses immediately became the benchmark for local painters. Murillo and Zurbarán seem to have drawn the same conclusion from Herrera's accomplishment: that they should go to Madrid to study the new artistic techniques and practices. In 1658, both painters traveled north and attempted, with varying degrees of success, to remake their art.

Zurbarán's move to Madrid was motivated by financial as well as artistic considerations.[15] In the 1650s, he had continued to rely on the export market and his rental properties to support his large family. Then, in 1656, he experienced severe financial problems and was soon in debt. At about the same time, he stopped sending pictures to America. Behind these abrupt reversals was the destruction by the English of the returning Indies fleets in 1656 and 1657, a catastrophe that ruined Zurbarán and many citizens of Seville who depended on the remittances from over-

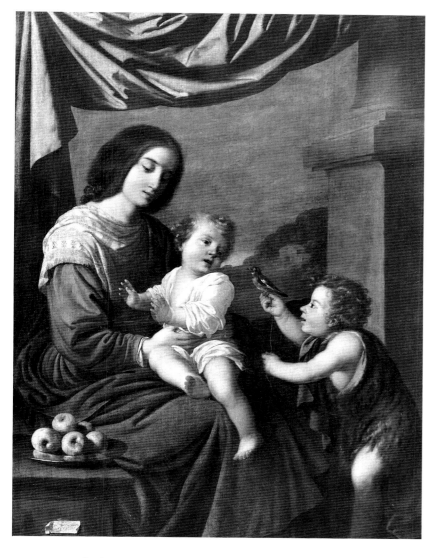

232. Francisco de Zurbarán, *Virgin and Child with St. John the Baptist*, 1658. San Diego, Museum of Art, canvas, 1.37 × 1.04m.

seas to settle loans and replenish capital. Thus, in 1657, he was in trouble: the English had captured his money and the younger painters had stolen his fame.

The decision to leave Seville now seems like the act of a desperate man. In 1658, Velázquez still reigned supreme at court, and if Zurbarán had hoped to capitalize on their friendship, he would be disappointed. Colonna and Mitelli had arrived in the same year, and Rizi and Carreño were hired to assist them. Zurbarán also faced competition from a rival of earlier days, Alonso Cano, who had returned from Granada in 1657 and would remain in Madrid until 1660. In 1658, both painters executed pictures for the Franciscan monastery of San Diego in Alcalá de Henares, and this is the only documented commission obtained by Zurbarán during his final years in Madrid.[16]

Otherwise, Zurbarán made a living by producing pictures that attempt to reflect the prevailing changes in artistic taste and devotional practice. He softened his style, lightened his palette, and heightened the intensity of expression, but the results are often equivocal. The *Virgin and Child with St. John the Baptist* (pl. 232), a representative work of the period, combines the palpable materiality of his earlier style with gentler, more delicate poses and expressions. A dramatic note is introduced by the young St. John, who frightens the Christ Child with a goldfinch, a traditional symbol of the Passion. This is a lovely, gentle painting, yet it is clearly no match for the brilliant, theatrical setpieces of Rizi, Carreño, and Herrera.

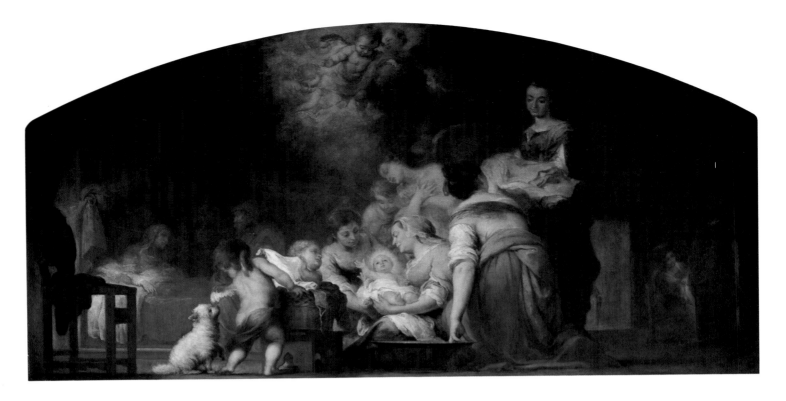

233. Bartolomé Murillo, *Birth of the Virgin*, 1660. Paris, Louvre, canvas, 1.84 × 2.60m.

Zurbarán supported himself as best he could, but when he died in 1664, his fame and fortune were greatly diminished.

As a younger artist with a more supple mind, Murillo had greater success in assimilating the new art. His stay in Madrid was fairly short; he is first documented there in late April of 1658, and is known to have been in Seville again by early December. However, in those seven months he learned what he needed to know. The changes in Murillo's style are evident in the first dated work executed after his return, the *Birth of the Virgin* (pl. 233), which was intended for the chapel of the Immaculate Conception in the cathedral.[17] This chapel was sponsored by Captain Gonzalo Núñez de Sepulveda, a city councillor who in 1654, a year prior to his death, donated the magnificent sum of 150,000 ducats to the church.[18] The endowment, which also financed a sumptuous annual mass in honor of the Virgin Immaculate, is of interest for showing how important individual fortunes had survived the hard times and were still available for pious purposes and to support the art market. On 15 January 1661, Murillo received a payment of 2,600 reales for his altarpiece from Captain Gonzalo's legacy.

In the *Birth of the Virgin*, Murillo abandons the hard-edged technique of his youth and adopts the open, sketchy brushwork learned in Madrid. Under the glow of soft light, the figures dissolve into the ambient space, intensifying the tender sentiment of the narrative. St. Anne lies in a canopied bed, attended by Joachim, while the newborn infant is removed from the bath by a rotund, matronly woman. The baby is handed for drying to a helper, with assistance from two putti, who remove toweling from a wicker basket. A young woman carrying the clothing emerges from the shadows, and two angels sweetly genuflect before the radiant child. Murillo's attempts to narrow the gap between the mortal and the divine are at last crowned with success. The exuberant energy of Herrera the Younger has been domesticated and transformed into an art that is calm, soothing, and reassuring. Murillo conveyed the mood and moment of the new religiosity in Seville and, following Herrera's return to Madrid in 1660, became the leading painter.

His only rival was an artist of compelling but uneven gifts, Juan de Valdés Leal.[19]

Valdés, a native of Seville, was baptized on 4 May 1622. There are no further records of his life until his marriage, which occurred in Córdoba in 1647, but the earliest surviving works suggest that he had been inspired by the roughcut realism and crusty technique of the elder Herrera.

Valdés appears to have moved to Córdoba only a year or two before his marriage, although his reasons for leaving Seville are not known. However, the mid-1640s were not a propitious time to launch an artistic career. Córdoba, a much smaller place, was large enough to support some thirty-three monasteries and convents (half the number of Seville) as well as numerous parish churches, which provided institutional commissions for a little, but not undistinguished community of painters. In addition, Valdés had a family connection: an uncle called Simón Rodríguez de Valdés, who was a prominent silversmith. Simon Rodríguez was also the father-in-law of an aspiring young artist who played a part in the career of Valdés Leal.

Antonio del Castillo y Saavedra (1616–68) is one of the few distinctive painters of the epoch who lived outside Madrid or Seville.[20] He was born in Córdoba, the son of a minor painter named Agustín del Castillo, and was orphaned at about the age of ten. In 1631, he became an apprentice and after his marriage in 1635, began his career as a painter and polychromer.

The first identifiable pictures by the artist, which date from the early 1640s, demonstrate a rather unsettled mixture of the local style and that of certain painters from Seville, with bits and pieces of Flemish art thrown in for good measure. Cordoban painting of the early seventeenth century had followed its own course. The dry, reform mannerist style brought to town by Pablo de Céspedes in the 1580s had been kept alive by followers such as José Luis Zambrano, Juan de Peñalosa, and Castillo's father, and their imprint on the young Antonio is obvious (*Virgin of the Immaculate Conception*, Córdoba, Santa Marina). In his first major commission, the *Martyrdom of St. Pelagius* of 1645 (Córdoba, cathedral), there is also evidence that he was acquainted with the output of the younger Frans Francken and his prolific workshop, examples of which were known in Seville. The imprint of Francken and his followers is even stronger in Castillo's best-known work, the six paintings of Joseph's life, which were probably done in the later 1640s.[21] The *Triumph of Joseph* (pl. 234), with its colorful costumes, theatrical setting, and exotic buildings, is a clear reflection of the stock-in-trade of the Francken workshop. At the same time, Castillo worked in a tenebrist style, as seen in the *Adoration of the Shepherds* (Málaga, Museo de Bellas Artes), the sources of which seem to lie generically in Sevillian painting of the 1620s and 1630s, and specifically in the version by Pablo Legot in Santa María de Oliva, Lebrija.

The number and diversity of these influences suggest that Castillo occasionally spent time in nearby Seville. Despite an evident eclecticism, he developed a recognizable, engaging individual manner characterized by sculpturesque, yet lively figures. Castillo was also a dedicated and inventive draftsman, who depicted a wide range of themes, including numerous drawings of peasants in rustic country settings which are unique in seventeenth-century Spain.[22] Valdés Leal was understandably impressed by Castillo's art, after the two painters became acquainted in 1647.

Valdés's production of the late 1640s has largely disappeared, although the style of these years can be measured in the *Virgin of the Immaculate Conception with Sts. Andrew and John the Baptist* (pl. 236), which probably was executed around 1650–52. The principal figures, with their powerfully individualized features, heavy drapery, and vigorous brushwork, are still indebted to Herrera the Elder. However, the upper part of the picture is derived from Castillo, especially the broad-faced putti who juggle the attributes of the Virgin Immaculate and have been charged by Valdés with greater movement and energy.

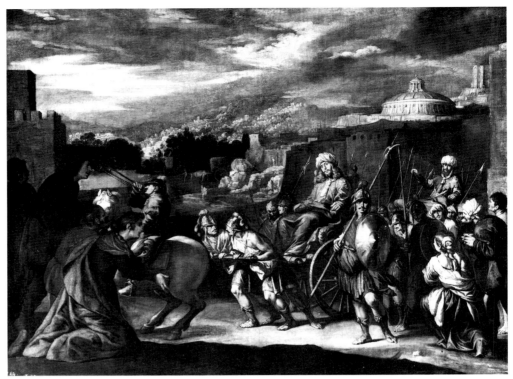

234. Antonio del Castillo, *Triumph of Joseph*, 1645–50. Madrid, Prado, canvas, 1.09 × 1.45m.

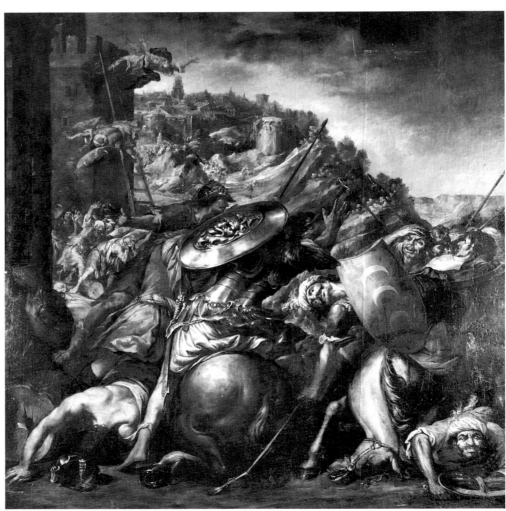

235. Juan de Valdés Leal, *Miraculous Defeat of the Saracens*, 1652–53. Seville, Museo de Bellas Artes, canvas, 3.30 × 3.25m.

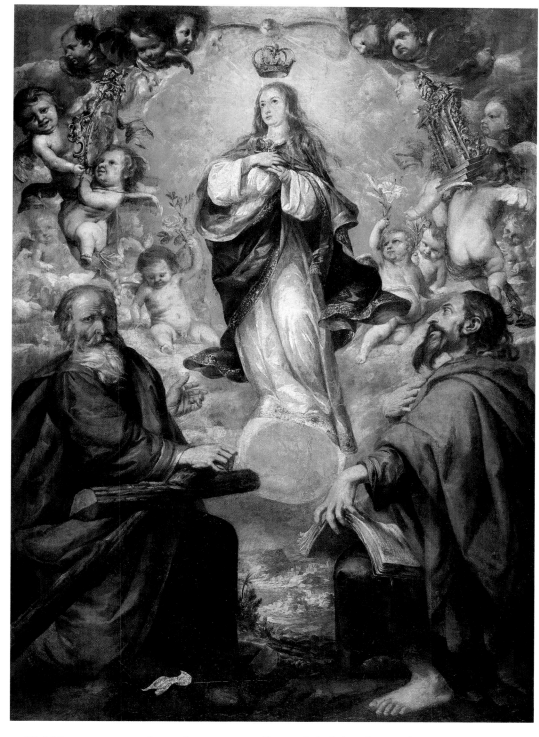

236. Juan de Valdés Leal, *Virgin of the Immaculate Conception with Sts. Andrew and John the Baptist*, ca. 1650–52. Paris, Musée du Louvre, canvas, 2.34 × 1.67m.

Valdés appears to have been away from Córdoba from about 1650 to 1654, spending at least part of the time in Seville, and during this period, he received an important commission from the convent of Santa Clara in Carmona, a town between Seville and Córdoba. The major part of this work is six scenes of the life of St. Clare, the founder of the female branch of the Franciscan order, one of which is dated 1653.[23]

The Carmona series required Valdés to paint on a new scale and order of compositional complexity, presenting him with a challenge that he groped his way to meet. The early episodes are somewhat static and forced, with disjointed compositions and stilted poses. But by the time he reached the *Miraculous Defeat of the Saracens* (pl. 235), he was beginning to find his voice as a history painter. The canvas depicts the most famous event in the life of St. Clare: the rout of the infidel troops of the emperor Frederick II, who attacked the convent of San Damiano in 1240. Desperately ill when the assault began, St. Clare was carried to the gates, where she prayed before the Host for the safety of the convent. The painting shows the dramatic answer to her prayers.

The *Miraculous Defeat of the Saracens* forms a pair with the scene of the saint's brandishing a monstrance against the invaders (Seville, Museo de Bellas Artes). The madcap retreat of the troops makes little sense when seen by itself; even when placed beside the companion picture, it is a bizarre work of art. In the foreground, the infidels fall over one another as they hastily withdraw in spectacular disarray from the convent walls. Cavalry troops tumble down, crushing the hapless foot soldiers beneath the weight of their horses. In the lower right corner, a desperate, almost comic figure grimaces in pain as he attempts to wriggle out from under a fallen animal, while in the distance, two soldiers fly through the air, having been abruptly dislodged from the heights of a siege ladder. All hell is breaking loose, and Valdés is in his element at last.

The concluding scene represents the *Death of St. Clare* (pl. 237), and for the composition Valdés turned to the version created by Murillo for San Francisco el Grande, which he appropriated with only a few changes. Despite the obvious borrowing, the pictures could not be less alike. In Murillo's work (pl. 238), the passing of the saint is infused with dignity and quiet grief. Members of her order cluster around the deathbed, their faces and gestures bespeaking grief and desolation, while Christ and the Virgin Mary, accompanied by a procession of lovely virgin martyrs, arrive to escort St. Clare to heaven. Valdés destabilizes this ordered composition by cramming the deathbed scene into a corner and individualizing the virgin martyrs with almost blatantly unappealing faces. Here the artist takes his stand and expresses allegiance to the studied ugliness of Herrera the Elder. Murillo entices the viewer with visions of celestial loveliness; Valdés attacks the senses by exaggerating the dramatic aspects of the story.

Valdés went back to Córdoba in 1654 for a final two-year stay and began one of his greatest creations, the altarpiece for the church of the Shod Carmelites (*in situ*).[24] Although the contract signed on 18 February 1655 called for an unspecified number of paintings to be completed in a year's time, the work eventually would comprise twelve pictures and take three years to finish (two canvases are dated 1658). One reason for the delay might have been the painter's decision to leave Córdoba and settle permanently in Seville, where he rented a house on 15 July 1656.

Valdés's return coincided with the appearance in Seville of Herrera the Younger, who profoundly affected him. Herrera's impact is first noticeable in the Carmelite altarpiece. Most of the smaller pictures were done in Valdés's early manner, before he had settled definitively in Seville; the image of *St. Apollonia and the Blessed Juana Scopeli*, which is in the predella, features two very plain women as the leading actors. St. Apollonia, whose martyrdom entailed the extraction of her teeth, is unflinchingly presented as an overdressed peasant wearing a fancy gown. On a table covered with a white cloth, her molars and bicuspids are displayed with the blood still clinging to the roots. In the three scenes of Elijah, on the other hand, two of which are dated 1658, the new aesthetic is at work, especially in the centerpiece, the monumental *Ascension of Elijah*, one of the greatest Spanish pictures of the period (pl. 239).

The Ascension of Elijah plays a central role in the imagery of the Carmelite order, which claimed to have been founded by the Hebrew prophet. In 2 Kings 2:11, Elijah

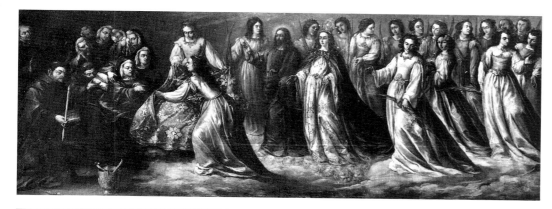

237. Juan de Valdés Leal, *Death of St. Clare*, 1653. Spain, private collection, 2.65 × 2.92m.

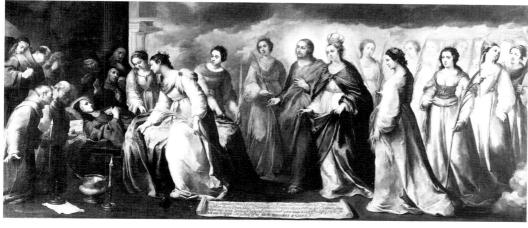

238. Bartolomé Murillo, *Death of St. Clare*, ca. 1646. Dresden, Gemäldegalerie, canvas, 1.89 × 4.46m.

was assumed into heaven from Mount Carmel in a fiery chariot. As he ascended, his mantle fell to the ground and was received by Elisha, an act that symbolizes the succession of the Carmelites to the prophet's legacy. In Valdés's painting, a spirited team of horses pulls the chariot toward heaven, while a yellow mantle drifts down into Elisha's outstretched arms.

Valdés has conceived the scene with an almost explosive theatricality. Fire bursts from the wheels and adornments of the chariot; flames are ignited by the impact of the horses' hooves. Even Elijah's beard seems ablaze as it is swept aside by the rush of the wind. On the ground below, a cool, placid landscape, filled with exquisite flora and fauna, is painted in subdued greens and grays that contrast with the riotous reds, oranges, and yellows of the flaming chariot.

The *Ascension of Elijah* is the start of another phase of Valdés's art. The brilliant colors, slashing brushwork, and high-keyed emotionalism are unprecedented in his previous work, suggesting that Valdés, like Murillo, was moved by the innovations of the younger Herrera. Indeed, there is a noticeable resemblance in the distribution of compositional masses between the *Ascension of Elijah* and Herrera's *Stigmatization of St. Francis* (pl. 231), especially in the poses of the central figures with their outstretched arms.

Herrera thus emerges as the catalyst for important changes in the styles of Murillo and Valdés, although they responded differently to their encounters with his work. Murillo tamed Herrera's exuberance to serve a placid, intimate vision of Christianity; Valdés whipped it up in order to express an intense, overwrought interpretation of the life of Christ and the saints. For Murillo, salvation was the Savior's glorious gift to man; for Valdés, it was the triumphant conclusion of awful struggle and sacrifice.

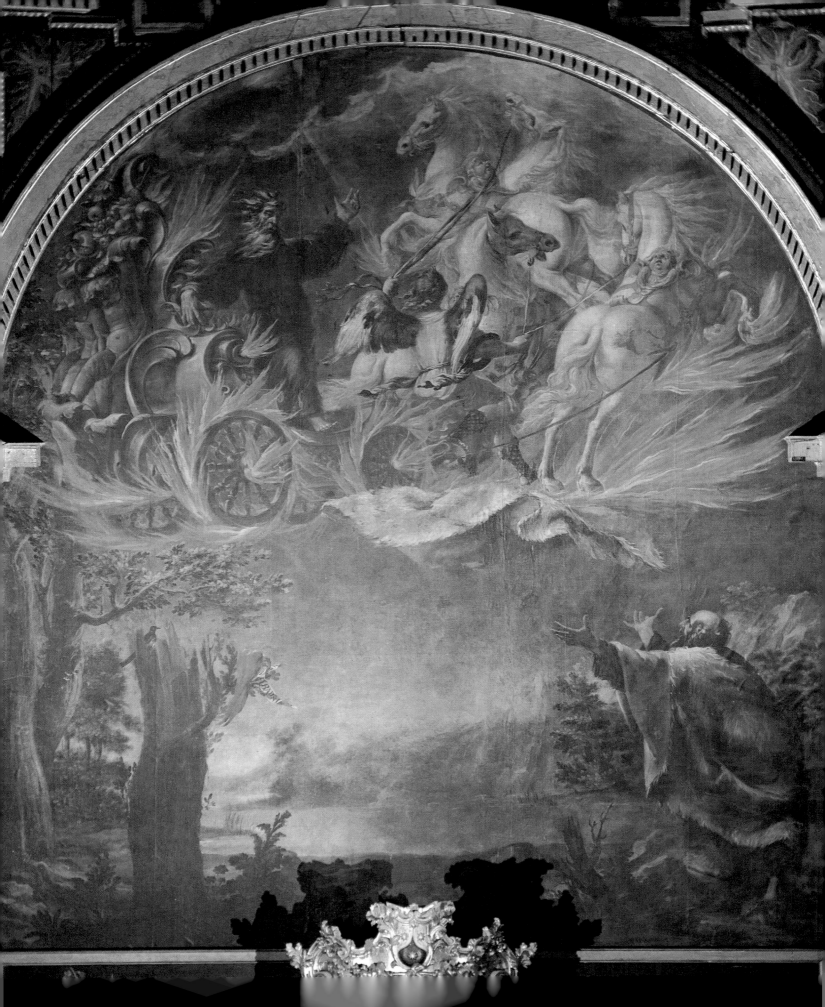

Before departing for Madrid in 1660, Herrera was involved in another enterprise that helped to alter artistic life in Seville: a drawing academy founded on 11 January 1660 under the leadership of Herrera and Murillo.[25] As revealed by the constitution, the academy did not have the lofty pedagogical ambitions of the Accademia di San Luca in Rome or the Académie Royale in Paris. It belonged to the older tradition of the drawing academy, in which aspiring artists drew from live models and were informally instructed by experienced masters. Although its purposes were limited, the Seville academy of drawing is an important event in the history of Spanish art. From time to time, as has been seen, Spanish painters attempted to launch academic programs, only to have them thwarted by opposition from within their own ranks. The Seville academy, however, succeeded in becoming the first formally constituted artistic academy in Spain.

The academy's success is probably to be explained by its limited aims. Instead of trying to supplant the system of apprenticeship, it sought merely to supplement it. Even the most dedicated enemy would have found difficulty in opposing the notion that practice in drawing was a good thing. Also, the leadership was put on a rotating basis, which prevented an authoritarian artist from taking control. There were enough secondary offices to go around, allowing numerous academicians to participate in the governance.

Yet perhaps the Seville academy was not merely a neutral element in the world of artistic practice. Following Herrera's departure, Murillo continued as president until 1661, when he was succeeded by Sebastián de Llanos, who served until 1663. In that year, Valdés Leal was elected for four years, although he resigned in 1666, after completing three-quarters of his term. By then, more than a decade had passed since Herrera's return to Seville, and Murillo and Valdés Leal had become the dominant painters. It may be an exaggeration to say that the academy was conceived with the intention of promoting innovation, but in the process of change that occurred after 1655, it helped to codify the emerging consensus about the purposes of painting. When it dissolved in 1674, apparently the victim of inertia, the new style had infiltrated every workshop in town.

239. Juan de Valdés Leal, *Ascension of Elijah*, ca. 1658. Córdoba, Carmen Calzado, canvas, 5.67 × 5.08m.

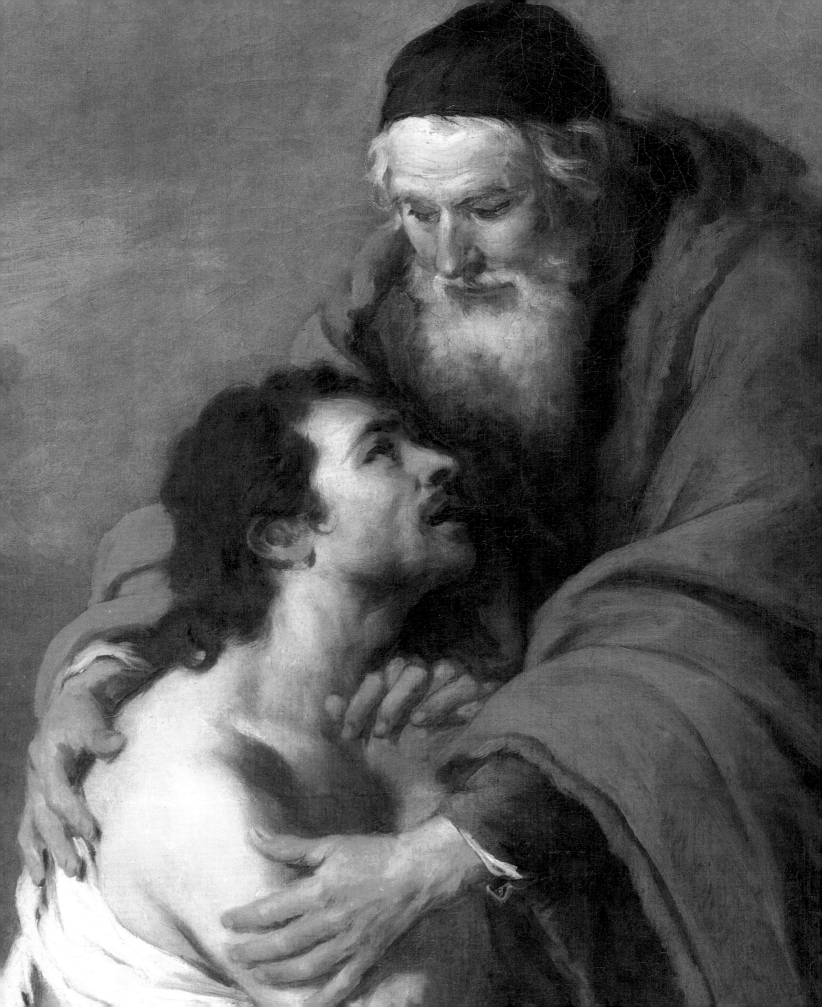

12

The New Era in Andalusia
1660–1700

DESPITE THE ACCELERATING decline of its economy, Seville remained the predominant artistic center in Andalusia during the second half of the seventeenth century. However, Granada, which had stagnated after the death of Sánchez Cotán in 1627, experienced a surge of activity after 1650. The revitalization of Granadine painting was sparked by the arrival of Alonso Cano, who had decided to return to his birth place, hoping to find the peace and security that had eluded him in Madrid.[1] In February 1652, he occupied his recently granted benefice, in exchange for which he had agreed to create such works for the cathedral as were needed. The other, more difficult, condition was that he become ordained within a year.

Almost from the start, Cano ran into trouble because the canons tended to treat him as an employee instead of a colleague, and the situation was aggravated because he failed to keep his promise about ordination. In addition, a faction that had opposed his appointment worked ceaselessly to undermine his position. The lack of mutual trust and understanding finally provoked a rupture: on 6 October 1656, the canons declared his position vacant and an unordained, unrepentant Cano left for the court to present his grievance to the king.

He arrived in Madrid in 1657 and on 13 February of the following year, petitioned Philip IV to revalidate his appointment. The king was ready to help, and arranged for Cano to be examined by the nuncio, who approved his qualifications. One month later, on 14 March, he was ordained by the bishop of Salamanca, after which the king ordered the chapter to restore his benefice. The artist delayed his return to Granada until June 1660.

Cano undoubtedly was an independent spirit and a slow worker, qualities that would not have endeared him to the canons of Granada. He seems, however, to have made a diligent effort to uphold his part of the agreement. He designed and fabricated liturgical furniture, which is still in use today, and began to produce seven large paintings of the life of the Virgin, which constitute a major element in the decoration of the cathedral.

These pictures were to be placed in the principal chapel at a height of some twenty-five meters above the floor, a distance that required Cano to create un-cluttered, legible compositions. In the initial work, the *Presentation of the Virgin*, he struggled unsuccessfully with the problem: the figures are too small and are overwhelmed by the monumental architectural setting. Comparable difficulties plague the *Purification of the Virgin*, probably the next work to be designed. In the two successive paintings, the *Annunciation* and the *Visitation*, which were finished before his dismissal, Cano found a way to meet the challenge.

The *Annunciation* (pl. 241) is one of Cano's most successful pictures, synthesizing the new taste for compositional movement and drama with consummate draftsman-

240. Detail of pl. 247.

259

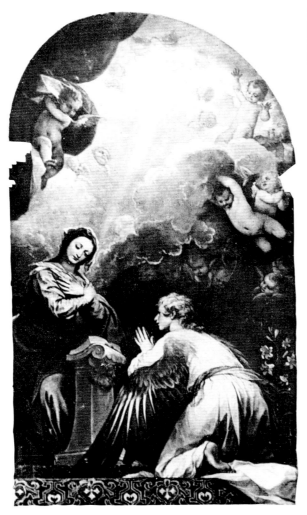

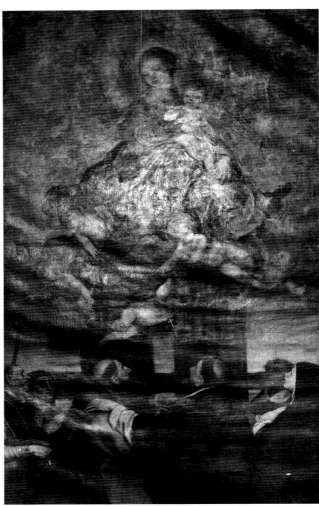

241. Alonso Cano, *Annunciation*, 1652–56. Granada, cathedral, canvas, 4.51 × 2.52m.

242. Alonso Cano, *Virgin of the Rosary with Saints*, 1665–67. Málaga, cathedral, canvas, 3.50 × 2.13m.

ship. The communication between Gabriel and the Virgin Mary is economically rendered by corresponding poses of genuflection and response, while a blaze of glorious light dramatically illuminates the scene from above, where putti fly through the clouds. Here, and in the *Visitation*, Cano once again demonstrates what can only be called the instinctive Italianism of his style through his masterful figure drawing, the quality that distinguishes him both from his contemporaries and from the painters of the succeeding generation.

During the three-year interval in Madrid, Cano continued to work. In addition to collaborating with Zurbarán for the Franciscans of Alcalá de Henares in 1658, he executed both a picture and a statue for Charles II of England, which he was finishing just prior to his return to Granada in late June 1660.

Once back at the cathedral, his first task was to finish the series of the Virgin's life, which was accomplished by November 1664. Cano relied heavily on assistants for the last three works – the *Birth of the Virgin*, the *Immaculate Conception*, and the *Assumption* – none of which equals the quality of those executed during the first campaign. No sooner had the canvases been put in place than the canons took their revenge and evicted the artist from his rooms in the cathedral tower. At this point, Cano understandably decided to leave Granada, and took up residence in Málaga to work for the bishop. There he created a final masterpiece, the *Virgin of the Rosary with Saints* (pl. 242), a mellifluous composition in which the Virgin, Child, and putti form an almost perfect triangle, superimposed above the oval grouping of saints.

Yet Cano's career was not over. Almost incredibly, he was lured back to Granada by the repentant canons, who, on 4 May 1667, appointed him chief architect of the cathedral. Just enough time remained to draft a design for the façade before his death on 3 September. Cano bequeathed a legacy of beautiful works to the cathedral and left behind a competent group of followers who perpetuated his style until the end of the century. These included Juan de Sevilla (1643–95), Pedro de Bocanegra (1638–89), and Juan Niño de Guevara (1632–93), the last of whom worked in Málaga. Although they could not match the refinement or sophistication of their master, Cano's pupils demonstrate how an excellent painter could make a big difference in a small place.

In Seville, this sort of artistic monopoly was almost impossible to achieve, owing to a much greater demand for altarpieces and devotional works. However, there is no doubt that Murillo gradually outdistanced all other painters, including his closest competitor, Juan de Valdés Leal. Around the year 1660, Murillo and Valdés Leal enjoyed roughly equal status with their clientele; but by the end of the decade, Murillo's leading position was unquestioned. Murillo's fame was consolidated by several commissions executed in rapid succession in the second half of the decade, starting with the altarpiece for the monastery of San Agustín, painted around 1664–65. Even more important were the pictures for Santa María la Blanca finished in 1665, the most publicized church decoration of the 1660s.[2]

Santa María la Blanca had been built originally as a synagogue and later converted into a church, which was refurbished and redecorated between 1662 and 1665 at the expense of Justino de Neve (ca. 1625–85), a canon who was to become one of Murillo's principal patrons. Neve was the son of a prosperous Flemish merchant who had married a Spaniard,[3] and like many members of Seville's colony of foreigners, he sought assimilation into the local elite through an ecclesiastical career. He entered the service of the cathedral chapter around 1646 and became a canon in 1658. Neve's inherited wealth and acquired social standing were matched by an interest in the visual arts, and in time he became pre-eminent among the art patrons of the city.

The commission for Santa María la Blanca consisted of four paintings, two in the arched spaces beneath the small dome of the nave and two more in the same format placed at the head of the aisles. The nave paintings represent the pious legend of the founding of Santa Maria Maggiore, Rome, the mother church of Santa María la Blanca. According to this story, a Roman patrician, John, and his wife had pledged their wealth to the Virgin. She rewarded their piety by appearing in a dream and instructed them to build a church in her name on the Esquiline Hill, in accordance with a plan that would be traced on the surface of a miraculous summertime snowfall. The couple rushed to report their vision to Pope Liberius (352–66), who had also been visited by the Virgin, and all proceeded to the designated place, where they witnessed the miraculous fall of snow. Following the heaven-sent plan, they built the church and named it Santa Maria della Neve, the Italian word for "snow," which neatly coincides with the name of the Sevillian canon. In the two lunettes dedicated to this story (pls. 243 and 244), Murillo intensified the sketchy, sfumato technique first used in the *Birth of the Virgin* (pl. 233). The consonance between the gentle narrative and the warm, intimate style seems effortless, so much so that it is easy to overlook the confident artistry of the complicated poses and the dextrous brushwork in the backgrounds.

Santa María la Blanca was inaugurated on 5 August 1665, with a spectacular public festival, the details of which are recorded in a commemorative publication.[4] All Seville came to see the church and its new decoration. In addition, the square and adjacent buildings were sumptuously adorned with temporary altars and a gallery of

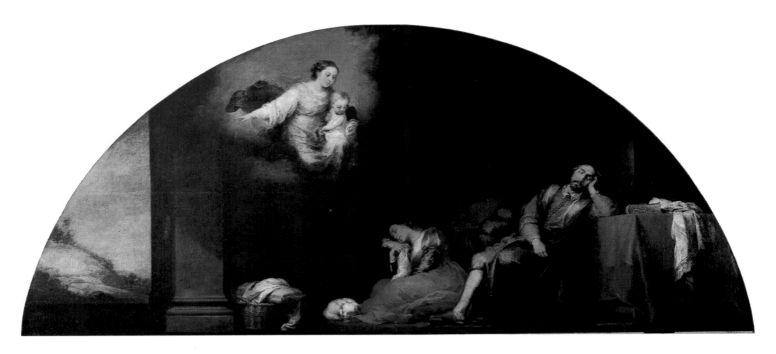

243. Bartolomé Murillo, *Dream of Patrician John*, 1665. Madrid, Prado, canvas, 2.32 × 5.22m.

famous pictures from local collections. The chronicler mentions works ascribed to Rubens, Ribera, Artemisia Gentileschi, and Orazio Borgianni, among the non-Spanish artists, and there was even a picture given to Rembrandt (called "Reblan"), which may have been owned by a Dutch merchant. Among the Spaniards, Murillo was triumphant. He created three pictures for the principal temporary altar and also displayed his scenes of the life of Jacob, painted for the marquis of Villmanrique. These beautiful pictures, originally five in number, contain the artist's most developed landscapes, which provide the settings for the episodes from Genesis. Murillo had never painted such ambitious landscapes before (nor would he do so again), and therefore he took his inspiration from northern examples, particularly the works in the style of Joos de Momper.[5] In *Jacob Laying the Peeled Rods before the Flock of Laban* (pl. 245), Murillo relies on de Momper for motifs such as the steep, rocky formations and the theatrical use of trees, as well as for the predominant tonalities of greenish brown and grayish blue.

The inauguration of Santa María la Blanca was a great day in the religious life of Seville and a revealing one for understanding its art. Seville was famous as an international mercantile bazaar; it is not surprising that paintings from foreign places were found there. If Murillo's works could hold their own in this company, perhaps it is because he had deliberately situated his style within a broad European tradition in order to satisfy his cosmopolitan clientele. Murillo is often considered to be the quintessential Sevillian painter, but in fact his art was decisively shaped by foreigners and foreign influences.

The importance of the year 1665 is confirmed by another major commission, from the Capuchinos of Seville, which included ten paintings for the main altar and one picture for each of eight lateral altars of the church.[6] The guardian, or head, of the monastery was called Fray Francisco de Jerez, and he was another second-generation Sevillian who had followed an ecclesiastical career. Fray Francisco's father belonged to a distinguished Irish Catholic family from Dublin named Gough and had settled in Jerez de la Frontera, where he married a member of a prominent Anglo-Spanish family, María Fletcher Morgan Cabeza de Vaca. Although it seems incredible, the family name of Murillo's patron was Gough y Fletcher Morgan Cabeza de Vaca!

Murillo worked on this, his largest commission, through most of 1666, complet-

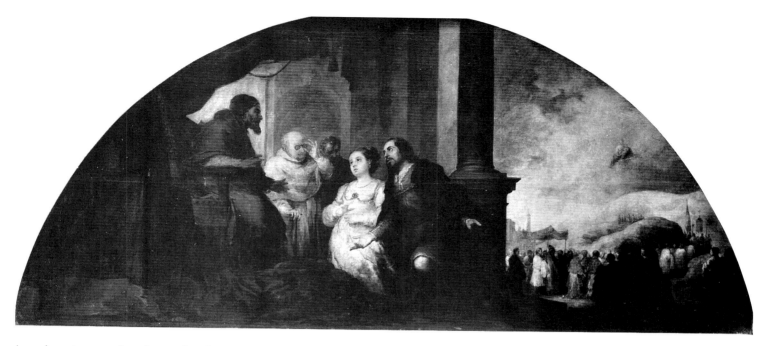

ing the pictures for the main altar and two of the side chapels. Then Fray Francisco left for Rome, where he became an important official of the Franciscan order. The next two guardians showed no interest in finishing the project and the work stopped until 1668, when their successor, Fray Antonio de Ondarroa, raised the money needed to bring it to completion.

The altarpieces for the Capuchinos contain some of Murillo's most eloquent, lyrical paintings, as exemplified by the tender *St. Francis Embracing the Crucified Christ* (pl. 246). Following the dictates of the text from the Gospel of Luke, which is held aloft by putti, St. Francis pushes away the globe symbolizing worldly pursuits and gently embraces the body of Christ, looking lovingly into His eyes. Christ draws St. Francis near and returns his devotion by placing a reassuring arm on his shoulder. This touching but apparently simple composition was in fact carefully thought through in two preparatory studies (London, Courtauld Institute of Art and

244. Bartolomé Murillo, *Patrician John Reveals His Dream to Pope Liberius*, 1665. Madrid, Prado, canvas, 2.32 × 5.22m.

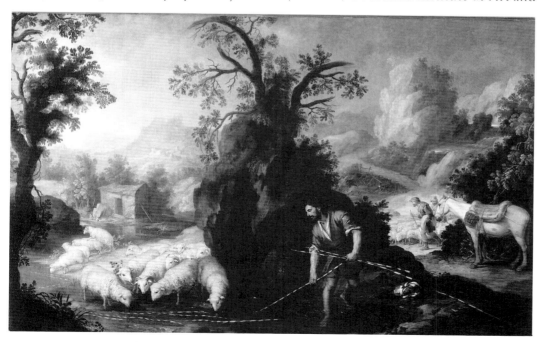

245. Bartolomé Murillo, *Jacob Laying the Peeled Rods before the Flock of Laban*, 1665–70. Dallas, Meadows Museum, Southern Methodist University, canvas, 2.13 × 3.58m.

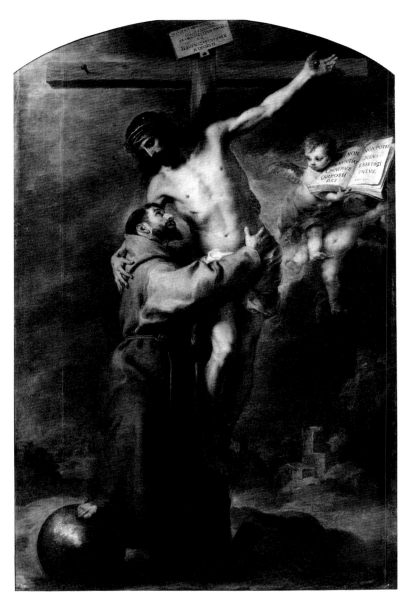

246. Bartolomé
Murillo, *St. Francis
Embracing the Crucified
Christ*, 1668–70. Seville,
Museo de Bellas Artes,
canvas, 2.83 × 1.88m.

Hamburg, Kunsthalle), in which the artist made the many small changes that enhance the expression of feeling.

On other occasions, however, Murillo was content to copy an existing composition by another artist, following the time-honored practice of Sevillian painters. For example, the *Pietà* (Seville, Museo de Bellas Artes), originally in one of the lateral chapels, is based on an engraving of the picture by Annibale Carracci (Naples, Capodimonte). Murillo's frequent recourse to prints for compositional sources is more complicated than it seems and will be discussed below.

In the final years of the 1660s, Murillo increased his already considerable productivity. In 1667–68, he supplied paintings for the chapter room of the cathedral, including eight roundels with portraits of Seville's patron saints and a *Virgin of the Immaculate Conception*, which are still in place. And in 1667, he began to work for the Brotherhood of Charity, one of the city's major lay confraternities.[7]

The Caridad, as it is known, was founded in 1565 with the mission of providing a decent burial for paupers. Following the plague of 1649, the brotherhood's charitable work became an urgent social necessity, and its membership began to increase.

Then, in 1662, the Caridad accepted a remarkable new member who would lead it to unprecedented heights of activity and prestige: Miguel de Mañara (1627–79).

Mañara was yet another of the newly rich class of foreign merchants who had inherited a fortune made by his father, a native of Corsica, in the Indies trade. During his early years, the younger Mañara lived an idle life, enjoying the fruits of his inheritance, until he was roused from complacency by the sudden death of his wife in 1661. This tragic event awakened his latent religiosity and revealed extraordinary organizational talents, which he placed at the service of the Caridad. He was elected leader of the confraternity (*hermano mayor*) in 1663 and governed it until his death in 1679. Under Mañara's direction, the Caridad expanded its charitable activities to provide care for the needy sick and built a hospital on the grounds adjacent to the chapel. In due course, Mañara decided to enlarge and renovate this small chapel.

Mañara had known Murillo since 1650, when he became the godfather of his son José, named after José de Veitia. Veita was one of Mañara's closest friends and may have had a hand in establishing the contact between the artist and the merchant. Thus, when Mañara began to plan the decoration of the new chapel, he naturally turned to Murillo. The painter had applied for membership in the Caridad as early as 1660, but was made to wait five years before acceptance, probably because his occupation made him seem unworthy in the eyes of the aristocratic members. When it became clear that Murillo's services would be needed, he was admitted to the confraternity (14 June 1665).

The reconstruction of the chapel was concluded in June 1667, and Murillo immediately went to work on the first of eight pictures, finishing the last of them in 1672. Mañara's scheme for the decoration is a tripartite exposition of Christian charity as the way to salvation. The first part comprises two memorable paintings by Valdés Leal, demonstrating the futility of earthly pursuits and honors (pls. 250 and 251). A life devoted to accumulating wealth, power, and even learning is shown to lead only to the grave. Charity, which constitutes the second part of the program, provides the way to salvation, as seen in the seven acts of mercy, six of which are depicted by Murillo; the seventh, burying the dead, the Caridad's foundation charity, is embodied in a sculptural group, the *Entombment of Christ*, placed in the altarpiece. The third component consists of two paintings by Murillo for lateral altars, depicting St. Elizabeth of Hungary and St. John of God, both of whom illustrated the efficacy of good works and the necessity of personal participation in charitable deeds.

Murillo's paintings of the acts of mercy have long been recognized as among his greatest; in Victorian Britain, they were considered the acme of the art. In order to impart maximum authority to the message, each of the acts is performed by Christ or a biblical character and reflects the emotional tenor of Mañara's own writings on charity and salvation. For example, in the *Return of the Prodigal Son* (pl. 247), which represents clothing the naked, Murillo emphasizes the protective embrace of the forgiving father and underscores the good deed by showing a pile of fresh clothes held by a servant. The vaporous clouds that invade the background unobtrusively reinforce the warm sentiments of the joyful reunion.

The acts of feeding the hungry and giving drink to the thirsty appear in the *Feeding of the Five Thousand* (pl. 248) and *Moses Sweetening the Waters of Mara* (pl. 249). For these multi-figured compositions, Murillo depended on pictures by Herrera the Elder and the Genoese, Giovanchino Assereto (1600–49).[8] (Herrera's painting was then in the refectory of the Jesuit college of San Hermenegildo; Assereto's work seems to have been in a private collection, perhaps belonging to a Genoese trader.) Murillo freely adapted these models by repositioning figures and altering the group-

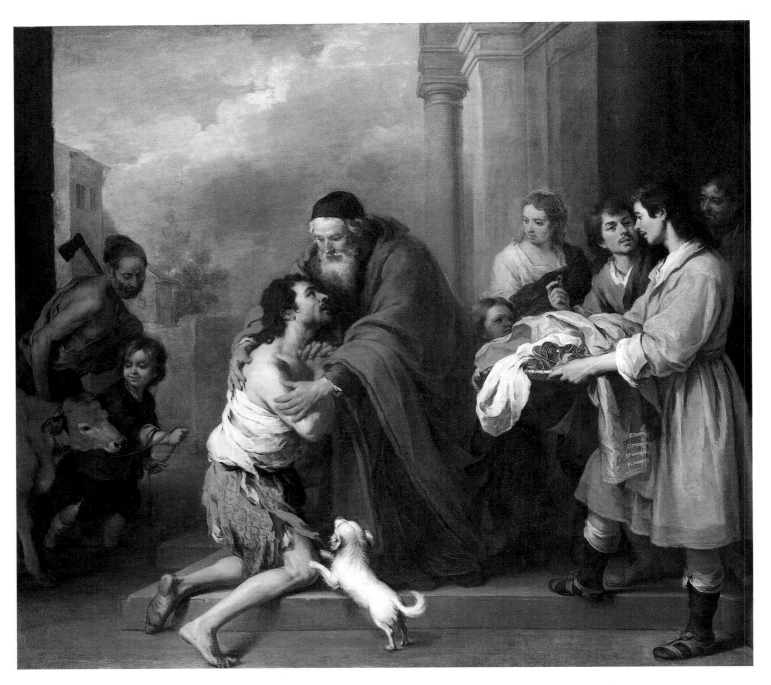

247. Bartolomé Murillo, *Return of the Prodigal Son*, 1667–70. Washington, National Gallery of Art, Gift of the Avalon Foundation, canvas, 2.36 × 2.62m.

ings; nevertheless, his preference for copying instead of inventing a multi-figure composition should be noted.

Murillo's acts of mercy, which were installed on the walls of the chapel, were prefaced by Valdés Leal's two most famous paintings (pls. 250 and 251), completed by 1672.[9] These relentlessly gruesome pictures are located just inside the entrance, so that visitors to the church must experience the agony of Valdés's Hell before entering the promised land of Murillo's acts of mercy. The first, entitled *In Ictu Oculi* (*In the Twinkling of an Eye*, pl. 250), is a highly charged representation of the futility of worldly goals and pursuits. A menacing skeleton, carrying a scythe, a coffin, and a shroud, extinguishes the flame of life, causing darkness and oblivion to descend over the attributes of wealth, power, and learning. The paths of glory lead but to the grave, which is unflinchingly rendered in the companion picture, *Finis Gloriae Mundi* (*The End of Worldly Glory*, pl. 251), where vile bugs feast on the rotting remnants of

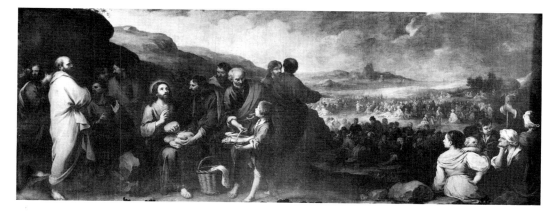

248. Bartolomé Murillo, *Feeding of the Five Thousand*, 1667–70. Seville, La Caridad, canvas, 2.50 × 5.90m.

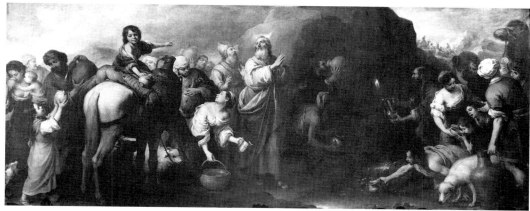

249. Bartolomé Murillo, *Moses Sweetening the Waters of Mara*, 1667–70. Seville, La Caridad, canvas, 2.50 × 5.90m.

human flesh. The choice of salvation or damnation is graphically offered in the scale that appears above the corpses: nothing more ("ni mas") than worldly pursuits is needed for perdition. On the other side of the balance are instruments of prayer and penance: nothing less ("ni menos") is needed to save the soul. However, the scale is in equilibrium and the additional weight for salvation can only be provided by performing the acts of mercy represented in the clear light of the chapel.

Mañara's division of labor between the two painters proves that he was a knowing connoisseur. The shrill, nervous art of Valdés was suited to evoke the terror of death and decay, while the calm, soothing art of Murillo was just right for depicting the sweetness and light of salvation. As the prices demonstrate, however, Mañara did not value their talents equally: Valdés received 5,740 reales for his two paintings; Murillo, 8,000 reales for each of the four smaller acts of mercy, 13,300 for the story of Moses, and 15,975 for the *Feeding of the Five Thousand*. The lateral altarpieces dedicated to St. John of God and St. Elizabeth of Hungary were each valued at 8,425 reales. The discrepancy in these prices is astounding and indicates that by this date Valdés was no longer able to compete with Murillo for the favor of Seville's patrons.

Yet the start of Valdés's career in Seville some sixteen years earlier had been marked by great promise. In 1656, when he moved to Seville from Córdoba, he received a major commission from the Hieronymite monastery of Buenavista, just outside the city walls, which included episodes from the life of St. Jerome and several full-length portraits of brothers of the order. The *Temptation of St. Jerome* (pl. 252), dated 1657, follows the composition of Zurbarán's painting for Guadalupe (pl. 153), but is endowed with energy and refinement that do not appear either in the model or in Valdés's earlier works.

The same excited theatricality is evinced in other pictures of the 1650s. In the *Liberation of St. Peter* (pl. 253), painted for the cathedral in 1656, Valdés creates a dramatic composition around the electrifying figure of the angel, who strides into

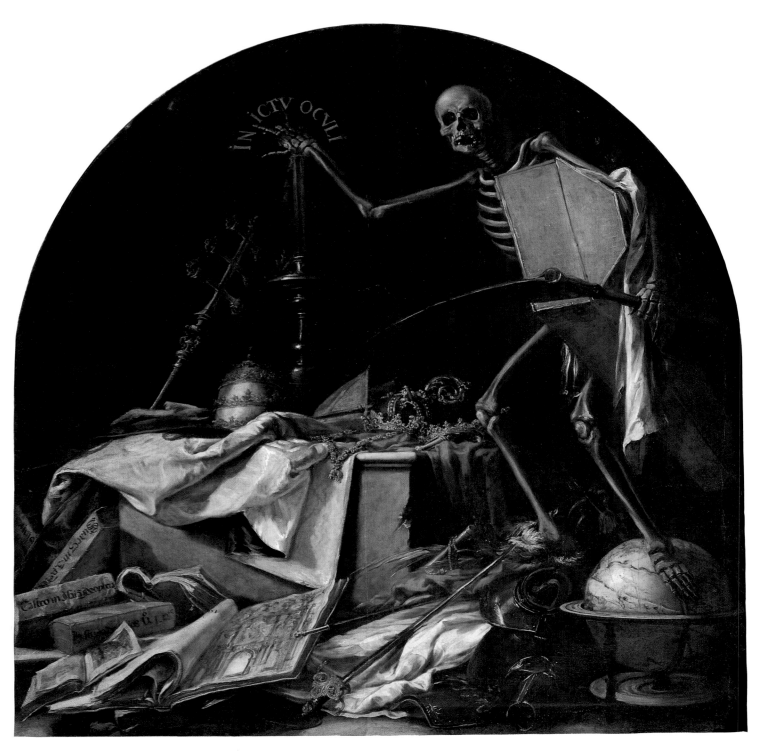

250. Juan de Valdés Leal, *In Ictu Oculi*, 1670–72. Seville, La Caridad, canvas, 2.20 × 2.16m.

the apostle's prison, wings fully spread and drapery swirling in the wind. *St. John the Evangelist Leading the Virgin and the Three Marys to Golgotha* (pl. 254) demonstrates how the Gospel text inspired the artist to invent a new episode in the history of the Passion. The scene occurs offstage from Christ toiling up the road to Calvary; the holy figures, having learned of the Savior's impending fate, hasten to the site of the crucifixion. In this moving image, Valdés communicates the fear, anxiety, and incipient grief of those who are about to witness a great tragedy.

Another example of the artist's weird, ecstatic style is the *Miracle of St. Ildephonsus* (pl. 257), dated 1661. St. Ildephonsus, a seventh-century archbishop of Toledo, wrote

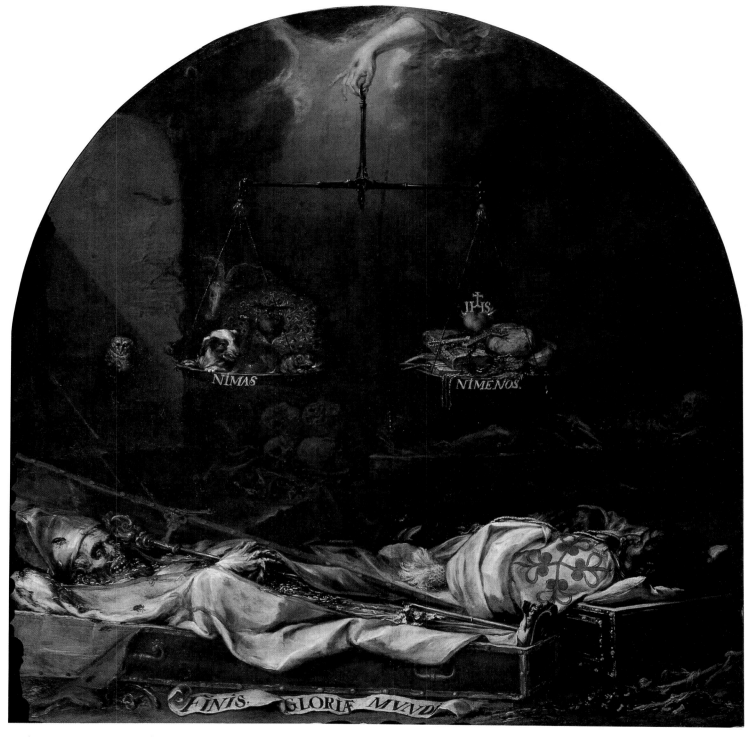

In the painting, the banner reads: FINIS GLORIÆ MVNDI

an important treatise defending the purity of the Virgin, who, as a reward for his devotion, presented him with a priestly vestment. In this high-strung version of the miracle, Valdés allows his imagination to run riot. Under the chill glare of an unreal light, the gaunt, hollow-cheeked St. Ildephonsus rapturously fingers the vestment that falls in a cascade onto his face. Every inch of the canvas is crowded with frenetic activity, as putti fill the sky and angels jockey for position around the enthroned Virgin Mary. In a surprising and shocking change of mood, three putti in the foreground struggle for possession of the archbishop's crozier.

Valdés Leal, who brought this excitable manner of religious painting to its highest

251. Juan de Valdés Leal. *Finis Gloriae Mundi*, 1670–72. Seville, La Caridad, canvas, 2.20 × 2.16m.

269

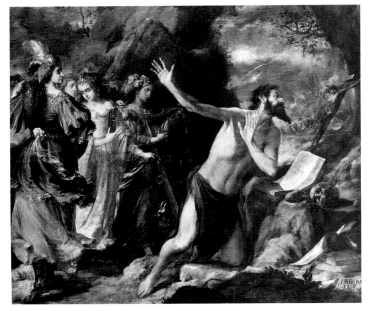

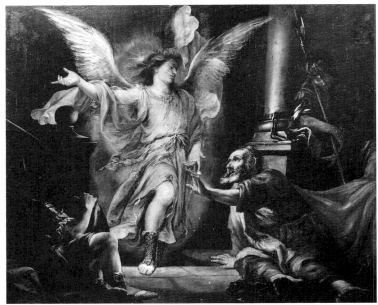

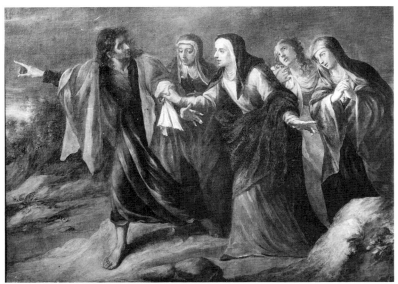

252 (above left). Juan de Valdés Leal, *Temptation of St. Jerome*, 1657. Seville, Museo de Bellas Artes, canvas, 2.22 × 2.47m.

253 (above right). Juan de Valdés Leal, *Liberation of St. Peter*, 1656. Seville, cathedral, canvas, 1.88 × 2.21m.

254. Juan de Valdés Leal, *St. John the Evangelist Leading the Virgin and the Three Marys to Golgotha*, ca. 1657–60. Seville, Museo de Bellas Artes, canvas, 1.44 × 2.04m.

pitch in the 1660s, unfortunately misjudged the mood of his clients, who increasingly preferred Murillo's serene promises of salvation without suffering and sainthood without martyrdom or penance. Just a few years earlier, Murillo had produced his own version of the miracle of St. Ildephonsus (pl. 258), which minimizes the visionary aspects, making it seem as though the saint were negotiating the purchase of a fancy cloak instead of receiving a miraculous reward from heaven. Valdés re-creates all the intensity of a visionary experience, but the picture-buying public was looking elsewhere for inspiration.

The differences in approach are more apparent in paintings of the Virgin of the Immaculate Conception, a theme of unsurpassed importance to the faithful of Seville. The dispute over the immaculacy of the Virgin Mary was one of the most divisive in the history of the Renaissance church.[10] In simple terms, there were two parties to the debate: the immaculists, led by the Franciscan order, who believed that the Virgin had been miraculously conceived without original sin, and the sanctification party, led by the Dominicans, who held that Mary had been conceived in sin and subsequently sanctified, or purified, in the womb of her mother.

270

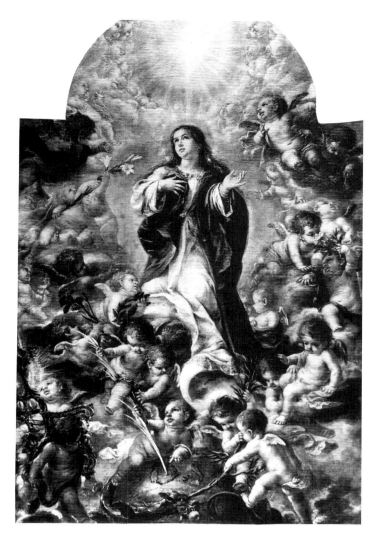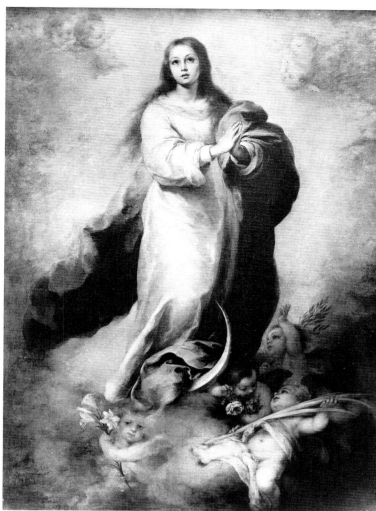

From the late Middle Ages, the crown and church of Castile had been ardent proponents of the immaculist doctrine and repeatedly had attempted to persuade the popes to elevate it to the status of a dogma. If little progress was made in Rome, the advocacy of the Virgin's immaculacy had a powerful effect on the faithful of Spain, who adopted the cause as their own, and nowhere with greater fervor than in Seville, where Mariolatry ran deep. Public spectacles and observances in support of the *Inmaculada* were staged at frequent intervals; it was for this purpose that Captain Gonzalo Núñez de Sepulveda had endowed the chapel where Murillo's *Birth of the Virgin* was placed in 1661. In fact, 1661 proved to be a triumphant year for the immaculists, because it was then that Pope Alexander VII issued a constitution ("Solicitudo omnium Ecclesiarum") declaring the immunity of Mary from original sin and forbidding further discussion of the issue.

News of the papal ruling was received in Seville with unbridled joy and intensified the demand for images of the Virgin Immaculate. Now that the theological issue had been resolved, it was possible to approach the subject in a different way. In the early years of the century, painters had depicted the *Inmaculada* accompanied by a full complement of Marian symbols that expressed the eternal purity of the Virgin. Once the doctrine had been clarified and the opposition stifled, the theological apparatus became redundant and could be replaced by the Virgin Immaculate triumphant, shorn of all but the most decorative attributes.

Valdés painted this indispensable subject of Sevillian devotion only a few times – a

255. Juan de Valdés Leal, *Immaculate Conception*, ca. 1665–70. Seville, Museo de Bellas Artes, canvas, 3.19 × 2.01m.

256. Bartolomé Murillo, *Immaculate Conception*, ca. 1665–70. Madrid, Prado, canvas, 2.06 × 1.44m.

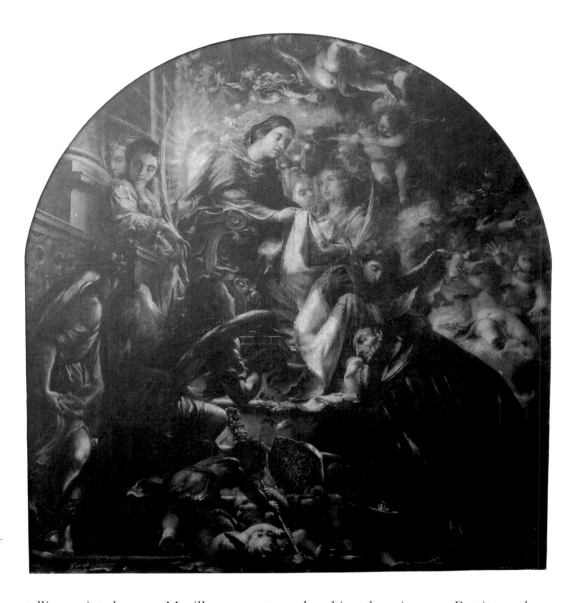

257. Juan de Valdés Leal, *Miracle of St. Ildephonsus*, 1661. Spain, private collection, canvas, 2.70 × 2.50m.

telling point, because Murillo never stopped making these images. But it was here that Valdés's peculiar talent failed – his was not an art of joy. The most ambitious version, datable to the mid-1660s, was probably part of an altarpiece for a local church (pl. 255). Simply as a technical performance, the work is splendid: the loose brushwork, the scintillating colors, and the variety of poses are admirable. The composition, however, is less felicitous: the Virgin has to fight for attention with the crowd of putti who surround her; even more disconcerting, her triumphant surge toward heaven seems to sputter as she stumbles on a cloud.

A contemporary rendition by Murillo (pl. 256) is more faithful to the spirit of the times. The youthful Virgin is a lovely creation, her physical beauty a sufficient expression of her purity; only a few putti are needed as supporting players. It is no surprise that Murillo's appealing vision of the Immaculate Conception became canonical, while Valdés never painted the subject again after 1670.

By the mid-1660s, Valdés must have sensed that the tide of public taste was running against him, because it was then that he began to work as a decorative painter. Some of these jobs can only be regarded as menial, such as gilding ironwork and inscriptions on bronze plaques. Much more important, although still little appreciated, are his mural paintings, which are executed in tempera, not fresco. Valdés began to paint murals in 1664 and devoted a good part of his later career to

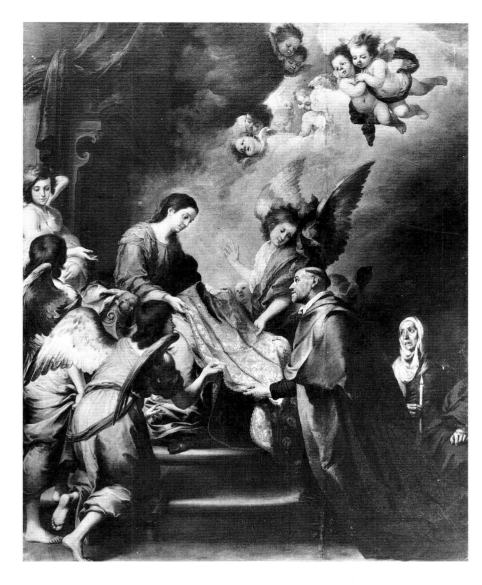

258. Bartolomé Murillo, *Miracle of St. Ildephonsus*, ca. 1655–60. Madrid, Prado, canvas, 3.09 × 2.51m.

this endeavor. The best examples are the vaults and cupola of the Caridad, done from 1680 to 1682, and the interior of the church of the Venerable Sacerdotes, a joint commission undertaken with his son and successor, Lucas (1661–1725), executed in the late 1680s.[11] Using a whitewash background, Valdés and his son created elaborate ornamental frameworks that surround narrative scenes. This aspect of Valdés's work, more than his easel paintings, proved to have a lasting influence on artists of Andalusia.

The most spectacular of Valdés's decorative works was executed in 1671 for the celebrations of the canonization of St. Ferdinand of Castile (1199–1252), who had reconquered Seville from the Moslems in 1248 and was a venerated figure in local history and devotion. His body, which had been entombed in the cathedral, was exhumed in 1668 and found to be incorrupt. This was taken as as sign of his sanctity, and he was duly canonized in 1671. To celebrate the event, the chapter staged a festival of impressive splendor, which included the construction of a gigantic temporary structure, known as the "triunfo." The monument, made of wood and decorated with paintings and sculpture, was designed and decorated by Valdés and the leading sculptor Bernardo Simón de Pineda, and built in little more than two months. Although the structure was just as quickly dismantled, its appearance is preserved in a large print produced by Valdés himself, which was used to illustrate a

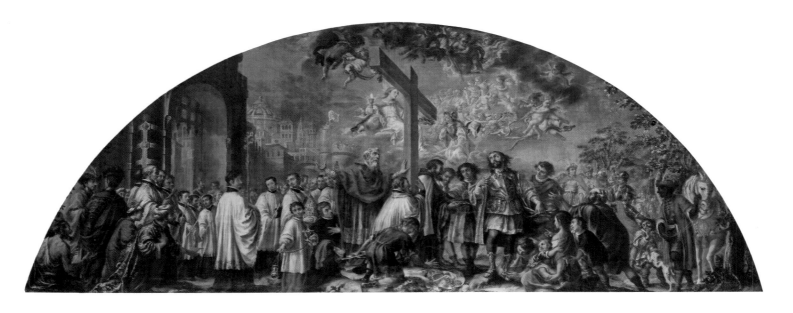

259. Juan de Valdés Leal and assistants, *Exaltation of the Cross*, 1685. Seville, La Caridad, canvas, 4.20 × 9.90m.

festival book published later in the year (pl. 260).[12] As this spirited, complex etching shows, Valdés had made a virtue of necessity and become not only an inventive decorative artist but also a skilled printmaker.

It was just as well that he had extended his artistic range, because commissions for paintings were increasingly rare and decreasingly lucrative after 1670. In 1673, he executed seven paintings of St. Ambrose for the archbishop, Ambrosio Spinola, as part of the decoration of the oratory in the archepiscopal palace.[13] In addition, Valdés painted and gilded the chapel, receiving a total of one thousand ducats for all this work. Murillo's contribution to the project was a *Virgin and Child in Glory* (Liverpool, Walker Art Gallery), for which he was paid the identical amount.

Thereafter, the demand for oil paintings petered out almost entirely. Only Miguel de Mañara remained a faithful client. In addition to employing Valdés to decorate the vaults and cupola of the Caridad chapel, he ordered what would be his last major work, the peculiar *Exaltation of the Cross* (pl. 259), which is still in the choir, where it was placed in 1685.[14]

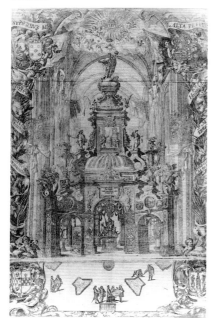

260. Juan de Valdés Leal, *Monument to St. Ferdinand*, 1671. Etching, 56 × 35mm.

This legendary subject was chosen because the brotherhood celebrated the Exaltation as its special feast day. According to the story, the Roman emperor Heraclius rescued the True Cross from the Persian king, Chosroes, and brought it to Jerusalem. As the king prepared to enter the city in triumph with his trophy, the stone gate collapsed and blocked his way. An angel informed him that he could not bring the cross into the city with imperial pomp and ceremony, but would have to imitate the action of Christ and mount a lowly donkey. Mañara understandably was devoted to the story, which proved that a rich man could not enter the kingdom of heaven, thereby encouraging the brothers to divest themselves of their wealth to assist the poor.

After the sluggish works of the early seventies, the *Exaltation* shows a revival of Valdés's pictorial imagination. More than fifty figures are crowded into the composition (some of which were executed by Lucas Valdés), representing a diverse spectrum of physical types. In the center, the emperor removes his splendid robes while the patriarch Zacharias motions toward the city. The ecclesiastical and imperial retinues stand on either side, their ranks filled with freakish types; above, there is a busy allegorical scene with a personification of State paying homage to the Church. Full of incident and dissonance alike, the *Exaltation of the Cross* is the last flash of Valdés Leal's idiosyncratic genius. He lived until 1690, plagued by ill health

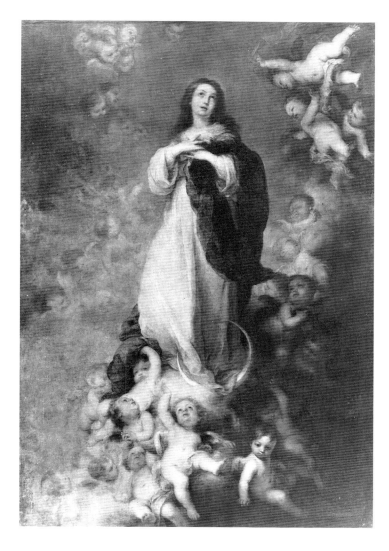

261. Bartolomé Murillo, *Immaculate Conception*, ca. 1676–80. Madrid, Prado, canvas, 2.74 × 1.90m.

and debt, surviving Murillo by eight years but otherwise losing the longtime competition between them.

Murillo, it must be said, was likewise not overwhelmed by new church commissions in the 1670s. In fact, only the hospital of Venerable Sacerdotes ordered a significant group of pictures from the painter.[15] This institution had been started by Justino de Neve in 1676 as an asylum for retired members of the clergy. Although it was not completed until 1698, Murillo was asked to paint three pictures soon after construction was started. One of these proved to be his culminating version of the Virgin Immaculate (pl. 261), a glorious picture in which the last of the traditional attributes is eliminated except for the crescent moon, and the putti, now freed of symbolic baggage, flutter all around the triumphant Virgin, some painted so thinly they seem to dissolve into the fluffy clouds.

The noticeable reduction in institutional patronage that occurred during the 1670s is related to the progressive decline of the local economy, which was losing more ground to Cádiz.[16] Beginning around 1670, while the population of Cádiz began to grow rapidly, Seville, although remaining considerably larger, experienced stagnation. Nature was also unkind to the city. Crop failures were frequent in the 1670s, which led to a severe famine in 1678. Two years later, an earthquake caused heavy damage in Seville, and, once again, ecclesiastical revenues had to be diverted to feed the poor and alleviate the general misery, leaving little to improve the appearance of churches.

Murillo was able to minimize the impact of these misfortunes through his connections with the foreign merchants, whose skill in trade and finance insulated them from human follies and the assaults of nature. The number of foreigners resident in Seville in 1665 has been estimated at around seven thousand. Not all were involved in trade or managed to avoid economic reversals, and certainly only a minority were interested in owning pictures. There were enough people of wealth and taste, however, to support Murillo even in the hardest times, thus sheltering him from the adversity experienced by many of his colleagues. At this point, his relations with José de Veitia may have proved helpful. Murillo's reputation was more than sufficient to attract this clientele, but Veitia's involvement in the world of commerce seems at times to have been instrumental in arranging contacts between the artist and the merchant-princes.

The most intriguing member of this group was Francisco Báez Eminente,[17] a Portuguese Jew who had converted to Catholicism and had emerged as a powerful financial operator in 1663, when he had leased the right to collect an important tax on merchandise from the Indies. This brought him into constant contact with Veitia, who administered the receipt of this tax for the crown. Eminente and his sons held the concession, with some interruptions, until the end of the century. In due course, the financier moved to Madrid, where his enemies exploited his Jewish ancestry to destroy his wealth. In December 1689, he was arrested by the Inquisition and his goods in Madrid, Seville, and other places were sequestered. Among the possessions seized in Seville were five paintings by Murillo, three of which are known today – the *Glory of Angels* (Woburn Abbey), a perfect subject for a crypto-Jew, lacking as it does any figure identifiable with the Christian religion; *St. Francis Xavier* (Hartford, Wadsworth Atheneum); and *St. Francis of Paula* (Princess Labia).

Another of Murillo's merchant clients was Joshua van Belle, a Dutch ship owner.[18] Van Belle, who was born in Rotterdam in 1635, is first documented in Seville on 16 June 1663. He stayed in the city for eight years, after which he returned home, settling first in Amsterdam, then in Rotterdam, where he joined the town council and eventually became burgomaster. Besides his civic and commercial activities, van Belle was a notable collector, a fact that emerges from the circumstances surrounding the dispersal of his possessions. He died in 1710, having bequeathed his collection to his son, who sold it in Rotterdam on 6 September 1730.[19] At that date, it comprised 106 lots, with attributions to such important artists as Titian, van Dyck, Rubens, and Veronese. Also included were five paintings by Murillo: the portrait of van Belle himself (Dublin, National Gallery of Ireland), which, according to an inscription on the verso, was painted in 1670; an *Ecce Homo*; a *St. John and the Lamb*; a *Virgin Mary Enthroned*; and a *Portrait of a Gentleman* (all unidentified).

It was toward the end of the 1660s that Nicolas Omazur, the most important of Murillo's private collectors, arrived in Seville. Omazur, the descendant of a prestigious old Flemish family, was born in Antwerp around 1630 and on 2 July 1669, was recorded in Seville as a "resident."[20] His purpose was to open a branch of the family's silk manufactory, which he managed until his death on 2 June 1698.

Omazur is in a class by himself as a collector of paintings by Murillo. By 1690, the date of the first inventory of his collection, he owned no fewer than thirty-one examples, some of which, however, were bought after the artist's death. Among these were such masterpieces as the *Marriage at Cana* (Birmingham, Barber Institute), one of Murillo's most accomplished history paintings, and the artist's *Self-Portrait* (pl. 262), which Omazur sent to Antwerp to be engraved by Richard Collin in 1682. And, needless to say, he had commissioned portraits of himself (Prado) and his first wife, Isabel de Malcampo (copy, Glasgow, Stirling-Maxwell Collection), both of

262. Bartolomé Murillo, *Self-Portrait*, ca. 1670–72. London, National Gallery, canvas, 1.22 × 1.07m.

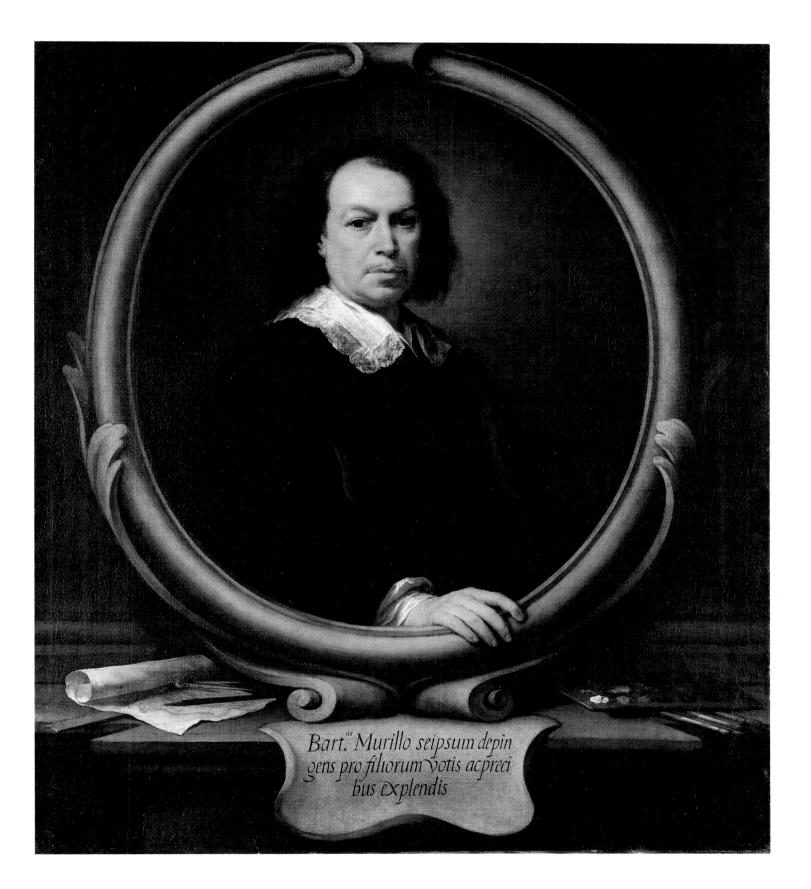

Bart.ᵘˢ Murillo seipsum depin
gens pro filiorum votis acpreci
bus explendis

which use a standard format of northern painting, placing the figure in an illusionistic frame.

Omazur collected Murillo's paintings with an almost scientific passion. For example, he owned two unusual depictions of Old Testament scenes – the *Sacrifice of Isaac* and *Tobias and the Angel* (Aynhoe, William C. Cartwright) – and several genre paintings, among them the pair of a *Young Girl with Basket of Fruit* and a *Young Boy with Dog* (Leningrad, Hermitage). More unusual was a set of the Four Seasons, two of which, *Spring* and *Summer*, were bought from the estate sale of Justino de Neve. Rarest of all was an unfinished composition of *Music, Bacchus and Love*, a type of subject otherwise unknown in Murillo's oeuvre. Rounding out the collection was an important group of drawings. At his death, Omazur owned the largest, most representative collection of the artist's work ever assembled. Other merchants of Seville may have been richer, but none could surpass Omazur's wealth of pictures by Murillo.

The fashion for Murillo among the foreign merchants took an interesting turn in the 1660s, when his clientele followed the Indies trade down the Guadalquivir to Cádiz, a logical consequence of the city's rising economic fortunes. The most important of these new patrons was the Genoese merchant Giovanni Bielato, about whom unfortunately little is known.[21] The earliest mention of his activity in Cádiz dates to 1662, and he seems to have remained in the city for roughly ten years, before returning to Genoa, where he drafted his last will and testament in 1674. Bielato died in November or December 1681, shortly before which he had donated his paintings by Murillo to the Capuchinos of his native city. This collection numbered seven splendid works: *Joseph and His Brothers* (London, Wallace Collection); the *Immaculate Conception* (Kansas City, Nelson-Atkins Museum of Art); the *Adoration of the Shepherds* (London, Wallace Collection); *Rest on the Flight* (Wrotham Park); *Penitent Magdalene* (Cologne, Wallraf-Richartz Museum); *St. John the Baptist* (Rochester, Mich., Mrs. Alfred G. Wilson); and *St. Thomas of Villanueva* (London, Wallace Collection). In his will, Bielato made a further bequest to the Capuchinos of Cádiz, who used the money to commission an altarpiece by Murillo for their church. The artist was working on this painting (*in situ*) when he died on 3 April 1682, and it was finished by his assistant Francisco Meneses Osorio.

Another foreign client in Cádiz was Pedro Colarte Dowers, the first marquis of El Pedroso, a member of a Dunkirk family which had distinguished itself in the Spanish Navy.[22] He had come to Cádiz as a youth and from there had journeyed to the Indies; after returning briefly to Flanders, he settled in Cádiz as a merchant in 1649. Over the next fifty years, Colarte amassed fame and fortune, culminating in the concession of his title in 1690. One of his daughters, María Leonor, married Bartolomé Bozán Bielato, the nephew of Giovanni, who probably provided the link between Colarte and the artist. At his death in 1701, Colarte owned the picture now known as the "*Pedroso Holy Family*" (London, National Gallery), which was valued at the considerable sum of eight hundred escudos de plata.

The implications of the patronage by foreign merchant families are by no means clear-cut, but this does not mean that they are negligible. In some cases, it is easy to detect motifs that resulted from catering to the preferences of the merchant population, as in the half-length portraits in illusionistic frames. This format, of which the *Self-Portrait* is the best example (pl. 262), was a commonplace in Flemish painting and, as has already been seen, was used in the portraits of Nicolas Omazur and Isabel Malcampo, where the sitters also hold symbols that are part and parcel of the language of Dutch and Flemish painting.

More subtle traces of Murillo's knowledge of northern painting are evident in his genre paintings. These enchanting pictures seemingly appear out of nowhere; they are without precedent in Sevillian, or, indeed, in all Spanish painting. But scenes of everyday life were a staple in the repertory of Dutch and Flemish painters, and were certainly familiar to Murillo's merchant clientele. In particular, Murillo seems to have known the work of the *bamboccianti*, a group of northerners who went to Italy and created a distinctive type of genre scene. The most famous was Pieter van Laer, a Dutch painter, one of whose early patrons had been the duke of Alcalá, although it is not certain whether his paintings by the artist were sent back to Seville. However, Joshua van Belle had one painting by van Laer and two by his most important Italian follower, Michelangelo Cerquozzi, proving that their works were owned by Murillo's patrons.

The best evidence that Murillo knew northern genre paintings is found in the works themselves. For instance, the *Old Woman and Young Boy* (pl. 263), datable to around 1670, reinterprets a Dutch theme that symbolizes the virtue of cleanliness (see the version by Quirijn van Brekelenkam, Leiden, Stedelijk Museum, dated 1648). Murillo also painted a few erotic genre pictures, the most remarkable of which, done around 1660, is misleadingly called *Group of Figures* (pl. 264).[23] The clue to its meaning is the bespectacled hag and the young girl, who are stock characters in scenes of prostitution. To cite one instance, they occur in a painting by Michael Sweerts (Rome, Accademia di San Luca), a Flemish painter who worked in Rome in the 1640s, where they obviously represent a prostitute and a procuress. At first, the eroticism of Murillo's composition appears subdued, but the glimpse of the little boy's backside through the hole in his trousers is suggestive of forbidden sexual practices that obviously titillated one of the artist's patrons.

Except for this one libidinous painting, Murillo's genre pictures – there are about twenty in existence – are entirely innocent and even incongruously poetic, given the impoverished condition of the subjects – usually young boys and girls wearing tattered, old clothing. For the most part, the compositions follow a pattern: two or three figures are involved in an idle pastime, such as playing games or eating bread, fruit, or sweet confections. In the background there are vaguely defined ruins and one or two notional landscape motifs, all bathed in soft light and enveloped in hazy clouds.

While it is true that this precise compositional type is unique to Murillo, the con-

263. Bartolomé Murillo, *Old Woman and Young Boy*, ca. 1670. Munich, Alte Pinakothek, canvas, 1.47 × 1.13m.

264. Bartolomé Murillo, *Group of Figures*, ca. 1660. Fort Worth, Kimbell Art Museum, canvas, 1.10 × 1.43m.

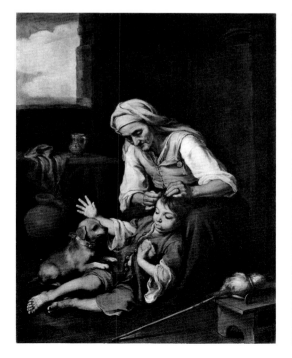

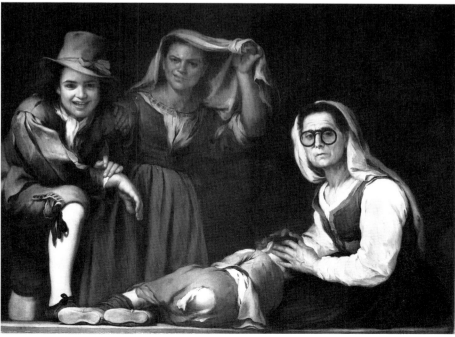

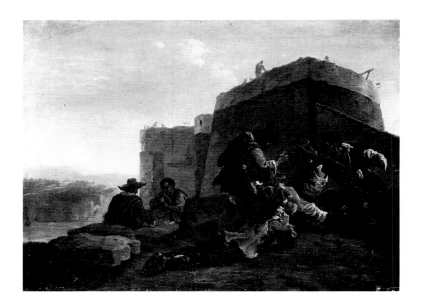

265. Pieter van Laer, *Landscape with Mora Players*, ca. 1636–37. Munich, Alte Pinakothek, panel, 0.30 × 0.41m.

stituent parts are often encountered in paintings by the *bamboccianti*. A good example is Pieter van Laer's *Landscape with Mora Players* (pl. 265), which can be instructively compared with Murillo's *Young Boys Playing Dice* (pl. 266). Despite the differences in composition, the motifs are quite similar – the boys in ragged clothes playing simple games in the open air, the irregular architectural forms, and the poetic landscape with delicately tinted clouds. Murillo's interpretation of this formula subordinates the landscape to the figures and permits him to infuse a stronger sentiment into his subjects. The origins of these pictures in the realm of northern art seem to be beyond all reasonable doubt.

Murillo's foreign clients also acquired devotional works, and here they followed the prevailing fashion. Recent research in the notarial archives of Seville has produced eighty-seven inventories compiled between 1650 and 1700, which list 241 paintings attributed to Murillo.[24] Judging by the descriptions, a high percentage can be classified as devotional images rather than narrative compositions.

The popularity of Murillo's devotional pictures right up to the end of the last century was no accident: Murillo was one of the great devotional artists of all time, especially in his later years, when he produced ingratiating compositions that inspire gentle, pious feelings. The *Infant Christ Offering a Drink of Water to St. John* (pl. 267) is a superb example of the sort of imagery that established Murillo's reputation in the seventeenth century and demolished it in the twentieth. The appeal of these pictures to the devout – and Seville's merchants were among them – is self-evident. The patronage of these businessmen provides important clues for understanding the artist. As would be expected, they habitually made careful inventories of their possessions which open a window into their physical and mental worlds.[25] They show, for example, that the traders lived in spacious houses decorated with luxurious furnishings and tapestries. Murillo's paintings, with their soft expression, subdued mood and movement, warm colors, and rich textures, would have blended into these comfortable surroundings. The avoidance of the violent side of Christian history would also have enhanced the artist's appeal to this materialistic clientele. The inventories further reveal that the merchants were apparently neither collectors nor readers of books. Their talents and energies were directed toward the world of affairs, not the world of the mind. Thus, it is natural that they were drawn to pictures that were unencumbered by recondite allegorical allusions and easily comprehended.

Despite their penchant for lush, uncomplicated pictures, these clients were not unsophisticated. As natives of foreign lands, they were acquainted with artists and

266. Bartolomé Murillo, *Young Boys Playing Dice*, ca. 1665–75. Munich, Alte Pinakothek, canvas, 1.45 × 1.08m.

280

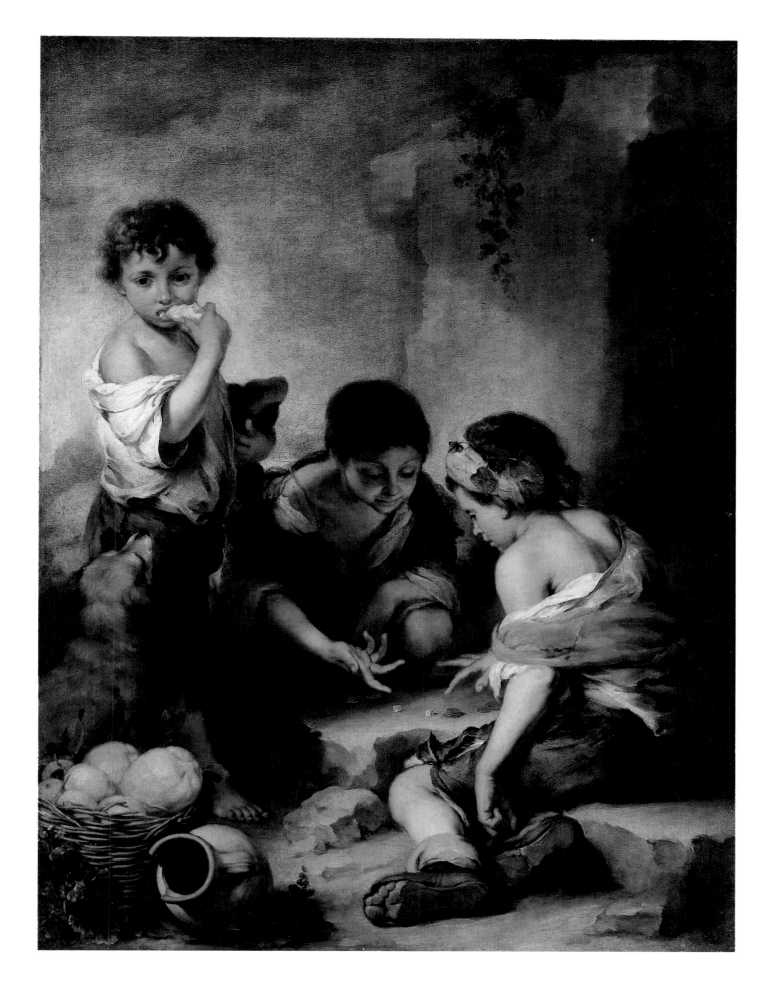

connoisseurs from Flanders, Holland, and Italy. For that matter, so were other patrons of Seville, who had access to representative works from diverse artistic cultures, such as the ones that were displayed during the festivities of Santa María la Blanca. However, among the painters of Seville, Murillo alone was capable of satisfying this cosmopolitan taste. Although he did not leave the city until 1658, and never traveled in Europe at all, he absorbed a variety of foreign sources through the study of paintings and especially prints. His canvases include compositions derived from engravings and etchings by or after Rubens, Annibale Carracci, Stefano della Bella, and Jacques Callot.[26] By borrowing ideas from these artists, Murillo applied a veneer of internationalism to his own works.

Murillo, of course, was hardly alone in appropriating compositions invented by other artists. What sets him apart from his colleagues is his superb draftsmanship and technical virtuosity, which allowed him to analyze his sources and express his ideas with maximum effect.[27] Murillo had a lifelong interest in drawing: his earliest sheets are preparatory studies for the paintings of San Francisco el Grande; his latest are for his final work, the *Mystic Marriage of St. Catherine*, for the Capuchinos of Cádiz. He produced drawings in almost every medium, including pen, ink, and wash, and colored chalk, sometimes mixing ink and crayon together. Among these drawings are many preliminary studies that demonstrate how he imitated the working procedures of Italian artists, who carefully planned their compositions and experimented with posing the figures.

A good example is the study for a painting of the Virgin and Child (pl. 269), the last of approximately twenty versions of this subject. Instead of repeating an earlier idea, Murillo started over with a new composition, which he first tried out in a

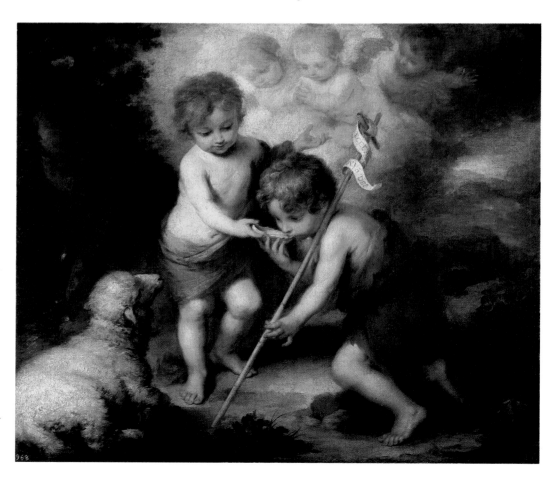

267. Bartolomé Murillo, *Infant Christ Offering a Drink of Water to St. John*, ca. 1675–80. Madrid, Prado, canvas, 1.04 × 1.24m.

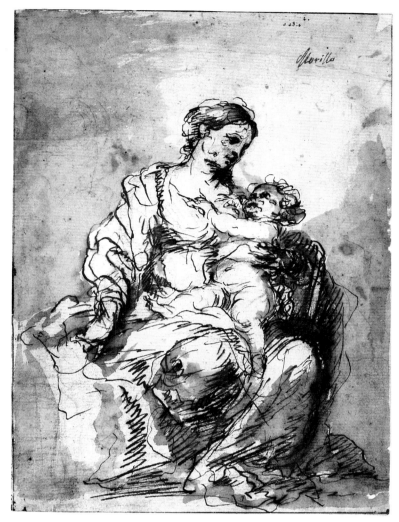

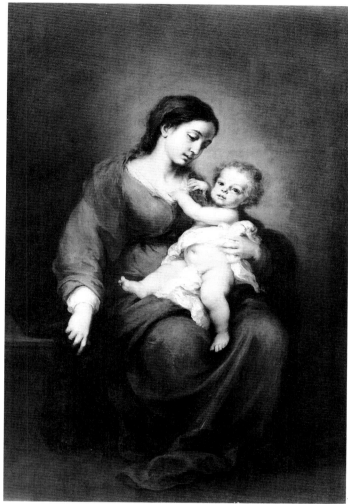

drawing (pl. 268). After considering the results, he amended the poses and in the finished work turned the Child's head outward, reducing the diagonal movement and obtaining direct communication with the viewer. More subtle is the increased complexity of the Child's pose, seen in the superb foreshortening of the legs, the twisting motion of the upper body, and the counterplay of drapery that sinuously winds around the figure. The soft colors, applied with broad brushstrokes, impart a glow to the radiant image of Mother and Child.

Obviously, for Murillo, good drawing was the foundation of good art, a point explicitly made in his *Self-Portrait* (pl. 262). On the ledge supporting the frame, he displayed the tools of his profession, palette and brushes on one side and drawing instruments on the other. These can be read as a sign that the practice of drawing was crucial to his art. More to the point, his study sheets allowed him to achieve the seemingly effortless grace that pleases his admirers and deceives his critics, and that above all makes his pictures so effective for their purpose – to inspire devotion to Christ, the Virgin, and the saints, and to show that their love makes salvation possible.

Murillo's commitment to the art of drawing had another important implication. It aligned his paintings with the foreign styles familiar to his patrons: to Canon Federigui, who had been at the court of Urban VIII; to Nicolas Omazur, who owned Flemish paintings; to Giovanni Bielato, the merchant from Genoa; to the Hispano–

268. Bartolomé Murillo, *Virgin and Child*, ca. 1675–80. Cleveland, Museum of Art, Mr. and Mrs. Charles G. Prässe Collection, pen and brown ink with brown wash, 214 × 154mm.

269. Bartolomé Murillo, *Virgin and Child*, ca. 1675–80. New York, Metropolitan Museum of Art, Rogers Fund (1943), canvas, 1.63 × 1.09m.

Irish Catholic called Fray Francisco de Jerez. The polish and sophistication resulting from his superb draftsmanship surely explain why Murillo was one of only two Spanish painters of the Golden Age who achieved a European reputation in their own lifetime (the other being Ribera).

These same qualities were decisive in the rivalry with Valdés Leal. Valdés worked for many of the same ecclesiastical patrons, but his powerful religious sentiment and the raw energy of his style were more effective in dimly lit churches, where the rough edges were lost in the shadows, than in the houses of rich private collectors, where the harsh realities of life were meant to be forgotten. The images of Valdés Leal belonged to the mystical, militant phase of Spanish Catholicism, an era that had come to a close. A tranquil dialogue between heaven and earth had now commenced, and in his soothing, seductive paintings, Murillo spoke the new language of the faith.

This idiom soon became universal in Seville, as painter after painter learned how to use it.[28] Murillo's closest imitators were products of his workshop, such as Francisco Meneses Osorio (ca. 1640–1721). But even those who had little or no direct contact with the master fell into line. Esteban Márquez (died 1696), Juan Simon Gutiérrez (1643–1718), and Cristóbal López (ca. 1671–1730) may now have few admirers, but in their time they worked hard to satisfy the demand for paintings in Murillo's manner which still showed no signs of abating in the first quarter of the eighteenth century.

By then, Murillo had been installed in the ranks of the world's greatest painters. Palomino observed this phenomenon, soon to become a craze, with misgivings: "Thus today, outside of Spain, a picture by Murillo is esteemed more than one by Titian or van Dyck. That is how much the flattery of color can coax the layman's favor!"[29] Murillo's fame went unchallenged until the end of the nineteenth century, when it was undermined by the growing secularism of western society and the rise of modernism in the arts. He may never again be mentioned in the same breath as Titian and van Dyck, but undoubtedly he deserves to be recognized as the greatest religious painter of the late seventeenth century.

13

A Grand Finale

ON 17 SEPTEMBER 1665, Philip IV died at the age of sixty-two, having ruled the Spanish monarchy for almost forty-five years. His corpse was duly removed to the Royal Pantheon of the Escorial, where it was interred with a minimum of ceremony. As was customary, the exequies were celebrated later in a splendid observance at the convent of the Encarnación, near the palace. In front of the main altar, the royal architect Sebastián de Herrera Barnuevo had designed a colossal funerary monument that reached high into the cupola above the crossing.[1] The baldacchino was a gigantic candelabrum, which held hundreds of candles. As mass was intoned, the candles were lit and the monarch who had brought his kingdom close to ruin went out in a blaze of glory.

By this time, the royal architects and artists had become more adept at manipulating political symbols than their masters at manipulating political reality. An emblem devised for the occasion showed one sun setting as a new one rose: Philip IV, the old sun king, was dead, but his successor, Prince Charles, would now illuminate the firmament.[2] Never before or since has a symbol been so much at variance with reality.

In 1649, five years after the death of his first wife, Isabella of Bourbon, Philip had married his niece Mariana of Austria, the daughter of his sister, Mary of Hungary, and the emperor Ferdinand III of Austria. This marriage set a new standard for inbreeding among the royal families of Europe, and the consequences were lethal for the couple's offspring. Of their five children, only two survived childhood, one of whom was to be the last Habsburg king of Spain, Charles II, born on 6 November 1661. Although no one expected this debilitated infant to last any longer than his ill-fated siblings, he managed to survive for thirty-nine years and presided over the final phase of the decline of Habsburg Spain.

Philip IV had bequeathed a sad inheritance to his misfit son: Spain was a country exhausted by war, impoverished by taxes, and crippled by plague and famine. Charles, who was frail of mind and body, became a hapless spectator of the machinations of his ministers and favorites, none of whom could arrest the terminal losses of power, prestige, and wealth.[3] Spain fought an intermittent war with France, which was lost, and endless war against bankruptcy, which was no more successful. A weak revival of the economy is thought to have occurred in the northeastern region of the peninsula, but in Castile misery ruled in the absence of effective government.

And yet the visual arts flourished as never before: not only were great quantities of altarpieces and easel pictures created, but private and public spectacles were undiminished in splendor. Theatrical representations with elaborate sets and complicated machinery had been introduced into court life at the Buen Retiro and continued to be performed well into the reign of Charles II. In December 1672, the musical play (zarzuela), *Los celos hacen estrellas*, by Juan Vélez de Guevara, was staged in the Gilded Hall of the Alcázar. The scenery was devised by Herrera the Younger, who later executed a beautiful series of watercolors showing how the play unfolded (pl. 270).[4]

Public spectacles were rarer, but nonetheless brilliant. One of the most elaborate was organized in 1680, when the king's first wife, Marie Louise of Orléans, entered Madrid.[5] In most respects, 1680 was a dreadful year for the country, coming on the heels of a harvest failure in 1677, which was followed by severe shortages and a soaring inflation of food prices. The news from abroad was no better. In 1678, Spain signed the Peace of Nijmegen, ceding the Franche-Comté to France. These disasters culminated in 1680 with a devaluation of the currency, which wreaked havoc on the economy and ruined many important fortunes. Yet the gigantic triumphal arches on the royal route from the Retiro through the Puerta del Sol to the Alcázar were decorated with paintings and sculpture that proclaimed the undiminished glory of Spain (pl. 271).

A more solemn event occurred on 30 June 1680, when the Inquisition staged a grandiose auto-da-fé in the Plaza Mayor of Madrid. It lasted from seven o'clock in the morning until nine in the evening and was presided over by the king, accompanied by dozens of grandees and nobles. A painting by Francisco Rizi (pl. 272) scrupulously records this bizarre ritual of stagecraft and fanaticism.[6]

Religion was never far from the minds of Spanish kings, even when their prayers manifestly went unheeded. If no longer able to defend the faith with his armies, Charles still felt obliged to uphold the inherited title of Catholic Majesty through devotions like the one recorded by Pedro Ruiz González in 1683 (pl. 273). Here the king takes communion before an ornate altar and presents himself as the defender of the sacrament of the Eucharist. The definitive statements of the king's faith were to come still later in the reign in paintings of considerably greater consequence: Claudio Coello's "*Sagrada Forma*" (pl. 288) and Luca Giordano's decoration of the Imperial Staircase of the Escorial (pl. 290).

270. Francisco de Herrera the Younger, set for *Los celos hacen estrellas*, 1673. Vienna, Oesterreichische Nationalbibliothek, pen and ink with watercolor, 208 × 150mm.

271. Anonymous, *Triumphal Arch for Solemn Entry of Marie Louise of Orléans into Madrid*, 1680. Madrid, Museo Municipal, etching, 748 × 490mm.

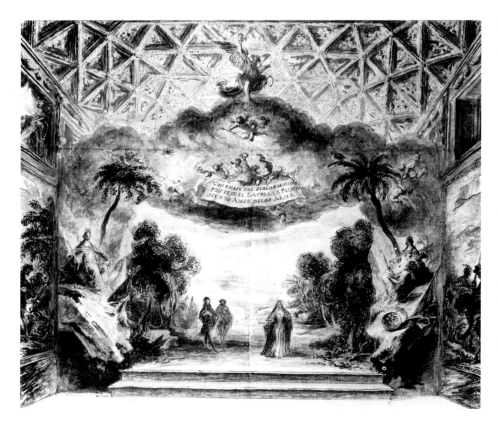

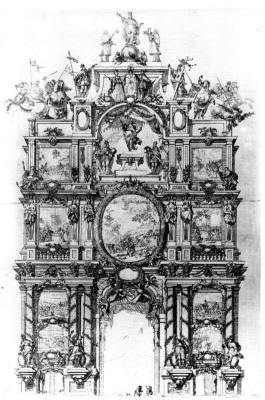

286

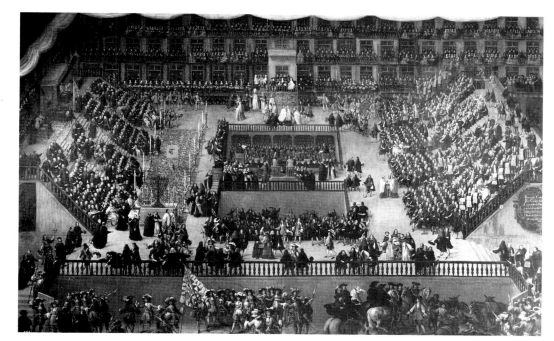

272. Francisco Rizi, *Auto-da-fé of 1680*, 1683. Madrid, Prado, canvas, 2.77 × 4.38m.

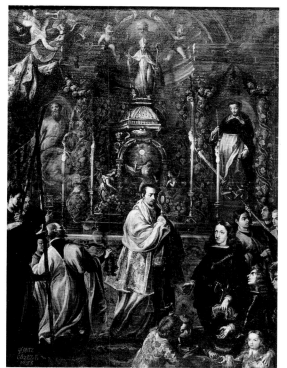

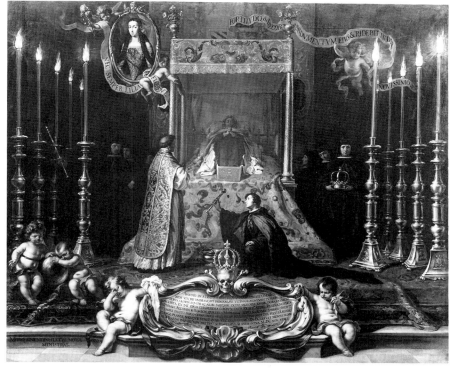

Exequies for members of the royal family offered another opportunity for ceremonial events. Marie Louise of Orléans died on 12 February 1689 and was laid in state in the palace. Sebastián Múñoz (1637–90) rendered the solemn splendor of the occasion in an excellent picture (pl. 274), one of the few in existence by his hand. The exequies, which occurred on 22–23 March in the Encarnación, featured a monumental catafalque designed by José de Churriguera. A year later, when the new queen, Mariana of Neuberg, arrived in Madrid, she was greeted with the customary triumphal procession.

The impression of great artistic activity at the court of Charles II is not an illusion,

273. Pedro Ruiz González, *Charles II Before the Sacrament*, 1683. Ponce, Puerto Rico, Museo de Arte, canvas, 2.32 × 1.66m.

274. Sebastián Múñoz, *Marie Louise of Orléans Lying in State*, 1689–90. New York, Hispanic Society of America, canvas, 2.07 × 2.52m.

however unlikely it may seem.[7] It is true that there was no figure of the magnitude of Velázquez, but the number of excellent painters, it can be argued, exceeded those who practiced during the reign of Philip IV. The causes of this creative upsurge in an epoch of drastic decline are far from clear, but a few hypotheses can be formulated.

Some credit should be attributed to Philip IV, whose lifelong affection for painting did much to encourage artists and patrons alike. Thus, several major artists of Charles's reign had emerged during the later years of Philip's rule. Carreño, Rizi, and Herrera the Younger all were established at court, although without official appointments, when the new king ascended the throne. And of these painters, two – Carreño and Rizi – proved to be effective teachers of younger artists, who filled the ranks of royal painters in the closing years of the century.

The supply of painters proved to be more than abundant; but what about the demand? The apex of the demand pyramid was occupied, of course, by the king, that is to say, by a slow-witted, poorly educated prince, whose inability to govern was conspicuous even by the standards of the later Spanish Habsburgs. But Charles was not a simpleton. Although no one has ever attempted to measure the monarch's intelligence, it may be a more rewarding task than his biographers have been willing to admit. Despite the evidence of appearances (pl. 275), there is reason to believe that the dynastic love of pictures was somehow included in the reduced package of genes received by the prince.[8]

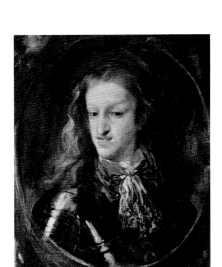

275. Claudio Coello, *Charles II*, ca. 1675–80. Madrid, Prado, 0.66 × 0.56m.

The best testimony comes from a contemporary, if prejudiced, source, Antonio Palomino, who was in Madrid from 1678 to the end of the reign (and beyond). Palomino was named royal painter in 1688 and thus was able to observe the king at first hand. Admittedly, Palomino held the monarchy in great reverence, but even after allowance is made for his bias, enough remains to show that poor Charles felt at home in the protected world of painting and painters.

Fortunately, Palomino's testimony can be confirmed by independent evidence. For instance, the documentation concerning Luca Giordano's fresco decorations at the Escorial, carried out from 1692 to 1694, demonstrates that the king closely monitored the progress, involving himself in even the smallest details.[9] Equally revealing is a letter from the baroness von Berlepsch, a member of the retinue of Mariana of Neuberg, to the duke of Neuberg, the Elector Palatine and uncle of the queen. The letter is dated 6 June 1697, when the king's health had begun its final decline, and deals with the problems caused by the elector's failure to send an ambassador to Madrid. Without an ambassador, the baroness complained, there were difficult problems that could not be solved, some of which were very difficult indeed. As an example, she mentioned a painting by Veronese in the royal collection, which the queen was supposed to obtain as a gift for her uncle: "The queen has asked for it twice, but the king denies the request, saying that it has been where it is for a long time."[10] Unable to defend his monarchy or perpetuate his dynasty, the king at least was determined to keep his hereditary picture collection intact.

Another measure of his devotion to painting is the expansion in the number of royal painters appointed during the reign. These statistics are difficult to interpret, but even as raw data they are striking. In 1668, according to a memorandum from the Committee of Works, there were three painters on the books, one of whom was not receiving remuneration.[11] This low number reflects the policy of Philip IV, who reduced the corps of royal painters inherited from his father and kept it small. Charles, on the other hand, appointed a minimum of fifteen artists to the rank between 1668 and 1698. A majority of these nominations were honorary, and those to whom a salary was granted were hard pressed to collect. Still, it is an impressive record and, up to a point, shows that Charles was cognizant of his role as a protector of the arts.

Exactly how the king deployed his small army of painters is still not very well studied, like much else in this twilight period of Spanish history. The prolific career of Luca Giordano, who served as court painter from 1692 to 1702, is hardly representative in terms of production, but in general he worked on projects of a kind that were commissioned throughout the reign. His frescoes at the Escorial continue a program of new decoration initiated by Claudio Coello's major altarpiece for the sacristy (pl. 288), while his decorative work at the Alcázar again follows in Coello's footsteps. In 1686, Coello designed ceiling paintings of Cupid and Psyche for a gallery in the queen's quarters, which were executed by Palomino, Sebastián Múñoz, and Isidoro Arredondo. Giordano, for his part, executed frescoes and oil paintings in the royal chapel.

As always, portraiture was a key requirement of royal painters, a tradition that was continued by Carreño, Coello, and the now-forgotten Venetian artist Francesco Leonardoni, who succeeded as royal portraitist upon Coello's death. Not all the tasks were quite so elevated; the still-life painter Bartolomé Pérez, who was a royal painter from 1688 to his death in 1693, received six hundred reales in 1692 for embellishing the case of a table clock. In earlier reigns, such decorative painters were paid on a piecework basis and never given fixed appointments. The documentation of his promotion helps to explain this apparent departure from tradition, but also why more and more artists were dignified with this most desired position. It was done as compensation for his work on the decorations for a festival, in lieu of payment in specie. The army of painters thus to some extent was a captive army, unpaid or underpaid, yet content to capitalize on the advantages that only a royal appointment could confer.

Outside the palace, the principal consumers of painting in Madrid were, as before, the aristocracy and the church. Aristocratic patronage during Charles's reign has never been studied in any way, although Palomino's biographies provide reason to believe that it was more reliable than it had been during the time of Philip IV. Palomino refers to the count of Benavente as his protector and has a good deal to say about the patronage of Velázquez's assistant Juan de Alfaro by the admiral of Castile, Juan Gaspar Enríquez de Cabrera.[12] It may be that the Spanish nobility was starting to be weaned from its preference for foreign artists. However, major collections of European painting were still being formed or enlarged in the period, the most important of which belonged to the admiral of Castile, Gaspar de Haro, and the duke of Medinaceli.[13]

As ever, the patronage of the church was paramount, although it has not been examined except in the context of the careers of individual artists. The quantity of altarpieces produced in and around Madrid leaves no doubt that, in one way or another, the church escaped relatively unscathed from the economic disasters of the reign. It is not surprising that ecclesiastical institutions in the city commissioned works of art; they could rely for funds on private donations as well as their annual revenues. But how rural towns like Burguillos and Orgaz found the wherewithal to engage the services of Francisco Rizi, or Calzada de Oropesa those of Claudio Coello, is still to be discovered. Whatever the causes, the effect was a booming market for the painters of Madrid.

Prince Charles was only four years old when his father died, leaving the government in the hands of the queen, who ruled, or rather misruled, until 1677 when she was temporarily banished to Toledo. Therefore, patronage at court was under her control during the first part of the reign, and she used the power to upset the established order of preference among the aspirants to favor. By right of seniority, the position of court painter should have gone to Rizi, who had been a royal painter since 1656. However, Mariana's favor alighted upon Carreño. On 27 September

1669, he was appointed by the queen to the rank of royal painter over the objections of the Committee of Works,[14] and three months later, he received a further appointment as *ayuda de furriera*. His rise to the top culminated in the appointment as court painter in 1671. During this period, Rizi's fortunes seem to have descended by equal measures. His application for a position at the Escorial in 1669 was denied, and by 1673, he was complaining that he had been "shoved into a corner" ("arrinconado"). The consequences of the gain and loss of favor for these artists naturally were significant.

Once installed as court painter, Carreño, like his illustrious predecessor Velázquez, devoted himself principally to portraiture.[15] Carreño's raw material was not inspiring: the physiognomy of Charles II remorselessly revealed the consequences of six generations of inbreeding (he had had only 46 forebears over this period instead of the normal 126). And the queen mother, while normal in appearance, insisted on being portrayed in the habit of a nun, which was worn by high-born widows as a costume of mourning. Trapped between the bleak and the black, Carreño did his job with skill and dignity.

The secret of his success is a compositional format adopted from the royal portraits of Mazo (pl. 209), in which the sitters are depicted within a state room of the palace, most frequently the famous Hall of Mirrors. This device allowed the artist to

276. Juan Carreño, *Charles II*, 1671. Oviedo, Museo de Bellas Artes de Asturias, canvas, 2.10 × 1.47m.

277. Juan Carreño, *Charles II as Grandmaster of the Golden Fleece*, 1677. Rohrau, Harrach Collection, canvas, 2.17 × 1.41m.

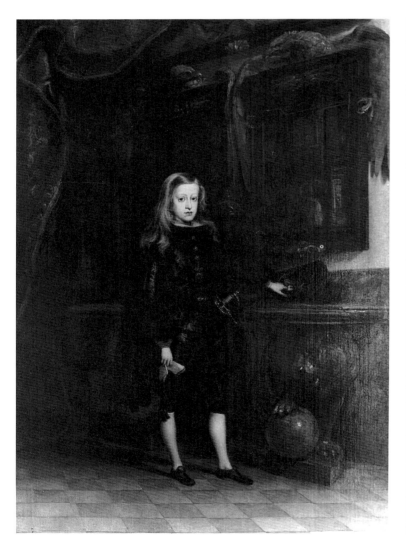

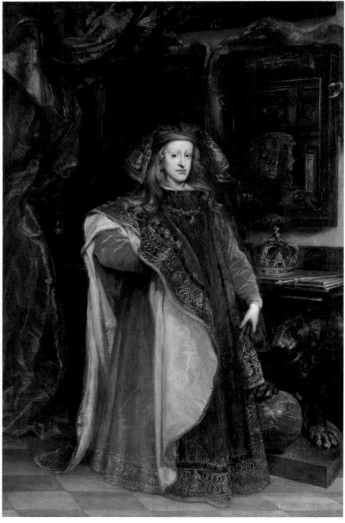

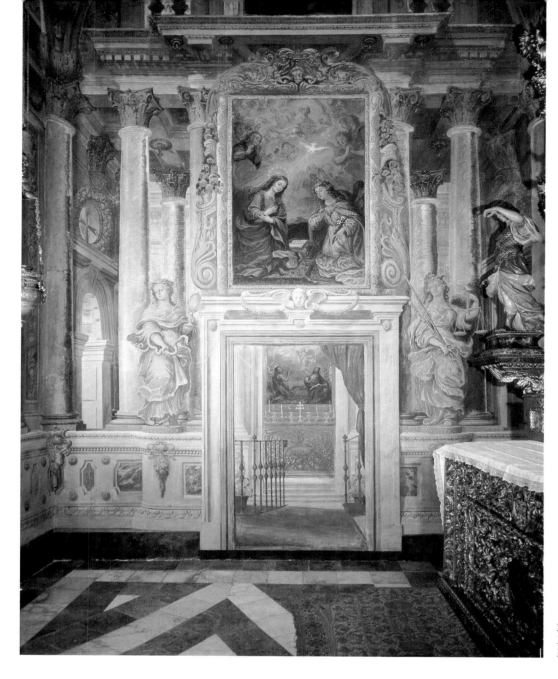

278. Francisco Rizi, Capilla del Milagro, convent of Descalzas Reales, Madrid, 1678, fresco.

soften the impact of the king's appearance by drawing attention to the surroundings, especially the fascinating reflections of the pictures in the room, as seen in a portrait of 1671, the first in the series (pl. 276). It was admittedly a trick done with mirrors, but it worked at least for a while. However, as the king aged, he grew inexorably uglier. In the flamboyant portrait of Charles as grandmaster of the Golden Fleece (pl. 277), the disparity between the regal trappings and the lost soul encased within them is profoundly unsettling. The very brilliance of execution only heightens the impression of the king's inadequacy for his lofty office.

More appealing are the portraits of non-royal sitters, in which Carreño's close study of van Dyck's masterpieces is apparent. The stylish portrait of the duke of Pastrana (1666; Prado) and the opulent rendition of the Russian ambassador Peter Ivanovich Potemkin (1681–82; Prado) testify to the overpowering influence of Flemish portraiture on artists of the period.

During much of the 1670s, Francisco Rizi was in virtual exile from the court and

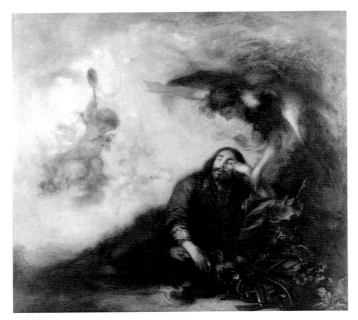

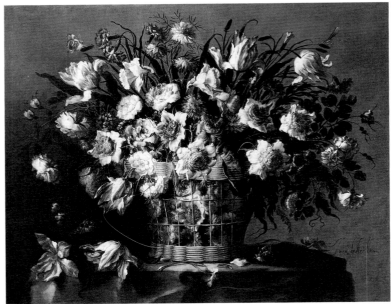

279. Francisco de Herrera the Younger, *Dream of Joseph*, ca. 1672. Madrid, private collection, canvas, 2.08 × 1.96m.

280. Juan de Arellano, *Basket of Flowers*, ca. 1670–76. Fort Worth, Kimbell Art Museum, 0.84 × 1.05m.

occupied with numerous commissions for provincial churches and monasteries.[16] His position as painter to the cathedral of Toledo provided him with some work, and from this base of operations he branched out into other towns of the archdiocese. He also attracted the patronage of the Carmelites, who ordered altarpieces for their churches in Avila and Alba de Tormes. As a group, these pictures show that Rizi's talent for theatrical composition and effective massing of figures was undiminished; but the execution is sometimes careless, as if he believed that the finer points of the art would be wasted on farmers and friars.

Rizi returned to favor around 1677, when Juan José de Austria, the illegitimate son of Philip IV, became the chief minister. During the first part of the reign, this prince had schemed to take control of the government, only to back away when he had nearly accomplished his objective. In 1677, he finally resolved to make his move and banished the queen mother to Toledo. Juan José hardly had time to assert himself before he died in September 1679, with little to show for his efforts, unless it be the restitution of Rizi at court.

In 1678, Rizi started to fresco in a chapel founded by Juan José in the convent of the Descalzas Reales, where the prince's illegitimate daughter (born of a union with the niece of Jusepe de Ribera) had taken vows. The Capilla del Milagro, although tiny in scale, is replete with every device of pictorial illusionism. In order to impart a feeling of expansiveness to the space, Rizi painted a fictional colonnade, beyond which there is a view into an illusionistic, columned hall (pl. 278). On one wall, the artist created a false door, with a distant altar visible through a painted gate. In the cupola, he depicted the Assumption of the Virgin, an event observed by the gesticulating apostles who are ranged around a balustrade. With this display of virtuosity, Rizi regained his due place at court.

The third royal painter of this vintage is Herrera the Younger, who returned to Madrid from Seville in 1660, hoping no doubt to resume the career begun so auspiciously with the paintings for the Carmelite church (pl. 215). However, the progress of Herrera's later career is difficult to follow.[17] While Palomino mentions his activity as a fresco painter, all his works in this medium have been destroyed, and the altarpieces and easel paintings have not fared much better. From the few surviving pictures, and from the more numerous drawings, it can be seen that he developed into an ever more brilliant artist. The special qualities of his art can be gauged in the *Dream of Joseph* (pl. 279), executed for the Colegio de Santo Tómas, Madrid, perhaps in the early 1670s. This painting contains all the distinctive features of the artist's later works: pastel colors, warm, hazy light, and amazingly loose brushwork. Herrera's lyrical style is seductive and gentle, although the man himself was famously irascible and combative. Herrera gained the appointment as royal painter in 1672, but almost at once began to shift his interests to architecture. He was appointed master of the royal works in 1677 and thereafter divided his time between Madrid and Zaragoza, where he created the design and supervised the construction of the basilica of El Pilar until bitter quarrels with the canons forced him to leave.

Beyond the confines of the court, there was a diverse group of painters who serviced the steady demand of ecclesiastical clients. Some were long-lived survivors of the previous reign, like Antonio de Pereda, who died in 1678. Francisco Camilo (1615–73), like Pereda, had been an apprentice of Pedro de las Cuevas, but proved to be more amenable to the innovations of Carreño, Rizi, and Herrera, particularly their sketchy brushwork.[18] His fusion of the stable, voluminous forms of Carducho with the more advanced technique of the post-Rubens generation is a hallmark of his style.

A third member of this transitional group is the still-life painter Juan de Arellano (1614–76), the best of the numerous practitioners of this genre who worked in Madrid during the second part of the century.[19] During the forties and fifties, still lifes from Flanders and Naples were imported in increasing quantities, gradually displacing the approach formulated by Sánchez Cotán and developed by van der Hamen. Arellano was inspired by the Antwerp school of flower painting, represented by Jan Brueghel the Elder and the Younger and Daniel Seghers, whom he effectively imitated (pl. 280). The artist sold his pictures directly to the public from a shop he maintained for over forty years outside San Felipe el Real, in the Puerta del Sol.

The succeeding group of painters was born and bred into the High Baroque style; by a macabre coincidence, the best of them died young, dramatically thinning the ranks of successors to Rizi and Carreño, who had been their teachers. Among the best of Carreño's pupils were Juan Martín Cabezalero and Mateo Cerezo. The former was born in Almadén around 1633 and lived only until 1673.[20] After his arrival in Madrid, he entered Carreño's studio and remained in his household until 1666. Despite his training, Cabezalero had a distinct style from his master. His figures are drawn with crisp outlines and carefully modeled with firm, controlled brushstrokes, qualities that are different from the broken, impasto technique employed by Carreño. These characteristics are evident in one of his few surviving works, the *Assumption of the Virgin* (pl. 281), probably executed in the late 1660s and more indebted to Italian than Flemish sources.

Cerezo, by contrast, follows right in Carreño's path. He was born in Burgos in 1637 and died in 1666, when not yet thirty years old.[21] Palomino dates his arrival in Madrid around 1652, which is when he probably began to study with Carreño. He spent the later years of the decade in Valladolid, returning definitively to the capital around 1660. Over the next six years, his development was rapid as a religious painter and as one of the most appealing still-life artists of the period. These abilities are already evident in a painting dated 1660, the *Mystic Marriage of St. Catherine* (pl. 282), where the bright colors, sparkling textures, and harmonious composition show his precocious talent.

Like Carreño, Francisco Rizi was an inspiring teacher, and the earliest of his pupils was Juan Antonio Escalante, who continued to collaborate with his master after becoming an independent artist. Escalante was born in Córdoba in 1633.[22] He arrived in Madrid around 1650 and lived only until 1669, when he succumbed to tuberculosis. Like the other painters of his generation, Escalante was overwhelmed by the

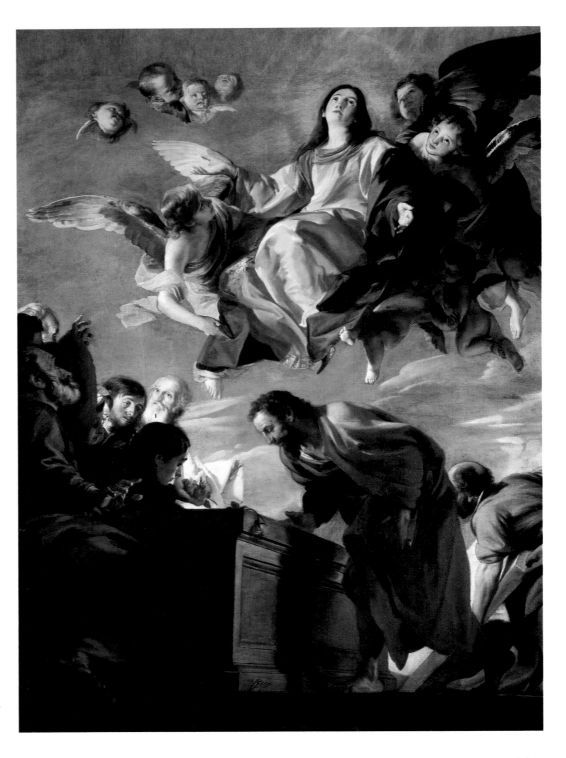

281. Juan Martín Cabezalero, *Assumption of the Virgin*, ca. 1665–70. Madrid, Prado, canvas, 2.37 × 1.69m.

great Venetian and Flemish pictures in Madrid collections, but he interpreted his sources in an individualistic way, devising a manner that is closer to an oil sketch than a finished painting. A typical example of his spirited style is *Elias and the Angel* (pl. 283), part of a series he executed in 1667–68 for the Merced Calzada, Madrid. The cool, varied colors, swirling movement of drapery, and air of excited communication between the prophet and the angel are representative of the artist at his best.

The last of these short-lived masters is José Antolínez, one of the few painters of his generation to be born in Madrid (1635–75).[23] Palomino describes Antolínez as a

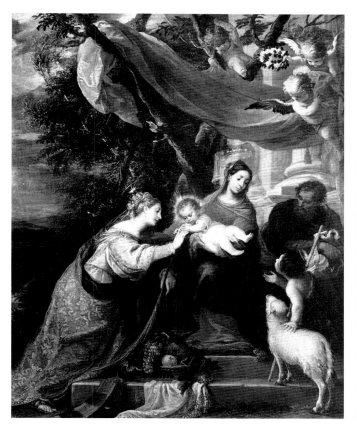

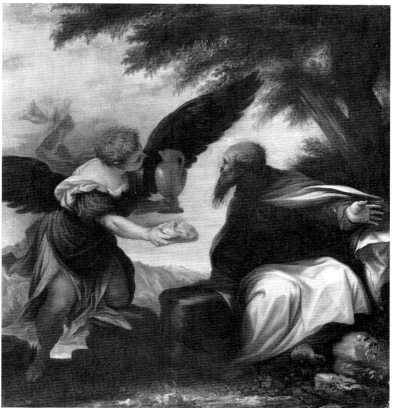

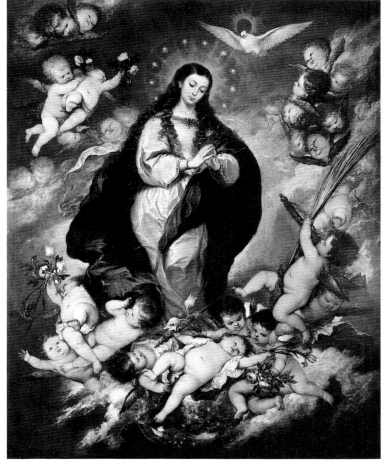

282 (above left). Mateo Cerezo, *Mystic Marriage of St. Catherine*, 1660. Madrid, Prado, canvas, 2.07 × 1.63m.

283 (above right). Juan Antonio Escalante, *Elias and the Angel*, 1667–68. Madrid, Prado, canvas.

284. José Antolínez, *Immaculate Conception*, ca. 1665–70. Oxford, Ashmolean Museum, canvas, 2.11 × 1.70m.

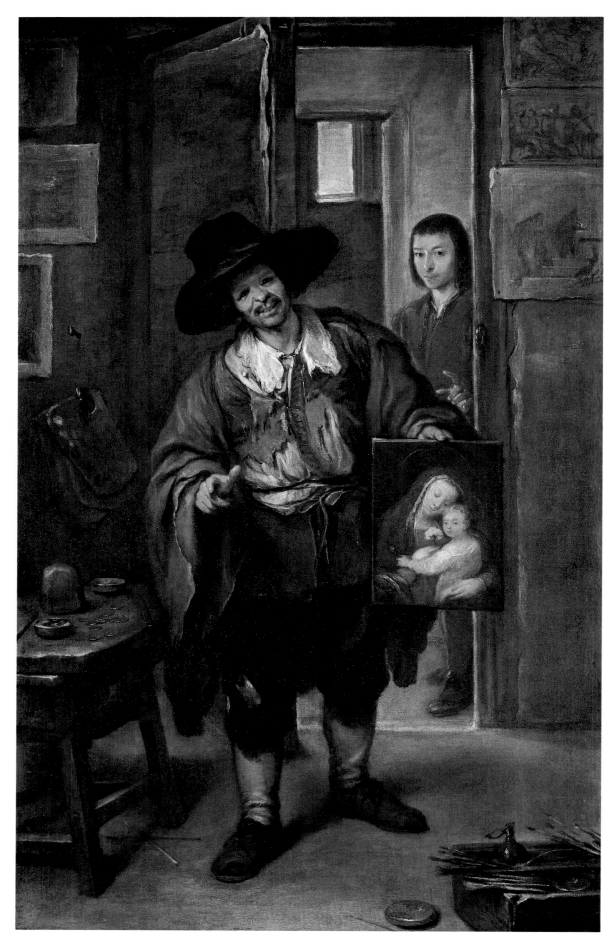

285. José Antolínez,
Picture Merchant, ca. 1670.
Munich, Alte Pinakothek,
canvas, 2.01 × 1.25m.

colorful although not very likeable character, as vain as he was talented. Perhaps for this reason, he was an outsider to the established art world and received only a few church commissions. Antolínez was thus compelled to earn a living from devotional paintings, especially of the Virgin of the Immaculate Conception. Despite his boasts and pretensions, Antolínez probably lived like the humble painter seen in his own extraordinary work, the *Picture Merchant* (pl. 285), which can be interpreted as a self-mocking representation of his marginal existence. But the artist's overweening pride was not entirely unfounded. Although his versions of the Immaculate Conception follow a set formula, including a peculiar, ovoid facial type, they are painted with deep, delicious colors and a richly textured brushwork (pl. 284).

The consequences of the early deaths of these promising artists were forestalled by the continued vitality of the older royal painters. But almost as if by prearrangement, they all disappeared at once. Rizi died on 2 August 1685 and was followed by Herrera on 25 August. Carreño attended Herrera's funeral with a sense of grim humor and foreboding; Palomino quotes him as saying: "This is just so he can be a little ahead of us," an ironic reference to their longstanding rivalry.[24] His presentiments were not unfounded, and on 3 October, he died too, bringing to a close a vital period of the Spanish Golden Age. Fortunately, new talent was by then on hand.

The leader of this group, and one of the best painters of the seventeenth century, is Claudio Coello, who was born in Madrid early in 1642.[25] Coello was trained by Rizi in the mid-1650s and soon developed a distinctive personal style. From Rizi, he acquired the talent for scenographic compositions that employ a framework of classical architecture. The balanced but active disposition of figures was another part of Rizi's legacy, as was the skill in fresco painting, a major part of Coello's activity. However, Coello is a more careful, assured draftsman, who avoids the hasty abbreviation of extremities and the agitated surface effects by which Rizi disguised his lack of interest in rendering anatomy. The most distinctive feature of Coello's style is a soft, opalescent light that imparts a warm patina to his canvases. In his mature works, Coello sometimes surprisingly approximates followers of Pietro da Cortona such as Ciro Ferri and especially Carlo Maratta.

This similarity might be more than mere chance because, around 1660, two painters arrived in Madrid fresh from lengthy stays in Rome. Both are now little known, their works having either vanished or been misidentified. Of the two, Andries Smidt is the more elusive. He was a native of Antwerp, born around 1625, who was in Rome by 1650 and who arrived in Madrid about 1660, where he lived until his death twenty years later.[26] Only one work by the artist is known, the *Virgin of Atocha with Saints* (Madrid, Museo Lázaro Galdiano), which is dated 1663 and unmistakably resembles Coello's treatment of light and forms. Indications of a relationship between Smidt and Coello are still too fragile to support any weighty theories about an artistic connection between them.

It is quite a different matter as far as José Jiménez Donoso is concerned.[27] Born in Consuegra (Toledo) around 1632, Donoso was apprenticed in Madrid to Francisco Fernández, a pupil of Carducho. According to Palomino, he then went to Rome, where he remained for several years. Although this long stay is not otherwise documented, his paintings make it credible. Donoso returned to Madrid in the late 1650s and began an active career as a painter and frescoist, of which little survives. A rare painting of the *Foundation of the Lateran Basilica* (pl. 286), executed around 1666 for the Valencian Order of Mercy, is comparable to the early work of Cortona's follower Lazzaro Baldi (active in Rome from the mid-1650s). From the early 1670s on, Donoso and Coello shared numerous fresco commissions and were probably in contact in the preceding years as well, when Claudio could have acquired the Roman veneer that is apparent in these years.

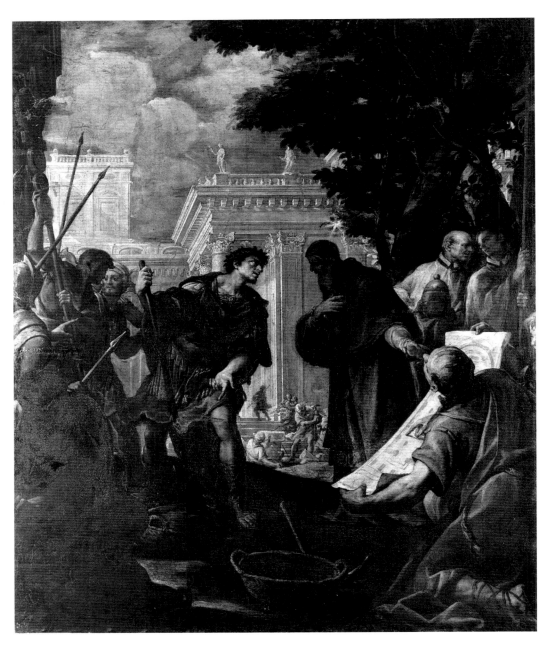

286. José Jiménez Donoso, *Foundation of the Lateran Basilica*, ca. 1666. Valencia, Museo de Bellas Artes, canvas, 2.42 × 2.00m.

287. Claudio Coello, *Triumph of St. Augustine*, 1664. Madrid, Prado, canvas, 2.70 × 2.03m.

Coello was a highly productive artist, but the most significant part of his output, the frescoes, virtually disappeared in the wholesale destruction of Madrid's Baroque churches and chapels. Still, the numerous oil paintings are sufficient to track his development and assess his achievement. By 1664, the year of the *Triumph of St. Augustine* (pl. 287), Coello, although only twenty-two, was a self-assured master of his art. While it is true that the composition probably stems from Herrera's *Triumph of St. Hermengild* (pl. 215), Coello has simplified and anchored the scheme through the introduction of a classical colonnade. The bishop's crozier runs parallel to the body like a road sign, indicating the upward, diagonal movement of the saint. Coello's chromatic sense, refined as always, blends many hues of blue and red, which are burnished by the soft light.

Over the next ten years, Coello produced paintings at a prodigious pace for churches all over the heartland of Castile, until at last, on 30 March 1683, he was rewarded with the appointment of royal painter. The parlous state of the crown's finances prevented payment of his salary for two years, although Coello had as

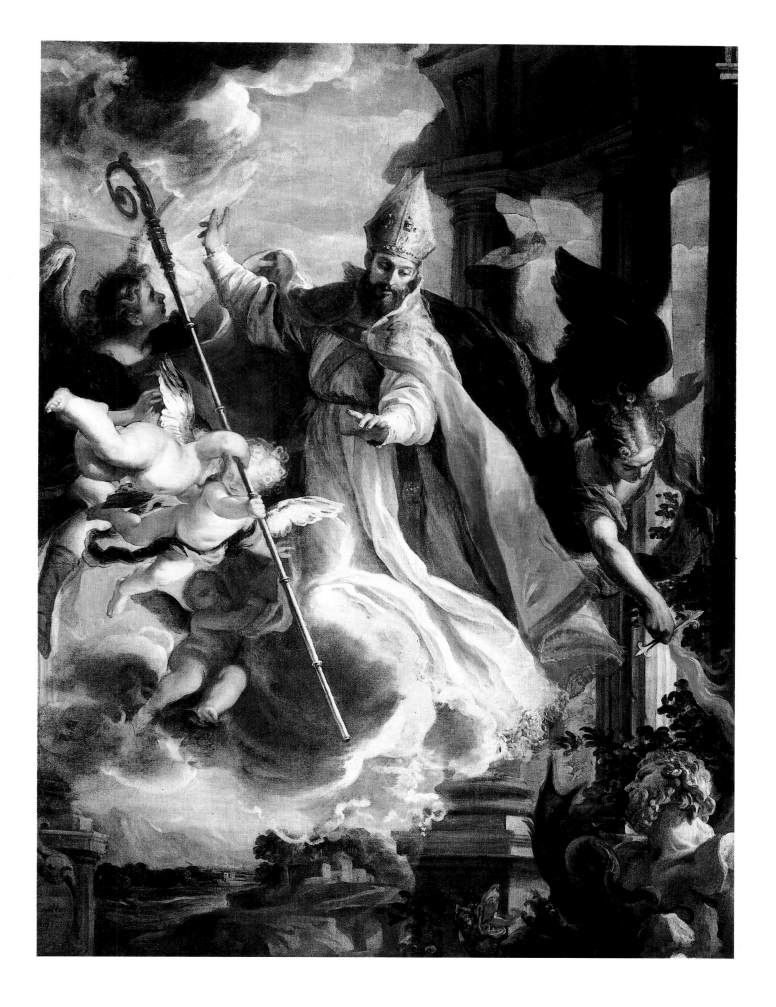

much to do for other patrons as he could handle. From July 1683 to July 1684, he was in Zaragoza, executing a large fresco for the Augustinian college of Santo Tomás de Villanueva (now San Roque, and known as "La Mantería"). Part of the fresco survives and, although heavily restored, affords the best example of Coello's work in this medium. In 1684–85, the artist was occupied with several church commissions in Madrid. There is little to indicate that he did much for the crown, which was only fair considering what he was being paid. Finally, in 1685, his salary was initiated, although it quickly fell into arrears, and in January 1686, he was appointed court painter, filling the vacancy created by the death of Carreño.

In 1685, Coello began his first important picture for the king, known as "*La Sagrada Forma*," a highpoint in Spanish Baroque painting (pl. 288).[28] This large, ambitious work has a complex history, which is rooted in the endless political intrigues of the reign. In the early 1670s, the dowager queen Marianna had promoted a young commoner, Fernando Valenzuela, to the position of favorite. This appointment dismayed certain grandees who expected one of their number to fill the office. Valenzuela lasted a couple of years in power and then was banished, but in 1676 he returned for another period that ended when the *junta de gobierno* (the ruling committee, which advised the king) decided to overthrow him. Charles sent Valenzuela to a supposedly safe refuge at the Escorial late in 1676, but his hiding place was discovered. On 17 January 1677, the duke of Medina Sidonia led a group of nobles and a company of soldiers into the monastery to capture Valenzuela, violating the privilege of sanctuary. The prior watched in horror as the soldiers tore through the building in search of the artless dodger and promptly excommunicated Medina Sidonia and his collaborators. As a result, the leaders of His Catholic Majesty's government were no longer members of the church that he was sworn to uphold.

A way out of this untenable situation was sought by the king, who petitioned Pope Innocent XI to pardon the sinners. This was granted on condition that the guilty parties pay for a new altar in the monastery, which, in the event, was sponsored by the king. The site for the altar was in the sacristy, one wall of which was transformed into a composition of colored marbles and sculpture with Coello's picture as the centerpiece.

This enormous work, which measures about five by three meters, is in fact a movable screen, which can be lowered by a pulley into the floor below, revealing the miraculous host of Gorkum, the "Sagrada Forma," a monstrance that had shed blood when defiled by the Protestants in 1572. This precious object was transferred to the new altar in an expiatory ceremony held on 19 October 1684 and attended by the king, the offending noblemen, and members of the court, and it is this event that is represented in Coello's picture.

The "*Sagrada Forma*" is at once a documentary, a ceremonial group portrait, a religious allegory, and a statement of political propaganda, all conjoined in a masterpiece of illusionistic painting. Large-scale group portraits are very rare in Spanish art; the *Surrender of Breda* (pl. 130) and *Las Meninas* (pl. 198) are the obvious forerunners, and Coello's invention is worthy of their company. As a documentary, it records the ceremony of 19 October 1684, when Charles and members of the junta expunged the penalty of excommunication through the prescribed act of penitence. The king kneels in devotion before the host of Gorkum, which is held by the prior, Fray Francisco de los Santos, the author of an important book on the Escorial. In the right corner are the offenders, including the dukes of Medina Sidonia, of Pastrana, and of Medinaceli, the marquis of La Puebla, and others. Members of the religious community fill the rest of the space, which is depicted with literal accuracy, to the pictures on the wall, the same ones installed by Velázquez in the 1650s.

288. Claudio Coello, "*La Sagrada Forma*," 1685–90. El Escorial, sacristy, canvas, approx. 5.00 × 3.00m.

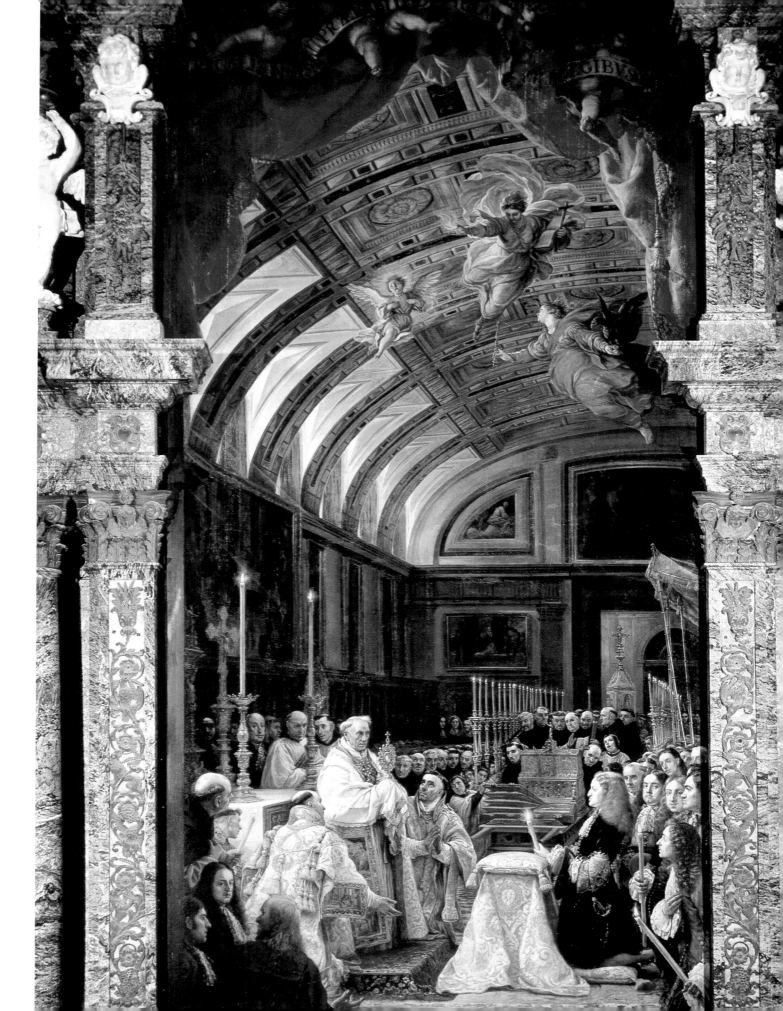

The picture was intended to be more than an artistic "snapshot" of an important event. It also has an allegorical dimension, which is introduced by the inscription and by the winged personifications that soar in the upper reaches of the high-vaulted room. The inscription, held aloft by putti, reads: REGALIS MENSA PRAEBIT DELICIAS REGIBUS (the table of the king shall provide delights for kings), a reference to the altar, the Holy Eucharist, and the king's piety. The personifications, which are derived from Cesare Ripa's emblem book, *Iconología*, symbolize, from left to right, Divine Love, Religion, and Royal Majesty – the tripartite components of the Habsburg dynasty. By inserting these textual and allegorical references, Coello sought to shift the focus from a specific, and fundamentally shameful, event in the history of the monarchy to an age-old Habsburg theme – the dynasty as the temporal defender of the faith. In effect, the picture absorbs the resonant echoes of royal piety still heard within the Escorial and recycles them to glorify the faith of Charles II. Coello has not only made the best of a bad thing; he has turned an act of religious contrition into a moment of secular triumph. This may now seem a dubious accomplishment, but it certainly represented exemplary service to the crown of Spain.

Following the completion of his masterpiece, Coello's health began to fail, and his end supposedly was hastened by the arrival of the Neapolitan master Luca Giordano, who started to work at the Escorial in the autumn of 1692. Whether it was disappointment or disease that delivered the final blow, Coello died in the summer of 1693, leaving Giordano in a commanding position amidst the large army of newly appointed Spanish royal painters.

Coello's appointment as royal painter in 1683 seems to mark a change in attitude toward this jealously guarded honor. From that year to the end of the reign, at least eleven new appointments were made (twelve if Coello is included) to the ranks.[29] In fact, in 1703, three years after the Bourbons had succeeded the Habsburgs on the throne, the committee of Royal Works confessed that it had lost count of the painters employed by the crown. Many of these were unsalaried and had been awarded their positions as a means to obtain free labor or settle outstanding debts. Yet not all were negligible artists; one was a significant figure indeed, the painter-theorist Antonio Palomino.

Palomino has long been known as the "Spanish Vasari," a reputation earned as the author of the biographies of 226 artists published in 1724 in a treatise entitled *Museo pictórico y escala óptica*. The biographical section, subtitled "El Parnaso español pintoresco laureado," is deserving of its great reputation and continues to be a valuable source of information about painters of the Golden Age. It may be that its very usefulness as an historical source has overshadowed the first two parts of the treatise, not to mention Palomino's career as a painter.

Asisclo Antonio Palomino de Castro y Velasco was baptized with this lengthy name on 1 December 1655, in the Cordoban town of Bujalance.[30] About ten years later, his family, who were *hidalgos*, moved to Córdoba and enrolled the young boy in the Dominican college of Santo Tomás. Here Palomino began to acquire the extraordinary and varied erudition that was later decanted into his treatise. He finished his schooling and took holy orders, but by then he had discovered a talent for painting, to which he devoted his life. Although nothing is known of his early studies, he did receive encouragement from a local painter, Juan de Alfaro y Gámez, who had worked in Velázquez's shop in the 1650s. At the urging of Alfaro, and with his support, Palomino moved to Madrid in 1678.

Once settled in the capital, the artist became a close friend of Carreño and studied with Coello, who may have taught him the technique of fresco, at which he later excelled. In addition, he continued his studies of mathematics and optics with Padre Jacobo Kresa, a professor at the Colegio Imperial.

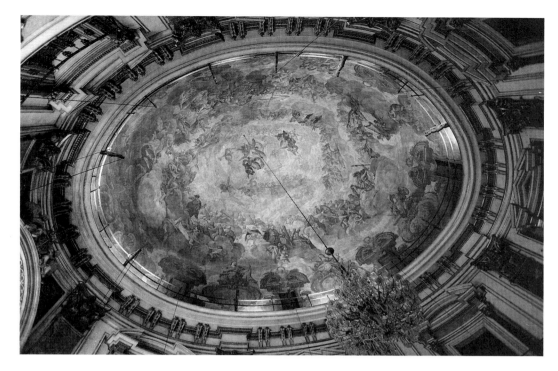

289. Antonio Palomino, cupola,
Nuestra Señora de los Desamparados,
Valencia, ca. 1700, fresco.

Equipped with a formidable education and accomplished technique, Palomino gradually began to build his career, finally gaining the appointment as honorary royal painter on 23 June 1688. During the 1690s, he painted frescoes in Madrid and became acquainted with Luca Giordano, whom he greatly admired. But Palomino was to do his best work outside Madrid, where he developed a devoted and far-flung clientele.

Palomino's move to the provinces was timed well. In 1699, he left for Valencia to paint frescoes in Santos Juanes (known as San Juan del Mercado); one year later, on 1 November 1700, Charles II died, having bequeathed the monarchy to the grandson of Louis XIV, who would rule as Philip V, although without full authority until the French had defeated the Austrian Habsburg pretender, the archduke Charles, in the War of the Spanish Succession (concluded in 1714). In the interim, the court was in a state of flux and Madrid was unsettled by the invasion of the Austrian forces in 1706. It was a good moment to be out of town, and Palomino prospered, despite the hard times, thanks to his provincial clients.

After completing the work at Santos Juanes (now destroyed), Palomino accepted a fresco commission from another Valencian church, Nuestra Señora de los Desamparados, where he displayed his mastery of Italian Baroque fresco decoration (pl. 289). In succeeding years, the artist executed frescoes in Salamanca (San Esteban, 1705), Granada (Cartuja, 1711–12), Córdoba (cathedral, 1712–13), and El Paular (Cartuja, 1723), as well as a full complement of altarpieces and easel paintings, becoming the leading Spanish exponent of what might be called the international style of late Baroque painting. At his death, on 12 August 1726, he could look back upon a long and prosperous career, although it might be called more successful than brilliant.

His treatise, however, is a different matter; it is indisputably the most important theoretical work produced in the Spanish Golden Age and the equal of any treatise written by a painter up to the date of its publication.[31] *Museo pictórico y escala óptica* was published in two installments: the first part, consisting of the theory of painting, appeared in 1715; the second, with the section on practice and the biographies, in

1724, that is to say, two years before the artist's death. Although publication did not occur until well into the first quarter of the eighteenth century, the book has its origins in the mental and practical world of the seventeenth.

Palomino's treatise is distinguished from its predecessors in Spain by the scope of its material and the rigor of its organization. Unlike Pacheco and Carducho, who were learned painters, Palomino was both learned and a painter. His studies with the Dominicans in Córdoba and the Jesuits in Madrid had provided him with a thorough education in religious and humanistic letters, so that even when he takes up the traditional topics of theoretical writing – the origin of painting and its claims to the status of a liberal art, the subjects of Books One and Two – he is able to make the arguments with unprecedented erudition and thoroughness.

Similarly, in the technical section, which is contained in Book Three, his careful study of mathematics and geometry comes to the fore. Pacheco had dealt with practice as technique, while Carducho had preferred to ignore it entirely, fearing to undermine his defense of painting as a liberal art. But Palomino, like Andrea Pozzo, whose treatise on perspective had been published a couple of decades earlier, was a geometer and mathematician, and his disquisitions on technique leave no doubt that painting is a serious scientific pursuit. Much more could be said about this enormously rich work of artistic literature, which raised the discourse on painting to a new level and was crucial in spreading knowledge of the Spanish school to other parts of Europe.

The final chapter in the history of Golden Age painting in Spain, like the first, was written by a foreign artist, the prodigious Luca Giordano (1634–1705).[32] As a Neapolitan, Giordano was nominally a Spanish subject, although he had lived and worked in Italy all his life. However, his paintings had been admired in Madrid since the reign of Philip IV, who twice attempted to lure the painter to his court. Giordano resisted the invitations and meanwhile created a European reputation as a brilliant frescoist and the world's fastest painter.

Charles succeeded where his father had failed by exploiting Giordano's famous lust for lucre. In 1690, Giordano petitioned the king to renew his son's appointment in the government of Naples.[33] Charles agreed only on condition that the painter, then approaching sixty years of age, come to Spain as his court painter. The offer was sweetened by the promise of immense rewards in the form of royal appointments for his relatives, including his father-in-law, who was a notorious smuggler.

Giordano, it must be said, gave good value for the money. He arrived in Spain in 1692 and stayed for ten years. According to Palomino, he put his brush down only to eat, sleep, and take an occasional ride in a carriage put at his disposal by the king. He started by creating extensive frescoes at the Escorial, which occupied him from September 1692 to July 1694. Then he moved to Madrid, where he painted frescoes in the royal chapel (destroyed) and in the churches of Nuestra Señora de Atocha (destroyed) and San Antonio de los Portugueses, restoring the work of Rizi and Carreño. In the Casón of the Buen Retiro, he composed a grandiloquent fresco glorifying the Order of the Golden Fleece and the Spanish monarchy (in situ).[34] And in Toledo, again at the king's behest, he decorated the ceiling of the cathedral sacristy with the Bestowal of the Chasuble on St. Ildephonsus (1698; in situ). When Giordano was not on a scaffold, he was in front of an easel, cranking out uniformly fine pictures for private patrons and churches as well as for the king. To this day, the patrimonial collections of the Spanish crown contain over two hundred paintings by his hand.

Giordano was brought to Spain for a specific purpose, to execute the frescoes at the Escorial, which may be taken as a representative commission. Charles's desire to leave his artistic mark on the Escorial is understandable: this great building was the

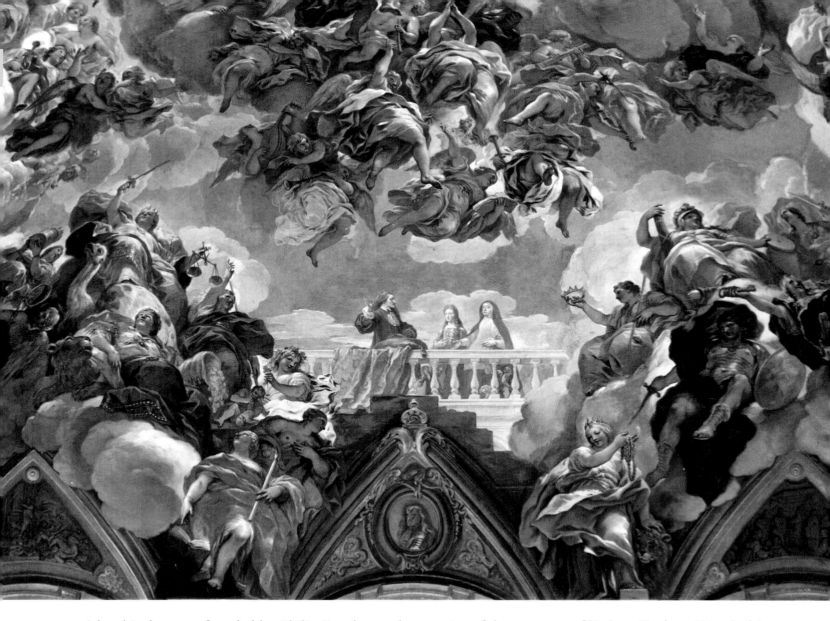

memorial to his dynasty, founded by Philip II to house the remains of the emperor
Charles V. It was here that all of Charles's ancestors had been buried and where one
day soon he would be laid to rest. By 1692, it had become apparent that the king
would die without an heir, thus bringing to a close almost two hundred years of
Habsburg rule in Spain. Charles, attentive as ever to the use of art for royal propaganda, hired the greatest fresco painter of the age to cast his valedictory into a
magnificent pictorial statement.

Most of Giordano's frescoes are in the basilica, where they complement the themes
expounded by the artists of Philip II. But above the Imperial Staircase, located in the
courtyard of the Evangelists, he deployed his inexhaustible store of pictorial rhetoric
to offer a final tribute to the Habsburg dynasty.[35] In the lower register, on the wall
beneath the vault, Giordano depicted three episodes of the battle of St. Quentin, the
first victory of the reign of Philip II, which inspired him to build the Escorial. A
fourth section shows Philip directing the construction of the edifice. In the vault,
there is a resplendent vision of the Adoration of the Trinity by the heavenly host,
which includes martyrs, saints, and also the persons of Charles V and Philip II, who
offer their crowns to the triple godhead. This imagery is a deliberate reprise of the
icon of the Spanish Habsburgs, Titian's *Gloria* (pl. 34), which had been with the

290. Luca Giordano, *Triumph of the
Spanish Habsburgs*, 1692–94. El
Escorial, Imperial Staircase, fresco.

305

emperor when he died at Yuste and subsequently transferred by his devoted son to the Escorial. This allusion is another way of invoking the grandeur of the founders; Titian had shown the kings kneeling at the gate of heaven, and Giordano was able to confirm that they had been granted entry. Behind a balustrade, at a respectful but unbridgeable distance, the last of the line, accompanied by his overbearing mother and his detestable second wife, points to the vision of glory that was now only a sacred memory (pl. 290).

With the death of Charles in 1700, the Golden Age of painting in Spain came to a close. The advent of the Bourbons was by no means unpropitious for the arts; indeed, a new cycle of foreign influence and native assimilation was initiated, which brought to Spain such important painters as Giaquinto, Tiepolo, and Mengs, and culminated in the emergence of Goya in the 1780s. However, the Bourbon reform of Spanish institutions attempted to level the differences with the rest of Europe, and the realities of the changing balance of power sapped the confidence and conviction of the Habsburg era, when the patrons and painters of Spain received artistic ideas from abroad and transformed them into a Hispanocentric vision of human and universal history.

Epilogue
Masters or Servants?
Spanish Painters of the Golden Age

ALMOST FROM ITS ORIGINS, the history of art has been studied according to nation and chronology. Even today, books are routinely written and courses taught on subjects such as French Gothic, Italian Renaissance, Spanish Baroque, and English Neo-Classicism, to mention just a few examples. Despite the widespread acceptance of this convention, historians of art tend to be reluctant to define the intrinsic features of a national or regional style and, when they venture to do so, often resort to uncritical generalizations. Few would deny that these differences can be readily perceived; an experienced eye can tell at a glance whether a painting of the seventeenth century was done in Holland or Italy, or even in Amsterdam or Naples. The difficulties arise when it is time to put these differences into words and to identify the conditions that fostered a particular mode of pictorial expression.

It is reasonable to suppose that the issue of national styles is skirted because, more often than not, it has inspired facile formulations based on unproven, and sometimes dangerous, assumptions. However, such errors ought not to condemn the enterprise since, in principle, the differences between the art of various regions of Europe, if carefully analyzed, can help in understanding broader historical experiences as well as in answering significant questions concerning artistic production.

The distinctive character of Spanish painting of the sixteenth and seventeenth centuries was already apparent to observers at the time, as indicated by examples drawn at random from Italian sources. For instance, in 1502, the painter Antoniazzo Romano, who was patronized by Spanish prelates in Rome, was commissioned to execute two canvases for San Giacomo degli Spagnoli, which were to be done *ad modum ispanje*, "in the Spanish manner."[1] What is meant by the phrase is not explained, but obviously some sort of empirical distinction was understood by the parties to the contract.

In 1590, another perception of "Spanish taste" is encountered in a commission by the count of Chinchón. The count was planning to augment the decoration of a chapel in his town and decided to order two paintings from Florence, using the Florentine ambassador as his intermediary. In the instructions to his correspondent at the grand-ducal court, the ambassador wrote as follows:

> Advise the discreet painter [he is not mentioned by name] that in Spain they like devotional paintings with quiet attitudes and without elaboration. And in the Adoration of the Magi, he should try to show the Madonna with an honest expression, with a blue mantle covering her head or at least over both shoulders, and well composed. And, above all, he should not let any naked foot be seen....[2]

The third example is drawn from the seventeenth century and from the biography of no less an artist than Bernini. During his visit to France in 1665, Bernini conversed with the collector Paul Fréart de Chantelou and made unkind remarks about Spanish patrons, which he illustrated with anecdotes.[3] One story he told was of a Spanish nobleman traveling to Naples who fell off his mule and rolled down a hillside with his animal. Threatened with death, he prayed to the Virgin and was saved.

Upon arriving in Naples, he commissioned Filippo Angeli to paint a votive picture of his miraculous escape and carefully described where it occurred. When the painting was completed, the Spaniard found it generally to his liking, but complained that the incident had taken place on the other side of the mountain. After much discussion, Filippo bowed to his patron's insistence that the story should not be falsified. He eliminated the figure, leaving nothing in view but the mountain, and delivered the painting to his satisfied client. The butt of Bernini's joke had made a fool of himself because he placed accuracy above art, not to mention common sense.

From these examples, it might be inferred that the distinctive features of Spanish painting were its doctrinaire religiosity and verism. There is a superficial plausibility to this formulation which, like all simple generalizations, disguises a complex phenomenon. From 1475 to 1700, Spanish painting underwent significant changes, changes that make it unlikely that any unitary definition could be sufficient to account for artists as diverse as Pedro Berruguete and Claudio Coello. It seems more logical to examine the period by stages and attempt to define the broader contexts in which artists and patrons had to operate before analyzing their responses to the circumstances they encountered and how these conditions compare with certain developments in other parts of Europe.

It has been argued above that Spanish painting of the Golden Age was shaped by the dynamic relations between the crown and the church. While the pre-eminence of the church would never diminish, the conception of its temporal mission was shaped by larger political currents as well as by specific local conditions. In a Europe divided by struggles of conscience, only Spain and Italy kept the faith pure. Whereas Italy was fragmented into small, relatively impotent political units, Spain emerged not only as the most powerful monarchy in Europe, but as a Catholic monarchy. The Spanish crusade against Islam, triumphantly completed with the conquest of Granada in 1492, was readily converted into a crusade against Protestantism, and the rulers of the monarchy, who inherited the northern lands most troubled by the Reformation, became its natural leaders.

During the first half of the sixteenth century, Spain was governed by Charles V, who spent little time in his Spanish realms, as he traveled across Europe, attempting to pacify the subjects of his empire. In his absence, the bishops of Castile and Aragon were unchallenged as artistic patrons. To some extent, their position resembles that of the rulers of the petty fiefdoms in Italy, such as Mantua, Ferrara, and Urbino, but there are crucial differences. The Italian dukedoms were hereditary and thus fostered a degree of continuity between generations. In the Spanish bishoprics, a change in leadership sometimes meant a change in style. Another important difference was the dearth of patronage by aristocrats, many of whom were abroad in the service of the crown, and of civic humanists, who never emerged as a potent force in Spanish society. Above all, the lack of a permanent court prevented secular patronage from coalescing into a major force.

The high-ranking ecclesiastics of this period were not necessarily narrow-minded zealots. Many of them belonged to aristocratic families, had received a sound education, and some had lived in Italy or Flanders. With this experience behind them, they were aware of artistic fashions and employed both painters from abroad as well as Spaniards who had studied in other parts of Europe. The constant traffic of these artists imparts a special quality to the period, much as it does to the France of François I, who implanted Italian art in French soil at Fontainebleau, patronizing such distinguished artists as Primaticcio, Rosso Fiorentino, and Niccolò dell' Abate. As also occurred in the northern regions of Europe, the imported Italian styles mingled with the prevailing Gothic manner, called Hispano-Flemish in Spain, producing surprising combinations of diverse, even opposing, artistic conventions. The pull of the Hispano-Flemish was strong enough to carry along the most Italianate painters – San Leocadio, Llanos, and Yáñez – and they gradually accommodated its features into their art.

Right from the start, Spanish patrons were profoundly concerned with doctrinal orthodoxy. As the paintings created for the churches and monasteries have gradually been removed and placed in the secular environment of art museums, it has been easy to forget that their original purpose was to instruct and inspire the faithful who prayed before them. Confronted with the spiritual power of the faith and the temporal authority of its ministers, Spanish painters could only follow instructions. It was not until much later that they attempted to establish equal footing with their patrons by promoting the sense of professional vocation that was articulated by Leon Battista Alberti's *Della pittura*, published in 1435–36. In these circumstances, a concern for the correct expression of sacred history and doctrine was only to be expected. It was not until the second half of the century that this concern became obsessive.

Painting in this period was indelibly stamped by the personality of Philip II, the most powerful patron of the epoch. Philip established the first permanent court when he settled in Madrid in 1561. Thus anchored to a fixed site, royal patronage finally became a counterbalance to the preponderance of the church. This is not to say that court patronage was entirely secular. Philip had inherited a dangerous situation in his northern realms where heresy, as Protestantism was considered in Spain, seemed to gain ground every day. The king sought to prevent the spread of the Reformation by installing a *cordon sanitaire* around his peninsular realms. In 1558, the importation of foreign books was banned, and a year later, Spanish students were recalled from foreign universities. The Inquisition intensified its pursuit of "Lutherans" (a supposed cell was discovered in Seville and purged between 1558 and 1561) and false converts. When the United Provinces revolted against the authority of the crown in 1566, for reasons as much political as religious to be sure, the militance of Spanish Catholicism was bound to intensify.

The Escorial is the perfect expression of this complex man and his temporal and spiritual aspirations. Spanish hegemony and the Catholic faith had become one and inseparable in the king's mind, and this fusion was projected in the decoration of his great monument, where a new attitude toward painting was imposed upon its practitioners. Decency, decorum, and doctrine were the watchwords of this art – shepherds adoring the newborn Christ were not to carry a basket of eggs; frisky dogs were forbidden to the Holy Family; the feet of the Virgin Mary had to be decently shod (in his picture of 1619 [pl. 99], Velázquez showed her wearing the sturdy shoes of a laborer).

What makes Philip hard to understand is that he was as much a connoisseur as a zealot; he himself seems to have found it difficult to reconcile these two traits of his personality. His quest for artistic excellence led him to import foreign painters on a scale never before imagined, but he did not give them much freedom. Some managed to satisfy their exigent master, while others did not, but all of them helped to reorient and modernize the art of painting in Spain.

Thus modernized, painting at Philip's court at first seems little different from painting at the papal court during the pontificates of Pius IV and Pius V. There are, in fact, important differences that need to be stressed. Philip and his religious advisers zealously monitored the style and content of their artists, and the results at times have a distinctly impersonal flavor. The insistence on verisimilitude, all the same, gradually opened the way to greater verism. (Much the same phenomenon can be perceived in Italian painting of the period.) Sigüenza's praise of Navarrete's *Martyrdom of St. James* (pl. 55) illustrates the point: "The attitude and movement of the knife passing through the neck of the apostle [is done] with such propriety and naturalism that those who see it will swear that he is already starting to expire."[4]

On the whole, Philip's Spanish painters took greater liberties in this direction than the Italians, perhaps because the latter were charged with providing the decoration of the principal areas of the monastery. In the shadowy spaces of the lateral chapels of the basilica, Navarrete, Sánchez Coello, and, at times, Luis de Carvajal represented commonplace human types and garbed them as saints. The credible detail, that small touch of the familiar, had long been a part of the repertory of Spanish painters, who in this respect were conforming to a widespread predilection of late medieval artists. However, the monumental figure style learned from the Italians allowed a closer approximation to reality than was possible before.

Although religious art at court and in the cathedrals expressed the attitudes of the official Counter Reformation, it tended to minimize the spiritual renovation that is equally a part of this movement. Philip and his bishops were wary of the excesses of private devotion, which they feared, when carried to an extreme, could threaten the authority and solidarity of the Roman church. The more ecstatic aspects of Spanish spirituality found only an occasional outlet in the visual arts. Luis de Morales and El Greco, each an eccentric painter in his own way, succeeded best in expressing the powerful emotions awakened by the revival of Catholic spirituality in Spain. Morales, as a devotional painter pure and simple, comes closest to reproducing the emotions of private prayer. El Greco, a far more sophisticated artist, effected a unique synthesis between piety and dogma. Yet neither made an impact on the next generation; Morales was isolated by his geographical location, El Greco, by his inimitable, abstracting, intellectual style. The future lay in another direction, which led to the expression of the new spirituality in an immediate, earthbound way, while continuing to observe to the requirements of correct doctrine.

In the early 1600s, the evolution of Spanish painting again mirrors certain developments in Italian painting, which remained its primary source of inspiration. Indeed, the superficial similarities between Caravaggio and some of the Spanish artists result from the pursuit of common aims, although they are not otherwise connected. The genesis of the style known as Spanish naturalism was considerably more complex.

A crucial ingredient, as has been seen, was supplied by the Italians at the Escorial, who changed the rules of composition and figure style, opening the way for the use of large-scale figures deployed in calm, measured compositions. Also important were paintings imported from Italy by collectors and dealers, of whom the best known is Bartolomé Carducho. These paintings came principally from two places – Florence and Venice – and consisted of religious works by the so-called reformers, on the one hand, and paintings from the Bassano workshop, on the other. Genre scenes from Flanders also began to arrive at this time, notably by followers of Pieter Aertsen. These works were carefully studied and adapted by the naturalist painters in Madrid and Seville.

As the number of imported paintings increased after 1600, the traffic of painters declined considerably. The reduction of direct contact between the two peninsulas meant that certain important developments in Italian painting reached Spain in attenuated form, if at all. For instance, there are hardly any Spanish counterparts to the numerous followers of Caravaggio who came to Rome from France and the Netherlands and transported this newest pictorial fashion back to their native lands. And the classical style, as reinvigorated by Annibale Carracci and his school, remained largely unknown until later in the century, when it attracted a certain interest among collectors but was largely ignored by painters. Most important of all, the Spaniards did not have the opportunity to talk with innovative Italian painters or study their most ambitious works, which were painted for churches and palaces. They had access only to the surfaces, not the systems, of Italian painting and thus were free to interpret it without inhibition, choosing what was useful or compatible with their habitual way of working. The result might be called Italianizing rather than Italianate.

During the reign of Philip III, Spanish painters in Madrid and Seville, now the prevailing centers of artistic activity, adapted their chosen Italian sources to serve the changing religious convictions and tastes of their patrons. They devised spare compositions populated by monumental figures and, following the dictates of a faith that required verisimilitude, kept an eye glued to appearances, portraying a seamless universe in which all things great and small were infused with the heavenly spirit.

This mode of expression continued to prevail during the early part of the reign of Philip IV, when another shift in direction, inspired in part by the predilections of the monarch himself, began to occur. Since the time of Philip II, Spanish collectors, who had constituted a growing presence in the European art market, increasingly turned to foreign specialists to satisfy their appetite for such important subject categories as mythology, landscape, and genre. Philip, as voracious a collector as the period would know, followed this trend, to the disadvantage of his Spanish painters, except, of course, Velázquez.

The king made another choice of fateful consequence. In 1628, he met the greatest painter of his non-Spanish realms, Peter Paul Rubens, and immediately became his devoted client. During the 1630s, Rubens was a sort of royal painter *in absentia*, much as Titian had been to Philip II, and and supplied pictures for the decoration of the principal palaces. This patronage turned the eyes of Spanish painters away from Italy and toward Flanders. The Flemish "takeover" of Spanish painting is paralleled by developments at the court of Charles I of England, another of Rubens's important royal patrons, who used his power to change the direction of the visual arts. Charles went so far as to employ Rubens's greatest disciple, van Dyck, while Philip kept his distance, undoubtedly because he had found a great painter among his Spanish subjects, Velázquez. But Velázquez was used primarily as a portraitist; in history painting, Rubens would become supreme.

In the later part of the seventeenth century, Spanish painting was again dominated by Flanders, as it had been in the days of Ferdinand and Isabella. The contrast with the policy of the French court at this moment is instructive. Under Louis XIV, France co-opted the grand manner of central-Italian painting and effectively politicized it. In Spain, a more passive policy prevailed, and the adaptation of a foreign style was played out in a distinctive way. The verve, color, and energy of Rubens's style were eagerly imitated; his underlying classicism, hard-won from the dedicated study of ancient and modern masters, was found to be less compelling in a country where classicism had never been at home.

Thus summarized, the development of Spanish painting appears to lack any kind of uniform or fundamental character. However, the appearance of heterogeneity and sudden change is somewhat deceptive. To be sure, foreign styles came and went in various regions, often at the whim of powerful individuals. Nevertheless, it is this very process and procedure of change that gives Spanish painting from 1475 to 1700 a special character.

The dynamic of artistic reception and assimilation is hardly unique to Golden Age Spain; in fact, it could be argued that it is the most salient characteristic of non-Italian painting of this period. Within Italy itself, important centers such as Milan, Genoa, and Naples experienced comparable processes of transformation, inspired by the exercise of patronage and the effects of the migration of painters and paintings from other places.

If the process of change in all these places is comparable, the results were profoundly affected by differing local circumstances. For instance, the underlying history of painting in Spain and England during the seventeenth century is surprisingly similar in that both countries acted simultaneously as receivers and transmitters of artistic impulses beyond their borders, with the king and courtiers serving as the relay station. In each case, the model of Flemish painting was fundamental, although there was an awareness of Italian art. Yet once these styles had been adapted, they were transformed again, and even more drastically, when they were shipped to the respective colonies in north and south America. At every step along the way, choices were made, sometimes knowingly, sometimes unconsciously, that reshaped the initial message, and it is these choices that produced new and characteristic variations.

The difficulties of identifying the complicated filtering mechanisms of cultural transmission can hardly be exaggerated and involve the broadest range of factors, from psychological and sociological to political and economic or, to put it another way, from personal to societal. As such, hypotheses about the experience of Spanish painters of the Golden Age are bound to be tentative. Yet it is probably worth launching a few speculative notions, if only to stimulate discussion of this crucial issue.

The painters of Golden Age Spain operated within fairly narrow boundaries. Unable, and at times unwilling, to declare independence from their patrons, they were frequently in a servile position. This, of course, was typical of artistic conditions throughout most of Europe, but Spanish painters seem to have had fewer market options than, say, Italian, Dutch, or Flemish artists. The predominance of the Catholic church as a social and political institution, unmatched in any other major European state, bound the painters to serve a cautious, conservative clientele that was unleavened by free spirits such as Cardinal Francesco Barberini or Cardinal Jules Mazarin. The changes in Spain's spiritual climate are thus graphically recorded in its paintings because the artists were continually compelled to adapt their sources to fit the prevailing requirements and even to choose them with this in mind. Although the temper of religious practice changed, the requirements of decency, orthodoxy, and clarity remained paramount. Thus, when Pacheco wrote that the principal end of painting was to "induce men to piety and bring them to God," he was not mouthing a platitude but voicing a conviction universally held in his society. And the consensus was that this goal was best achieved through direct, unambiguous, dogmatic imagery that inspired intense involvement in the events of the New Testament, the lives of saints, and the doctrines of the church.

The operational consequences of this attitude are perhaps what impart a degree of consistency beneath the changing appearances of religious painting of the Golden Age. One of these is the preference for narration over allegory. The painters who enthusiastically embraced Rubens's style had little need for his complex language of allegory, just as their predecessors in the sixteenth century all but ignored the abstruse compositions of the Italian mannerists. A concomitant of this attitude was the preference for simple compositions designed to enhance legibility, with the principal figures deployed along the front plane, where their actions and reactions were communicated to the viewer with solemn clarity and without distraction or interference. The concern for "correctness," a combination of the plausible and the decent, coupled with the relatively weak hold of classicism on artistic tradition, encouraged painters to approximate natural appearances, in detail if not always in general effect. Some of these preferences had obviously filtered into the consciousness of the Florentine ambassador when he advised that the paintings for the count of Chinchón be executed "with quiet attitudes and without elaboration."

The part played by secular patronage is equally important but more difficult to define. It seems clear that the members of this sector became the arbiters of taste, with consequences that were not always favorable for Spanish painters. Beginning with Ferdinand and Isabella, who brought Michel Sittow and Juan de Flandes to their court, Spanish rulers frequently bestowed their favor on foreign artists. And where the kings led, the high nobility followed. The imperial destiny of Spain provided the opportunity for the top echelon of society to travel abroad and cultivate the taste for painting in foreign places. This diversion of wealth and favor had a profound impact on the professional and artistic opportunities of the painters of Spain.

The patronage of foreign artists by the monarchs was carried out largely by remote control. That is to say, the rulers normally did not bring the painters to reside at court, although there are exceptions, notably in the reign of Philip II. This meant that there was little personal contact between foreign and Spanish painters, thus sealing off a major conduit of artistic transmission. Hence, the native artists had to instruct themselves in the styles that came from abroad, selecting not only what was most readily accessible, but also what could be most easily integrated into their habitual manner of practice.

Another consequence was that the king and his nobles became accustomed to relying on foreigners for the production of entire categories of painting, which deprived Spanish painters of the opportunity to expand their artistic horizons. Secular patronage could be relied on for religious commissions, but this type of work, while abundant, was confined by the criteria established by the church. Thus, the circle of possibilities was drawn ever tighter.

The foreign orientation of secular clients exacted another if more subtle toll on Spanish artists – it wounded their self-esteem and put them on the defensive, making them timid about taking risks. As soon as painters began to write, they sounded this note of injured pride and false prejudice. In the early 1600s, Eugenio Cajés complained bitterly about those "*señores* who go abroad from Spain and attempt to bring back great quantities of pictures from foreign provinces," and in 1693, Claudio Coello supposedly died of melancholy precipitated by the arrival of Luca Giordano at the court of Charles II. Palomino harbored no uncertain resentment about the inferior status of the Spanish painter as against the foreigner, and voiced his feelings, with some exaggeration, in the preface of the biographical section of his treatise:

It is to our nation's discredit that we bring to the public forum of the world the lives of our eminent artists, since most of them lived in extremely straitened circumstances, and those who attained old age, became destitute, having to seek their last refuge in the charity of a hospice, whereas in the lives of foreign artists we see them full of riches and with numerous good connections, ending up in magnificent sepulchers with epitaphs that honor them.[5]

Occasionally, a few painters would try to rally support for their profession, as Carducho's persistent but futile attempts to organize a royal academy show. However, the ground was not fertile for such an enterprise. It may even have been risky to travel abroad on a study trip; those who were absent might be forgotten and lose their place in line. Spain, as Jusepe de Ribera is quoted as saying, was "a loving mother to foreigners and a very cruel stepmother to her own sons."

Although the character of Spanish painting in the Golden Age was shaped by the continual dialogue with art in other regions of Europe, it was not always a conversation between equals. Forces beyond the control of artists limited their options and favored established interests. But if Spanish painting was powerfully affected by Italy and Flanders, it cannot be considered a regional school of Italian or Flemish art, and not only because societal forces channeled production in different directions. Individual artists also made individual choices according to their abilities and opportunities. The greatest of them, Velázquez and El Greco, through supreme efforts of intellect and imagination, exploited their positions on the margin to declare independence from the grand manner of classicism and invented truly original ways of painting. Others, like Zurbarán and Murillo, cannily infused local artistic traditions and spiritual values with new life and meaning. And still others, such as Juan Correa de Vivar and Luis Tristán, while content to treat their models as repertories of motifs, nevertheless combined them in unexpected ways with a vernacular style.

The richness and vitality of the Golden Age were generated by this complex interplay of forces and personalities. The painters of Spain, like painters in many other parts of Europe, found themselves working in a crucible in which different artistic cultures were fused, and from this meltingpot they fashioned images representing the collective experience of their society, images that continue to reverberate with grandeur and emotion.

Notes

Introduction

1. Palomino, ed. Mallory 1987.
2. Cited by Brown 1987, 4. For contracts and other economic facets of artistic life, see Martín González 1984.
3. Cited by the seventeenth-century writer Jusepe Martínez, ed. Gállego 1988, 279.
4. Trans. Brown in Enggass and Brown 1970, 179–80.
5. This is surveyed in the anthology compiled by Calvo Serraller 1981.
6. Calvo Serraller 1981, 161.
7. Martín González 1984, 17–24.

Chapter 1

1. For surveys of the period, see Angulo 1954, Camón Aznar 1970, and Checa 1983. Marías 1989 appeared after this book had gone to press.
2. Cited by Trizina 1976, 18.
3. Trizina 1976.
4. Vandevivère 1986.
5. Vandevivère 1967.
6. Post 1947, vol. 9, part 1, 17–161. A modern study is needed.
7. Clough 1973 casts considerable doubt on the Urbino stay and the collaboration with Justus van Ghent, the case for which is stated by Lavalleye 1964.
8. Post 1947, vol. 9, part 1, 162–234; Gómez-Menor 1968; Marías, "Datos," 1976; Sterling 1988. Borgoña is in need of a new, comprehensive study.
9. Condorelli 1960.
10. Condorelli 1963; Bologna 1977.
11. Company 1985.
12. Post 1953, 175–276; Garín 1978.
13. D. Brown in J. Brown and Mann 1990.
14. Tormo 1924, 33.
15. Ibáñez Martínez 1986.
16. Giusti and Leone de Castris 1985, 5–9; Naldi 1986, 72–75.
17. Freixas 1984.
18. Sebastián 1988.
19. Angulo 1946; Martín Cubero 1988 reviews the documentation and bibliography.
20. Gómez-Moreno (1941) 1983, 121–62. A new study of his career is badly needed.
21. Longhi 1953; Dacos 1985.
22. Cited in Gómez-Moreno (1941) 1983, 229.
23. Mazariegos Pajares 1979.
24. Gómez-Moreno (1941) 1983, 99–119.
25. Rosenthal 1985.
26. Dacos 1984 exemplifies the expansionist tendency in recent studies of Machuca's Italian period.
27. Avila 1987.
28. Sánchez Cantón 1950.
29. Eisler 1985; Checa 1987.
30. Boom 1935, 135–61.
31. Duverger 1969.
32. Steppe 1985, 254–55.
33. Steppe 1985, 256–60.
34. Hope 1980, 76–78, 86–89, 109–16, 119–23.

Chapter 2

1. Brown, "Philip II," 1989.
2. Mateo 1983
3. Avila 1979.
4. Avila 1985, 76–77.
5. Albi 1979, vol. 1, 33–311.
6. Benito, "Sobre la influencia," 1988.
7. Albi 1979, vol. 1, 313–493; vol. 2, 1–417.
8. Albi 1979, vol. 2, 111–20.
9. Valdivieso 1986, 67–73.
10. For the much-debated production and chronology of the Italian period, see Serrera 1989, with earlier references.
11. Serrera 1985, 388–90.
12. Serrera 1985, 391–84.
13. Bologna 1953.
14. Serrera 1983; Dacos 1983–84.
15. Serrera 1983, 43–54.
16. Serrera 1983, 50.
17. Bäcksbacka 1962 and Trapier 1953 are now inadequate.
18. Solís Rodríguez 1977–78.
19. Pérez Sánchez 1974.
20. Rodríguez G. de Ceballos 1987.
21. Rodríguez G. de Ceballos 1987, 200–201.
22. Trapier 1953, 25.
23. Cited by Trapier 1953, 33.
24. Brown, "Philip II," 1989.
25. Dacos 1980.
26. Friedländer 1975 and Groeneveld 1981.
27. San Román 1938. An exhibition of his work at the Prado was scheduled to be held in 1990. Kusche's important article on Anguissola (1989) appeared after this book went to press.
28. Kubler 1982.

29. Gérard 1984.
30. Post, ed. Wethey 1966, 148–80; Martín González 1969.
31. Gérard 1984, 96.
32. Rosso Del Brenna 1975; Gérard 1984, 96–101.
33. Wilkinson 1975; Bustamante and Marías 1982.
34. Brown, "Philip II," 1989.
35. Antonio Sáenz 1987.
36. Sigüenza, ed. Sánchez Cantón 1923, 390–91.
37. Mulcahy 1980.
38. Zarco Cuevas 1931, 40.
39. Sigüenza, ed. Sánchez Cantón 1923, 400.
40. Zarco Cuevas 1931, 153–72.
41. Zarco Cuevas 1931, 75–98; Barrio Moya, "El pintor," 1982; Antonio Sáenz 1987.
42. Zarco Cuevas 1932, 57–88.
43. Zarco Cuevas 1932, 1–27; Marías 1979.
44. Sigüenza, ed. Sánchez Cantón 1923, 409.
45. Cloulas 1968; Mulcahy 1980.
46. Sigüenza, ed. Sánchez Cantón 1923, 400–401.
47. Sigüenza, ed. Sánchez Cantón 1923, 424.
48. Zarco Cuevas 1932, 217–69; Scholz 1984 and 1987, 161–204.
49. See Scholz 1987 for one interpretation of the library decoration.
50. Morán and Checa 1985, 107–27; Brown, "Felipe II," 1986.
51. Matilla Tascón 1988.
52. Ollero Butler 1975.
53. Zarco Cuevas 1930.

Chapter 3

1. Wethey 1962; Brown, "El Greco and Toledo," 1982 and "El Greco: Between the Renaissance," 1986.
2. Panagiotakis 1986.
3. *From Byzantium to El Greco*, 1987, 190–91.
4. Martínez de la Peña 1967.
5. Salas, "Un exemplaire," 1967, *Miguel Angel y El Greco*, 1967 and 1984.
6. Salas, *Miguel Angel y El Greco*, 1967, 38.
7. Andrés 1983.
8. Brown, "El Greco and Toledo," 1982, 95–98, where the documentation is cited. The interpretation of the subject

was suggested to me by Catherine Wilkinson, who plans to publish her ideas in due course.

9. Kagan, "El Greco and the Law," 1982.
10. Cloulas 1984; Bury 1984.
11. Sigüenza, ed. Sánchez Cantón 1923, 424.
12. Mann 1986, 1–45.
13. San Román 1934, 3–4.
14. San Román (1910) 1982, 209.
15. Kagan, "The Toledo of El Greco," 1982, 35–73.
16. Kagan 1984.
17. For the identification, see Martínez Caviró 1988; for the quotation, see Kagan, "The Toledo of El Greco," 1982, 60.
18. Schroth 1982.
19. Cited in Schroth 1982, 1.
20. Marías and Bustamante 1981; Marías, "El Greco," 1986.
21. Mann 1986, 47–110.
22. Cited in Mann 1986, 88.
23. Kagan 1982, 59–61.
24. Hadermann-Misguich 1987 discusses the Byzantine elements in El Greco's art.
25. Kagan 1982, 53–61; Rodríguez G. de Ceballos 1984.
26. Material for the study of the relationship between art and sermons is gathered in Dávila Fernández 1980.

Chapter 4

1. For information on Lerma's patronage and art collection I have relied on the doctoral dissertation in progress by Sarah Schroth. Morán Turina 1989 offers a more positive evaluation of Philip III's artistic activities.
2. Magurn 1955, 33.
3. Jacob 1967–68.
4. Angulo and Pérez Sánchez 1969, 14–46; Pérez Sánchez, "Pintura madrileña," 1976, 294.
5. Baldinucci 1812, vol. 8, 334–35 (Pagano); vol. 9, 410 (Passignano).
6. Baldinucci 1812, vol. 9, 432; *Itinerario di Pietro Sorri*, 1983, 18–19.
7. Pérez Sánchez 1964, 10–19; Wethey 1964; Pérez Sánchez 1982, 285.
8. Martín González 1988.
9. Angulo and Pérez Sánchez 1969, 271–98.
10. Angulo and Pérez Sánchez 1969, 86–189. Pérez Sánchez 1976, 294–307. The baptismal document published by Gambacorta 1967, dated 16 August 1570 (cited by Pérez Sánchez 1976, 294), is now generally thought to refer to another person of the same name.
11. Martín González 1958, 133–39.
12. Brown, "Academies of Painting," 1986–87 and Ubeda de los Cobos 1989.
13. Gállego 1976, 11–28.
14. Carducho, ed. Calvo Serraller 1979.
15. Angulo and Pérez Sánchez 1969, 212–59; Pérez Sánchez, "Pintura madrileña," 1976, 307–14.

16. Kusche 1964.
17. Schroth 1985, 29.
18. *El Toledo de El Greco*, 1982, 155–57; Serrera 1986.
19. Angulo and Pérez Sánchez 1972, 39–102; Pérez Sánchez 1983, 28–29, 31–34; Jordan 1985, 43–63.
20. Marías, "La obra artística," 1986. For the disputed identification of El Greco's portrait see Brown and Carr 1982 and 1984.
21. *El Toledo de El Greco*, 1982, 192–95.
22. Angulo and Pérez Sánchez 1969, 299–325; Marías, "Juan Bautista Maino," 1976.
23. Junquera 1977.
24. Pérez Sánchez 1973, nos. 1–7; Brown and Kagan 1987, 240–41.
25. Pérez Sánchez 1964.
26. Angulo and Pérez Sánchez 1972, 111–99.
27. Angulo and Pérez Sánchez 1972, 227–358; Pérez Sánchez 1980.
28. Pérez Pastor 1914, 39.
29. Benito Domenech 1980.
30. López Torrijos 1978.
31. Kowal, *Francisco Ribalta*, 1985 and *Ribalta y los Ribaltescos*, 1985; Benito Domenech 1987 and 1988.
32. Darby 1967 and Benito Domenech 1987, 92–111.
33. Benito Domenech "Sobre la influencia," 1988, 15–26.
34. Benito Domenech 1987, 122–23.
35. Benito Domenech "Sobre la influencia," 1988, 25–26.
36. Pérez Sánchez 1972.
37. Brown, "Academies of Painting," 1986–87.

Chapter 5

1. The period under discussion is surveyed in Valdivieso 1986, 87–153.
2. Serrera 1987.
3. Serrera 1987, 206.
4. Domínguez Ortiz 1984, 68; 227–33.
5. Serrera 1987, 222–25.
6. Mesa and Gisbert 1972; Gere 1973.
7. Brown 1978, 44–48.
8. Serrera 1976.
9. Serrera 1985, 395–97; Valdivieso 1986, 96–102.
10. Valdivieso and Serrera 1985, 16–116; Bassegoda i Hugas, "Adiciones," 1988.
11. Brown 1978, 21–43.
12. Brown 1978, 77–80; Lleó Cañal 1979, 45–50.
13. Pacheco, ed. Sánchez Cantón 1956; Brown 1978, 44–62; Pacheco, ed. Fallay d'Este 1986; Bassegoda, "Observaciones," 1988.
14. Veliz 1986, 31–106; McKim Smith et al. 1988, 7–11.
15. Brown 1978, 70–71.
16. Pacheco, ed. Piñero Ramírez and Reyes Cano 1985.

17. Valdivieso and Serrera 1985, 189–227.
18. Valdivieso and Serrera 1985, 303–69.
19. Valdivieso and Serrera 1985, 117–73.
20. Previtali 1978, 100–15.
21. This discussion is based on Brown, *Velázquez*, 1986, 7–35. For a catalogue of individual works, see López-Rey 1979.
22. Cited in Schroth 1985, 32–33.
23. Brown and Kagan 1987, 238.

Chapter 6

1. Elliott 1986.
2. The discussion of Velázquez from 1622–29 is based on Brown, *Velázquez*, 1986, 36–68.
3. Angulo and Pérez Sánchez 1969, 126–51.
4. Angulo and Pérez Sánchez 1977, 32–36.
5. *Varia Velazqueña*, 1960, vol. 2, 228–29.
6. Angulo and Pérez Sánchez 1969, 239–348 and 260–65.
7. Angulo and Pérez Sánchez 1969, 326–34 and 260–65.
8. Jordan 1985, 103–46.
9. Jordan 1985, 135; Brown and Mann 1990, s.v. van der Hamen.
10. Harris 1970, 364.
11. Pacheco, ed. Sánchez Cantón 1956, vol. 1, 157.
12. Palomino, ed. Mallory 1987, 146.
13. Brown and Elliott 1980, 44–45; Marías and Bustamante 1984, 109–10; Spezzaferro 1985.
14. Brown, *Velázquez*, 1986, 66–67.
15. Brown, *Velázquez*, 1986, 65–68.
16. Brown, *Velázquez*, 1986, 69–79.
17. Brown and Elliott 1980.
18. Brown and Elliott 1980, 254; Brown, *Velázquez*, 1986, 96.
19. Brown and Elliott 1980, 141–92.
20. Angulo and Pérez Sánchez 1983, 78–103.
21. Angulo and Pérez Sánchez 1983, 138–239.
22. Pérez Sánchez 1983–84, 107; Jordan 1985, 212.
23. Brown and Elliott 1980, 184–90.
24. Brown and Elliott 1980, 178–84.
25. Alpers 1971.
26. Brown, *Velázquez*, 1986, 129–38.
27. Brown, *Velázquez*, 1986, 274–77.
28. Brown, *Velázquez*, 1986, 168.
29. Angulo and Pérez Sánchez 1983, 13–34.
30. Angulo and Pérez Sánchez 1983, 268–312.
31. Tormo et al. 1930, vol. 1, 109–10.
32. Angulo and Pérez Sánchez 1983, 295–98.

Chapter 7

1. Martínez Ripoll 1978.
2. Valdivieso 1986, 163. For another early work, see Ayala Mallory 1987.
3. Martínez Ripoll 1976.
4. Martínez Ripoll 1978, 145–52.

5. Guinard 1960; Baticle 1987, 53–68.
6. Baticle 1987, 71–73.
7. Domínguez Ortiz 1984, 233.
8. Cited in Brown, "Patronage and Piety," 1987, 2.
9. Baticle 1987, 76–79.
10. Baticle 1987, 97–100.
11. Baticle 1987, 104–6.
12. Baticle 1987, 81–93.
13. Cited in Brown, "Patronage and Piety," 1987, 6.
14. Baticle 1987, 56.
15. Brown and Elliott 1980, 138.
16. Brown and Elliott 1980, 156–61; López Torrijos, *La mitología*, 1985, 137–46; Baticle 1987, 161–65.
17. Baticle 1987, 173–201; Pemán 1989, 95–118, 271–74.
18. Spear 1982, 151.
19. Valdivieso and Serrera 1985, 260–302.
20. Brown 1978, 111–27; Cherry 1985.
21. Guinard 1960, 191–92.
22. Pérez Sánchez 1978.
23. Brown and Kagan 1987.
24. Wethey 1983.
25. Baticle 1979; Wethey 1983, 113–15.

Chapter 8

1. Spinosa 1979; Felton and Jordan 1982.
2. Chenault 1969.
3. Bottari and Ticozzi 1822, vol. 1, 289.
4. Brown 1973.
5. Mancini ed. Salerno 1956–57, 249–51.
6. Felton and Jordan 1982, 92–101.
7. Giustiani, ed. Holt 1947, 331–32; Salerno 1960, 96, 102–3.
8. Chenault 1969.
9. Delfino 1986, 114.
10. Bologna and Pacelli 1980, 29.
11. Pérez Sánchez 1978.
12. Brown 1973 and *Jusepe de Ribera*, 1989.
13. Ceci 1920.
14. Brown 1984, 142–44; Brown and Kagan 1987, 242–43.
15. Felton and Jordan 1982.
16. Pérez Sánchez, "Las colecciones," 1977; Brown and Elliott 1980, 123.
17. Spear 1982, 286–302.
18. Cited in Spear 1982, 289.
19. Brown and Elliott 1980, 268, n. 41; Madruga Real 1983.
20. Aguirre y Ortiz de Zárate 1984.
21. Burke 1989.
22. *Testamentaría*, vol. 1, 1975 (Alcázar, Madrid), vol. 2, 1981 (Buen Retiro); Archivo de Palacio, Madrid, registro 242, fols. 122–29 (El Escorial).
23. Faraglia 1892, 669–78.
24. Ruffo 1916, 44–45.
25. Faraglia 1885, 449.
26. Nappi 1983, 48.
27. Ruffo 1916, 29, 32–33.
28. Faraglia 1892, 671.
29. Martínez, ed. Julián Gállego 1988, 100.
30. Brown, *Jusepe de Ribera*, 1989, 42–44.

Chapter 9

1. Cited in Brown and Elliott 1980, 115.
2. The following discussion of Philip IV is based on and to some extent repeats Brown, "Felipe IV," 1987, where further references are cited. See also Morán and Checa 1985, 251–82.
3. Orso 1986, 32–80.
4. Brown and Elliott 1980, 105–40; von Barghahn 1986, for identification of surviving pictures.
5. Brown and Elliott 1987.
6. Alpers 1971.
7. Muller 1989.
8. Orso 1986, 153–62; Balis 1986, 218–64.
9. Orso 1986, 60–74.
10. Burke 1984, 101–23; Brown, *Velázquez*, 1986, 210–13.
11. Cited in Brown, "Felipe IV," 1987, 12.
12. Harris 1982.
13. Orso 1986, 74–87.
14. Vannugli 1989.
15. Cited in Brown, "Felipe IV," 1987, 17–18.
16. Cited in Brown and Elliott 1980, 114.
17. Volk 1980. For aristocratic collections in general, see Morán and Checa 1985, 283–306.
18. Pérez Sánchez, "Las colecciones," 1977; Brown and Elliott 1980, 123.
19. Burke 1989.
20. Burke 1984, 101–23; Brown, *Velázquez*, 1986, 210–13.
21. Andrés 1975; Burke 1984, 131–201.
22. For a list of more than 500 seventeenth-century Spanish collections, see Frederickson 1989, 145–52.
23. Barrio Moya, "Las colecciones artísticas," 1982.
24. Barrio Moya 1979.
25. Caturla 1948; Burke 1984, 227–47.
26. Matilla Tascón 1984.
27. Angulo and Pérez Sánchez 1983, 36–62.
28. Valdivieso 1986, 231.
29. Luna 1984, 58, 156–61.
30. Haraszti-Takács 1983.
31. Young 1976; Angulo and Pérez Sánchez 1983, 255–67.
32. López Torrijos, *La mitología*, 1985 assembles the evidence for mythological subjects by Spanish painters of the period.

Chapter 10

1. This section follows Brown, *Velázquez*, 1986, chapters VI-X.
2. Brown, *Velázquez*, 1986, 173–74.
3. Brown, "Enemies of Flattery," 1986.
4. McKim Smith et al. 1988, 81–96.
5. Bull and Harris 1986.
6. Brown, *Velázquez*, 1986, 188–240.
7. Gállego 1976; Brown 1978, 93–94.
8. Gállego 1976, 119–48.
9. Harris 1960; Brown, *Velázquez*, 1986, 195–209.
10. Harris, 1981; Brown, *Velázquez*, 1986, 204–5.
11. Brown 1978, 107–9.
12. Brown, *Velázquez*, 1986, 252–53.
13. Brown, *Velázquez*, 1986, 253–64. The literature on this painting is vast and growing steadily.
14. See Orso 1986, 163–82, for the identification of the room and the relationship of its pictorial decoration to the interpretation of the picture.
15. Calvo Serraller 1981, 287.
16. Angulo and Pérez Sánchez 1983, 141–64.
17. Angulo and Pérez Sánchez 1983, 199.
18. Wethey 1983, 27–31, 51–65.
19. In *Velázquez*, 1986, 271–73, I attribute the *Temptation of St. Thomas Aquinas* (Orihuela) to Cano. However, I now believe that it is by Velázquez.
20. Gaya Nuño 1960.
21. Pérez Sánchez, "Rubens," 1977.
22. Poorter 1978.
23. Pacheco, ed. Sánchez Cantón 1956, vol. 1, 154.
24. *Pedro Pablo Rubens*, 1977–78, 99–102.
25. Pérez Sánchez, "Presencia," 1976.
26. McKim-Smith et al. 1988.
27. Angulo and Pérez Sánchez 1983, 240–52.
28. Pérez Sánchez 1986, 58–90.
29. Pérez Sánchez 1986, 92–101.
30. Sancho Gaspar 1987.
31. Pérez Sánchez 1985, 63–64 and 1986, 18–55.
32. Baticle 1964.

Chapter 11

1. Domínguez Ortiz 1984, 22–34.
2. Domínguez Ortiz 1984, 68–74.
3. Domínguez Ortiz 1984, 233.
4. Baticle 1987, 59–62.
5. Serrera 1988, 63–83.
6. Martínez Ripoll 1978, 32–37.
7. Martínez Ripoll 1978, 158–61.
8. Angulo 1981. Murillo's career to 1660 is covered in vol. 1, 3–67. See also *Bartolomé Murillo (1617–1682)*, 1982–83.
9. Angulo 1981, vol. 2, 3–18.
10. Veitia Linaje, ed. Solano 1981.
11. Angulo 1981, vol. 2, 128.
12. Angulo 1981, vol. 2, 258.
13. Ortiz de Zúñiga, ed. Espinosa y Carzel 1796, vol. 5, 332–35.
14. Kinkead, "Francisco de Herrera," 1982.
15. Kinkead 1983.
16. *Zurbarán*, 1988, 327–31.
17. Kinkead 1979.
18. Kinkead 1978, 608–12.
19. Kinkead 1979; Valdivieso 1988.
20. Valverde Madrid 1986.
21. *Antonio del Castillo y su época*, 1986, 66–77.
22. Muller 1966.
23. Valdivieso 1988, 41–49.

24. Valdivieso 1988, 57–68.
25. Brown 1975, 44–48; *El manuscrito*, 1982.

Chapter 12

1. Wethey 1983, 67–73, 81–92.
2. Angulo 1981, vol. 2, 41–47.
3. Braham 1980; Angulo 1981, vol. 1, 323, 463–5.
4. Angulo 1981, vol. 1, 339–47.
5. Valdivieso in *Bartolomé Murillo (1617–1682)*, 1982–83, 170.
6. Angulo 1981, vol. 1, 351–75.
7. Brown 1978, 128–46; Valdivieso and Serrera 1980.
8. Angulo 1981, vol. 2, 79–83.
9. Brown 1978, 136–9; Kinkead 1978; Valdivieso and Serrera 1980, 63–76.
10. Stratton 1988.
11. Valdivieso 1988, 195–96; 200–205.
12. Kinkead 1978, 219–223.
13. Kinkead, "The Altarpiece," 1982.
14. Kinkead 1978, 295–97.
15. Angulo 1976.
16. García Fuentes 1980.
17. Ravina Martín 1982.
18. Angulo 1981, vol. 2, 314–15.
19. Hoet 1752, vol. 1, 352–60.
20. Kinkead 1986.
21. Angulo 1981, vol. 2, 94–95.
22. Saltillo 1916.
23. Brown, "Murillo," 1982.
24. Courtesy of Duncan T. Kinkead.
25. Sanz and Dabrio 1977.
26. For examples, see Ayala Mallory 1982 and Serrera 1982.
27. Brown 1975; Mena Marques 1982, 53–63; Brown 1983.
28. For Murillo's followers, see Valdivieso 1986, 237–55.

29. Palomino, ed. Mallory 1987, 281. For the history of Murillo's fame, see García Felguera 1989.

Chapter 13

1. Bonet Correa 1961, Orso 1989, 65–70.
2. Orso 1989, 83, fig. 11.
3. Kamen 1980.
4. Vélez de Guevara, ed. Varey and Shergold 1970, xxxvii–xliii; Orso 1982.
5. López Torrijos, "Grabados y dibujos," 1985.
6. Pérez Sánchez 1986, 262–63.
7. For an overview of the period, see Sullivan 1986, 1–35.
8. López Torrijos, *La mitología*, 1985, 74–75.
9. Carr 1987, 18.
10. Adalberto de Baviera and Maura Gamazo 1930, 407.
11. Sánchez Cantón 1916, 97. All the following data on appointments at the court of Charles II come from this source.
12. Palomino, ed. Mallory 1987, 251.
13. Fernández Duro 1903; Burke 1984, 131–201; Lleó Cañal 1989.
14. Pérez Sánchez 1986, 22–23, 59, 78.
15. Pérez Sánchez 1986, 47–52.
16. Pérez Sánchez 1986, 78–88.
17. Pérez Sánchez 1986, 93–94, 97–101.
18. Angulo 1959 and 1965; Sullivan 1986, 20–22.
19. Pérez Sánchez 1983–4, 98–99, 118–22.
20. Pérez Sánchez 1986, 288–89.
21. Buendía and Gutiérrez Pastor 1986; Pérez Sánchez 1987.
22. Pérez Sánchez 1986, 306–9; Sullivan 1986, 18–20.

23. Angulo 1957; Sullivan 1986, 22–26.
24. Palomino, ed. Mallory 1987, 274.
25. Sullivan 1986.
26. Pérez Sánchez 1986, 342–43.
27. Sullivan 1986, 81–83.
28. Sullivan 1986, 62–79.
29. Sánchez Cantón 1916, 103–8.
30. León Tello and Sanz Sanz 1979, 99–114; Flórez Martín 1988.
31. León Tello and Sanz Sanz 1979, 120–254; Palomino, ed. Mallory 1987, vii–xviii.
32. Ferrari and Scavizzi 1966, 135–74. Giordano's Spanish career requires further study.
33. Carr 1987, 9–10,
34. Carr 1982; López Torrijos, *Lucas Jordán*, 1985.
35. Carr 1987, 47–64.

Epilogue

1. Gregory Hedberg, "Antoniazzo Romano and His School," (Ph.D. dissertation, New York University, 1980), 19.
2. This reference from the Archivio di Stato, Florence, was kindly provided by Richard L. Kagan.
3. Paul Fréart de Chantelou, *Diary of the Cavaliere Bernini's Visit to France*, ed. Anthony Blunt, trans. Margery Corbett (Princeton, 1985), 23–4. James Clifton drew attention to this story in a paper entitled "Spanish Patrons in Seventeenth-Century Italy: Perception and Reality," read at the annual meeting of the American Society for Hispanic Art-Historical Studies, February, 1989.
4. Cited above, p. 59.
5. Palomino, Mallory ed. 1987, 3.

Bibliography

Adalberto de Baviera and Carlos Maura Gamazo. "Documentos referentes a las postrimerías de la Casa de Austria en España." *Boletín de la Real Academia de la Historia* 96 (1930), 356–515.

Aguirre y Ortiz de Zárate, Jesús, Duke of Alba. *Discursos leídos ante la Real Academia de Bellas Artes de San Fernando en la recepción pública del Excmo. Sr. Don Jesús Aguirre y Ortiz de Zárate, Duque de Alba.* Madrid, 1984.

Albi, José. *Joan de Joanes y su círculo artístico.* Valencia, 1979.

Alpers, Svetlana. *The Decoration of the Torre de la Parada.* Corpus Rubenianum Ludwig Burchard, vol. 9. London, 1971.

Andrés, Gregorio de. *El marqués de Liche: bibliófilo y coleccionista de arte.* Madrid, 1975.

———. "El Arcediano de Cuenca D. Luis de Castilla (+1618) protector del Greco y su biblioteca manuscrita." *Hispania Sacra* 35 (1983), 87–141.

Angulo, Diego. *Alejo Fernández.* Seville, 1946.

———. *Pintura del Renacimiento.* Ars Hispaniae, vol. 12. Madrid, 1954.

———. *José Antolínez.* Madrid, 1957.

———. "Francisco Camilo." *Archivo Español de Arte* 32 (1959), 89–107.

———. "Nuevas obras de Francisco Camilo." *Archivo Español de Arte* 38 (1965), 59–61.

———. "Casa de Venerables Sacerdotes." *Boletín de Bellas Artes* 4 (1976), 44–96.

———. *Murillo. Su vida, su arte, su obra.* Madrid, 1981.

Angulo, Diego and Alfonso E. Pérez Sánchez. *Historia de la pintura española. Escuela madrileña del primer tercio del siglo XVII.* Madrid, 1969.

———. *Historia de la pintura española. Escuela toledana de la primera mitad del siglo XVII.* Madrid, 1972.

———. *A Corpus of Spanish Drawings.* Vol. 2, *Madrid 1600–1650.* London, 1977.

———. *Historia de la pintura española. Escuela madrileña del segundo tercio del siglo XVII.* Madrid, 1983.

Antonio del Castillo y su época. Córdoba, 1986.

Antonio Sáenz, T. de. "Pintura española del último tercio del siglo XVI en Madrid. Juan Fernández de Navarrete, Luis de Carvajal y Diego de Urbina." Ph. D. dissertation. Universidad Complutense, Madrid, 1987.

Avila, Ana. "Juan Soreda y no Juan de Pereda." *Archivo Español de Arte* 52 (1979), 405–24.

———. "Influencia de Rafael en la pintura española del siglo XVI a través de los grabados." In *Rafael en España.* Madrid, 1985, 43–85.

———. "Notas sobre el Descendimiento de Pedro Machuca." *Boletín del Museo del Prado* 8 (1987), 151–60.

Ayala Mallory, Nina. "Rubens y Van Dyck en el arte de Murillo." *Goya* nos. 169–71 (1982), 92–104.

———. "Una obra desconocida de Francisco de Herrera 'El Viejo.'" *Archivo Español de Arte* 60 (1987), 357–64.

Bäcksbacka, Ingjald. *Luis de Morales.* Helsinki, 1962.

Baldinucci, Filippo. *Notizie de' profesori del disegno.* Milan, 1812.

Balis, Arnout. *Rubens' Hunting Scenes.* Corpus Rubenianum Ludwig Burchard, part 17, vol. 2. Oxford, 1986.

Barrio Moya, José L. "La colección de pinturas de Don Francisco de Oviedo, secretario del rey Felipe IV." *Revista de Archivos, Bibliotecas y Museos* 82 (1979), 163–71.

———. "El pintor Luis de Carvajal y sus bienes." *Boletín del Seminario de Estudios de Arte y Arqueología, Universidad de Valladolid* 48 (1982), 414–20.

———. "Las colecciones artísticas de Don Juan Alvarez, funcionario del rey Felipe IV." *Analecta Calasanctiana* 24 (1982), 257–69.

Bartolomé Murillo (1617–1682). Madrid-London, 1982–83.

Bassegoda i Hugas, Bonaventura. "Adiciones y complementos al catálogo de Francisco Pacheco." *Boletín del Museo e Instituto Camón Aznar* 31–32 (1988), 151–65.

———. "Observaciones sobre el *Arte de la Pintura* de Francisco Pacheco como tratado de iconografía." *Cuadernos de Arte e Iconografía* 2 (1988), 185–96.

Baticle, Jeannine. "*La Fundación de la Orden Trinitaria,* de Carreño de Miranda." *Goya* no. 63 (1964), 140–53.

———. "Deux tableaux d'Alonso Cano au Musée du Louvre." *Revue du Louvre* 29 (1979), 123–24.

———. *Zurbarán.* New York, 1987.

Benito Domenech, Fernando. *Pinturas y pintores en el Real Colegio de Corpus Christi.* Valencia, 1980.

———. *Los Ribalta y la pintura valenciana de su tiempo.* Madrid, 1987.

———. *The Paintings of Ribalta, 1565–1628.* New York, 1988.

———. "Sobre la influencia de Sebastiano del Piombo en España: A propósito de dos cuadros suyos en el Museo del Prado." *Boletín del Museo del Prado* 9 (1988), 5–28.

Bologna, Ferdinando. "Osservazioni su Pedro de Campaña." *Paragone* 4, no. 43 (1953), 27–49.

———. *Napoli e le rotte mediterranee della pittura da Alfonso il Magnanimo a Ferdinando il Cattolico.* Naples, 1977.

Bologna, Ferdinando and Vincenzo Pacelli. "Caravaggio, 1610: La 'Sant' Orsola confitta del Tirano' per Marcantonio Doria." *Prospettiva* 23 (1980), 24–44.

Bonet Correa, Antonio. "El túmulo de Felipe IV de Herrera Barnuevo y los retablos baldaquinos del barroco español." *Archivo Español de Arte* (1961), 285–96.

Boom, Ghislaine de. *Marguerite d'Autriche-Savoie et la Pré-Renaissance.* Paris-Brussels, 1935.

Bottari, Giovanni and Stefano Ticozzi. *Raccolta di lettere sulla pittura, scultura ed architettura.* Milan, 1822–25.

Braham, Allan. "Murillo's Portrait of Don Justino de Neve." *Burlington Magazine* 122 (1980), 192–94.

Brown, David. "Yáñez de la Almedina, *Madonna and Child with the Infant Saint John.*" In Jonathan Brown and Richard G. Mann, *Spanish Painting of the Fifteenth through Nineteenth Centuries.* The Collections of the National Gallery of Art, Systematic Catalogue. Washington, 1990.

Brown, Jonathan. *Jusepe de Ribera. Prints and Drawings.* Princeton, 1973.

———. *Murillo and His Drawings.* Princeton, 1975.

———. *Images and Ideas in Seventeenth-Century Spanish Painting.* Princeton, 1978.

———. "El Greco and Toledo." In *El Greco of Toledo.* Boston, 1982, 75–147.

———. "Murillo, pintor de temas eróticos. Una faceta inadvertida de su obra." *Goya* nos. 169–71 (1982), 35–43.

———. "Murillo: New Drawings, Old Problems." *Master Drawings* 21 (1983), 160–62.

———. "Mecenas y coleccionistas españoles de Jusepe de Ribera. *Goya* no. 183 (1984), 140–50.

———. "Felipe II, coleccionista de pintura y escultura." *IV Centenario del Monasterio de El Escorial. Las colecciones del rey. Pintura y escultura.* Madrid, 1986, 19–31.

———. *Velázquez. Painter and Courtier.* New Haven and London, 1986.

———. "El Greco: Between the Renaissance and the Counter Reformation." In *Art and Religion: Faith, Form and Reform.* 1984 Paine Lectures in Religion. Columbia (Missouri), 1986, 40–66.

———. "Enemies of Flattery: Velázquez' Portraits of Philip IV." *Journal of Interdisciplinary History* 17 (1986), 137–54.

———. "Academies of Painting in Seventeenth-Century Spain." *Leids Kunsthistorisch Jaarboek* 5–6 (1986–87), 177–85.

———. "Patronage and Piety: Religious Imagery in the Art of Francisco de Zurbarán." In Jeannine Baticle, *Zurbarán.* New York, 1987.

———. "Philip II as Art Collector and Patron." In *Spanish Cities of the Golden Age. The Views of Anton van den Wyngaerde.* Ed. Richard L. Kagan. Berkeley, 1989, 14–39.

———. "Felipe IV, el rey de coleccionistas." *Fragmentos* no. 11 (1987), 4–20.

———. *Jusepe de Ribera, grabador.* Valencia and Madrid, 1989.

Brown, Jonathan and Dawson Carr. "*Portrait of a Cardinal*: Niño de Guevara or Sandoval y Rojas?" *Studies in the History of Art* 11 (1982), 33–42.

———. "El 'Retrato de un cardenal:' ¿ simbolo o simulacro?" In *Visiones del pensamiento. El Greco como intérprete de la historia, la tradición y las ideas.* Madrid, 1984, 59–73.

Brown, Jonathan and John H. Elliott. *A Palace for a King. The Buen Retiro and the Court of Philip IV.* New Haven and London, 1980.

———. "The Marquis of Castel Rodrigo and the Landscape Paintings in the Buen Retiro." *Burlington Magazine* 129 (1987), 104–7.

Brown, Jonathan and Richard L. Kagan. "The Duke of Alcalá: His Collection and Its Evolution." *Art Bulletin* 69 (1987), 231–55.

Brown, Jonathan and Richard G. Mann. *Spanish Painting of the Fifteenth through Nineteenth Centuries.* The Collections of the National Gallery of Art, Systematic Catalogue. Washington, 1990.

Buendía, José R. and Ismael Gutiérrez Pastor. *Vida y obra del pintor Mateo Cerezo (1637–1666).* Burgos, 1986.

Bull, Duncan and Enriqueta Harris. "The Companion of Velázquez's *Rokeby Venus* and a Source for Goya's *Naked Maja.*" *Burlington Magazine* 128 (1986), 643–54.

Burke, Marcus B. "Private Collections of Italian Art in Seventeenth-Century Spain." Ph.D. dissertation. New York University, 1984.

———. "Paintings by Ribera in the Collection of the Duque de Medina de las Torres." *Burlington Magazine* 131 (1989), 132–35.

Bury, John. "A Source for El Greco's 'St. Maurice.'" *Burlington Magazine* 126 (1984), 144–48.

Bustamante, Agustín and Fernando Marías. "La estela de El Viso del Marqués: Esteban Perolli." *Archivo Español de Arte* 55 (1982), 173–85.

Calvo Serraller, Francisco. *La teoría de la pintura en el siglo de oro.* Madrid, 1981.

Camón Aznar, José. *La pintura española del siglo XVI.* Summa Artis, vol. 24. Madrid, 1970.

Carducho, Vicente. *Diálogos de la pintura.* Ed. Francisco Calvo Serraller. Madrid, 1979.

Carr, Dawson W. "The Fresco Decorations of Luca Giordano in Spain." *Record of The Art Museum, Princeton University* 41, no. 2 (1982), 42–55.

———. "Luca Giordano at the Escorial. The Frescoes for Charles II." Ph.D. dissertation. New York University, 1987.

Caturla, María L. "El coleccionista madrileño Don Pedro de Arce, que poseyó 'Las Hilanderas,' de Velázquez." *Archivo Español de Arte* 21 (1948), 292–304.

Ceci, Giuseppe. "Un mercante mecenate del secolo XVII: Gaspare Roomer." *Napoli Nobilissima* 1 (1920), 160–64.

Checa, Fernando. *Pintura y escultura del renacimiento en España, 1450–1600.* Madrid, 1983.

———. *Carlos V y la imagen del héroe en el Renacimiento.* Madrid, 1987.

Chenault, Jeanne. "Ribera in Roman Archives." *Burlington Magazine* 109 (1969), 561–62.

Cherry, Peter. "The Contract for Francisco de Zurbarán's Paintings of Hieronymite Monks for the Sacristy of the Monastery of Guadalupe." *Burlington Magazine* 127 (1985), 374–81.

Clough, C.H. "Pedro Berruguete and the Court of Urbino. A Case of Wishful Thinking." *Notizie da Palazzo Albani* 3 (1974), 17–24.

Cloulas, Annie. "Les peintures du grand rétable au Monastère de l'Escurial." *Mélanges de la Casa de Velázquez* 4 (1968), 175–202.

———. "Le Greco à l'Escurial: *Le martyre de Saint Maurice.*" *Studies in the History of Art* 13 (1984), 49–54.

Company i Climent, Ximó. *Pintura del Renaixement al Ducat de Gandía. Imatges d'un temps i d'un país.* Valencia, 1985.

Condorelli, Adele. "Il problema di Juan de Borgoña." *Commentari* 11 (1960), 46–59.

———. "Paolo da San Leocadio." *Commentari* 14 (1963), 134–50, 246–53.

Dacos, Nicole. "Pedro Campaña dopo Siviglia: Arazzi e altre inediti." *Bolletino d'Arte* 65, no. 8 (1980), 1–45.

———. "Ferdinand Storm, da Ysenbrant a Campaña." *Prospettiva* 33–6 (1983–4), 175–80.

———. "Pedro Machuca en Italie." In *Scritti di storia dell'arte in onore di Federico Zeri.* Milan, 1984, vol. 1, 332–61.

———. "Alonso Berruguete dans l'atelier de Raphaël." *Arte Cristiana* 73 (1985), 245–57.

Darby, Delphine F. *Juan Sariñena y sus colegas.* Valencia, 1967.

Dávila Fernández, María del Pilar. *Los sermones y el arte.* Valladolid, 1980.

Delfino, Antonio. "Documenti inediti tratti dall Archivio Storico del Banco di Napoli." *Ricerche sul '600 napoletano dedicato a Ulisse Prota-Giurleo nel centenario della nascità.* Milan, 1986, 111–16.

Domínguez Ortiz, Antonio. *La Sevilla del siglo XVII.* 3rd ed. Seville, 1984.

Duverger, Jozef. "Marie de Hongrie, gouvernante des Pays-Bas, et la Renaissance." *Actes du XXIIᵉ Congrès International d'Histoire de l'Art.* Budapest, 1969, vol. 1, 715–26.

Eisler, William. "Arte y estado bajo Carlos V." *Fragmentos* 3 (1985), 21–39.

Elliott, John H. *The Count-Duke of Olivares: The Statesman in an Age of Decline.* New Haven and London, 1986.

El manuscrito de la Academia de Murillo. Seville, 1982.

El Toledo de El Greco. Toledo, 1982.

Enggass, Robert and Jonathan Brown. *Italy and Spain 1600–1750. Sources and Documents in the History of Art.* Englewood Cliffs, 1970.

Faraglia, Nunzio F. "Notizie di alcuni artisti che lavorarono nella chiesa di S. Martino e nel Tesoro di S. Gennaro." *Archivio Storico per le Province Napoletane* 10 (1885), 435–61.

———. "Notizie di alcuni artisti che lavorarono nella chiesa di S. Martino sopra Napoli." *Archivio Storico per le Province Napoletane* 17 (1892), 657–78.

Felton, Craig and William B. Jordan, eds. *Jusepe de Ribera, lo Spagnoletto, 1591–1652.* Fort Worth, 1982.

Fernández Duro, Cesareo. *El último*

Almirante de Castilla. Don Juan Tomás Enríquez de Cabrera. Madrid, 1903.

Ferrari, Oreste and Giuseppe Scavizzi. *Luca Giordano*. Naples, 1966.

Flórez Martín, Carmen. "Noticias sobre Antonio Palomino y su familia." *Academia* 66 (1988), 237–56.

Frederickson, Burton. "List of New Spanish and Italian Inventories Available at the Getty Provenance Index." *Burlington Magazine* 13 (1989), 137–52.

Freixas, Pere. "Documents per l'art renaixcentista català. La pintura a Girona durant el primer terç del segle XVI." *Annals de l'Institut d'Estudis Gironins* 27 (1984), 165–88.

Friedländer, Max J. *Early Netherlandish Painting*. Vol. 13, *Antonis Mor and His Contemporaries*. Leyden-Brussels, 1975.

From Byzantium to El Greco. Greek Frescoes and Icons. London, 1987.

Gállego, Julián. *El pintor de artesano a artista*. Granada, 1976.

García Felguera, María de los Santos. *La fortuna de Murillo (1682–1900)*. Seville, 1989.

García Fuentes, Lutgardo. *El comercio español con América, 1650–1700*. Seville, 1980.

Garín Ortiz de Taranco, Felipe M. *Yáñez de la Almedina*. Valencia, 1978.

Gaya Nuño, Juan A. "Juan Bautista del Mazo, el gran discípulo de Velázquez." *Varia Velázqueña*. Madrid, 1960, vol. 1, 471–81.

Gérard, Veronique. *De castillo a palacio. El Alcázar de Madrid en el siglo XVI*. Madrid, 1984.

Gere, John A. "A Drawing by Matteo Perez da Leccio." *Master Drawings* 1 (1973), 150–54.

Giusti, Paola and Pierluigi Leone de Castris. *"Forastieri e regnicoli." La pittura moderna a Napoli nel primo cinquecento*. Naples, 1985.

Giustiniani, Vincenzo. "Letter to Signor Teodoro Amideni." In ed. Elizabeth Holt. *Literary Sources of Art History*. Princeton, 1947.

Gómez-Menor, José. "Algunos documentos sobre Juan de Borgoña y otros artífices toledanos de su tiempo." *Anales Toledanos* 2 (1968), 167–71.

Gómez-Moreno, Manuel. *Las águilas del renacimiento español*. 2nd ed. Madrid, 1983.

Groeneveld, E. E. H. "Een kerziene biographie van Anthonis Mor." *Jaarboek van het Koninklijk Museum voor Schone Kunsten-Antwerpen*, 1981, 97–117.

Guinard, Paul. *Zurbarán et les peintres espagnols de la vie monastique*. Paris, 1960.

Hadermann-Misguich, Lydie. "Le byzantinisme du Greco à la lumière de découvertes récentes." *Bulletin de la Classe des Beaux-Arts, Academie Royale de Belgique* 69 (1987), 42–64.

Haraszti-Takács, Marianna. *Spanish Genre Painting in the Seventeenth Century*. Budapest, 1983.

Harris, Enriqueta. "La misión de Velázquez en Italia." *Archivo Español de Arte* 33 (1960), 109–36.

____. "Cassiano dal Pozzo on Velázquez." *Burlington Magazine* 112 (1970), 364–73.

____. "Velázquez and the Villa Medici." *Burlington Magazine* 123 (1981), 537–41

____. "Velázquez as Connoisseur." *Burlington Magazine* 124 (1982), 436–40.

Hoet, Gerard. *Catalogus of Naamlyst van Schildereyn met derzelver pryzen*. s'Gravenhage, 1752.

Hope, Charles. *Titian*. New York, 1980.

Ibáñez Martínez, Pedro M. "Un nuevo documento sobre Fernando Yáñez de la Almedina." *Boletín del Museo e Instituto Camón Aznar* no. 26 (1986), 111–22.

Itinerario di Pietro Sorri (1556–1622). Genoa, 1983.

Jacob, Sabine. "Florentinische Elemente in der Spanischen Malerei des frühen 17. Jahrhunderts." *Mitteilungen des Kunsthistorischen Institutes in Florenz* 13 (1967–8), 115–64.

Jordan, William B. *Spanish Still Life in the Golden Age*. Fort Worth, 1985.

Junquera, Juan J. "Un retablo de Maino en Pastrana." *Archivo Español de Arte* 50 (1977), 129–40.

Kagan, Richard L. "The Toledo of El Greco." In *El Greco of Toledo*. Boston, 1982, 35–73.

____. "El Greco and the Law." *Studies in the History of Art* 11 (1982), 79–90.

____. "Pedro de Salazar de Mendoza as Collector, Scholar and Patron of El Greco." *Studies in the History of Art* 13 (1984), 85–93.

Kamen, Henry. *Spain in the Later Seventeenth Century, 1665–1700*. London and New York, 1980.

Kinkead, Duncan T. *Juan de Valdés Leal (1622–1680). His Life and Work*. New York and London, 1978.

____. "Bartolomé Esteban Murillo: New Documentation." *Burlington Magazine* 121 (1979), 35–37.

____. "The Altarpiece of the Life of Saint Ambrose by Juan de Valdés Leal." *Art Bulletin* 64 (1982), 472–81.

____. "Francisco de Herrera and the Development of the High Baroque Style in Seville." *Record of the Art Museum, Princeton University* 41, no. 2 (1982), 12–23.

____. "The Last Sevillian Period of Francisco de Zurbarán." *Art Bulletin* 65 (1983), 305–11.

____. "The Picture Collection of Don Nicolás Omazur." *Burlington Magazine* 128 (1986), 132–44.

Kowal, David M. *Francisco Ribalta and His Followers. A Catalogue Raisonné*. New York and London, 1985.

____. *Ribalta y los Ribaltescos: La evolución del estilo barroco en Valencia*. Valencia, 1985.

Kubler, George. *Building the Escorial*. Princeton, 1982.

Kusche, Maria. *Juan Pantoja de la Cruz*. Madrid, 1964.

____. "Sofonisba Anguissola en España." *Archivo Español de Arte* 62 (1989), 391–420.

Lavalleye, Jacques. *Le Palais Ducal d'Urbin*. Les Primitifs Flamands. Corpus de la peinture des anciens Pays-Bas meridionaux au quinzième siècle. Brussels, 1964.

León Tello, Francisco J. and María M. V. Sanz Sanz. *La teoría española en la pintura en el siglo XVIII. El tratado de Palomino*. Madrid, 1979.

Lleó Cañal, Vicente. *Nueva Roma: Mitología y humanismo en el Renacimiento sevillano*. Seville, 1979.

____. "The Art Collection of the Ninth Duke of Medinaceli." *Burlington Magazine* 131 (1989), 108–16.

Longhi, Roberto. "Comprimari spagnoli della maniera italiana." *Paragone* no. 43 (1953), 3–15.

López-Rey, José. *Velázquez. The Artist as Maker*. Lausanne-Paris, 1979.

López Torrijos, Rosa. "Bartolomé Matarana y otros pintores italianos del siglo XVII." *Archivo Español de Arte* 51 (1978), 184–85.

____. *Lucas Jordán en el Casón del Buen Retiro. La alegoría del Toisón de Oro*. Madrid, 1985.

____. "Grabados y dibujos para la entrada en Madrid de María Luisa de Orléans (1680)." *Archivo Español de Arte* 58 (1985), 239–50.

____. *La mitología en la pintura española del siglo de oro*. Madrid, 1985.

Luna, Juan J. *Claudio de Lorena y el ideal clásico del paisaje en el siglo XVII*. Madrid, 1984.

Madruga Real, Angela. *Arquitectura barroca Salamantina. Las Agustinas de Monterrey*. Salamanca, 1983.

Magurn, Ruth S. ed., *The Letters of Peter Paul Rubens*. Cambridge, 1955.

Mancini, Giulio. *Considerazioni sulla pittura*. Ed. Luigi Salerno. Rome, 1956–57.

Mann, Richard G. *El Greco and His Patrons. Three Major Projects*. Cambridge, 1986.

Marías, Fernando. "Datos sobre la vida y la obra de Juan de Borgoña." *Archivo Español de Arte* 49 (1976), 180–82.

____. "Juan Bautista Maino y su familia." *Archivo Español de Arte* 49 (1976), 468–70.

____. "Luca Cambiaso: Testamento escurialense e inventario de bienes." *Archivo Español de Arte* 52 (1979), 83–88.

____. "El Greco and the Eyes of Reason." *El Greco Exhibition*. Tokyo, 1986, 65–72.

____. "La obra artística y arquitectónica del Cardenal Sandoval y Rojas." In *El Toledo de Felipe II y El Greco*. Toledo, 1986.

321

_____. *El largo siglo XVI.* Madrid, 1989.

Marías, Fernando and Agustín Bustamante. *Las ideas artísticas de El Greco.* Madrid, 1981.

_____. "La herencia de El Greco, Jorge Manuel Theotocópuli y el debate arquitectónico en torno a 1620." *Studies in the History of Art* 13 (1984), 101–11.

Martín Cubero, María L. *Alejo Fernández.* Madrid, 1988.

Martínez Caviro, Balbina. "El convento toledano de las Benitas, don Francisco de Pisa y El Greco." *Archivo Español de Arte* 61 (1988), 116–20.

Martínez, Jusepe. *Discursos practicables del noblísimo arte de la pintura.* Ed. Julián Gállego. Madrid, 1988.

Martínez de la Peña. "El Greco, en la Academia de San Lucás." *Archivo Español de Arte* 45 (1967), 97–105.

Martínez Ripoll, Antonio. *La iglesia del Colegio de San Buenaventura.* Seville, 1976.

_____. *Francisco de Herrera "El Viejo."* Seville, 1978.

Martín González, Juan J. "Arte y artistas del siglo XVII en la corte." *Archivo Español de Arte* 31 (1958), 125–42.

_____. "Precisiones sobre Gaspar Becerra." *Archivo Español de Arte* 42 (1969), 327–56.

_____. *El artista en la sociedad española del siglo XVII.* Madrid, 1984.

_____. "Bienes artísticos de Don Rodrigo Calderón." *Boletín del Seminario de Estudios de Arte y Arqueología. Universidad de Valladolid* 54 (1988), 267–92.

Mateo, Isabel. *Juan Correa de Vivar.* Madrid, 1983.

Matilla Tascón, Antonio. "Comercio de pinturas y alcabalas." *Goya* no. 178 (1984), 180–81.

_____. "Felipe II adquiere pinturas del Bosco y Patinir." *Goya* no. 203 (1988), 258–61.

Mazariegos Pajares, Jesús. "Alonso Berruguete, pintor." *Publicaciones del Instituto Tello Téllez de Meneses* no. 42 (1979), 31–131.

McKim-Smith, Gridley, Greta Anderson-Bergdoll and Richard Newman. *Examining Velázquez.* New Haven and London, 1988.

Mena Marques, Manuela. "Murillo dibujante." In *Bartolomé Murillo (1617–1682).* Madrid and London, 1982–83, 77–89.

Mesa, José de and Teresa Gisbert. *El pintor Mateo Pérez de Alesio.* La Paz, 1972.

Morán Turina, J. Miguel. "Felipe III y las artes." *Anales de Historia del Arte,* no. 1 (1989), 159–79.

Morán Turina, J. Miguel and Fernando Checa. *El coleccionismo en España. De la cámara de maravillas a la galería de pinturas.* Madrid, 1985.

Mulcahy, Rosemarie. "The High Altarpiece of the Basilica of San Lorenzo de El Escorial." *Burlington Magazine* 122 (1980), 188–92.

Muller, Jeffrey M. *Rubens. The Artist as Collector.* Princeton, 1989.

Muller, Priscilla. "Antonio del Castillo and the Rustic Style." *Apollo* 84 (1966), 380–83.

Murillo (1617–1682). Madrid and London, 1982–83.

Naldi, Riccardo. "Pseudo Bramantino." In Giovanni Previtali, *Andrea da Salerno nel Rinascimento Meridionale.* Florence, 1986.

Nappi, Eduardo. "I vicerè e l'arte a Napoli." *Napoli Nobilissima* 22 (1983), 41–57.

Ollero Butler, Jacobo. "Miguel Coxcie y su obra en España." *Archivo Español de Arte* 48 (1975), 165–98.

Orso, Steven N. "Francisco de Herrera the Younger: New Documentation." *Source. Notes in the History of Art* 1, no. 2 (Winter 1982), 29–32.

_____. *Philip IV and the Decoration of the Alcázar of Madrid.* Princeton, 1986.

_____. *The Royal Exequies for Philip IV of Spain: A Study of Habsburg Art and Propaganda.* Columbia, Mo., 1989.

Ortiz de Zúñiga, Diego. *Anales eclesiásticos y seculares de la muy noble y muy leal ciudad de Sevilla.* Ed. Antonio M. Espinosa y Carzel. Madrid, 1796.

Pacheco, Francisco. *Arte de la pintura.* Ed. Francisco J. Sánchez Cantón. Madrid, 1956.

_____. *Libro de descripción de verdaderos retratos de ilustres y memorables varones.* Ed. Pedro M. Piñero Ramírez and Rogelio Reyes Cano. Seville, 1985.

_____. *L'Art de la peinture.* Ed. Lauriane Fallay D'Este. Paris, 1986.

Palomino, Antonio. *Lives of the Eminent Spanish Painters and Sculptors.* Ed. Nina Ayala Mallory. Cambridge, 1987.

Panagiotakis, Nikolaos. *The Cretan Period of the Life of Domenikos Theotokopoulos* (in Greek). Athens, 1986.

Pedro Pablo Rubens (1577–1640). Exposición homenaje. Madrid, 1977–78.

Pemán, César. *Zurbarán y otros estudios sobre pintura del XVII español.* Madrid, 1989.

Pérez Pastor, Cristóbal. *Noticias y documentos relativos a la historia y literatura española.* Memorias de la Real Academia Española, vol. 11. Madrid, 1914.

Pérez Sánchez, Alfonso E. *Borgianni, Cavarozzi y Nardi en España.* Madrid, 1964.

_____. *Jerónimo Jacinto de Espinosa.* Madrid, 1972.

_____. *Caravaggio y el naturalismo español.* Seville, 1973.

_____. *El retablo de Morales en Arroyo de la Luz.* Madrid, 1974.

_____. "Pintura madrileña del siglo XVII: Addenda." *Archivo Español de Arte* 49 (1976), 293–325.

_____. "Presencia de Tiziano en la España del Siglo de Oro." *Goya* no. 135 (1976), 140–59.

_____. "Las colecciones del conde de Monterrey (1653)." *Boletín de la Real Academia de la Historia* 174 (1977), 417–59.

_____. "Rubens y la pintura barroca española." *Goya* nos. 140–41 (1977), 86–109.

_____. *Los Ribera de Osuna.* Seville, 1978.

_____. "En el centenario de Orrente. 'Addenda' a su catálogo." *Archivo Español de Arte* 53 (1980), 1–18.

_____. "La academia madrileña de 1603 y sus fundadores." *Boletín del Seminario de Estudios de Arte y Arqueología. Universidad de Valladolid* 48 (1982), 281–89.

_____. *Pintura española de bodegones y floreros de 1600 a Goya.* Madrid, 1983–84.

_____. *Juan Carreño de Miranda (1614–1685).* Madrid-Avilés, 1985.

_____. *Carreño, Rizi, Herrera y la pintura madrileña de su tiempo (1650–1700).* Madrid, 1986.

_____. "Revisión de Mateo Cerezo. A propósito de un libro reciente." *Archivo Español de Arte* 60 (1987), 281–97.

Poorter, Nora de. *The Eucharist Series.* Corpus Rubenianum Ludwig Burchard, vol. 2. London, 1978.

Post, Chandler R. *A History of Spanish Painting.* Vol. 9, *The Beginning of the Renaissance in Castile and Leon.* Cambridge, 1947.

_____. *A History of Spanish Painting.* Vol. 11, *The Valencian School in the Early Renaissance.* Cambridge, 1953.

_____. *A History of Spanish Painting.* Vol. 14, *The Later Renaissance in Castile.* Ed. Harold E. Wethey. Cambridge, 1966.

Previtali, Giovanni. *La pittura del cinquecento a Napoli e nel vicereame.* Turin, 1978.

Ravina Martín, Manuel. "El pintor Murillo y la familia Eminente." *Symposium Internacional Murillo y su época.* Seville, 1982 (unpublished).

Rodríguez G. de Ceballos, Alfonso. "La repercusión en España del decreto del Concilio de Trento acerca de las imágenes sagradas y las censuras al Greco." *Studies in the History of Art* 13 (1984), 153–59.

_____. "El mundo espiritual del pintor Luis de Morales." *Goya* no. 196 (1987), 194–203.

Rosenthal, Earl. *The Palace of Charles V in Granada.* Princeton, 1985.

Rosso Del Brenna, Giovanna. "Il ruolo di G. B. Castello il Bergamasco." In *Galeazzo Alessi e l'architettura del '500.* Genoa, 1975, 619–24.

Ruffo, Vincenzo. "Galleria Ruffo nel secolo XVII in Messina (con lettere di pittori ed altri documenti inediti)." *Bollettino d'Arte* 10 (1916), 21–64, 95–128, 165–92,

232–56, 369–88.

Salas, Xavier de. *Miguel Angel y El Greco.* Madrid, 1967.

———. "Un exemplaire des *Vies* de Vasari annoté par le Greco." *Gazette des Beaux-Arts* 69 (1967), 178–81.

———. "Las notas del Greco a la 'Vida de Tiziano,' de Vasari." *Studies in the History of Art* 13 (1984), 161–68.

Salerno, Luigi. "The Picture Gallery of Vincenzo Giustiniani." *Burlington Magazine* 102 (1960), 21–27, 93–104, 135–48.

Saltillo, Marqués del. "La nobleza andaluza de origen flamenco. Los Colarte." *Revista de Historia y de Genealogía Española* 5 (1916), 495–500.

Sánchez Cantón, Francisco J. *Los pintores de cámara de los reyes de España.* Madrid, 1916.

———. *Fuentes literarias para la historia del arte español.* Vol. 1. Madrid, 1923.

———. *Libros, tapices y cuadros que coleccionó Isabel la Católica.* Madrid, 1950.

Sancho Gaspar, José Luis. "El 'boceto' de Colonna-Mitelli para el techo de la Ermita de San Pablo." *Boletín del Museo del Prado* 8 (1987), 32–38.

San Román, Francisco. "Documentos del Greco, referentes a los cuadros de Santo Domingo el Antiguo." *Archivo Español de Arte y Arqueologia* 10 (1934), 1–13.

———. *Alonso Sánchez Coello.* Lisbon, 1938.

———. *El Greco en Toledo.* (Madrid, 1910) Toledo, 1982.

Sanz, María J. and María T. Dabrio. "Bibliotecas del periodo barroco. Datos para su estudio." *Archivo Hispalense* 60 (1977), 113–55.

Scholz, Michael. "New Documents on Pellegrino Tibaldi in Spain." *Burlington Magazine* 126 (1984), 766–68.

———. *Eine spanische Wissenschaftsutopie am Ende des 16: Jahrhunderts. Die Bibliotheksfresken von Pellegrino im Escorial.* Münster, 1987.

Schroth, Sarah. "*Burial of the Count of Orgaz.*" *Studies in the History of Art* 11 (1982), 1–17.

———. "Early Collectors of Still-Life Painting in Castile." In William B. Jordan, *Spanish Still Life in the Golden Age, 1600–1650.* Fort Worth, 1985, 28–39.

Sebastián, Santiago. "Joan de Burgunya." In *L'època dels genis Renaixement, Barroc.* Gerona-Barcelona, 1988, 107–12.

Serrera, Juan M. *Pedro de Villegas Marmolejo.* Seville, 1976.

———. "Murillo y la pintura italiana de los siglos XVI y XVII. Nuevas relaciones y concomitancias." *Goya* nos. 160–71 (1982), 126–32.

———. *Hernando de Esturmio.* Seville, 1983.

———. "Pinturas y pintores del siglo XVI en la Catedral de Sevilla." In *La Catedral de Sevilla.* Seville, 1985, 353–404.

———. "El viaje a Marruecos de Blas de Prado. Constatación documental." *Boletín del Museo e Instituto Camón Aznar* 25 (1986), 23–26.

———. "Vasco Pereira, un pintor portugués en la Sevilla del último tercio del siglo XVI." *Archivo Hispalense* 213 (1987), 197–239.

———. "Zurbarán y América." In *Zurbarán.* Madrid, 1988, 63–83.

———. "Pedro de Campaña: obras dispersas." *Archivo Español de Arte* 62 (1989), 1–14.

Sigüenza, José de. Historia de la Orden de San Jerónimo (Madrid, 1600). Ed. Francisco J. Sánchez Cantón. *Fuentes literarias para la historia del arte español.* Vol. 1. Madrid, 1923.

Solis Rodríguez, Carmelo. "Luis de Morales. Nuevas aportaciones documentales." *Revista de Estudios Extremeños* 33 (1977), 571–652; 34 (1978), 49–137.

Spear, Richard E. *Domenichino.* New Haven and London, 1982.

Spezzaferro, Luigi. "Un imprenditore del primo seicento: Giovanni Battista Crescenzi." *Ricerche di Storia dell'Arte* no. 26 (1985), 50–73.

Spinosa, Nicola. *La obra pictórica completa de Ribera.* Barcelona, 1979.

Steppe, Jan Karel. "Mêcénat espagnol et art flamand au XVIᵉ siècle." In *Splendeurs d'Espagne et les villes belges.* Brussels, 1985, vol. 1, 247–82.

Sterling, Charles. "Du nouveau sur Juan de Borgoña: son tableau le plus ancien connu." *L'Oeil* no. 401 (1988), 24–31.

Stratton, Suzanne. "La Inmaculada Concepción en el arte español." *Cuadernos de Arte e Iconografia* 1, no. 2 (1988), 3–127.

Sullivan, Edward J. *Baroque Painting in Madrid. The Contribution of Claudio Coello, with a Catalogue Raisonné of His Works.* Columbia, Mo., 1986.

Testamentaría del Rey Carlos II, 1701–1703. Ed. Gloria Fernández Bayton. Vol. 1, Madrid, 1975. Vol 2, Madrid, 1981.

Tormo, Elías. "Obras conocidas y desconocidas de Yáñez de la Almedina." *Boletín de la Sociedad Española de Excursiones* 32 (1924), 32–39.

Tormo y Monzo, Elías, Celestino Gusi and Enrique Lafuente Ferrari. *La vida y la obra de Fray Juan Ricci.* Madrid, 1930.

Trapier, Elizabeth Du G. *Luis de Morales and Leonardesque Influences in Spain.* New York, 1953.

Trizina, Jazeps. *Michel Sittow. Peintre revalais de l'école brugeoise (1468–1525/26).* Brussels, 1976.

Ubeda de los Cobos, Andrés. "Consideración social del pintor y academicismo artístico en Madrid en el siglo XVII." *Archivo Español de Arte* 62 (1989), 61–74.

Valdivieso, Enrique. *Historia de la pintura sevillana. Siglos XIII al XX.* Seville, 1986.

———. *Juan de Valdés Leal.* Seville, 1988.

Valdivieso, Enrique and Juan M. Serrera. *El Hospital de la Caridad de Sevilla.* Seville, 1980.

———. *Historia de la pintura española. Escuela sevillana del primer tercio del siglo XVII.* Seville, 1985.

Valverde Madrid, José. "Antonio del Castillo: su vida y obra." In *Antonio del Castillo y su época.* Córdoba, 1986, 19–54.

Vandevivère, Ignace. *La Cathédrale de Palencia et l'église paroissale de Cervera de Pisuerga. Les Primitifs Flamands. Corpus de la peinture des anciens Pays-Bas meridionaux aux quinzième siècle.* Brussels, 1967.

———. *Juan de Flandes.* Madrid, 1986.

Vannugli, Antonio. *La Collezione Serra di Cassano.* Salerno, 1989.

Varia Velazqueña. Homenaje a Velázquez en el III centenario de su muerte. Madrid, 1960.

Veitia Linaje, José, *Norte de la Contratación de las Indias Occidentales.* Ed. Francisco Solano. Madrid, 1981.

Vélez de Guevara, Juan. *Los celos hacen estrellas.* Ed. J. E. Varey and N. D. Shergold. London, 1970.

Veliz, Zahira, ed. *Artists' Techniques in Golden-Age Spain: Six Treatises in Translation.* New York, 1986.

Volk, Mary Crawford. "New Light on a Seventeenth-Century Collector: The Marquis of Leganés." *Art Bulletin* 62 (1980), 56–68.

Von Barghahn, Barbara. *Philip IV and the "Golden House" of the Buen Retiro: In the Tradition of Caesar.* New York, 1986.

Wethey, Harold E. *El Greco and His School.* Princeton, 1962.

———. "Orazio Borgianni in Italy and Spain." *Burlington Magazine* 106 (1964), 147–59.

———. *Alonso Cano. Pintor, escultor y arquitecto.* Madrid, 1983.

Wilkinson, Catherine. "Il Bergamasco e il Palazzo a Viso del Marqués." In *Galeazzo Alessi e l'architettura del '500.* Genoa, 1975, 625–30.

Young, Eric. "Antonio Puga, His Place in Spanish Painting, and the Pseudo-Puga." *The J. Paul Getty Museum Journal* 3 (1976), 47–65.

Zarco Cuevas, Julián. "Inventario de las alhajas, estatuas, pinturas, tapices y otros objetos de valor y curiosidad donados por el rey don Felipe II al Monasterio de El Escorial. Años de 1571 a 1598." *Boletín de la Real Academia de la Historia* 96 (1930), 545–668; 97 (1930), 35–144.

———. *Pintores españoles en San Lorenzo el Real de El Escorial (1566–1613).* Madrid, 1931.

———. *Pintores italianos en San Lorenzo el Real de El Escorial (1575–1613).* Madrid, 1932.

Zurbarán. Madrid, 1988.

Index